Personality Disorder and Serious Offending

Personality Disorder and Serious Offending

Hospital treatment models

Edited by

Chris Newrith MB ChB, MRCPsych, MSc
Consultant Psychiatrist in Psychotherapy
Main House Therapeutic Community
Birmingham Personality Disorder Service
Birmingham, UK

Clive Meux MB BS, FRCPsych
Consultant Forensic Psychiatrist
Oxford Clinic Medium Secure Unit
Littlemore Mental Health Centre
Oxford, UK

Pamela J. Taylor MB BS, MRCP, FRCPsych, FMedSci
Professor of Forensic Psychiatry
Wales College of Medicine
Cardiff University
Cardiff, UK

Hodder Arnold

A MEMBER OF THE HODDER HEADLINE GROUP

First published in Great Britain in 2006 by
Hodder Arnold, an imprint of Hodder Education and a member of the Hodder Headline Group,
338 Euston Road, London NW1 3BH

http://www.hoddereducation.com

Distributed in the United States of America by
Oxford University Press Inc.,
198 Madison Avenue, New York, NY10016
Oxford is a registered trademark of Oxford University Press

Hodder Headline's policy is to use papers that are natural, renewable and recyclable products and made from wood grown in sustainable forests. The logging and manufacturing processes are expected to conform to the environmental regulations of the country of origin.

Whilst the advice and information in this book are believed to be true and accurate at the date of going to press, neither the author[s] nor the publisher can accept any legal responsibility or liability for any errors or omissions that may be made. In particular (but without limiting the generality of the preceding disclaimer), every effort has been made to check drug dosages; however, it is still possible that errors have been missed. Furthermore, dosage schedules are constantly being revised and new side-effects recognized. For these reasons the reader is strongly urged to consult the drug companies' printed instructions before administering any of the drugs recommended in this book.

British Library Cataloguing in Publication Data
A catalogue record for this book is available from the British Library

Library of Congress Cataloging-in-Publication Data
A catalog record for this book is available from the Library of Congress

ISBN-10   0 340 763 85X
ISBN-13   978 0 340 763 858

1 2 3 4 5 6 7 8 9 10

Commissioning Editor: Clare Christian and Philip Shaw
Project Editor: Clare Patterson
Production Controller: Karen Tate
Cover Design: Sarah Rees

Typeset in 10/13 pts Sabon by Charon Tec Ltd, Chennai, India
www.charontec.com
Printed and bound in Malta.

What do you think about this book? Or any other Hodder Arnold title?
Please send your comments to www.hoddereducation.com

CONTENTS

CONTRIBUTORS

Zubin Bhagwagar MD, MRCPsych, DPhil
Assistant Professor, Yale University School of Medicine, Connecticut, USA

Ronald Blackburn MA (Cantab), MSc, PhD, CPsychol, FBPsS
Emeritus Professor of Clinical and Forensic Psychological Studies, Division of Clinical
Psychology, University of Liverpool, Liverpool, UK

Robert James Richard Blair PhD
Unit Chief, Unit of Affective Cognitive Neuroscience, Mood and Anxiety Disorders Program,
National Institute of Mental Health, Bethesda, Maryland, USA

Christopher Cordess MB BChir, MA, MPhil, FRCP, FRCPsych
Psychoanalyst; and Emeritus Professor of Forensic Psychiatry, University of Sheffield, and
Honorary Consultant and Director of Research, Rampton Hospital, Nottingham, UK

Philip Cowen MD, FRCPsych
Professor, Psychopharmacology Research Unit, Department of Psychiatry, University of
Oxford, Oxford, UK

Sophie Davison MB BChir, MA, MRCPsych, MPhil, DFP
Consultant Forensic Psychiatrist, York Clinic, Guy's Hospital, London, UK

Conor Duggan BSc, PhD, MD, FRCPsych
Professor of Forensic Mental Health, University of Leicester, and Honorary Consultant
Psychiatrist, East Midlands Centre for Forensic Mental Health, Leicester, UK

Anselm Eldergill BSc(Economics in Government)
Solicitor; Visiting Professor of Mental Health Law, Northumbria University,
Newcastle Upon Tyne, UK

Tim Exworthy MB, MS, LLM, MRCPsych, DFP
Consultant Forensic Psychiatrist, Redford Lodge, London, UK

George W. Fenton MB ChB, BAO, FRCPsych (deceased)
Formerly Emeritus Professor of Psychiatry, Department of Psychiatry, Ninewells Hospital
and Medical School, Dundee, UK

Peter Gottlieb
Formerly Head of the Forensic Psychiatric Unit, St Hans Hospital, Copenhagen; Consultant Psychiatrist, Ministry of Justice, Clinic of Forensic Psychiatry, Copenhagen, Denmark

Peter Greeven PhD
Programme Director and Consultant Psychotherapist, Expertise Centre for Forensic Psychiatry, Utrecht, The Netherlands

Don Grubin MB BS, MD, FRCPsych
Professor of Forensic Psychiatry, University of Newcastle, and (Honorary) Consultant Forensic Psychiatrist, Newcastle, North Tyneside, Northumberland NHS Trust, Newcastle Upon Tyne, UK

Rex Haigh MA (Cantab), BM BCh (Oxon), MRCGP, MRCPsych, Memb Inst GA
Consultant Psychiatrist in Psychotherapy and Programme Director, Thames Valley Initiative, Warneford Hospital, Oxford, and Clinical Lead, Nottinghamshire Personality Development Network and Mandala Therapeutic Community, Nottingham, UK

Rob Hale FRCPsych
Consultant Psychotherapist–Psychoanalyst, Portman Clinic, London, UK

Grant T. Harris PhD
Director of Research, Mental Health Centre, Penetanguishene, and Associate Professor of Psychiatry (Adjunct), University of Toronto, and Associate Professor of Psychology (Adjunct), Queen's University, Ontario, Canada

Tracey Heads MB ChB, MD, MRCPsych, DFP
Consultant Forensic Psychiatrist, North Wales Forensic Psychiatry Service, Conway, UK

N. Zoe Hilton PhD
Senior Research Scientist, Mental Health Centre, Penetanguishene, and Assistant Professor of Psychiatry (Adjunct), University of Toronto, Ontario, Canada

Tim Howard BM MS, MRCPsych
Consultant Forensic Psychiatrist, Northgate Hospital, Northumberland, UK

Gill McGauley BSc, MB BS, FRCPsych
Senior Lecturer and Consultant in Forensic Psychotherapy, Division of Mental Health, St George's, University of London, and West London Mental Health Trust, Broadmoor Hospital, UK

Tim McInerny BA, MB BS, MRCPsych, Dip For Psych
Honorary Consultant Forensic Psychiatrist, Professorial Unit, Broadmoor Hospital, Crowthorne, Berkshire, UK

Elaine McNicholas RMN
Forensic Community Psychiatric Nurse, Oxford Clinic Medium Secure Unit, Littlemore
Mental Health Centre, Oxford, UK

Fiona L. Mason MB BS, MRCPsych, DFP
Consultant Forensic Psychiatrist, St Andrew's Hospital, Northampton, UK

Barbara Maughan BA, MSc, PhD
Reader in Developmental Psychopathology, MRC Social, Genetic and Developmental
Psychiatry Centre, Institute of Psychiatry, King's College London, London, UK

Clive Meux MB BS, FRCPsych
Consultant Forensic Psychiatrist, Oxford Clinic Medium Secure Unit, Littlemore Mental
Health Centre, Oxford, UK

Estelle Moore BSc (Hons), MSc, PhD, C.Psychol, AFBPsS
Consultant Clinical and Forensic Psychologist, Broadmoor Hospital, Crowthorne, Berkshire,
and Honorary Lecturer in Clinical Psychology, Institute of Psychiatry, London, UK

Chris Newrith MB ChB, MSc, MRCPsych
Consultant Psychiatrist in Psychotherapy, Main House Therapeutic Community, Birmingham
Personality Disorder Service, Birmingham, UK

Marie Quayle MA, MSc, CPsychol, AFBPsS
Consultant Clinical Psychologist, West London NHS Mental Health Trust, Southall,
Middlesex, UK

David Reiss MA, MB BChir, MPhil, MRCPsych, DFP
Director of Forensic Psychiatry Education, West London Mental Health NHS Trust, and
Honorary Clinical Senior Lecturer, Department of Psychological Medicine, Imperial College,
London, UK

Marnie E. Rice PhD, FRSC
Director of Research Emerita, Mental Health Centre, Penetanguishene, and Professor of
Psychiatry and Behavioural Neurosciences, McMaster University, and Professor of Psychiatry
(Adjunct), University of Toronto, and Associate Professor of Psychology, (Adjunct), Queen's
University, Ontario, Canada

Alla Rubitel MD MRCPsych
Specialist Registrar in Forensic Psychotherapy, Portman Clinic, The Tavistock and Portman
NHS Trust, London, UK

R. Rosner MD
Clinical Professor, Forensic Psychiatric Clinic, New York, USA

Wilhelm Skogstad MD (Munich), MRCPsych
Psychoanalyst (British Psychoanalytical Society), Consultant Psychiatrist, Cassel Hospital, Richmond, Surrey, UK

Pamela J. Taylor MB BS, MRCP, FRCPsych, FMedSci
Professor of Forensic Psychiatry, Wales College of Medicine, Cardiff University, Cardiff, UK

Brian Toone MB BS, MPhil, FRCP, FRCPsych
Consultant Neuropsychiatrist, Maudsley Hospital, London, UK

Peter Tyrer MD, FRCPsych, FRCP, FFPH, FMedSci
Professor of Community Psychiatry, and Head of the Department of Psychological Medicine, Imperial College, London, UK

Stephen Tyrer MA, MB BChir, DPM, LMCC, FRCPsych
Consultant Psychiatrist, Prudhoe Hospital, Prudhoe, Northumberland, UK

Susan Young BSc(Hons), PhD, DClinPsy
Clinical Neuropsychologist and Chartered Clinical Psychologist, Bethlem Royal Hospital, Beckenham, Kent, and Honorary Lecturer in Clinical Psychology, Institute of Psychiatry, London, UK

FOREWORD

One of the strengths of forensic psychiatry in the UK is the emphatic focus on the nature of the therapeutic care and treatment of persons held in the custody of the justice system. For example, in a foundational textbook of British forensic psychiatry, *Forensic Psychiatry: clinical, legal and ethical issues* (Gunn and Taylor, 2000), great attention is paid to treatment of the mental disorders that one is likely to encounter in the clinical practice of psychiatry in forensic settings. The present book, by Newrith, Meux and Taylor, *Personality Disorder and Serious Offending: hospital treatment models*, is very much in keeping with the therapeutic focus of British forensic psychiatry.

In contrast, in the USA forensic psychiatry has largely addressed the non-therapeutic assessment and disposition of individuals in both criminal and civil law cases. For example, on 20 May 1985, the American Academy of Psychiatry and the Law (AAPL) adopted the following definition: 'Forensic psychiatry is a subspecialty of psychiatry in which scientific and clinical expertise is applied to legal issues in legal contexts embracing civil, criminal, correctional or legislative matters; forensic psychiatry should be practiced in accordance with guidelines and ethical principles enunciated by the profession of psychiatry' (AAPL, 2004). AAPL's definition included 'correctional' legal matters, i.e. issues related to jail and prison confinement, but did not specifically include the provision of therapeutic treatment as one of those 'correctional' matters. Similarly, in *Principles and Practice of Forensic Psychiatry* (Rosner, 2003), produced for the AAPL's Tri-State Chapter, the focus is on the legal regulation of care and treatment, rather than on the nature of the care and treatment to provide to persons detained in the justice system. Even in *Correctional Psychiatry* (Rosner and Harmon, 1989), an earlier book prepared under the auspices of AAPL's Tri-State Chapter, there is only one chapter on therapy: 'Treatment of Antisocial and Other Personality Disorders in a Correctional Setting' (Weinstock, 1989).

In the USA throughout most of the twentieth century, treatment of persons held in detention in secure hospitals and correctional facilities was widely regarded as peripheral to the core of forensic psychiatry; that core was considered to be the examination and evaluation of persons for potential and actual report writing and testimony in court cases. In the late 1980s and early 1990s, as the price for formal recognition as a subspecialty of psychiatry, organized American forensic psychiatry was obliged to designate the special population forensic psychiatrists treat: persons in the custody of the justice system. In the 1990s, the American Psychiatric Association (APA) formally acknowledged forensic psychiatry as a subspecialty; the American Board of Psychiatry and Neurology (ABPN) replaced the American Board of Forensic Psychiatry as the organization to assess and certify the competence of practitioners of forensic psychiatry; and the Accreditation Council for Graduate Medical Education (ACGME) replaced the Accreditation Council on Fellowships in Forensic Psychiatry as the organization to assess and certify training programmes for forensic psychiatrists. The APA, ABPN, and ACGME made treatment of persons detained in the justice system move from the periphery into the core of American forensic psychiatry (Prosono, 2003). Treatment in secure hospitals and correctional facilities is now part of mainstream US forensic psychiatry, but it remains a relatively new and under-addressed field.

From the point of view of public health administration, one of the peculiarities of the USA is that the government does not have an affirmative obligation to identify persons at large in the community who are in need of mental health services, let alone to provide treatment for those persons. On the other hand, as soon as a person is involuntarily confined in a police lock-up, a jail or a prison, the government is required to quickly determine if the person has a diagnosable mental or physical disorder and is responsible for the provision of services to such a person. Thus, for Americans who lack the education, insight, motivation, or funding to seek mental health evaluation and treatment, being arrested and detained in the justice system may provide assessment and therapy for here-to-fore unknown and unattended mental disorders. Secure facilities in the USA now house and provide treatment for large numbers of mentally ill persons, who otherwise might be unidentified and untreated in the community.

In the USA, starting in the 1950s, with the introduction of effective neuroleptic medications, there began a process of de-institutionalization, i.e. the discharge from mental hospitals into the community of chronically mentally ill persons, in the hope that community-based outpatient mental health services would monitor and treat them. Alas, in accordance with the proverb, 'There is many a slip between the cup and the lip', many of the chronically mentally ill persons discharged into the community did not receive the ongoing community-based support and treatment that they needed. As a result, untreated mentally ill persons moved from the civil law mental health system to the criminal law mental health system. These chronically mentally ill patients, often with co-morbid personality disorders and superimposed substance abuse problems, moved into the domain of forensic psychiatry. Secure hospitals and correctional facilities now offer the only free, long-term, institutional care and treatment for the mentally ill in the USA.

The population in such facilities constitutes a public health challenge. The challenge is to find treatments that address all of the components of the chronic and multiple bio-psycho-social needs of these patients, are effective in real world settings, make the most therapeutic use of the period of institutional confinement, find ways to engage the competent informed cooperation of these patients, maximize compliance with treatment, bridge the post-discharge gap between institutional treatment and community-based treatment, and do so with the limited economic resources that society allocates to this population. Because our British colleagues in forensic psychiatry have long been addressing the therapeutic needs of persons held in the justice system, forensic psychiatrists in the USA have much to learn from them.

During the past five years, the AAPL's Tri-State Chapter, in co-operation with the Royal College of Psychiatrists' section on forensic psychiatry, has planned and implemented a series of international conferences on forensic psychiatry. These conferences, alternately meeting in London and New York, have provided an opportunity to explore commonalities and contrasts in the practice of forensic psychiatry in the UK and the USA. It has become clear that we can learn from one another's experience and strengths in different facets of our field. Because it is unrealistic for all of us personally to meet and share our knowledge and skills, it is important to use the exchange of written materials to foster our mutual education. One excellent example of what British forensic psychiatry has to teach American practitioners is the present volume, Newrith, Meux and Taylor's *Personality Disorder and Serious Offending: hospital treatment models*. Those in the UK will find this book of immediate relevance to the traditional focus of forensic psychiatry in their nation. Those in the USA will find it of importance to the therapeutic mission that has become an increasing concern of American forensic psychiatry. I commend this book to the attention of forensic psychiatrists on both sides of the Atlantic!

REFERENCES

American Academy of Psychiatry and the Law (2004). *Membership Directory*. Bloomfield, CT: AAPL.

Gunn J and Taylor PJ (eds) (2000). *Forensic Psychiatry: clinical, legal and ethical issues*. Oxford: Butterworth-Heinemann.

Prosono M (2003). History of Forensic Psychiatry. In Rosner R (ed.), *Principles and Practice of Forensic Psychiatry*, Second Edition. London: Hodder Arnold, 14–30.

Rosner R (ed.) (2003). *Principles and Practice of Forensic Psychiatry*, Second Edition. London: Hodder Arnold.

Rosner R and Harmon R (eds) (1989). *Correctional Psychiatry*. New York: Plenum.

Weinstock R (1989). Treatment of Antisocial and Other Personality Disorders in a Correctional Setting. In Rosner R and Harmon R (eds), *Correctional Psychiatry*. New York: Plenum, 41–59.

Richard Rosner
January 2006

ACKNOWLEDGEMENTS

We would not have been able to complete this book without the sterling support of our secretaries Lyn Taylor, Christine Tonks and Joanne Buswell. Initially, Lyn took a major co-ordinating role; each slaved with her editorial partners on the respective sections. Christine Tonks and Gerrie Gane provided additional invaluable help with the references.

We are also grateful to Jan Lees and Nicola Singleton for information from their research additional to that in their wonderfully rich reports, and to David Cooke for his advice for statistically challenged clinicians on the interpretation of meta-analysis. Gopi Krishnan contributed to some of the description of services and an update on plans for the Rampton Hospital personality disorder service for the chapter by Christopher Cordess, and we are duly grateful.

Sadly, George Fenton died before the book was complete. His research on behalf of offender patients, including Broadmoor Hospital patients, had been conducted over many years and he continued to advise on neurophysiological research almost until his death. His chapter illustrates the wealth of his knowledge. We are grateful to his widow for allowing us to publish it, even though he could not check our editing.

Our particular thanks go to the residents and staff of Woodstock, in Broadmoor Hospital, without whom the book would never have been written. All staff members are over-stretched, as they have to continue demanding work while under-resourcing bites, but many gave support and advice and some wrote substantial contributions for us. The patients often complain that we do not consistently live up to our philosophies and ideals and, unfortunately, they are right. This is generally due to the combination of short staffing and bureaucracy inherent in this kind of work, but sometimes simply to our own failings as human beings. Nevertheless, as others have shown, Woodstock has had considerable success, and the generosity of most of the patients belies the pejorative labels they have acquired over the years. They regularly contribute to research, whether ours or that of others. Finally, when we asked for help with the cover design, most of the patients made pictorial images for us that they considered represented something of the pain and stigma of having a personality disorder or the work involved in trying to do something about it. We have used one image on the cover, and others appear throughout the book. These are just tiny examples of the creativity that can emerge if we provide a stable framework and facilitate healing and growth through specific treatments.

Chris Newrith
Clive Meux
Pamela Taylor

CHAPTER 6

The authors are grateful to the National Programme on Forensic Mental Health Research and Development whose grant funded Dr Alla Rubitel's post during the preparation of this chapter.

CHAPTER 7

This work was supported by a Wellcome Trust grant.

CHAPTER 10

Barbara Maughan is supported by the Medical Research Council.

CHAPTER 27

This chapter first appeared as a section in the *New Oxford Textbook of Psychiatry*, edited by Gelder, Lopez-Ibor and Andreasen, Oxford: Oxford University Press (2001). Reproduced by kind permission of the publisher.

LIST OF ABBREVIATIONS USED

AAI	adult attachment interview
ADHD	attention deficit hyperactivity disorder
BPD	borderline personality disorder
CAT	cognitive analytic therapy
CBT	cognitive behavioural therapy
CFI	Camberwell Family Interview
CI	confidence interval
CMRG	cerebral metabolic rates of glucose
CNV	contingent negative variation
CPA	Care Programme Approach, a structured approach to continuing clinical care required by the British government (see www.healthcarecommission.org.uk/informationforserviceproviders/guidanceforNHS)
CPN	community psychiatric nurse
CS	conditioned stimulus
CSF	cerebrospinal fluid
CT	computerized tomography
DBT	dialectical behavioural therapy
DIPD	diagnostic interview for personality disorders
DSM-IIIR	Diagnostic and Statistical Manual, Third Edition, Revised
DSM-IV	Diagnostic and Statistical Manual, Fourth Edition
DSPD	dangerous and severe personality disorder
ECHR	European Convention on Human Rights
EEG	electroencephalography
EFP	Expertise Centre for Forensic Psychiatry (Netherlands)
ERP	event related potentials
5-HIAA	5-hydroxyindoleacetic acid
5-HT	5-hydroxytryptophan (also called serotonin)
HVA	homovanillic acid
ICD-9	International Classification of Diseases, Ninth Revision
ICD-10	International Classification of Diseases, Tenth Revision
IPDE	International Personality Disorder Examination
IQ	intelligent quotient
MAO-A	monoamine oxidase A
MAPPP	Multi Agency Public Protection Panel
MCMI	Million Clinical Multiaxial Inventory
m-CPP	metachlorophenyl piperazine
MDMA	3, 4 methylenedioxymethamphetimine
MHA 1983	Mental Health Act 1983

MHAC	Mental Health Act Commission
MHPG	3-methoxy 4-hydroxy phenylglycol
MHRT	Mental Health Review Tribunal
MMPI	Minnesota Multiphasic Personality Inventory
MRI	magnetic resonance imaging
NHS	National Health Service
NVQ	National Vocational Qualification
OPD	operationalized psychodynamic diagnostics
OR	odds ratio
PAS	personality assessment schedule
PCL	psychopathy checklist
PCL-R	revised psychopathy checklist
PCL-SV	psychopathy checklist – screening version
PD	personality disorder
PET	positron emission tomography
PTSD	post-traumatic stress disorder
RCT	randomized control trial
RMO	responsible medical officer
RTS	rehabilitation therapy staff
SAP	standardized assessment of personality
SCR	skin conductance response
SPECT	single positron emission computerized tomography
SPET	single positron emission tomography
SSRI	selective serotonin reuptake inhibitor
TBS	Terbeschikkingstelling or Special Hospital Order (Netherlands)
TLE	temporal lobe epilepsy
UCS	unconditioned stimulus
VIM	violence inhibition model

INTRODUCTION

PERSONALITY DISORDER AND ITS TREATMENT: STARTING IS NOT DIFFICULT

Chris Newrith, Clive Meux and Pamela J. Taylor

Look ... I've got an unfortunate character. I don't know how I came by it, whether it was the way I was brought up or whether it's just the way I'm made. All I know is that if I make other people unhappy, I'm no less unhappy myself. Not much comfort for them, perhaps, but there it is.

Let it suffice that the malady has been diagnosed – heaven alone knows how to cure it!

Lermontov, 1840

If we were to accept completely Willie Bosket's version of his life, in which racism alone turned him against society and the law, then we would have to believe, as some professed during the Sixties, that men like him are the vanguard of resistance to racism. But, experience and human nature argue against that completely heroic reading. When we consider Bosket's criminal career, it is his impulsiveness and readiness for maximum violence that strike us most ...

As restless and impulsive as his father and grandfather and great grandfather,

introduced to sodomy by his grandfather, he never has much of a chance ...

[Willie's father had begun to function more normally in the same school to which his son later went, but he was discharged.] *That meant to a home that was not a home, and streets where the first law is survival. At home was his father, a violent alcoholic, and his mother, a prostitute.*

Fox Butterfield, 1995

The dilemmas associated with the treatment of someone who has a personality disorder and who offends are perhaps encapsulated in these two accounts. The first is fictional, but at least partly autobiographical; the second is factual. Of all mental disorders, personality disorder (of whatever type) is most readily recognized by its impact on both individual relationships and the collective relationship with society. How, then, can there be certainty about where exactly the disorder lies, or even if there is a disorder?

When individuals who have acquired a diagnosis of personality disorder state that others are hostile, critical and denying them various positive experiences, or perhaps that 'the system' is against them, it is often true. Does the fact that others may indeed be hostile, or that health, social or criminal justice systems may be truly suspicious or rejecting, invalidate the concept of a primary disorder? The determination of critical timings can be helpful in trying to establish how mental illness relates to behaviour; that is less so in the case of personality disorder. Whether apparent disorder or apparent rejection came first is rarely a useful guide to how the presenting dynamic has emerged. There will probably have been lack of care in earlier life in most cases and, as children, many will have suffered prolonged physical or sexual abuse, or both. In circumstances of neglect and/or abuse, it is doubtful whether parents or others in the individual's early social circle will be able to give an accurate account of birth and early development. Some sufferers may have sustained physical damage, including brain damage, during mother's pregnancy or at birth; others may have acquired developmental delays for other physical reasons, such as early central nervous system infections. Under what circumstances is deprivation or abuse sufficient to instigate lifelong patterns of adverse relationships? What circumstances are necessary to give rise to innate vulnerabilities? By the time of presentation, it is often difficult or impossible to unravel the developmental pathways, yet people present in a position of being unable to make or maintain relationships, or as a party to habitually unhealthy and damaging relationships. They are generally, like Lermontov's hero, deeply unhappy. Suicide rates are at least as high as for other major mental disorders, but, not uncommonly, the misery and aggression are also projected onto others, and it is this that tends to lead to exclusion from sustained supportive or therapeutic services. Brief service contacts, with a general practitioner, in accident and emergency departments or in a brush with the criminal justice system, are common. Treatment for the personality disorder is not.

Sources of potential help for individuals suffering the effects of personality disorder are few, and those that exist are uneven in quality. Diagnostic confusion surrounding this disorder does not help the situation, and some service providers use it to deny services. There are important limits, however, to systems which simply operationalize description of what can be observed by interviewing clinicians. The 'disease classification' model supplied by the *International Classification of Diseases* (World Health Organization, 1992) or the US-based *Diagnostic and Statistical Manual* (American Psychiatric Association, 1994) provides a label for 'the malady' that may serve only to reinforce clinical nihilism. This labelling is a long way from the true medical concept of 'diagnosis', which implies understanding of the cause of the condition, its probable course if untreated, and the likely effect on that course of well-defined interventions. The term 'personality disorder', therefore, has much the same value as the term 'anaemia'. It denotes little more than recognition of some consistencies in unhealthy presentations that limit the individual concerned in some predictable ways. It should perhaps also put the clinician in mind of a list of treatments that may be helpful, but, on the basis of such labelling alone, treatment choice would largely be a process of trial and error. For it to be otherwise, a causal mechanism or developmental pathway would have to be known. In other words, while some basic clinical interventions might maintain the status quo, change is likely to depend on matching the treatment to the primary problem. Is the latter an external deficiency – or an internal inability to process the material being fed in? We also need to know whether, if a deficiency is prolonged, for example a deficiency in attachment, simple replacement therapy will, in itself, be insufficient.

So, Lermontov's tantalizing challenge 'Heaven alone knows how to cure it!' still holds some bite 150 years later in the twenty-first century. Even clinical optimists in the field tend to think of treatment in terms of the phrases still enshrined in English mental health legislation: 'prevention of deterioration' or 'alleviation' rather than 'cure'. Even if it is accepted that an operational definition of what can be observed is possible, and 'the malady' can be diagnosed, is there any theoretical basis for it? There is no personality disorder virus, nor is there any consistently recognizable and specific deficit or reconfiguration of the brain that investigative techniques currently available can identify as uniquely indicative of a personality disorder. Indeed, some would argue that the greatest objection to the very concept of personality disorder is that the label is not indicative of specific and unequivocal primary pathology.

This book aims to acknowledge these dilemmas, but also to find a way of working that makes it possible to avoid therapeutic paralysis. At the centre of the book is a description of an evolving service in a high-security hospital setting. It is founded on the richness and complexity of the current evidence base concerning pathways into personality disorder and is, therefore, a complex, multi-modular approach. Before we describe this service, we explore in turn each of the aspects that may contribute to the development of personality disorder. The rationale for the therapeutic approach in this unit, which draws on many schools of thought, but has a clear and replicable framework, in which this knowledge is applied. The service aims to provide an environment that minimizes the repetition of early adverse experiences and disorder-maintaining practices. Within that context, assessments of the men described in subsequent chapters can be completed, and repeated as treatment progresses. An eclectic mix of established treatments is offered in a way that engages these residents in the standard framework, but allows for individual variation. Needless to say, the service does not always succeed in its lofty ideals. After the central chapter setting out this

approach, we explore ways of extending or modifying it to accommodate variations in the disorder and its co-morbidities, and variations in the situational needs of subgroups of those who suffer with it.

If this sort of clinical eclecticism can be more or less justified in theory by pulling together a collection of partly understood pathways, such a solution does, in turn, raise further questions. For example, is there any evidence of an overall advantage in having individuals with such disorders living and working together, being in specified therapies together, and receiving additional individual treatments? Is coercion, such as compulsory detention in hospital, a barrier to or a brake on treatments, or an essential enabler of therapy? Is coercion of most value for specified subgroups of people with, say, a greater number of certain problems? Does sequencing in treatment matter? Does the individualized approach, which allows for different needs in varying the treatment menu, including timing of some of the elements, really provide an advantage for some over a systematic, tightly timed programme that is easier to run to measurable clinical standards? If so, who does better in which system? It will come as no surprise that we have to leave many of the questions unanswered, but we hope that the process of formulating them by bringing clinical and research experience together may in itself be helpful.

BAD AND DANGEROUS, MAD AND DANGEROUS – JUST DESERTS OR SAFETY?

Treatment for any condition has to take place within its wider social context of resource availability and perceived worthiness of the group to be treated. Even in richer societies, resources are finite. It is not difficult to understand how meeting the needs of a premature baby could be seen as more important than meeting the needs of, say, a heroin addict. Provision for those who do not have the respect of society becomes more complex when, in a democratic society, the ruling body endorses populist but treatment-hostile views. A former British Prime Minister (John Major), for example, suggested, in a debate on law and order, that we should be ready to 'condemn a little more and understand a little less'. For the offender with personality disorder, this requires that we confront a perhaps unforeseen risk. Failure to understand the problems that such people are experiencing or their derivation, increases the risk that society's response will be to use punitive measures that would probably result in the maintenance or even exacerbation of their pathology. This in turn is likely to confirm the sufferer's early experiences that power and authority are only ever improperly used, and that survival lies in fighting them. Approaches that do not involve an understanding of this group are, therefore, likely to increase the risk of harm to others.

Middle ways between embracing understanding and offering an entirely therapeutic response on the one hand and crude enclosure or punishment on the other can create further tensions between practice, terminology and reality. Introducing a 'treatment' that 'works' into the penal and probation system might lead to people being rejected from treatment in an evidence-based health service because 'treatment' is better provided elsewhere. Is it proper to call some of the programmes offered by correctional services 'treatment programmes', or would it be clearer to refer to them as 'training programmes'? Perhaps it does not matter, though, so long as an individual receives practical, helpful interventions, what these interventions are called. Does society prefer a punitive tone in the language and better accept interventions that include it? How can we engage in a more open dialogue about which treatment provides the best chance of improving the individual's condition and decreasing the risk to public safety?

RIGHTS AND TREATMENT MORALITIES

We may all regress at times of severe stress, but, for the person who suffers with personality disorder, regression is an almost permanent state of affairs. The tension between recognizing an adult's chronological maturity, while simultaneously allowing for their arrested or regressed emotional development can make for difficult ethical dilemmas. Do such people have capacity? They may have a better understanding than most of their legal rights and how to exercise them, but this does not necessarily mean that they have reached a developmental stage of being able to judge the realities of their mental state and its implications. To what extent are they able to take responsibility for their actions in this context? To what extent can they understand, in any useful sense, the proposed treatment and its implications? To what extent do they have the capacity – here meaning the volitional and motivational state – to maintain treatment once started? Being free to abandon treatment on the kind of impulse that necessitated it does not necessarily equate with being in a position to make a free and informed choice.

On the other side of the debate are questions such as what level of confidence in the effectiveness of treatment is necessary before coercion of an individual specifically in order to undergo it is justified? A related question is about the level of confidence in the effects of treatment that is needed in order to insist that certain levels of service are made widely available? In Britain, the government has set up a number of bodies – for example the National Institute for Clinical Excellence (NICE) – to review the evidence-based treatments provided in the health service. It has also set up a body called the Clinical Health Improvement and Audit (CHIA) Inspectorate to review the services responsible for the implementation of treatments. The evidence accumulated to date for the effectiveness of treatments is reviewed in later chapters. More is known than is sometimes claimed, but still the evidence base is weaker by current standards than for many other disorders, even other major mental disorders. With respect to personality disorder, however, it may be important to question the extent to which reviews or bodies should set the randomized, controlled trial as the gold standard. Is the randomized, controlled trial really the best way of evaluating the treatment of a disorder that has complex causative pathways and, almost by definition, substantial individual variation, even within recognized sub-categories. Truly honest researchers might find it impossible to claim that they can identify a sufficiently homogenous sample for these kinds of group comparisons. If so, what are the alternatives?

Then there is the matter of cost effectiveness. Psychological and social treatments are labour intensive and appear expensive, if only as mental health treatments go. Who, though, has costed failures to treat offenders with personality disorder – whether in terms of institutional havoc or community tragedy? We know of only one US-based effort in this direction (Cohen et al., 1994). Then, too, although there has long been concern about inter-generational cycles in the development of personality disorder, the costs of interventions to minimize the cycles and of failing to intervene have barely been considered. The Bosket story is presented as one of social abuse, from which no generation of the family has yet escaped. The depth of the problem for this family is undoubted; the breadth of the problem is currently being investigated in birth cohort studies (e.g. Moffit et al., 2001).

Varying degrees of coercion into assessment and/or the treatment of personality disorder are permissible in most countries. In the UK, such coercion is explicit and subject to regular appeal, at least annually if the patient so wishes. When mental health legislation is used to detain the sufferer in hospital, such review applies most robustly to the fact of detention, and to any physical (drug) treatments; the effectiveness of psychological treatment in the individual is, in effect, only indirectly tested by an independent body called a Tribunal, when it reviews the evidence that the individual is proving 'treatable'. It is widely accepted that there must be some indication of consent and cooperation for psychological assessments and treatments to occur at all; this may be why, in legal terms, in the UK they are designated as 'treatments which do not require consent'. This refers to formal legal consents not real consent. In the criminal justice system, coercion is often more covert, perhaps allowing people to serve a sentence in the community if they cooperate in a treatment scheme, or to leave prison early for the same reason.

To date, proposals for mental health legislative reform in the UK have united all interested parties – patients and their organizations, carers and theirs, clinicians and civil rights lawyers. The exceptionally broad definition of mental disorder (of which personality disorder could be one unspecified component), explicit limits to clinical confidentiality, and concepts of preventive detention without treatment are just three of the many concerns about the proposed reforms. Legislation in such a difficult area is coercive of clinicians and patients alike. It may threaten the trust between them, and could place insurmountable barriers in the way of treatment, although perhaps less so for those with personality disorder who have been convicted of a criminal offence. It could deter treatment seeking by those who have not yet offended and might have been prevented through treatment.

THE WORK AND THE BOOK

Belief systems are powerful in the field covered by this book. We have them too, and doubtless they will break through in the writing from time to time. There is now more substance than mere belief to support the treatment of offenders with personality disorder, but there is still a long way to go. The dilemmas and difficulties raised by working in this field make it rewarding as well as frustrating. We think that the contributors to this text have conveyed in their writing both evidence-based knowledge and their enthusiasm for their respective areas of expertise. We certainly wanted them to bring that combination. We would like the book to stimulate questions and debate. Clinical work and evidence will continue to develop as the book goes through the publishing process.

REFERENCES

American Psychiatric Association (1994). *Diagnostic and Statistical Manual of Mental Disorders*, fourth edition. Washington, DC: American Psychiatric Association.

Butterfield F (1995). *All God's Children*. New York: Knopf.

Cohen MA, Miller TR and Rossman SB (1994). The costs and consequences of violent behavior in the United States. In: Reiss AJ and Roth JA (eds), *Understanding and Preventing Violence. Consequences and Control*, Vol. 4. Washington, DC: National Academy Press, 67–166.

Lermontov M (1840). *A Hero of Our Time*. Translated by Foote B (1966). Harmondsworth: Penguin Classics.

Moffitt TE, Caspi A, Rutter M and Silva PA (2001). *Sex Differences in Antisocial Behaviour*. Cambridge: Cambridge University Press.

World Health Organisation (1992). *The ICD-10 Classification of Mental and Behavioural Diorders*. Geneva: World Health Organization.

Part 1

DEFINING AND DIAGNOSING

the societies in which they live,

Chapter 1

PRESENTING CHARACTERISTICS OF PERSONALITY DISORDER

Sophie Davison

INTRODUCTION

The management of offenders with personality disorder remains a controversial area. A number of factors contribute to the underdiagnosis and misdiagnosis of personality disorder in clinical practice (Paris, 1996). Many clinicians are sceptical that personality can be assessed reliably and often consider patients with personality disorder to be 'untreatable'. Some have argued that personality disorder is an ill-defined concept used to stigmatize those individuals whose behaviour deviates from social norms and to exclude them from services. Some have even suggested that the diagnosis should be abandoned on these grounds (Lewis and Appleby, 1988).

However, denying the existence of personality disorders will not make them or their associated problems go away. Personality disorders place a huge burden on individuals and the societies in which they live. Uncertainty about the response to the available treatments and lack of appropriate services are invalid reasons for failing to diagnose and assess personality disorders properly.

Professionals throughout the mental health, general medical and criminal justice systems and the associated public and voluntary agencies deal regularly with individuals whose longstanding difficulties in the way they think, feel, behave and relate to others (i.e. who suffer from a personality disorder) make their management a particular challenge. There is evidence that individuals with personality disorder are amongst the heaviest users of mental health services (Reich et al., 1989; Menzies et al., 1993; Saarento et al., 1997; Williams et al., 1998). Many present repeatedly, take up disproportionate time, effort and resources and often do not complete treatment. Understanding their difficulties is crucial in planning appropriate services and managing individual cases.

Despite all the debate, practitioners dealing with individuals with personality disorder are generally very good at identifying them, even if they do not all use the same theoretical frameworks or nomenclature in their approach to management.

This chapter concentrates on the practical identification and assessment of personality disorder in a clinical setting. It describes some of the many ways in which personality disorder may present in practice and the features that may alert a practitioner to its presence. First and foremost, it demonstrates that the principles involved in identifying and assessing individuals with personality disorder are no different from those used in good clinical practice to assess any individual presenting with mental health problems and associated psycho-social difficulties.

DEFINITIONS

This section concentrates on the key features that are useful for recognizing individuals with personality disorder when they present. In Chapter 3, Professor Blackburn discusses the problem of defining when personality traits (that run along a continuum from normal to abnormal) constitute a disorder. This debate is not unique to disorders of personality; it applies to many other mental and physical disorders.

Although the debate about where the cut-off point should be is interesting for research purposes, practitioners rarely have problems in their everyday work identifying what constitutes a disorder and what does not. In clinical practice, where the aim is to decide whether or not an intervention is necessary, the cut-off point used is a functional and pragmatic one. A set of problems and symptoms is usually considered to constitute a disorder when the individual suffers as a result of it or when the problems interfere with social functioning. This is reflected in the *International Classification of Diseases – 10* (ICD-10) classification system (World Health Organization, 1992), in which a mental disorder is defined as '... a clinically recognisable set of symptoms or behaviour associated in most cases with distress and with interference with personal functions. Social deviance or conflict alone without personal dysfunction should not be included in mental disorder as defined here.' Personality disorders are no exception. Thus deviant behaviour in the absence of personal distress or impairment of personal functioning is not considered a disorder, nor are personality traits that differ from the norm but do not lead to distress or impairment of functioning.

Most classification systems differentiate between those disorders that have a defined onset after a period of normality – often referred to as 'mental illness' within British psychiatry, or Axis I disorders in the case of *Diagnostic and Statistical Manual of Mental Disorders*, fourth edition (DSM-IV) (American Psychiatric Association, 1994) – and those that are persistent and can be identified as having arisen out of a developmental process – personality disorders and learning disability. The official classification systems, DSM-IV and ICD-10, differ slightly in their wording of the definition of personality disorder, but they and almost all other definitions include several key concepts, one of which is that the onset is usually in childhood or adolescence and the disorder is persistent over a long time into adulthood. This is the key feature in differentiating personality disorders from Axis I mental disorders.

The following are other features common to all definitions.

- There are enduring maladaptive and inflexible patterns of thinking (i.e. ways of perceiving and interpreting self, other people and events), feeling (i.e. the range, intensity, lability and appropriateness of emotional responses), behaving (e.g. impulse control) and relating to others. These differ from the way the average person in the same culture thinks, feels and acts.
- Several of these different areas of psychological functioning are abnormal.
- The disorder is pervasive. This means it is manifest across a broad range of personal and social situations.
- The disorder is associated with a substantial degree of personal distress and/or problems in occupational and social performance (De Girolamo and Reich, 1993).

IDENTIFYING PERSONALITY DISORDER IN CLINICAL PRACTICE

It is the associated distress and impairment in personal functioning that bring individuals with personality disorder to the attention of services. The task for a practitioner is then to recognize whether or not the distress and functional impairment are caused by a personality disorder.

Some of the presentations discussed below may raise the index of suspicion that an individual has a personality disorder, but the only way to be sure is to take a longitudinal approach. A one-off assessment is just a snapshot in time of a person's functioning. Without taking a thorough life history, it is impossible to determine whether the problems presenting at that time are tendencies to feel, think or behave in particular ways that have been present since adolescence and are manifest in many areas of the individual's life, or whether they have arisen as a result of a mental illness with a specified onset following a period of normal functioning.

Research has shown that most experienced clinicians make the diagnosis of personality disorder by taking a systematic history and listening to patients' narratives of their lives (Westen, 1997). Patients tell the story of their relationships with family, loved ones, friends, authorities and colleagues at home, at work, at leisure and at school. Clinicians look for recurring patterns of behaviour and interpersonal interactions from which they draw inferences about characteristic patterns of relating to others, behaviour patterns, coping mechanisms, belief patterns, hopes, fears and emotional responses (Perry, 1992; Westen, 1997).

It is also important to obtain information from as many different sources as possible, as an individual's current mental state may confound an assessment. For example, individuals who are severely depressed may re-interpret their whole history and feel they have always been this way, whereas close relatives will say that they used to be cheerful and function well. This additional information will also shed light on which areas of a patient's life are affected.

DESCRIBING PERSONALITY DISORDER IN CLINICAL PRACTICE

The psychiatric classification systems (ICD-10 and DSM-IV) divide personality disorders into various discrete categories (see Chapter 4). Trying to pigeonhole individuals into categories is useful for research purposes to ensure like is being compared with like. It may also provide a convenient shorthand for communicating in very broad terms the sorts of problems an individual is likely to have. However, the categories have been criticized for their lack of specificity, the fact that they overlap and because reliability between clinicians is very poor in identifying the individual categories (Perry, 1992; Livesley et al., 1994). In addition, providing personality disorder category labels does not provide the accurate information about the individual's actual difficulties and circumstances that is required to plan and prioritize interventions.

Everyone has to develop their own way of organizing the information they collect about personality disorders. Allnutt and Links (1996) have suggested that clinicians be aware of the factors that raise suspicion that there might be a personality disorder and then ask a few brief screening questions to establish whether the individual has any features suggestive of each type of personality disorder.

However, research has confirmed that clinicians do not find a checklist of direct questions about particular traits very useful in the clinical setting (Westen, 1997). For practical purposes, it has been suggested that it is more useful to undertake a functional assessment of personality. This is essentially a case formulation addressing the relevant areas of abnormal functioning (Gunn, 1993; Westen and Arkowitz-Westen, 1998). Gunn (1993) suggests listing the abnormal traits and the functional impairment or distress they cause under the headings 'thinking', 'feelings and emotions', 'behaviour', 'social functions' and 'insight'. The 'thinking' heading would include any beliefs people have about themselves (e.g. low self-esteem) and their beliefs about others (e.g. everyone is hostile and untrustworthy). The 'feelings and emotions' heading would include any abnormalities in the quality or intensity of emotions. Gunn (1993) argues that setting out a functional analysis in this way gives a clearer picture of the therapeutic task by separating out different problems, each of which can be tackled in its own right.

PERSONALITY DISORDER PRESENTING AS PSYCHOLOGICAL DISTRESS AND PSYCHIATRIC SYMPTOMS

Individuals with personality disorder may present with psychiatric symptoms similar to those of people with other mental disorders. These symptoms can be distressing and relate to their abnormal ways of thinking and feeling or to social difficulties. Examples of the symptoms sometimes complained of include low mood, anxiety, insomnia, irritability, labile mood, feelings of emptiness and episodes of sudden intense rage.

The level of personal distress experienced by a patient cannot be used to distinguish whether that patient is suffering from a personality disorder or an Axis I disorder, despite suggestions that personality disorders may be less likely to present as a result of personal distress (Paris, 1996). Many individuals with personality disorder experience considerable distress as a result of their disorder, and not all patients with Axis I disorders experience distress (for example, the early stages of hypomania may be experienced as very pleasant by a patient).

PERSONALITY DISORDER PRESENTING WITH CO-MORBID AXIS I PSYCHIATRIC DISORDERS

Sometimes, presenting psychiatric symptoms may be due to a co-occurring Axis I psychiatric

disorder. A large proportion of individuals with personality disorder present with Axis I disorders as their primary problem (Casey and Tyrer, 1990). Individuals with personality disorder are at greater risk of developing affective disorders, anxiety disorders, eating disorders, and substance misuse disorders (de Girolamo and Reich, 1993; Gunderson and Sabo, 1993; Links, 1996). It has also been suggested that patients with borderline personality disorder are particularly vulnerable to developing post-traumatic stress disorders in response to what for others would be sub-threshold stressors (Gunderson and Sabo, 1993). Less has been written about the co-occurrence of psychosis and personality disorder, but this is of particular relevance in forensic psychiatry in which a proportion of patients have a history of anti-social personality traits pre-dating the onset of their schizophrenic illness. (This is dealt with in more detail in Chapter 14.)

It is important to explore whether the distress or functional impairment experienced by an individual with personality disorder is being exacerbated by a superimposed Axis I disorder. Successful treatment of the Axis I disorder might improve the patient's functioning and quality of life.

Conversely, recognizing an underlying personality disorder has important implications for the management of Axis I disorders: having a personality disorder increases the severity of the symptoms; worsens the prognosis of treatment, especially of depression, anxiety disorder and obsessive–compulsive disorders; increases the likelihood of episodes of incomplete treatment; and is associated with longer and costlier treatments (Reich and Green, 1991; Tyrer et al., 1990).

Finally, it has been suggested that occasionally individuals with antisocial personality disorder may present with feigned mental symptoms in order to avoid the consequences of their law breaking by obtaining patient status rather than law-breaker status (Turkat, 1990). One must, however, be extremely cautious about labelling someone as feigning, as it is possible to be genuinely distressed as well as to have difficulties accepting responsibility for one's own behaviour. In addition, if individuals repeatedly feign psychological symptoms, this itself may be a manifestation of an abnormal personality (Mullen, 1993).

PERSONALITY DISORDER PRESENTING AS PROBLEM BEHAVIOUR

Maladaptive and abnormal behaviours frequently bring individuals with personality disorders, especially Cluster B disorders, to the attention of professionals. These behaviours may or may not cause distress to the individual, but always lead to impairment of social and interpersonal functioning and may make others suffer.

Individuals with personality disorder tend to find maladaptive ways of reducing their psychological distress and bolstering their fragile self-esteem, for example with illicit or prescribed drugs, alcohol, self-harm or impulsive behaviours, including sexual promiscuity, binge eating, impulsive spending and reckless driving. Individuals may present as a result of any of the adverse consequences of these behaviours.

Self-harm is of particular concern, as it is often repeated and is associated with a higher risk of completed suicide. Patients with antisocial personality disorder have a much higher accidental and violent death and suicide rate than patients with other disorders (Martin et al., 1985). Patients with borderline personality disorder have been found to have a 3–9 per cent suicide rate on 15–20-year follow-up, which increased to 19 per cent if they were also alcohol dependent, and to 38 per cent if they were alcohol dependent and suffering from major affective disorder (Stone, 1993; de Girolamo and Reich, 1993).

The most common behaviours associated with personality disorder that present to services involved in the criminal justice system are criminal and antisocial behaviours. These may take the form of sexual or physical violence and aggression or repeated offences of other natures. Some definitions of antisocial personality disorder have been criticized for placing too great an emphasis on antisocial behaviour without including other abnormal traits. However, antisocial personality disorder is not synonymous with criminality: not all criminals have a personality disorder. It is not only antisocial personality disorder that is associated with antisocial behaviour. Many people with antisocial personality disorder also have features of other personality disorders, and individuals with other personality disorders but not antisocial personality disorder may engage in criminal behaviour. This is borne out by studies of populations of offenders in prison and special hospitals (Coid, 1992; Singleton et al., 1998).

Although maladaptive and problem behaviours may be one of the more common presentations of personality disorder, they are not diagnostic, and other mental disorders may present with problem behaviour. Taking a snapshot view and assuming that a patient presenting with a behaviour problem automatically has a personality disorder can lead to misdiagnosis. For some patients with Axis I disorders such as schizophrenia, schizoaffective disorder and bipolar disorder, symptoms such as behavioural disturbance, aggression and uncooperativeness may be associated with relapse of their illness. It is only by taking a longitudinal approach, and discovering that patients have episodes of normal behaviour when well, that misdiagnosis can be avoided.

PERSONALITY DISORDER PRESENTING WITH PHYSICAL SYMPTOMS AND DISORDERS

Individuals with personality disorder have high rates of physical morbidity as well as of psychiatric morbidity, which have significant public health implications (Norton, 1992). This is because many dysfunctional behaviours may have adverse physical as well as psychological and social consequences. Substance misuse places individuals at risk of the physical consequences of acute intoxication, withdrawal, chronic use and the complications of injecting. Addictive behaviour may also place them at risk from tobacco-related illnesses. Sexual disinhibition may increase the risk of sexually transmitted disease. Self-harm and suicidal behaviour may have physical consequences. Individuals with personality disorder may present with head or other injuries due to accidents and violence. In addition, somatization disorder, characterized by multiple and recurrent physical complaints for which medical attention is sought and that are not due to any apparent physical cause, has been linked with personality disorder in women (Emerson et al., 1994; see Dowson, 1995a, for overview).

PERSONALITY DISORDER PRESENTING WITH SUFFERING OF OTHERS AND DYSFUNCTION IN INTERPERSONAL RELATIONSHIPS

Some of the most prominent features of personality disorder are profound interpersonal difficulties manifest in intimate, family, social and occupational relationships that cause the individual and those around him or her to suffer. Individuals with personality disorder may present in a number of ways as a result of these difficulties, for example, in crisis following the break-up of a relationship, contemplating suicide and self-harm or drinking heavily; causing concern by showing morbid jealousy or harassing a former partner; having relationship difficulties resulting from violent behaviour; suspected of child abuse or neglect; or in crisis having lost their accommodation or their job.

Individuals with antisocial personality disorder are more likely to be divorced,

unemployed and engage in spouse or child abuse than the general population, and antisocial personality disorder is especially prevalent among the unemployed, homeless, wife batterers and child abusers. Antisocial personality disorder in parents is associated with psychiatric disorders in their children, which may be mediated, at least in part, by poor parenting (see Dowson, 1995a, and Moran, 1999, for overviews).

Individuals with personality disorder may present seeking help for themselves or under pressure from someone else. It is often useful to reflect on why an individual is presenting at a particular time and who suggested they seek help or brought them to the attention of services. This may provide a clue as to the areas of the individual's life that may be affected and to who else might be suffering.

WHERE PERSONALITY DISORDERS PRESENT

Personality disorders may result in a great deal of distress and behaviour that inevitably causes others to intervene (Dolan and Coid, 1993). This means that the sufferers present to a wide range of agencies in a wide range of settings.

PERSONALITY DISORDER PRESENTING TO HEALTH SERVICES

About one in ten of the general population are thought to have a personality disorder (de Girolamo and Reich, 1993). In primary care settings, Casey and Tyrer (1990) found that about a third of people attending general practitioners (GPs) had a personality disorder, even though for the vast majority it was not assessed by the GPs as the primary reason for presenting. Many of these patients had other co-morbid primary diagnoses such as anxiety, depression and alcohol misuse. Cluster C personality disorders are the commonest personality disorders encountered in primary care attenders (Moran et al., 2000). Patients with personality disorder are more likely to be frequent GP attenders (Moran et al., 2001), and may present to accident and emergency departments or to general medical and surgical specialties with the physical and psychiatric symptoms described above.

Studies have confirmed that individuals with personality disorder are frequent users of in-patient, out-patient and emergency psychiatric services (Reich et al., 1989; Menzies et al., 1993; Saarento et al., 1997; Williams et al., 1998) and those with co-morbid Axis I disorders are amongst the heaviest users (Kent et al., 1995). It has been reported that, in England and Wales in 1985, only 7.6 per cent of psychiatric admissions had a personality disorder diagnosis (Department of Health and Social Security, 1985). However, these figures only included those patients for whom personality disorder was the only and main diagnosis. Studies using research diagnostic instruments have found that 20–40 per cent of psychiatric out-patients and about half of psychiatric in-patients fulfil the diagnostic criteria for a personality disorder, often in addition to other Axis I disorders (see de Girolamo and Dotto, 2000, Dowson, 1995b, and Moran, 1999, for overviews).

PERSONALITY DISORDERS PRESENTING TO CRIMINAL JUSTICE AGENCIES

Individuals with personality disorder do not present exclusively to medical services; those engaging in antisocial behaviour frequently present to the criminal justice system. Spence and McPhillips (1995) found that individuals with personality disorder accounted for the largest numbers of assessment of patients detained by police under Section 136 of the Mental Health Act 1983 in an area of London.

A survey of psychiatric morbidity in prisons estimated that 78 per cent of male remand prisoners, 64 per cent of male sentenced prisoners and 50 per cent of female prisoners had a personality disorder (Singleton et al., 1998). Coid (1992) found that 98 per cent of prisoners on special units for the management of dangerous and disruptive prisoners had a personality disorder. It is likely that individuals with personality disorder are over-represented amongst those prisoners presenting management problems, who often spend long periods in segregation or are moved frequently around the system because of the disruption they cause (Gunn et al., 1991).

In practice, it is apparent that a number of individuals with personality disorder are being managed by the probation service, which may be providing interventions for certain aspects of their disordered behaviour. For example, Dolan et al. (1995) found that 67 per cent of offenders attending an intensive probation programme that aimed to divert offenders from custody, reduce offending and facilitate change in psychological functioning and problems associated with offending behaviour fulfilled the diagnostic criteria for a personality disorder.

PERSONALITY DISORDER PRESENTING TO OTHER STATUTORY AND VOLUNTARY AGENCIES

In addition, individuals with personality disorder may present to a range of other agencies as a result of their social dysfunction. This includes agencies involved in child care, housing, employment, family law and debt collection. Those with paranoid personality disorder may present in the courts, litigating against their neighbours and others.

HOW PERSONALITY DISORDERS PRESENT AT INTERVIEW

Observation of patients' interactions and behaviours at interview can reveal much about the patients, their experiences and habitual ways of interacting and how these lead them into difficulties. Individuals may relate to professionals in the same problematic way that they relate to others, which Westen (1997) found to be useful diagnostically to experienced clinicians. Patients with personality disorder often invite rejection and punitive reactions from others. Clinicians may feel they are being coerced or manipulated by patients who present as helpless and wanting the clinician to take control. The patients then frustrate the clinicians' attempt to do so, leaving the latter feeling angry, frustrated and helpless. Patients may appear ambivalent about treatment or present in crisis in a chaotic, unplanned way. Those with personality disorder may also provoke different reactions in different professionals, causing disagreements amongst them (referred to as splitting). Monitoring one's own reaction can thus alert one to the possibility that an individual who is presenting has a personality disorder.

Dowson (1995c) described in more detail the different ways that individuals with particular types of personality disorder may interact with clinicians. He suggested that patients with paranoid personality disorder may be guarded and suspicious and have concerns about confidentiality. Patients with borderline personality disorder often demand urgent help in a crisis and may present inconsistently and react catastrophically to changes in arrangements. Histrionic traits may be suspected if patients show dramatic mood variations during the interview and draw attention to themselves in the way they dress or behave. Individuals with narcissistic traits may appear to be trying to impress the clinician, and may be difficult to interview because of their condescending manner, demands for special treatment and questioning of the ability of the professional. Patients with obsessive–compulsive personality traits may be difficult to interview because their rigidity and attention to detail may make it difficult for them to get to the point, thus frustrating and irritating

the clinician. Those with dependent traits may illicit impatience and irritation as an emotional response to their passive helplessness or, conversely, may induce some to provide extra help and become overly involved.

Whilst monitoring and reflecting on these reactions to patients is extremely useful in alerting one to the possibility of personality disorder, it is important to remember that not all patients who elicit negative reactions in clinicians have a personality disorder, and that not all patients with a personality disorder elicit negative reactions. As discussed earlier, a diagnosis of personality disorder can only be made when a longitudinal approach to the individual's life reveals that the way he or she is interacting in the clinical situation is part of a longstanding pattern that has been manifest for many years in a wide range of situations and relationships. Observing the patient longitudinally over time and in a number of settings is also particularly helpful. Jumping to conclusions on the basis of a one-off snapshot leads to misdiagnosis. Patients with mania or schizophrenia who are uncooperative and manifest behavioural disturbance as part of their illness are sometimes mislabelled as having a personality disorder and are rejected from services.

CONCLUSIONS

Individuals with personality disorder present in a range of ways to a range of agencies. They usually present as a result of personal distress, physical disorders, problematic behaviour, dysfunction in social, family, intimate and occupational relationships and/or as a result of the suffering of others. Personality disorders often present in association with co-morbid Axis I psychiatric disorders. Diagnosis is made on the basis of a longitudinal assessment of the presenting problems and the individual's life history. The correct identification and assessment of personality disorder have important implications for service planning and individual case management. Lack of adequate knowledge about effective interventions and lack of adequate services are not valid reasons for failing to diagnose personality disorder.

REFERENCES

Allnutt S and Links P (1996). Diagnosing specific personality disorders and the optimal criteria. In: Links P (ed.), *Clinical Assessment and Management of Severe Personality Disorder.* Washington DC: American Psychiatric Press, 21–47.

American Psychiatric Association (1994). *Diagnostic and Statistical Manual of Mental Disorders,* fourth edition. Washington DC: American Psychiatric Association.

Casey P and Tyrer P (1990). Personality disorder and psychiatric illness in general practice. *British Journal of Psychiatry* **156**:261–5.

Coid J (1992). DSM-III diagnosis in criminal psychopaths: a way forward. *Criminal Behaviour and Mental Health* **2**:78–94.

De Girolamo G and Dotto P (2000). Epidemiology of personality disorders. In: Gelder MG, Lopez-Ibor JJ and Andreasen NC (eds), *New Oxford Textbook of Psychiatry*, Vol. 1. New York: Oxford University Press, 959–64.

De Girolamo G and Reich JH (1993). *Epidemiology of Mental Disorders and Psychosocial Problems: Personality Disorders.* Geneva: World Health Organization.

Department of Health and Social Security (1985). *Mental Illness in Hospitals and Units in England. Results from the Mental Health Inquiry Statistical Bulletin. Government Statistical Service.* London: HMSO.

Dolan B and Coid J (1993). *Psychopathic and Antisocial Personality Disorders. Treatment and Research Issues.* London: Gaskell.

Dolan B, Evans C and Norton K (1995). Multiple Axis II diagnoses of personality disorder. *British Journal of Psychiatry* **166**:107–12.

Dowson JH (1995a). Personality disorders: less specific presentations and epidemiology. In: Dowson JH and Grounds AT (eds), *Personality Disorders, Recognition and Clinical Management.* Cambridge: Cambridge University Press, 128–58.

Dowson JH (1995b). Personality disorders: basic concepts and clinical overview. In: Dowson JH and Grounds AT (eds), *Personality Disorders, Recognition and Clinical Management.* Cambridge: Cambridge University Press, 1–42.

Dowson JH (1995c). Assessment of personality disorders. In: Dowson JH and Grounds AT (eds), *Personality Disorders, Recognition and Clinical Management.* Cambridge: Cambridge University Press, 195–230.

Emerson J, Pankrantz L, Joos S and Smith S (1994). Personality disorders in problematic medical patients. *Psychosomatics* **35**:469–73.

Gunderson JG and Sabo AN (1993). The phenomenological and conceptual interface between borderline personality disorder and PTSD. *American Journal of Psychiatry* **150**:19–27.

Gunn J (1993). Personality disorders. In: Gunn J and Taylor PJ (eds), *Forensic Psychiatry: Clinical, Legal and Ethical Issues.* London: Butterworth Heinemann, 373–406.

Gunn J, Maden T and Swinton M (1991). *Mentally Disordered Prisoners.* London: Home Office.

Kent S, Fogarty M and Yellowlees P (1995). Heavy utilisation of inpatient and outpatient services in a public mental health service. *Psychiatric Services* **46**:1254–7.

Lewis G and Appleby L (1988). Personality disorder: the patients psychiatrists dislike. *British Journal of Psychiatry* **153**:44–9.

Links P (1996). Comprehending co-morbidity: a symptom disorder plus a personality disorder. In: Links P (ed.), *Clinical Assessment and Management of Severe Personality Disorder.* Washington DC: American Psychiatric Press, 93–108.

Livesley WJ, Schroeder ML, Jackson DN and Lang KL (1994). Categorical distinctions in the study of personality disorder: implications for classification. *Journal of Abnormal Psychology* **103**:6–17.

Martin RL, Cloninger CR, Guze SB et al. (1985). Mortality in a follow-up of 500 psychiatric outpatients. Part II. Cause-specific mortality. *Archives of General Psychiatry* **42**:58–66.

Menzies D, Dolan B and Norton K (1993). Are short-term savings worth long-term costs? Funding treatment for personality disorders. *Psychiatric Bulletin* **17**:517–19.

Moran P (1999). *Antisocial Personality Disorder: an Epidemiological Perspective.* London: Gaskell.

Moran P, Jenkins R, Tylee A et al. (2000). The prevalence of personality disorder among UK primary care attenders. *Acta Psychiatrica Scandinavica* **102**:52–7.

Moran P, Rendu A, Jenkins R et al. (2001). The impact of personality disorder in UK primary care: a 1-year follow-up of attenders. *Psychological Medicine* **31**:1447–54.

Mullen P (1993). Deception, self-deception and dissociation. In: Gunn J and Taylor PJ (eds), *Forensic Psychiatry: Clinical, Legal and Ethical Issues.* London: Butterworth Heinemann, 407–34.

Norton K (1992). The Health of the Nation: the impact of personality disorder on key areas. *Postgraduate Medical Journal* **68**:350–4.

Paris J (1996). *Social Factors in the Personality Disorders. A Biopsychosocial Approach to Etiology and Treatment.* Cambridge: Cambridge University Press.

Perry JC (1992). Problems and considerations in the valid assessment of personality disorders. *American Journal of Psychiatry* **149**:1645–53.

Reich J, Boerstler H, Yates W and Nduaguba M (1989). Utilization of medical resources in persons with DSM-III personality disorders in a community sample. *International Journal of Psychiatry in Medicine* **19**:1–9.

Reich J and Green AI (1991). Effect of personality disorders on outcome of treatment. *Journal of Mental and Nervous Diseases* **179**:74–82.

Saarento O, Niementen P, Hakko H et al. (1997). Utilization of psychiatric in-patient care among new patients in a comprehensive community-care system. *Acta Psychiatrica Scandinavica* **95**:132–9.

Singleton N, Meltzer H and Gatward R (1998). *Office of National Statistics Survey of Psychiatric Morbidity Among Prisoners in England and Wales.* London: The Stationery Office.

Spence SA and McPhillips MA (1995). Personality disorder and police Section 136 in Westminster: a retrospective analysis of 65 assessments over six months. *Medicine, Science and the Law* **35**:48–52.

Stone MH (1993). Long-term outcome in personality disorders. *British Journal of Psychiatry* **162**:299–313.

Turkat ID (1990). *The Personality Disorders. A Psychological Approach to Clinical Management.* New York: Pergamon Press.

Tyrer P, Seivewright N, Ferguson B et al. (1990). The Nottingham Study of Neurotic Disorder: relationship between personality status and symptoms. *Psychological Medicine* **20**:423–31.

Westen D (1997). Divergences between clinical and research methods for assessing personality disorders: implications for research and the evolution of Axis II. *American Journal of Psychiatry* **154**:895–903.

Westen D and Arkowitz-Westen L (1998). Limitations of Axis II in diagnosing personality pathology in clinical practice. *American Journal of Psychiatry* **155**:1767–71.

Williams W, Weiss TW, Edens A, Johnson M and Thornby JI (1998). Hospital utilization and personality characteristics of veterans with psychiatric problems. *Psychiatric Services* **49**:370–5.

World Health Organization (1992). The ICD-10 classification of Mental and Behavioural disorders. Clinical Descriptions and Diagnostic Guidelines. Geneva: World Health Organization.

Chapter 2

DIAGNOSTIC CATEGORIES OF PERSONALITY DISORDER

Peter Tyrer

INTRODUCTION

Ever since modern medicine began at the dawn of the nineteenth century, it has been realized that medicine cannot progress unless it has clear definitions of the conditions that it purports to treat. Classification in psychiatry has lagged behind that in medicine and related disciplines and to some extent has been scorned because of its failures in this regard. This is unfair because psychiatric disorders are extremely difficult to classify and we do not have the advantages of our medical colleagues in being able to draw on a great deal of additional independent information that enables our classifications to be validated. Nevertheless, psychiatrists have been slow to accept the principles of formal diagnosis and classification and have been all too ready to dismiss these notions as relics of some out-dated 'medical model' of psychiatry that should have no place in a humane and understanding mental health care system. This view fails to take account of the importance of classifying all conditions for purposes of efficiency and communication. If every problem we come across in practice is unique, we have to spend a very long time communicating our accounts of each person to others and spend an even longer time treating them as we go through the process of trial and error in testing all known

remedies. Labelling patients is not necessarily dehumanizing; it can be a great aid to selecting treatment, predicting prognosis and maintaining proper care across a variety of settings.

Although many of these comments may be self-evident, they are worth repeating because, in the context of personality disorder, the criticisms of classification in general are often more pronounced. Because all personalities are unique, any form of classification will fail to do justice to their tremendous variety, but to abandon the task of sorting them out into some reasonable order merely leads to anarchy. What follows in this account is like the first response to the teacher's whistle in the school playground: the children have been called to order, but are still largely engaged in their own activities. The external observer only sees a semblance of order developing and is not particularly impressed; the same can be true about the present classification and diagnosis of personality disorder. However, when one considers that 40 years ago the classification of these conditions was almost totally ignored, one realizes how much progress we have made in a relatively short time.

Throughout this chapter, the principles of a good classification system are addressed: a valid and reliable measure that commands broad agreement, a system that is clinically useful and that, ideally, cleanly divides each disorder so that there is no overlap between them.

CLASSIFICATION SYSTEMS

DICHOTOMOUS VERSUS CATEGORICAL CLASSIFICATION

Although doctors and decision makers in all fields of medicine prefer categorical classifications to dimensional ones, there is increasing evidence from research studies in personality disorder that the dimensional system of classifying personality disorder is more valid and reliable (Livesley et al., 1994; Clark et al., 1995). The major problem appears to be with the specific personality disorder diagnoses rather than with the broad concept of personality disorder as a whole. Thus the *International Classification of Diseases*, 10th edition (ICD-10; World Health Organization, 1992) and the *Diagnostic and Statistical Manual of Mental Disorders*, 4th edition (DSM-IV, American Psychiatric Association, 1994) definition of personality disorder as 'deviations of personal characteristics and behaviour patterns from the norm', manifest mainly as dysfunctional behaviour that is 'pervasive' and that leads to distress or impairment in social, occupational and personal function, is more reliably rated than any of the individual personality disorders (Bronisch, 1992; Bronisch and Mombour, 1994). The inadequacy of the specificity of the individual personality disorders is demonstrated by the degree of overlap between them, particularly for disorders within the flamboyant personality cluster (Pfohl et al., 1986; Fyer et al., 1988; Flick et al., 1993). This overlap is often inflated with the description of 'co-morbidity', implying that two or more separate disorders exist in the same person, when it is more likely that the person has one disorder that is inadequately defined.

Nevertheless, the fact remains that categorical diagnosis is still the preferred option for clinicians and, in the field of forensic psychiatry in particular, this is often imperative since the presence of a specific defined disorder has been the cornerstone of treatment and detention decisions ever since the introduction of the Lunacy Act of 1890. The diagnostic importance of personality disorder became even more important with the introduction of 'psychopathy' as a reason for special management of mental disorder (Dolan and Coid, 1993). It is therefore unfortunate that the criteria for making these diagnostic decisions were, until so recently, so poorly defined that the diagnosis of personality disorder was influenced more by subjective judgement than by any independent assessment.

The first section of this chapter describes the main principles underlying the diagnosis of personality disorder; this is followed by a description of categories of personality disorder and their assessment, in which special attention is paid to those disorders that are common in forensic psychiatric practice; and the last section discusses the dimensional assessment of severity of personality disorder.

GENERAL PRINCIPLES OF DIAGNOSIS AND ASSESSMENT

A good diagnosis is one that should be relatively easy to obtain, preferably in the course of a clinical interview. Increasingly, formal means of obtaining diagnoses in all parts of psychiatry are being recommended, usually in the form of structured or semi-structured interviews, but it is important to realize that these only consist of good comprehensive clinical interviews together with a formal scoring system. There are several important differences between the assessment of personality disorder and that of mental state disorders (Table 2.1).

In the case of personality disorder, the assessor is not primarily interested in recording symptoms and clinical features in a standardized way, as is the case with most mental disorders, but in assessing maladaptive behaviour and its effects on the subject and others,

Table 2.1 Differences in the assessment of mental state and personality disorders

Mental state disorders	Personality disorders
Temporary (usually)	Permanent (or at least longstanding)
Reactive	Generative
Dominated more by symptoms than behaviour	Dominated mainly by behaviour and relationships with others
Diagnosed mainly on present state	Diagnosed on basis of long-term function
May develop into other mental state disorders	Tends to remain 'stable'

attitudes and relationships with other people, and social functioning in all its areas (at work, at home, with family and friends, and with society in general). The second important difference is that in assessing personality disorder the present state is not necessarily important; the normal functioning of the subject over a much longer time scale (ideally since adolescence) is being determined.

These differences immediately give rise to problems that make it more difficult to diagnose personality disorder than mental state disorders. The reliability and validity of assessment are clearly more difficult when a hypothetical norm is being determined instead of present state, and the important elements of observation of the subject and the phenomenology of the mental state are denied to the clinician assessing personality disorder. The reliability problems are accentuated by the tendency for those with some forms of personality disorder, particularly in the flamboyant group, to exaggerate, minimize or deny aspects of their personality.

Because of these problems, there are arguments for using much more than an interview with the patient in order to make a diagnosis of personality disorder. This may be true, but unfortunately there is no good way of deciding which source of information is more reliable

when different sources disagree. Informants are often considered on theoretical grounds to be more accurate assessors than subjects, but unfortunately there is no fundamental evidence that they are more valid assessors (Zimmerman et al., 1988). However, in comparisons of types of informant, there are important differences, and women, particularly if they are closely involved with the subject and spend much time with him or her, are generally superior to other sources (Brothwell et al., 1992; Pilgrim et al., 1993).

Most of the instruments used for assessing personality disorder are subject based and, bearing in mind that the assessment covers a long period, it is understandable that subjects are generally preferred by investigators. There remains a worry that in the most severe cases of personality disorder the subject is inherently inaccurate or deliberately deceitful in an interview situation, and that other forms of data are needed to corroborate the information obtained. Such information should always be examined if a comprehensive assessment of personality is to be made.

CATEGORICAL DIAGNOSIS OF PERSONALITY DISORDER

The current categorical diagnoses of personality disorder are shown in Table 2.2. Although these are well known to most clinicians, in the current language of medical science they have little evidence base. They illustrate the best and the worst of current classification procedures. Because they are created through consensus by a democratic process (best summarized by the statement, 'a camel is a horse created by a committee'), they command broad acceptance and are used internationally, but the process also means that contradictory elements are commonplace and there is no overall integration of the classification.

The personality disorders are generally less well described in the classification than any other group of disorders (Sartorius et al.,

Table 2.2 Current categorical classification of personality disorder

	ICD-10 (World Health Organization, 1992)	DSM-IV (American Psychiatric Association, 1994)	
Code			**Code**
F 60.0	Paranoid – excessive sensitivity, suspiciousness, preoccupation with conspiratorial explanation of events, persistent tendency to self-reference	Paranoid – interpretation of people's actions as deliberately demeaning or threatening	301.0
F 60.1	Schizoid – emotional coldness, detachment, lack of interest in other people, eccentricity and introspective fantasy	Schizoid – indifference to social relationships and restricted range of emotional experience and expression	301.20
	No equivalent	Schizotypal – deficit in interpersonal relatedness with peculiarities of ideation, odd beliefs and thinking, unusual appearance and behaviour	301.22
F 60.5	Anankastic – indecisiveness, doubt, excessive caution, pedantry, rigidity and need to plan in immaculate detail	Obsessive–compulsive – preoccupation with orderliness, perfectionism and inflexibility that leads to inefficiency	301.4
F 60.4	Histrionic – self-dramatization, shallow mood, egocentricity and craving for excitement with persistent manipulative behaviour	Histrionic – excessive emotionality and attention-seeking, suggestibility, and superficiality	301.50
F 60.7	Dependent – failure to take responsibility for actions, with subordination of personal needs to those of others, excessive dependence with need for constant reassurance and feelings of helplessness when a close relationship ends	Dependent – persistent dependent and submissive behaviour	301.60
F 60.2	Dyssocial – callous unconcern for others, with irresponsibility, irritability and aggression, and incapacity to maintain enduring relationships	Antisocial – pervasive pattern of disregard for and violation of the rights of others occurring since the age of 15	301.7
	No equivalent	Narcissistic – pervasive grandiosity, lack of empathy, arrogance, and requirement for excessive admiration	301.81
F 60.6	Anxious – persistent tension, self-consciousness, exaggeration of risks and dangers, hypersensitivity to	Avoidant – pervasive social discomfort, fear of negative evaluation, and timidity, with feelings of inadequacy in social	301.82

(*Continued*)

Table 2.2 (*Continued*)

	ICD-10 (World Health Organization, 1992)	DSM-IV (American Psychiatric Association, 1994)	
	rejection, and restricted lifestyle because of insecurity	situations	
F 60.3	Impulsive – inability to control anger, to plan ahead, or to think before acts, with unpredictable mood and quarrelsome behaviour Borderline – impulsivity with uncertainty over self-image, liability to become involved in intense and unstable relationships, and recurrent threats of self-harm	Borderline – pervasive instability of mood, interpersonal relationships and self-image associated with marked impulsivity, fear of abandonment, identity disturbance and recurrent suicidal behaviour	301.83

1993). This is largely because, although each disorder has face validity when considered separately, the degree of overlap between them is so great that there is little value in each diagnosis individually. This phenomenon is reified in the literature by the word 'co-morbidity', which is a respectable term to describe the presence of two or more co-existing diseases (Feinstein, 1970). In the case of personality disorders, co-morbidity is more often consanguinity: the same basic disorder described in different forms and by different titles (Tyrer, 1992, 1996).

The research evidence is different. Personality disorders, and personality variation in normal subjects, naturally fall into three or four major groups: a risk-taking, irresponsible group with a tendency to behaviour which, in colloquial terms, is 'over the top'; a converse group which is withdrawn and avoids social contact; a third group which is timid, fearful and lacking in confidence; and the last (sometimes incorporated into the previous group) which is abnormally rigid and fastidious in its dealings with the world (Walton and Presly, 1973; Tyrer and Alexander, 1979; Cloninger, 1987). These groupings have now been formalized into a three-cluster system in the DSM classification: Cluster A, consisting of the 'odd' or 'eccentric' cluster

(comprising schizoid, schizotypal and paranoid personality disorders); Cluster B, consisting of the flamboyant or dramatic group (antisocial, borderline, impulsive, narcissistic, and histrionic personality disorders); and Cluster C, comprising anxious or avoidant, anankastic or obsessive–compulsive, and dependent personality disorders (Reich and Thompson, 1987). However, some put the anankastic group into a separate Cluster D (Tyrer and Alexander, 1979).

There have also been arguments in favour of abandoning all forms of categorization of personality disorder in favour of a global concept of persistent abnormality in social functioning and impaired relationships (Rutter, 1987). This has led to the development of an interview schedule that records all personality in terms of social function, the Adult Personality Functioning Assessment (APFA) Interview (Hill et al., 1989). Although this approach has its merits, the notion of equating all personality variation within a common framework is not generally popular and, in the field of forensic psychiatry in particular, it would seem unhelpful to equate the kinds of personality disturbance seen in institutions such as Broadmoor Hospital with the very different personality disturbance of conditions such as the typical anankastic personality disorder.

Table 2.3 Commonly used instruments for diagnosing categorical personality disorders

Main purpose	Questionnaires	Interview schedules	Comments
Identification of personality disorders in general	• Millon Clinical Multiaxial Inventory-III (MCMI-III) • Personality Disorder Questionnaire-IV (PDQ-IV)	• International Personality Disorder Examination (IPDE) • Personality Assessment Schedule (PAS) • Diagnostic Interview for DSM-IV Personality Disorders (DIPD-IV) • Structured Clinical Interview for DSM-IV Axis II Personality Disorders (SCID-II) • Structured Interview for DSM-IV Personality (SIDP)	The Standardised Assessment of Personality (SAP) may also be used in cases where patients either refuse assessment or are unreliable; this uses informants only
Identification of antisocial (and psychopathic) personality disorders	Psychopathy Checklist – Revised (HPCL-R)	Criminal Profile Scale	Specific instruments for forensic populations

FORMAL ASSESSMENTS OF CATEGORICAL PERSONALITY DISORDER

There is an increasing number of instruments for recording the presence or absence of personality disorders (Table 2.3). These are particularly focused on the DSM personality disorders and so their success is largely dependent on the validity of this classification. Questionnaires are always more convenient than other measures in the assessment of personality, but their value is limited by the tendency for those with severe personality disorder to answer dishonestly.

The Personality Diagnostic Questionnaire (PDQ), an instrument that has followed the four revisions of DSM (Hyler and Reider, 1984; Hyler et al., 1988; Hyler, 1994), is frequently used because of its convenience in administration. The latest version (PDQ-IV) asks subjects to rate their personality in 85 questions with a time frame of several years. A total score of 50 or more suggests personality disorder, but no more, as there is evidence that the instrument is too free in its attribution of personality disorder and may be assisted by an informant version (Dowson, 1992). In many studies, the PDQ is used as a screening instrument.

Structured interview schedules are now the instruments of choice in assessing personality disorder, mainly because their reliability and differing types of validity are superior to those of questionnaires. In recognizing this, it is also important to note that the level of agreement between the diagnosis of personality disorder made by both interviews and self-report is remarkably poor, with overall agreement being little better than chance (Perry, 1992). Although agreement between interview schedules is a little better than self-report/interview comparisons, it seldom reaches the modest level of 0.50 agreement, illustrating that although these interviews achieve better internal reliability, their failure to generalize indicates fundamental problems.

There are more than ten personality interview schedules in current use and more are being developed every year. The earliest is the Personality Assessment Schedule (PAS) developed in 1976 and first published in 1979 (Tyrer and Alexander, 1979; Tyrer et al., 1979). This identifies the personality traits that create the most severe social dysfunction when present to excessive degree. The computer-driven diagnosis derived from the scores is similar, but not identical to, the DSM-III and ICD-10 personality disorders and includes other subgroups of personality disorder such as dysthymic and hypochondriacal personality disorder (Tyrer et al., 2000). The Adult Personality Functioning Assessment (APFA) (Hill et al., 1989) and a modified form of the PAS with additional questions (M-PAS) (Piven et al., 1994), have focused specifically on social dysfunction as the key consequence of personality disorder and these are only suitable for assessments in dimensional form.

The other instruments have all pinned their hopes on the definition of personality disorder through the identification of prototypical behaviours that can be fashioned into operational criteria (Blashfield et al., 1985) in the same way that the Research Diagnostic Criteria identified the core features of depressive illness and began the reform of psychiatric classification with the introduction of DSM-III. Five schedules currently compete for priority in assessing DSM personality disorders: the International Personality Disorder Examination (IPDE), the Structured Interview for DSM-IV Personality (SIDP-IV), the Diagnostic Interview for DSM-IV Personality Disorders (DIPD-IV), the Wisconsin Personality Disorders Interview (WISPI) (Klein et al., 1993) and the Structured Clinical Interview for DSM-IV Axis II Personality Disorders (SCID-II).

The IPDE (Loranger et al., 1987, 1994) is a semi-structured clinical interview available in two versions: a DSM-IV module and an ICD-10 module. It scores each question on a three-point scale (absent, exaggerated or pathological)

and can therefore be used for dimensional scoring (although the range is somewhat restricted). The SIDP-IV (available in three versions; Pfohl et al., 1995) also allows both categorical and dimension assessments of DSM-IV and ICD-10 personality disorders and enables better dimensional assessments to be made.

The DIPD-IV is a semi-structured clinical interview designed to assess DSM-IV personality disorders (Zanarini et al., 1994). The SCID-II (First et al., 1995) is a development of Structured Clinical Interview for DSM-III, which was developed first with mental state diagnoses before being adapted for personality disorders (Spitzer et al., 1987). The schedule is available in screening and full versions and, as the screening version has cut-off points, the schedule may only take 20 minutes to complete.

The Diagnostic Interview for Borderlines (DIB) (Gunderson et al.,1981) and other similar measures for borderline patients or those with specific personality disorders are now much less often used. This is mainly because of the large degree of overlap between different personality disorders, which is most marked for borderline conditions (Fyer et al., 1988). Finally, as Dowson and Grounds (1995) have emphasized, when patients do not agree to being interviewed with one of these instruments, which can take between 30 and 180 minutes to administer, other methods will have to be used. One of the most frequently used of these is the Standardised Assessment of Personality (SAP) (Mann et al., 1981), which assesses ICD personality disorders (disorder, abnormal personality or no abnormal personality) using informants. Evidence from the comparison of informant data suggests that close informants (e.g. spouses and cohabitees) are judged to be better assessors of personality than more distant informants, and that women are generally superior to men in the validity of their assessments (Brothwell et al., 1992; Pilgrim et al., 1993). A very short, simple, self-rated screen derived from the Standardised

Assessment of Personality (SAPAS) (Moran et al., 2003) has also just been introduced.

Developments in the assessment of personality include the assessment of personality entirely from documentary evidence (e.g. written notes, reports, inquiries). Although at first sight this information might be deemed to be inadequate, it does have the advantage of being contemporaneous and informant derived, and also gives descriptions of behaviour that are relatively unbiased. One instrument, the Document-Derived Personality Assessment Schedule (PAS-DOC) (Tyrer, 2004) has been developed and is currently being tested.

DIMENSIONAL ASSESSMENT OF PERSONALITY DISORDER

Personality was assessed dimensionally long before any attempt was made to categorize it into disorders. The Maudsley Personality Inventory (MPI) (Eysenck, 1959) and the later Eysenck Personality Inventory (EPI) (Eysenck and Eysenck, 1964) and Eysenck Personality Questionnaire (EPQ) (Eysenck and Eysenck, 1975) have been widely used in personality research and demonstrate the stability of the concepts of extraversion and neuroticism, although the third dimension (psychoticism),

measured in the EPQ, is a less satisfactory measure of what others call psychopathy. The Karolinska Scales of Personality (KSP) (Weinryb et al., 1992) also measure a similar set of dimensions, and these are felt to be fundamental to the biological basis of personality. The Millon Clinical Multiaxial Inventory (MCMI) is a popular self-rated instrument in the United States in particular (Millon et al., 1997).

Although many of the structured interviews for the DSM personality disorders maintain that they can score all the personality disorders dimensionally, their main use is for categorical diagnosis, and the dimensional measures are really afterthoughts. However, the Personality Disorder Interview (PDI-IV) (Widiger et al., 1995) is a semi-structured clinical interview of 93 sets of questions. It has the advantage of being scored both categorically and on a dimensional scale, with greater scope than the other DSM structured interviews. The Schedule for Normal and Abnormal Personality (SNAP) (Clark, 1990) is also a useful dimensional system, which is best used with the less severe personality disorders (Table 2.4).

The Psychopathy Checklist (PCL) (Hare, 1980), now in revised form (HPCL-R) (Hare, 1991), is commonly used with offenders with

Table 2.4 Commonly used instruments for diagnosing dimensional personality disorders

Main purpose	Questionnaires	Interview schedules	Comments
Identification of personality characteristics in general	• Eysenck Personality Inventory and Questionnaire (EPI and EPQ) • Karolinska Scales of Personality (KSP) • Personality Assessment Inventory (PAI) • Schedule for Normal and Abnormal Personality (SNAP) • Dimensional Assessment of Personality Pathology – Basic Questionnaire (DAPP-BQ) (Schroeder et al., 1992)	• Personality Assessment Schedule (PAS) • Personality Disorder Interview-IV (PDI-IV)	

personality disorder as it aims to assess the concept of psychopathy categorically and dimensionally. The HPCL-R measure of psychopathy is a checklist of 20 items that includes the standard features of psychopathy; glibness and superficial charm, self-grandiosity, risk-taking behaviour, manipulative behaviour, pathological lying, lack of guilt, callousness and insensitivity, impulsiveness, promiscuity and irresponsibility. It is important to emphasize that psychopathy so defined is different from antisocial personality disorder, but this is not necessarily important, particularly if one wishes to chart progress in treatment over time. The ratings may be reinforced by information derived from clinical notes and reports and it could be argued that these need to be studied in all cases because of the plausibility of such individuals.

CLASSIFICATION OF SEVERITY OF PERSONALITY DISORDER

The notion of severe personality disorder is central to much of the work of forensic psychiatrists and yet there is no standard way of recording this from the DSM-IV and ICD-10 classifications. However, it has been noticed in many studies that the more severe personality disordered patients tend to have a much greater number of personality disorders diagnoses than those with less severe disorders (Kass et al., 1985; Oldham et al., 1992; Dolan et al., 1995).

This therefore leads to the suggestion that co-morbidity (or, more strictly speaking, overlap) of personality disorder is a measure of severity. There has also been considerable debate about the classification of sub-threshold levels of personality disorder. In the initial draft of the ICD-10 guidelines for personality disorder, 'personality accentuation' was included as a category, but subsequently omitted in the final description. However, the notion of personality difficulty or accentuation making patients more vulnerable to stresses is a well-established one (Leonhard, 1968) and could have a place in formal classifications. The proposal below (Table 2.5) combines these approaches and also allows the existing classification systems to be adapted for measuring severity (Table 2.6).

Five levels of severity of classification are allowed, the first four of which were included in the original description (Tyrer and Johnson, 1996), the last (or severe category) being added for a special group characterized by 'gross societal disturbance', in which there is gross severity of personality disorder within the

Table 2.5 New classification of severity of personality disturbance

Level	
0	No personality disorder (i.e. good capacity to form relationships, reasonable personal resources to draw on at times of adversity)
1	Personality difficulty (tendency for enduring patterns of behaviour to interfere with social functioning at times of particular stress and vulnerability but not at other times)
2	Simple personality disorder – particular and persistent personality abnormalities that create significant problems in occupational, social and/or personal relationships (present cut-off point for personality disorder in both ICD-10 and DSM-IV)
3	Diffuse personality disorder – widespread personality abnormalities covering more than one cluster of personality disorder
4	Severe personality disorder – widespread personality abnormalities covering more than one cluster of personality disorder and leading to gross societal disturbance

Table 2.6 Procedure for converting categorical personality disorders to levels of severity

Level of severity	ICD-10	DSM-IV	Structured interview schedules
0 – no personality abnormality	No personality abnormality	No personality abnormality	No personality abnormality
1 – personality difficulty	Personality difficulty recorded when general criterion for personality disorders is met and three diagnostic criteria present for paranoid, schizoid, histrionic, anankastic and\or anxious personality disorders or two criteria present for dissocial, impulsive or borderline personality disorders	Personality difficulty recorded when any of the following are present: four diagnostic criteria for schizotypal, borderline, histrionic, narcissistic or dependent personality disorder; three diagnostic criteria for paranoid, schizoid, avoidant or obsessive–compulsive personality disorders; or two criteria present for antisocial personality disorder in section 3 of the criteria	Sub-threshold criteria for personality disorder met according to criteria of interview schedule
2 – simple personality disorder	Either a single personality disorder or, if more than one, all personality disorders are within the same cluster (cluster 1 – schizoid and paranoid; cluster 2 – dissocial, impulsive, borderline or histrionic; cluster 3 – anankastic anxious and dependent)	Either a single personality disorder or, if more than one, all personality disorders are within the same cluster (cluster A – schizotypal, schizoid and paranoid; cluster B – antisocial, borderline, histrionic and narcissistic; cluster C – avoidant, dependent and obsessive–compulsive)	One or more personality disorders within the same ICD-10 or DSM-IV cluster
3 – diffuse personality disorder	Two or more personality disorders from different clusters	Two or more personality disorders present from different clusters as for ICD-10	Two or more personality disorders present from different clusters as for ICD-10
4 – severe personality disorder	Two or more personality disorders from different clusters that create gross societal disturbance	Two or more personality disorders from different clusters that create gross societal disturbance	Two or more personality disorders from different clusters that create gross societal disturbance

Derived from Tyrer and Johnson (1996).

flamboyant group and a personality disorder in at least one other cluster also. The system has the merit of allowing the existing ICD-10 and DSM-IV systems to be adapted for this new classification of severity.

In deciding which method of assessing personality disorder to choose, several issues need to be addressed (Table 2.7). Whatever their imperfections, the DSM and ICD classifications are the current gold standard in personality diagnosis and so must be chosen for purposes of official statistics and international comparisons (e.g. epidemiological surveys). One of the important advantages of the categorical

Table 2.7 Choice of categorical or dimensional diagnosis of personality disorder

Categorical diagnosis	Dimensional diagnosis
Hypothesis testing about a specific diagnostic category (e.g. impulsive personality disorder)	Measurement of change in patients with personality disturbance over time
Official statistics	When testing the validity of categorical diagnosis
To select a treatment or management based on diagnosis	When studying personality disturbance in whole populations
For international comparisons	When examining relationships between personality and other continuous variables
Grant applications	When examining populations at the extremes of the range of personality disturbance
When studying co-morbidity with mental state disorders (dual and triple diagnoses)	Long-term follow-up studies

diagnosis in psychiatry is that many management decisions are dichotomous. Therefore, if one of the necessary prerequisites of treatment in a special institution or using a new type of therapy is the possession of a diagnosis of personality disorder, an assessment that allows categorical assessment is essential.

Categorical diagnosis is also necessary when planning treatment or services for patients with mental state and personality disorders (now commonly called dual diagnosis). Although it is possible to use dimensional measures for most practical purposes, it is more useful to use categories for ease of communication and efficiency. Lastly, and by no means flippantly, for research workers wishing to obtain grants, the merits of the dimensional approach have not yet penetrated to the personality disorder establishment in most countries, and so it is unwise to plump for the assessment of dimensional personality disorders alone.

REFERENCES

American Psychiatric Association (1994). *Diagnostic and Statistical Manual of Mental Disorders,* 4th edition. Washington DC: American Psychiatric Association.

Blashfield R, Sprock J, Pinkston K and Hodgin J (1985). Exemplar prototypes of personality disorder diagnoses. *Comprehensive Psychiatry* **26**:11–21.

Bronisch T (1992). Diagnostic procedures of personality disorders according to the criteria of present classification systems. *Verhaltungstherapie* **2**: 140–50.

Bronisch T and Mombour W (1994). Comparison of a diagnostic checklist with a structured interview for the assessment of DSM-III-R and ICD-10 personality disorders. *Psychopathology* **27**:312–20.

Brothwell J, Casey PR and Tyrer P (1992). Who gives the most reliable account of a psychiatric patient's personality? *Irish Journal of Psychological Medicine* **9**:90–3.

Clark LA (1990). *Schedule for Normal and Abnormal Personality (SCAN).* Iowa: Department of Psychiatry, University of Iowa.

Clark LA, Watson D and Reynolds S (1995). Diagnosis and classification of psychopathology: challenges to the current system and future directions. *Annual Review of Psychology* **46**:121–53.

Cloninger CR (1987). A systematic method for clinical description and classification of personality variants. *Archives of General Psychiatry* **44**:573–88.

Dolan B and Coid J (1993). *Psychopathic and Antisocial Personality Disorders: Treatment and Research Issues.* London: Gaskell Books, Royal College of Psychiatrists.

Dolan B, Evans C and Norton K (1995). Multiple axis-II diagnoses of personality disorder. *British Journal of Psychiatry* **166**:107–12.

Dowson JH (1992). Assessment of DSM-III-R personality disorders by self-report questionnaires: the role of informants and a screening test for comorbid personality disorders. *British Journal of Psychiatry* **161**:344–52.

Dowson JH and Grounds AT (1995). *Personality Disorders: Recognition and Clinical Management*. Cambridge: Cambridge University Press.

Eysenck HJ (1959). *The Maudsley Personality Inventory*. London: University of London Press.

Eysenck HJ and Eysenck SBG (1964). *Manual of the Eysenck Personality Inventory*. London: University of London Press.

Eysenck HJ and Eysenck SBG (1975). *The Eysenck Personality Questionnaire*. London: University of London Press.

Feinstein A (1970). The pre-therapeutic classification of comorbidity in chronic disease. *Journal of Chronic Diseases* **23**:455–62.

First MB, Spitzer RL, Gibbon M and Williams JBW (1995). The Structured Clinical Interview for DSM-III-R Personality Disorders (SCID-II): Part 1: Description. *Journal of Personality Disorders* **9**:83–91.

Flick SN, Roy-Byrne PP, Cowley DS, Shores MM and Dunner DL (1993). DSM-III-R personality disorders in a mood and anxiety disorders clinic: prevalence, comorbidity and clinical correlates. *Journal of Affective Disorders* **27**:71–9.

Fyer MR, Frances AJ, Sullivan T, Hurt SW and Clarkin J (1988). Co-morbidity of borderline personality disorder. *Archives of General Psychiatry* **45**:348–52.

Gunderson JG, Kolb JE and Austin V (1981). The Diagnostic Interview for Borderline Patients. *American Journal of Psychiatry* **138**:896–903.

Hare RD (1980). A research scale for the assessment of psychopathy in criminal populations. *Personality and Individual Differences* **1**:111–17.

Hare RD (1991). *The Hare Psychopathy Checklist – Revised*. Toronto: Multi-health Systems.

Hill J, Harrington R, Fudge H, Rutter M and Pickles A (1989). Adult Personality Functioning Assessment (APFA): an investigator-based standardised interview. *British Journal of Psychiatry* **155**:24–35.

Hyler SE (1994). *Personality Diagnostic Questionnaire-4*. New York: New York State Psychiatric Institute.

Hyler SE and Reider RO (1984). *Personality Diagnostic Questionnaire – Revised*. New York: New York State Psychiatric Institute.

Hyler SE, Rieder RO, Williams JBW, Spitzer RL, Hendier J and Lyons M (1988). The Personality Diagnostic Questionnaire: development and preliminary results. *Journal of Personality Disorders* **2**:229–37.

Kass F, Skodol AE, Charles E, Spitzer RL and Williams JBW (1985). Scaled ratings of DSM-III personality disorders. *American Journal of Psychiatry* **143**:627–30.

Klein MH, Benjamin LS, Rosenfeld R, Treece C, Husted J and Greist JH (1993). The Wisconsin Personality Disorders Interview: development, reliability and validity. *Journal of Personality Disorders* **7**:285–303.

Leonhard K (1968). *Akzentuierte Personlichkeiten*. Berlin: Verlag Volk und Gesundheit.

Livesley WJ, Schroeder ML, Jackson DN and Jang KL (1994). Categorical distinctions in the study of personality disorder: implications for classification. *Journal of Abnormal Psychology* **103**:6–17.

Loranger AW, Sartorius N, Andreoli A et al. (1994). The International Personality Disorder Examination: the WHO/ADAMHA international pilot study of personality disorders. *Archives of General Psychiatry* **51**:215–24.

Loranger AW, Susman VL, Oldham JM and Russakoff LM (1987). *International Personality Disorder Examination (PDE). A Structured Interview for DSM-III-R and ICD-10 Personality Disorders. WHO/ADAMHA Version*. White Plains, NY: The New York Hospital, Cornell Medical Center, Westchester Division.

Mann AH, Jenkins R, Cutting JC and Cowen PJ (1981). The development and use of a standardized assessment of abnormal personality. *Psychological Medicine* **11**:839–47.

Millon T, Davis R and Millon C (1997). *MCMI-III Manual*. Minneapolis, MN: National Computer Systems.

Moran P, Leese M, Lee T, Walters P, Thornicroft G and Mann A (2003). Standardised Assessment of Personality – Abbreviated Scale (SAPAS): preliminary validation of a brief screen for personality disorder. *British Journal of Psychiatry* **183**:228–32.

Oldham JM, Skodol AE, Kellman HD, Hyler SE, Rosnick L and Davies M (1992). Diagnosis of DSM-III-R personality disorders by two semistructured interviews: patterns of comorbidity. *American Journal of Psychiatry* **149**:213–20.

Perry JC (1992). Problems and considerations in the valid assessment of personality disorders. *American Journal of Psychiatry* **149**:1645–53.

Pfohl B, Blum N and Zimmerman M (1995). *Structured Interview for DSM-IV Personality: SIDP-IV*. Iowa: Department of Psychiatry, University of Iowa.

Pfohl B, Coryell W, Zimmerman M and Stangl D (1986). DSM-III personality disorders: diagnostic overlap and internal consistency of individual DSM-III criteria. *Comprehensive Psychiatry* **27**:21–34.

Pilgrim JA, Mellers JD, Boothby HA and Mann AH (1993). Inter-rater and temporal reliability of the Standardized Assessment of Personality and the influence of informant characteristics. *Psychological Medicine* **23**:779–86.

Piven J, Wzorek M, Landa R et al. (1994). Personality characteristics of the parents of autistic individuals. *Psychological Medicine* **24**:783–95.

Reich J and Thompson WD (1987). DSM-III personality disorder clusters in three generations. *British Journal of Psychiatry* **150**:471–5.

Rutter M (1987). Temperament, personality and personality disorder. *British Journal of Psychiatry* **150**: 443–58.

Sartorius N, Kaelber CT, Cooper JE et al. (1993). Progress toward achieving a common language in psychiatry. Results from the field trial of the clinical guidelines accompanying the WHO classification of mental and behavioral disorders in ICD-10. *Archives of General Psychiatry* **50**:115–24.

Schroeder ML, Wormsworth JA and Livesley WJ (1992). Dimensions of personality disorder and their relationship to the big five dimensions of personality. *Psychological Assessment* **4**:47–58.

Spitzer R, Williams JBW and Gibbon M (1987). *Structured Interview for DSM-III Personality Disorder*. New York: Biometrics Research Department, New York State Psychiatric Institute.

Tyrer P (1992). Flamboyant, erratic, dramatic, borderline, antisocial, sadistic, narcissistic, histrionic and impulsive personality disorders: who cares which? *Criminal Behaviour and Mental Health* **2**:95–104.

Tyrer P (1996). Comorbidity or consanguinity? *British Journal of Psychiatry* **168**:669–71.

Tyrer P (2004). *Personality Assessment Schedule – Document-Derived Version (PAS-DOC)*. London: Department of Psychological Medicine, Imperial College.

Tyrer P and Alexander J (1979). Classification of personality disorder. *British Journal of Psychiatry* **135**:163–7.

Tyrer P, Alexander MS, Cicchetti D, Cohen MS and Remmington M (1979). Reliability of a schedule for rating personality disorders. *British Journal of Psychiatry* **135**:168–74.

Tyrer P, Alexander J and Ferguson B (2000). Personality Assessment Schedule. In: Tyrer P (ed.), *Personality Disorders: Diagnosis, Management and Course*. London: Arnold/Wright, 133–59.

Tyrer P and Johnson T (1996). Establishing the severity of personality disorder. *American Journal of Psychiatry* **153**:1593–7.

Walton HJ and Presly AS (1973). Use of a category system in the diagnosis of abnormal personality. *British Journal of Psychiatry* **122**:259–68.

Weinryb RM, Gustavsson JP, Åsberg M and Rössel RJ (1992). Stability over time of character assessment using a psychodynamic instrument and personality inventories. *Acta Psychiatrica Scandinavica* **86**: 179–84.

Widiger TA, Mangine S, Corbitt EM, Ellis CG and Thomas GV (1995). *Personality Disorder Interview-IV: A Semistructured Interview for the Assessment of Personality Disorders*. Odessa, FL: Psychological Assessment Resources.

World Health Organization (1992). *ICD-10: Classification of Mental and Behavioural Disorder*. Geneva: World Health Organization.

Zanarini MC, Frankenburg FR, Sickel AE and Yong L (1994). *Diagnostic Interview for DSM-IV Personality Disorders (DIPD-IV)*. Belmont MA: McLean Hospital.

Zimmerman M, Pfohl B, Coryell W, Stangl D and Corenthal C (1988). Diagnosing personality disorder in depressed patients: a comparison of patient and informant interviews. *Archives of General Psychiatry* **45**:733–7.

Chapter 3

DESCRIBING PERSONALITY AND ITS ABNORMAL DEVIATIONS

Ronald Blackburn

INTRODUCTION

Personality disorder has something to do with the way a person 'really is'. Unlike the symptoms of mental illness, the traits defining personality disorder do not signal a discontinuity of individual functioning, nor do they represent some separate disease or illness affecting an entity that exists independently of it (Millon, 1996). Personality and personality disorder are therefore inseparable concepts.

Current concepts are rooted in nineteenth century European typologies and the clinically based theories of Freud, Jung and McDougall. These theories attempted to encompass both normal and abnormal functioning from analyses of problems encountered in the clinical setting, but during the 1930s, academic psychologists identified a need for a scientific analysis of the characteristics of healthy individuals. Psychiatric and psychological approaches to personality henceforth diverged. Psychiatrists continued to prefer a clinical and intuitive approach, relying on descriptive concepts of the earlier typologists and psychoanalysts (Tyrer, 1988). Within psychology, however, the study of personality incorporated the experimental and quantitative methods of the natural sciences, and has relied on measurement through psychological tests.

This academic split is reflected in the American Psychiatric Association's *Diagnostic and Statistical Manual of Mental Disorders* (DSM) classifications of personality disorder, which ignore several decades of research into personality in the general population (Livesley, 1995). However, attempts to integrate these two traditions have increased in recent years. This chapter examines the nature of personality as it has been conceptualized in psychological theory and research, and how this relates to recent concepts of personality disorder.

PERSONALITY AND PERSONALITY THEORY

WHAT IS PERSONALITY?

In everyday usage, the term personality refers to a person's distinctive and typical social attributes as they impact on others. For example, people may be said to have a 'friendly' or 'interesting' personality. In this context, personality is simply a global evaluation. Personality theories are concerned with individual distinctiveness, but because the psychological phenomena involved can be conceptualized from different perspectives, theorists have offered a wide array of definitions of personality.

Strictly speaking, there is no such 'thing' as personality and, from a psychological perspective, it is more appropriately viewed as an area of inquiry. McAdams (1997) identifies this area as the study of the whole person or the self, the dynamics of human motivation, and the identification and measurement of differences between individuals in terms of behavioural regularities (i.e. dispositions or traits). Although early theories aimed to account for the uniqueness of the individual person (the idiographic approach), recent work has emphasized individual differences. This approach draws on research with large samples of the normal population, derives assessment strategies from psychometric theory, and aims to establish general principles for understanding variations between people (the nomothetic approach). The last of these approaches is emphasized here.

TRAITS AS DESCRIPTORS OF PERSONALITY

Traits are consistent patterns of actions, thoughts or feelings that distinguish between people. Traits differ from specific acts or temporary mood states in denoting a tendency or *disposition* to behave in certain ways under relevant conditions. They are abstractions based on observations of behaviour, including self-reports or observations. They nonetheless denote properties that people carry around with them.

Language is replete with trait terms (e.g. 'sociable', 'aggressive'), some being context dependent (e.g. 'aggressive' assumes interpersonal confrontation), while others describe the style or the 'how' of behaviour (e.g. 'methodical', 'energetic'). Trait language reflects the folk-wisdom of personality description, and even the most ardent academic opponents of trait psychology freely write references on their students indicating how 'conscientious', 'lazy' or 'stable' they are!

Traits are the basic unit in the study of personality and also in the DSM classification of personality disorders ('... enduring patterns of perceiving, relating to, and thinking about the environment and oneself ...'). Although common language traits are not tied to any theory, many trait terms used in research and clinical practice originate from particular theories (e.g. 'open to experience', 'over-controlled', 'field-dependent') and depend on particular measurement operations. Structured psychological assessments that focus on specific characteristics also provide a shortcut to inferences about traits that would otherwise require extensive observations.

THE UTILITY OF TRAITS

Despite the widespread use of trait terms, their conceptual and empirical status have been widely debated (Alston, 1975; Johnson, 1997). Two recurring questions are briefly considered. The first concerns the *consistency* of behaviour, and the second is whether traits *explain* behaviour. The 'person–situation' debate addresses the question of how far the behaviours from which traits are inferred are generalized across situations. Because we usually observe people in a limited range of settings, our ascriptions of particular traits assume that these will also be manifest in other situations. However, some psychologists have argued that the features we observe are more the product of a specific situation than of a personal disposition. Taking this view, a person's behavioural repertoire consists of largely unconnected response dispositions rather than broad regularities.

During the 1970s, trait psychology came under attack following an influential review by Mischel (1968), who concluded that the research evidence on the cross-situational consistency of behaviour did not justify conceptualizing personality in terms of 'broad response dispositions'. Subsequent reviewers highlighted the evidence for consistency, for example in the area of aggression and antisocial behaviour (e.g. Olweus, 1979), and more recent evidence indicates that assumptions about the cross-situational and long-term stability of trait-relevant behaviours are justified (Kenrick and Funder, 1988).

The debate has now largely subsided, but it served to highlight conceptual issues in the use of traits (Alston, 1975). For example, to describe someone as 'aggressive' implies only a greater than average probability of aggressive behaviour in relevant situations, not that the person invariably takes the opportunity to behave in that way. Traits therefore describe average behaviour over many settings and occasions. Conversely, we cannot infer a trait from a single act. For example, some offenders who commit acts of extreme aggression are timid or over-controlled, and do not exhibit a generalized aggressive disposition (Blackburn, 1996).

Situations are not wholly independent of persons. Some settings, such as formal meetings, clearly control behaviour because of social roles and norms, but disposition determines the situations people choose and create. Nevertheless, the limitations of trait description must be emphasized. The consistency of behaviour across situations is merely relative, and domineering executives are sometimes putty in the hands of their families.

The second issue is whether traits explain behaviour. In everyday language, traits may have at least a low-level explanatory power. For example, the statement that 'Joe hit Fred because Joe is aggressive' might seem to be circular, but insofar as it informs us that Joe's behaviour was usual for him, it pre-empts the need for further explanation (Johnson, 1997). However, although traits as tendencies are *real* properties of persons, and not merely 'in the eye of the beholder', the attribution of an act of aggression to a trait of aggressiveness falls short of a scientifically acceptable explanation because the trait itself needs to be explained. Moreover, if traits describe probable and not invariant behaviour, they cannot provide a *fundamental* explanation of particular acts. This requires reference to a person's beliefs and desires (Alston, 1975).

Some writers therefore distinguish traits that are observable from those that are non-observable. Alston (1975) distinguishes dispositions denoting frequency of behaviour given certain conditions (e.g. aggressive, industrious), and those that are 'purposive-cognitive' (e.g. personal constructs, expectancies, unconscious needs). The latter are explanatory, but are less detectable in observable behaviour. Others similarly distinguish between surface and source traits. Source, or 'genotypic', traits are the more basic constituents of personality and reflect theories concerning motives or goals. They can account for surface (or phenotypic) traits, but also for inconsistencies, for example when a situation arouses competing goals.

THE STRUCTURE OF PERSONALITY

Personality theorists conceptualize traits as part of a hierarchy. Traits (e.g. dominance) are inferred from specific response dispositions or 'habits' (e.g. taking the lead in group activities). In turn, when certain traits occur together in many individuals, we may identify types or categories of people. The DSM categories of personality disorder are type constructs of this kind. However, psychologists have been more concerned to identify how relationships between traits form dimensions, using the statistical method of factor analysis. Dimensions summarize the interrelationships between traits lower in the hierarchy, and represent higher-order dispositions.

Research has established that relationships between the vast number of normal-range traits denoting behavioural, emotional and cognitive dispositions reflect a few robust dimensions. For many years, there was disagreement about the optimal number of dimensions (Watson et al., 1994). Some workers suggested that three dimensions are sufficient (e.g. Eysenck's neuroticism, extraversion and psychoticism), while others argued for at least seven. However, convergent findings across methods, samples and cultures now indicate that most variation in personality is accounted for by the 'Big

Five' factors (John, 1990; Costa and McCrae, 1992) of:

- neuroticism vs. stability
- extraversion vs. introversion
- agreeableness vs. antagonism
- conscientiousness vs. lack of self-discipline
- openness to experience vs. rigidity.

These dimensions (or domains) represent the covariation of traits (or facets) lower in the hierarchy. The main facets of neuroticism, for example, are anxiety, hostility, depression, self-consciousness, impulsiveness and vulnerability, while agreeableness contrasts trust and co-operativeness with cynicism, callousness and aggression.

The five-factor model integrates several apparently divergent dimensional models. For example, Eysenck's neuroticism and extraversion dimensions coincide with their counterparts in the five-factor model, while psychoticism is a composite of low agreeableness and low conscientiousness (Watson et al., 1994). McCrae and Costa (1996) argue that 'Standing on these factors is as basic to the description of a person as age, sex, and education, and no personality psychologist can afford to ignore them' (p. 65). They propose that the five factors represent biologically derived basic tendencies that, through dynamic processes of cognition, affect and volition, determine characteristic adaptations (attitudes, goals, relationships), objective biography and the self-concept, and our interactions with the social and physical environment.

PERSONALITY AND PERSONALITY DISORDER

There are no absolute or culture-free criteria by which behaviour can be defined as abnormal and, as is noted in DSM-IV (American Psychiatric Association, 1994), there are no sharp boundaries between normality and abnormality. Behaviour may be described as abnormal if it is statistically unusual or rare, socially inappropriate or undesirable, subjectively distressing, deviates from optimal social or psychological functioning, or fails to meet some ideal standard of 'health'. Most of these enter into conceptions of what constitutes personality disorder, but the most common criteria are the statistical and the functional.

ABNORMALITY OF PERSONALITY AS STATISTICAL DEVIATION

Trait theorists generally see normality and abnormality as falling on a quantitative continuum. A trait is abnormal when its manifestation is extreme relative to the population average, extremeness commonly being defined arbitrarily in psychological tests by the statistical criterion of two standard deviations from the mean (a position occupied by less than 2 per cent of the population). In these terms, disorders of personality are extreme variants of normal personality, and can hence be described by reference to dimensions of personality, such as the five-factor model. Moreover, studies of traits defining personality disorder reveal that their structure follows that of the five-factor model (Clark et al., 1996). We therefore do not need a separate trait language for describing disorders of personality.

However, statistical abnormality seems insufficient to identify disorder. The DSM asserts that 'Only when personality traits are inflexible and maladaptive and cause significant functional impairment or subjective distress do they constitute Personality Disorders' (American Psychiatric Association, 1994, p. 630). This clearly suggests that unusual or rare characteristics are not in themselves a criterion of personality disorder. The question is whether 'inflexibility', 'functional impairment' and 'subjective distress' are necessarily implied by, or inevitable consequences of, certain statistically deviant traits.

ABNORMALITY OF PERSONALITY AS DYSFUNCTION

Many writers propose inflexibility as a hallmark of maladjustment (Leary, 1957; Mischel, 1968; Millon, 1996). Adaptation to one's environment assumes a repertoire of skills or strategies that permit varying responses to changing circumstances. When a person has a limited range of such skills, and actions are reproduced rigidly across a variety of situations for which they may be inappropriate, negative consequences are likely for the person and others. Mischel (1968) also noted that extreme consistency of behaviour indicates poor situational discrimination, and is therefore probably a sign of maladjustment. However, if inflexibility describes the predominance of certain traits and lack of others, it is essentially reducible to statistical deviation. This is explicit in *interpersonal theory* (Leary, 1957; Blackburn, 1998), in which personality disorders are equated with inflexible interpersonal styles whose inflexibility is defined by their extremeness. Also, insofar as 'subjective distress' refers to the frequent experience of anxiety, mood lability or poor self-esteem, it is reflected directly in an extreme position on the dimension of neuroticism.

Functional impairment is indicated by failure to perform social and occupational roles or, at a more abstract level, by failure in 'the universal tasks of establishing identity, attachment, intimacy, or affiliation' (Livesley et al., 1994). Dysfunction is not, however, necessarily expressed in extreme traits, because it depends on the context. Some people may have extreme traits but function adequately because their characteristics are not an impediment for a particular role or setting. This is recognized in the notions of discordant personality (Foulds, 1971) or personality accentuation (Tyrer, 1988), which fall short of disorder.

The DSM-IV criteria for personality disorder are inconsistent in terms of whether or not they indicate dysfunction. For example, 'shows arrogant or haughty behaviours or attitudes' (narcissistic personality disorder) and 'lacks close friends or confidants other than first degree relatives' (schizoid and schizotypal personality disorders) are behavioural indicators of traits that may be unusual, but that do not preclude adequate functioning. In contrast, 'shows perfectionism that interferes with task completion' (obsessive–compulsive personality disorder) refers to the conditions under which an extreme trait is dysfunctional.

Parker (1997) suggests that the dysfunctional component of disorder is 'somewhat independent' of extremes of personality and that the personality and disorder components need to be evaluated separately. Nestadt (1997), on the other hand, argues that the distinction is artificial and that the *potential* to manifest impairment is implied by certain dispositions. Their role becomes apparent when emotional and behavioural problems bring the person to clinical attention. Nestadt draws a parallel with mental handicap, which is not identified by low intelligence alone but by dysfunctional adaptation under conditions requiring intellectual ability, and notes that 'disorder is situation specific'. This argument, however, seems to reinforce the view that statistical abnormality of a disposition is not itself sufficient to define disorder.

CATEGORICAL AND DIMENSIONAL REPRESENTATIONS OF PERSONALITY DISORDER

There is a longstanding debate about whether disorders of personality are appropriately represented as categories (or types) or by dimensions. Although DSM-IV disavows any assumption that the categories of mental disorder are discrete entities, categorical classification of personality disorder follows a medical model that implies qualitative distinctions between normality and abnormality and clear boundaries between categories. A dimensional approach, on the other hand, assumes only quantitative distinctions.

Description by categories has advantages in conceptualization and communication, uses familiar labels, and facilitates clinical decision making (Widiger and Costa, 1994). The advantages of description by dimension lie in the retention of information, flexibility, lack of boundary dilemmas, and greater statistical power in research. Dimensions can be converted into categories by specifying cut-off points. This is implicit in the diagnosis of the category of personality disorder, where the cut-off is simply presence or absence. Dimensional and categorical descriptions are not, then, incompatible, but dimensions are held to describe the essential underlying structures.

The *Diagnostic and Statistical Manual*, third edition (American Psychiatric Association, 1980) aimed to identify a set of mutually exclusive and independent disorders of personality, but in the light of evidence that multiple or co-occurring (co-morbid) diagnoses are the rule rather than the exception, it has been increasingly argued that a few common dimensions underlie the current categories (Livesley et al., 1994; Widiger and Costa, 1994; Livesley, 1995). Empirical data support a dimensional representation of personality pathology. For example, a similar structure underlies traits of personality in both personality disordered and non-disordered samples (Tyrer, 1988), suggesting that any differences are quantitative rather than qualitative. Similarly, the genetic contributions to personality disorders are comparable to those of normal personality dimensions (Livesley et al., 1994). There are therefore good grounds for construing personality disorders as extreme positions on dimensions of human variation identified through research into the structure of normal personality. The five-factor model is currently regarded as the most relevant dimensional system.

It should be noted that a dimensional representation does not provide a classification in the traditional sense. It is nevertheless possible to translate the current classes of personality disorder into a dimensional system. For example, avoidant personality disorder appears to be primarily a combination of extreme neuroticism and extreme introversion, while borderline personality disorder represents extreme neuroticism and low agreeableness (Widiger and Costa, 1994). The common element of neuroticism can account for the finding that many patients meet the criteria for both borderline and avoidant disorders, as well as for others.

However, the validity of the current categories as independent disorders is questionable, and a more promising approach is to identify the most commonly occurring patterns of traits or dimensions empirically, using the methods of cluster analysis (Tyrer, 1988; Livesley and Jackson, 1992; Livesley, 1995). Among mentally disordered offenders, this approach consistently reveals four broad classes in self-reports of personality deviation, these being described as *primary psychopath*, *secondary psychopath*, *controlled personalities* and *inhibited personalities* (Blackburn, 1996, 1998). These show a significant relationship to the DSM categories of personality disorder: primary psychopaths are, for example, identified by antisocial, narcissistic, histrionic and paranoid traits.

CONCLUSION

The description of dispositions is the starting point for a clinical understanding of personality disorders, but the limitations of traits in predicting and explaining individual behaviour need to be recognized. Given that traits are probabilistic descriptions, it is to be expected that there will always an upper limit to their power to predict future behaviours, such as dangerous acts. Short of being able to forecast situations, however, they provide the best first attempt at prediction. Nevertheless, in understanding how abnormal personality contributes to a specific act, such as a serious crime, we must determine not only the relation of the act to observable traits, but also its *meaning* in terms of the person's generalized goals and beliefs. This kind of idiographic analysis is always dependent on the observer's theory.

REFERENCES

Alston WP (1975). Traits, consistency, and conceptual alternatives for personality theory. *Journal for the Theory of Social Behaviour* **5**:17–48.

American Psychiatric Association (1980). *Diagnostic and Statistical Manual of Mental Disorders,* third edition. Washington DC: American Psychiatric Association.

American Psychiatric Association (1994). *Diagnostic and Statistical Manual of Mental Disorders*, fourth edition. Washington DC: American Psychiatric Association.

Blackburn R (1996). Replicated personality disorder clusters among mentally disordered offenders and their relation to dimensions of personality. *Journal of Personality Disorders* **10**:68–81.

Blackburn R (1998). Psychopathy and personality disorder: implications of interpersonal theory. In: Cooke DJ, Hart SJ and Forth AE (eds), *Psychopathy: Theory, Research and Implications for Society.* Amsterdam: Kluwer, 269–301.

Clark LA, Livesley WJ, Schroeder ML and Irish SL (1996). Convergence of two systems for assessing specific traits of personality disorder. *Psychological Assessment* **8**:294–303.

Costa PT and McCrae RR (1992). Normal personality assessment in clinical practice: the NEO personality inventory. *Psychological Assessment* **4**:5–13.

Foulds GA (1971). Personality deviance and personal symptomatology. *Psychological Medicine* **1**:222–33.

John OP (1990). The 'Big Five' factor taxonomy. Dimensions of personality in the natural language and in questionnaires. In: Pervin LA (ed.), *Handbook of Personality Theory and Research.* New York: Guilford Press, 66–100.

Johnson JA (1997). Units of analysis for the description and explanation of personality. In: Hogan R, Johnson J and Briggs S (eds), *Handbook of Personality Psychology.* New York: Academic Press, 73–93.

Kenrick DT and Funder DC (1988). Profiting from controversy: lessons from the person–situation debate. *American Psychologist* **43**:23–34.

Leary T (1957). *Interpersonal Diagnosis of Personality.* New York: Ronald Press.

Livesley WJ (1995). Past achievements and future directions. In: Livesley WJ (ed.), *The DSM-IV Personality Disorders.* New York: Guilford Press, 497–505.

Livesley WJ and Jackson D (1992). Guidelines for developing, evaluating, and revising the classification of personality disorders. *Journal of Nervous and Mental Disease* **180**:609–18.

Livesley WJ, Schroeder ML, Jackson DN and Jang KL (1994). Categorical distinctions in the study of personality disorder: implications for classification. *Journal of Abnormal Psychology* **103**:6–17.

McAdams DP (1997). A conceptual history of personality psychology. In: Hogan R, Johnson J and Briggs S (eds), *Handbook of Personality Psychology.* New York: Academic Press, 3–39.

McCrae RR and Costa PT (1996). Toward a new generation of personality theories: theoretical contexts for the five-factor model. In Wiggins JS (ed.), *The Five-Factor Model of Personality: Theoretical Perspectives.* New York: Guilford Press, 51–87.

Millon T (1996). *Disorders of Personality: DSM IV and Beyond.* New York: John Wiley & Sons.

Mischel W (1968). *Personality and Assessment.* New York: John Wiley & Sons.

Nestadt G (1997). Response to Dr Gordon Parker's paper: an epidemiological perspective. *Journal of Personality Disorders* **11**:375–80.

Olweus D (1979). Stability of aggressive reaction patterns in males: a review. *Psychological Bulletin* **86**:852–75.

Parker G (1997). The etiology of personality disorders: a review and consideration of research models. *Journal of Personality Disorders* **11**:345–69.

Tyrer P (1988). *Personality Disorders: Diagnosis, Management and Course.* London: Wright.

Watson D, Clark LA and Harkness AR (1994). Structures of personality and their relevance to psychopathology. *Journal of Abnormal Psychology* **103**:18–31.

Widiger TA and Costa PT (1994). Personality and personality disorders. *Journal of Abnormal Psychology* **103**:78–91.

Chapter 4

CLINICAL ASSESSMENT OF INDIVIDUALS WITH PERSONALITY DISORDER IN THE SECURE HOSPITAL

Estelle Moore

INTRODUCTION

Central to any discussion regarding the assessment of personality disorder is the difficulty of conceptualizing and describing the nature of the disturbance (Taylor, 1986). Description is, nevertheless, an essential task in the process of clinical assessment.

The extensive international research literature on personality disorder, with respect to its aetiology, amenability to intervention, outcome and, particularly, assessment, highlights the diversity of options for describing and making sense of what personality is, and when its manifestations might be considered 'disordered'. This diversity is embodied in the different traditions (e.g. psychoanalytic, object relations, and self psychology theories) that have contributed to the evolution of the classification systems of specific personality disorder diagnoses (Jackson and Livesley, 1995). Since classification depends on the appearance of consensus (Tyrer, 1995), lack of consensus poses a fundamental problem, which tends to materialize in a number of ways (e.g. 'diagnostic co-occurrence', Blackburn, 2000) during the process of clinical assessment.

As an example of one of these systems, Axis II of the *Diagnostic and Statistical Manual of Mental Disorders,* fourth edition (DSM-IV, American Psychiatric Association, 1994)

represents a hybrid of clinical and research observations, but has been criticized for failing to meet the needs of both research and clinical taxonomists (Westen and Shedler, 1999). It is perhaps even less helpful to the clinician faced with a detained person who appears hostile and distressed (Howard et al., 1994). Add to this the fact that the individual does not wish to be talking to the clinician, but has been required to do so following court proceedings, and herein lie some of the challenges encountered by mental health professionals seeking to assess personality (disorder) in forensic settings.

THEORY AND EMPIRICAL VALIDATION IN PERSONALITY ASSESSMENT

It is not possible within the scope of this chapter to offer anything but the briefest of references to the history of personality assessment and theory, a field of enquiry to which whole texts have been devoted, and for which the status 'comprehensive clinical science' has been proposed (Millon, 2002). It seems important, nevertheless, to attempt to place in some context contemporary formulations of what might constitute good practice in the clinical assessment of personality disorder in forensic settings, which can draw on a combination of general personality theory, clinical judgement and cumulative research knowledge (Jackson and Livesley, 1995).

The idea of 'personality' holds a central place in our understanding of ourselves and others, fundamental to our concept of what it means to be a person (Burr, 1995). The possibilities for words that refer to a person's personality are endless (e.g. kind, controlling, generous, etc.), and would not be useful if they referred to merely transient phenomena. The term personality is generally associated with 'traits' (longstanding tendencies), as distinguished from 'states' (temporary conditions), interpreted within a multivariate model that includes situational variables and interaction terms (Westen, 1995). Our notion of personality thus incorporates ideas of individual difference (uniqueness), stability, general coherence (i.e. that personality characteristics are consistent with one another), and the notion that 'personality' bears some relationship to our behaviour (Burr, 1995). However, it would be a mistake to assume that people apply generalized traits irrespective of the situation in which they find themselves. The DSM-IV directs the diagnostician to pay attention to personality traits as 'disordered' only under certain conditions: when they appear inflexible, stable, of determinable duration, maladaptive, cause significant functional impairment, and are not better accounted for by anything else (American Psychiatric Association, 1994, p. 630).

Widely shared ('essentialist') notions of personality encourage us to think of ourselves and others as having a particular nature, both as individuals and as a species, a model of personality in which biological givens may be modified by environmental influence. As a 'commonsense' view, this model can serve us reasonably well in making sense of behaviour in everyday life. In clinical practice it might most usefully be understood as a theory we use to make sense of the patterns we see in our experience, rather than as a 'fact' of human nature (Burr, 1995).

The five-factor model of personality is the product of years of research and debate between scientists (e.g. Cattell, Eysenck and Guilford) and psychometricians (McCrae and John, 1992). This working model of personality (the five factors include: neuroticism, extraversion, openness to experience, agreeableness and conscientiousness) has been referred to as an 'interim treaty', which has served to provide a platform for collaboration in the exploration of empirical and conceptual possibilities across diverse realms of inquiry (Wiggins, 1992). As a version of trait theory, the five factors provide a dimensional model in which Axis II personality disorders might be interpreted as maladaptive variants of *normal* personality traits. This is conceptually important, because the less arbitrary the cut-off between normality and abnormality, the better. It has been argued that the dimensional approach to personality disorder diagnosis is 'not only superior theoretically, but also yields more precise information about the specific associations with criminal behaviour' (Ulrich et al., 2001). However, informed observation of the lives and narratives of those who struggle in their interactions with the world also highlights a range of limitations of the 'big-five' model, (indeed, any nomothetic, or group norm-based, approach) when applied to the individual as a member of a clinical population (Westen, 1996). Principally, whilst it may offer a description of the outcome of various personality processes, the five-factor model does not offer explanations as to *why* a person might behave in particular ways. Making sense of confusing clinical presentations is one of the tasks of clinical assessment.

Similarly, the categorical classificatory systems – e.g. the *International Classification of Diseases,* tenth revision (ICD-10, World Health Organization, 1992) and DSM-IV – have a number of well-documented limitations, including failure to encapsulate the wide variety of personality variance (Tyrer, 1995) and to reflect severity of disorder (Norton and Dolan, 1995). Such systems are compromised by a heterogeneity of definition that ensures that the majority of individuals with a personality disorder diagnosis receive more than one such diagnosis (Tyrer, 1992; Dolan et al., 1995; Shea, 1995). This phenomenon is no less true for mentally disordered offender populations, who typically meet criteria for more than one personality disorder (Coid, 1992).

The optimal diagnostic system is one that links problems, outcomes and proposed processes of change (Koerner et al., 1996). Thus, guidelines for comprehensive personality assessment, which can be applied across individuals, are to be found at the interface of the nomothetic and idiographic traditions, with the capacity both to identify individual differences and to organize them theoretically within domains of functioning (Westen, 1996). Translated into principles for the clinician, this means paying attention not only to the individual's internal world, but also to how this interacts with the external, and how usual, or unusual, this is, both for this person and for people in general. Psychological formulation of non-intellectual aspects of behaviour thus incorporates a notion of personality in its broadest sense, including the interacting emotional adjustments, interpersonal relations, motivation, interests and attitudes of the individual in a variety of contexts (Anastasi, 1976). Personality disorders are not 'immutable givens', but a product of 'the dynamic between temperamental endowments and the individual's social and personal progress through life' (Mullen, 1993).

With this background as a foundation, what follows is an outline of possibilities for the goals of assessment with a clientele at the extreme end of the population: those with offence histories and 'severe' personality disorder who are admitted to the high-security hospital.

THE HIGH-SECURITY POPULATION

Mentally disordered offenders are an extremely diverse group in terms of both their offending and the extent of their psychological needs (Vaughan and Badger, 1995). Those admitted to maximum security typically present with challenging behaviours that are underscored by multiple psychological vulnerabilities, and a documented past history of difficulty in benefiting from formal/informal helping agencies (Taylor, 1997). The prevalence of birth trauma, head injury and previous abuse of alcohol and drugs is higher in this group than in the general population (Quayle et al., 1996, 1998; Lumsden et al., 1998; Taylor et al., 1998).

A substantial subgroup of those in high-security hospitals has experienced significant social damage during childhood, including physical, emotional and sexual abuse, instability within the family, and sudden changes in parenting (Taylor, 1997). For a variety of reasons, case-note records of childhood sexual abuse often underestimate the true prevalence of such incidents for male in-patients (Lab and Moore, 2005). Histories of severe deprivation, abuse and institutional care often parallel those of delinquency (Kruppa et al., 1995; Heads et al., 1997).

Interpersonal trauma involves the shattering of links and affective bonds, of attachment to others, and of the capacity to think (Adshead and Van Velsen, 1996). Thus presentations of distress in the in-patient population can be very extreme and overwhelming in their impact (Derksen, 1995). Witnessing incapacity for thought and reflection can invoke a sense of helplessness in the observer (Welldon, 1997). Skills in observation and analysis can enable mental health workers to manage their own feelings as witnesses in such circumstances (Theilgaard, 1996).

WHEN TO ASSESS?

Clinical assessment is a process that takes place in and over time. At the point at which potential candidates for high-security services have been considered for possible admission, they will already have passed through a series of filters that evaluate the urgency (i.e. danger posed) and need for intervention. If admission is recommended (the purpose of which may be to arrive at a more reliable decision regarding the person's potential to benefit from intervention, and may not result in a recommendation for treatment), clinical assessment is undertaken by staff from a range of disciplines, including medical doctors, forensic psychiatrists, nurses, social workers, occupational therapists, psychotherapists, speech and language therapists, neuropsychologists and clinical and/or forensic psychologists.

The individual is observed in the 'here and now', in interaction with different people and in different settings: 'context' includes all of the circumstances that give a particular behaviour meaning (Cronbach, 1990). Individuals may disclose something of their immediate or more distant past in clinical interview, and other accounts (i.e. written records) can be placed alongside the emerging narrative of their life experience to date. Clinical history taking is a crucial tool in forensic assessment (Browne et al., 1993).

It can be difficult 'accurately' to assess personality disorder at the point of entry to a healthcare system, since this is a time when Axis I disorders are often influencing the overall picture. Re-assessment of personality during a period of remission or over time is likely to be important (Davidson, 2000). It might be anticipated that approximately one-third of admissions to forensic units will be unable to collaborate in a 'standard' way within the first 3 months of admission, although those with a diagnosis of personality disorder tend to be under-represented in this group (Moore and Gudjonsson, 2002).

With regard to observation of behaviour, the massive influence of incarceration as a context will need to be borne in mind continually (Megargee, 1995). Concurrently, staff will be required to assist in the defusing of the 'numerous domestic sources of frustration' (Cox, 1986) encountered by those who are detained

without imminent prospect of release. Given this reality, it is infinitely more productive to engage in (rather than resist) exploration of these frustrations as a component part of the clinical assessment process.

The observations of the team members are subsequently shared in multi-disciplinary meetings within a specified time period (e.g. 3 months) following admission. Differences of opinion are likely to be expressed at such a meeting, as each discipline tends to favour its own preferred set of 'predictor variables' (Monahan and Steadman, 1994). Patients are likely to present to different members of the team in different ways, which are a product of what each brings to their interactions over time: differences in power, both real (e.g. to detain versus to be detained) and perceived, are typically highly influential.

The outcome of the assessment in this setting will include diagnosis of the presenting disorder(s), a detailed summary of the information used to arrive at this conclusion, and clear recommendations for the most appropriate placement for the individual within the healthcare or criminal justice system. Importantly, a range of perspectives and experiences of the person in question is embodied from the outset in the assessment process. When risk of violence is part of the equation, this breadth of skill is a fundamental requirement (Steadman et al., 1994). Incorporating more than one viewpoint (or using more than one rater) may safeguard against some of the biases that can impact in detrimental ways on decisions about an individual's future (Hare, 1998).

THE GOALS OF CLINICAL ASSESSMENT

Clinical assessment is intimately linked with therapeutic intervention: the clinical formulation leads to ideas about how to introduce change. Piecemeal assessment is a poor basis for clinical decision making (Blackburn, 2000): interventions that are not founded upon a clear description of the needs of the individual are likely to lack purpose and direction, and will be difficult to justify to the recipient. The central objective of all clinical assessment is to gather information that will ultimately be useful in implementing therapy and increasing a patient's well-being (Millon, 1999). For the goals of treatment planning, monitoring and prediction in forensic services, the relationship(s) between (a) clinical syndromes, (b) personality and (c) dangerousness need to be understood as far as is possible for each individual.

Assessment at the outset of an admission for treatment provides a baseline against which future behaviour can be compared, and subsequent evaluations may be used as a measure of 'outcome' (Hughes et al., 1997; Newton, 1998; Quayle and Moore, 1998). The majority of those who remain in high-security hospitals will require a range of further assessments (e.g. psycho-sexual, anger management, repeat neuropsychological, detailed drug and alcohol evaluations), as determined by ongoing treatment plans.

WHAT TO ASSESS?

A distinguishing feature for many in the high-security hospital is that patients arrive *in spite of* previous attempts to treat or contain their problems (Taylor, 1997). The complexity of the problems with which both men (Grounds et al., 1987) and women (Bland et al., 1999) with personality disorder in secure settings typically present underscores the rationale for a wide-ranging exploration of need organized within a developmental framework, which can track continuities and discontinuities over time. What constitutes a needs assessment in high security?

NEUROPSYCHIATRIC/PSYCHOLOGICAL INDICES OF FUNCTIONING

Establishing the cognitive parameters of the individual's functioning is of clinical importance with respect to diagnostic formulation. Neurophysiological (Howard, 1984; Lumsden and Howard, 1999), neuroimaging (Chesterman et al., 1994; Wong et al., 1997), and neuropsychological assessment, including intellectual, performance and verbal skills, and memory functioning (Hill et al., 1997) serve to highlight pathology resulting from birth trauma, head injury and drug and sustained alcohol misuse. Such factors, particularly when combined with other stressors such as maternal deprivation, have been implicated in the aetiology of abnormal personality (Coid, 1999). Bremner and colleagues (1995) have reported anatomical changes in individuals following exposure to stress, associated with neuropsychological dysfunction and altered personality development.

The results of these assessments require interpretation for individual patients in the context of their life experience, as Miller (1999) points out with reference to the evaluation of the impact of head injury. Investigation of possible physical causation identifies individuals with biological or neurological deficits, which may be treatable using a combination of mood-stabilizing drugs and other psychological treatments.

PERSONALITY AND MOTIVATION

Three broad questions inform Westen's (1996) 'theory- and data-driven guide' to personality assessment.

1. What are this person's psychological resources?
2. What motivates them?
3. What is their experience of themselves, of others, and their capacity to relate?

Armed with answers to such questions, it may then be possible to relate patterns of personality characteristics to typologies (e.g. under-controlled, over-controlled, inhibited, etc.) derived from taxonomic research with similar populations (Blackburn, 1999), and to delineate need that can be addressed via clinical intervention.

Westen has proposed that psychological resources comprise cognitive functions, affective experience, (usefully distinguished from) affect regulation, and behavioural coping skills. Intensity of affect, its regulation, and thinking style reflect an interaction of temperament, socialization and experience. These variables have been most frequently described for individuals with a diagnosis of borderline personality disorder (Derksen, 1995), and represent primary targets for intervention in the internationally recognized psychological treatment programmes (Layden et al., 1993; Linehan, 1993; Young, 1994; Ryle, 1997). There is evidence to support the relationship between specific maladaptive beliefs and at least five of the personality disorders as predicted by cognitive theory (Beck et al., 2001).

In his research on the interpersonal expectations of offenders in maximum security, Blackburn (1999) has shown how extreme interpersonal styles are maintained by specific patterns of biased expectations, which foster 'self-fulfilling prophecies' for the individual (e.g. expectations of criticism attract hostility, expectations of trust attract sincerity, etc.). It has been proposed that construing the interactional pattern (particularly as it stabilizes in relationships) as the problem rather than the person(ality) might potentially enable the person to separate from the problem and generate other possibilities for themselves (Tomm, 1992; Dickerson and Zimmerman, 1995). The idea of changing the environment to better suit the person as a management possibility for some personality disorders is emerging as an alternative mode of intervention (Tyrer, 2002).

Westen (1995) proposes that motivation, comprising wishes, fears and values, can be hierarchically organized, such that specific objectives might be embedded within broader goals (e.g. 'I wish I was strong'; 'I'm afraid that people are out to get me'; 'I value being in control'). Lack of goal direction and affective deficit are associated with a clinical diagnosis of psychopathy (Howard et al., 1984; Lösel, 1998). Equally, criminality may be the product of calculated risk taking (Welldon, 1997), and such attitudes require monitoring and challenge. The particular combination of motives and the conflicts that these engender are of interest with respect to describing people's experience of themselves, the world and others. The articulation and documentation of such conflict may be a crucial first step in unravelling associated distress (Ryle, 1997).

DANGEROUSNESS AND RISK

The relationship between dangerous behaviour and personality disorder is inevitably complex and indirect (Blackburn, 1999). It is very difficult to establish causation for adult disorders from particular childhood or adolescent experiences (Porter, 1996), although early victimization and violence are risk factors for subsequent psychological disturbance (Follette et al., 1996; Luntz-Weiler and Widom, 1996).

The ongoing assessment and management of risk is perhaps the most important function of forensic services (Rose, 1998). Dispositional, historical, situational and clinical factors should inform risk analysis (Steadman et al., 1994; Webster et al., 1994; O'Rourke et al., 1997): the broader the information base, the less uncertainty is likely to compromise decision making (Carson, 1994). The more salient pieces of information have then to be selected and simplified so that they can be incorporated into treatment plans for individuals with personality disorder. Members of the team should be alert to the bias of clinical anecdotes and myths, which can create unwarranted emphases in the decision-making process (Bjorkly, 1997). 'Negative' predictions and prognoses (e.g. 'He won't be able to cope with that'; 'She'll never change') can easily trump the more positive (but hopefully not naïve) observations (e.g. 'He was supportive of others in the group today') of experienced professionals in the forensic setting (Price, 1997).

Whilst a focus on the potential to harm is perhaps inevitable, several authors point out the need to document the individual's personal strengths and the protective factors that can serve to ameliorate the impact of interactional problems (Lösel, 1993). The clinical approach to risk assessment is thus based on functional analysis of the situational and individual risks posed in different contexts, generating a set of probabilities associated with specified dangerous behaviours (Beck-Sander and Clark, 1998). On the basis of a systematic analysis of a set of clinical indicators, what triggers aggression? What inhibits it? What is the impact of a change in mental state on the individual's self-regulatory mechanisms (Bjorkly, 1997)?

Risk prediction has been dominated by the maxim that past behaviour most reliably predicts future behaviour (Walker, 1991); diagnostic and mental state variables are seen as much less reliable predictors (Monahan, 1988). Generally, global descriptors create a static impression of the individual and his/her behaviour, and do not reflect possible changes over time and circumstances (Sloore, 1988; Hall, 1989; Towl and Crighton, 1995). The clinical challenge is therefore to find ways of measuring factors that are neither 'tarnished by circularity' nor dependent on past offending (Lumsden and Howard, 1999), but that are potentially changeable by intervention (Strand et al., 1999).

Recent initiatives for services for the 'dangerous and severely personality disordered' (DSPD) recommend the use of a 'battery of standardized procedures' during the assessment process, and routine inclusion of the Psychopathy Checklist – Revised (PCL-R) (Hare, 1991) on the basis of its reliability as a predictor of violent recidivism (Serin and Amos, 1995). Research supports the notion that risk of violence can be understood in terms of four fundamental personality dimensions:

1. impulse control
2. affect regulation
3. narcissism
4. paranoid personality style.

The last two dimensions increase the risk of violence in people with schizophrenia spectrum disorders (Nestor, 2002). Patients with histories of violence towards others and personal victimization are at increased risk of being assaultative and requiring restraint (Flannery et al., 2002). As quoted from Josephine Hardy: 'Damaged people are dangerous: they know they can survive' (see Adshead, 1994). Acknowledging actuarial realities (i.e. high-risk status) whilst creating and capitalizing upon opportunities for change can support a therapeutic focus.

FORMULATING TREATABILITY

As a term, like personality disorder, 'treatability' tends to imply that there is something internal to the individual that has the potential or otherwise for change. This can be misleading, because, in practice, treatability rests upon the interaction between the patient's potential to move from whatever position he or she starts from and our ability to measure this. Adshead (2001) has delineated a seven-factor model of treatability, including the nature and severity of pathology, previous health/ill-health, the timing of intervention, and the knowledge and availability of relevant treatments. For personality disorder specifically, information from a series of steps will need to be integrated by the clinical team in arriving at a view of treatability for each individual (Kosky and Thorne, 2001).

- The first involves diagnosis. Treatment goals for those with personality disorder are often more modest (e.g. raise self-esteem, reduce self-harm) than the amelioration of 'personality disorder' itself.
- The second possible step involves assessment of the person's capacity to engage with others, since this forms the basis of the therapeutic alliance. The extent to which any individual can enter into intimate relationships with others is

likely to be dependent on his or her representations of past relations; early experience thus provides the 'intrapsychic substrate' for interpersonal behaviour (Westen, 1995). Derksen (1995) has compiled accounts of the characteristic experience of others in interaction with those who meet the criteria for a personality disorder diagnosis: for those with psychotic traits (e.g. paranoid), trust can only be won very gradually, and for those who are described as schizoid, intimacy is hard to maintain. The self-absorbed (narcissistic) tend to be reluctant to engage in dialogue about themselves, and expect little from their relationships. Problems with excessive dependency and avoidance (Cluster C) typically emerge through indirect means once a relationship is established. Rage tends to surface quickly during interactions with those who meet the criteria for Cluster B (borderline, antisocial, histrionic) disorders. Whilst intolerable instability and personal suffering are associated with a 'borderline' diagnosis, suffering in the person's surroundings tends to be associated with 'antisocial' traits (Derksen, 1995). As a crucial step in articulating realistic expectations and goals for therapy from staff and patient perspectives, treatment contracts may be usefully introduced at this stage.

- A third step might involve assessment of the patient's functional level. Information gleaned from colleagues in different parts of the service will be important to integrate with the overall picture; the ability to operate in other placements (e.g. at education, in occupational therapy) can be a proxy for the ability to engage in therapy, since these activities will require interactional and other skills.
- Motivation and commitment to change can be assessed within models of the stages of change (Prochaska et al., 1994).

Motivational interviewing techniques can then be used to encourage reflection on the possible benefits of change and to formulate plans to support the process of maintaining new behaviours.

- A fifth component of treatability might include articulation of the psychological difficulties but also the strengths that individuals can bring to bear in their immediate circumstances and in facing the future (Meux, 2000).
- In forensic services in particular, the importance of the index (and other) offence(s) needs to be integrated in the formulation of treatability. The monitoring of 'parallel behaviours' and offence-specific beliefs (e.g. violent fantasy, subversive attitudes, minimization, denial, sexual preferences, etc.) will provide priorities for treatments to reduce risk.

THE ASSESSMENT OF PERSONALITY DISORDER

Comprehensive clinical assessment of personality disorder within forensic in-patient populations thus rests upon multi-disciplinary, and also multi-modal, approaches. Some of the tools available to the researcher in this enterprise are discussed by Blackburn in Chapter 3 of this text. Personality questionnaire measures yield research findings at a remarkable rate, but studies that facilitate the incorporation of assessment information into the treatment process are less well documented (Butcher and Rouse, 1996). The emphasis below is on the *range* of possible methods available to clinicians rather than on any systematic evaluation of their relative merits.

FACE-TO-FACE INTERVIEWS

The reliability of unstandardized clinical evaluations of personality disorder generally falls within the 'poor to fair' range, but can be greatly improved if joint interviews are conducted by those with similar ideas about what they want to ask (Zimmerman, 1994). A number of semi-structured interview schedules are available – e.g. the Structured Clinical Interview for DSM-III, Axis II (SCID-II, Spitzer et al., 1989), PDE (Loranger et al., 1987) and its latest versions – to enable clinicians to approach the diagnostic task in a more systematic way.

In a study of the divergence between clinical and research methods for assessing personality disorders, Westen (1997) found that clinicians of 'every theoretical persuasion' perceived direct questions (e.g. 'Have you ever been told that you seemed like a shallow or superficial kind of person?') to be less helpful in the diagnostic process than *observation* of the person's behaviour, and *listening* to descriptions of his or her relationships with others. Aside from the (potentially adverse) impact on the recipient's self-esteem of asking direct questions of this kind, what assumptions do such measures make about the person's ability to respond to such a question? Westen (1997) has outlined a number of limitations of the 'direct question' method, including the extent to which people have cognitive access to such information about themselves, and the defensive biases (e.g. detachment as a coping strategy) that are likely to be invoked by this method of enquiry. Thus, typically, diagnosis of personality disorder is arrived at on the basis of information about the history of the person's relationships and functioning *and* his or her responses in clinical interviews.

SELF-REPORT QUESTIONNAIRES

Psychological 'testing' has been used as an adjunct to psychiatric diagnosis since the nineteenth century (Patrick, 1996). Zimmerman (1994) provides a useful outline of some of the factors (e.g. coverage, correspondence to DSM-IV, the clinical experience required of the interviewer) that might be taken into consideration in choosing a questionnaire to assess personality disorder. Other factors may need to be taken into consideration for the high-security population. What is the respondent's level of literacy? Are the questions culturally applicable (Ballard, 1989)? Are the norms applicable? What difference does the gender of the respondent make (Nikelly, 1996)? How many items does the measure include? Although one of the most widely used and researched personality inventories (Walsh and Betz, 1995), particularly in early research with offender populations (Megargee and Bohn, 1979), the length of the (566-item) Minnesota Multiphasic Personality Inventory (MMPI, Hathaway and McKinley, 1967) is sometimes prohibitive for even the most motivated new arrival on the secure hospital admission unit.

Self-report measures – e.g. Millon Clinical Multiaxial Inventory (MCMI-III, Millon, 1984), Personality Diagnostic Questionnaire (PDQ, Hyler et al., 1988) – are very useful as an opportunity for patients to endorse or deny aspects of their experience of themselves and others. Interpretation of the profiles generated by this method should always be situated within a more comprehensive clinical formulation of the person's interpersonal presentation (Westen, 1995). Why? Because questionnaires designed to index Axis II diagnoses tend to evidence weak validity: if the operational criteria (i.e. DSM-IV) against which the validity of instruments designed to diagnose personality disorder are measured are themselves invalid, how are findings to be interpreted (Zimmerman, 1994)? Is it the criteria that are invalid, or the instrument designed to measure them?

As with the semi-structured interview schedules, self-report measures are reliant on direct questions, and (erroneously) assume that the respondents can, or will be able to, report reliably on their psychological functioning. Whilst suitable for establishing conscious beliefs, questionnaire measures yield unreliable data in situations where there is low self-knowledge and high defensiveness (Westen, 1995). Psychodynamic theory generates the hypothesis that defence mechanisms, as internal moderators of conflict, serve to maintain an intrapsychic equilibrium (Bateman, 1996). It may be developmentally necessary that the vulnerable self is protected, via defences, from uncomfortably discrepant incoming information, such that the individual can only answer from a position of developmental arrest, even if he or she is trying to be 'honest and open'.

Personality disorder is associated with affective and cognitive avoidance (Young, 1999). Researchers (e.g. Shedler et al., 1993) have shown that those who report an absence of psychological symptoms but show a pattern of cardiac reactivity indicative of distress associated with early memories do not tend to obtain high 'lie' scores on self-report scales. Consistent with this phenomenon, 'floor' effects (i.e. depressed score profiles) are commonly noted in questionnaire findings with secure hospital participants who are perceived by others to be functioning outside the 'normal' range (Quayle and Moore, 1998). As an adaptation to this type of presentation, experiential techniques (e.g. imagery and role-play) can be introduced in therapy to generate higher levels of affect and gain access to habitually avoided material (McGinn et al., 1995). Conversely, studies consistently find evidence that patients over-report pathology when they are acutely ill (Zimmerman, 1994) or perhaps are seeking to secure a transfer from prison to hospital.

With these provisos in mind, measures designed to tap Axis I disorders (e.g. the Beck Depression Inventory, Beck and Steer, 1987), specific attitudes towards offending (e.g. the Gudjonsson Blame Attribution Inventory, Gudjonsson and Singh, 1989), and (albeit self-reported) behavioural outcomes (e.g. developments in anger control, Renwick et al.,

1997) can be useful for assessing specific issues in the process of intervention. Scores must be interpreted in the context of the person's characteristic presentation and motivation to change. Overall, self-report inventories and semi-structured interviews have been recommended for systematic, replicable and objective assessments of personality disorder, and are considered less susceptible to gender, cultural and ethnic biases than unstructured assessments (Widiger and Axelrod, 1995).

OBSERVATION OF INTERPERSONAL BEHAVIOUR AND THE USE OF INFORMANT RATINGS

Direct observation by staff of the individual's response to others is afforded by the in-patient environment (e.g. with peers on the ward, at a social function, in occupational therapy). The Chart of Interpersonal Reactions in Closed Living Environments (CIRCLE, Blackburn and Renwick, 1996) is a rating scale with norms for hospitalized male forensic patients that can be completed by staff familiar with the patient. Circumplex models of interpersonal characteristics have a long history in the study of personality assessment (Haslam et al., 2002). Nurse assessment of interpersonal style is gaining empirical support as a comparatively simple yet useful tool in the high-security setting, capable of distinguishing between different diagnostic groups (McCartney et al., 1999) and of generating cognitive–interpersonal targets for intervention (Blackburn, 1999). Again, incorporating the ratings of more than one observer might protect against (counter-transferential) biases that foster and maintain the rejection of those with 'malignant' reputations (Watts and Morgan, 1994).

The defining features of the personality disorders are based on an extended longitudinal perspective of how individuals interact with a constantly changing environment (Zimmerman, 1994). The experience of relatives, or other people who have had contact over time with the individual, will also be an important source of information for the clinical team. Fundamental discrepancies in the accounts of perpetrators and victims (and some family members may have played *both* roles in relation to the identified patient; Bentovim, 1996) highlight the need to obtain information from people other than the offender (and sometimes people other than family members) regarding interpersonal violence (Estroff and Zimmer, 1994). Building partnerships with relatives, who are likely to be suffering, or to have suffered in numerous ways as a consequence of the patient's admission, is also a clinical priority from the point of admission (McGann and McKeown, 1995).

There are measures designed to capture at least patients' perspectives on their early years – e.g. the Family Relations Test (FRT, Bene, 1965), Young's Parent Inventory (YPI-1, Young, 1994), the Adult Attachment Interview (AAI, Main and Goldwyn, 1989) – which, if administered with adaptations for the high-security population (see Turton et al., 2001), can complement the social history in providing a foundation for understanding some of the critical features of the individual's socialization experience. Research has shown that people with a diagnosis of borderline personality disorder have a tendency to view others negatively when compared with 'normal' controls (Arntz and Veen, 2001).

The Q-sort method has an established history in the study of personality (Westen, 1996), and is an alternative method for capturing complex clinical impressions (Block, 1961). Stimulated by a comprehensive critique of Axis II measurement instruments, the Shedler–Westen Assessment Procedure (SWAP-200; Westen and Shedler, 1999) relies on the judgements of a clinician observer when presented with personality descriptive statements. The use of clinicians as informants can by-pass the problems inherent in self-report tools, and maintain an

element of clinical expertise in the observation and inferential process.

TASK PERFORMANCE, PROJECTIVE AND IPSATIVE MEASURES

Tests of performance involve the recording of response to a standard task, usually one that is designed to generate evidence of a specific response style, ability or characteristic (Cronbach, 1990). Such tests range from being highly structured (e.g. the Wechsler Adult Intelligence Scale, Revised (WAIS-R), Wechsler, 1981) to almost totally unstructured (e.g. the Rorschach Inkblot technique, Exner, 1993). The purpose of the latter (i.e. tasks with 'projective' qualities) has been argued to be non-transparent, and therefore less open to manipulation in the assessment of some of the personality disorders. The inherent ambiguity in these assessments can be particularly useful in highlighting individual features of special interest, such as defence mechanisms and possible motives for criminal acts (Hill et al., 1996).

Task approach and error analysis are widely recognized as a component part of neuropsychological assessment, and can be used to discriminate between diagnostic categories. For example, Hill and colleagues (1997) report a significant association between the tendency to display cognitive inflexibility (perseveration) and a case-note diagnosis of antisocial personality disorder. Elevated rates of cognitive disturbance and indications of associated neurological abnormality have been found in offenders with psychopathic traits (Lapierre et al., 1995), as reviewed by Blair in Chapter 7.

Advocates of idiographic approaches – in which each person is treated as a lawful, integrated system to be studied in his or her own right (Aiken, 1989) – emphasize the fact that the individual produces data that can be generalized to other individuals. This represents an advantage over aggregate (group-based) data (Brown, 1998), especially in the search for interventions that reliably produce change. Tasks that involve ipsative measurement (i.e., a format in which the variables being measured are compared with each other) might include the (unstructured) use of personal records (e.g. biographies, diary keeping), repertory grid (Houston, 1998) and card-sorting (Canter et al., 1985) techniques.

PSYCHODYNAMIC DIAGNOSIS

During clinical assessment, psychotherapists are trained to organize their conceptualization of case history in terms that describe the links between a patient's symptoms and the disorders of his or her emotional and cognitive development. Historically, psychological constructs derived from psychoanalysis provided the basis for the classification of mental phenomena. A recent initiative led by German researchers and clinicians has set out to operationalize these diagnostic classes in terms of observable and testable descriptions of the patient's experience of sickness, relationships, conflict and structure (OPD Task Force, 2001). An example of one element of this system would be the description of the patient's habitual interpersonal behaviour (e.g. 'The patient time and again experiences himself in such a way that he is ...') and the reaction of others (e.g. 'The patient time and again experiences others in such a way that they are ...').

The concept of conflict (defined as fixed patterns in an individual's experience, outside of his or her awareness) is another very useful one in clinical work with personality disorder. The hypothesis that internalised unconscious and long-term conflict will find expression via behaviour and symptoms, and emerge in the transference and counter-transference, provides an important added dimension in the overall diagnostic and needs assessment. In order to complete the interpersonal picture, the therapist rater must also record his or her experience

as follows: 'Time and time again, others, including the therapist, experience that the patient is ...', and 'Time and time again, others, including the therapist, experience themselves in their interaction with the patient as ...'.

THE PATIENT'S PERSPECTIVE

What about the person, designated the 'patient', who is the object of this level of scrutiny? For some, such a range of input and attention is unprecedented in their life history, and utterly overwhelming as a consequence. Refusal to participate should not be confused with clinical denial: comparatively few high-security hospital patients refuse to participate in any form of assessment, particularly if the purpose of the initiative is genuine, in their interests and appropriately explained to them (Theilgaard, 1996). Patients with 'ego-centric' disorders rarely initially share the clinician's perspective as to what might need to change, and can often feel very discouraged, even habituated to disappointment (Young, 1999). If co-operation between the assessors and the person being assessed breaks down, the professionals' task is to shift to assessment of what might have contributed to the impasse. It is important to 'leave the door open' for therapeutic windows of opportunity to re-emerge.

Clinical pathways that facilitate the introduction of a range of therapies following the initial assessment process are essential if the motivation (of staff and patients) fostered by the tasks of admission is to be maintained. A problem-centred assessment process facilitates the prioritization of needs to be addressed within treatment. Disillusionment can quickly set in if promised interventions do not materialize, and it might be all too easy to 'pathologize' expressions of disappointment as evidence of disorder. Equally, rushing into and 'surviving' interventions without engaging any more than is necessary can constitute psychological avoidance (at which individuals with traumatic histories are likely to be particularly adept).

The tone in which members of the clinical team communicate their 'findings' to the patient during the assessment process is of pivotal importance in the establishment (or otherwise) of therapeutic alliances that will enable the patient to contemplate collaborative goal-setting and change. Empathic exploration provides the foundation for therapy (Cox, 1986). Feedback to the individual is essential: space and time for this aspect of the assessment are now a core component of the Care Programme Approach (CPA), which has been described as the cornerstone for managing individual clinical risk. In the past, it has been the case that the person at the centre of inquiry has not been appropriately included in discussion as to what might be done about his or her problems. Equally, some clinical risk discussions must be held in confidential meetings. Getting the balance right for different patients is the clinical team's task.

In his outline of methods of 'taking the plunge' and talking with patients with personality disorder about their diagnosis, Tyrer (1998) reports that the outcomes of his provision of feedback have included improved diagnostic accuracy and more active participation by patients in their treatment. Others have sounded a note of caution: the personality disorder label still carries pejorative connotations in many services (Ramon et al., 2001). Personality disorder does not enhance the prognosis for change; on the contrary, it is typically associated with impediments to the remission of mental health problems (Tyrer and Simmonds, 2003). There is evidence that co-morbid personality disorder is associated with an increased risk of violence in psychosis (Moran et al., 2003), and patients have the right to be made aware of the implications of diagnoses by their clinical and legal teams. Davidson (2000) recommends that clinicians consider what this diagnosis might mean to the person. She argues that assessment of their problems (both current and historical) provides the opportunity to explain why the term

'personality disorder' organizes some understanding of their experiences in such a way that it: (a) makes sense, (b) is non-pejorative, and (c) allows the possibility that change is possible. Proper collaboration inevitably requires clinical sensitivity, time and perseverance (Feldbrugge, 1992; McGinn et al., 1995; Millon, 1999).

CONCLUSIONS

Ideally, the clinical assessment of personality disorder will generate useful, practical suggestions for potential opportunities to intervene and at least disrupt the maintenance of pervasively destructive interpersonal patterns. In this sense it can be an exercise that generates (realistic) enthusiasm and breathes life into otherwise seemingly hopeless narratives. Some of its components will necessarily not be completely rigorous or possible to short cut: how long does it take to 'get to know' another person? Standardization of the framework of assessment affords benefits, including objectivity and the potential for systematic evaluation.

Behaviour on locked wards is governed by a multiplicity of messages of reward and punishment that also shape actions and restrict abilities to engage in new roles. Many of the constraints of the secure hospital setting, if misapplied, can aggravate the challenging behaviour it is designed to contain (Davies, 1996). Thus a range of descriptors (e.g. developmental, multi-variate, comprehensive) is needed to capture the type of information that is used in the process of formal assessment, and patients have the right to challenge the conclusions via tribunal etc.

There is clearly much scope for refinement of the process of the assessment of personality disorder in forensic services. Is there a supervisory framework in place to enable clinicians working with offenders to listen to and record that which is unbearably difficult to hear (Cox, 1996)? How do we weight the importance of the information we gather? Whose views are given precedence within the clinical team, and with what consequence? What do we do with discrepant information? In clinical practice, it can seem to be the case that the assessment process is more readily conducted than the treatment phases of a forensic patient's admission, which creates the dilemma that there is as yet a limited basis on which to recommend with confidence the interventions that systematically address the needs of those who have been assessed as having the potential to benefit.

REFERENCES

Adshead G (1994). Damage: trauma and violence in a sample of women referred to a forensic service. *Behavioural Sciences and the Law* **12**:235–49.

Adshead G (2001). Murmurs of discontent: treatment and treatability of personality disorder. *Advances in Psychiatric Treatment* **7**:407–16.

Adshead G and Van Velsen C (1996). Psychotherapeutic work with victims of trauma. In: Cordess C and Cox M (eds), *Forensic Psychotherapy: Crime, Psychodynamics and the Offender Patient*, Vol. II: *Mainly Practice*. London: Jessica Kingsley, 355–69.

Aiken LR (1989). *Assessment of Personality*. Boston: Allyn and Bacon.

American Psychiatric Association (1994). *Diagnostic and Statistical Manual of Mental Disorders,* fourth edition. Washington, DC: American Psychiatric Association.

Anastasi A (1976). *Psychological Testing*, fourth edition. New York: MacMillan.

Arntz A and Veen G (2001). Evaluations of others by borderline patients. *Journal of Nervous and Mental Disease* **189**:513–21.

Ballard BL (1989). Ethnocultural issues in the assessment of psychopathology. In: Wetzler S (ed.), *Measuring Mental Illness: Psychometric Assessment for Clinicians*. Washington, DC: American Psychiatric Press, Inc., 259–65.

Bateman A (1996). Defence mechanisms. General and forensic aspects. In: Cordess C and Cox M (eds), *Forensic Psychotherapy: Crime, Psychodynamics and the Offender Patient*, Vol. I: *Mainly Theory*. London: Jessica Kingsley, 41–51.

Beck AT, Butler AC, Brown GK, Dahlsgaard KK, Newman CF and Beck JS (2001). Dysfunctional beliefs discriminate personality disorders. *Behaviour, Research and Therapy* **39**:1213–25.

Beck AT and Steer RA (1987). *Beck Depression Inventory: Manual*. New York: Harcourt Brace Jovanovich.

Beck-Sander A and Clark A (1998). Psychological models of psychosis: implications for risk assessment. *Journal of Forensic Psychiatry* **9**:659–71.

Bene E (1965). *Manual for the Adult Version of the Family Relations Test: An Objective Technique for Exploring Recollected Childhood Feelings*. Buckinghamshire: NFER Nelson.

Bentovim A (1996). The trauma organised system of working with family violence. In: Cordess C and Cox M (eds), *Forensic Psychotherapy: Crime, Psychodynamics and the Offender Patient*, Vol. II: *Mainly Practice*. London: Jessica Kingsley, 291–311.

Bjorkly S (1997). Clinical assessment of dangerousness in psychotic patients: some risk indicators and pitfalls. *Aggression and Violent Behaviour* **2**:167–78.

Blackburn R (1999). Violence and personality: distinguishing among violent offenders. In: Curran D and McCarney W (eds), *Psychological Perspectives on Serious Criminal Risk*. Leicester: British Psychological Society, 109–27.

Blackburn R (2000). Classification and assessment of personality disorders in mentally disordered offenders: a psychological perspective. *Criminal Behaviour and Mental Health* **10**(Suppl.):8–32.

Blackburn R and Renwick SJ (1996). Rating scales for measuring the interpersonal circle in forensic psychiatric patients. *Psychological Assessment* **8**:76–84.

Bland J, Mezey G and Dolan B (1999). Special women, special needs: a descriptive study of female Special Hospital patients. *Journal of Forensic Psychiatry* **10**:34–45.

Block J (1961). *The Q-sort Method in Personality Assessment and Psychiatric Research*. Springfield, IL: Charles C Thomas.

Bremner JD, Krystal JH, Southwick SM and Charney DS (1995). Functional anatomical correlates of the effects of stress on memory. *Journal of Traumatic Stress* **8**:527–37.

Brown JF (1998). Clinical training dissertations: some fundamental design issues that we seldom talk about. *Clinical Psychology Forum* **116**:30–3.

Browne F, Gudjonsson GH, Gunn J, Rix G, Sohn L and Taylor PJ (1993). Principles of treatment for the mentally disordered offender. In: Gunn J and Taylor PJ (eds), *Forensic Psychiatry: Clinical, Legal and Ethical Issues.* Oxford: Butterworth-Heinemann, 646–90.

Burr V (1995). Where do you get your personality from? In: *An Introduction to Social Constructionism.* London, New York: Routledge, 17–31.

Butcher JN and Rouse S (1996). Personality: individual differences and clinical assessment. *Annual Review of Psychology* **47**:87–111.

Canter D, Brown J and Groat L (1985). A multiple sorting procedure for studying conceptual systems. In: Brown J and Canter D (eds), *The Research Interview.* London: Academic Press, 79–114.

Carson D (1994). Dangerous people: through a broader conception of 'risk' and 'danger' to better decisions. *Expert Evidence* **3**:51–69.

Chesterman P, Taylor PJ, Cox T, Hill M and Lumsden J (1994). Multiple measures of cerebral state in dangerous mentally disordered inpatients. *Criminal Behaviour and Mental Health* **4**:228–39.

Coid JW (1992). DSM-III diagnosis in criminal psychopaths: a way forward. *Criminal Behaviour and Mental Health* **2**:78–94.

Coid JW (1999). Aetiological risk factors for personality disorders. *British Journal of Psychiatry* **174**:530–8.

Cox M (1986). The 'holding function' of dynamic psychotherapy in a custodial setting: a review. *Journal of the Royal Society of Medicine* **79**:162–4.

Cox M (1996). A supervisor's view. In: Cordess C and Cox M (eds), *Forensic Psychotherapy: Crime, Psychodynamics and the Offender Patient*, Vol. II: *Mainly Practice.* London: Jessica Kingsley, 199–223.

Cronbach LJ (1990). *Essentials of Psychological Testing*, fifth edition. New York: Harper and Row.

Davidson K (2000). *Cognitive Therapy for Personality Disorder.* Oxford: Butterworth-Heinemann.

Davies R (1996). The inter-disciplinary network and the internal world of the offender. In: Cordess C and Cox M (eds), *Forensic Psychotherapy: Crime, Psychodynamics and the Offender Patient*, Vol. II: *Mainly Practice.* London: Jessica Kingsley, 133–44.

Derksen J (1995). *Personality Disorders: Clinical and Social Perspectives. Assessment and Treatment Based on DSM-IV and ICD-10.* Chichester: John Wiley & Sons.

Dickerson V and Zimmerman J (1995). A constructionist exercise in anti-pathologising. *Journal of Systemic Therapies* **14**:33–45.

Dolan B, Evans C and Norton K (1995). Multiple Axis-II diagnoses of personality disorder. *British Journal of Psychiatry* **166**:107–12.

Estroff SE and Zimmer C (1994). Social networks, social support and violence among persons with severe, persistent mental illness. In: Monahan J and Steadman HJ (eds), *Violence and Mental Disorder: Developments in Risk Assessment Research.* Chicago: University of Chicago Press, 259–95.

Exner JE (1993). *The Rorschach: A Comprehensive System*, Vol. I: *Basic Foundations*, second edition. New York: John Wiley & Sons.

Feldbrugge JTTM (1992). Rehabilitation of patients with personality disorders: patient–staff collaboration used as a working model and tool. *Criminal Behaviour and Mental Health* **2**:169–77.

Flannery RB Jr, Rachlin S and Walker AP (2002). Characteristics of assaultive patients with schizophrenia versus personality disorder: six year analysis of the Assaulted Staff Action Program (ASAP). *Journal of Forensic Sciences* **47**:558–61.

Follette VM, Polunsy MA, Bechtle AE and Naugle AE (1996). Cumulative trauma: the impact of child sexual abuse, adult sexual assault, and spouse abuse. *Journal of Traumatic Stress* **9**:25–35.

Grounds AT, Quayle M, France J, Brett T, Cox M and Hamilton JR (1987). A unit for 'psychopathic disorder' patients in Broadmoor Hospital. *Medicine, Science and Law* **27**(1):21–31.

Gudjonsson GH and Singh KK (1989). The revised Gudjonsson Blame Attribution Inventory. *Personality and Individual Differences* **10**:67–70.

Hall GCN (1989). WAIS-R and MMPI profiles of men who have sexually assaulted children: evidence of limited utility. *Journal of Personality Assessment* **53**:404–12.

Hare RD (1991). The Hare Psychopathy Checklist–Revised. Toronto: Multi-Health Systems.

Hare RD (1998). The Hare PCL-R: some issues concerning its use and misuse. *Legal and Criminological Psychology* **3**:99–119.

Haslam N, Reichert T and Fiske AP (2002). Aberrant social relations in the personality disorders. *Psychology and Psychotherapy* **75**:19–31.

Hathaway SR and McKinley JC (1967). *Manual for the Minnesota Multiphasic Personality Inventory.* New York: Psychological Corporation.

Heads TC, Taylor P and Leese M (1997). Childhood experiences of patients with schizophrenia and a history of violence: a special hospital sample. *Criminal Behaviour and Mental Health* **7**:117–30.

Hill GM, Chesterman P, Lumsden J and Bishopp D (1996). Neuropsychiatric indices in a maximum secure admission sample: an experimental analysis of Rorschach responding. *British Journal of Projective Psychology* **41**:33–44.

Hill GM, Chesterman P, Murphy D, Tidmarsh D and Lumsden J (1997). Neuropsychiatric indices in a maximum secure sample: DSM-III-R psychiatric diagnosis and the analysis of error in WMS visual design recall. In: Deu N and Roberts L (eds), *Dangerous, Disordered and Doubly Deviant: Issues in Criminological and Legal Psychology* **27**:40–8.

Houston J (1998). *Making Sense with Offenders. Personal Construct Therapy and Change.* Chichester: John Wiley & Sons.

Howard KI, Orlinsky DE and Leuger RH (1994). Clinically relevant outcome research in individual psychotherapy: new models guide the researcher and clinician. *British Journal of Psychiatry* **165**:4–8.

Howard RC (1984). The clinical EEG and personality in mentally abnormal offenders. *Psychological Medicine* **14**:569–80.

Howard R, Bailey R and Newman A (1984). A preliminary study of Hare's 'Research Scale for the Assessment of Psychopathy; in mentally-abnormal offenders. *Personality and Individual Differences* **5**:389–96.

Hughes G, Hogue T, Hollin C and Champion H (1997). First-stage evaluation of a treatment programme for personality disordered offenders. *Journal of Forensic Psychiatry* **8**:515–17.

Hyler SE, Rieder RD, Williams JBW, Spitzer RL, Hendler J and Lyons M (1988). The Personality Diagnostic Questionnaire: development and preliminary results. *Journal of Personality Disorders* **2**:229–37.

Jackson DN and Livesley WJ (1995). Possible contributions from personality assessment to the classification of personality disorders. In: Livesley WJ (ed.), *The DSM-IV Personality Disorders.* New York: Guilford Press, 459–81.

Koerner K, Kohlenberg RJ and Parker CR (1996). Diagnosis of personality disorder: a radical behavioural alternative. *Journal of Consulting and Clinical Psychology* **64**:1169–76.

Kosky N and Thorne P (2001). Personality disorder – the rules of engagement. *International Journal of Psychiatry in Clinical Practice* **5**:169–72.

Kruppa I, Hickey N and Hubbard C (1995). The prevalence of post traumatic stress disorder in a special hospital population of legal psychopaths. *Psychology, Crime and Law* **2**:131–41.

Lab D and Moore E (2005). Prevalence and denial of sexual abuse in a male psychiatric in-patient population. *Journal of Traumatic Stress* **18**:323–30.

Lapierre D, Braun CMJ and Hodgins S (1995). Ventral frontal deficits in psychopathy: neuropsychological test findings. *Neuropsychologia* **33**:139–51.

Layden MA, Newman CF, Freeman A and Byers Morse S (1993). *Cognitive Therapy of Borderline Personality Disorder.* Boston, MA: Allyn and Bacon.

Linehan M (1993). *Cognitive Behavioral Treatment of Borderline Personality Disorder.* New York: Guilford Press.

Loranger AW, Susman VL, Oldham JM and Russakoff LM (1987). The Personality Disorder Examination: a preliminary report. *Journal of Personality Disorders* **1**:1–13.

Lösel F (1993). The effectiveness of treatment in institutional and community settings. *Criminal Behaviour and Mental Health* **3**:416–37.

Lösel F (1998). Treatment and management of psychopaths. In: Cooke DJ, Forth A and Hare R (eds), *Psychopathy: Theory, Research and Implications for Society.* Dordrecht: Kluwer Academic Publishers, 303–54.

Lumsden J, Chesterman LP and Hill GM (1998). Neuropsychiatric indices in a high security admission sample. I: Estimating the prevalence. *Criminal Behaviour and Mental Health* **8**:285–310.

Lumsden J and Howard R (1999). The contingent negative variation as a predictor of reoffending behaviour. In: Curran D and McCarney W (eds), *Psychological Perspectives on Serious Criminal Risk.* Leicester: British Psychological Society, 88–108.

Luntz-Weiler B and Widom C (1996). Psychopathy and violent behaviour in abused and neglected young adults. *Criminal Behaviour and Mental Health* **6**:253–71.

Main M and Goldwyn R (1989). *Adult Attachment Rating and Classificatory System.* Berkeley, CA: Department of Psychology, University of California at Berkeley.

McCartney M, Collins M, Park B, Larkin E and Duggan C (1999). The assessment and meaning of the legal classification of offenders in a special hospital using observer ratings of interpersonal style. *Journal of Forensic Psychiatry* **10**:17–33.

McCrae RR and John OP (1992). An introduction to the five-factor model and its applications. *Journal of Personality* **60**:175–215.

McGann G and McKeown M (1995). Applying psychosocial interventions. The Thorn initiative in a forensic setting. *Psychiatric Care* **2**:133–6.

McGinn LK, Young JE and Sanderson WC (1995). When and how to do longer term therapy without feeling guilty. *Cognitive and Behavioural Practice* **2**:187–212.

Megargee EI (1995). Assessment research in correctional settings: methodological issues and practical problems. *Psychological Assessment* **7**:359–66.

Megargee EI and Bohn MJ (1979). *Classifying Criminal Offenders. A New System Based on the MMPI.* Beverley Hills, CA/London: Sage Publications.

Meux C (2000). Exploring the assessment of personality disorder. *Criminal Behaviour and Mental Health* **10**(Suppl.):1–7.

Miller E (1999). Head injury and offending. *Journal of Forensic Psychiatry* **10**:157–66.

Millon T (1984). *Millon Clinical Multiaxial Inventory*, third edition. Minneapolis, MI: National Computer Systems.

Millon T (1999). *Personality Guided Therapy.* Chichester: John Wiley & Sons.

Millon T (2002). Assessment is not enough: the SPA should participate in constructing a comprehensive clinical science of personality. *Journal of Personality Assessment* **78**:209–18.

Monahan J (1988). Risk assessment of violence amongst the mentally disordered: generating useful knowledge. *International Journal of Law and Psychiatry* **11**:249–57.

Monahan J and Steadman H (1994). Towards a rejuvenation of risk assessment research. In: Monahan J and Steadman HJ (eds), *Violence and Mental Disorder: Developments in Risk Assessment.* Chicago/London: University of Chicago Press, 1–17.

Moore E and Gudjonsson GH (2002). Blame attribution in relation to index offence on admission to secure hospital services. *Psychology, Crime and Law* **8**:131–43.

Moran P, Walsh E, Tyrer P, Burns T, Creed F and Fahy T (2003). Impact of comorbid personality disorder on violence in psychosis: report from the UK700 Trial. *British Journal of Psychiatry* **182**:129–34.

Mullen P (1993). Care and containment in forensic psychiatry. *Criminal Behaviour and Mental Health* **3**:212–25.

Nestor PG (2002). Mental disorder and violence: personality dimensions and clinical features. *American Journal of Psychiatry* **159**:1973–8.

Newman JP and Wallace JF (1993). Psychopathy and cognition. In: Dobson KS and Kendall PC (eds), *Psychopathology and Cognition.* New York: Academic Press, 293–349.

Newton M (1998). Changes in measures of personality, hostility and locus of control during residence in a prison therapeutic community. *Legal and Criminological Psychology* **3**:209–23.

Nikelly AG (1996). Alternatives to the androcentric bias of personality disorders. *Clinical Psychology and Psychotherapy* **3**:15–22.

Norton K and Dolan B (1995). Assessing change in personality disorder. *Current Opinion in Psychiatry* **8**:371–5.

OPD Task Force (2001). *Operationalised Psychodynamic Diagnostics. Foundations and Manual.* Seattle: Hogrefe and Huber Publishers.

O'Rourke MM, Hammond SM and Davies J (1997). Risk assessment and risk management: the way forward. *Psychiatric Care* **4**:132–8.

Patrick J (1996). The use of psychological tests in the diagnosis and treatment of personality disorders. In: Links PS (ed.), *Clinical Assessment and*

Management of Secure Personality Disorders. Washington, DC: American Psychiatric Press, 49–76.

Porter S (1996). Without conscience or without active conscience? The etiology of psychopathy revisited. *Aggression and Violent Behavior* **1**:179–89.

Price R (1997). On the risks of risk prediction. *Journal of Forensic Psychiatry* **8**:1–4.

Prochaska JO, Norcross JC and DiClimente CC (1994). *Changing for Good.* New York: Avon Books.

Quayle M, Clark F, Renwick SJ, Hodge J and Spencer T (1998). Alcohol and secure hospital patients: I. An examination of the nature and prevalence of alcohol problems in secure hospital patients. *Psychology, Crime and Law* **4**:27–41.

Quayle M, Darling P, Perkins D, Lumsden J, Forshaw D and McKeown O (1996). The assessment of patients in a forensic addictive behaviours unit within a special hospital setting. *Journal of Substance Misuse* **1**:160–4.

Quayle M and Moore E (1998). Evaluating the impact of structured groupwork with men in maximum security. *Criminal Behaviour and Mental Health* **8**:77–91.

Ramon S, Castillo H and Morant N (2001). Experiencing personality disorder: a participative research. *International Journal of Social Psychiatry* **47**:1–15.

Renwick SJ, Black L, Ramm M and Novaco RW (1997). Anger treatment with forensic hospital patients. *Legal and Criminological Psychology* **2**:103–16.

Rose N (1998). Living dangerously: risk-thinking and risk management in mental health care. *Mental Health Care* **1**:263–6.

Ryle A (1997). *Cognitive Analytic Therapy and Borderline Personality Disorder: The Model and the Method.* Chichester: John Wiley & Sons.

Serin RC and Amos NL (1995). The role of psychopathy in the assessment of dangerousness. *International Journal of Law and Psychiatry* **18**:231–8.

Shea MT (1995). Interrelationships among categories of personality disorders. In: Livesley WJ (ed.), *The DSM-IV Personality Disorders.* New York: Guilford Press, 397–406.

Shedler J, Mayman M and Manis M (1993). The illusion of mental health. *American Psychologist* **48**:1117–31.

Sloore H (1988). Use of the MMPI in the prediction of dangerous behaviour. *Acta Psychiatrica Belgica* **88**:42–51.

Spitzer RL, Williams JBW, Gibbon M and First MB (1989). *Structured Interview for DSM-III-R Personality Disorders (SCID-II).* New York: New York State Psychiatric Institute, Biometrics Research.

Steadman HJ, Monahan J, Appelbaum P et al. (1994). Designing a new generation of risk assessment research. In: Monahan J and Steadman HJ (eds), *Violence and Mental Disorder: Developments in Risk Assessment.* Chicago/London: University of Chicago Press, 297–318.

Strand S, Belfrage H, Fransson G and Levander S (1999). Clinical and risk management factors in risk prediction of mentally disordered offenders – more important than historical data? *Legal and Criminological Psychology* **4**:67–76.

Taylor PJ (1986). Psychopaths and their treatment. *Journal of the Royal Society of Medicine* **12**:693–5.

Taylor PJ (1997). Damage, disease and danger. *Criminal Behaviour and Mental Health* **7**:19–48.

Taylor PJ, Leese M, Williams D, Butwell M, Daly R and Larkin E (1998). Mental disorder and violence: a special (high security) hospital study. *British Journal of Psychiatry* **172**:218–26.

Theilgaard A (1996). A clinical psychological perspective. In: Cordess C and Cox M (eds), *Forensic Psychotherapy*, Vol. II: *Mainly Practice.* London: Jessica Kingsley, 47–62.

Tomm K (Karl, Cynthia, Andrew and Vanessa) (1992). Therapeutic distinctions in an on-going therapy. In: McNamee S and Gergen KJ (eds), *Therapy as Social Construction.* Newbury Park, CA: Sage, 116–35.

Towl G and Crighton D (1995). Risk assessment in prisons: a psychological critique. *Forensic Update* **40**:6–14.

Turton P, McGauley G, Marin-Avellan L and Hughes P (2001). The Adult Attachment Interview: rating and classification problems posed by non-normative samples. *Attachment and Human Development* **3**:284–303.

Tyrer P (1992). Flamboyant, erratic, dramatic, borderline, antisocial, sadistic, narcissistic, histrionic and impulsive personality disorders: who cares which? *Criminal Behaviour and Mental Health* **2**:95–104.

Tyrer P (1995). Are personality disorders well classified in DSM-IV? In: Livesley WJ (ed.), *The DSM-IV Personality Disorders.* New York: Guilford Press, 29–42.

Tyrer P (1998). Feedback for the personality disordered. *The Journal of Forensic Psychiatry* **9**:1–4.

Tyrer P (2002). Nidiotherapy: a new approach to the treatment of personality disorder. *Acta Psychiatrica Scandinavica* **105**:469–71.

Tyrer P and Simmonds S (2003). Treatment models for those with severe mental illness and comorbid personality disorder. *British Journal of Psychiatry* **182**(Suppl. 44):S15–S18.

Ulrich S, Borkenau P and Marneros A (2001). Personality disorder in offenders: categorical versus dimensional approaches. *Journal of Personality Disorders* **15**:443–9.

Vaughan PJ and Badger D (1995). *Working with the Mentally Disordered Offender in the Community.* London: Chapman and Hall.

Walker N (1991). Dangerous mistakes. *British Journal of Psychiatry* **158**:752–7.

Walsh WB and Betz NE (1995). *Tests and Assessment*, third edition. Englewood Cliffs, NJ: Prentice Hall.

Watts D and Morgan G (1994). Malignant alienation: dangers for patients who are hard to like. *British Journal of Psychiatry* **164**:11–15.

Webster CD, Harris G, Rice M, Cormier V and Quinsey V (1994). *The Violence Prediction Scheme: Assessing Dangerousness in High Risk Men.* Toronto: University of Toronto, Centre of Criminology.

Wechsler D (1981). *Wechsler Adult Intelligence Scale – Revised Manual.* New York: The Psychological Corporation.

Welldon E (1997). To treat or not to treat: the therapeutic challenge. In: van Marle H (ed.), *Challenges in Forensic Psychotherapy.* London: Jessica Kingsley, 31–42.

Westen D (1995). A clinical–empirical model of personality: life after the Mischelian Ice Age and the NEO-lithic era. *Journal of Personality* **63**:495–524.

Westen D (1996). A model and a method for uncovering the nomothetic from the idiographic: an alternative to the five-factor model? *Journal of Research in Personality* **30**:400–13.

Westen D (1997). Divergences between clinical and research methods for assessing personality disorders: implications for research and the evolution of Axis II. *American Journal of Psychiatry* **154**:895–903.

Westen D and Shedler J (1999). Revising and assessing Axis II. Part I: Developing a clinically and empirically valid assessment method. *American Journal of Psychiatry* **156**:258–72.

Widiger T and Axelrod SR (1995). Recent developments in the clinical assessment of personality disorders. *European Journal of Psychological Assessment* **11**:213–21.

Wiggins JS (1992). Have model, will travel. *Journal of Personality* **60**:527–32.

Wong MTH, Fenwick PBC, Lumsden J, Fenton GW, Maisey M and Stevens J (1997). Repetitive and non-repetitive violent offending in male patients in a maximum security hospital: clinical and neuroimaging findings. *Medicine, Science and Law* **37**:150–60.

World Health Organization (1992). *ICD-10 Classification of Mental and Behavioural Disorders: Clinical Descriptions and Diagnostic Guidelines.* Geneva: World Health Organization.

Young JE (1994). *YPI-1.* New York: Cognitive Therapy Center.

Young JE (1999). *Cognitive Therapy for Personality Disorders: A Schema-Focused Approach*, third edition. Sarasota, FL: Professional Resource Press.

Zimmerman M (1994). Diagnosing the personality disorders. A review of issues and research methods. *Archives of General Psychiatry* **51**:225–45.

Chapter 5

PERSONALITY DISORDER IN MENTAL HEALTH LEGISLATION

Tim Exworthy

INTRODUCTION

This chapter aims to provide a brief overview of mental health legislation as it relates to personality disorder in England and Wales. It concentrates on the principal piece of legislation in this area, the Mental Health Act 1983. The legal concept of psychopathic disorder is described in general terms, along with the broad criteria for compulsory admission to hospital and the accompanying 'treatability test' for psychopathic disorder, and the criteria engaged when Mental Health Review Tribunals (MHRTs) consider the discharge of a patient from hospital. The principal provisions for compulsory admission to hospital are also outlined.

It is also important to recognize that personality disorders, as psychiatric conditions, may be relevant within other pieces of legislation. For example, under the Homicide Act 1957, a personality disorder is recognized as an 'abnormality of mind', and if this is considered to have 'substantially impaired' the person's 'mental responsibility for his acts', the charge of murder will be reduced to one of manslaughter on the grounds of diminished responsibility.

MENTAL HEALTH ACT 1983

The Mental Health Act 1983 (MHA; the Act) relates to the 'reception, care and treatment of mentally disordered patients' and comprises a number of Parts. This chapter is mostly concerned with Parts I (Application of Act: definition of mental disorder), II (compulsory admission to hospital and guardianship), III (patients concerned with criminal proceedings or under sentence) and V (MHRTs). The Act is complemented by the Code of Practice (Department of Health and Welsh Office, 1999), which provides guidance to practitioners and has recently had its status enhanced (cases of *Munjaz* and *S*). The implementation of the Act is kept under review by the Mental Health Act Commission, which also makes regular visits to hospitals where patients are detained, investigates complaints and provides independent psychiatrists (second opinion appointed doctors) under the consent to treatment provisions of the Act (Part IV).

PERSONALITY DISORDER AND PSYCHOPATHIC DISORDER

Personality disorder, as a phrase, does not feature in the MHA. Instead, the term 'psychopathic disorder' is employed as one of the four types of mental disorder (the others being mental illness, mental impairment and severe mental impairment). Psychopathic disorder is defined in section 1 of the Act as:

a persistent disorder or disability of mind (whether or not including significant impairment of intelligence) which results in abnormally aggressive or seriously irre-sponsible conduct on the part of the person concerned.

Psychopathic disorder is thus a legal con-struct rather than a clinical entity and it includes a behavioural component: 'abnormally aggres-sive or seriously irresponsible conduct'. This phrase is not defined further in the MHA, although it also features in the definitions of mental impairment and severe mental impair-ment. The Code of Practice to the MHA (Department of Health and Welsh Office, 1999), in the chapter 'People with learning disabilities', offers a definition of 'abnormally aggressive behaviour' as being:

actions ... outside the usual range of aggres-sive behaviour and which cause actual dam-age and/or real distress occurring recently or persistently or with excessive severity.

'Irresponsible conduct' refers to (paragraph 30.5):

behaviour which shows a lack of responsi-bility, a disregard of the consequences of action taken and where the results cause actual damage or real distress, either recently or persistently or with excessive severity.

Seriously irresponsible conduct would need to be proportionately more severe.

There has been a longstanding dissatisfac-tion with the term 'psychopathic disorder' (for example, Home Office and Department of Health & Social Security, 1975). More recently, the Reed Committee (Department of Health and Home Office, 1994) acknowl-edged the limited utility of the term, but rec-ognized it embraced a heterogeneous range of (paragraph 2.2):

severe personality disorders, which con-tribute to the person committing anti-social acts, usually of a recurrent or episodic type.

One important feature may be an inability to relate to others, and to take account of their feelings and safety.

The committee suggested 'psychopathic dis-order' be replaced with 'personality disorder' in the statute but not defined further.

DETENTION UNDER THE MENTAL HEALTH ACT 1983

The most recent figures available reveal that on 31 March 2004, of the 14 000 people detained under the MHA in England, 686 (4.9 per cent) were classified under the category of psy-chopathic disorder and two-thirds of them were men (Department of Health, 2004a). In the year 2003–4, there were just over 24 800 formal admissions under the MHA and of these, 117 were under the category of psycho-pathic disorder; 38.5 per cent (45) were under the provisions of Section 3, and the remainder were under Part III of the Act, with 68 per cent of them (49) being transfers of sentenced prisoners to hospital. On 31 March 2002, the last time it was reported, approximately half the patients detained under the category of psychopathic disorder were to be found in the high-security hospitals, where they made up 27 per cent of the patient population. By com-parison, in other National Health Service (NHS) facilities, such patients accounted for less than 2 per cent of in-patients (Department of Health, 2002a).

Patients assessed as (or thought to be) meet-ing the criteria for psychopathic disorder can be admitted to hospital under the provisions of the MHA. Part II of the Act sets out the provisions for the civil detention of such patients, either from the community or hav-ing been voluntary patients in hospital. It also includes the provision for guardianship, which is not a form of detention, as it does not involve a deprivation of liberty, but has criteria similar to the other provisions. Part III of the Act relates to patients involved in criminal proceedings and permits their admission to hospital during the remand period, at the time of sentencing or from prison, while serving a term of imprisonment.

Each of the relevant provisions requires two (in some cases only one) medical recommendations. In general terms, the medical recommendation includes a brief description of the clinical features of the patient's medical condition and provides reasons why the detaining power of the Act has to be employed on that occasion. In addition, the statutory criteria have to be addressed when completing the form. The exact criteria vary depending on the particular provision being applied, but must relate the type(s) of mental disorder considered present (it is possible to classify a patient as suffering from more than one form of mental disorder), specify that the particular form of mental disorder is considered to be above a threshold where treatment in hospital is considered justified (the so-called 'appropriateness test'), and that detention in hospital is necessary for at least one of the following reasons: the patient's own health or the patient's safety or for the protection of other people (the 'necessity (or safety) test'). In addition, there is a 'treatability test', which is discussed below.

The various provisions have different life spans. Some are for single use, whereas others can be renewed, some to an overall maximum period and others have no limit to the number of times they can be renewed.

DETENTION UNDER PART II, MHA

The existence of psychopathic disorder is no bar to the use of any of the provisions for hospital detention under Part II, MHA. In the provisions whose duration is limited to 72 hours or less, there is no need to distinguish between the four forms of mental disorder. Similarly, the power permitting 'admission for assessment' (Section 2), which lasts for a maximum of 28 days, requires only that the patient 'is suffering from mental disorder of a nature or degree which warrants the detention of the patient in a hospital for assessment … for at least a limited period'. As the Code of Practice (Department of Health and Welsh Office, 1999) makes clear, one of the reasons for employing Section 2 may be because 'the diagnosis and prognosis of (the) patient's condition is unclear' and so it is not possible to state with certainty which form of mental disorder the patient is suffering from.

Section 3 (admission for treatment) is the primary treatment provision in the MHA for civilly detained patients. It permits the compulsory detention in hospital for treatment, which could be enforced subject to the provisions covering consent to treatment in the MHA. Section 3 can be initiated while the patient is already detained under one of the shorter assessment orders in Part II of the Act or an application for admission under Section 3 can be made while the patient is still in the community or resides as a voluntary patient in hospital.

DETENTION UNDER PART III, MHA

In this part of the Act, the presence of psychopathic disorder, as the sole form of mental disorder, invalidates the use of either Section 36 ('remand of accused person to hospital for treatment') or Section 48 ('removal to hospital of other prisoners' – that is, those not serving terms of imprisonment), as these both apply only to patients suffering from mental illness or severe mental impairment. By contrast, psychopathic disorder is the only form of mental disorder permitted for the use of the hospital and limitation direction under Section 45A. This provision, sometimes known as a hybrid order, is an amendment to the MHA by the Crime (Sentences) Act 1997. It permits the Crown Court to pass a term of imprisonment on an offender but to direct that the person be immediately admitted to a specified hospital. In the year 2003–4 there were two recorded uses of Section 45A (Department of Health, 2004a).

The main treatment provision in Part III of the Act is the hospital order (Section 37), which permits the compulsory admission of a person convicted of an offence punishable with imprisonment. The same provision allows the court to make a guardianship order as the disposal for a criminal conviction. The hospital order is an alternative to a custodial disposal, which the court makes on the basis of two medical recommendations, and having had 'regard to all the circumstances including the nature of the offence and the character and antecedents of the offender, and to the other available methods of dealing with him'. The existence of the order relies on the presence of at least one of the forms of mental disorder at the time of sentencing. It does not require there to be any association between the commission of, or motivation for, the offence and the offender's mental state. The making of the hospital order concludes the criminal proceedings and the offender passes from the criminal justice system to the health system and becomes a patient. The court has no further involvement with the patient, and the power to discharge the patient from the order is with the patient's consultant, known as the Responsible Medical Officer (RMO) in the terminology of the MHA, or an MHRT (see below).

In cases of serious offending, or more precisely when there is a future risk of serious offending, the court may decide additionally to impose a restriction order (under Section 41, MHA) with the hospital order (and so create a 'restricted patient'). The restriction order, which can only be made by the Crown Court or higher courts, is made on public safety grounds when it is considered 'necessary for the protection of the public from serious harm' (Section 41, MHA). It has the effect of requiring Home Office authority prior to granting discharge, trial leave or transfer to another unit. The MHRT has the power to order discharge, but is limited to making recommendations with regard to transfer or leave.

In some cases it may not be clear that a hospital order is appropriate. For example, the person's apparent willingness to engage in therapy may be considered to be motivated by a wish to avoid a prison sentence. In such instances, admission to hospital under an interim hospital order (Section 38, MHA) allows for a prolonged assessment (of up to a year if necessary) in which to consider a patient's ability to engage and benefit from treatment. This provision operates in the period between conviction and sentencing in the criminal court and is premised on the belief 'that the mental disorder from which the offender is suffering is such that it may be appropriate for a hospital order to be made'. There is evidence of its use being directed towards assessing the treatability of patients suffering from psychopathic disorder (Kaul, 1994). However, the court retains sentencing discretion at the termination of the interim hospital order, and it is not inevitable that a hospital order will follow, even if recommended by the hospital psychiatrist.

Finally, it may be necessary to transfer a sentenced prisoner to hospital for psychiatric treatment. Such a scenario could arise when a prisoner becomes unwell for the first time while in prison. In the case of a psychopathically disordered prisoner, it is more likely to be the case that, although the disorder was recognized prior to sentencing, there was no offer of a hospital bed at that stage. If the index offence was serious and a lengthy term of imprisonment is anticipated, it may be calculated that it is preferable not to recommend admission, under a hospital order, at the time of sentencing, but to transfer the prisoner at a later stage in the sentence for treatment of discrete aspects of the psychopathic disorder. From the hospital's point of view, this has the advantage that the person can be transferred back to prison when that phase of treatment is completed or if treatment proves to be impossible to deliver.

If the person is still in hospital at the time the prison sentence would have been completed, detention in hospital continues as if the person had been admitted under a hospital order (a so-called 'notional hospital order'). Occasionally, prisoners are transferred very close to their prison release date and thereafter remain detained, albeit in hospital. Such a practice would attract judicial censure if its sole purpose were simply to delay the person's release. However, it is a legitimate use of Section 47 if the transfer process is part of a 'staged discharge under medical supervision' leading to eventual discharge into the community (*South West London and St George's Mental Health NHS Trust v. W [2002] EWHC 1770 Admin*).

TREATABILITY

The treatment orders of the MHA that apply to psychopathic disorder (Sections 3, 37, 47) contain a 'treatability' clause or 'test' as part of the statutory criteria for detention. This states that the medical treatment the patient will receive in hospital is 'likely to alleviate or prevent a deterioration of his condition'. In other words, the proposed treatment is likely to lead to greater stabilization in the patient's condition (in these cases, psychopathic disorder) but a cure is not required, and nor is complete prevention of any further deterioration, to satisfy the treatability test. Moreover, there are no time limits as to when the treatment should take effect. The Court of Appeal in the *Canons Park* case suggested the treatability test can still be satisfied 'provided that alleviation or stabilisation is likely in due course'.

The statutory definition of 'medical treatment' (Section 145, MHA) 'includes nursing, and also includes care, habilation and rehabilitation under medical supervision'. In *Reid*, the House of Lords held that the term 'medical treatment' was 'wide enough to include treatment which alleviates or prevents a deterioration of the symptoms of the disorder, not the disorder itself which gives rise to them'. In practice, this means the threshold for satisfying

the treatability test is set so low that once a patient has been admitted to hospital it may be very difficult subsequently to establish that it cannot be met.

Treatability is a different concept from the 'consent to treatment' provisions contained within Part IV of the Act. Those provisions do not distinguish between the different types of mental disorder, but provide a series of arrangements permitting the compulsory treatment of detained patients subject to certain safeguards. The House of Lords held in the case of *R (B) v. Ashworth Hospital Authority* that clinicians are not restricted to providing treatment only for the mental condition the patient is classified (under the MHA) as suffering from.

DISCHARGE FROM DETENTION

Patients, irrespective of which category of mental disorder they have been classified as suffering from, can be discharged from the MHA provision detaining them in hospital in a variety of ways. The 'section' can be allowed to expire, the RMO can discharge the patient (unless subject to restrictions), in some situations the patient's 'nearest relative' can apply for discharge or the patient can make an application to the Mental Health Act managers of the unit responsible for detention or to the MHRT. For restricted patients, only the Home Office or the MHRT can order the patient's discharge.

Mental Health Review Tribunals are established under the MHA (Section 65) and consider whether there is a need for continuing the legal restrictions on the patient, as well as making recommendations regarding future care. They are considered an important safeguard of patients' rights against inappropriate detention. In human rights' terms, Article 5 (the right to liberty and security) of the European Convention on Human Rights (ECHR) has particular significance in framing the state's obligations towards the detained patient (*Winterwerp v. Netherlands (1979); X v. U.K. (1981)*). However, MHRTs do not review the lawfulness of the original detention under the MHA, but consider the patient's situation at the time of the hearing. Patients are entitled to apply for a tribunal hearing at a specified frequency, for example once during every period of detention under (Section 3) treatment orders. In addition, in certain situations, patients can be 'referred' to the MHRT for a hearing (without applying themselves) by the hospital managers, the Home Secretary or the Secretary of State for Health. Those on short-term orders (of 72 hours or less) and those for whom the criminal courts have passed assessment orders (Sections 35, 36 and 38) are ineligible for MHRTs.

In practice, MHRTs consist of one legal, one medical and one lay member, all of whom have been appointed by the Government Department of the Lord Chancellor (now known as the Department for Constitutional Affairs). The tribunal functions as a 'court' and its procedure is set out in the Mental Health Review Tribunal Rules 1983, which is a form of subordinate legislation. In general terms, the MHRT has four options at the hearing: it can elect not to discharge the patient; it can adjourn because further reports or inquiries need to be made; it can discharge the patient (and, in the case of a restricted patient, this can be subject to particular conditions – a conditional discharge); or it can delay the discharge until particular arrangements, such as for supervised accommodation, have been made. Certain categories of detained patients are entitled (under Section 117, MHA) to the provision of aftercare arrangements upon discharge from hospital. This is coordinated through the Care Programme Approach (CPA) (Department of Health, 1990; see also Department of Health, 1995).

The tribunal must order the discharge of an unrestricted patient if it is not satisfied that the patient is suffering from at least one of the four forms of mental disorder (Section 72, MHA):

of a nature or degree which makes it appropriate for him to be … detained in a

hospital for medical treatment; or that it is necessary for the health or safety of the patient or for the protection of other persons that he should receive such treatment.

In the *Canons Park* case, the Court of Appeal held that, in the case of a patient suffering from psychopathic disorder, the tribunal did not have to consider the treatability test. This decision was later effectively overturned by the House of Lords in the *Reid* case. As a result, the criteria for compulsory admission to hospital are now said to be mirrored in the criteria to be applied when considering discharge from detention.

In the cases of patients subject to restriction orders, the criteria to be employed by the tribunal reflect Section 72 (above). In addition, if discharge is being considered, the tribunal has to decide whether or not the patient should 'remain liable to be recalled to hospital for further treatment' (Section 73, MHA). If this point is answered in the affirmative, the patient is granted a conditional discharge (if not, the discharge is absolute). The MHRT has discretion as to what conditions, if any, it will impose, but generally has regard to the need for ongoing treatment in the community as part of managing any risk the patient may continue to pose. Typically, conditions relate to supervision (by both a psychiatrist and a social worker or probation officer), residence and medical treatment, although this does not amount to compulsory community treatment.

A conditionally discharged patient remains subject to their restriction order and the Home Secretary may issue a warrant for their recall to hospital at any time. In practice, and except in an emergency, the decision to recall a patient will be based on objective medical evidence indicating a relapse in the patient's mental disorder or otherwise of a heightened level of risk posed by the patient. There is an automatic referral to the MHRT within a month of the recall, in order to avoid violation of Article 5, ECHR.

The term 'restricted patient' also refers to those subject to restriction directions (under Section 49 – i.e. remand or convicted prisoners transferred to prison) or limitation directions (under Section 45A). An MHRT also has the power to conditionally or absolutely discharge such patients. However, if the authority to detain in hospital is seen as no longer appropriate, the pre-existing authority to detain in prison is revived unless the Home Secretary (in the case of patients transferred after conviction) agrees to their release into the community.

PROPOSED REFORM OF THE MENTAL HEALTH ACT 1983

Over recent years, there has been extensive consultation with regard to establishing a new mental health act. The current proposals (Department of Health, 2004b) contain radical proposals affecting those suffering from personality disorders. A new definition of mental disorder is proposed: 'an impairment of or a disturbance in the functioning of the mind or brain resulting from any disability or disorder of the mind or brain' (clause 2(5)). Particular categories of mental disorder, such as psychopathic disorder, will not be identified or defined. The new, inclusive definition will encompass all types of personality disorder. In addition, the current behavioural criterion of 'abnormally aggressive or seriously irresponsible conduct' required for the categorization of psychopathic disorder will be lost. The result is a widening of the net of those potentially subject to compulsory detention.

Furthermore, the concept of 'treatability' for detention under the Act for patients suffering from psychopathic disorder or mental impairment looks set to be abandoned. 'Treatability' was regarded as a 'narrow concept' (Department of Health and Home Office, 2000), which was a 'problem' as it 'prevented' people with psychopathic disorder 'from being treated under statutory powers

for their own benefit or to protect the safety of others' (Department of Health, 2002b). As case law has evolved, it has become increasingly apparent that the courts have not seen 'treatability' in limited terms.

REFERENCES

Department of Health (1990). *The Care Programme Approach for People with a Mental Illness Referred to the Specialist Psychiatric Services.* HC(90)23/LASSL(90)11. London: Department of Health.

Department of Health (1995). *Building Bridges. Guide to Arrangements for Inter-agency Working for the Care and Protection of Severely Mentally Ill People.* London: Department of Health.

Department of Health (2002a). *In-patients Formally Detained in Hospitals under the Mental Health Act 1983 and Other Legislation, England: 1991/1992 to 2001/2002.* Bulletin 2002/26. London: Department of Health.

Department of Health (2002b). *Draft Mental Health Bill.* Cm 5538-I. London: Stationery Office.

Department of Health (2004a). *In-patients Formally Detained in Hospitals under the Mental Health Act 1983 and Other Legislation, England: 1993/1994 to 2003/2004.* Bulletin 2004/22. London: Department of Health.

Department of Health (2004b). *Draft Mental Health Bill.* Cm 6305. London: Stationery Office.

Department of Health and Home Office (1994). *Report of the Department of Health and Home Office Working Group on Psychopathic Disorder (Chair Dr John Reed).* London: Department of Health and Home Office.

Department of Health and Home Office (2000). *Reforming the Mental Health Act. Part I: The New Legal Framework.* Cm 5016–I. London: Stationery Office.

Department of Health and Welsh Office (1999). *Code of Practice Mental Health Act 1983.* London: Stationery Office.

Home Office and Department of Health and Social Security (1975). *Report of the Committee on Mentally Abnormal Offenders (The Butler Report).* Cmnd 6244. London: HMSO.

Kaul A (1994). Interim hospital order – a Regional Secure Unit experience. *Medicine, Science and the Law* **34**:233–6.

CASE LAW

R (on the application of B) v. Ashworth Hospital Authority [2005] All ER(D)279.

R (on the application of Munjaz) v. Mersey Care NHS Trust and R (on the application of S) v. Airedale NHS Trust [2003] EWCA Civ 1036.

R v. Canons Park Mental Health Review Tribunal, ex parte A [1994] 2 All ER 659.

Reid v. Secretary of State for Scotland [1999] 1 All ER 481.

South West London and St George's Mental Health NHS Trust v. W [2002] EWHC 1770 Admin.

Winterwerp v. Netherlands (1979) 2 EHRR 387.

X v. U.K. (1981) 4 EHRR 188.

Part 2

THE THEORETICAL FRAMEWORK

Chapter 6

ATTACHMENT THEORY AND PERSONALITY DISORDERED PATIENTS

Gill McGauley and Alla Rubitel

INTRODUCTION

Patients with severe personality disorder who have offended are among the most disturbed and complex people requiring professional care and treatment. Attention frequently focuses on two main questions: whether these people are treatable, and which system (health or criminal justice) should take responsibility for their management (Cawthra and Gibb, 1998). Dolan and Coid (1993), after an extensive review of the literature on psychopathic and antisocial personality disorders, concluded with respect to the first issue that these patients cannot be said to be untreatable until all possible treatment options have been tried and, after rigorous evaluation, shown to have failed. Although further, more stringent, research is awaited, clinical evidence suggests that while some personality disordered offenders are clearly treatable, others present a much more challenging treatment proposition. Furthermore, a person's capacity to engage in and use treatment may fluctuate. One of the greatest difficulties is identifying those patients who are most likely to be treatable and under what conditions. Whichever system or organization ultimately provides containment and care, this group is a costly one, not only in terms of their use of resources, but also because of the cost to the community of their antisocial behaviour and the level of public distress they generate.

One of the most striking characteristics of individuals within this group is their highly disturbed pattern of interpersonal relationships, within the context of which their offending behaviour has often occurred. This observation suggests that attachment theory may have a particular relevance to both the understanding and the management of these patients. This chapter sets out how attachment processes and the related capacity to think about mental states in the self and others – referred to by Fonagy and Target (1997) as reflective function – not only contributes to the care and treatment of these patients, but also offers a way of linking the mental processes involved in attachment relationships with those involved in interpersonal violent offences.

ATTACHMENT THEORY – A SYNOPSIS

THE ORIGINS OF ATTACHMENT THEORY

The foundations for the study of human attachment organization were laid down by John Bowlby and Mary Ainsworth (Ainsworth and Bowlby, 1991). Bowlby (1977), drawing on concepts from ethology, developmental psychology, psychoanalysis, cybernetics and information processing, formulated attachment theory as a body of explanations concerned with:

> Conceptualising the propensity of human beings to make strong affectional bonds to particular others and of explaining the many forms of emotional distress and personality disturbances, including anxiety, anger, depression and emotional detachment to which unwilling separation and loss give rise.

The formation of an attachment bond between the human infant and its primary caregiver (most often the mother) is necessary to protect the vulnerable infant and promote its security and survival. Bowlby postulated that this bond forms during the first year of life and continues as part of the normal repertoire of child and adult behaviour. Attachment behaviour is most obvious when there is a threat, real or perceived, to this attachment bond. In these situations, the child, distressed on the withdrawal of the attachment figure, shows a strong tendency to seek proximity with the attachment figure, especially when in pain or frightened (Bowlby, 1982). Disruption or the threat of disruption of these bonds through separation, deprivation or bereavement stimulates painful affective states and in some cases leads to psychopathology. In Bowlby and Ainsworth's view, a child uses the attachment figure as a secure base from which to explore the world.

A crucial concept in attachment theory is that of internal working models (Bowlby, 1973). Bowlby used this term to describe individuals' representation of the world, of their attachment figures and of themselves and the relationships between these representations. Internal working models are acquired by the infant through internalization of the characteristic interpersonal interactions of his or her major attachment figures. If the attachment figure has been sensitive to the infant's needs, the child is likely to develop an internal working model of self as valued. If, however, the parent has been rejecting or neglecting of the child's attempts to elicit comfort or to explore the world, Bowlby postulated that the child is likely to construct internal working models of the self as unworthy or incompetent (Bretherton, 1995). The type of internal working models a child constructs is therefore of great importance. These structures not only integrate past experiences, but also regulate the child's behaviour with attachment figures and come to organize (and predict) behaviour in future attachment relationships.

EMPIRICAL OBSERVATIONS OF ATTACHMENT

Mary Ainsworth's work made it possible to test some of Bowlby's work experimentally. The Baltimore Study, which she undertook in the 1960s, involved direct observation of children's interactions with their parents at 18 stages throughout their first year of life. Ainsworth's methodology emphasized observing meaningful behaviour patterns in context rather than merely counting specific behaviours. This research yielded two major contributions to the field of attachment theory.

First, Ainsworth formulated the concept of maternal sensitivity to infant signals and its crucial role in the development of infant–mother attachment patterns. The sensitivity of the caregiver's response to the infant is considered a major psychic organizer in shaping the internal models that a child builds, influencing the child's future developmental pathway. Sensitive responsiveness, or maternal sensitivity, calls on the caretaker's ability both to access the child's mental state and then to attribute meaning to it. The attribution of meaning necessarily involves the caretaker's own internal working models and capacity to think about the mental state of others. Second, Ainsworth identified three principal patterns of infant attachment and devised a laboratory-based procedure known as the Strange Situation for classifying infant security at 1 year (Ainsworth and Wittig, 1969). In the Strange Situation, children, upon reunion with their primary attachment figure, react in one of three ways. Infants who actively seek contact with their caregiver on reunion, communicate their feelings of stress and distress openly and then readily return to exploratory play are classified as secure in their attachment to that caregiver. Children who do not appear distressed and ignore or avoid their caregiver on reunion (although, like secure children, they are physiologically aroused during the separation) are classified as insecure – avoidant. Children who combine strong proximity seeking with resistance to contact, or who remain unsoothable, without being able to return to explore and play are classified as insecure – ambivalent attached. When faced with having to modulate between attachment and exploration, ambivalent infants maximize attachment behaviours, whereas avoidant infants minimize or deactivate attachment behaviours and conceal their distress. Secure infants achieve a balance between activating attachment behaviours on reunion and subsequently returning to explorative play (van IJzendoorn and Bakermans-Kranenburg, 1997).

Main and Solomon (1990) identified a fourth category, that of disorganized/disorientated behaviour during the Strange Situation. These children showed contradictory or undirected behaviour such as freezing or stereotypic movements or signs of apprehension regarding the parent. Further research shows that the parents of these children were in a state of unresolved mourning in relation to earlier losses or traumas (Main and Hesse, 1990; Ainsworth and Eichberg, 1991) or had abused or neglected their children (Crittenden 1985; Carlson et al., 1989).

ATTACHMENT AT THE REPRESENTATIONAL LEVEL

The next developmental milestone in attachment theory came from Mary Main's reconceptualization of Ainsworth's patterns of infant

attachment as corresponding adult patterns. This led to the development of the Adult Attachment Interview (AAI) (Main and Goldwyn 1984, 1998; George et al., 1985). Just as an infant's behaviour in the Strange Situation reflects the child's current internal working models of attachment, so an adult's AAI classification is thought to reflect their current attachment representations and internal models of attachment.

The AAI is a semi-structured interview consisting of a series of questions and probes designed to elicit as full a story as possible about the individual's childhood attachment experiences and evaluates the effect of these experiences on present functioning. The interviews are recorded, transcribed verbatim and coded to yield a four-way classification in the Main Goldwyn system. Autonomous–secure subjects give a clear and coherent account of early attachments even if these were negative. Dismissing–insecure subjects demonstrate an inability to remember much about attachment relations from childhood and emphasize their independence. They appear cut off from the emotional component of their attachment experiences. Their current state of mind is characterized by idealization or derogation of their attachment figures. Like insecure–avoidant children in the Strange Situation, their strategy is to limit the influence of attachment relationships and experiences in their feelings. Subjects classified as preoccupied–insecure on the AAI can neither dismiss nor coherently describe the influence of attachment experiences. Their narratives suggest that their past experiences still continue to preoccupy their attention, either in a vague inchoate way or suffused with current anger with respect to their attachment figures. Both dismissing and preoccupied subjects are considered to be insecurely attached. In addition, a fourth, overarching classification of unresolved for loss or for trauma is used for those subjects whose narratives show incoherence and disorganization when discussing loss or abuse experiences.

Not only do these AAI classifications correspond to Ainsworth's secure, ambivalent and avoidant infant patterns at a conceptual level, but they also correlate empirically, so a dismissing parent tends to have an avoidant child. Many studies of non-clinical populations have now confirmed this transgenerational concordance between the AAI assessments of parents and the attachment status of their children (Fonagy et al., 1991).

More recently, a new category of 'cannot classify' has emerged (Hesse, 1996). This category is not a collection of cases that do not fit into the other categories, but contains subjects who reveal two disparate attachment strategies and would indicate a placement in two opposing insecure categories (i.e. preoccupied and dismissing). This category has been found to include subjects with histories of psychiatric disorder, marital and criminal violence and experiences of sexual abuse. Hesse suggested that 'cannot classify' subjects show a complete breakdown of coherent discourse about attachment experiences, whereas dismissing and preoccupied subjects display an insecure, but consistent, strategy in their attachment narratives. 'Unresolved' subjects show a breakdown in their discourse strategy only when discussing loss or trauma.

ATTACHMENT AND PERSONALITY DISORDER

The life histories and current problems of patients with diagnoses of borderline and antisocial personality disorder (American Psychiatric Association, 1994), with their numerous disruptions to attachment processes, evidence of failed parental sensitivity and current interpersonal difficulties, strongly suggest the relevance of attachment theory for this population. The early experiences of these patients frequently include separations, losses, neglect, rejection and physical and sexual abuse. Researchers have found that histories of sexual abuse, physical abuse and neglect differentiate between various groups of borderline and non-borderline personality disordered patients (Ogata et al., 1990; McClellan et al., 1995). Child abuse has also been found to be a significant predictor of antisocial (Luntz and Widom, 1994) and borderline personality disorder (Brown and Anderson, 1991).

From the above associations, it is reasonable to hypothesize that, as the early lives of personality disordered patients frequently contain experiences that are also associated with the development of insecure attachments, insecure attachment status will be over-represented in personality disordered populations. Indeed, there is evidence that in clinical populations there is a strong over-representation of both dismissing and preoccupied attachment status, as measured by the AAI, compared to the distribution in non-clinical samples (van IJzendoorn and Bakermans-Kranenburg, 1996).

More specifically, in relation to personality disorder, it was found, albeit in a small sample, that the rate of insecure attachment was increased in borderline patients compared with a matched depressed group (Patrick et al., 1994). Indeed, in their sample of 12, all borderline patients were classified as 'preoccupied'. In a larger study it was found that a highly significant difference existed in the distribution of the three principal types of attachment pattern between a psychiatric group of patients with borderline, antisocial or paranoid personality disorders compared with a matched control group (Fonagy et al., 1995). In the latter group, 62 per cent of the 85 controls were rated as secure–autonomous, 21 per cent as dismissive and 16 per cent as preoccupied. By contrast, 22 per cent of the personality disordered group were classified as secure–autonomous, 18 per cent as dismissive and 22 per cent as preoccupied. However, there is no simple relationship between patterns of attachment and personality disorder, and specific styles of attachment classification have not been shown reliably to map onto particular personality disorders.

THE PREDICTION OF PSYCHOPATHOLOGY FROM ATTACHMENT INSECURITY

Several studies have linked attachment insecurity in early life with the development of behavioural problems and psychopathology in childhood and adult life (Scolnick, 1986; Urban et al., 1991; Belsky and Cassidy, 1994). The majority of studies have concentrated on examining the association between early attachment insecurity and the development of disruptive behaviour and conduct disorder in childhood. Two studies report that insecurely attached boys are more aggressive, disruptive and attention seeking than securely attached boys both at pre-school and at the age of 6 (Cohn, 1990; Turner, 1991).

In general, longitudinal studies have failed to identify a straightforward relationship between early attachment status and conduct problems or other psychopathology in childhood. However, these studies have made explicit both the link and the complexity of the link between attachment and disturbance. This point is well illustrated by one study that showed that attachment security as measured at 1 year could be used to predict the presence of neurotic disorder at 6 years old (Lewis et al., 1984). In particular, insecurely attached boys showed significantly more internalizing behaviours (anxiety, depression) than their secure counterparts. However, the authors found that the strength of the prediction from attachment security to behaviour disorder depended not only on the child's sex, but also on a number of other variables such as birth order, the number of friends the child had, and the occurrence of stressful family events.

There are both methodological and theoretical problems still to be resolved in this research area. Methodologically, the assessment of attachment security in childhood using a modified version of the Strange Situation may be influenced by disruptive behaviour. The outcome measure cannot therefore be considered independent of the diagnosis. Theoretically, although attachment status is stable in low-risk, non-clinical samples (Bretherton, 1985), it is much less so in clinical, high-risk populations (Vaughn et al., 1979; van IJzendoorn and Bakermans-Kranenburg, 1997) such as in a personality disordered offender group. In particular, the disorganized classification that is fairly strongly linked to psychopathology is relatively unstable (Lyons-Ruth et al., 1993). Researchers cannot therefore assume continuity of a particular attachment status from infancy through to adolescence and adulthood in high-risk samples with the same certainty as in low-risk samples. An indirect developmental pathway has been described linking insecure attachment with later delinquency, antisocial personality disorder and offending. Research showing that childhood conduct disorder is predictive of later offending and antisocial behaviour has been noted in many studies (Zoccolillo et al., 1992; Farrington, 1994). In addition, empirical evidence shows that insecure attachment status is over-represented in antisocial personality disorder. Some studies have reported more specific links between attachment representations and later psychopathology in adolescent populations. Rosenstein and Horowitz (1996) found a high rate of dismissing attachment styles in adolescents with conduct disorder and substance abuse. In a further group of adolescents co-morbid for conduct and affective disorder, half were classified as dismissing of attachment and half as unresolved with regard to loss or trauma.

Allen et al. (1996) assessed attachment status in adolescents who were psychiatric in-patients and a control group of high-school students. Ratings from the adolescents' attachment interviews predicted criminal behaviour 10 years later, even when previous hospitalizations were accounted for. The subgroup of subjects whose interviews were coded as 'cannot classify', because they met criteria for more than one incompatible attachment category, reported the most criminal behaviour. Dismissing subjects and those unresolved for loss and trauma had higher levels of criminal behaviour compared with either the preoccupied or secure group. In particular, scales for derogation of attachment and lack of resolution of trauma predicted criminal behaviour.

Fonagy comments that it is perhaps more realistic to conceive of insecure attachment as a risk factor in the development of disruptive behaviour and conduct disorder (Fonagy et al., 1997), and Sroufe (1988) cautions against over-extending predictive claims from attachment status in early life in relation to adult functioning. It should be remembered that there are many other aspects that contribute to interpersonal functioning within relationships. However, links, albeit of moderate strength, have been found between insecure attachment in infancy and later personality disorders, but the complexities of these links need to be much more clearly investigated by empirical research in order to support the theoretical model of attachment security and disturbance.

ATTACHMENT AND BORDERLINE PERSONALITY DISORDER

Attachment concepts have made an important contribution to the understanding of the impaired interpersonal relationships in borderline personality disordered patients.

In their review of attachment research in psychiatric populations, Dozier et al. (1999) outline some theoretical links between borderline pathology and characteristics of the preoccupied attachment classification. They note that borderline pathology is generally associated with the exaggeration of symptomatology and negative affect and a 'preoccupation'

with concerns about current and previous relationship difficulties. The authors point out that the readiness of borderline patients to report distress, as an example of maximizing the expression of attachment needs, is also a characteristic of adults who are preoccupied with respect to attachment. Adults with a preoccupied attachment classification have internal working models of caregivers as either incompetent or inconsistently available and of the self as inconsistently valued – also central features of borderline personality disorder.

Fonagy et al. (1995) have proposed a model of borderline personality disorder using formulations derived from attachment theory and the concept of reflective function. They then link this model, outlining a pathway through to offending behaviour. Reflective function describes the psychological processes underlying the capacity to mentalize, that is to represent behaviour of the self and others in terms of mental states. It is the developmental process that allows children not only to respond to another person's behaviour, but also to conceptualize the beliefs, feelings, intentions, attitudes, knowledge and hopes of others (Fonagy and Target, 1997). Thus reflective function involves both a self-reflective and an interpersonal component. By accurately attributing mental states to others, the behaviour of others becomes meaningful and predictable to the child.

Fonagy and Target (1997) locate the acquisition of reflective function in the child's early social and attachment relationships. They suggest that common mechanisms underpin attachment organization in the caregiver and infant and the emergence of the capacity to mentalize in the child, and propose a model of how attachment may directly relate to the development of reflective function. They propose that the 'disorganized/disorientated' attachment pattern is a particular vulnerability factor for the development of borderline personality disorder (Fonagy et al., 2002).

In their model (Fonagy et al., 2002), it is assumed that in normal development there is a degree of integration and generalization of a mentalizing model of behaviour. In some severe personality disorders, the normal coordination and integration of reflective functioning across different domains of the mind does not occur. As a result, non-reflective functioning dominates the behaviour of personality disordered individuals in affectively charged situations. In line with this hypothesis, there is evidence that family maltreatment impairs the development of the child's reflective capacities and sense of self (Beeghly and Cicchetti, 1994). In the proposed model, maltreatment interacts with the development of reflective function in two ways. First, maltreatment presents the child with a strong disincentive for taking the perspective of the other person, as to do so would expose the child to the hostility in the abuser's mind that is directed towards him/her. Second, the child is not able to develop the capacity to understand traumatic interpersonal situations that would be likely to limit their impact and act as a protective factor. The authors conclude that maltreated children are vulnerable because the long-term effect of their reaction to maltreatment leads them to adopt a predominantly non-mentalizing (and therefore handicapping) stance, which may come to dominate their interpersonal relationships and leave them with reduced resilience in the face of future trauma.

Empirical evidence from the AAIs of borderline patients rated for reflective function tends to support the proposed model. Compared to matched controls, the borderline patients' AAI interviews were differentiated by three characteristics (Fonagy et al., 1996):

- a higher prevalence of sexual abuse reported in their AAI narratives,
- significantly lower ratings on the reflective function scale,
- a significantly higher rating on lack of resolution of abuse.

The authors comment that these findings are consistent with their assumption that individuals who have experienced severe maltreatment in childhood and who respond to this experience by an inhibition of reflective function are less likely to resolve their abuse and more likely to manifest borderline psychopathology. If, however, maltreated children have access to a meaningful attachment relationship that allows them to develop reflective function, they have a better chance of resolving their earlier experiences and are less likely to develop borderline personality disorder. Thus unresolved abuse experiences reduce the likelihood of future meaningful relationships and consequently limit possible development of reflective function.

ATTACHMENT AND OFFENDING

The existence of a relationship between attachment and crime was probably first proposed by Bowlby (1944) in his paper 'Forty-four juvenile thieves: Their characters and home-life'. Bowlby postulated that the anti-social behaviour in a subgroup of patients referred to a child guidance clinic, who he described as having an affectionless character, had its origins in early disorders of attachment, arising from the pathological effects of prolonged and early separation. Subsequently, Bowlby discussed violence as a disorder of attachment and care-giving systems. Indeed, attachment theory can shed light on many of the variables considered relevant in offending behaviour, such as self-esteem, mastery, control and interpersonal and social relating.

Farrington (1995) showed that the best predictors of subsequent offending in 8 year olds were hyperactivity, impulsivity, conduct disorder, marital discord between the parents, harsh or erratic parenting and separation from a parent for reasons other than by death or illness. Some of these factors contribute to the development of insecure attachment, while others, such as conduct disorder, occur more frequently in insecurely attached boys.

Although there is some continuity from early conduct problems and delinquency through to later offending, there is, of course, considerable discontinuity, as many adult offenders have no history of juvenile delinquency and the vast majority of children with an insecure attachment pattern do not become serious offenders. Within the context of early delinquency, insecure attachment is probably best thought of as one of a host of predisposing factors towards later offending.

Although not all offenders carry a diagnosis of personality disorder, a significant proportion of offenders do meet the diagnostic criteria. In one study, 63 per cent of remanded men, 49 per cent of sentenced men and 31 per cent of women in both groups were considered to have an antisocial personality disorder (Singleton et al., 1998).

In a study of 40 Dutch men who had committed serious crimes such as murder, child sexual abuse and rape and were detained in a secure forensic facility, it was found that 55 per cent of the sample were personality disordered (van IJzendoorn et al., 1997). The distribution of attachment classifications greatly deviated from a non-clinical population: secure attachments were present in only 5 per cent of subjects and the unresolved and 'cannot classify' categories were over-represented. Although specific personality disorders did not correspond to discrete attachment classifications, in part due to a high degree of Axis II co-morbidity, the data suggested that dismissing category subjects showed fewer personality disorder symptoms than those in the preoccupied category, while the 'cannot classify' subjects appeared to be the most disturbed in terms of personality disorder pathology. Such findings may well have a predictive value for treatment response.

In a small controlled study of offenders, Levinson and Fonagy (2004) investigated the possibility that certain criminals who had committed interpersonal violent offences were unable to envision their victim's state of mind. This hypothesis arose from Fonagy's model linking borderline psychopathology to early maltreatment, which in turn leads to an inhibition of reflective function and capacity to envision another's mental state. The latter capacity is thought to be a crucial inhibitory factor in interpersonal violence. The researchers found that, as in other studies, offenders had a significantly higher rate of insecure attachment, especially in the dismissing category, compared with matched psychiatric in-patient and normal control groups. As predicted, prisoners had significantly lower ratings of reflective function compared with other groups. Furthermore, those with violent index offences had much lower ratings of reflective function than those with non-violent offences. Their pattern of results is consistent with an assumption that some criminality arises in the context of disturbed attachment relationships when both individuals and social institutions can be readily dismissed as attachment objects and antisocial violent acts may be facilitated by a non-reflective stance with respect to the victim. Failure to envision the mental states of others may reduce an individual's sense of responsibility for his or her own actions, as well as permitting offenders to disregard or misinterpret the psychological consequences of their actions on others. In addition, limited reflective function also permits offenders to dehumanize their victims and treat them as a thing rather than a person. However, Fonagy (Fonagy et al., 2002) cautions that linking some violent behaviour and borderline states to dismissive and preoccupied forms of non-mentalizing self-organizations would be too simplistic, as there are both wide situational variations and differences in the types of relationships.

In a recent uncontrolled study, Frodi et al. (2001) examined the mental representations of early attachment relationships in 14 Swedish psychopathic criminal offenders detained in either a forensic psychiatric unit or a medium secure prison. Although all participants scored between 12 and 16 on Hare's Psychopathy Checklist Revised Screening Version (Hart et al., 1995), only 11 met the DSM criteria for personality disorder (nine had antisocial personality disorder, one had borderline and one schizoid personality disorder). As in other studies (van IJzendoorn et al., 1997; Levinson and Fonagy, 2004), this study also reported an over-representation of individuals who were dismissing of attachment. There was no association between the distribution of AAI classifications and degree of psychopathy. The authors note that this may be due to too narrow a range in psychopathy scores (9–19 on the 0–24 scale).

CONCLUSIONS AND FUTURE DIRECTIONS

This chapter provides a brief resume of attachment theory and the related concept of reflective function. In particular, the authors describe research in which the AAI has been conducted in psychiatric populations (Dozier et al., 1999) and, to a lesser extent, with forensic personality disordered populations (van IJzendoorn et al., 1997; Frodi et al., 2001). The AAI was first developed for use with a non-clinical group, and its use in a severely personality disordered group such as those patients detained in forensic institutions can pose procedural and coding challenges to interviewers and raters of the transcripts (see Turton et al., 2001, for a review).

At a specific level, attachment theory provides some tentative models for the genesis of certain personality disorders (e.g. borderline personality disorder) and some offending behaviour.

Attachment theory and reflective function can also contribute to the care and management of personality disordered offender patients in several areas. At the most general level, attachment theory provides a framework for thinking about the impact of the adversity that personality disordered patients have endured in their early attachment relationships. It allows professionals to understand the nature of the developmental problems that have subsequently arisen and the current manifestation of these problems in the patients' interpersonal relationships, not only with peers and staff, but also with their institutions. Adshead (1998) has focused on how relationships between patients, psychiatric caregivers and institutions may resemble attachment relationships. An attachment perspective may help staff understand some of their patients' behaviours, such as self-harm and aggressive outbursts.

An understanding of how insecure early attachments leave personality disordered patients with fragile affect regulation and a reliance on a more punitive and less flexible range of internal working models (which in turn govern their responses in their current interpersonal interactions) is likely to increase the care team's therapeutic effectiveness and minimize unthinking, anti-therapeutic responses. The elucidation of attachment styles and the capacity for reflective function in adult personality disordered offender patients hold the potential for both directing more tailored psychotherapeutic treatments and an increase in the efficacy of these interventions. Psychotherapy may bolster diminished reflective capacity. Preliminary data (Fonagy et al., 1995) suggest that psychodynamic treatment is associated with both a significant increase in the proportion of secure classifications compared to pre-treatment status and improvement in reflective function. Dozier (1990) found that secure attachment status in a severely ill psychiatric population was associated with greater treatment compliance and less rejection of the healthcare professionals involved.

A further study, building on Dozier's work, examined whether attachment classifications at the beginning of treatment predicted a response to in-patient psychotherapeutic interventions in a personality disordered in-patient population. The proportion of patients who improved was high amongst those with an initial insecure–dismissing classification (Fonagy et al., 1996).

It is clear that longitudinal studies, some of which are currently underway, are needed to test the predictive power of adult attachment classification further. However, initial results indicate the usefulness of the AAI as a measure of change, in terms of predicting and assessing a patient's capacity to engage in treatment and in forecasting either treatment dropout or improvement.

REFERENCES

Adshead G (1998). Psychiatric staff as attachment figures. *British Journal of Psychiatry* **172**:64–9.

Ainsworth MDS and Bowlby J (1991). An ethological approach to personality development. *American Psychologist* **46**:333–41.

Ainsworth MDS and Eichberg C (1991). Effects on infant–mother attachment of mother's unresolved loss of an attachment figure or other traumatic experience. In: Parkes CM, Stevenson-Hinde J and Marris P (eds), *Attachment Across the Life Cycle.* London: Tavistock/Routledge, 160–83.

Ainsworth MDS and Wittig BA (1969). Attachment and the exploratory behaviour of one year olds in a strange situation. In: Foss BM (ed.), *Determinants of Infant Behaviour*, Vol. 4. London: Methuen, 113–36.

Allen JP, Hauser ST and Borman-Spurrell E (1996). Attachment theory as a framework for understanding sequelae of severe adolescent psychopathology: an 11-year follow-up study. *Journal of Consulting and Clinical Psychology* **64**:254–63.

American Psychiatric Association (1994). *Diagnostic and Statistical Manual of Mental Disorders,* fourth edition, revised. Washington, DC: American Psychiatric Association.

Beeghly M and Cicchetti D (1994). Child maltreatment, attachment and the self system: emergence of an internal state lexicon in toddlers at high social risk. *Development and Psychopathology* **6**:5–30.

Belsky J and Cassidy J (1994). Attachment: theory and evidence. In: Rutter M and Hay D (eds), *Development Through Life: A Handbook for Clinicians.* Oxford: Blackwell Scientific Publications, 373–402.

Bowlby J (1944). Forty-four juvenile thieves: their characters and home-life. *International Journal of Psycho-Analysis* **25**:19–52.

Bowlby J (1973). *Attachment and Loss*, Vol. II: *Separation.* New York: Basic Books.

Bowlby J (1977). The making and breaking of affectional bonds. I: Aetiology and psychopathology in the light of attachment theory; II: Some principles of psychotherapy. *British Journal of Psychiatry* **130**: 201–10; 421–31.

Bowlby J (1982). *Attachment and Loss*, Vol. I: *Attachment,* second edition. New York: Basic Books.

Bretherton I (1985). Attachment theory: retrospect and prospect. In: Bretherton I and Waters I (eds), *Growing Points in Attachment Theory and Research.* Monographs of the Society for Research in Child Development, 50 (Serial No. 209, Nos 1–2). Chicago, IL: University of Chicago Press, 3–36.

Bretherton I (1995). The origins of attachment theory. In: Goldberg S, Muir S and Kerr J (eds), *Attachment Theory, Social, Developmental and Clinical Perspectives.* Hillsdale, NJ: The Analytic Press, 45–84.

Brown GR and Anderson B (1991). Psychiatric morbidity in adult inpatients with childhood histories of sexual and physical abuse. *American Journal of Psychiatry* **148**:55–61.

Carlson J, Cicchetti D, Barnett D and Barunwald KG (1989). Finding order in disorganization: lessons from research on maltreated infants' attachments to their caregivers. In: Cicchetti D and Carlson V (eds), *Child Maltreatment. Theory and Research on the Causes and Consequences of Child Abuse and Neglect.* Cambridge: Cambridge University Press, 494–528.

Cawthra R and Gibb R (1998). Severe personality disorder – whose responsibility? *British Journal of Psychiatry* **173**:8–10.

Cohn DA (1990). Child–mother attachment of six year olds and social competence at school. *Child Development* **61**:152–62.

Crittenden P (1985). Maltreated infants: vulnerability and resilience. *Journal of Child Psychology and Psychiatry* **26**:85–96.

Dolan B and Coid J (1993). *Psychopathic and Antisocial Personality Disorders: Treatment and Research Issues.* London: Gaskell.

Dozier M (1990). Attachment organisation and treatment use for adults with serious psychopathological disorders. *Development and Psychopathology* **2**:47–60.

Dozier M, Chase Stovall K and Albus KE (1999). Attachment and psychopathology in adulthood. In: Cassidy J and Shaver PR (eds), *Handbook of Attachment: Theory, Research and Clinical Applications.* New York: Guilford Press, 497–519.

Farrington DP (1994). Early developmental prevention of juvenile delinquency. *Criminal Behaviour and Mental Health* **4**:209–27.

Farrington DP (1995). Preventing crime and violence. *British Medical Journal* **310**:271–2.

Fonagy P, György G, Jurist LE and Target M (2002). The roots of borderline personality disorder in disorganised attachment. In: *Affect Regulation, Mentalisation, and the Development of the Self.* New York: Other Press, 343–73.

Fonagy P, Leigh T, Kennedy R et al. (1995). Attachment, borderline states and the representation of emotions and cognitions in self and other. In: Cicchetti D and Toth S (eds), *Emotion, Cognition and Representation.* Rochester Symposium on Developmental Psychopathology, Vol. 6. Rochester, NY: University of Rochester Press, 371–414.

Fonagy P, Leigh T, Steele M et al. (1996). The relation of attachment status, psychiatric classification and response to psychotherapy. *Journal of Consulting and Clinical Psychology* **64(1)**:22–31.

Fonagy P, Steele M and Steele H (1991). Intergenerational patterns of attachment: maternal representations during pregnancy and subsequent infant–mother attachments. *Child Development* **62**:891–905.

Fonagy P and Target M (1997). Attachment and reflective function: their role in self-organisation. *Development and Psychopathology* **9**:679–700.

Fonagy P, Target M, Steele M et al. (1997). Morality, disruptive behaviour, borderline personality disorder, crime and their relationships to security of attachment. In: Atkinson L and Zucker KJ (eds), *Attachment and Psychopathology.* New York/London: Guilford Press, 223–74.

Frodi A, Dernevik M, Sepa A, Philipson J and Bragesjö M (2001). Current attachment representations of incarcerated offenders varying in degree of psychopathy. *Attachment and Human Development* **3(3)**:269–83.

George C, Kaplan N and Main M (1985). Adult Attachment Interview. Unpublished manual. Berkeley, CA: Department of Psychology. University of California at Berkeley.

Hart SD, Cox D and Hare R (1995). *Manual for the Screening Version of the Hare Psychopathy Checklist – Revised (PCL:SV).* Toronto: Multi-Health Systems.

Hesse E (1996). Discourse, memory and the Adult Attachment Interview: a note with emphasis on the emerging cannot classify category. *Infant Mental Health Journal* **17**:4–11.

Levinson A and Fonagy P (2004). Offending and attachment: the relationship between interpersonal awareness and offending in a prison population with psychiatric disorder. *Canadian Journal of Psychoanalysis* **12(2)**:225–51.

Lewis M, Feiring C, McGuffog C and Jaskir J (1984). Predicting psychopathology in six year olds from early social relations. *Child Development* **55**:123–36.

Luntz BK and Widom CS (1994). Antisocial personality disorder in abused and neglected children grown up. *American Journal of Psychiatry* **151**:670–4.

Lyons-Ruth K, Alpern L and Repacholi B (1993). Disorganised infant attachment classification and maternal psychosocial problems as predictors of hostile aggressive behaviour in the preschool classroom. *Child Development* **64**:572–85.

Main M and Goldwyn R (1984). Adult attachment scoring and classification system. Unpublished manuscript. Berkeley, CA: Department of Psychology, University of California at Berkeley.

Main M and Goldwyn R (1998). Adult attachment scoring and classification system. Unpublished manuscript. Berkeley, CA: Department of Psychology, University of California at Berkeley.

Main M and Hesse E (1990). Parents' unresolved traumatic experiences are related to infant disorganized attachment status: Is frightened and/or frightening parental behaviour the linking mechanism? In: Greenberg MT, Cicchetti D and Cummings EM (eds), *Attachment in the Pre-school Years: Theory, Research and Intervention*. Chicago, IL: University of Chicago Press, 161–84.

Main M and Solomon J (1990). Procedures for identifying disorganized/disoriented infants in the Ainsworth Strange Situation. In: Greenberg MT, Cicchetti D and Cummings EM (eds), *Attachment in the Pre-school Years: Theory, Research and Intervention*. Chicago, IL: University of Chicago Press, 121–60.

McClellan J, Adams J, Douglas D, McCurry C and Storck M (1995). Clinical characteristics related to severity of sexual abuse: a study of seriously mentally ill youth. *Child Abuse and Neglect* **19**:1245–54.

Ogata SN, Silk KR, Goodrich S, Lohr NE, Western D and Hill E (1990). Childhood sexual abuse and physical abuse in adult patients with borderline personality disorder. *American Journal of Psychiatry* **147**:1008–13.

Patrick M, Hobson RP, Castle P, Howard R and Maughan B (1994). Personality disorder and the mental representation of early social experience. *Development and Psychopathology* **5**:763–83.

Rosenstein DS and Horowitz HA (1996). Adolescent attachment and psychopathology. *Journal of Consulting and Clinical Psychology* **64(2)**:244–53.

Scolnick A (1986). Early attachment and personal relationships across the life course. In: Baltes P, Featherman D and Lerner R (eds), *Lifespan Development and Behavior*. Hillsdale, NJ: Lawrence Erlbaum, 173–206.

Singleton N, Meltzer H, Gatward R, Coid J and Deasy D (1998). *Psychiatric Morbidity among Prisoners*. London: Stationery Office.

Sroufe LA (1988). The role of infant care-giver attachments in development. In: Belsky J and Nezworski T (eds), *Clinical Implications of Attachment*. Hillsdale, NJ: Lawrence Erlbaum, 18–38.

Turner P (1991). Relations between attachment, gender and behaviour with peers in the preschool. *Child Development* **62**:1475–88.

Turton P, McGauley G, Marin-Avellan L and Hughes P (2001). The Adult Attachment Interview: rating and classification problems posed by non-normative samples. *Attachment and Human Development* **3(3)**:284–303.

Urban J, Carlson E, Egeland B and Sroufe LA (1991). Patterns of individual adaptation across childhood. *Development and Psychopathology* **3**:455–560.

van IJzendoorn MH and Bakermans-Kranenburg MJ (1996). Attachment representations in mothers, fathers, adolescents and clinical groups: a meta-analytic search for normative data. *Journal of Consulting and Clinical Psychology* **64**:8–21.

van IJzendoorn MH and Bakermans-Kranenburg MJ (1997). Intergenerational transmission of attachment: a move to the contextual level. In: Atkinson L and Zucker KJ (eds), *Attachment and Psychopathology*. New York: Guilford Press, 135–70.

van IJzendoorn MH, Feldbrugge JTTM, Derks FCH et al. (1997). Attachment representations of personality disordered criminal offenders. *American Journal of Orthopsychiatry* **67(3)**: 449–59.

Vaughn B, Egelard B, Sroufe LA and Waters E (1979). Individual differences in infant–mother attachment at twelve and eighteen months: stability and change in families under stress. *Child Development* **50**:971–9.

Zoccolillo M, Pickles A, Quinton D and Rutler M (1992). The outcome of childhood conduct disorder: implications for defining adult personality disorder and conduct disorder. *Psychological Medicine* **22**:971–86.

Chapter 7

THEORY OF MIND AND ANTISOCIAL BEHAVIOUR

Robert James Richard Blair

INTRODUCTION

Theory of mind refers to the ability to represent the mental states of others, i.e. their thoughts, desires, beliefs, intentions and knowledge (Premack and Woodruff, 1978; Leslie, 1987; Frith, 1989). It allows the attribution of mental states to self and others in order to explain and predict behaviour. However, the term 'theory of mind' is misleading. It should not be conceptualized as a theory that is available to conscious access; instead, it should be thought of as an innately specified cognitive mechanism that allows the representation of the mental states of others.

The classic measure of theory of mind is the Sally–Anne task (Wimmer and Perner, 1983; Baron-Cohen et al., 1985). In this task, the child is shown two dolls, Sally and Anne, a basket and a box. The child watches as Sally places her marble in the basket and then leaves the room. While Sally's out, naughty Anne moves Sally's marble from the basket to the box. Then she, too, leaves the room. Now Sally comes back into the room. The child is asked the test question: 'Where will Sally look for her marble?'. In order to pass this task, the child must represent Sally's mental state, her belief that the marble is in the basket. Without this representation, the child will answer on the basis of the marble's real location, i.e. the

box. Most children from the age of 4 years pass this task (Wimmer and Perner, 1983).

As a model, the theory of mind hypothesis has some similarities with the earlier ideas of role-taking and perspective-taking (e.g. Chandler et al., 1974; Selman, 1976, 1980). For example, role-taking is defined as the ability to recognize another person's expectations and desires, predicting how they might react, and understanding what they mean to communicate. In particular, Selman (1976, 1980) proposed a developmental model of social role-taking, which is a description of five stages through which the child develops. Essentially, it suggests that the child shows a gradual, qualitative progress from egocentric reasoning to an eventual understanding of the complexities of mutual perspective-taking. For example, Selman (1976) suggests that the child aged 3 to 6 years is at Stage 0, an egocentric viewpoint. The child is considered to have a sense of differentiation of self and other, but fails to distinguish between the social perspective (thoughts, feelings) of the other and of the self. By the age of 12 years, the child should have reached Stage 4, social and conventional system role-taking. At this stage, the child is able to appreciate that even mutual perspective-taking may not always lead to complete understanding.

Theory of mind has been linked to antisocial behaviour in several ways. There have been suggestions that the processes of theory of mind, and particularly the related concepts of role-taking and perspective-taking, allow the inhibition of antisocial behaviour and foster moral reasoning (e.g. Feshbach, 1987). It is argued that representations of the inner states of others either allow the suppression of aggression directly or are necessary for empathic responding (e.g. Feshbach, 1987; Gibbs, 1987). Empathic responding is also thought to inhibit aggression (e.g. Eisenberg, 1986; Feshbach, 1987): 'the painful consequences of an aggressive act through the vicarious response of empathy should function as inhibitors of the instigator's own aggressive tendencies' (Eisenberg, 1986, p. 194).

Empathy is defined as 'an affective response more appropriate to someone else's situation than to one's own' (Hoffman, 1987, p. 48). It is an emotional reaction in an observer to the affective state of another. According to these positions, it is this empathic response to the victim that inhibits antisocial behaviour (e.g. Eisenberg, 1986). According to some empathy theorists, the capacity to empathize requires the ability to represent the mental states of others (e.g. Batson et al., 1987; Feshbach, 1987; Hoffman, 1987; Frith, 1989). Representations of the internal mental state of another are assumed to act as stimuli for the activation of the affective, empathic response (Batson et al., 1987). For example, Feshbach (1975, 1978, 1987) considers empathy to be a function of three processes:

- the cognitive ability to discriminate affective cues in others,
- the more mature cognitive skills entailed in assuming the perspective and role of another person,
- emotional responsiveness – that is, the affective ability to experience emotions.

According to Feshbach (1987, p. 273), 'empathy is conceived to be the outcome of cognitive and affective processes that operate conjointly'.

Theory of mind, or at least the related concepts of role-taking and perspective-taking, has not only been linked to the inhibition of aggression. In addition, role-taking and perspective-taking have also been considered crucial for the development of morality (e.g. Kohlberg, 1981; Turiel, 1983). For example, Kohlberg (e.g. 1981) argued that the capacities for more complex perspective-taking allow developmental 'advances' in the child's stage of moral reasoning. Perspective-taking is viewed as underlying advances in moral judgement (e.g. Colby et al., 1983; Eisenberg, 1986; Keller and Edelstein, 1991). Moreover, perspective-taking has also been viewed as underlying some types of prosocial behaviour (Underwood and Moore, 1982). The suggestion has been that prior to helping another, the individual must engage in perspective-taking in order to represent the other's need.

Thus, in summary, theory of mind and the related concepts of role-taking and perspective-taking have been linked to four core areas of social functioning:

1. the inhibition of antisocial behaviour,
2. empathic responding,
3. moral development,
4. prosocial behaviour.

There are two main ways in which the relationship between theory of mind and the above four core areas of social functioning can be explored.

1. Relating performance on measures of the various functions in normal individuals.
2. Taking a developmental neuropsychological approach (see Morton and Frith, 1993).

The first approach typically involves correlational analyses of performances on tests designed to assess different functions. The major problem with this approach is that the validity of the tasks is often uncertain. Thus, for example, many of the tests of role-taking and perspective-taking are scored according to the complexity of the participant's responses (e.g. Selman, 1980). However, it is uncertain whether the participant's increasing score with age reflects a developmental progression in role-taking or in verbal comprehension. Moreover, the extent to which the tasks assess different functions is frequently unclear. For example, both Selman's measure of perspective-taking and Kohlberg's measure of moral development are heavily influenced by intelligence quotient (IQ) and educational background. Thus, correlations obtained between role-taking and moral reasoning may not reflect a causal relationship between role-taking and these variables, but instead may simply index the child's IQ and educational background across tasks.

Because of the above problem, this chapter primarily considers evidence gathered through the developmental neuropsychological approach, which does not face the major problem outlined above. Within this approach, populations of patients are identified who lack a particular cognitive capacity and are then studied to determine the implications of this lack. So, if we could identify a population of patients who lacked theory of mind, we could determine the implications of this lack. Patients with autism constitute such a population, as they lack the ability to represent the mental states of others.

THE CASE OF AUTISM

Autism is a severe developmental disorder, described by the American Psychiatric Association's *Diagnostic and Statistical Manual* fourth edition (DSM-IV; American Psychiatric Association, 1994, p. 66) as 'the presence of markedly abnormal or impaired development in social interaction and communication and a markedly restricted repertoire of activities and interests'. The main criteria for the diagnosis in DSM-IV can be summarized as qualitative

impairment in social communication and restricted and repetitive patterns of behaviour and interests. These criteria must be evident before 3 years of age. The incidence rate has been estimated as approximately 4 in 10 000 (Lotter, 1966).

Children with autism have been consistently reported to show a theory of mind impairment, originally observed by Baron-Cohen et al. (1985). Children with autism and two comparison groups, a mildly retarded population to match for mental age and a chronologically (to mental age) matched population of normally developing children, were presented with the Sally–Anne task described above. While most of the members of both comparison groups passed this test, 80 per cent of the children with autism failed it. This finding has now been replicated in a number of studies, using real people instead of toys, using a 'think' question rather than a 'look' question, and using a control group of specifically language-impaired children to rule out a language deficit explanation (e.g. Leslie and Frith, 1988; Perner et al., 1989).

If theory of mind is necessary for the inhibition of antisocial behaviour, empathic responding, prosocial behaviour and moral development, we can make several predictions about the behaviour of individuals with autism. If theory of mind is a prerequisite for the development of these behaviours, a population who lacks theory of mind – individuals with autism – should show high levels of aggression, reduced empathy, impaired moral development and reduced prosocial behaviour. The first prediction is difficult to address. Some children with autism do present with aggressive episodes, but they are not habitually violent (Scragg and Shah, 1994). However, given that their social interactions are so dysfunctional, their relative lack of aggression cannot really be considered to be informative.

Do individuals with autism show reduced empathy? The suggestion that children with autism lack empathy is certainly an old and widespread idea (e.g. Kanner, 1943; Frith, 1989; Gillberg, 1992; American Psychiatric Association, 1994). According to Kanner's (1943, p. 38) description, people 'figured in about the same manner as did the desk, the bookshelf, or the filing cabinet'. There have been some demonstrations that children with autism have difficulty recognizing the emotional expressions of others (e.g. Hobson, 1986; Tantam et al., 1989; Bormann-Kischel et al., 1995). In addition, children with autism have been found to show difficulties in detecting intermodal correspondence of facial and vocal/linguistic affect (e.g. Hobson et al., 1988; Loveland et al., 1995).

However, there are contrasting reports that indicate that children with autism are not entirely unresponsive to the socio-affective cues of those around them. According to Wing and Gould (1979), the social impairment of the autistic child need not manifest itself in the avoidance of social contact as Kanner (1943) described. They noted that some children with autism were merely passive or even actively sociable in a peculiar fashion. Phillips et al. (1995) found that children with autism did not treat people as objects when problem solving, and Yirmiya et al. (1992) found that autistic children performed 'surprisingly well' on the Feshbach and Powell Audiovisual Test for Empathy (Feshbach, 1982), although they were impaired relative to normally developing controls. Also, children with autism have been found to be unimpaired in facial affect recognition when the control group was matched on verbal mental age (e.g. Ozonoff et al., 1990; Prior et al., 1990). In addition, several studies have found the emotion-processing impairment to be pronounced only when the emotion is a complex 'cognitive' emotion such as surprise or embarrassment (e.g. Capps et al., 1992; Baron-Cohen et al., 1993; Bormann-Kischel et al., 1995). Finally, while Davies et al. (1994) found that high-ability children with autism did show difficulties in facial affect-matching tasks relative to controls, they also showed

difficulties on non-facial stimuli-matching tasks. Davies et al. (1994) suggested that this indicates that there may be a general perceptual deficit in children with autism that is not specific to faces or emotions.

I decided to investigate whether individuals with autism show emotional responses to the distress of others and autonomic activity in response to other individuals displaying sad expressions. This was done by investigating the psychophysiological responsiveness of children with autism and comparison groups to distress cues (sad faces), threatening (angry faces and threatening animals) and neutral stimuli (neutral faces and objects). Twenty children with autism and two mental-age-matched comparison groups consisting of 20 children with moderate learning difficulty and 20 normal developing children were shown slides of these three types of stimuli and their electrodermal responses were recorded (Blair, 1999a). The children with autism, like those in the two comparison groups, showed significantly greater autonomic responses to the distress cues than to the neutral stimuli. Thus, theory of mind is not a prerequisite for generating autonomic responses to the distress of others.

In line with this finding, Bacon et al. (1998) investigated the behavioural responses to simulated distress of high-functioning and low-functioning children with autism and three comparison populations (developmental language disordered, mentally retarded, and normally developing). Specifically, they explored the extent to which each of these populations orientated (stopped playing and paid attention to) both to the sound of a loud, unfamiliar noise and to the sight and sound of simulated distress in an adult. Interestingly, both groups of children with autism showed reduced social referencing relative to the comparison groups following the sound of the loud, unfamiliar noise, i.e. they did not look towards an adult in the presence of the ambiguous noise. However, the high-functioning children with autism were as likely as the comparison groups to look at the adult when the adult simulated distress. These results indicated that while children with autism did not look towards adults as a source of information in an ambiguous context (i.e. the loud, unfamiliar noise), they automatically orientated to adults when presented with a basic emotional stimulus (the sound of distress).

However, perhaps theory of mind is crucial for generating a sense of aversion to the distress of others. One of the markers of a developing sense of aversion to the distress of others in the normal developing child is the emergence of the moral/conventional distinction (Smetana, 1985; Blair, 1995). The moral/conventional distinction is the distinction that children and adults make in their judgements between moral and conventional transgressions (Turiel, 1983; Smetana, 1993). This distinction is made from the age of 39 months (e.g. Smetana and Braeges, 1990) and is found across cultures (e.g. Nucci et al., 1983; Song et al., 1987). Within the literature, moral transgressions (e.g. hitting another, damaging another's property) are defined by their consequences for the rights and welfare of others. Conventional transgressions (e.g. talking in class, dressing in opposite-sex clothes) are defined by their consequences for the social order. Children and adults generally judge moral transgressions to be more *serious* than conventional transgressions (e.g. Nucci, 1981; Smetana and Braeges, 1990). In addition, and more importantly, modifying the rule conditions (by an authority figure removing the prohibition against the act, for example) only affects the permissibility of conventional transgressions. Even if there is no rule prohibiting the action, subjects generally judge moral transgressions as non-permissible. In contrast, if there is no rule prohibiting a conventional transgression, subjects generally judge the act as permissible. While subjects do not always make the moral/conventional distinction in their seriousness judgements, they do always make it in their modifiability judgements.

Thus, children have been found to judge some conventional transgressions as being as serious as some moral transgressions at some ages (Turiel, 1983; Stoddart and Turiel, 1985). However, even those children who judged the conventional transgressions as being as serious as the moral transgressions judged the moral transgressions as being less rule contingent and less under authority jurisdiction than the conventional transgressions.

It is crucial to note here that it is the presence of victims that distinguishes moral and conventional transgressions. If a subject considers that a transgression will result in a victim, he or she will process that transgression as moral. If a subject does not consider that a transgression will result in a victim, he or she will process that transgression as conventional. Thus, Smetana (1982) has shown that whether an individual treats abortion as a moral transgression or conventional transgression is determined by whether or not he or she judges the act to involve a victim. Similarly, Smetana (1985) has found that unknown transgressions (specified by a nonsense word, e.g. 'X has done dool') were processed as moral or conventional according to the specified consequences of the act. Thus, 'X has done dool and made Y cry' would be processed as moral, whereas 'X has done dool and the teacher told him off' would be processed as conventional. Thus, if an individual is responsive to the presence of victims, he or she should make the moral/conventional distinction. On the other hand, if an individual is not sensitive to the distress of victims, he or she will not make the moral/conventional distinction.

So, do children with autism make the moral/conventional distinction? I investigated the ability to make the moral/conventional distinction in two groups of ten children with autism (one group that failed all false-belief tasks and one group that passed first-order tasks) and two comparison groups (ten children with moderate learning difficulty and ten typically developing children). All four groups of children, even the least able group of children with autism, made the moral/conventional distinction (Blair, 1996). That is, they were less likely to permit the moral transgressions than the conventional transgressions under normally and, crucially, modified rule conditions. The children with autism – even those who, according to their false-belief test results, showed no ability to represent the mental states of others – still prohibited the moral, but not the conventional, transgressions in the absence of prohibitory rules. Thus, not only do children with autism generate appropriate autonomic responses to the distress of others, they also appear to generate appropriate aversion to acts that typically result in harm to others. Therefore theory of mind does not appear to be crucial for either the generation of appropriate autonomic responses to the distress of others or the generation of appropriate aversion to moral transgressions, acts that typically result in harm to others.

Theory of mind may, however, be necessary for the development of prosocial behaviour. Sigman et al. (1992) and Bacon et al. (1998) investigated the behaviour of children with autism following the simulation of distress by an adult actor. Both studies report significantly reduced prosocial behaviour towards the distressed adult in the children with autism. So, given that children with autism show autonomic responses to the distress of others (Blair, 1999a), orientated to the sound of adult's distress (Bacon et al., 1998), and appear to find the distress of others aversive (Blair, 1996), what does their lack of prosocial behaviour mean? Perhaps only that the children with autism did not know what to do in the prosocial situations. In order to show prosocial behaviour, it is crucial both to notice/respond to the distressed other and to be able to formulate a strategy to help the other that is appropriate to his or her needs. Children with autism should be less able to represent the needs of others because of their theory of mind impairment.

The above evidence implies that theory of mind is not crucial for the generation of empathic responses to the distress of others or for moral socialization. However, this does not necessarily imply that impairments in theory of mind could not result in antisocial personality. It is possible that antisocial personality might reflect some impairment in theory of mind. The fact that individuals with autism are not usually aggressive may reflect the same difficulties in the formations of appropriate behavioural strategies that may be the cause of their lack of prosocial behaviour. So is there any evidence of a theory of mind impairment in the antisocial personality?

ANTISOCIAL PERSONALITY

Three main forms of antisocial personality are distinguished in current diagnostic practice: conduct disorder, antisocial personality disorder and psychopathy. Conduct disorder and antisocial personality disorder are both DSM-IV diagnoses. Conduct disorder can be considered to be the child form of antisocial personality disorder, since the diagnosis of antisocial personality disorder is not applied to antisocial individuals younger than 18 years. Both conduct disorder and antisocial personality disorder are diagnosed on the basis of behaviour. For example, for an individual to be considered to be presenting with conduct disorder, he or she must have shown a disturbance of conduct lasting at least 6 months that features at least three different forms of antisocial behaviour. Individuals considered to have antisocial personality disorder must present with a pervasive pattern of disregard for, and violation of, the rights of others that begins in childhood or early adolescence and continues into adulthood (American Psychiatric Association, 1994).

Classifications of psychopathy are not synonymous with diagnoses of conduct disorder or antisocial personality disorder, but represent an extension. The psychopathic child and adult are currently defined by high scores on clinically based rating scales. For children, this is the Psychopathy Screening Device (PSD; Frick and Hare, 2001), and for adults, the Revised Psychopathy Checklist (PCL-R; Hare, 1991). Factor analyses of behaviours rated on both the PSD and PCL reveal two independent factors:

1. an emotion dysfunction factor defined largely by emotional shallowness and lack of guilt (Factor 1),
2. an antisocial behaviour factor defined largely by impulsive aggression and the commission of a wide variety of offence types (Factor 2: Harpur et al., 1989; Hare et al., 1991; Frick et al., 1994).

High scores on Factor 2 of the PSD and PCL are closely associated with the diagnosis of conduct disorder and antisocial personality disorder, respectively (Frick et al., 1994). However, high scores on Factor 1, while highly correlated with scores on antisocial behaviour factor, are less closely associated with the DSM diagnoses. More interestingly, scores on Factor 1 appear to be determined, to a certain extent, by different influences from scores on Factor 2. Thus, both socio-economic status and IQ are correlated with Factor 2 scores, but neither is associated with scores on Factor 1 (Hare et al., 1991). Moreover, while Factor 2 score declines with age, Factor 1 score remains constant (e.g. Harpur and Hare, 1994). This persistence suggests that Factor 1, the emotion dysfunction factor, may more closely reflect the neurocognitive impairment(s) thought to result in the development of psychopathy. Factor 2, and by implication the diagnoses of conduct disorder and antisocial personality disorder, may more accurately reflect the interaction between this neurocognitive impairment and the individual's social environment.

THE CASE OF PSYCHOPATHY

So do psychopathic individuals have a theory of mind impairment? Three studies can be considered to have investigated this question. The first two of these, however, were primarily investigations of the related capacity of role-taking (see above), e.g. Reed and Cuadra (1957) and Widom (1976, 1978). Moreover, these first two studies investigated the relationship between psychopathic personality and role-taking before Hare provided the present formalized descriptions of the disorder (Hare, 1981, 1993). In addition, they proved inconclusive: whereas Reed and Cuadra (1957) and Widom (1976) reported impaired role-taking in the psychopath, Widom (1978) did not.

I investigated this question with 25 psychopathic individuals, defined according to the PCL-R, and a comparison group of 25 non-psychopathic age-matched and IQ-matched individuals who were resident in the same forensic institutions (Blair et al., 1996). Both groups of subjects were submitted to the Advanced Theory of Mind Test (Happé, 1994). This test is a more naturalistic measure of mentalizing ability. Other tasks, such as, for example, the Sally–Anne task described above (e.g. Wimmer and Perner, 1983), are not naturalistic and are principally designed for work with young children. Performance on the Advanced Theory of Mind Test has been found to correlate directly with performance on standard false-belief tasks. Moreover, it is sufficient to discriminate even those highly able autistic subjects who pass standard false-belief tasks (Happé, 1994). Recently, this task has also been used to identify the neural substrate of mentalizing through functional neuroimaging. (Fletcher et al., 1995).

The performances of the psychopathic individuals and the non-psychopathic comparison group did not differ. However, the performance of the psychopathic individuals was significantly better than that of a high-functioning population of individuals with autism of comparable IQ. Even this highest functioning population of individuals with autism had been shown to have a theory of mind impairment (Happé, 1994). Thus it can be concluded that psychopathic individuals generally do not have a theory of mind deficit.

However, irrespective of their theory of mind deficit, do psychopathic individuals have empathy impairment? Certainly, the clinical picture of the psychopathic individual describes someone who has dysfunctional empathy (e.g. Cleckley, 1976; Hare, 1991). However, as stated above, empathy is a very under-specified concept with a plethora of different definitions (see Eisenberg and Strayer, 1987). A more precise model of empathy, the violence inhibition mechanism (VIM) model, has recently been developed couched in information-processing terms (see Blair, 1995). This model was prompted by the work of the ethologists Eibl-Eibesfeldt (1970) and Lorenz (1981), who proposed that most social animals possess mechanisms for the control of aggression. They noted that submission cues displayed to an aggressor terminate attacks: an aggressor dog will cease fighting if its opponent bares its throat. I proposed the existence of a functionally similar mechanism in humans, the VIM. This was done by speculating that a deficit within, or a failure to develop, this mechanism might, under certain social conditions, result in the development of psychopathic behaviour: the individual without this mechanism would not inhibit his aggression when the victim displayed distress cues.

It is suggested that when the VIM is activated by distress cues, it initiates a withdrawal response that results in the interruption of ongoing behaviour and the activation of the autonomic nervous system (Blair, 1995). It is suggested that it is the activation of VIM by distress cues that initiates arousal in normally developing individuals (e.g. Bandura and Rosenthal, 1966; Eisenberg et al., 1990). Moreover, it should be noted that the VIM is thought to be activated whenever distress cues are displayed; it is not reliant upon contextual information about ongoing violence for activation. In line with this, the display of distress cues has been found to result in the inhibition not only of aggression (e.g. Perry and Perry, 1974), but also of non-violent disputes over property ownership (e.g. Camras, 1977) and sexual activity (Chaplin et al., 1995). If the psychopathic individual lacks, or has a dysfunctional, VIM, he or she should not show (or should show reduced) arousal responses specifically to distress cues.

Five studies have examined the responsiveness of psychopathic individuals to distress cues (Sutker, 1970; House and Milligan, 1976; Aniskiewicz, 1979; Blair et al., 1997; Blair, 1999b). Three of these studies involved a similar design: subjects had to observe confederates who they thought were being given electric shocks. Skin conductance responses to the sight of the apparently shocked confederates were recorded. Of these three studies, two reported less responsiveness in the psychopath relative to controls (House and Milligan, 1976; Aniskiewicz, 1979), while one did not (Sutker, 1970). In the fourth study, 18 adult psychopaths and 18 incarcerated controls were shown slides of distress cues, threatening and neutral stimuli and their electrodermal responses were recorded (Blair et al., 1997). The threatening stimuli included images of angry expressions. This study found that the psychopaths showed, relative to the controls, reduced electrodermal responses to the distress cues. In contrast, the two groups did not differ in their electrodermal responses to the threatening stimuli (including the angry face) and to the neutral stimuli. A fifth study utilized an identical design to the fourth but examined the responses of three groups of 16 children (Blair, 1999b). Two groups were children with emotional and behavioural difficulties, divided according to their Antisocial Process Screening Device scores (Frick and Hare, 2001). A further 16 normal developing children in mainstream education were also presented with these stimuli. The high Antisocial Process Screening Device scoring children showed, relative to the controls (and like the adult psychopathic individuals), reduced electrodermal responses to the distress cues. These results indicate that psychopathic individuals do not have a global empathy impairment – they respond appropriately to angry expressions (Blair et al., 1997); rather, they show a specific impairment in their response to distress cues.

At the anatomical level, there have been suggestions that amygdala dysfunction is a prerequisite for the development of psychopathy (see Patrick, 1994; Blair and Frith, 2000; Blair, 2003). There is considerable overlap of impairment following acquired lesions to the amygdala in previously healthy patients and individuals with the developmental disorder of psychopathy. Thus, patients with acquired lesions to the amygdala show impairments in aversive conditioning paradigms (Bechara et al., 1995; La Bar et al., 1995), as do patients with psychopathy (e.g. Lykken, 1957). Patients with amygdala lesions fail to show augmented startle reflexes (Angrilli et al., 1996), as do patients with psychopathy (e.g. Patrick et al., 1993). Moreover, as regards processing facial expressions, the amygdala has been implicated in processing the facial affects of others; specifically, individuals with acquired lesions to the amygdala show an inability to recognize the facial affect of fear (e.g. Calder et al., 1996). A positron emission tomography (PET) functional imaging study in normal volunteers has shown that there is a specific neural response in the left amygdala that is proportional to the intensity of sad facial affect (Blair et al., 1999).

Thus, to summarize, the above research on patients with psychopathy suggests three main conclusions:

1. that the psychopathic individual has no theory of mind impairment,
2. that the psychopathic individual does have a precise impairment in the processing of sad facial expressions,
3. that the psychopathic individual may be a potential developmental consequence of early amygdala dysfunction.

The third conclusion is important as regards the issue of theory of mind. Theory of mind functioning is not associated with the amygdala, but rather with the functioning of the medial frontal cortex, specifically Brodmann's area 8 (e.g. Fletcher et al., 1995; Goel et al., 1995).

RELATIONSHIPS BETWEEN THEORY OF MIND AND ANTISOCIAL BEHAVIOUR

This chapter presents data indicating that a global theory of mind impairment, as is seen in the developmental disorder of autism, does not result in a lack of empathy or impoverished moral development. Data are also presented indicating that the psychopathic individual has no theory of mind dysfunction. However, are there any ways in which theory of mind dysfunction might lead to either antisocial personality disorder or aspects of this disorder? The work of Ken Dodge suggests that there are (e.g. Dodge, 1980; Dodge et al., 1990). Specifically, he has indicated that highly aggressive boys show 'hostile attribution biases'. The essence of his hypothesis is that the social cognition of aggressive children is biased. These children tend to over-attribute hostile intentions to peers, even in circumstances in which a hostile attribution is not warranted. Dodge (1980) exposed aggressive and non-aggressive boys to a frustrating outcome instigated by an ambiguously intentioned peer. In response to the ambiguous provocation, aggressive boys demonstrated a bias towards attributing a hostile intention to the peer. Also, this attributional bias directly mediated the retaliatory aggressive behaviour of these boys. As a result, they displayed retaliatory aggressive behaviour more frequently than did non-aggressive boys. It has been found that aggressive boys tend to over-attribute hostile intentions to others in response to photographs of peers and in response to actual ambiguous situations (Steinberg and Dodge, 1983).

It is crucial to note here that the hostile attribution biases of aggressive children are very specific. Aggressive children are not globally impaired in their attributions of intent. While they are more likely to attribute hostile intent to another's ambiguous behaviour that is directed at themselves, they show no such bias if the ambiguous behaviour is directed at a third individual (Dodge and Frame, 1982). This clearly implies that highly aggressive children do not have a theory of mind deficit in the classic sense of the word. Their ability to attribute intention remains intact. Their dysfunction is, as Dodge (e.g. 1980) argues, a bias, which results in them attributing hostile intent to others who are directing ambiguous behaviour at them. At present, the developmental origins of this bias are unclear. There has been some suggestion that it may be associated with early physical abuse (Dodge et al., 1995) or a product of an earlier propensity to be aggressive in these individuals (e.g. Dodge and Frame, 1982). Moreover, a hostile attribution bias is not only seen in aggressive children, but also in children with depression (Quiggle et al., 1992). Thus hostile attribution biases may be a consequence of development in an environment appreciated to be hostile.

Theory of mind and antisocial behaviour need not only be linked within models that presuppose a theory of mind dysfunction causes antisocial behaviour. Indeed, some forms of antisocial behaviour may only be possible if the individual is fully able to represent the mental states of others. One of the reasons why a theory of mind was unlikely to be causally involved in the development of psychopathy was that the symptomatology of psychopathy includes a tendency to con and manipulate others (see Hare, 1991). To be able to con and manipulate others is possible only if you are able to represent their mental states. If you cannot represent what another might think, it is very difficult to manipulate their behaviour (see Blair et al., 1996). A second form of behaviour that is only possible if

you are able to represent the mental states of others is the capacity to lie (e.g. Morton, 1988). Without the ability to represent that another might have a different belief from your own, there can be no motivation to lie: you will always believe that they hold your belief.

CONCLUSION

This chapter considers the relationship between theory of mind and antisocial personality disorder, beginning with a discussion of why theory of mind has been linked to the development of antisocial behaviour. Representations produced by an individual's theory of mind (role/perspective-taking system) have been considered to inhibit aggression either directly or through empathy. The evidence produced, however, indicates that this position is incorrect. Individuals without the capacity to represent the mental states of others – individuals with autism – do not appear to be at heightened risk for aggression and are certainly capable of showing particular forms of empathic reactions to others.

This chapter also considers whether there is any relationship between theory of mind impairment and the most extreme form of antisocial personality, the psychopath. The reviewed data indicate that there is no theory of mind impairment present in adults with psychopathy. However, this population does have a disorder of empathy: they do not respond to the distress of others. At the anatomical level, their empathic disorder suggests damage to the amygdala.

Finally, this chapter considers further potential relationships between theory of mind and antisocial behaviour, with reference to Dodge's work on 'hostile attribution biases'. However, it is necessary to conclude that Dodge is not identifying a theory of mind impairment: the children are able to represent intentions appropriately in interactions that do not involve hostility. Moreover, it is unclear whether the hostile attribution biases result in an increased risk of antisocial behaviour or whether, given that these biases are also shown by children with depression, they are a developmental result of growing up in hostile environments.

Currently, treatment is difficult. The goal of future research is to enable more direct interventions.

REFERENCES

American Psychiatric Association (1994). *Diagnostic and Statistical Manual of Mental Disorders*, fourth edition. Washington, DC: American Psychiatric Association.

Angrilli A, Mauri A, Palomba D et al. (1996). Startle reflex and emotion modulation impairment after a right amygdala lesion. *Brain* **119**:1991–2000.

Aniskiewicz AS (1979). Autonomic components of vicarious conditioning and psychopathy. *Journal of Clinical Psychology* **35**:60–7.

Bacon AL, Fein D, Morris R, Waterhouse L and Allen D (1998). The responses of autistic children to the distress of others. *Journal of Autism and Developmental Disorders* **28**:129–42.

Bandura A and Rosenthal TL (1966). Vicarious classical conditioning as a function of arousal level. *Journal of Personality and Social Psychology* **3**:54–62.

Baron-Cohen S, Leslie AM and Frith U (1985). Does the autistic child have a 'theory of mind'? *Cognition* **21**:37–46.

Baron-Cohen S, Spitz A and Cross P (1993). Do children with autism recognise surprise? A research note. *Cognition and Emotion* **7**:507–16.

Batson CD, Fultz J and Schoenrade PA (1987). Adults' emotional reactions to the distress of others. In: Eisenberg N and Strayer J (eds), *Empathy and its Development*. Cambridge: Cambridge University Press, 163–85.

Bechara A, Tranel D, Damasio H, Adolphs R, Rockland C and Damasio AR (1995). Double dissociation of conditioning and declarative knowledge relative to the amygdala and hippocampus in humans. *Science* **269**:1115–18.

Blair RJR (1995). A cognitive developmental approach to morality: investigating the psychopath. *Cognition* **57**:1–29.

Blair RJR (1996). Brief Report: Morality in the autistic child. *Journal of Autism and Developmental Disorders* **26**:571–9.

Blair RJR (1999a). Psycho-physiological responsiveness to the distress of others in children with autism. *Personality and Individual Differences* **26**:477–85.

Blair RJR (1999b). Responsiveness to distress cues in the child with psychopathic tendencies. *Personality and Individual Differences* **27**:135–45.

Blair RJR (2003). Neurobiological basis of psychopathy. *British Journal of Psychiatry* **182**:5–7.

Blair RJR and Frith U (2000). Neuro-cognitive explanations of the antisocial personality disorders. *Criminal Behaviour and Mental Health* **10**:S66–S82.

Blair RJR, Jones L, Clark F and Smith M (1997). The psychopathic individual: a lack of responsiveness to distress cues? *Psychophysiology* **34**:192–8.

Blair RJR, Morris JS, Frith CD, Perrett DI and Dolan R (1999). Dissociable neural responses to facial expressions of sadness and anger. *Brain* **122**:883–93.

Blair RJR, Sellars C, Strickland I et al (1996). Theory of Mind in the psychopath. *Journal of Forensic Psychiatry* **7**:15–25.

Bormann-Kischel C, Vilsmeier M and Baude B (1995). The development of emotional concepts in autism. *Journal of Child Psychology and Psychiatry and Allied Disciplines* **36**:1243–59.

Calder AJ, Young AW, Rowland D and Perrett DI (1996). Facial emotion recognition after bilateral amygdala damage: differentially severe impairment of fear. *Cognitive Neuropsychology* **13**:699–745.

Camras LA (1977). Facial expressions used by children in a conflict situation. *Child Development* **48**:1431–5.

Capps L, Yirmiya N and Sigman M (1992). Understanding of simple and complex emotions in non-retarded children with autism. *Journal of Child Psychology and Psychiatry and Allied Disciplines* **33**:1169–82.

Chandler MJ, Greenspan S and Barenboim C (1974). Assessment and training of role-taking and referential communication skills in institutionalised, emotionally disturbed children. *Developmental Psychology* **10**:546–53.

Chaplin TC, Rice ME and Harris GT (1995). Salient victim suffering and the sexual responses of child molesters. *Journal of Consulting and Clinical Psychology* **63**:249–55.

Cleckley H (1976). *The Mask of Sanity.* St Louis, MO: Mosby.

Colby A, Kohlberg L, Gibbs J and Lieberman M (1983). A longitudinal study of moral judgement. *Monographs of the Society for Research in Child Development* **48**:124.

Davies S, Bishop D, Manstead ASR and Tantam D (1994). Face perception in children with autism and Asperger's syndrome. *Journal of Child Psychology and Psychiatry and Allied Disciplines* **35**:1033–57.

Dodge KA (1980). Social cognition and children's aggressive behaviour. *Child Development* **51**:162–70.

Dodge KA and Frame CL (1982). Social cognitive biases and deficits in aggressive boys. *Child Development* **53**:620–35.

Dodge KA, Pettit GS, Bates JE and Valente E (1995). Social information-processing patterns partially mediate the effect of early physical abuse on later conduct problems. *Journal of Abnormal Psychology* **104**:632–43.

Dodge KA, Price JM, Bachorowski JA and Newman JP (1990). Hostile attributional biases in severely aggressive adolescents. *Journal of Abnormal Psychology* **99**:385–92.

Eibl-Eibesfeldt I (1970). *Ethology: The Biology of Behavior.* New York: Holt, Rinehart and Winston.

Eisenberg N (1986). *Altruistic Cognition, Emotion, and Behavior.* Hillsdale, NJ: Erlbaum.

Eisenberg N, Fabes R, Miller PA, Shell R, Shea C and May-Plumlee T (1990). Pre-schoolers' vicarious emotional responding and their situational and dispositional prosocial behaviour. *Merrill–Palmer Quarterly* **36**:507–29.

Eisenberg N and Strayer J (eds) (1987). Critical issues in the study of empathy. In: *Empathy and its Development.* New York: Cambridge University Press, 3–13.

Feshbach ND (1975). Empathy in children: some theoretical and empirical considerations. *Counselling Psychologist* **5**:25–30.

Feshbach ND (1978). Studies of empathic behavior in children. In: Maher BA (ed.), *Progress in Experimental Personality Research.* New York: Academic Press, 1–47.

Feshbach ND (1982). Sex differences in empathy and social behaviour in children. In: Eisenberg N (ed.), *The Development of Prosocial Behavior.* New York: Academic Press, 315–38.

Feshbach ND (1987). Affective processes and academic achievement. *Child Development* **58**:1335–47.

Fletcher PC, Happé F, Frith U et al. (1995). Other minds in the brain: a functional imaging study of 'theory of mind' in story comprehension. *Cognition* **57**:109–28.

Frick PJ and Hare RD (2001). *The Antisocial Process Screening Device.* Toronto: Multi-Health Systems.

Frick PJ, O'Brien BS, Wootton JM and McBurnett K (1994). Psychopathy and conduct problems in children. *Journal of Abnormal Psychology* **103**:700–7.

Frith U (1989). *Autism: Explaining the Enigma.* Oxford: Blackwell.

Gibbs JC (1987). Social processes in delinquency: the need to facilitate empathy as well as sociomoral reasoning. In: Kurtines WM and Gewirtz JL (eds), *Moral Development Through Social Interaction.* New York: John Wiley & Sons, 301–21.

Gillberg C (1992). The Emanual Miller Lecture, 1991. Autism and autistic-like conditions: subclasses among disorders of empathy. *Journal of Child Psychology and Psychiatry* **33**:813–42.

Goel V, Grafman J, Sadato N and Hallet M (1995). Modeling other minds. *Neuroreport: An International Journal for the Rapid Communication of Research in Neuroscience* **6**:1741–6.

Happé FGE (1994). An advanced test of Theory of Mind: understanding of story characters' thoughts and feelings in able autistic, mentally handicapped, and normal children and adults. *Journal of Autism and Developmental Disorders* **24**:129–54.

Hare RD (1981). Psychopathy and violence. In: Hayes JR, Roberts TK and Solway KS (eds), *Violence and the Violent Individual.* Jamaica, NY: Spectrum, 53–74.

Hare RD (1991). *The Hare Psychopathy Checklist – Revised.* Toronto: Multi-Health Systems.

Hare RD (1993). *Without Conscience: The Disturbing World of the Psychopaths Among Us.* New York: Simon and Schuster.

Hare RD, Hart SD and Harpur TJ (1991). Psychopathy and the DSM-IV criteria for antisocial personality disorder. *Journal of Abnormal Psychology* **100**:391–8.

Harpur TJ and Hare RD (1994). Assessment of psychopathy as a function of age. *Journal of Abnormal Psychology* **103**:604–9.

Harpur TJ, Hare RD and Hakstian AR (1989). Two-factor conceptualisation of psychopathy: construct validity and assessment implications. *Psychological Assessment: A Journal of Consulting and Clinical Psychology* **1**:6–17.

Hobson P (1986). The autistic child's appraisal of expressions of emotion. *Journal of Child Psychology and Psychiatry* **27**:321–42.

Hobson RP, Ouston J and Lee A (1988). Emotion recognition in autism: co-ordinating faces and voices. *Psychological Medicine* **18**:911–23.

Hoffman ML (1987). The contribution of empathy to justice and moral judgement. In: Eisenberg N and Strayer J (eds), *Empathy and its Development.* Cambridge: Cambridge University Press, 47–80.

House TH and Milligan WL (1976). Autonomic responses to modeled distress in prison psychopaths. *Journal of Personality and Social Psychology* **34**:556–60.

Kanner L (1943). Autistic disturbances of affective contact. *Nervous Child* **2**:217–50.

Keller M and Edelstein W (1991). The development of socio-moral meaning making: domains, categories, and perspective-taking. In: Kurtinez WM and Gewirz JL (eds), *Handbook of Moral Behavior and Development*, Vol. 1: *Theory*, Vol. 2: *Research*, Vol. 3: *Application.* Hillsdale, NJ: Lawrence Erlbaum, 89–114.

Kohlberg L (1981). *The Philosophy of Moral Development: Moral Stages and the Idea of Justice.* San Francisco, CA: Harper and Row.

La Bar KS, Le Doux JE, Spencer DD and Phelps EA (1995). Impaired fear conditioning following unilateral temporal lobectomy in humans. *Journal of Neuroscience* **15**:6846–55.

Leslie AM (1987). Pretense and representation: the origins of 'Theory of Mind'. *Psychological Review* **94**:412–26.

Leslie AM and Frith U (1988). Autistic children's understanding of seeing, knowing and believing. *British Journal of Developmental Psychology* **6**:315–24.

Lorenz K (1981). *The Foundation of Ethology.* New York: Springer-Verlag.

Lotter V (1966). Epidemiology of autistic conditions in young children: I. Prevalence. *Social Psychiatry* **1**:124–37.

Loveland KA, Tunali-Kotoski B, Chen R, Brelsford KA, Ortegon J and Pearson DA (1995). Intermodal perception of affect in persons with autism or Down

syndrome. *Development and Psychopathology* **7**:409–18.

Lykken DT (1957). A study of anxiety in the sociopathic personality. *Journal of Abnormal and Social Psychology* **55**:6–10.

Morton J (1988). When can lying start? *Issues in Criminological and Legal Psychology* **13**:35–6.

Morton J and Frith U (1993). Causal modelling: a structural approach to developmental psychopathology. In: Cicchetti D and Cohen DH (eds), *Manual of Developmental Psychopathology.* New York: John Wiley & Sons, 357–90.

Nucci L (1981). Conceptions of personal issues: a domain distinct from moral or societal concepts. *Child Development* **52**:114–21.

Nucci L, Turiel E and Encarnacion-Gawrych GE (1983). Social interactions and social concepts: analysis of morality and convention in the Virgin Islands. *Journal of Cross Cultural Psychology* **14**:469–87.

Ozonoff S, Pennington B and Rogers S (1990). Are there emotion perception deficits in young autistic children? *Journal of Child Psychology and Psychiatry* **31**:343–63.

Patrick CJ (1994). Emotion and psychopathy: startling new insights. *Psychophysiology* **31**:319–30.

Patrick CJ, Bradley MM and Lang PJ (1993). Emotion in the criminal psychopath: startle reflex modulation. *Journal of Abnormal Psychology* **102**:82–92.

Perner J, Frith U, Leslie AM and Leekam SR (1989). Exploration of the autistic child's theory of mind: knowledge, belief and communication. *Child Development* **60**:689–700.

Perry DG and Perry LC (1974). Denial of suffering in the victim as a stimulus to violence in aggressive boys. *Child Development* **45**:55–62.

Phillips W, Gomez JC, Baron-Cohen S, Laa V and Riviere A (1995). Treating people as objects, agents, or 'subjects': how young children with and without autism make requests. *Journal of Child Psychology and Psychiatry and Allied Disciplines* **36**:1383–98.

Premack D and Woodruff G (1978). Does the chimpanzee have a 'theory of mind'? *Behaviour and Brain Sciences* **4**:515–26.

Prior M, Dahlstrom B and Squires T (1990). Autistic children's knowledge of thinking and feeling states in other people. *Journal of Autism and Developmental Disorders* **31**:587–602.

Quiggle NL, Garber J, Panak WF and Dodge KA (1992). Social information processing in aggressive and depressed children. *Child Development* **63**:1305–20.

Reed CF and Cuadra CA (1957). The role-taking hypothesis in delinquency. *Journal of Consulting Psychology* **5**:386–90.

Scragg P and Shah A (1994). Prevalence of Asperger's syndrome in a secure hospital. *British Journal of Psychiatry* **165**:679–82.

Selman RL (1976). Social–cognitive understanding: a guide to educational and clinical practice. In: Lickona T (ed.), *Moral Development and Behavior.* New York: Holt, Rinehart and Winston, 299–316.

Selman RL (1980). *The Growth of Interpersonal Understanding.* New York: Academic Press.

Sigman MD, Kasari C, Kwon J and Yirmiya N (1992). Responses to the negative emotions of others by autistic, mentally retarded, and normal children. *Child Development* **63**:796–807.

Smetana JG (1982). *Concepts of Self and Morality: Women's Reasoning about Abortion.* New York: Praeger.

Smetana JG (1985). Preschool children's conceptions of transgressions: effects of varying moral and conventional domain-related attributes. *Developmental Psychology* **21**:18–29.

Smetana JG (1993). Understanding of social rules. In: Bennett M (ed.), *The Child as Psychologist: An Introduction to the Development of Social Cognition.* New York: Harvester Wheatsheaf, 111–41.

Smetana JG and Braeges JL (1990). The development of toddlers' moral and conventional judgements. *Merrill–Palmer Quarterly* **36**:329–46.

Song M, Smetana JG and Kim SY (1987). Korean children's conceptions of moral and conventional transgressions. *Developmental Psychology* **23**:577–82.

Steinberg MS and Dodge KA (1983). Attributional bias in aggressive adolescent boys and girls. *Journal of Social and Clinical Psychology* **1**:312–21.

Stoddart T and Turiel E (1985). Children's concepts of cross-gender activities. *Child Development* **56**:1241–52.

Sutker PB (1970). Vicarious conditioning and sociopathy. *Journal of Abnormal Psychology* **76**:380–6.

Tantam D, Monaghan L, Nicholson H and Stirling J (1989). Autistic children's ability to interpret faces: a research note. *Journal of Child Psychology and Psychiatry* **30**:623–30.

Turiel E (1983). *The Development of Social Knowledge: Morality and Convention.* Cambridge: Cambridge University Press.

Underwood B and Moore B (1982). Perspective-taking and altruism. *Psychological Bulletin* **91**:143–73.

Widom CS (1976). Interpersonal and personal construct systems in psychopaths. *Journal of Consulting and Clinical Psychology* **44**:614–23.

Widom CS (1978). An empirical classification of female offenders. *Criminal Justice and Behaviour* **5**:35–52.

Wimmer H and Perner J (1983). Beliefs about beliefs: representation and the constraining function of wrong beliefs in young children's understanding of deception. *Cognition* **13**:103–28.

Wing L and Gould J (1979). Severe impairments of social interaction and associated abnormalities in children: epidemiology and classification. *Journal of Autism and Developmental Disorders* **9**:11–29.

Yirmiya N, Sigman MD, Kasari C and Mundy P (1992). Empathy and cognition in high-functioning children with autism. *Child Development* **63**:150–60.

Chapter 8

NEUROCHEMICAL BASIS OF AGGRESSION AND IMPULSIVITY IN PERSONALITY DISORDER

Zubin Bhagwagar and Philip Cowen

I was not a little surprised to find many maniacs who at no period gave any evidence of any lesion of understanding, but who were under the dominion of instinctive and abstract fury, as if the faculties of affect alone had sustained injury.

Philippe Pinel (1962)

INTRODUCTION

While Pinel was obviously writing about the category of patients who he thought exhibited signs of *manie sans delire*, he could well have been, and probably was, writing about patients who would currently be diagnosed as having a personality disorder. Since Pinel's time, there has been a vast body of work suggesting that personality disorders can be understood in developmental and cognitive terms. However, the above lines are still relevant to this chapter in an age when it is becoming increasingly clear from various neurobiological studies that the 'faculties of affect' have indeed 'sustained injury'.

Over the last two decades, there has been a growing body of evidence linking various neurotransmitter abnormalities with aggression and impulsivity in personality disorders. These neurobiological formulations are not meant to undermine the importance of developmental and social explanations of aggressive behaviour; both lines of thought, as with so much else in psychiatry, complement each other.

Following the trend set by earlier reviews of the subject (Volavka, 1996; Coccaro, 1998), this chapter concentrates on the evidence of involvement of a number of separate neurotransmitter systems in the expression of aggressive behaviour. While the bulk of the evidence concerns the ubiquitous neurotransmitter serotonin (5-HT), other neurotransmitters have also been implicated, albeit without the strength of evidence accompanying the former. It is therefore understandable that the bulk of this chapter is devoted to the 5-HT system. Arguments about the nosology of personality disorders are discussed elsewhere in the book and not reviewed in this chapter.

SEROTONIN

BASIC NEUROPHYSIOLOGY

Serotonin is synthesized from the essential amino acid tryptophan, which is present in the diet. Conversion by the enzyme tryptophan hydroxylase to 5-hydroxytryptophan is the initial and rate-limiting step in the synthesis of

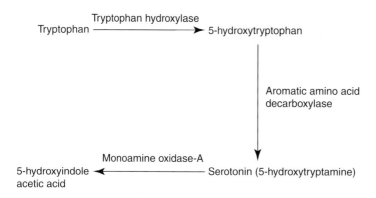

Fig. 8.1 Biosynthetic and catabolic pathway for serotonin (5-HT)

5-HT (Fig. 8.1). Unlike the first step in the metabolism of the catecholamines, dopamine and noradrenaline (norepinephrine), the ambient level of the 5-HT precursor tryptophan does not saturate tryptophan hydroxylase. Therefore fluctuations in the availability of tryptophan to the brain can alter the amount of 5-HT synthesized by the 5-HT neurons. After hydroxylation of tryptophan, 5-HT is produced by decarboxylation through aromatic acid decarboxylase. Synaptic 5-HT is rapidly removed by a specific transporter mechanism, the 5-HT transporter (5-HTT), a primary site of action for the selective serotonin reuptake inhibitors (SSRIs) and, to a lesser degree, tricyclic antidepressants. Intracellular 5-HT not protected by vesicular storage is catabolized by the enzyme monoamine oxidase A (MAO_A) to 5-hydroxyindoleacetic acid (5-HIAA).

Serotonin neurons are principally located in the midline or the raphe of the brainstem. They project in a diffuse manner to all regions of the brain. While there is much overlap in projections from the dorsal and median raphe, selective activation of dorsal raphe neurons causes 5-HT release in the ventral hippocampus, frontal cortex, globus pallidus and striatum; median raphe stimulation results in 5-HT release in the ventral and dorsal hippocampus. Morphologically fine projections from the dorsal raphe nucleus are particularly liable to degenerate following the administration of substituted amphetamines such as 3,4-methylenedioxymethamphetamine (MDMA; 'Ecstasy').

THE ROLE OF SEROTONIN IN AGGRESSIVE BEHAVIOUR

Preliminary evidence of an association between impaired brain 5-HT function and aggression comes from preclinical studies. Animal studies show that damage to the 5-HT cell bodies in the dorsal and median raphe nuclei (Grant et al., 1973) or pharmacological treatments that impede the synthesis of 5-HT (Valzelli et al., 1981) increase the incidence of the aptly named phenomenon of 'muricide' (mouse-killing behaviour) by rats. An interesting study also showed abnormally lower levels of the 5-HT metabolite 5-HIAA in the cerebrospinal fluid (CSF) of a small ($n = 26$) aggressive subset of a large ($n = 4500$), free-ranging population of primates (Mehlman et al., 1994).

Studying the link between 5-HT function and aggression in humans is more problematic because of difficulties in assessing 5-HT function in the living human brain. The various measures employed are shown in Table 8.1.

'CENTRAL' SEROTONERGIC FUNCTION

Brain imaging

The most direct means of measuring brain 5-HT function comes from studies using positron emission tomography (PET) and single photon emission tomography (SPET). Ligands for a number of 5-HT receptor subtypes as well as

Table 8.1 Studies of serotonergic function and aggression

	Parameters studied
Studies measuring indices of 'central' serotonergic function	PET/SPET imaging of serotonin receptors Neuroendocrine challenge tests CSF metabolite levels (5-HIAA etc.)
Studies of 'peripheral' serotonergic mechanisms	Serotonin levels in blood Tryptophan levels in blood Platelet 5-HT transport Platelet 5-HT receptor binding
Molecular genetic studies of the serotonergic system	Serotonin receptor polymorphisms Serotonin transporter polymorphisms

PET, positron emission tomography; SPET, single photon emission tomography; CSF, cerebrospinal fluid; 5-HIAA, 5-hydroxyindoleacetic acid; 5-HT, serotonin.

5-HTT are available and have been used in clinical studies. However, little work looking specifically at aggression has yet been done.

Tiihonen et al. (1997) used SPET to measure 5-HTT binding in 21 impulsive violent offenders (17 of whom had an antisocial personality disorder). Serotonin-specific binding in the midbrain of impulsive violent offenders was lower than that of healthy control subjects. The patient group also had a significant history of alcoholism, but the findings are consistent with the reported reduction in blood platelet 5-HTT binding in aggressive individuals (see below). It is generally believed that aggressive behaviour is linked to decreased 5-HT neurotransmission, and presumably the decrease in transporter binding may be an attempt to compensate for lowered 5-HT release. Another possibility is that decrease in transporter binding might mark a reduction in the density of 5-HT nerve terminals. Interestingly, a PET study indicated that 5-HTT binding in cortical regions was lowered in subjects with longstanding use of MDMA (McCann et al., 1998). In an interesting development, positron [^{11}C] α-methyltryptophan has been used to measure the rates of brain 5-HT synthesis in vivo in human subjects, and the results of these studies are awaited.

Cerebrospinal fluid measures of serotonergic function

In the mid-seventies, initial evidence began to appear relating 5-HT to violent aggression/impulsivity in humans. In their seminal study, Asberg et al. (1976) were able to demonstrate a bi-modal distribution of 5-HIAA in the CSF of patients with unipolar major depression. In essence, patients with the lowest levels of the metabolite were the most likely to have attempted or succeeded in committing suicide in a violent manner. Though a diagnosis of depression was an obvious confounding variable, this study nevertheless set the stage for the hypothesis that aggression/violence is related to low levels of CSF 5-HIAA.

This observation was replicated in a later publication (Brown et al., 1979) when a strong inverse correlation ($r = -0.78$, $p < 0.001$) was shown between a life history of aggressive behaviour and CSF 5-HIAA concentrations in 24 US Navy recruits diagnosed as having a variety of personality disorders. However, the same group (Brown et al., 1982) further demonstrated that in a group of 12 males with borderline personality disorder, CSF 5-HIAA and a life history of aggression showed a weak inverse correlation that did not reach statistical significance.

At that stage, the work did not clarify what specific behaviour or associated feature correlated measures of self-reported violence with low CSF 5-HIAA levels. More evidence for the inverse relationship between CSF 5-HIAA and aggression/impulsivity emerged from work on a group of 36 patients with personality disorder and a history of alcoholism (Linnoila et al., 1983). A relatively low 5-HIAA concentration was found in the group who had committed impulsive violent offences compared with those who had committed premeditated acts of violence. Of the groups studied, impulsive violent offenders who had tried to commit suicide had the lowest 5-HIAA levels. The obvious implication of this study was that impulsivity might be the factor closely associated with serotonergic dysfunction rather than aggression per se. A similar pattern of low CSF 5-HIAA was seen in a subsequent study of impulsive arsonists who had a diagnosis of borderline personality disorder (Virkkunen et al., 1987). Virkkunen goes on to suggest that abnormal brain 5-HT metabolism may occur in early-onset, type 2 alcoholism in men who are prone to exhibit impulsive behaviour under the influence of alcohol (Virkkunen et al., 1990). Low CSF 5-HIAA was found to be correlated with a history of paternal alcoholism and abnormal glucose tolerance tests in such patients.

Coccaro (1998) makes the interesting observation that the pattern of low CSF 5-HIAA associated with aggression is seen in subjects with personality disorders who have a criminal history. However, when subjects with personality disorders without a history of criminal activity were studied, CSF 5-HIAA analysis was equivocal in terms of a relationship with aggression. Coccaro points out a discrepancy in that no correlations were seen either between CSF 5-HIAA levels and lifetime history of aggression in subjects with personality disorder (Gardner et al., 1990; Coccaro et al., 1997a) or between CSF 5-HIAA levels and measures of aggression or impulsivity (Simeon

et al., 1992). He postulates that the differential findings could be explained by the fact that CSF 5-HIAA levels are a relatively insensitive index of brain 5-HT function. Arguably, in a cohort of less severely aggressive patients there would be fewer subjects with low CSF 5-HIAA levels, which could lead to a type I error.

On balance, it would appear that there is a case for the hypothesis that there is an inverse relationship between the end product of 5-HT metabolism as measured in CSF 5-HIAA levels and a past history of aggression or longstanding impulsivity, or perhaps both. However, as a cautionary note, one can speculate on the type of subject who might volunteer for the sort of invasive study involving CSF assays. Gustavsson et al. (1997) describe an elegant experiment in which subjects volunteering in a psychobiological study that included a lumbar puncture were compared with those who had declined to participate, with regard to scores on personality scales. Significant differences were found on the Eysenck Personality Questionnaire and the Karolinska Scales of Personality Impulsiveness. The results suggested an over-representation of impulsive individuals in the volunteers who agreed to have the lumbar puncture. This effect might explain why some studies have failed to find a difference in CSF 5-HIAA levels between patients and controls, as both groups might share characteristics such as impulsiveness and a tendency towards risk-taking behaviours.

Preclinical studies have demonstrated that centrally acting arginine vasopressin facilitates aggression in hamsters (Ferris et al., 1997) and rats (Haller et al., 1996). A relationship between central vasopressin and 5-HT and aggressive behaviour has also been suggested in anatomical and behavioural studies (Haller et al., 1996). To examine the relationship in humans, Coccaro et al. (1998) studied CSF vasopressin, CSF 5-HIAA and the prolactin d-fenfluramine challenge (a neuroendocrine marker of brain 5-HT function) in 26 subjects with a wide variety of *Diagnostic and Statistical Manual* of *Mental Disorders*, fourth edition (DSM-IV, American Psychiatric Association, 1994) personality disorders.

The CSF vasopressin level correlated directly with a life history of general aggression and aggression against persons, and correlated inversely with prolactin d-fenfluramine responses. Cerebrospinal fluid vasopressin did not correlate with CSF 5-HIAA levels. Prolactin d-fenfluramine responses correlated inversely with a life history of aggression. The authors suggest that vasopressin may play a role in enhancing, while serotonin plays a role in inhibiting, aggressive behaviour in personality disordered individuals. However, the possibility also remains that vasopressin may influence aggressive behaviour in such individuals independent of its interaction with 5-HT.

Neuroendocrine challenge tests

Evidence for an association between 5-HT and aggression in personality disorders is probably the most robust in the area of 5-HT neuroendocrine challenge tests. These tests measure the functioning of central 5-HT neurons by quantifying the change in a known variable (a plasma hormone level) after the administration of selective pharmacological challenges that increase 5-HT neurotransmission either pre-synaptically or by activating post-synaptic receptors.

The prolactin response to fenfluramine The prolactin response to the 5-HT-releasing agents dl-fenfluramine and d-fenfluramine is probably the most widely studied in the field of aggressive behaviour. Fenfluramine releases pre-synaptic stores of 5-HT, blocks 5-HT reuptake and thus indirectly stimulates post-synaptic 5-HT receptors. This enhancement of central 5-HT activity is reflected by increased secretion of prolactin-releasing factor in the hypothalamus, which facilitates the release of prolactin from pituitary lactotrophs. This results in elevated concentrations of prolactin in peripheral blood. In both animals and humans, the prolactin response to d-fenfluramine can be blocked by the 5-HT$_2$ receptor antagonist ritanserin but not by pindolol, a β-adrenoceptor antagonist with 5-HT$_{1A}$ receptor antagonist properties (Goodall et al., 1993; Park and Cowen, 1995). This suggests that fenfluramine-mediated prolactin release is mediated by indirect stimulation of post-synaptic 5-HT$_2$ receptors.

Coccaro et al. (1989) found a reduction in the prolactin response to d-fenfluramine in male subjects with borderline personality disorder compared with patients with other personality disorders and controls but not patients with mood disorders. The group differences appeared to be attributable to the impulsive/aggressive criteria for borderline personality disorder. The blunted prolactin responses were associated with factors such as anger dyscontrol, self-damaging behaviour and impulsivity, relevant to the diagnosis of borderline personality disorder, but not to other diagnostic features such as affective or interpersonal difficulties. Prolactin responses were also negatively correlated with the assault and irritability subscales of the Buss Durkee Hostility Inventory. When assaultiveness and irritability were controlled for statistically, patients who were positive for either of the two no longer appeared to have a lower prolactin d-fenfluramine response, suggesting that the strongest behavioural correlate of the challenge test was impulsive aggression. The same authors later replicated the finding of an inverse correlation between the prolactin d-fenfluramine response and assaultiveness as measured by the Buss Durkee Questionnaire (Coccaro et al., 1997b). While interpreting the results of these studies, one has to remember that blunting of the prolactin response to fenfluramine has been noted in about half the studies involving depressed patients (Park et al., 1996). One wonders, therefore, whether co-morbid depression, even if not to a clinically significant degree, could account for some of the lowering of the fenfluramine-induced pro-lactin release.

A dissenting note was added to the results of the above study when a positive relationship was observed between the prolactin d-fenfluramine response and self-reported impulsiveness in a group of 22 patients with drug abuse and anti-social personality disorder (Fishbein et al., 1989). Clearly, the history of drug abuse may be a confounding factor, although the authors mention that the subjects had been drug free for 5 days. In an extension of an earlier report (Coccaro et al., 1989), the inverse relationship between the prolactin d-fenfluramine response and self-reported assaultiveness was confirmed (Siever et al., 1993). Coccaro went on to repli-cate the finding of an inverse correlation between the prolactin d-fenfluramine response and a life history of aggression (Coccaro et al., 1996a, 1997a) and laboratory measures of aggression (Coccaro et al., 1996a,b). Patients with specific personality disorders have also been studied, and a reduced prolactin d-fenflu-ramine response has been noted in antisocial personality disorders (O'Keane et al., 1992) and compulsive personality disorders (Stein et al., 1996).

It is obvious that there is a robust body of evidence that shows an inverse relation-ship between the prolactin response to d-fenfluramine and measures of aggression in a wide variety of patients with differing per-sonality disorders. Interestingly, very few stud-ies have compared the nature and magnitude of the relationship between aggression and the CSF 5-HIAA concentration response with the relationship between aggression and the prolactin d-fenfluramine response. Mann et al. (1992b) found a positive correlation between CSF 5-HIAA and prolactin response to d-fenfluramine challenge in suicidal sub-jects with mood disorders. Another study (Coccaro, 1992) compared the relative mag-nitude of the correlations with a measure of aggression in subjects with personality disor-ders. Prolactin responses to d-fenfluramine

were inversely correlated with self-reported aggression and irritability, whereas CSF 5-HIAA concentrations were not. Despite this, the correlations of the two measures of serotonergic function with aggression were not significantly different from each other.

Coccaro et al. (1997a) further showed that the neuroendocrine challenge test was more sensitive in detecting a relationship between aggression and central serotonergic function. Twenty-four subjects with personality dis-orders had their Life History of Aggression scores correlated with the two measures of serotonergic function. Aggression was signifi-cantly and inversely correlated with prolactin responses to d-fenfluramine challenge but not with CSF 5-HIAA concentrations. The two measures of serotonergic function did not correlate with each other. The authors specu-late that CSF 5-HIAA would be a sensitive correlate of aggression only in those subjects with impulsive aggressive behaviour severe enough to constitute criminal acts. In a com-parison of three indicators of central seroton-ergic functioning, CSF 5-HIAA levels, prolactin response to metachlorophenylpiperazine (m-CPP) and prolactin response to d-fenfluramine, the latter two neuroendocrine tests correl-ated equally and inversely with a measure of assaultiveness, whereas CSF 5-HIAA did not (Coccaro et al., 1997b).

Prolactin response to m-CPP Another neuro-endocrine challenge test to assess the functioning of the central serotonergic system uses m-CPP, which probably involves the direct activation of 5-HT$_{2C}$ receptors (Cowen, 1993). Moss et al. (1990) studied 15 men with antisocial personal-ity disorder and found a significantly reduced prolactin response and a significantly greater cortisol response to m-CPP when compared with 12 control subjects. Prolactin but not cortisol responses showed a significant inverse correlation with measures of assaultiveness, aggression, negative affect and increased needs. However, in contrast to the fenfluramine challenge data, impulsivity did not correlate with the prolactin response. The inverse correlation between the prolactin m-CPP response and the Buss Durkee Assault factor was later demonstrated in a group of subjects with personality disorder (Coccaro et al., 1997b).

If the prolactin response to m-CPP is blunted in patients with aggression and impulsivity, this would indicate lowered sensitivity of post-synaptic 5-HT_{2C} receptors. This abnormality could also explain the blunted, lowered prolactin response to fenfluramine seen in such individuals. However, other lines of work, for example lowered CSF 5-HIAA, would suggest that aggressive behaviour is linked to decreased pre-synaptic availability of 5-HT. It is possible, therefore, that aggression and impulsivity are associated with impaired 5-HT function at both pre-synaptic and post-synaptic sites.

Other neuroendocrine challenge tests Coccaro et al. (1990) reported an inverse correlation between the prolactin response to the 5-HT_{1A} agonist buspirone and self-reported irritability and assaultiveness in ten subjects with personality disorder. Coccaro also reported a further study in which the administration of ipsapirone, another selective 5-HT_{1A} agonist, resulted in an inverse correlation between the subsequent cortisol and thermal response and measures of aggression in eight male subjects with personality disorder (Coccaro, 1998).

PERIPHERAL SEROTONERGIC FUNCTION

Serotonin/tryptophan levels

As described above, tryptophan hydroxylase (the rate-limiting enzyme in 5-HT metabolism) is not saturated by levels of its substrate tryptophan. Thus one could argue that the metabolism of 5-HT in the brain is dependent on the level of tryptophan available from plasma. Tryptophan has to be actively transported across the blood–brain barrier to reach the brain. During this process, it is in competition with other large neutral amino acids (LNAAs), all of which use the same carrier. Thus it is the concentration of tryptophan relative to other LNAAs that determines the availability of tryptophan to the brain and the rate of 5-HT synthesis.

Eriksson and Lidberg (1997) examined amino acid concentrations in 89 subjects with personality disorder who had committed various (violent and non-violent) crimes and compared the results with those of 14 healthy controls. The median plasma tryptophan concentration was higher in all crime groups when compared with the group of controls, and the results were significantly higher for groups in which a greater degree of violence was used (rape, arson, homicide and manslaughter). When compared with the non-violent group, significantly higher concentrations of tryptophan were found in the groups in which subjects had committed rape, arson and homicide or manslaughter. The ratio of tryptophan to the other LNAAs did not show any statistically significant differences in the groups studied, although, in general, the concentrations of the LNAAs were higher in the group of patients who had committed violent crimes when compared with the controls. The findings suggested a relationship between tryptophan levels and violent and aggressive behaviour. However, the fact that the ratio of tryptophan relative to other LNAAs was not significantly altered makes the functional significance of this abnormality difficult to evaluate.

Serotonin in whole blood is mainly contained in platelets, which have an active transport system to take up 5-HT from plasma. Previous studies of blood 5-HT have reported it to relate positively to aggression in groups of in-patients with depression (Mann et al., 1992a,b), hyperactivity (Cook et al., 1995), conduct disorder (Pliszka et al., 1988) and episodic problem behaviour (Brown et al., 1989). The only study to look at the relationship between aggression and personality disorders (Mann et al., 1992a) found that depressed patients with co-morbid personality disorder had higher whole-blood 5-HT levels than controls. The matter was further clarified by an epidemiological study of whole-blood 5-HT in a birth cohort ($n = 781$) of 21-year-old youths in Dunedin, New Zealand (Moffitt et al., 1998). Violence was measured using cumulative court conviction records and participants' self-report. Whole-blood 5-HT related to violence among men but not women. Violent men's blood 5-HT level was 0.48 standard deviation (SD) above the male population norm and 0.56 SD above the mean of non-violent men. The finding was specific to violence, as opposed to general crime, and it was robust to two different methods of measuring violence. Taken together, the intervening variables (gender, diurnal variation, medication, drug abuse etc.) accounted for 25 per cent of the relationship between blood 5-HT and violence.

As the authors correctly point out, this association of high blood 5-HT and violence could be indirect and possibly coincidental: 5-HT in the blood is largely produced in the gut, is contained in platelets and does not cross the blood–brain barrier. However, the study is useful insofar as it is probably the first epidemiological study of whole-blood 5-HT levels in relation to violence.

Platelet serotonin receptors

Increased serotonergic transport into blood platelets and serotonergic neurons has been postulated as one of the possible explanations for the paradox whereby both low CSF 5-HIAA and high blood 5-HT are related to aggression (Cook et al., 1993, 1995). The 5-HTT responsible for the uptake of 5-HT into blood platelets appears very similar to that found on 5-HT neurons. Blood platelets therefore provide an accessible model of neuronal 5-HT uptake. However, studies looking at the number of 5-HTT binding sites in patients with personality disorders provide results that are not in keeping with the above hypothesis. In such patients, an inverse

correlation has been reported between the number of platelet 5-HTT binding sites on the one hand and self-mutilation and impulsivity on the other (Simeon et al., 1992).

Further confirmation of this hypothesis was observed when, in a group of 24 patients with personality disorders, the maximum binding (B_{max}) values of platelet tritiated paroxetine (5-HTT) binding was inversely correlated with the Life History of Aggression total score and aggression score when compared with 12 healthy volunteers (Coccaro et al., 1996b). The B_{max} values of platelet tritiated paroxetine binding were also inversely correlated with the Buss Durkee Hostility Inventory assault score in patients (Buss and Durkee, 1957). It is unclear how decreased numbers of 5-HTT sites on the platelet found in some studies of aggressive subjects could relate to increased levels of blood 5-HT found in other investigations. What is needed is a study that measures both variables simultaneously.

The platelet also possesses membrane receptors of the 5-HT$_{2A}$ subtype that pharmacologically resemble those seen in the brain. McBride et al. (1994) reported no differences in measures of platelet 5-HT$_{2A}$ receptor function in depressed patients with and without a co-morbid borderline personality disorder. However, Coccaro et al. (1997a,b) found that the density of platelet 5-HT$_{2A}$ receptor binding sites in patients with personality disorders was directly correlated with a self-reported propensity for aggression.

MOLECULAR GENETIC STUDIES OF THE SEROTONIN SYSTEM

The genes encoding 5-HT receptors are suitable candidates for molecular genetic linkage and association studies, and much work has been carried out along these lines in patients with mood disorders. The data in the latter area are somewhat inconsistent, and the same is true of the more limited number of studies in patients with aggression-related disorders.

Nielsen et al. (1994) studied tryptophan hydroxylase polymorphisms and CSF 5-HIAA levels in 56 impulsive violent offenders with a personality disorder (28 had antisocial personality disorder, 27 had intermittent explosive personality disorder and 1 had a conduct disorder), 14 non-impulsive offenders and 20 healthy volunteers. The obvious point of studying the tryptophan hydroxylase gene was its position as the rate-limiting step in the synthesis of 5-HT.

The impulsive violent offenders with at least one copy of the 'L' allele (i.e. LL or LU) had significantly lower CSF 5-HIAA concentrations compared with those impulsive violent offenders with a UU genotype. However, no association between impulsive violent behaviour and the tryptophan hydroxylase polymorphism was noted. The presence of the L allele was, however, associated with an increased rate of past suicide attempts across all categories of the violent offenders. This association was independent of impulsivity status and CSF 5-HIAA concentrations.

Tryptophan hydroxylase polymorphisms continued to be the focus of attention in a later study in which 40 male subjects with personality disorder were genotyped for the polymorphism (New et al., 1998). As opposed to the previous study, subjects with the LL genotype had higher scores of self-reported aggression than those with either the LU or UU genotype. No correlation was observed between specific genotypes and a history of suicide.

EFFECTS OF SEROTONIN MANIPULATION

The data demonstrating the possible relationship between the 5-HT system and aggression make it of interest to assess the effects of manipulations of brain 5-HT function in healthy subjects and selected patient groups. It is possible to lower brain 5-HT synthesis abruptly by using a dietary manipulation that acutely decreases the availability of tryptophan to the brain. This manoeuvre may potentiate aggressive responding in normal control subjects (Cleare and Bond, 1995; Moeller et al., 1996), particularly those with high trait aggression. This suggests that lowering brain 5-HT function can potentiate aggressive behaviour in humans.

Although various drugs have been used in the management of aggression, for the purposes of this chapter it is important to take note of the work done in this area with SSRIs, because these drugs produce large selective increases in brain 5-HT function.

In 26 healthy volunteers treated for 4 weeks with the SSRI paroxetine, there was a reduction in focal indices of hostility mediated via a more general decrease in negative affect. There was also an increase in social affiliation as measured by a behavioural task (Knutson et al., 1998). Further, with regard to clinical populations, a number of open and controlled trials have shown that the fluoxetine is able to reduce measures of aggression in patients with personality disorders (Markovitz et al., 1991; Heiligenstein et al., 1992; Fava et al., 1993; Salzman et al., 1995; Coccaro and Kavoussi, 1997) and there is also some evidence for sertraline (Kavoussi et al., 1994).

OVERVIEW

The balance of evidence suggests that there is an inverse correlation between measures of 5-HT function and ratings of aggression and the incidence of suicide attempts. This correlation is consistent across several measures of 5-HT function, particularly neuroendocrine challenge tests and measures of CSF 5-HIAA concentration. It is arguable that the reduced 5-HT activity may be closer to the heritable substrate than the impulsive behaviour, as a blunted prolactin response to fenfluramine in personality disordered probands was a better predictor of impulsivity in their relatives than were impulsive traits in the probands themselves (Coccaro et al., 1994).

NORADRENALINE

The noradrenergic system is activated when an organism is confronted by a novel or threatening situation that requires increased vigilance in preparation for active responses (Siever, 1987). Noradrenaline is synthesized from the non-essential amino acid tyrosine and its end product of metabolism is 3-methoxy-4-hydroxy phenyl glycol (MHPG).

Studies have looked at both the starting point and end product of noradrenaline metabolism. Siever and Trestman (1993) showed a slight positive correlation between plasma noradrenaline and self-reported impulsivity in male subjects with personality disorders. Brown et al. (1979) reported a positive correlation between CSF MHPG concentrations and a life history of aggression in male subjects with a personality disorder; however, a multiple regression analysis showed that CSF 5-HIAA accounted for 80 per cent of the variance in aggression scores in that study. Weighted against these findings, Virkkunen et al. (1987) reported a significant reduction in CSF MHPG concentration in impulsive violent offenders. In addition, Coccaro (1998) found a significant reduction in plasma free MHPG in male patients with borderline personality disorder when compared with patients with non-borderline personality disorders and normal controls. Further, Coccaro reported a slight inverse correlation between plasma free MHPG and a life history of aggression in patients with personality disorders.

Neuroendocrine challenges for the noradrenergic system have used clonidine, an α_2-adrenergic receptor agonist, which would normally cause an increase in the concentration of growth hormone (GH). Coccaro et al. (1991) reported a positive correlation between the GH response to clonidine and self-reported irritability in male patients with personality disorders.

The results of available studies linking noradrenaline to aggression or impulsivity are not concordant. Although more work needs to be done to clarify the situation, it is wholly possible that there is a complex inter-relationship between the neurotransmitters that is difficult for the present studies, with their single neurotransmitter hypothesis, to detect.

DOPAMINE

Although there is some evidence linking increased dopaminergic functioning to schizotypal personality disorder (Siever et al., 1991, 1993), the available evidence linking dopamine with aggression in personality disorder is limited. Brown et al. (1979) found no relationship between CSF homovanillic acid (HVA), the end product of dopamine metabolism. However, Linnoila et al. (1983) reported a reduction in CSF HVA in antisocial violent offenders. In an extension of this work, Virkkunen et al. (1987) reported a lower CSF HVA concentration in repetitive violent offenders as opposed to non-repetitive violent offenders. More work is needed to clarify the relationship between dopamine and aggression in personality disorder.

OTHER NEUROTRANSMITTERS

In perhaps the only study of its sort, patients with borderline personality disorder were infused with the acetylcholinesterase inhibitor physostigmine, which would have the net effect of increasing acetylcholine functioning (Steinberg et al., 1997). Peak physostigmine-induced dysphoria did not correlate with impulsive aggressive borderline personality disorder traits. As mentioned above, Coccaro et al. (1998) reported a positive correlation between CSF vasopressin and a life history of aggression and aggression against persons.

CONCLUSIONS

All the above data, when taken together, underline the fact that it is possible to link the function of certain neurotransmitters with aggressive and impulsive behaviour in patients with personality disorder. The evidence seems to be strongest for 5-HT, and the most commonly studied personality disorders are of the antisocial or borderline type. Instruments used in the assessment and quantification of aggression and impulsivity vary across studies and may account for some proportion of the divergent results. Measures of neurotransmitter function also vary, and in turn lend their proportion of noise to the results.

Clearly, more work is needed to establish relationships between different neurotransmitters and the expression of aggression. It is to be hoped that such studies, combined with the availability of more selective and better tolerated pharmacological agents, might lead to badly needed improvements in possible drug treatments. Future research in this area will be able to employ brain imaging to define more clearly and directly the neurochemical changes involved in aggressive behaviours. In combination with other kinds of brain functional imaging and neuropsychology, we may eventually be able to understand the neurobiological basis of aggression and its disorders.

REFERENCES

American Psychiatric Association (1994). *Diagnostic and Statistical Manual of Mental Disorders*, fourth edition. Washington, DC: American Psychiatric Association.

Asberg M, Traskman L and Thoren P (1976). 5-HIAA in the cerebrospinal fluid: a biochemical suicide predictor? *Archives of General Psychiatry* **38**:1193–7.

Brown CS, Kent TA, Bryant SG et al. (1989). Blood platelet uptake of serotonin in episodic aggression. *Psychiatry Research* **27**:5–12.

Brown GL, Ebert MH, Goyer PF et al. (1982). Aggression, suicide and serotonin: relationship to CSF amine metabolites. *American Journal of Psychiatry* **139**:741–6.

Brown GL, Goodwin FK, Ballenger JC et al. (1979). Aggression in humans correlates with cerebrospinal fluid amine metabolites. *Psychiatry Research* **1**:131–9.

Buss AH and Durkee A (1957). An inventory for assessing different kinds of hostility. *Journal of Consulting Psychology* **21**:343–9.

Cleare AJ and Bond AJ (1995). The effect of tryptophan depletion and enhancement on subjective and behavioural aggression in normal male subjects. *Psychopharmacology (Berl)* **118**:72–81.

Coccaro EF (1992). Impulsive aggression and central serotonergic system function in humans: an example of a dimensional brain–behavioural relationship. *International Clinical Psychopharmacology* **7**:3–12.

Coccaro E (1998). Neurotransmitter function in personality disorders. In: Silk KR (ed.), *Biology of Personality Disorders.* Washington, DC: American Psychiatric Press, 1–25.

Coccaro EF, Gabriel S and Seiver LJ (1990). Buspirone challenge: preliminary evidence for a role for 5-HT$_{1A}$ receptors in impulsive aggressive behaviour in humans. *Psychopharmacology Bulletin* **26**:393–405.

Coccaro EF and Kavoussi RJ (1997). Fluoxetine and impulsive aggressive behaviour in personality disordered subjects. *Archives of General Psychiatry* **54**:1081–8.

Coccaro EF, Kavoussi RJ, Berman ME et al. (1996a). Relationship of prolactin response to d-fenfluramine to behavioural and questionnaire assessments of aggression in personality disordered males. *Biological Psychiatry* **40**:157–64.

Coccaro E, Kavoussi RJ, Cooper TB et al. (1997a). Central serotonin and aggression: inverse relationship with prolactin response to d-fenfluramine, but not with CSF 5-HIAA concentration in human subjects. *American Journal of Psychiatry* **154**:1430–5.

Coccaro EF, Kavoussi RJ, Hauger RL, Cooper TB and Ferris CF (1998). Cerebrospinal fluid vasopressin levels: correlates with aggression and serotonin in personality disordered subjects. *Archives of General Psychiatry* **55**:708–14.

Coccaro EF, Kavoussi RJ, Sheline YI, Lish JD and Csernansky JG (1996b). Impulsive aggression in personality disorder correlates with tritiated paroxetine binding in the platelet. *Archives of General Psychiatry* **53**:531–6.

Coccaro EF, Kavoussi RJ, Trestman RL, Gabriel SM, Cooper TB and Siever LJ (1997b). Serotonin function in human subjects: intercorrelations among central 5-HT indices and aggressiveness. *Psychiatry Research* **73**:1–14.

Coccaro EF, Lawrence T, Trestman R et al. (1991). Growth hormone responses to intravenous clonidine challenge correlates with behavioural irritability in psychiatric patients and health volunteers. *Psychiatry Research* **39**:129–39.

Coccaro EF, Seiver LJ, Klar HM et al. (1989). Serotonergic studies in affective and personality disorder patients: correlates with suicidal and impulsive aggression. *Archives of General Psychiatry* **43**:587–99.

Coccaro EF, Silverman JM, Klar HM, Horvath TB and Seiver LJ (1994). Functional correlates of reduced central serotonergic function in patients with personality disorders. *Archives of General Psychiatry* **51**:318–24.

Cook EH, Arora RC, Anderson GM et al. (1993). Platelet serotonin studies in hyperserotonemic relatives of children with autistic disorder. *Life Sciences* **52**:2005–15.

Cook EH, Stein MA, Ellison T, Unis AS and Levinthal BL (1995). Attention deficit hyperactivity disorder and whole blood serotonin levels: effects of comorbidity. *Psychiatry Research* **57**:13–20.

Cowen P (1993). Serotonin receptor sub-types in depression: evidence from studies in neuroendocrine regulation. *Clinical Neuropharmacology* **16**:S16–S18.

Eriksson T and Lidberg L (1997). Increased plasma concentrations of the 5-HT precursor amino acid tryptophan and other large neutral amino acids in violent criminals. *Psychological Medicine* **27**:477–81.

Fava M, Rosenbaum JF, Pava JA, McCarthy MK, Steingard RJ and Boufiddes E (1993). Anger attacks in unipolar depression. 1. Clinical correlates and response to fluoxetine treatment. *American Journal of Psychiatry* **150**:1158–63.

Ferris CF, Meloni RH, Koppel G, Perry KW, Fuller RW and Delville Y (1997). Vasopressin/serotonin interactions in the anterior hypothalamus control aggressive behaviour in golden hamsters. *Journal of Neurosciences* **17**:4331–41.

Fishbein DH, Lozovsky D and Jaffe J (1989). Impulsivity, aggression and neuroendocrine responses to serotonergic stimulation in substance abusers. *Biological Psychiatry* **25**:1049–66.

Gardner DL, Lucas PB and Cowdrey RW (1990). CSF metabolites in borderline personality disorder compared with normal controls. *Biological Psychiatry* **28**:247–54.

Goodall EM, Cowen PJ, Franklin M and Silverstone PJ (1993). Ritanserin attenuates anorectic, endocrine and thermic responses to d-fenfluramine in human volunteers. *Psychopharmacology* **112**:461–6.

Grant LD, Coscine DV, Grossman SP and Freedman DX (1973). Muricide after serotonin depleting lesions of the midbrain raphe nuclei. *Pharmacology Biochemistry and Behaviour* **1**:77–80.

Gustavsson JP, Asberg M and Schalling D (1997). The healthy control subjects in psychiatric research: impulsiveness and volunteer bias. *Acta Psychiatrica Scandinavica* **96(5)**:325–8.

Haller J, Makara GB, Barbna I, Kovacs K and Nagy J (1996). Compression of the pituitary stalks elicits chronic increases in CSF vasopressin, oxytocin as well as in social investigation and aggression. *Journal of Neuroendocrinology* **8**:361–5.

Heiligenstein JH, Coccaro EF, Potvin JH, Beasley CM, Dornseif BE and Mascia DN (1992). Fluoxetine not associated with increased violence or aggression in controlled clinical trials. *Annals of Clinical Psychiatry* **4**:285–9.

Kavoussi RJ, Liu J and Coccaro EF (1994). An open trial of sertraline in personality disordered patients with aggression. *Journal of Clinical Psychiatry* **55**:137–41.

Knutson B, Wolkowitz OM, Cole SW et al. (1998). Selective alteration of personality and social behaviour by serotonergic intervention. *American Journal of Psychiatry* **155**:373–9.

Linnoila M, Virkkunnen M, Scheinin M et al. (1983). Low cerebrospinal fluid 5-hydroxyindoleacetic acid concentration differentiates impulsive from non-impulsive behaviour. *Life Sciences* **33**:2609–14.

Mann JJ, McBride A, Anderson GM and Mieczkowski TA (1992a). Platelet and whole blood serotonin content in depressed inpatients: correlations with acute and lifetime psychopathology. *Biological Psychiatry* **32**:243–57.

Mann JJ, McBride PA, Brown RP et al. (1992b). The relationship between central and peripheral serotonin indices in depressed and suicidal psychiatric inpatients. *Archives of General Psychiatry* **49**:442–6.

Markovitz PJ, Calabrese JR, Schulz SC and Meltzer HY (1991). Fluoxetine in borderline and schizotypal personality disorder. *American Journal of Psychiatry* **148**:1064–7.

McBride PA, Brown RP, DeMeo M et al. (1994). The relationship of platelet 5-HT$_2$-receptor indices to major depressive disorder, personality traits and suicidal behaviour. *Biological Psychiatry* **35**:295–308.

McCann UD, Szabo Z, Scheffel U, Dannals RF and Ricaurte GA (1998). Positron emission tomographic evidence of toxic effects of MDMA ('Ecstasy') on brain serotonin neurons in human beings. *Lancet* **352**:1433–7.

Mehlman PT, Higley JD, Faucher I et al. (1994). Low CSF 5-HIAA concentrations and severe aggression and impaired impulse control in non-human primates. *American Journal of Psychiatry* **151**:1485–91.

Moeller FG, Dougherty DM, Swann EC, Collins D, Davis CM and Cherek DR (1996). Tryptophan depletion and aggressive responding in healthy males. *Psychopharmacology (Berl)* **126**:97–103.

Moffitt TE, Brammer GL, Caspi A et al. (1998). Whole blood serotonin relates to violence in an epidemiological study. *Biological Psychiatry* **43**:446–57.

Moss HB, Yao JK and Panzak GL (1990). Serotonergic responsivity and behavioural dimensions in antisocial personality disorder. *Biological Psychiatry* **28**: 325–38.

New AS, Gerlenter J, Yovell Y et al. (1998). Tryptophan hydroxylase genotype is associated with impulsive aggression measures: a preliminary study. *American Journal of Medical Genetics* **81**:13–17.

Nielsen DA, Goldman D, Virkkunen M, Tokola R, Rawlings R and Linnoila M (1994). Suicidality and 5-hydroxyindoleacetic acid associated with a tryptophan hydroxylase polymorphism. *Archives of General Psychiatry* **51**:34–8.

O'Keane V, Moloney E, O'Neill H et al. (1992). Blunted prolactin responses to d-fenfluramine in sociopathy: evidence for subsensitivity of central serotonergic function. *British Journal of Psychiatry* **160**:643–6.

Park SBG and Cowen PJ (1995). Effect of pindolol on the prolactin response to d-fenfluramine. *Psychopharmacology* **118**:471–4.

Park SBG, Williamson DJ and Cowen PJ (1996). 5-HT neuroendocrine function in major depression: prolactin and cortisol responses to d-fenfluramine. *Psychological Medicine* **26**:1191–6.

Pinel P (1962). *A Treatise on Insanity* (Davis D, trans.). New York: Hafner, 9. (Original work published 1801.)

Pliszka SR, Graham AR, Rogeness MD, Renner P, Sherman J and Broussard T (1988). Plasma neurochemistry in juvenile offenders. *Journal of the American Academy of Child and Adolescent Psychiatry* **27**:588–94.

Salzman C, Wolfson AN, Schatzberg A et al. (1995). Effect of fluoxetine on anger in symptomatic volunteers with borderline personality disorder. *Journal of Clinical Psychopharmacology* **15**:23–9.

Siever LJ (1987). The role of noradrenergic mechanisms in the aetiology of affective disorders. In: Meltzer HY (ed.), *Psychopharmacology: The Third Generation of Progress*. New York: Raven Press, 493–504.

Siever LJ, Amin F, Coccaro EF et al. (1991). Plasma homovanillic acid in schizotypal personality disorder. *American Journal of Psychiatry* **148**:1246–8.

Siever LJ, Amin F, Coccaro EF et al. (1993). CSF homovanillic acid in schizotypal personality disorder. *American Journal of Psychiatry* **150**:149–51.

Siever LJ and Trestman RL (1993). The serotonin system and aggressive personality disorder. *International Clinical Psychopharmacology* **8**:33–9.

Simeon D, Stanley B, Frances A et al. (1992). Self mutilation in personality disorders: psychological and biological correlates. *American Journal of Psychiatry* **149**:221–6.

Stein DJ, Trestman RL, Mitroupoulou V et al. (1996). Impulsivity and serotonergic function in compulsive personality disorder. *Journal of Neuropsychiatry and Clinical Neurosciences* **8**:393–8.

Steinberg BJ, Trestman R, Mitropoulou V et al. (1997). Depressive response to physostigmine challenge in borderline personality disorder patients. *Neuropsychopharmacology* **17**:264–73.

Tiihonen J, Kuikka JT, Bergstrom KA et al. (1997). Single photon emission tomography imaging of monoamine transporters in impulsive violent behaviour. *European Journal of Nuclear Medicine* **24**:1253–60.

Valzelli L, Bernasconi S and Dalessandro M (1981). Effect of tryptophan administration on spontaneous and p-CPA induced muricidal aggression in laboratory rats. *Pharmacological Research communications* **13**:891–7.

Virkkunen M and Linnoila M (1990). Serotonin in early onset male alcoholics with violent behaviour. *Annals of Medicine* **22(5)**:327–31.

Virkkunen M, Nuutila A, Goodwin FK et al. (1987). Cerebrospinal fluid monoamine metabolite levels in male arsonists. *Neuropsychopharmacology* **1**:55–62.

Volavka J (1996). Neurochemistry of violence. In: Volavka J (ed.), *Neurobiology of Violence*. Washington, DC: American Psychiatric Press, 49–76.

Chapter 9

NEUROPSYCHIATRY OF PERSONALITY DISORDER

George W. Fenton

INTRODUCTION

This chapter reviews the neuropsychiatry of personality change and personality disorder, discussing the difference between the two and reviewing *The International Classification of Mental and Behavioural Disorders* (ICD-10; World Health Organization, 1992) definitions. It presents the clinical features of the common causes of organic personality change, which include the frontal lobe syndrome, the limbic personality syndromes, postencephalitic personality changes, organic personality syndromes due to vascular pathology, and personality alterations associated with degenerative brain diseases.

The traditional view is that the classical personality disorders are the final outcome of an interplay between genetic factors and psychosocial phenomena of developmental origin. With the advent of modern brain imaging, neuropharmacological, neurophysiological and neuropsychological investigation techniques, there is a growing area of research suggesting that dysfunction of certain brain systems contributes to behavioural dyscontrol in personality disorders in the absence of coarse brain disease. The neurochemical basis of aggression and impulsivity is discussed in Chapter 8.

CLINICAL DEFINITIONS

Brain disease, damage or dysfunction can lead to alteration of personality and behaviour. Such changes can follow either diffuse or local brain pathology. On occasion, the pattern of personality and behavioural change can have some localizing significance, but it should be noted this is not always the same; for example, the classical features of frontal lobe syndrome occur not only with frontal lobe lesions, but sometimes also with cerebral damage elsewhere. The ICD-10 distinguishes between personality disorder and personality change. Both types of condition manifest deeply ingrained and enduring behaviour patterns presenting as inflexible responses to a broad range of personal and social situations. They represent either extreme or significant deviations from the way the average individual in a given culture perceives, thinks, feels and particularly relates to others, and tend to be stable and often cause subjective distress.

Personality disorders differ from personality change in their timing and mode of presentation: they are developmental conditions with a genesis and early signs in childhood or adolescence and continue into adulthood. They are not secondary to another mental disorder or brain disease, although they may precede and co-exist with other disorders. In contrast, personality change is acquired, usually during adult life following severe or prolonged stress, extreme environmental deprivation, serious psychiatric disorder, brain disease or injury. This chapter deals exclusively with personality change due to brain disease or injury categorized as follows (fully described in ICD-10).

ORGANIC PERSONALITY DISORDER (F07.0)

This is characterized by a significant alteration of the habitual patterns of pre-morbid behaviour. The expression of emotions, needs and impulses is particularly affected. Cognitive functions may be defective, mainly or even exclusively in the areas of planning and anticipating likely personal and social consequences. There needs to be an established history or other evidence of brain disease, damage or dysfunction. Organic personality disorder includes frontal lobe syndrome (see below) and lobotomy or post-leucotomy syndrome.

POSTENCEPHALITIC SYNDROME (F07.1)

This includes residual behaviour change following recovery from encephalitis. Symptoms that are non-specific and vary include general malaise, apathy or irritability, learning difficulties, altered sleep and eating patterns, and changes in sexuality and social judgement. There may also be a variety of residual neurological dysfunctions (e.g. paralyses, deafness, aphasia etc.).

POSTCONCUSSIONAL SYNDROME (F07.2)

This occurs following head injury (usually mild, but sufficiently severe to result in transient loss of consciousness) and can include symptoms such as headache, dizziness, fatiguability, irritability, difficulty in concentration, impairment of memory, insomnia, reduced tolerance to stress, depression and anxiety.

OTHERS (F07.8, F07.9)

This category includes patients whose clinical picture does not fit well into the above categories. It includes mild degrees of cognitive impairment not yet amounting to dementia as in progressive disorders such as Alzheimer's disease.

THE FRONTAL LOBE SYNDROME

The prefrontal areas are concerned with the control of adaptive behaviour, abstract conceptual ability, set-shifting/mental flexibility, planning and problem solving, initiation and sequencing of behaviour, temporal order judgements, important aspects of personality including affect, drive, motivation and inhibition of behaviour, and social behaviour. To be effective, behaviour must be appropriate, modifiable, motivated and free from interference and disruptive impulsive responses. This requires monitoring and, if necessary, anticipating changes in the environment so that the subject's responses to the situation can be adjusted appropriately.

Frontal lobe patients fail to anticipate changes, show poor planning activity and do not learn from their errors. They are particularly poor at self-guided learning and goal setting. They perform normally on externally driven tasks but are poor at self-motivated learning, with a striking vulnerability to being distracted by irrelevant stimuli and the intrusion of unwanted responses. They tend to perseverate and have severe deficits in solving problems, deducing concepts and making analogies. The ability to initiate cognitive strategies and to generate words, and verbal fluency are impaired with frontal lobe damage.

Although not involved in the laying down and storage of long-term memory traces, the frontal lobes are important for memory retrieval related to temporal order judgements and are critical for the central executive component of working memory (the central executor). The central executor is a limited capacity, modality-free, attentional system that is of use in the act of processing of information and in its transient storage. It is involved in all attentionally demanding tasks, including problem solving, reasoning and learning.

Another characteristic of frontal lobe dysfunction is loss of inhibitory control, with a tendency to react immediately and usually inappropriately to external stimuli. Irascibility and verbal aggression are common. The capacity to cope with personal relationships is frequently affected and deterioration in social habits and hygiene may occur. A dulling of curiosity and vitality and a loss of capacity for empathy are common. Some patients may become inappropriately jocular and puerile. Many develop anergia or passivity.

Studies of personality changes observed in the very large number of patients treated by standard prefrontal leucotomy and soldiers who sustained major frontal lobe damage from penetrating gunshot injuries during the two world wars have provided a rich source of information about how frontal lobe damage relates to emotional disturbance. The major behavioural changes after prefrontal leucotomy consist of decreased drive, shallowness of affect, social unconcern with indifference for the opinions of others, inability to plan ahead and lack of self-criticism (Greenblatt and Solomon, 1966).

Differing patterns of cognitive and behaviour disturbance have been related to the site of the damage within the frontal lobes. The orbital frontal cortex, connected with the amygdala and hippocampus and, via the frontal dorsolateral convexity, with the rest of the brain, exerts higher control over the amygdala. Orbital frontal damage renders an individual overly responsive to environmental changes. Trivial stimuli elicit aggression normally kept in control by long distance judgement. The time, place and strategy of the aggressive response are inappropriate to the social context. Such individuals are impulsive, socially disinhibited and lack the capacity for self-criticism. They may be unable to anticipate the negative consequences of their behaviour and can be silly, hyperactive and excitable. Such individuals have been described as 'pseudopsychopathic' (Blumer and Benson, 1975). However, they are not 'classical psychopaths', because they are not vicious and predatory and lack the capacity to plan.

In contrast, damage to the dorsolateral complexity of the frontal lobe typically leads to apathy, with slowed psychomotor activity, lack of motivation and occasional brief aggressive outbursts. Such patients have been described as 'pseudodepressed' (Blumer and Benson, 1975). However, they do not show the depressive mood change and negative thinking characteristic of people with major depressive illness. They may also be helped by dopamine agonists such as bromocriptine or psychostimulants rather than conventional antidepressant medication.

Medial frontal damage involving the cingulate areas leads to apathy, decreased initiation and motor behaviour, decreased verbal output, decreased spontaneity, urinary incontinence and gait disturbance.

However, the division of the frontal syndromes into these three subtypes is of limited value, since frontal lobe damage in most cases does not respect such divisions. Most patients display features of all three syndromes. Bilateral damage is usually necessary, although milder forms of frontal lobe syndrome may be seen with unilateral dysfunction. In recent years, the localization perspective has been overtaken by the concept of a distributed frontal network involving frontal lobes, cordate nuclei and the dorsal medial nuclei of the thalamus (Mesulam, 1990). Aspects of the frontal lobe syndrome may develop from damage to any of the sites in this network.

Head injury is the most common contemporary cause of the frontal lobe syndrome. The damage is due to severe focal contusions and lacerations, usually associated with small haemorrhages from the blood vessels torn at the time of the injury. Sometimes the contusions are large, with large haemorrhagic contusion and/or intracerebral haemorrhage with haemotoma formation. Irrespective of the site of the blow, the commonest sites for contusion are the regions on either side of the sharp edge of the sphenoidal wing, so that the undersurfaces of the frontal lobes and the tips of the temporal lobes are damaged, often bilaterally (Adams et al., 1981). The frontal lobe damage is often part of generalized brain damage with diffuse axonal injury, especially when the head injury is a closed one. The duration of post-traumatic amnesia (PTA) correlates with outcome. For example, 97 per cent of patients with severe disability have PTAs of 28 days or more (Lishman, 1968).

Although post-traumatic personality change is usually easy to diagnose as it follows a severe head injury with a significant duration of PTA, it is important to be aware that the social and emotional consequences of frontal lobe injury sustained in early life may only become apparent in adolescence. Eslinger et al. (1992) reported the case of a 33-year-old woman who sustained a frontal lobe haemorrhage at the age of 7 years. Although she exhibited cognitive slowing after the injury, social disinhibition, interpersonal conflicts and affective instability did not appear until she was confronted with the problems of adolescence.

Frontal lobe tumours are associated with affective and personality disturbances in as many as one-third of cases. Personality change may be one of the earliest manifestations in about one-quarter. This presentation is especially characteristic of slow-growing meningiomas (Direkze et al., 1971). Irresponsibility, childishness and lack of reserve are the most frequent features, often with a tendency towards facetiousness and indifference. Disinhibition can lead to social lapses and out-of-character misdemeanours, e.g. the occurrence of sexual offences in a middle-aged man of previously exemplary character (Lishman, 1987). Lack of insight, with indifference to the impact the illness is having on the individual's life, even in the presence of an intact cognition, is a common feature. Tumours arising from the sphenoidal ridge (the borderline between the frontal and temporal lobes) show a high frequency of mental changes. Similar personality changes are sometimes seen with temporal lobe tumours.

LIMBIC SYSTEM AND PERSONALITY DISORDER

The limbic system, with functions subserving emotions, exerts control over the hypothalamus. The amygdala (located in the anteromedial temporal lobe) is an important link between sensory and sensory association signals and outflow to the hypothalamus, a sort of bridge between the externally perceived reality and basic drives. It may help define emotional valence to perceived objects (Bear, 1979). The amygdala also modulates hypothalamic-mediated aggressive behaviour. Stimulation of the dorsomedial amygdala of a cat undergoing lateral hypothalamic stimulation results in increased firing of the ventromedial hypothalamus, inhibiting cat attack behaviour towards rats. In contrast, stimulation of the ventrolateral amygdala decreases firing of the ventromedial hypothalmus and facilitates the cat's attack behaviour.

The Kluver–Bucy syndrome develops in monkeys following bilateral anterior temporal lobectomy, with hypermetamorphosis (a tendency towards increased exploration behaviour), increased orality or a tendency to use their mouths to examine objects, alteration of appetite and sexuality, and tameness and reduction in fear towards normally fear-inducing objects. The reduced fear is thought to be a form of psychic blindness or loss of emotional valence associated with perceived objects. A Kluver–Bucy-like syndrome occurs in humans following bilateral destruction of the amygdalae resulting from herpes encephalitis, Pick's disease, head trauma or advanced Alzheimer's disease. Affected individuals typically become apathetic and docile, tend to explore their environments with their hands, putting objects they encounter into their mouths, become bulimic and sexually preoccupied. Many develop agnosias and most show signs of aphasia and amnesia (Lilly et al., 1983).

In temporolimbic epilepsy, there is increased firing of the amygdala of one or both hemispheres. Over recent years, the concept of a specific temporal lobe neurobehavioural syndrome has been formulated (Bear, 1979; Geschwind, 1979; Blumer, 1995). The syndrome consists of three sets of neurobehavioural change: hyperemotionality, viscosity and hyposexuality. The heightened emotionality involves periods of irritability, dysphoria (irritable and distressed at the same time) and lability of affect in a setting of humourlessness, religiosity, an interest in spirituality and hypermoralism. Although highly emotional, the patients tend to be voluble in their speech, and a number, particularly those with right-sided temporal lobe lesions, tend to write excessively (hypergraphia). As a contrast to the intensity and lability of their emotionality, patients display viscosity, a lack of fluidity and slowing of psychomotor functioning. The patients tend to be meticulous about all details and, if allowed, they will persist on minor points in a circumstantial fashion, giving the impression of being perseverative. They often give the impression of being tangential, but in fact they pursue their lines of thought stubbornly if allowed to do so. Everything has to be very orderly, and the conversation flows in a circumstantial manner towards an ultimate conclusion. Overt viscosity, especially if combined with the verbosity, represents a substantial social handicap. Global hyposexuality occurs in many such patients.

It has been proposed that this constellation of behavioural traits results from a change in functioning of the nervous connections between the primary receiving areas of the cortex and the mesial temporal lobe limbic system structures. The function of these neural connections is to give emotional significance to stimuli that have been processed by the primary receiving areas of the cortex. Experimental work has demonstrated that structural lesions in the temporal lobe of primates may act to disconnect the emotion-mediating limbic structures, such as the amygdaloid complex and hippocampus, from the sensory association areas of the visual and auditory cortex. An extreme example of this destructive process is the Kluver–Bucy syndrome caused by bilateral temporal lobe excision. It has been suggested that abnormal electrical activity due to the epileptogenic process in the temporal lobes has a kindling effect on the medial limbic structures. The epileptic focus, as well as causing fits, acts as an electrode, discharging from time to time into the limbic structures, increasing their reactivity. This leads to the growth of new synaptic connections between the limbic system and the association cortices. Hence previously neutral stimuli, events or concepts are given an emotional labelling. According to this view, such a process leads to the development of many of the features of the temporal lobe behavioural syndrome. For example, continuously experiencing the environment with an unduly affective colouring will tend to lead to more intense emotionality and engender a mystically religious view of the world. If the person's immediate actions and thoughts are so coloured, the outcome may be an augmented sense of personal destiny and importance. Sensing emotional importance in even the most trivial events or acts will lead to these being performed ritualistically and repetitively, with lengthy circumstantial speech or writing (Bear, 1979). This syndrome is regarded as a sensory-limbic hyperconnection syndrome and a partial, inverse Kluver–Bucy syndrome. The frequency with which this syndrome occurs and its specificity to temporal limbic epilepsy are the subject of continuing debate.

OTHER CAUSES OF ORGANIC PERSONALITY CHANGE

Postencephalitic personality change was a common sequela of the encephalitis lethargica epidemics that occurred between 1917 and 1926, being observed mainly in children and young adolescents. It was frequently accompanied by other complications such as Parkinsonism, sleep disturbance, obesity or other evidence of hypothalamic dysfunction. Over-activity, impulsive antisocial behaviour through loss of impulse control and emotional lability were characteristic features. About one-third of cases improved by puberty and 50 per cent developed later Parkinsonism. Over the years since then, isolated cases have been reported, although the evidence of a link to encephalitis lethargica remains equivocal. However, other types of encephalitis, especially that due to herpes simplex infection, which causes damage to the mesial temporal and orbital frontal brain areas, can result in organic personality change.

Organic personality change may be a troublesome consequence of a stroke, usually a reflection of diffuse vascular ischaemia, which will progress to dementia even though the focal signs improve. After subarachnoid haemorrhage, Storey (1970) reported a moderate to severe degree of personality change in 19 per cent and mild changes in a further 22 per cent of patients, being most common after the rupture of middle cerebral aneurysms and usually occurring in parallel with the degree of intellectual and neurological disability. In contrast, people with anterior communicating aneurysm haemorrhage tended to show less intellectual impairment and more prominent personality change of the frontal lobe type, with disinhibited behaviour, more outspokenness but less anxiety and sometimes an increase in subjective well-being, with improvement in mood (Logue et al., 1968). Such changes are clearly a result of frontal lobe damage due to the bleeding or subsequent ischaemia. Paradoxically, in people with high levels of anxiety, tension or irritability, there may be 'improvement' in personality function following anterior communicating artery aneurysm rupture.

Features of the organic personality syndrome commonly occur in patients with degenerative brain diseases (reviewed in detail by Kauper and Cummings, 1995). Apathy and indifference occur in Alzheimer's disease, Parkinson's disease, progressive supranuclear palsy, olivopontocerebellar degeneration, Huntington's disease and diffuse Lewy body disease. Disinhibited behaviour can be a prominent feature of dementia of frontal lobe type, Huntington's disease, Wilson's disease and Fahr's disease. Agitation can be marked in Huntington's disease, in dementia of frontal lobe type and in the late stages of Alzheimer's disease.

PSYCHOPHYSIOLOGY OF PERSONALITY DISORDER

Psychophysiology is the study of the relationships between physiological measures and psychological states. The most commonly used psychophysiological measures recorded from antisocial populations have been skin conductance, heart rate, electroencephalography (EEG) and cognitive event-related potentials (ERPs) or evoked potentials.

SKIN CONDUCTANCE ACTIVITY FINDINGS IN RELATION TO ANTISOCIAL BEHAVIOUR

An increase in sweating of the skin reduces its electrical conductivity and is a measure of autonomic nervous system activity. Despite being so far from the brain, the skin conductance changes are a simple but powerful measure of central nervous system processing. Skin conductance responses (SCRs) tend to appear from 1 to 3 seconds from the onset of a stimulus (typically a tone) and provide a sensitive index of what is known as the orienting reflex or 'what is it?' response. The consensus of experimental research has shown that SCRs measure the allocation of attentional resources to the processing of a stimulus (Dawson et al.,

1990). The level of central nervous system arousal is measured by the resting skin conductance level (SCL) and the number of spontaneous SCRs recorded in a resting state when no external stimuli are presented. These are known as non-specific fluctuations (NSFs). Because skin conductance is a direct measure of sympathetic autonomic activity and since the sympathetic nervous system is sensitive to stress and emotional arousal, skin conductance activity can be used to index stress activity to aversive or arousing events.

In an early review of skin conductance activity in psychopathic individuals, Hare (1978) reported reduced tonic arousal as measured by the SCL (though not NSFs), reduced SCRs to aversive but not neutral tones, reduced SCRs in conditioning and quasi-conditioning paradigms, and longer SCR recovery times to aversive stimuli. Raine (1993) reviewed ten subsequent studies, four of which found significant reductions in either SCL or spontaneous NSFs in antisocial individuals collected from a variety of offending populations.

Four of the eight studies that have examined the skin conductance orienting reflex in psychopaths have found an orienting deficit: a reduced frequency of SCRs to neutral tone stimuli, especially in those with schizoid or schizotypal features. This may reflect frontal lobe dysfunction, since a significant relationship between reduced prefrontal cortex volume on magnetic resonance imaging (MRI) and fewer orienting responses have been reported (Scarpa and Raine, 1997). Eight studies have assessed SCRs to aversive stimuli, using auditory stimuli. Only two of these eight studies showed evidence of lower responsivity to aversive stimuli in antisocial individuals.

It may be more productive to use more socially relevant or meaningful aversive stimuli rather than tones, which are relatively neutral events. This has certainly been demonstrated in frontal lobe lesion patients with psychopathic behaviour (Dalasio et al., 1990). Dalasio et al. measured skin conductance responsivity to

pictures depicting mutilation, social disasters or nudity, which they regarded as socially significant stimuli, in five patients who had bilateral lesions of the orbital frontal and lower mesial frontal cortex and who showed psychopathic behaviour defined as severe deficits in social conduct, judgement and planning following brain damage. The latter showed reduced SCR amplitudes to social stimuli compared with six control patients with non-frontal lesions. In contrast, the frontal lobe lesion patients showed normal responses to neutral tone stimuli. The subsequent work of Blair et al. (1997; and see Chapter 7) emphasized the importance of investigating meaningful stimuli. Blair et al. selected 18 psychopathic individuals, identified using the revised Psychopathy Checklist, and compared their electrodermal responses to those of 18 incarcerated control subjects, who showed no evidence of psychopathy on the checklist. Subjects were shown slides containing material considered to be neutral, distressing or threatening. Relative to the controls, the psychopathic individuals showed reduced electrodermal responses to the distress cues. The two groups did not differ in their electrodermal responses to the threatening stimuli and to the neutral stimuli.

Classical conditioning has been assessed using a skin conductance paradigm: a neutral tone (conditioned stimulus or CS) is presented to the subject, followed a few seconds later by an unconditioned stimulus (UCS), either a loud tone or an electric shock. The key measure is the size of the SCR elicited by the CS after a number of CS/UCS pairings. Reviews by Hare (1978) and Raine (1993) found that 19 out of 20 studies reported significantly poor skin conductance conditioning in antisocial individuals. These findings are consistent with Eysenck's theory that antisocial individuals are characterized by poor classical conditioning, the socialization process and conscience development being facilitated by a set of classically conditioned negative emotional responses to situations that had previously led to punishment.

The skin conductance half recovery time is another measure used by psychophysiologists and refers to the time it takes for a SCR to reduce to half its peak value. The majority of studies of the skin conductance half recovery time have found significantly slower recovery rates in antisocial individuals, leading to the hypothesis that skin conductance half recovery time reflects the rate at which an emotional response particularly fear or anxiety dissipates. Antisocial individuals, because of their slower fear dissipation, experience less reinforcement for avoiding punishable acts (Mednick, 1977). However, the latter's interpretation of the half recovery time is not universally accepted. Others have suggested that recovery time reflects an openness or closedness to the environment, with longer recovery reflecting a shutting out of the environment stimuli (Venables, 1974; Siddle and Trasler, 1981). Regardless of interpretation, slower recovery rates relate to slower dissipation of autonomic activation.

To summarize the many skin conductance studies, there is evidence of reduced resting SCLs in some, but not all, populations of antisocial individuals. Reduced frequency of SCRs to neutral stimuli in orienting reflex paradigms does occur and seems to be relatively specific to those antisocial individuals with schizoid or schizotypal features. This may reflect frontal lobe dysfunction. The earlier studies reporting reduced skin conductance responsiveness to aversive tone stimuli have not been replicated. The use of socially meaningful stimuli to evoke SCRs indicates reduced responsiveness in psychopathic individuals. This may be specific for stimuli that have a distressing content. There is a little evidence to suggest that bilateral lesions of the orbital frontal and lower mesial frontal cortex are associated with lack of SCR to meaningful stimuli. Reduced skin conductance classical conditioning and longer skin conductance half recovery times are consistent features of the psychophysiology of antisocial personality.

HEART RATE AND ANTISOCIAL BEHAVIOUR

Heart rate reflects both sympathetic and parasympathetic nervous system activity, unlike skin conductance activity, which reflects sympathetic processes only. Resting heart rate and phasic changes in heart rate response to stimuli have been used to assess the degree of autonomic arousal and reactivity to both neutral and aversive events. A consistent finding has been significantly lower resting heart rate levels in children and adolescents displaying antisocial behaviour. This finding seems to be age specific, as it is not reported in adults with psychopathic personality or displaying antisocial behaviour. However, it does seem to have predictive value, as lower resting heart rates were one of a number of psychophysiological variables found to predict adult criminality in a prospective study of 15-year-old male schoolchildren (Raine et al., 1990).

There are two basic measures of phasic heart rate activity. In response to the onset of a neutral tone stimulus, the heart rate briefly decelerates and then accelerates. Aversive stimuli evoke prominent acceleration responses, which are thought to reflect sensory rejection or switching off from painful environmental events. In contrast, deceleration responses are considered part of the orienting response, reflecting increased attentional processing of the environment. Early studies suggested that psychopathic individuals displayed larger acceleration responses in anticipation of an aversive event, such as an electric shock or a loud (120 dB) tone. The paradigm used in these studies was the presentation of a neutral tone as a warning that an aversive event such as an electric shock or a loud tone was about to occur, and the magnitude of the heart rate acceleration after the warning tone was measured. Hare (1978) considered these findings to indicate that psychopathic individuals had the capacity to switch off from aversive events and were therefore less influenced by the experience of such events. However, it has not been possible to replicate these findings.

ELECTROENCEPHALOGRAPHY

A generalized excess of slower (theta/delta) background activity frequencies, most marked over the posterior quadrants of both hemispheres, especially in the posterior temporal regions, is found in some people in the absence of overt organic pathology. Such anomalous EEG changes are often known as non-specific abnormalities. They are common in populations of people manifesting antisocial behaviour. Indeed, their prevalence increases with the degree of maladjustment of the population studied: highest in aggressive psychopaths (50 per cent), and lowest in people selected for stability of personality, for example service personnel selected for air crew duties in the Second World War (5 per cent), as demonstrated by Williams (1941) and Hill (1951). They do occur in a minority (about 10 per cent) of quite healthy people.

Their significance remains unknown. The prevalence is at its peak in adolescence and early adult life, and declines dramatically in the thirties (Hill, 1951). The close relationship to age and the fact that such changes, anomalous in the adult EEG, are part of the normal developmental pattern in children have led to the hypothesis that their persistence into adult life is a reflection of failure of maturation of the brain. Such a view is attractive, as much of the behaviour of such individuals is 'immature'.

However, the relationship between the EEG and behavioural 'immaturity' is by no means a parallel one in any individual. Further, genetic factors have been shown to be important in their genesis (Knott et al., 1953). There is also some evidence linking their occurrence to perinatal brain damage (Volavka and Matousek, 1969). It may be that their occurrence in psychopaths is the outcome of an interaction between genetic predisposition and the presence of mild early brain damage that inter-act to retard the normal processes of brain maturation.

The early environment that breeds delinquency and psychopathic behaviour is often a socially disadvantaged one, in which poor socio-economic conditions prevail, with disrupted family life and poor standards of health care. Such poor social circumstances and inadequate parental supervision may also increase the risk of early brain damage due to the complications of pregnancy and childbirth, trauma or infection acquired in early childhood as a result of parental neglect or abuse. If only mild, this process may delay the maturation of brain activity and lead to immature EEG patterns. More severe early brain damage, on the other hand, will result in 'organic' EEG changes and/or epilepsy. This hypothesis remains to be tested.

In clinical practice, these EEG maturation phenomena can be ignored. However, they are often prominent in the posterior temporal regions and frequently have a sharpened waveform. Such sharply formed posterior slow waves can be mistaken for EEG sharp waves or the EEG sharp waves of temporal lobe epilepsy (TLE), which can lead to an erroneous clinical diagnosis of TLE. Fortunately, there are important differences in the location and physiological behaviour of the two waveforms. The posterior temporal slow waves are posterior in distribution, best seen in relaxed wakefulness with the eyes closed, are markedly attenuated by eye opening, and disappear during sleep. Hyperventilation significantly augments them. In contrast, TLE sharp waves are located over the anterior part of the temporal lobe.

Other studies have linked these types of EEG anomalies specifically to violent behaviour. In a series of EEG studies of prisoners charged with murder, Hill and Pond (1952) reported that abnormal EEGs predominated in those who had committed apparently motiveless crimes. In those offenders whose murders arose understandably, the EEGs were predominantly normal.

In a later study at the same hospital, Driver et al. (1974) was not able to confirm this finding using similar methods. It may be, of course, that in the intervening years between the work of Hill and Pond in the late 1940s and early 1950s and that of Driver and colleagues in the late 1960s and early 1970s, better forensic psychiatric assessments of homicide offenders led to early identification of mental disorder and admission to a high-security hospital rather than a prison.

A more recent high-security hospital study of 372 male patients indicates an association between temporal lobe dysfunction and the degree of violence manifest in their pre-admission offending behaviour (Wong et al., 1994). In the most violent group, 20 per cent had focal temporal electrical abnormalities on EEG (frequency slowing and/or sharp waves) and 41 per cent had structural abnormalities localized to the temporal lobe on computerized tomography (CT) scanning (dilated temporal horn and/or reduced size of the temporal lobe). The corresponding figures for the least violent group were 2.4 per cent and 6.7 per cent, respectively.

A different approach was used by Williams (1969), who studied the EEGs of 333 prisoners accused of violent crimes. He divided the subjects into 'habitual aggressiveness' ($n = 206$) and 'others' ($n = 127$), who were more likely to have committed a solitary act of violence. When subjects with histories of epilepsy, mental retardation or major head injury were excluded, 57 per cent of the habitually aggressive group compared to 12 per cent of the others ($\chi^2 = 37.5$, df[1], $p < 0.001$). Most of the abnormalities were localized over the frontotemporal areas.

Quantitative assessments of the EEG using frequency analysis techniques have consistently found an association between EEG frequency slowing and violence. In children and adolescents, a relative predominance of slow alpha activity (that is, slowing of the average frequency within the alpha range) with excessive amounts of theta activity in violent teenagers have also been reported. Similar phenomena (alpha frequency slowing and excess theta activity) have been reported in aggressive adults (Forssman and Frey, 1951; Kennard et al., 1956; Fishbein et al., 1989; Convit et al., 1991). In several studies, ratings of the level of violence have been positively related to the relative amount of delta activity present and negatively related to the amount of alpha activity, a relationship that is significantly stronger for the left hemisphere, particularly in the frontal regions. These results were independent of concurrent medication (Volavka, 1995).

The apparent link between violent behaviour and non-specific EEG abnormality requires explanation. The association is unlikely to be a direct one. The probability is that it reflects an interaction between a whole series of biological and social factors. For example, genetic factors may influence the EEG and the subject's behaviour in parallel. Being brought up in a socially disadvantaged family environment is likely to increase the risk of early brain damage due to adverse maternal or perinatal circumstances or trauma acquired as the result of parental neglect or abuse. Such brain damage, though often not severe enough to be clinically noticeable, may retard brain development or damage the neurosystems underlying impulse control. In parallel to the organic brain changes, environmental influences have a powerful effect on the person's future behaviour due to poor role modelling, abusive or inadequate parental supervision and negative school experiences with limited opportunities to learn socially appropriate ways of handling aggression. Volavka (1995) presents such a multidimensional model in detail.

An alternative hypothesis is that the EEG frequency slowing reflects reduced levels of resting arousal, an observation that is compatible with the skin conductance work. Avoidance of aggressive behaviour must be learned, but low arousal levels inhibit the learning process. The prospective study of 15-year-old schoolboys followed up to the age of 24 years, reported by Raine et al. (1990), is consistent with this hypothesis. Low SCLs and EEG frequency slowing at 15 years predicted criminality of a non-violent nature, mostly burglary and theft. However, the evidence that the low arousal hypothesis applies to severe or persistently aggressive behaviour is less convincing. The type of pattern of EEG slowing recorded from the latter subjects is not that usually associated with drowsiness or hypo-arousal, and fits better with the organic brain damage/disinhibition model.

EVENT-RELATED POTENTIALS

The electrical response of the cerebral cortex evoked by a sensory stimulus measures only a few microvolts in amplitude and is therefore buried in the background of the ongoing EEG. To extract the response (or signal) from the noise of the ongoing EEG, the constantly changing EEG activity is sampled and the voltage values stored at discrete intervals just before and after the stimulus onset. This procedure is repeated a fixed number of times, identical sensory stimuli being used on each occasion. The transient changes in voltage elicited by each of the repeated stimuli are summated or averaged. The positive and negative voltage samples of the background EEG tend to cancel each other out, while a response to the series of stimuli evokes a consistent pattern of potential change that can be displayed as a series of positive and negative waves following the stimulus. The latency from stimulus onset of each of these waves and their amplitude above the pre-stimulus baseline can be measured.

Certain components of the ERP vary systematically with the physical parameters of the stimulus and depend on the structural integrity of the sensory receptors and pathways, but are relatively impervious to transient changes and psychophysiological state. Such responses have been termed exogenous and consist of the early ERP component occurring within 50–100 ms of the stimulus regardless of stimulus modality. Brainstem responses occur even earlier – within 10 ms of stimulus onset. These are a result of the electrical changes created by the signal as it passes through the brainstem tracts and nuclei. Such responses are especially stable and stimulus bound. In contrast, the ERPs associated with perceptual phenomena are far more sensitive to subjective state. The perceptual experience of a stimulus depends not only on its physical characteristics, but also on the state of the observer – his or her level of alertness, direction of attention, memories of past experience, expectation and motivation. The late ERP components, i.e. after 200 ms, are those most susceptible to psychological influence. They are known as endogenous or cognitive evoked potentials. They are influenced much more by the subject's psychological or cognitive state than by the physical characteristics of the external stimuli used to evoke them.

One study has reported an association between aggressiveness and longer latencies of waves 1, 2 and 3 of the brainstem auditory evoked potential, which are a consequence of the transient electrical changes in the auditory pathways from the proximal end of the acoustic nerve (wave 1) to the higher brainstem structures (waves 6 and 7), following a tone stimulus. This has been interpreted as evidence of reduced arousal and excessively high filtering of environmental stimuli. A behavioural consequence of such under-arousal and filtering would be stimulus deprivation and chronically low levels of arousal (Fischbein et al., 1989; Raine, 1989).

In contrast, there has been a whole series of studies examining how subjects process sensory input based on the observation that, in general, more intense sensory stimuli evoke larger ERP amplitudes. It is possible to plot an amplitude/intensity graph to demonstrate how ERP amplitude measures vary with increasing stimulus intensity. Subjects showing a steep rise in amplitude of the response to increasing stimulus intensity are known as augmentors; those who show a drop in amplitude of response at high levels of stimulation are called reducers. The augmenting/reducing phenomenon is influenced by genetic factors. Augmenting has been consistently linked with measures of sensation seeking. Middle-latency ERP waveforms are used as amplitude measures of the augmenting/reducing process. psychopaths have been shown to be augmentors, presumably because of their propensity for sensation seeking (Raine, 1989; Raine et al., 1995).

The two types of cognitive evoked response that have been extensively studied in relation to personality disorder are the P_{300} wave and the contingent negative variation (CNV). The P_{300} is a positive wave occurring at a latency of around 300 ms, which is emitted when a subject recognizes an unexpected but important stimulus. The classical P_{300} paradigm involves the subject being presented with a series of tones of a certain frequency (e.g. 1000 Hz). This sequence of frequent tones is interrupted at random intervals by target tones at another frequency (e.g. 1000 KHz). The rare tones are interspersed into the sequence of frequent tones about 20 per cent of the time. The subject is instructed to listen carefully to the tones and carry out a response to the rare tones such as counting them or pressing a button to measure reaction time. The normal auditory evoked potential waveform develops in response to the frequent tones, while a positive wave developing 300 ms after the stimulus is recorded in response to the rare tone occurrence. The latency of the P_{300} is generally agreed to be a measure of stimulus evaluation time. A number of cognitive processes, including attention, stimulus probability, arousal, reducing uncertainty and memory context upgrading, have been associated with the P_{300} amplitude. It is probably a measure of the extent of cerebral resources used in processing the signal. Thus a reduced amplitude reflects less efficient cognitive functioning.

Reduced P_{300} amplitudes have been found in both schizotypal and borderline personality disorder patients (Kutcher et al., 1989). The former have P_{300} amplitudes that are intermediate between those of normal controls and schizophrenic patients (Trestman et al., 1996). In contrast, one of the few P_{300} studies of psychopaths reports higher P_{300} amplitudes, indicating enhanced attention to the stimuli of interest (Raine, 1989). This increased attention may well be a consequence of higher levels of stimulus or sensation seeking in these individuals. In a more complex recording paradigm, Barratt et al. (1997) examined two groups of prison inmates and matched non-inmate controls. All the inmates met *Diagnostic and Statistical Manual of Mental Disorders*, third edition, revised (DSM-III-R; American Psychiatric Association, 1987) criteria for antisocial personality disorder, but otherwise were free from mental disorder. The behaviour of both inmate groups was characterized by recurrent, overt aggressive behaviour. In one group, the aggression was rated as predominantly impulsive in nature, and in the other group the aggression was largely non-impulsive and premeditated. All subjects were tested for levels of impulsivity, verbal and performance intelligence quotient (IQ), verbal and visual memory, and reading ability. The two inmate groups did not differ in terms of ratings of impulsivity, but the impulsive aggressive group had significantly lower verbal skills. They showed a particular type of verbal information-processing difficulty, namely a developmental dyslexia. Though their reading comprehension did not differ from that of the non-impulsive aggressive group, they had problems in the decoding of reading symbols. This verbal symbol-decoding deficit correlated positively with the impulsivity ratings. The latter were inversely related to the P_{300} amplitudes. In contrast, verbal skills, in particular verbal symbol-decoding ability, were positively correlated with the amplitudes. These findings indicate complex relationships between impulsive behaviour, personality disorder, verbal skills and information processing at cortical level, which require further careful study.

The CNV is a slow negative potential developing in the cerebral cortex during an experimental situation that requires a person to process a pair of time-related signals. The first (S_1) is a warning that the subject should perform a certain course of action in response to the second signal (S_2/imperative stimulus). The CNV develops in the interval between the two signals as the subject prepares to respond to the second one. After completion of the response, it rapidly resolves. Early attempts to identify a specific psychological process such as arousal, attention, motivation, mental state, expectancy and conation as the generator of the CNV have proved unsuccessful. The CNV appears to develop in a variety of experimental situations. These include the following: holding a motor response in readiness; preparing for a perceptual judgement; anticipation of a reinforcer positive or negative; and preparing for a cognitive decision.

Gray-Walter, who first described the CNV phenomenon in 1964, initially considered it to reflect an underlying conditioning process, during which an association between the warning and the second stimulus requiring a response was established. This led to the first work carried out in his laboratory by McCallum (1973), reporting that psychopaths had unduly low-amplitude CNV responses – regarded as evidence of impaired learning ability in psychopaths. Two studies carried out at Broadmoor Hospital failed to replicate this finding (Fenton et al., 1978, 1984). However, both demonstrated significant differences between mentally disturbed offenders in the mental illness category and those legally labelled psychopathic disorder; the mental illness patients had consistently smaller CNV amplitudes. The Broadmoor studies showed that extraversion is an important factor in determining CNV amplitude. This may have accounted for the differences between the psychopathic disorder group and those with mental illness.

Later, a Go–NoGo CNV paradigm was developed at Broadmoor Hospital (Howard et al., 1982). In the Go condition, the warning stimulus (S_1) instructs the subject to prepare to

respond to the presentation of the second stimulus (S_2) 3.5 s later by pressing a button within a certain time window in order to avoid 'punishment' by a burst of aversive white noise. The NoGo condition also involves two paired (S_1/S_2) stimuli: S_1 tells the subject to expect S_2 3.5 s later and that no response to S_2 is required. An inappropriate button-press response to S_2 leads to the same white noise 'punishment' as used in the Go condition. The Go CNV is invariably of higher amplitude than the NoGo CNV. The difference between the Go and NoGo amplitudes (the Go–NoGo differentiation) is considered to be a reflection of the balance between excitatory and inhibitory neural processes within the underlying cerebral cortex. The degree of Go–NoGo differentiation correlated with impulsivity in Broadmoor patients, regardless of diagnosis, low levels of Go–NoGo differentiation being associated with high impul-sivity. These findings suggest a possible neural correlate of impulsivity (Howard et al., 1982). Long-term follow-up showed that those patients with poor Go–NoGo differentiation had significantly higher reconviction rates and more violent offences (Howard and Lumsden, 1996, 1997).

NEUROIMAGING

As might be expected, there are relatively few neuroimaging studies that focus on personality disorder. Most investigate the possible associations between brain dysfunction and violence. Because of the hypothesized relationship between schizotypal personality disorder and schizophrenia, some of the first neuroimaging studies of personality disorders have looked for the structural brain changes of schizophrenia in schizotypal personality disorder. Siever (1991) reported enlarged ventricles in patients with schizotypal personality disorder. Raine et al. (1992) found that a group of non-patients with high scores on a schizotypal scale had decreased prefrontal volume measurements on MRI. In contrast, structural imaging studies of borderline personality disordered patients have failed to find ventricular enlargement. In a single photon emission computerized tomography (SPECT) study of 40 chronic alcoholics, Kuruoglu et al. (1996) found that two-thirds showed reduced blood flow in both frontal lobes, which correlated with the rate of alcohol consumption but not with the amount of daily intake. In the sample of 40 were 15 patients with antisocial personality disorder. These 15 patients exhibited the most marked frontal hypoperfusion. It was therefore hypothesized that antisocial personality disorder patients are more sensitive to the toxic effects of alcohol. Alternatively, the frontal lobe dysfunction caused by the chronic alcoholism may contribute to the persistent antisocial behaviour.

Buchsbaum et al. (1997) carried out MRI on 12 patients with schizotypal personality disorder, 11 with chronic schizophrenia and 23 age-matched and sex-matched normal volunteers. Schizophrenic patients had larger left anterior and temporal horns than the normal controls. The size of the left anterior and temporal horns in the schizotypal personality disorder patients was intermediate between those of the controls and schizophrenic patients, and differed significantly from that of the schizophrenic patients. The left-minus-right difference was larger in schizophrenic patients than in the normal controls or schizotypal personality disorder subjects. Thus, in their structural brain characteristics as well as in their clinical symptomatology, the schizotypal personality disorder patients showed abnormalities resembling in attenuated form those found in fully fledged schizophrenia.

The first positron emission tomography study of psychiatric patients with aggressive behaviour was carried out as long ago as 1987. Four psychiatric patients displaying persistent aggressiveness had decreased blood flow to the left temporal lobes. Two of the four also had decreased frontal lobe blood flow (Volkow and Tancredi, 1987). Goyer et al. (1994) were the first to examine the cerebral metabolic rates

of glucose (CMRG) in a selected group of 17 patients with a DSM-III-R diagnosis of personality disorder. They were a heterogeneous collection, six being labelled antisocial, six borderline, two dependent and three narcissistic. The PET scans were carried out while the subjects were performing an auditory continuous performance task. Within the whole group, there was a significant inverse correlation between a life history of impulsive aggression and reduced glucose metabolism in the frontal cortex. The CMRG in the six antisocial patients and the six borderline patients was compared with that of a control group of 43 subjects. The borderline patients had altered rates of glucose metabolism. A further PET study compared 10 borderline patients with 15 age-matched controls and found a trend for increased glucose metabolism in the posterior part of the right temporal lobe (De la Fuente et al., 1994).

Although not explicitly studying patients with antisocial personality disorder, Raine et al. (1997) carried out PET scans on a group of murderers pleading not guilty by reason of insanity. The scanning was carried out while the subjects performed a standardized continuous performance task. There were lower rates of glucose metabolism in the lateral and mesial prefrontal cortex in the murderers compared with controls. Wong et al. (1997) recorded FDG PET brain scans from 31 offenders with schizophrenia in a high-security hospital and from 6 normal controls. They reported reduced FDG uptake in the anterior inferior temporal regions in the offender sample. In those displaying repetitive violence, the reduced uptake was restricted to the left side, whereas it was bilateral in the offenders with a history of either a single violent offence or only minor violence. How these differences in lateralization in violent offenders relate to their differing patterns of violent behaviour requires further study. Overall, the limited PET scan data support the hypothesis that low impulse control and aggression seem to correlate with decreased metabolic activity in the orbital frontal cortex and in the temporal lobes.

Finally, a very rigorously controlled brain imaging study is that of Intrator et al. (1997). They tested the hypothesis that psychopathy is associated with abnormal processing of affective verbal material using SPECT scanning to measure cerebral blood flow changes while the subjects were carrying out a lexical decision task. Two groups of male patients from a substance-abuse programme were selected according to their scores on the Psychopathy Checklist. Eight were high scorers and were regarded as psychopaths and eight scored within the normal range. Nine healthy volunteer control subjects were also studied. Compared with the normal controls and the non-psychopathic patients, the psychopaths had increased levels of cerebral blood flow in both frontotemporal regions during the processing of the emotional stimuli. Though this study has methodological problems, the most likely interpretation is that psychopaths require additional neural resources and therefore greater levels of blood flow to do the emotional task because of difficulties of understanding and using words that refer to emotional events and feelings. This may be part of a more general difficulty in processing affective information. Further imaging studies of psychopathy involving anatomical co-registration and a variety of linguistic and non-linguistic tasks are clearly needed to investigate this hypothesis further. Psychopaths may have functional anomalies in the brain mechanisms and circuitry involved in linguistic and affective processes. Recent research into the neurophysiology of emotion suggests that the ventromedial frontal cortex, medial temporal cortex and amygdala may be of particular importance.

REFERENCES

Adams JH, Graham DI, Scott G, Parker L and Doyle D (1981). Brain damage in fatal non-missile head injury. *Journal of Clinical Pathology* **33**:1132–45.

American Psychiatric Association (1987). *Diagnostic and Statistical Manual of Mental Disorders,* third edition, revised (DSM-III-R). Washington, DC: American Psychiatric Association.

Barratt ES, Stanford MS, Felthouse A and Kent TA (1997). The effects of phenytoin on impulsive and premeditated aggression: a controlled study. *Journal of Clinical Psychopharmacology* **17**:341–9.

Bear D (1979). Temporal lobe epilepsy: a syndrome of sensory–limbic hyperconnection. *Cortex* **15**:357–84.

Blair RJ, Jones L, Clark F and Smith M (1997). The psychopathic individual: a lack of responsiveness to distress cues? *Psychophysiology* **34(2)**:192–8.

Blumer D (1995). Personality disorders in epilepsy. In: Ratey JJ (ed.), *Neuropsychiatry of Personality Disorders.* Cambridge, MA: Blackwell, 230–63.

Blumer D and Benson DF (1975). Personality changes with frontal and temporal lobe lesions. In: Benson DF and Blumer D (eds), *Psychiatric Aspects of Neurologic Disease.* New York: Grune and Stratton, 151–69.

Buchsbaum MS, Yang S, Hizlett E et al. (1997). Ventricular volume and asymmetry in schizotypal disorder and schizophrenia assessed with magnetic resonance imaging. *Schizophrenia Research* **27**:45–53.

Convit A, Czobor T and Volavka J (1991). Lateralised abnormality in the EEG of persistent violent psychiatric inpatients. *Biological Psychiatry* **30**:363–70.

Dalasio AR, Tranel D and Dalasio H (1990). Individuals with sociopathic behavior caused by frontal damage failed to respond autonomically to social stimuli. *Behavioral Brain Research* **41**:81–94.

Dawson NV, Shell AM and Filion DL (1990). The electrodermal system. In: Cacioppo JT and Tassinary LG (eds), *Principles of Psychophysiology.* Cambridge: Cambridge University Press, 295–324.

De la Fuente JM, Lotstra S, Goldman S et al. (1994). Temporal glucose metabolism in borderline personality disorder. *Psychiatry Research* **55**:237–45.

Direkze M, Bayliss SG and Cutting JC (1971). Primary tumours of the frontal lobe. *British Journal of Clinical Practice* **25**:207–13.

Driver MV, West LR and Faulk M (1974). Clinical and EEG studies of prisoners charged with murder. *British Journal of Psychiatry* **125**:583–7.

Eslinger PJ, Grattan LM, Damasio H and Damasio AR (1992). Developmental consequences of childhood frontal lobe damage. *Archives of Neurology* **49**:764–9.

Fenton GW, Fenwick PBC, Ferguson W and Lam CT (1978). The contingent negative variation and antisocial behaviour: a pilot study of Broadmoor Hospital. *British Journal of Psychiatry* **132**:368–77.

Fenton GW, Howard R and Fenwick PBC (1984). The contingent negative variation, personality and anti-social behaviour. *British Journal of Psychiatry* **144**: 463–74.

Fischbein GH, Lozovsky D and Jaffe JH (1989). Impulsivity, aggression and neuroendocrine responses to serotonergic inhibition in substance abusers. *Biological Psychiatry* **25**:1049–66.

Forssman H and Frey TS (1951). Electroencephalograms of boys with behaviour disorders. *Acta Psychiatrica et Neurological Scandinavica* **28**:61–73.

Geschwind N (1979). Behavioural changes in temporal lobe epilepsy. *Psychological Medicine* **9**:217–19.

Goyer PF, Konicki PE and Schulz SC (1994). Brain imaging in personality disorders. In: Silk KR (ed.), *Biological and Neurobehavioral Studies of Borderline Personality Disorder.* Washington, DC: American Psychiatric Press, 109–26.

Greenblatt M and Solomon HC (1966). Studies of lobotomy. In: *Proceedings of the Association for Research in Nervous and Mental Disease. 36. The Brain and Human Behavior.* New York: Hafner, 19–34.

Hare RD (1978). Electrodermal and cardiovascular correlates of psychopathy. In: Hare RD and Schalling D (eds), *Psychopathic Behavior: Approaches to Research.* New York: John Wiley & Sons, 107–44.

Hill D (1951). EEG in episodic psychotic and psychopathic behaviour. *Electroencelpahlography and Clinical Neurophysiology* **4**:419–42.

Hill D and Pond DA (1952). Reflections on 100 capital cases submitted to electroencephalogy. *Journal of Mental Science* **98**:23–43.

Howard R, Fenton GW and Fenwick PBC (1982). *Event Related Brain Potentials in Personality and Psychopathology: a Pavlovian Approach.* Letchworth: John Wiley & Sons.

Howard R and Lumsden J (1996). A neurophysiological predictor of reoffending in special hospital patients. *Criminal Behaviour and Mental Health* **6**:147–56.

Howard R and Lumsden J (1997). CNV predicts violent outcomes in patients released from a special hospital. *Criminal Behaviour and Mental Health* **7**:237–40.

Intrator J, Hare R, Stritzke P et al. (1997). A brain imaging (single photon emission computerised tomography) study of semantic and affective processing in psychopaths. *Biological Psychiatry* **42**:96–103.

Kauper DI and Cummings JL (1995). Personality alterations in degenerative brain diseases. In: Ratey JJ (ed.), *Neuropsychiatry of Personality Disorders.* Cambridge, MA: Blackwell Science, 172–209.

Kennard MA, Rabinovic HMS and Schwartzman AE (1956). Factor of aggression as related to the electroencephalogram. *Diseases of the Nervous System* **17**:127–30.

Knott JR, Platt EB, Ashby MC and Gottlieb JSA (1953). A familial evaluation of the electroencephalogram of patients with primary behaviour disorder and psychopathic personality. *Electroencephalography and Clinical Neurophysiology* **5**:363.

Kuruoglu AC, Arikan Z, Vural G, Karakas M, Arac M and Isika E (1996). Single photon emission computerised tomography in chronic alcoholism. Antisocial personality disorder may be associated with decreased frontal profusion. *British Journal of Psychiatry* **169**:348–54.

Kutcher SP, Blackwood DH, Gaskell DF, Muir WG and StClair DM (1989). Auditory P$_{300}$ does not differentiate borderline personality disorder from schizotypal personality disorder. *Biological Psychiatry* **26**:766–74.

Lilly R, Cummings JL, Benson DF and Frankel K (1983). The human Kluver–Bucy syndrome. *Neurology* **33**:1141–5.

Lishman WA (1968). Brain damage in relation to psychiatric disability after head injury. *British Journal of Psychiatry* **114**:373–410.

Lishman WA (1987). *Organic Psychiatry*, second edition. Oxford: Blackwell.

Logue V, Durward M, Pratt RTC, Piercy M and Nixon WLB (1968). The quality of survival after a rupture of an anterior cerebral aneurysm. *British Journal of Psychiatry* **114**:137–60.

McCallum WC (1973). The CNV and conditionability of psychopaths. In: McCallum WC and Knott JR (eds), Event related slow potentials of the brain: their relations to behaviour. *Electroencephalography and Neurophysiology* Supplement 33.

Mednick SA (1977). A bio-social theory of the learning of law abiding behaviour. In: Mednik SA and Christiansen

KO (eds), *Biosocial Bases of Criminal Behavior.* New York: Gardner Press, 1–8.

Mesulam M-M (1990). Large-scale neurocognitive networks and distributed processing for attention, language, and memory. *Annals of Neurology* **28**:597–613.

Raine A (1989). Evoked potentials and psychopathy. *International Journal of Psychophysiology* **8**:1–16.

Raine A (1993). *The Psychopathology of Crime: Criminal Behavior as a Clinical Disorder.* San Diego: Academic Press.

Raine A, Buchsbaum M and LaCasse L (1997). Brain abnormalities in murderers identified by positron emission tomography. *Biological Psychiatry* **42**: 495–508.

Raine A, Sheard C, Reynolds GP and Lencz T (1992). Prefrontal structural and functional deficits associated with individual differences in schizotypal personality. *Schizophrenia Research* **7**:237–47.

Raine A, Venables PH and Williams M (1990). Relationships between CAS and ANS measures of arousal at age 15 and criminality at age 20. *Archives of General Psychiatry* **47**:1003–7.

Raine A, Venables PH and Williams M (1995). High autonomic arousal and electrodermal orinting at age 15 years as protective factors against criminal behaviour at age 29 years. *American Journal of Psychiatry* **152**:1595–600.

Scarpa A and Raine A (1997). Psychophysiology of anger and violent behaviour. In: Fava M (ed.), *The Psychiatric Clinics of North America*, Vol. 20, No. 2. Philadelphia, PA: WB Saunders, 375–94.

Siddle DAT and Trasler G (1981). The psychophysiology of psychopathic behaviour. In: Christie MJ and Mellett PG (eds), *Foundations of Psychosomatics.* Chichester: John Wiley & Sons, 283–303.

Siever LJ (1991). The biology of the boundaries of schizophrenia. In: Tamminger CA and Schulz CS (eds), *Advances in Neuropsychiatry and Psychopharmacology,*. Vol. 1. *Schizophrenia Research.* New York: Raven Press, 181–91.

Storey PB (1970). Brain damage and personality change after subarachnoid haemorrhage. *British Journal of Psychiatry* **117**:129–42.

Trestman RL, Horvath T, Kalus O et al. (1996). Event-related potentials in schizotypal personality disorder. *Journal of Neuropsychiatry and Clinical Neuroscience* **8**:33–40.

Venables PH (1974). The recovery limb of the skin conductance response. In: Mednik FA, Schulsinger F and Higgins J (eds), *Genetics, Environment and Psychopathology.* Oxford: North Holland, 117–33.

Volavka J (1995). *Neurobiology of Violence.* Washington, DC: American Psychiatric Press.

Volavka T and Matousek M (1969). The relation of pre and perinatal pathology to the adult EEG. *Electroencephalography and Clinical Neurophysiology* **27**:667.

Volkow ND and Tancredi L (1987). Neural substrates of violent behaviour: a preliminary study with positron emission tomography. *British Journal of Psychiatry* **151**:668–73.

Williams D (1941). Significance of an abnormal electroencephalogram. *Journal of Neurology and Psychiatry* **4**:257–68.

Williams D (1969). Neural factors related to habitual aggression. Consideration of differences between those habitual aggressives and others who have committed crimes of violence. *Brain* **92(3)**:503–20.

Wong MT, Fenwick PBC, Lumsden J et al. (1997). Positron emission tomography in violent offenders with schizophrenia. *Psychiatry Research* **68**:111–23.

Wong MT, Lumsden J, Fenton GW and Fenwick PBC (1994). Electroencephalography, computed tomography and violence ratings of male patients in a maximum-security mental hospital. *Acta Psychiatrica Scandinavica* **90**:97–101.

World Health Organization (1992). *The International Classification of Mental and Behavioural Disorders. Clinical Descriptions and Diagnostic Guidelines (ICD-10).* Geneva: World Health Organization.

Chapter 10

EARLY PREVENTION AND TREATMENT

Barbara Maughan

INTRODUCTION

Most severely antisocial adults have long histories of behavioural difficulties reaching back to childhood (Robins, 1966, 1978). In addition, the early lives of offenders are often marked by chronic psychosocial adversity: social disadvantage, family disruption, inadequate parenting, harsh treatment and abuse are all too common features of the early histories of offender populations. These patterns are not, of course, without exceptions; equally importantly, in our current state of knowledge, even the best-established childhood predictors could not identify the small group of severely personality disordered offenders with any certainty. But the consistency of the links with adverse childhood factors, the heavy burdens imposed by serious offending, and the major challenges posed by the treatment of these groups in adulthood all combine to make a compelling case for early intervention.

The force of these arguments has long been recognized. The first randomized trial of a delinquency prevention programme was mounted in the 1940s (McCord, 1992), and since then a wide range of strategies has been explored in the attempt to avert or reduce rates of childhood antisocial behaviour. For many years, results seemed unpromising: many childhood problems appeared highly resistant

to change, and some interventions not only proved ineffective, but actually had deleterious effects. More recently, reviews and commentaries on early intervention efforts have begun to reflect a more cautiously optimistic note (Kazdin, 2001; Farrington and Coid, 2003). Though we are far from solving the problem of childhood antisocial behaviour, some interventions with more promising effects are beginning to be identified.

BUILDING ON RISK RESEARCH

To a large extent, this shift of view reflects an improved understanding of early risks for antisocial behaviour. To be effective, interventions need to be targeted on well-established risks that are both causal and modifiable. Though causality is inevitably difficult to determine, recent years have seen a vast expansion in research on both the childhood precursors of crime and antisocial behaviour in adulthood (e.g. Stoff et al., 1997; Rutter et al., 1998; Hill, 2002), and on factors that affect the persistence of aggressive and antisocial behaviours over time (Maughan and Rutter, 2001). The roles of genetic and other biological factors (including their interactions with psychosocial risks) are becoming more clearly understood (Raine et al., 1997; Rutter et al., 1998; Caspi et al., 2002; Raine, 2002), and a wide variety of studies have examined developmental and psychosocial precursors to adult offending. Each of these veins of research has influenced thinking on strategies for early intervention.

Developmentally, it now seems clear that early-onset conduct problems, beginning well before adolescence, carry the most serious risks for persistence to antisocial behaviour in adult life (Moffitt, 1993; Moffitt et al., 2002) and probably also for violent offending (Henry et al., 1996). Indeed, consistent though modest links to antisocial personality disorder have been traced from temperamental characteristics assessed as early as age 3 (Caspi et al., 1996). Therefore, to be effective, early interventions may need to begin very early indeed.

Among individual risks, hyperactivity/inattention and impulsivity have emerged as strong predictors of persistent antisocial behaviour (Farrington et al., 1990; Rutter et al., 1998), along with depressed intelligence quotient (IQ) scores (possibly reflecting neuropsychological deficits) and poor school achievements. Very young children who go on to develop conduct problems often show disorganized patterns of attachment to their carers (Lyons-Ruth, 1996), and there is extensive literature documenting links between childhood conduct problems and poor parental supervision, harsh or erratic discipline, cold or rejecting parental attitudes, parental discord and family breakdown (Loeber and Stouthamer-Loeber, 1986). Childhood victimization is associated with modestly increased risks for both conduct problems and later offending (Widom, 1997) and possibly more substantially increased risks of antisocial personality disorder (Kessler et al., 1997). Indeed, many aggressive children show biased patterns of social information processing that may have roots in abusive experiences and contribute to the persistence of their problems over time (Dodge et al., 1995). Poor peer relations constitute a further domain of risk, and disaffection from schooling, along with the development of

more generally antisocial lifestyles, seems likely to compound early difficulties.

In the main, these factors have been identified as risks for broad indicators of antisocial behaviour and offending in adulthood – albeit including serious and violent crime – rather than for severe personality disorder per se. This may be an important caveat. The early histories of very serious offenders have been less systematically documented, and investigators have only recently begun to examine factors such as psychopathic traits and their correlates in juvenile populations (Viding, 2004). At this stage, it is unclear whether early risks for severely personality disordered offending involve extreme versions of more generally identified risks, specific pathogenic factors, or particularly adverse combinations of biological, cognitive and psychosocial vulnerabilities (Hill, 2003). Until these questions are clarified, results from existing childhood studies need to be viewed in terms of the promise they may hold for reducing severe adult difficulties, rather than for known and proven gains.

EARLY PREVENTION AND TREATMENT

Early interventions for childhood conduct problems have been offered in a variety of settings, and using a wide spectrum of approaches: parent education and training, pre-school programmes, cognitive skills training, school-based interventions and multi-modal strategies. Farrington and Coid (2003) review recent evidence on these issues in detail. This chapter provides a brief overview of findings on some of the more promising approaches identified to date. The emphasis is on results from well-designed, experimental trials of psychosocial interventions for childhood conduct problems, involving either randomized controlled trials, comparisons with untreated or other-treated controls, or detailed pre-measurement and post-measurement. Prevention trials include universal programmes, applied to whole 'populations' of children in high-risk schools or communities, along with more selective strategies, targeting children at high environmental risk or already showing early signs of behaviour problems; here, the specific methods used often shade into those employed in treating clinic-referred groups. Outcome measures typically include parent, teacher or observer-ratings of disruptive behaviours; self-reports and official records of offending; measures of school adjustment and achievement; and, in some instances, measures of known risk factors for antisocial behaviour, such as parental drug or alcohol problems, or exposure to abuse. Well-designed evaluations of preventive experiments are still quite limited in number, and few prevention programmes have been independently replicated (LeMarquand et al., 2001). By contrast, the more promising treatment strategies are supported by extensive bodies of research and meta-analyses (Kazdin, 2001). A number of investigators have examined predictors of treatment response and also – a key issue in work with children and families who may be facing high levels of stress and disorganization – what predicts treatment drop-out. More recent studies have also begun to investigate mediating mechanisms; in most cases, however, we still know relatively little about the particular aspects of successful programmes that contribute to their effects.

IMPROVING PARENTING

Prenatal and infancy programmes

Because parenting problems figure so centrally as risks for childhood conduct disorder, many programmes have focused on improving parenting skills. Some – described in more detail below – are designed to help parents whose children have already become hard to manage. Others, aimed initially at reducing low birth weight and adverse infant outcomes among young, severely socially disadvantaged mothers, have also shown effects on later parenting and child behaviours.

Nurse home-visiting programmes beginning in pregnancy, and designed to improve the health-related behaviours, childcare skills, family planning, and educational and occupational status of disadvantaged young mothers, have shown an impressive range of benefits. The more successful approaches (e.g. Kitzman et al., 1997; Olds et al., 1997) combined social support with direct education in health-related behaviours and child care. High-risk mothers visited during pregnancy and for 2 years after birth had reduced rates of subsequent pregnancies, substance abuse problems and dependence on welfare and crime. Their skills in infant care were improved and their children were less likely to be identified as victims of abuse or neglect (4 per cent versus 19 per cent in an untreated control group). In a related programme, poor, unmarried, teenage mothers were visited from pregnancy onwards, and offered day care for their children up to the age of 5 (Lally et al., 1988). Followed to age 15, children in the experimental group showed better social behaviour and school achievements than a matched comparison sample; fewer had been referred to the courts for delinquency (2 per cent versus 17 per cent) and their recorded offences were less severe. A further study, beginning when infants were 1 year old, offered a 2-year programme designed to promote children's social and intellectual competence (Johnson and Walker, 1987). In the first year, home visits focused on child development and parenting skills; in the second, mothers and children came to the centre to learn child management, cognitive development and communication skills. Follow-ups 5–8 years later showed significant reductions in teacher-rated acting-out problems for the experimental group but, although a more extended follow-up to the teens failed to show differences in teacher-rated aggression, maternal ratings of externalizing behaviours did show positive effects (see LeMarquand et al., 2001).

Parent management training

For young children already showing behavioural problems, parent management training is among the most promising treatment strategies identified to date (Kazdin, 2001; Woolgar and Scott, 2005). Drawing heavily on social learning models (Patterson, 1982; Patterson et al., 1992), these programmes are designed to train parents in methods of reducing coercive interchanges with their children, promoting prosocial behaviours, and decreasing deviant ones (Forehand and McMahon, 1981; Webster-Stratton, 1996). Treatment is conducted primarily with the parent, and may be delivered in individual sessions, in groups, or through the use of videotapes. For young, mildly oppositional children, programmes usually last 6–8 weeks; for older children with more severe problems, they can extend from 3 to 6 months.

Parent management training has been extensively evaluated. Outcome studies show marked improvements on parent and teacher reports of deviant behaviour, direct observations and also, in some studies, on measures such as arrest rates. Gains are such as to place children within non-clinical levels of functioning and have been maintained in some follow-ups as far as 3 years post-treatment. These are important strengths. However, there are also some limitations: drop-out rates can be high and (perhaps not unsurprisingly) many of the same family factors that predict the onset of childhood conduct problems also predict treatment drop-out. In general, effectiveness seems greatest with younger children, and children with more severe or chronic problems may respond less well.

PRE-SCHOOL PROGRAMMES

Early educational programmes have provided a second avenue for intervention. The US Head Start programme of the 1960s prompted a massive investment in pre-school education designed to improve the intellectual skills of low-income and disadvantaged children. Participants in a number of the experimental programmes have been followed throughout their schooling, and results from one small study, the High/Scope Perry Preschool Project (Berrueta-Clement et al., 1984; Schweinhart et al., 1993), have attracted particular attention in the delinquency field. Here, children from very high-risk poor families were provided with a high-quality 'active learning' pre-school curriculum, encouraging independence, problem solving and task persistence, combined with weekly home visits to parents. As in other pre-school interventions, initial IQ gains washed out soon after the children entered formal schooling, but other benefits persisted. By contrast with controls, experimental children were less likely to be referred for special education, completed more years of schooling, and showed better attainments and classroom behaviour during the school years. More strikingly, follow-ups at ages 19 and 27 found higher levels of employment and home ownership, fewer teenage pregnancies, and lower dependence on welfare benefits in the experimental group. In addition, they had fewer lifetime arrests by age 27 (a mean of 2.3 versus 4.6), and only 7 per cent (compared to 35 per cent in the control group) had been arrested on five or more occasions. Although it by no means eliminated adult antisocial behaviour, this programme does appear to have had important effects on both participation in 'prosocial' institutions and on reduced risks of recidivist crime. By contrast, the Carolina Abecedarian Project (Campbell and Ramey, 1995), providing pre-school education for children at risk of suboptimal cognitive development, has reported a range of positive outcomes in IQ and school achievements, but no comparable effects on crime rates at age 18. The reasons for these differences are unclear; the lack of services to parents may have limited gains in the Abecedarian programme, or other factors in the wider social environment may have restricted its

intervention reduced teacher-rated conduct problems and contributed to a more positive classroom environment, while the high-risk interventions are associated with reductions in parent-rated oppositional aggressive behaviour up to grade three. Other ongoing projects include Communities that Care (Hawkins and Catalano, 1992; Farrington, 2003), a flexible programme building on local involvement, and currently being implemented in the UK and North America, and the Better Beginnings, Better Futures project (Peters and Russell, 1996), involving two separate universal interventions (one providing prenatal and infant development programmes and pre-schooling, the second providing pre-school and primary school programmes) delivered by social services personnel in high-risk communities in Canada.

CONCLUSIONS

As this brief overview suggests, a variety of approaches are now beginning to show some positive effects in early interventions for childhood conduct problems. At this stage, programmes beginning early in a child's life, which are sustained over time, and which directly address the range of risks implicated in the development of disruptive behaviours, seem likely to promise the greatest gains. From the perspective of those working with adult populations, and especially with offenders with more severe personality disorders, the emphasis must, of course, be on their 'promise' at this stage. Although a number of programmes have shown continuing benefits some years post-intervention, longer-term follow-ups are inevitably more limited; how far gains can be passed through to late adolescence and adulthood is still very much an open question. Many challenges clearly remain in attempts to avert poor outcomes for children most at risk. However, as these findings illustrate, the relevant issues are being tackled in imaginative and increasingly effective ways.

REFERENCES

Baer RA and Nietzel MT (1991). Cognitive and behavioral treatment of impulsivity in children: a meta-analytic review of the outcome literature. *Journal of Clinical Child Psychology* **20**:400–12.

Beelman A, Pfingsten U and Losel F (1994). Effects of training social competence in children: a meta-analysis of recent evaluation studies. *Journal of Clinical Child Psychology* **23**:260–71.

Berrueta-Clement JR, Schweinhart LJ, Barnett WS, Epstein AS and Weikart DP (1984). *Changed Lives.* Ypsilanti, MI: High/Scope.

Bierman KL, Coie JD, Dodge KA et al. (2002). Using the Fast Track randomized prevention trial to test the early-starter model of the development of serious conduct problems. *Development and Psychopathology* **14**:925–43.

Botvin GJ (1990). Substance abuse prevention: theory, practice and effectiveness. In: Tonry M and Wilson JQ (eds), *Drugs and Crime.* Chicago, IL: University of Chicago Press, 461–519.

Campbell FA and Ramey CT (1995). Cognitive and school outcomes for high-risk African-American students in middle adolescence: positive effects of early intervention. *American Educational Research Journal* **32**:743–72.

Caspi A, McClay J, Moffitt TE et al. (2002). Role of genotype in the cycle of violence in maltreated children. *Science* **297**:851–4.

Caspi A, Moffitt TE, Newman DL and Silva PA (1996). Behavioral observations at age 3 predict adult psychiatric disorders: longitudinal evidence from a birth cohort. *Archives of General Psychiatry* **53**:1033–9.

Conduct Problems Prevention Research Group (1992). A developmental and clinical model for the prevention of conduct disorder: The Fast Track Program. *Development and Psychopathology* **4**:509–27.

Consortium on the School-based Promotion of Social Competence (1994). The school-based promotion of social competence: theory, research, practice and policy. In: Haggerty RJ, Sherrod LR, Garmezy N and Rutter M (eds), *Stress, Risk and Resilience in Children and Adolescents: Processes, Mechanisms and Interventions.* Cambridge: Cambridge University Press, 268–316.

Crick NR and Dodge KA (1994). A review and reformulation of social information processing mechanisms in children's social adjustment. *Psychological Bulletin* **115**:74–101.

Dodge KA, Pettit GS, Bates JE and Valente E (1995). Social information-processing patterns partially mediate the effects of early physical abuse on later conduct problems. *Journal of Abnormal Psychology* **104**:632–43.

Farrington DP (2003). Advancing knowledge about the early prevention of adult antisocial behaviour. In: Farrington DP and Coid JW (eds), *Early Prevention of Adult Antisocial Behaviour.* Cambridge: Cambridge University Press, 1–31.

Farrington DP and Coid JW (2003). *Early Prevention of Adult Antisocial Behaviour.* Cambridge: Cambridge University Press.

Farrington DP, Loeber R and Van Kammen WB (1990). Long-term criminal outcomes of hyperactivity–impulsivity–attention deficit and conduct problems in childhood. In: Robins LN and Rutter M (eds), *Straight and Devious Pathways from Childhood to Adulthood.* New York: Cambridge University Press, 62–81.

Forehand RL and McMahon RJ (1981). *Helping the Non-compliant Child: A Clinician's Guide to Parent Training.* New York: Guilford Press.

Hawkins JD, Catalano RF, Kosterman R, Abbott R and Hill KG (1999). Preventing adolescent health-risk behaviours by strengthening protection during childhood. *Archives of Pediatric and Adolescent Medicine* **153**:226–34.

Hawkins JD and Catalano RF (1992). *Communities that Care.* San Francisco, CA: Josey-Bass.

Hawkins JD, Catalano RF, Morrison DM, O'Donnell J, Abbott RD and Day LE (1992). The Seattle Social Development Project: effects of the first four years on protective factors and problem behaviors. In: McCord J and Tremblay R (eds), *Preventing Antisocial Behavior.* New York: Guilford Press, 139–61.

Henggeler SW, Melton GB and Smith LA (1992). Family preservation using multisystemic therapy: an effective alternative to incarcerating serious juvenile offenders. *Journal of Consulting and Clinical Psychology* **60**:953–61.

Henry B, Caspi A, Moffitt TE and Silva PA (1996). Temperamental and familial predictors of violent and non-violent criminal convictions: from age 3 to 18. *Developmental Psychology* **32**:614–23.

Hill J (2002). Biological, psychological and social processes in the conduct disorders. *Journal of Child Psychology and Psychiatry* **43**:133–64.

Hill J (2003). Early identification of individuals at risk for antisocial personality disorder. *British Journal of Psychiatry* **182**(Suppl. 44):S11–S14.

Johnson DL and Walker T (1987). Primary prevention of behavior problems in Mexican American children. *American Journal of Community Psychology* **15**: 375–85.

Kazdin AE (1997). Psychosocial treatments for conduct disorder in children. *Journal of Child Psychology and Psychiatry* **38**:161–78.

Kazdin AE (2001). Treatment of conduct disorders. In: Hill J and Maughan B (eds), *Conduct Disorders in Childhood and Adolescence.* Cambridge: Cambridge University Press, 408–48.

Kellam SG, Rebok GW, Ialongo N and Mayer LS (1994). The course and malleability of aggressive behavior from early first grade into middle school: results of a developmental epidemiologically-based preventive trial. *Journal of Child Psychology and Psychiatry* **35**:259–81.

Kessler RC, Davis CG and Kendler KS (1997). Childhood adversity and adult psychiatric disorder in the US National Comorbidity Survey. *Psychological Medicine* **27**:1101–19.

Kitzman H, Olds DL, Henderson CR et al. (1997). Effect of prenatal and infancy home visitation by nurses on pregnancy outcomes, childhood injuries, and repeated childbearing. *Journal of the American Medical Association* **278**:644–52.

Lally JR, Mangione PL and Honig AS (1988). Long-range impact of an early intervention with low-income children and their families. In: Powell DR (ed.), *Parent Education as Early Childhood Intervention* Norwood, NJ: Ablex, 79–104.

LeMarquand D, Tremblay RE and Vitaro F (2001). The prevention of conduct disorder: a review of successful and unsuccessful experiments. In: Hill J and Maughan B (eds), *Conduct Disorders in Childhood and Adolescence.* Cambridge: Cambridge University Press, 449–77.

Loeber R and Stouthamer-Loeber M (1986). Family factors as correlates and predictors of juvenile conduct problems and delinquency. In: Tonry M and Morris N (eds), *Crime and Justice*, Vol. 7. Chicago, IL: University of Chicago Press, 29–149.

Lyons-Ruth K (1996). Attachment relationships among children with aggressive behavior problems: the role of disorganized attachment patterns. *Journal of Consulting and Clinical Psychology* **64**:64–73.

Maughan B and Rutter M (2001). Antisocial children grown up. In: Hill J and Maughan B (eds), *Conduct Disorders in Childhood and Adolescence.* Cambridge: Cambridge University Press, 507–52.

McCord J (1992). The Cambridge–Somerville Study: a pioneering longitudinal experimental study of delinquency prevention. In: McCord J and Tremblay RE (eds), *Preventing Antisocial Behavior: Interventions from Birth through Adolescence.* New York: Guilford Press, 196–206.

Moffitt TE (1993). Adolescence-limited and life-course-persistent antisocial behaviour: a developmental taxonomy. *Psychological Review* **100**:674–701.

Moffitt TE, Caspi A, Harrington H and Milne BJ (2002). Males on the life-course persistent and adolescence-limited antisocial pathways: follow-up at age 26 years. *Development and Psychopathology* **14**:179–207.

Olds DL, Eckenrode J, Henderson CR Jr et al. (1997). Long-term effects of home visitation on maternal life course and child abuse and neglect. *Journal of the American Medical Association* **278**:637–43.

Olweus D (1994). Bullying at school: basic facts and effects of a school based intervention programme. *Journal of Child Psychology and Psychiatry* **35**:1171–90.

Patterson GR (1982). *Coercive Family Process.* Eugene, OR: Castalia.

Patterson GR, Reid JB and Dishion TJ (1992). *Antisocial Boys: A Social–Interactional Approach.* Eugene, OR: Castalia.

Peters RD and Russell CC (1996). Promoting development and preventing disorder: the Better Beginnings, Better Futures Project. In: Peters RD and McMahon RJ (eds), *Preventing Childhood Disorders, Substance Abuse, and Delinquency.* Thousand Oaks, CA: Sage, 19–47.

Raine A (2002). Biosocial studies of antisocial and violent behavior in children and adults: a review. *Journal of Abnormal Child Psychology* **30**:311–26.

Raine A, Brennan P, Farrington DP and Mednick SA (1997). *Unlocking Crime: The Biosocial Key.* New York: Plenum Press.

Reynolds D, Sammons P, Stoll L, Barber M and Hillman J (1996). School effectiveness and school improvement in the United Kingdom. *School Effectiveness and School Improvement* **7**:133–58.

Robins LN (1966). *Deviant Children Grown Up.* Baltimore, MD: Williams and Wilkins.

Robins LN (1978). Sturdy childhood predictors of adult outcomes: replications from longitudinal studies. *Psychological Medicine* **8**:611–22.

Rutter M, Giller H and Hagell A (1998). *Antisocial Behaviour by Young People.* Cambridge: Cambridge University Press.

Rutter M and Maughan B (2002). School effectiveness findings 1979–2002. *Journal of School Psychology* **40**:451–75.

Schweinhart LJ, Barnes HV and Weikart DP (1993). *Significant Benefits.* Ypsilanti, MI: High/Scope.

Smith PK and Sharp S (1994). *School Bullying.* London: Routledge.

Stoff D, Breiling J and Maser JD (eds) (1997). *Handbook of Antisocial Behavior.* New York: John Wiley & Sons.

Stringfield S and Herman R (1996). Assessment of the state of school effectiveness research in the United States of America. *School Effectiveness and School Improvement* **7**:159–80.

Tremblay RE, Vitaro F, Bertrand L et al. (1992). Parent and child training to prevent early onset of delinquency: The Montreal Longitudinal–Experimental Study. In: McCord J and Tremblay R (eds), *Preventing Antisocial Behavior.* New York: Guilford Press, 117–38.

Viding E (2004). Annotation: Understanding the development of psychopathy. *Journal of Child Psychology and Psychiatry* **45**:1329–37.

Webster-Stratton C (1996). Early intervention with video-tape modeling: programs for families of children with oppositional defiant disorder or conduct disorder. In: Hibbs ED and Jensen P (eds), *Psychosocial Treatment Research of Child and Adolescent Disorders: Empirically Based Strategies for Clinical Practice.* Washington, DC: American Psychological Association, 435–74.

Widom CS (1997). Child abuse, neglect, and witnessing violence. In: Stoff D, Breiling J and Maser JD (eds), *Handbook of Antisocial Behavior.* New York: John Wiley & Sons, 159–70.

Woolgar M and Scott S (2005). Evidence–based management of conduct disorders. *Current Opinion in Psychiatry* **18**:392–6.

Chapter 11

MALADAPTIVE LEARNING? COGNITIVE–BEHAVIOURAL THERAPY AND BEYOND

Marie Quayle and Estelle Moore

PSYCHOLOGICAL INTERVENTION: EARLY CONCEPTS

When psychological explanations of mental disorder began to gain particular acceptance in the early part of the twentieth century, theorists of the psychodynamic tradition emphasized unconscious processes and dynamics of the psyche, character and personality (e.g. Freud, 1905; Abraham, 1927). Later, when the discipline of clinical psychology became established, the emphasis shifted to a strictly scientific approach involving only what was directly observable and measurable. The study of 'mentalistic' concepts, such as cognitions and affects, was ruled out on the grounds that theorizing about unseen entities is neither productive nor necessary. Thus, the human person was reduced to an observable body, equivalent to any other animal body, and principles derived from work with animals were assumed to be applicable to humans.

Animal experiments in Russia and the USA were establishing two fundamental principles of learning, with meticulous attention to objectivity and detailed measurement. Pavlov (1927), working in Russia, demonstrated the phenomenon of classical conditioning: that a behaviour, adaptive or maladaptive, can be conditioned and produced in response to a 'signal' associated with an original stimulus, even when that stimulus is no longer present. Thus fear may continue to be triggered by an image or sound associated with a traumatic situation, even when the situation itself is well past. In the USA, Thorndike (1931) and Skinner (1974) established the principle of operant learning: that behaviour that is rewarded and reinforced in some way is likely to occur more often. When it is not reinforced, it will eventually extinguish; when it is punished, it will tend to be suppressed.

Early behaviour therapy arose out of the application of these two learning principles and, in particular, from the two-factor model (Mowrer, 1947), which encompassed both classical and operant conditioning. Thus, if a fear response occurs when a person enters a small room (classically conditioned from previous frightening experiences) and avoidance of that room reduces the fear, avoidance is likely to continue (operant conditioning), and may extend to an increasing number of occasions and situations in life. Behaviour therapy is based on the premise that the 'maladaptively' learned fear response can be gradually extinguished by learning a new coping response of calmness and relaxation in the previously feared situation (Mowrer, 1960).

The establishment of these principles of learning and their successful application to human situations led some behaviourists to propose that a person's behaviour is determined only by the triggers and reinforcement schedules in the environment, and is thus totally situation specific. According to this theory, no consistent pattern of behaviour across different environments would occur, and therefore the concept of personality was judged to be meaningless. The former concepts of character and personality and, in particular, personality disorder were reformulated in terms of deficits in adaptive learning opportunities in early life. When Bandura (1969) introduced the further learning principle of imitation, or modelling, it became possible to explain maladaptive learning via the observation of the behaviour of significant others. Therefore a behavioural pattern of interpersonal violence may be established, not only through the direct experience of rewarding or punishing consequences of personal violence, but also through observation of the use of violence by others.

SCHOOLS OF THERAPY: THEIR EMERGENCE AND INTEGRATION

Despite the successful application of learning principles in behaviour therapy, the narrow focus on observable behaviour within a specific environment was criticized as inadequate in explaining human behaviour and problems, from two different perspectives.

Analyses confined to external behaviour and situations failed to account for the cognitive and affective responses of the person. Bandura (1986) demonstrated that a person's perception of his or her ability to handle situations is crucial to behavioural change and developed techniques to enhance self-efficacy and self-control. Cognitive therapists (Beck, 1970, 1976; Meichenbaum, 1977) highlighted the role of irrational beliefs and automatic negative thoughts in problems with a behavioural component such as depression and dysfunctional sexual behaviour. Personal construct therapists

(Kelly, 1955) argued that meaning is idiosyncratically constructed: we experience 'reality' through our interpretation of it. Cognitive–behavioural therapy (CBT) represented an effort to develop an integrated approach, incorporating these different emphases from the cognitive and behavioural traditions (Meichenbaum, 1985). Therapists using CBT assume an inter-dependence of multiple processes involving the person's thoughts, feelings, behaviour and environmental consequences. Thus beliefs, including distortions in perception, and external environmental events are hypothesized to be linked in complex causal pathways preceding behavioural problems.

Whilst the cognitive–behavioural approach widened the focus to include not only external behaviours and situations, but also internal processes and meanings, it nevertheless still represents a focus on the individual. Systems theorists have argued that the 'scientific' approach of concentrating in detail on the individual (including analysis of the acquisition and maintenance of maladaptive behaviours, be they actions, thoughts or feelings) results in a tendency to perceive problems as residing entirely within the person (Mikesell et al., 1995). This ignores the complex interplay of interactions, interpersonal relationships and reward/punishment schedules, both within the whole family and group and within the individual's general life context. Such interactions can be profoundly problem maintaining (Magnavita, 2000), but equally represent opportunities for intervention. If it is assumed that problems and symptoms reflect a systems adaptation to a total context at a point in time, the adaptive efforts of members of the system can be predicted to reverberate throughout many levels of the system, from the biological substrate, through relationships, to the wider community (McGoldrick and Gerson, 1985).

These two major critiques of early behavioural therapy led to the widening of the concept of 'maladaptive' learning to include attitudes, feelings, beliefs and schemas within relationships, and within the context of the environment as a whole. The cumulative effects of multiple factors that can lead to psychopathology are increasingly understood via multi-dimensional models. Biopsychosocial models incorporate risk factors for the exacerbation of problems, and protective factors that can buffer their effects (Paris, 1996).

As in the development of CBT for personality disorder, which has a history within (at least) two traditions (Beck et al., 1990; Layden et al., 1993), a wide range of therapeutic approaches has emerged over the last 10 years, which integrate the concepts and techniques of various methods of intervention. Focusing primarily on intervention with individuals, cognitive–analytic therapy (CAT) (Ryle, 1997) and psychodynamic–behavioural therapy (Wachtel, 1985) would be examples of such integrations. As a variant of CBT, dialectical behaviour therapy (DBT) (Linehan, 1993) makes explicit therapeutic use of dialectical polarities (e.g. change versus acceptance) in negotiating alliances with, and enhancing the interpersonal skills repertoires of, patients with borderline personality disorder. Young (1999) has documented his expansion of the cognitive model to account for the perceived rigidity of belief, avoidance and interpersonal difficulty that typically characterizes the presentation in therapy of individuals with personality disorder. The concepts of CBT are presented as widely applicable in a range of settings, e.g. with in-patients (Wright et al., 1993), with couples (e.g. Dattilio and Padesky, 1990) and with groups (e.g. Wessler and Hankin-Wessler, 1989).

Therefore the different therapeutic models, once in marked conflict with one another, have been integrated in more recent times in order to meet the challenge of highly complex and often contradictory clinical presentations. In the same way, the essential element that gave substance to 'personality' as a construct (the fact that people exhibit distinctive and abiding characteristics) survived the challenge of situation-specific behavioural theorists, and re-emerged. Erstwhile adversaries have discovered the merits of a biological, psychodynamic, cognitive, interpersonal synthesis in promulgating the efficacy of multi-dimensional interventions (Millon, 1995). The possibility of usefully integrating the different psychotherapies at a theoretical level has also emerged (Brewin and Power, 1997). In the meantime, the challenge to individual clinicians presented by integrational models is the accumulation of a knowledge base (Magnavita, 2000) that incorporates abnormal and developmental psychology, systems of classification (even if these are not applied beyond assessment), and treatment ideas for Axis I disorders (e.g. depression, addictive behaviours), in addition to the application of techniques that foster the maintenance of a working alliance. Inevitably, this work cannot be safely conducted without opportunities for regular supervision and support.

TRANSLATING THEORY INTO PRACTICE: WITH WHAT EFFICACY?

In his comprehensive reviews of the literature on intervention for personality disordered offenders, Lösel (1998) observes that structured behavioural, cognitive–behavioural, skills-oriented and multi-modal programmes, based in part on social learning principles, have evidenced robust and replicable effects in the reduction of antisocial behaviour. Some authors have concluded that 'nothing works' for those with extreme antisocial and narcissistic (self-entitled) traits, and even that problems (and therefore associated risks) 'get worse' in intensive (group) treatment programmes. Others conclude that there is no clear picture to date of the effectiveness of offender treatment packages (Hollin, 1993; Blackburn, 2000). It might be predicted that individuals with the most complex and disabling problems at the outset of any therapeutic regime are likely to be those who display difficulties in adjustment to the setting, but these may not be reliable predictors of overall outcome (Chiesa, 2000).

The considerable heterogeneity of the high-risk personality disordered patient group and specific barriers to successful programme design and implementation (e.g. resistances to treatment generated in part by insensitive institutional practices, and poor treatment integrity) have compromised meta-analytic research initiatives. Consequently, multi-modal, multi-disciplinary interventions for the inhabitants of secure facilities tend to be the clinical reality, within which it is very difficult to control for the interacting effects of incarceration, treatment content and process. Facing such realities, one approach might be to ask: what works, for whom, under what circumstances (Quayle and Moore, 1998)? It is the *flexible* delivery of the therapeutic programme, tailored to the needs of each individual, that is likely to assist those with complex needs to engage with sessions and sustain an interest in them.

Evaluations of specific typically multi-modal interventions with small in-patient/incarcerated offender populations are available (e.g. Truax et al., 1966; Hughes et al., 1997; Renwick et al., 1997; Newton, 1998; Quayle and Moore, 1998; Reiss et al., 1998; Moore et al., 2000; Newton et al., 2005), although constructive clinical outcomes are not achieved with every participant (see Watt and Howells, 1999). Less than optimal outcomes in an inner city sample of patients with borderline personality disorder were found to be associated with greater severity of these traits, histories of self-cutting, substance abuse and unemployment (Ryle and Golynkina, 2000).

It is likely to be some time before the relative effectiveness of specific techniques used in the treatment of the various personality disorders can be reliably compared and evaluated. There is emerging evidence of the benefits of cognitive–behavioural intervention (in terms of reduced Axis I symptomatology and suicidal behaviour) for individuals with borderline personality disorder (Turner, 1989; Linehan et al., 1991, 1993, 1994; Westen, 1991; Arntz, 1994), and for those with psychosis, considered to be 'intractably' violent and dangerous (Becker et al., 1997).

Padesky (1994) observed that cognitive therapy case descriptions of positive treatment outcome with personality disorders attribute such results to change in maladaptive core schemas and the construction of more adaptive schemas. Cognitive–behavioural models have been considered to afford some clarity regarding issues of responsibility, accountability and risk, which, in turn, can help offenders to identify the cognitive and emotional precursors that predict and support their offending (Laws, 1989; Wood et al., 2000).

GLOBAL PRINCIPLES

Without exception, the literature on clinical intervention with personality disorder across all three Axis II clusters attests to the importance of the development and maintenance of the therapeutic alliance in the process of change. Linehan (1993) has defined 'therapist characteristics' as the 'attitudes and pervasive interpersonal positions that the therapist takes in relationship to the patient'. Therapists of all persuasions have shared their experiences of the need for compassion, persistence, patience, a belief in the value of the intervention, and a willingness to take risks and to repair mistakes in their work in this area (Macphail and Cox, 1975; Cox, 1986; Linehan, 1993; Ryle and Beard, 1993; Dickerson and Zimmerman, 1995; Adshead and Van Velsen, 1996; Marshall et al., 1999; Young, 1999; Magnavita, 2000; Padesky, 2005). The tradition of post-structuralist thought and practice offers further fresh insights into taken-for-granted assumptions within professional discourse, and many ideas for ways in which therapists can be accountable to those who seek, or are required to seek, their help (White, 1997).

Thus different presentations (e.g. needs for interpersonal distance versus needs for close attachments and intimacy) require different responses from therapists. Linehan (1993) has articulated the central dialectical balance that therapists might seek to achieve: between an orientation to change and yet acceptance of how the person is presenting; between the belief that change is possible and a responsivity to set-backs; and between providing nurturance and promoting independence (taking care *for* the person, rather than taking care *of* them). Writing about immature defences, Vaillant (1992) argues a fundamentally similar ethos: the personality disorders 'respond better to our empathy and forbearance than to our confrontation and rejection'. He states: 'an effective way to alter a person's choice of defensive style under stress is to make his or her social milieu more predictable and supportive' – hence the potentially 'holding' function of the secure hospital (Cox, 1986).

Psychotherapies serve to free 'individuals from the limitations of their own construct systems, in part by changing and elaborating the way they may construe problematic experiences' (Brewin and Power, 1997). A key issue in therapy is often how to help individuals see that they may be treating themselves or others unreasonably, and yet not shame them in the process (Gilbert, 1997). Those whose lives have been scripted by violence are typically exceptionally sensitive to the intolerable emotion of shame: violence is the ultimate humiliation (Gilligan, 2000). The offending of patients with personality disorder raises special additional pressures within the working alliance. Sometimes unacceptable behaviour is conflated with personality, and triggers anxieties in staff about the ethics of providing treatment for offenders who are not 'mentally ill' (Blackburn, 2000; Coffey, 2000).

Clinical interventions for patients who have resorted to serious violence require delivery via a discourse that incorporates the moral aspects of psychological conflicts (Goldner, 1999). Criminological formulation (i.e. assessment of the factors that led to the development and maintenance of violence) plays a central role in offender treatment pathways (Howells et al., 1997). The implicit and explicit 'explanations' for offending behaviour we refer to can carry associated risks of *promoting* the avoidance of responsibility by perpetrators, who might be persuaded to attribute responsibility to external events, stressors, the actions of others and/or medical/psychological conditions that are not subject to their personal control (Jenkins, 1990). In working to reduce offending, we can decline to attribute responsibility for offending to factors beyond the person's influence, whilst inviting him or her to take responsibility for respectful action in the future.

A CASE EXAMPLE

By way of illustration, the following is a fictitious case of a patient who is not identical to any one person with whom we have worked, but whose story shares the features of several.

Daniel Rogers is a man of 29 years, who spent 8 of these living in a special unit within high hospital security, which provides services to young male offenders with personality disturbance.

Daniel was born with a hearing impairment and a club foot, which caused him to experience separations (via early hospital experiences and deafness) from his parents from an early age. He recalls being told that he would never walk. His mother went to hospital with him as a small child; later, his father (who worked in the local neighbourhood and was often at home during the day) became more involved. When his mother got a job working night shifts, Daniel's father encouraged his children to sleep with him. Daniel competed with his sisters for his father's love, especially at times when he had been in trouble for getting behind and into fights (usually he kicked out at people) at school. When the fights at school spilled over into life at home, Daniel's father tried to beat sense into him, this being the tradition for child management in his own family.

Daniel's anger started to take control of his life: it destroyed his friendships; his mother and sisters were afraid of him. Quietly, during the day whilst they were at school, he killed their guinea-pigs, the discovery of which placed an intolerable strain on relationships at home. Eventually, Mr and Mrs Rogers decided that the only solution would be for Daniel to move away to a place where other people could handle his behaviour.

Unfortunately for Daniel, he was moved quickly from one children's home to another, where the staff had the same ideas as Mr Rogers senior about how to beat sense into teenagers. Daniel's sense of injustice became so great that it could be triggered with the slightest misdemeanour. His mood swung between extremes of feeling; he often entertained thoughts of dramatic ways to end his life. When he was sent back to the family home, aged just 17, one evening Daniel and his father argued about whether or not Daniel could have a lift to the off-licence. On his return, having consumed several cans of strong lager (which he had learnt to drink at speed at the children's home), Daniel picked up a knife that was lying on the sideboard in the kitchen and stabbed his father to death, also attacking his older sister, who was present at the scene.

Daniel was admitted to a secure hospital from remand prison aged 18. On remand, he made a serious attempt to take his life by slitting his wrists. He was assessed in hospital to be severely depressed and to meet criteria for borderline (impulsive) and antisocial personality disorders. His interpersonal style was experienced as dominant and coercive at times. He had reading difficulties that were not entirely linked to absences in the education he had received, but there was no evidence of brain damage. His speech was often difficult to follow.

On admission, and for at least a further 12 months, he was consumed with grief over the loss of contact with his family, who had decided to disown him, and especially the death of his father (see Pollock, 1999). This was managed by referral to a male nurse therapist, who listened regularly to Daniel's experience of shock and anger about the losses in his life, and attempted to help him manage his distress via cognitive–behavioural strategies. These weekly sessions were alternated with a series of assessment and intervention sessions with a speech and language therapist, whose aim was to help Daniel practise techniques for lip reading and self-expression (Thacker, 2000). He joined an unstructured group with a psychotherapist trained as a group analyst, members of the nursing staff and five other young men, all of whom were relatively new to the unit. A recurrent theme in the group involved frustration with life on the unit. It seemed to staff on the ward that Daniel reserved his most challenging behaviour for them: he was prone to explosions of rage if he was kept waiting, or touched without warning, or in receipt of the answer 'No'.

At his second annual case conference, some gloom was aired about the likelihood of him being able to 'change'. Staff shared their weariness about the lack of usefulness of their attempts to monitor his needs, and the amount of damage he had done to the lockers in the kitchen area when he punched and kicked them. A referral to the ward-based anger management group (see Novaco, 1997) was agreed as a partial solution. Daniel consented to participate, not because he believed he had trouble with his anger, but because he had worked out in advance who else would be likely to be in the group – his best friend on the unit had already been referred. The group lasted for 12 months, during which time his nurse therapy sessions ended because the member of staff moved to a new post. Daniel had found the sessions helpful: this time *he* made the request for more individual work. Staff debated whether or not to support this request. Eventually, he was referred to a female clinical psychologist, whose brief was to explore issues of anger in parallel with the group sessions. Four months after these meetings commenced, Daniel disclosed to his primary nurse that he had been sexually abused by his father between the ages of 5 and 11 years. His mood appeared low for the subsequent 18 months. He nevertheless completed an anger management group and a group centred on interpersonal skills (Quayle and Moore, 1998).

At his fourth case conference, Daniel was transferred to another unstructured psychotherapy group, facilitated by a medical and nursing staff team, where he joined others who had also been on the ward for more than 2 years. They were talking openly about their attitudes towards their offending at the first session he attended. This was very challenging to Daniel, who was preoccupied with talking about the ways in which *he* had been victimized and how the revenge that he had exacted (his father's life) was a small, and reasonable, price to pay. With much encouragement from his primary nurse, he managed to keep attending the group sessions, despite often arriving late and saying little. He told the other group members that he was deaf, was not prepared to wear his hearing aid, and had no interest in reading their lips. Instead, for a short period, following assessment of his previous use of alcohol (Quayle et al., 1996, 1998), he put his energies into attending educational sessions on alcohol and drugs in the education centre. In his individual sessions, Daniel felt the need to re-visit the issue of his experience of abuse and its consequences. He explored the core beliefs and assumptions about himself, others and the world that were organizing his behaviour on a daily basis (Padesky, 1994).

Daniel began to appear much less angry to staff: they noticed that they had forgotten how intolerant of delay he used to be. He got involved in an art therapy group (Klugman, 1999) as part of his activities, and took up bricklaying. He was reporting that he was still interested in revenge as a way of dealing with the 'bad' behaviour of others, but he was also demonstrating a readiness to learn about other ways of expressing himself.

During his fifth year on the unit, Daniel got into an altercation with another patient, who had a history of sex offending. The resolution of this conflict took place over the course of the subsequent year, during which Daniel turned to his fellow group members for support. Initially, they agreed that his anger at the other patient was entirely justified; moreover, they shared it. Later, the group began to notice that they were 'going round in circles' with their anger. Advice poured in about how Daniel might take responsibility for *not* seeking revenge, and how he might 'let things go' instead. Initially this was mystifying and deeply uncomfortable to him. Gradually, he discovered that he had not lost the respect of his peers through tolerating the presence of the person who had committed sexual offences. In fact, his tolerance was commended by the clinical team, including his Responsible Medical Officer (RMO), whose opinion he particularly valued. Daniel began to feel as if he could succeed at things. He won an award in the education centre for his painting of 'life behind bars' at about this time, which he was allowed to attach to the wall of his room. This was the first certificate he had ever received. He experienced a strong desire to celebrate this news with members of his family.

At his seventh case conference, members of a new team from a medium-secure psychiatric unit were invited to meet Daniel. They listened to the story of his background, and the work he had done in the preceding year with the ward social worker, his primary nurse and mother, who had agreed, after several years of no contact, to meet with her son. Daniel had been attending a structured group about families and relationships (Moore et al., 2000) when he remembered that he was not the only person in his family to have experienced abuse. He established telephone contact with his sisters, and became a source of support to them, particularly his younger sister, who had recently had a baby with an older man who had been accused of indecent assault. He shared with his sisters the work he had done on abuse with the psychologist.

In the year before he moved to the medium-secure hospital unit, 8 years after his fatal stabbing of his father and his wounding of his sister, Daniel engaged in another anger management group (based off the ward), this time with a very different motivation and awareness of his need to control any tendency towards aggressive behaviour. He also participated in a group on victim empathy, which was attended by seven other patients, including those with a history of sex offending. After the session in which he role-played events during the evening of his offence from the viewpoint of his sister, Daniel cried for a long time in his room. He told the group the next day that he had mixed feelings for his father, which included something called love, and that this was a very difficult feeling to talk about. His fellow group members said little, but listened intently to his words. In their review of this group work, some of them said that they thought he was ready to leave the hospital.

The story of Daniel illustrates the need for persistence in the provision of services, introduced, and possibly re-introduced, at suitable times during a treatment programme that addresses both mental health and 'criminogenic' needs, informed by multi-disciplinary and peer review. It underlines the need for a true biopsychosocial approach in which targeted psychological therapies can complement occupational, educational and social opportunities in a safe and structured in-patient milieu.

Lengthy follow-up periods are required in this work.

> After nearly 3 years, Daniel successfully moved from a medium-secure hospital service to a room in a purpose-built hostel in an area at some distance from his town of origin. He experienced this latter move as the most challenging hurdle he had faced following his manslaughter of his father. He is fearful of isolation, and makes use of the support offered on a weekly basis by members of the community team who are closely linked with his hostel. Some members of his family visit from time to time. He is now very close to his younger sister, a single parent, who values his assistance in the task of raising her child.

FURTHER OBSERVATIONS

A comprehensive and effective treatment plan for a personality disordered offender patient is likely to require the integration of many therapeutic approaches, including behavioural, affective, cognitive, social and relational, insight and awareness-raising, usually via the collaboration of therapists from different disciplines and orientations. Each patient will require a different intervention plan, which affords him/her valued roles in advancing his/her own progress. Other patients can be insightful collaborators in this process and in the assessment of the risks that are inevitably involved (Cox, 1982).

The core of the change process constitutes a re-evaluation by the patient of well-rehearsed behaviours and cognitive schemas that have represented that which is familiar, whilst also being associated with discomfort or distress (e.g. 'I am dangerous, bad, lonely, unlovable' etc.). The change process may usefully be formulated as the reversal or 'unlearning' of 'maladaptive' patterns of thought and behaviour. This conceptualization invites the patient to conceive of his or her early life not merely in terms of missed opportunities for adaptive learning, but also with an emphasis on the learning of *mal*adaptive behaviours, feelings and thoughts, and of having, up to now, got many things 'wrong'. A possible consequence of this formulation may be that low or fragile self-esteem, so often noted in those with a diagnosis of personality disorder, will be further threatened, and a successful outcome to therapy (including the reduction of future risk) will be less likely, or slower to emerge. Motivation to change depends not only on an awareness and acceptance of the need to change, but also on the presence of sufficient self-esteem and self-efficacy to make it possible (Miller et al., 1988; McMurran and Hollin, 1993).

The process of change may well be slow and painful for both patients and clinicians, and many pitfalls can occur along the way. Well-established learned behaviours do not immediately extinguish when they are no longer reinforced: intermittent reinforcement (albeit inadvertently in many instances) is a particularly effective way of *maintaining* behaviour and increasing resistance to change. Different factors can control the reinforcers that occur for offender patients living together within a closed institution. Other patients may endorse the message that engagement in 'difficult' therapies and responsibility taking are not necessary for moving on, or may be perceived to 'get away with things', and still make progress towards discharge. Clinicians may find themselves characterized as 'nurturing' or 'critical' parent figures by patients or, indeed, other staff members, thus recreating reliance on defences (such as splitting) that have so often been a feature of the patient's past experience. Beyond the hospital, beliefs, often influenced by media stereotypes of 'psychopaths' as monsters who can never change, easily overwhelm competing feelings of self-worth and the desire to act in responsible ways.

Behaviour patterns reflect the social assumptions of the time, which, in contemporary society, can shift rapidly. Therapists and clinicians may be experienced as representing moral and social values that are outdated and worthless. Yet, whilst a powerful desire to leave secure conditions may be a sufficient reinforcer to facilitate change within the institution, if the patient does not internalize certain core social values (which reinforce non-offending behaviour), he or she is unlikely to maintain that change beyond its walls.

CONCLUSION

Learning theory has much to contribute to the process and maintenance of change, but itself presents a challenge to the conceptualization of that change as the reversal of 'maladaptive' learning. In order for a behaviour to be learnt and to become part of the person's repertoire, it must be more reinforcing than 'not behaving in that way'. Thus behaviours which in therapy are identified as 'maladaptive' and in need of change have been experienced, at least at some time in the person's life, as adaptive and perhaps the only possible survival strategies. Offending behaviours, which later come to be accepted as unreasonable and inexcusable, are likely to have been perceived at the time as justifiable and inevitable.

It is the understanding that violent offending behaviour can be identified both as a maladaptive response, if re-used to try to solve future problems, and as the seemingly only possible response to past dilemmas, that makes the practice of CBT workable in forensic settings. The (paradoxical) acknowledgement that offending behaviour may have had an adaptive function, whilst demanding and believing in the possibility of change, is a core element in the environment that enables offender patients to re-evaluate and abandon long-established patterns of thinking and behaviour.

REFERENCES

Abraham K (1927). *Selected Papers of Karl Abraham*. New York: Brunner/Mazel, reprinted 1979.

Adshead G and Van Velsen C (1996). Psychotherapeutic work with victims of trauma. In: Cordess C and Cox M (eds), *Forensic Psychotherapy: Crime, Psychodynamics and the Offender Patient*, Vol. II: *Mainly Practice*. London: Jessica Kingsley, 355–69.

Arntz A (1994). Treatment of borderline personality disorder: a challenge for cognitive–behavioural therapy. *Behaviour, Research and Therapy* **32**:419–30.

Bandura A (1969). *Principles of Behavior Modification*. New York: Holt, Rinehart and Winston.

Bandura A (1986). *Social Foundations of Thought and Action: A Social Cognitive Theory*. Englewood Cliffs, NJ: Prentice Hall.

Beck AT (1970). Cognitive therapy: nature and relation to behaviour therapy. *Behaviour Therapy* **1**:184–200.

Beck AT (1976). *Cognitive Therapy and the Emotional Disorders*. New York: International Universities Press.

Beck AT, Freeman A, Pretzer J et al. (1990). *Cognitive Therapy of Personality Disorders*. New York: Guilford Press.

Becker M, Love CC and Hunter ME (1997). Intractability is relative: behaviour therapy in the elimination of violence in psychotic forensic patients. *Legal and Criminological Psychology* **2**:89–101.

Blackburn R (2000). Treatment or incapacitation? Implications of research on personality disorders for the management of dangerous offenders. *Legal and Criminological Psychology* **5**:1–21.

Brewin CR and Power MJ (1997). Meaning and psychological therapy: overview and introduction. In: Power MJ and Brewin CR (eds), *The Transformation of Meaning in Psychological Therapies. Integrating Theory and Practice*. Chichester: John Wiley and Sons, 1–14.

Chiesa M (2000). Hospital adjustment in personality disorder patients admitted to a therapeutic community milieu. *British Journal of Medical Psychology* **73**:259–67.

Coffey M (2000). Working with sex offenders. In: Chaloner C and Coffey M (eds), *Forensic Mental Health Nursing: Current Approaches.* Oxford: Blackwell Science, 41–59.

Cox M (1982). The psychotic patient as co-therapist. In: Pines M and Rafaelsen L (eds), *The Individual and the Group.* New York: Plenum Press, 205–10.

Cox M (1986). The 'holding function' of dynamic psychotherapy in a custodial setting: a review. *Journal of the Royal Society of Medicine* **79**:162–4.

Dattilio F and Padesky C (1990). *Cognitive Therapy for Couples.* Sarasota, FL: Professional Resource Exchange.

Dickerson V and Zimmerman J (1995). A constructionist exercise in anti-pathologising. *Journal of Systemic Therapies* **14**:33–45.

Freud S (1905). Three essays on the Theory of Sexuality. In: Strachey J (ed.), *The Standard Edition of the Complete Psychological Works of Sigmund Freud.* London: Hogarth Press, 130–243.

Gilbert P (1997). The biopsychosociology of meaning. In: Power MJ and Brewin CR (eds), *The Transformation of Meaning in Psychological Therapies. Integrating Theory and Practice.* Chichester: John Wiley and Sons, 33–56.

Gilligan J (2000). *Violence. Reflections on Our Deadliest Epidemic.* London: Jessica Kingsley.

Goldner V (1999). Morality and multiplicity: perspectives on the treatment of violence in intimate life. *Journal of Marital and Family Therapy* **25**:325–36.

Hollin C (1993). Advances in the psychological treatment of delinquent behaviour. *Criminal Behaviour and Mental Health* **3**:142–7.

Howells K, Watt B, Hall G and Baldwin S (1997). Developing programmes for violent offenders. *Legal and Criminological Psychology* **2**:117–28.

Hughes G, Hogue T, Hollin C and Champion H (1997). First-stage evaluation of a treatment programme for personality disordered offenders. *Journal of Forensic Psychiatry* **8**:515–17.

Jenkins A (1990). *Invitations to Responsibility. The Therapeutic Engagement of Men who are Violent and Abusive.* Adelaide, South Australia: Dulwich Centre Publications.

Kelly GA (1955). *The Psychology of Personal Constructs,* Vols 1 and 2. New York: Norton.

Klugman S (1999). Art therapy and art education within a secure setting. *Journal of the British Association of Art Therapists* **4**:29–34.

Laws DR (ed.) (1989). *Relapse Prevention with Sex Offenders.* New York: Guilford Press.

Layden MA, Newman CF, Freeman A and Byers Morse S (1993). *Cognitive Therapy of Borderline Personality Disorder.* Boston, MA: Allyn and Bacon.

Linehan M (1993). *Cognitive Behavioral Treatment of Borderline Personality Disorder.* New York: Guilford Press.

Linehan MM, Armstrong HE, Suarez A, Allmon D and Heard HL (1991). Cognitive–behavioural treatment of chronically parasuicidal borderline patients. *Archives of General Psychiatry* **48**:1060–4.

Linehan MM, Heard H and Armstrong HE (1993). Naturalistic follow-up of a behavioural treatment for chronically parasuicidal borderline patients. *Archives of General Psychiatry* **50**:971–4.

Linehan MM, Tutek DA, Heard HL and Armstrong HE (1994). Interpersonal outcome of cognitive behavioral treatment for chronic suicidal borderline patients. *American Journal of Psychiatry* **151**:1771–6.

Lösel F (1998). Treatment and management of psychopaths. In: Cooke DJ, Forth A and Hare R (eds), *Psychopathy: Theory, Research and Implications for Society.* The Netherlands: Kluwer Academic Publishers, 303–54.

Macphail DS and Cox M (1975). Dynamic psychotherapy with dangerous patients. *Psychotherapy and Psychosomatics* **25**:13–19.

Magnavita JJ (2000). *Relational Therapy for Personality Disorders.* Chichester: John Wiley & Sons.

Marshall WL, Anderson D and Fernandez Y (eds) (1999). *Cognitive–Behavioural Treatment of Sexual Offenders.* Chichester: John Wiley & Sons.

McGoldrick M and Gerson R (1985). *Genograms in Family Assessment.* New York: Norton.

McMurran M and Hollin CR (1993). *Young Offenders and Alcohol Related Crime.* Chichester: John Wiley & Sons.

Meichenbaum D (1977). *Cognitive Behavior Modification: An Integrative Approach.* New York: Plenum Press.

Meichenbaum D (1985). Cognitive behavioral therapies. In: Lynn SJ and Garske JP (eds), *Contemporary Psychotherapies: Models and Methods.* Columbus, OH: Charles E. Merrill Publishing Company.

Mikesell RH, Lusterman DD and McDaniel SH (eds) (1995). *Integrating Family Therapy: Handbook of Family Psychology and Systems Theory.* Washington, DC: American Psychological Association.

Miller WR, Sovereign RG and Krege B (1988). Motivational interviewing with problem drinkers, II: The drinker's check-up as preventive intervention. *Behavioural Psychotherapy* **16**:251–68.

Millon T (1995). Foreword. In: Derksen J (ed.), *Personality Disorders: Clinical and Social Perspectives. Assessment and Treatment Based on DSM-IV and ICD-10.* Chichester: John Wiley & Sons.

Moore E, Manners A, Lee J, Quayle M and Wilkinson E (2000). Trauma in the family: groupwork on family awareness for men in high security hospital. *Criminal Behaviour and Mental Health* **10**:242–55.

Mowrer OH (1947). On the dual nature of learning: a reinterpretation of 'conditioning' and 'problem solving'. *Harvard Educational Review* **11**:102–48.

Mowrer OH (1960). *Learning Theory and Behavior.* New York: John Wiley & Sons.

Newton L, Coles D and Quayle M (2005). A form of relapse prevention for men in a high security hospital. *Criminal Behaviour and Mental Health* (in press).

Newton M (1998). Changes in measures of personality, hostility and locus of control during residence in a prison therapeutic community. *Legal and Criminological Psychology* **3**:209–23.

Novaco RW (1997). Remediating anger and aggression with violent offenders. *Legal and Criminological Psychology* **2**:77–88.

Padesky C (1994). Schema change processes in cognitive therapy. *Clinical Psychology and Psychotherapy* **1**:267–78.

Padesky C (2005). *Constructing a New Self: A Cognitive Therapy Approach to Personality Disorders.* London: Cognitive Workshops.

Paris J (1996). *Social Factors in the Personality Disorders. A Biopsychosocial Approach to Etiology and Treatment.* Cambridge: Cambridge University Press.

Pavlov IP (1927). *Conditioned Reflexes: An Investigation of the Physiological Activity of the Cerebral Cortex.* Oxford/New York: Oxford University Press.

Pollock PH (1999). When the killer suffers: post-traumatic stress reactions following homicide. *Legal and Criminological Psychology* **4**:185–202.

Quayle M, Clark F, Renwick SJ, Hodge J and Spencer T (1998). Alcohol and secure hospital patients: I. An examination of the nature and prevalence of alcohol problems in secure hospital patients. *Psychology, Crime and Law* **4**:27–41.

Quayle M, Darling P, Perkins D, Lumsden J, Forshaw D and McKeown O (1996). The assessment of patients in a forensic addictive behaviours unit within a special hospital setting. *Journal of Substance Misuse* **1**:160–4.

Quayle M and Moore E (1998). Evaluating the impact of structured groupwork with men in maximum security. *Criminal Behaviour and Mental Health* **8**:77–91.

Reiss D, Quayle M, Brett T and Meux C (1998). Dramatherapy for mentally disordered offenders: changes in levels of anger. *Criminal Behaviour and Mental Health* **8**:139–53.

Renwick SJ, Black L, Ramm M and Novaco RW (1997). Anger treatment with forensic hospital patients. *Legal and Criminological Psychology* **2**:103–16.

Ryle A (1997). *Cognitive Analytic Therapy and Borderline Personality Disorder: The Model and the Method.* Chichester: John Wiley & Sons.

Ryle A and Beard H (1993). The integrative effect of reformulation: cognitive–analytic therapy with a patient with borderline personality disorder. *British Journal of Medical Psychology* **66**:249–58.

Ryle A and Golynkina K (2000). Effectiveness of time-limited cognitive analytic therapy of borderline personality disorder: factors associated with outcome. *British Journal of Medical Psychology* **73**:197–210.

Skinner BF (1974). *About Behaviorism.* New York: Knopf.

Thacker A (2000). What can we learn from the deaf patient? In: France J and Kramer S (eds), *Communication and Mental Illness.* London: Jessica Kingsley, 251–61.

Thorndike EL (1931). *Human Learning.* New York: Appleton-Century-Crofts.

Truax CB, Wargo DG and Silber LD (1966). Effects of group psychotherapy with high adequate empathy and nonpossessive warmth upon female institution-alised delinquents. *Journal of Abnormal Psychology* **71**:267–74.

Turner RM (1989). Case study evaluation of a bio-cognitive–behavioural approach for the treatment of borderline personality disorder. *Behaviour Therapy* **20**:477–89.

Vaillant GE (1992). The beginning of wisdom is never calling a patient a borderline; or the clinical manage-ment of immature defences in the treatment of indi-viduals with personality disorders. *Journal of Psychotherapy Practice and Research* **1**:117–34.

Wachtel PL (1985). Integrative psychodynamic therapy. In: Lynn SJ and Garshe JP (eds), *Contemporary Psychotherapies: Models and Methods.* Columbus, OH: Charles E. Merrill Publishing, 287–329.

Watt BD and Howells K (1999). Skills training for aggression control: evaluation of an anger manage-ment programme for violent offenders. *Legal and Criminological Psychology* **4**:285–300.

Wessler RL and Hankin-Wessler S (1989). Cognitive group therapy. In: Freeman A, Simon KM, Beutler LE and Arnowitz H (eds), *Comprehensive Handbook of Cognitive Therapy.* New York: Plenum Press, 559–81.

Westen D. (1991). Cognitive–behavioural interventions in the psychoanalytic psychotherapy of borderline personality disorders. *Clinical Psychology Review* **11**:211–30.

White M (1997). *Narratives of Therapists' Lives.* Adelaide, South Australia: Dulwich Centre Publications.

Wood RM, Grossman LS and Fichtner CG (2000). Psychological assessment, treatment and outcome with sex offenders. *Behavioural Sciences and the Law* **18**:23–41.

Wright JH, Thase ME, Beck AT and Ludgate JW (eds) (1993). *Cognitive Therapy with Inpatients: Developing a Cognitive Milieu.* New York: Guilford Press.

Young JE (1999). *Cognitive Therapy for Personality Disorders: A Schema-Focused Approach*, third edition. Sarasota, FL: Professional Resource Press.

Chapter 12

DYNAMIC PSYCHOTHERAPY FOR SEVERE PERSONALITY DISORDER

Conor Duggan

... the treatment of the antisocial tendency is not psycho-analysis but management, a going to meet and match the moment of hope.

Winnicott (1956)

INTRODUCTION

At the Third European Congress for the Study of Personality Disorders, held in Sheffield in 1998, there was a symposium to discuss the most appropriate treatment for a range of personality disturbance. The participants were presented with a number of clinical vignettes depicting different types of personality disorder and their task was to rate the suitability of a number of psychological approaches for each disorder. The consensus view was a conclusive rejection of dynamic modes of treatment. This is in accord with the currently accepted view that a structured psychotherapeutic approach is more valuable for personality disordered individuals (McGuire, 1995). In addition, even among those who favour a dynamic approach, there is general agreement that the kinds of patients being considered in this volume (i.e. those with significant ego deficits) are the least likely to benefit from this form of treatment. (The term 'severe personality disorder' is used in this chapter to refer to those with a combination of personality disorder – largely of an antisocial or borderline type – together with an offending history.)

Alongside this conclusive rejection of dynamic therapy for those with severe personality disorder there is an equally strongly held but contradictory view expressed from the coalface. This states that when dealing with these very difficult individuals, a dynamic understanding is very helpful, perhaps even essential, if staff are to continue with their work. More specifically, many believe that in order to avoid the type of scandals that have occurred recently concerning in-patient personality disorder units in particular, the capacity of the staff to think about and make sense of their encounters through some form of dynamic understanding is important. This applies especially to those who act out in a violent manner, the very patients that dynamic therapists feel they are least able to help.

This chapter seeks to achieve a rapprochement between these two (on the surface at least) contradictory positions. Briefly, taking these two positions at face value, it is argued that a dynamic approach is generally of more direct benefit to the staff and only indirectly beneficial to the patient. That is to say, there are some real constraints to the direct delivery of dynamic treatment for a group for which persistent lying together with severe acting out are some of the defining features of their personality. To support this position, the chapter starts with a brief review of what evidence there is for the effectiveness of dynamic treatment for those with personality disorder of any type. It then discusses the nature of personality disorder from an interpersonal perspective that provides not only a justification for the importance of a dynamic understanding, but also a rationale for staff supervision and support. An interpersonal approach also allows for the rigorous evaluation of the effectiveness of an intervention that does not rely solely on randomized controlled trials. In an era in which there are ever-shrinking resources for mental health services, it is imperative that dynamic therapy be shown to be effective, and an interpersonal theory provides a context in which this might be established.

Before dealing with these issues, it is important that dynamic therapy is not seen to be in competition with more structured psychological techniques, or with drugs, for the treatment of personality disorder. This would be a grave mistake, for the field has moved on from sterile turf battles about which of the therapies is most appropriate to considering when and for whom a particular treatment or blends of treatments are most suitable. The author is taking it as a given, therefore, that some form of integration of different approaches is most useful for the treatment of personality disorder. There are three reasons for this belief. First, personality disorders are heterogeneous and thus no one form of intervention is likely to be equally effective for different individuals. Second, there is little evidence that one form of treatment is likely to be effective for any one personality disordered individual over a long period of time. Third, as personality disturbance is a long-term problem, it makes sense for the therapist to share the burden and to use different approaches at different times.

However, when these different approaches are combined, as inevitably they are in real life, the dynamic therapist has something specific and useful to say as he or she encourages the patient to reflect upon and understand what has just occurred. For instance, Otto Kernberg, who could be regarded as a proponent of a pure dynamic approach, has no reservation about involving outside agencies – 'with or without the patient's approval'– in the case of a borderline patient who becomes suicidal when depressed (Kernberg et al., 1997). Once the crisis has passed, however, the dynamic therapist needs to interpret the reasons that moved him or her away from a position of technical neutrality. Kernberg responds, in an example of dealing with a borderline patient who cuts, with the statement: 'Now that you no longer cut yourself, we can return to the question of why you chose to do this to yourself'. The point is that the dynamic therapist has to be flexible enough to involve outside agencies and treatments as appropriate, but, at the same time as re-establishing the therapeutic frame once the immediate crisis has been managed, the patient is encouraged to reflect upon the material, perhaps in a way that is unique among the psychotherapies.

THE EVIDENCE FOR DYNAMIC THERAPIES AND PERSONALITY DISORDER

Although there is little evidence from controlled research on the effectiveness of dynamic therapy for personality disorder, there is still a substantial body of evidence from other sources. This area has been usefully reviewed by Gabbard (1997), from which the following is a distillation. There are only two controlled trials using dynamic psychotherapy for individuals with personality disorder. Woody et al. (1985) studied the effects of either para-professional drug counselling alone or counselling plus psychotherapy (either supportive–expressive or cognitive–behavioural) on substance misusers (with co-morbid antisocial personality disorder) who were randomly assigned to one or other of these treatments. Those with antisocial personality disorder who were also depressed made significant improvement in terms of symptoms and employment, while their drug use and illegal activity were reduced. Winston et al. (1994) compared the effects of brief adaptive therapy (40 weeks) or short-term dynamic therapy (40 weeks) on a group of personality disordered subjects (predominantly cluster C personality disordered). They found no difference between the two treatment groups, with both improving compared with the controls in terms of target complaints, symptoms and social adjustment.

In addition to these two controlled studies, several longitudinal studies have produced encouraging findings. The Menninger Psychotherapy Research Project (Kernberg et al., 1972) has been one of the most important and influential of these because of the detail collected on the patients. Although this project antedated the development of diagnostic interviews, there is general agreement that the majority of patients had borderline personality disorder. The treatments evaluated included psychoanalysis, expressive psychotherapy and supportive psychotherapy. Although the initial report (Kernberg, 1972) – which depended on statistical and quantitative data – showed that expressive psychotherapy was superior to supportive therapy, subsequent reports that examined all the evidence came to the opposite conclusion; namely, that for those with significant ego weakness, supportive therapy was superior (Horwitz, 1974; Wallerstein, 1986). Two of the report's more general conclusions are especially pertinent: (a) the borderline patients in the study were not a homogeneous group, so that no single psychotherapeutic approach was especially suitable for all the patients; and (b) the therapists employed both expressive and supportive approaches when treating individual patients.

Stevenson and Meares (1992) reported on the outcome for 30 borderline patients who were treated with dynamic therapy twice weekly for 1 year. Compared with the patient's course in the year prior to the intervention, the treatment reduced the amount of time away from work (from 4.7 to 1.4 months/year), the number of visits to medical practitioners (decreased to one-seventh), the time spent as an in-patient in hospital (by 50 per cent), and the number of hospital admissions (decreased by 59 per cent). An important aspect of this study was a 5-year follow-up. Significantly, this showed that these gains were maintained and that approximately one-third were no longer diagnosable as borderline (Stevenson and Meares, 1995).

Another uncontrolled study with impressive effects was a prospective Norwegian outpatient study in which a range of personality disturbance was treated with dynamic therapy based on object relations theory and self-psychology (Monsen et al., 1995a). The mean duration of treatment was 2 years, with a 5-year follow-up. At termination, three-quarters of the sample no longer met the criteria for a personality disorder diagnosis. Again, these gains were maintained at the 5-year follow-up (Monsen et al., 1995b).

These studies show that dynamic therapy may be effective, although they are subject to three caveats. First, they are uncontrolled and, as personality matures with the passage of time, one could argue that it is this, rather than the impact of the intervention, that has produced the effect. However, as personality changes relatively slowly, these gains in the shorter term are unlikely to be due to maturation alone. Second, the absence of controls makes it impossible to identify which specific aspect of the treatment was effective. Third, the personality disorders subject to these interventions, with the exception of the Woody et al. (1985) trial, are largely of a borderline or cluster C (i.e. anxious) type and have excluded those with antisocial personality disorder. Therefore the findings of these studies have only some applicability to the content of this chapter.

One other issue deserves comment. As personality disorder is a long-term disturbance, one might expect that such individuals might require more treatment compared with those with other disorders. This is an issue that has been addressed by Howard et al. (1986), who showed that borderline personality disorder patients required more sessions of treatment compared with anxious or depressed patients. The same group examined the rate of change in acute and chronic symptoms and characterological change in a large group of outpatients treated mainly with dynamic therapy. With 1 year of treatment, patients with acute, chronic and characterological symptoms had a 68–98 per cent, 60–86 per cent and 50 per cent chance of recovery, respectively (Howard et al., 1986).

PERSONALITY DISORDER FROM AN INTERPERSONAL PERSPECTIVE

Although the evidence from these intervention studies is encouraging (albeit certainly not conclusive), additional support for the importance of a dynamic understanding of personality disorder is provided by interpersonal theory. Interpersonal theory in this context is a super-ordinate system within which one or more specific psychological approaches (including dynamic therapy) might be used either singly or in combination to effect change. Although interpersonal theory in that sense is not linked to any particular psychotherapeutic approach, there is a close relationship between this as a system and dynamic processes, as it has its genesis in the work of the Neo-Freudian Harry Stack Sullivan (1953).

The importance of interpersonal theory in the context of this chapter is its focus on interpersonal relationships. Many believe that the core disturbance of personality disorder lies in the area of interpersonal relationships.

Vaillant (1987), for instance, separates personality disorder from other types of psychopathology as follows.

Unlike psychosis and neurosis, personality disorders almost always occur within a social context. It is difficult to imagine a hypochondriac or paranoiac becoming symptomatic on a desert island. In some respects, personality disorder is a means of making painful truce with people we can neither live with nor live without. If neurotic symptoms are the modes by which we cope with unbearable instincts, personality disorder is the mode by which we cope with unbearable people – in past or present time.

Those who work with the personality disordered are only too aware of the disturbed nature of these relationships, as they are often at the receiving end of the dysfunctional process. Lorna Benjamin (1993) – an interpersonal theorist – gives a description of the interaction between the patient with borderline personality disorder and the therapist that will strike a responsive chord with many. After an initial phase during which the therapist is idealized, there is a rapid progression to a phase when the therapist is manoeuvred through various crises to a position in which he or she gradually withdraws from wishing to treat the patient. This withdrawal leads in turn to further attacks on the therapist for not caring and to an escalation of increasingly dangerous behaviour. After the crisis has resolved, the patient once again wishes for further contact. The therapist, frightened by his or her recent experience, acquiesces in order to prevent a further deterioration. However, when the patient returns, the therapist appears distant and resentful, having been traumatized by the previous experience. This is accurately perceived by the patient, who castigates the therapist for his or her hypocrisy and lack of caring. The therapist, feeling even more guilty and resentful, then finds it more difficult to

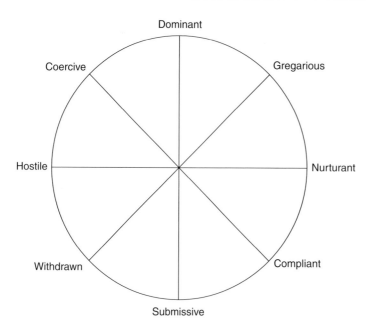

Fig. 12.1 The interpersonal circle

work with the patient. This in turn leads to further crises, and so on. Another important variation in this cycle, which Benjamin also mentions, is that the patient starts to get better but then begins to worry that doing so will lead to the termination of the therapy. Here again, the same cycle of crises and deterioration repeats itself, with the patient demanding more, the therapist feeling despondent and eventually 'burning out'.

We are tempted to focus on the psychopathology of the patient in such descriptions, but, in this vignette, what is interesting is the effect of the patient's behaviour on the therapist. Someone who initially is reasonable and benignly disposed to the patient becomes belittling, aloof and withdrawn. Interpersonal theory explains this transformation by claiming that interpersonal behaviour consists of one individual attempting to elicit specific responses from important others. As an understanding of interpersonal theory is important for much that follows, its essential elements are now described briefly. For more comprehensive coverage of these areas, interested readers are referred to the work of Benjamin (1993), Kiesler (1996), Wiggins (1985) and Blackburn (1998).

Interpersonal theory construes interpersonal behaviour to be a function of the two basic motivations: the need for control (power, dominance) and the need for affiliation (love, friendliness). Human interaction therefore consists of a continual negotiating on these two major relationship issues so that individuals can establish 'how friendly or hostile they will be with each other, and how much in charge or control each will be in their encounters' (Kiesler, 1996). Thus each of us develops an interpersonal style that describes the regularity with which we manage social encounters and relationships.

These two orthogonal dimensions of dominance and affiliation are the major axes around which a circular arrangement (or circumplex) of interpersonal dispositions and styles can be arranged (Fig. 12.1). The theory has two consequences. First, it suggests that a well-adjusted individual would have a wide repertoire of interpersonal styles that could be used appropriately depending on the situation. However, as a particular style becomes more pronounced, the individual is less able to adopt an alternative style. For instance, an individual who has a pronounced dominant interpersonal style will be unable to act in a submissive manner even when it is appropriate to do so. Consequently, the behaviour will be rigid, inflexible and maladaptive (i.e. it will approximate features of a personality disorder).

Second, interpersonal theory proposes that in every interpersonal exchange the particular interpersonal style of one individual has the function of eliciting a complementary response from the other. The basis behind this is that we all attempt to establish relationships with others that are comfortable and anxiety free. To do this, we manoeuvre others who interact with us in automatic and minimally aware ways to adopt positions that are complementary to the positions that we are offering (Kiesler, 1996). To give an example, an individual with a reasoned and not-extreme interpersonal style is likely to evoke a similar response from another; thus their interaction will be mutually rewarding. It also follows that an individual with an extreme and dysfunctional interpersonal style is likely to evoke a similar extreme complementary response, so that someone with a dominant style will be likely to 'pull' submissive responses from those with whom he or she interacts.

This theory has great relevance for the practice of psychotherapy with personality disordered individuals. It predicts, for instance, that the problematic relationship aspects of the disorder are likely to be re-enacted with the therapist. Kiesler (1996) expresses this as follows.

... the client will communicate to the therapist in the same duplicitous way that he or she communicates with other important persons in his or her life – will send the same rigid and evoking messages to the therapist that he or she sends to others. As a result, the therapist will experience 'live' in the sessions the client's distinctive interpersonal problems.

This is very similar to the psychoanalyst James Strachey's (1969) statement on transference, for which the re-enactment with the analyst is:

... far from being the misfortune that at first sight it might seem to be. In fact it gives us our great opportunity. Instead of having to deal as best we may with conflicts of the remote past, which are concerned with dead circumstances and mummified personalities, and whose outcome is already determined, we find ourselves involved in an actual and immediate situation in which we and the patient are the principal characters and the development of which is to some extent at least under our control.

The interpersonal difficulties that arise from managing such personality disordered individuals, far from being a catastrophe, rather provide us with 'our great opportunity', as long as they are handled correctly.

The problem for the therapist (and for others who have to live with a personality disordered individual) is that such an individual is very successful in obtaining self-confirming interpersonal data from those with whom he or she interacts. After all, this is what reaffirms that person's view of the world. Thus the therapist is manoeuvred into behaving in a way that confirms the patient's maladaptive schema. For instance, the borderline patient's fear of abandonment described in Benjamin's vignette is corroborated each time he or she is abandoned by the therapist. This is achieved by the patient creating crisis upon crisis, despite wishing desperately to avoid this very outcome. For the antisocial personality disorder patient, the pathology is different. In this case, the critical issue is not the fear of abandonment (about which the antisocial patient is relatively unconcerned), but rather the fear of not being in control. Just as the borderline patient increases the likelihood of abandonment despite wishing to avoid it, antisocial personality disordered patients often place themselves in a position in which they will be controlled (i.e. in confinement), despite their fear of that very outcome.

Looking at this process from the outside, one can observe an interpersonal dance in which both the patient and therapist are engaged and in which the pathology of one is complemented by the behaviour of the other. The systems therapist Watzlawick (1978) likens this process to a sailboat that is kept stabilized by two sailors, who are hanging out over opposite sides in equal measure. What neither realizes is that the boat would be quite steady were it not for the fact that they are trying so valiantly to steady it. He continues:

It is not difficult to see that in order to change this absurd situation, at least one of them has to do something quite unreasonable, to 'steady' less and not more, since this will immediately force the other to also do less of the same (unless he wants to finish up in the water), and they may eventually find themselves comfortably back inside a steady boat.

In order to break out from this recurrent cycle, it is the duty of the therapist to initiate the change. He or she does this by acting in a manner different from that expected; Murrell (1971) spells this out:

... the burden for initiating change lies primarily with the therapist. To effect change he must introduce new information, or negative feedback to the patient. ... This means, first, that he must respond to the patient in a way that is significantly different from the customary responses the patient receives in his social system.

In interpersonal language, this implies that (Kiesler, 1996):

Therapists should demonstrate the least complementarity in response to statements that are consistent with the problematic style of the patient. In order to discourage such behaviour, the therapist should respond with anticomplementarity. Conversely, therapists should offer complementary communications in response to client statements that represent the opposite of their identified problematic style, in order to encourage these types of behaviours (the goal of interpersonal therapy).

A characteristic of personality disorder is its rigidity, and the dysfunctional interpersonal exchanges of these cluster B personality disorders are maintained often by expressions of intense anger or aggression, particularly by those with an antisocial personality disorder. Thus the threat, if not the direct expressions of hostility, is often used to maintain the homeostasis. Being the object of this coercive control is extremely uncomfortable for staff, so that they in turn will have a tendency either to ignore the antisocial personality disordered individual or to become coercively controlling themselves. Either way, the personality disordered individual succeeds and is able to complain legitimately about being ignored or excessively controlled. This process also offers 'a great opportunity' in that it might allow for the possibility of a more benign experience in the exercise of that control than perhaps the antisocial adult experienced at the hands of his or her primary caregivers. The author believes that this is what Winnicott was referring to in his paper 'The antisocial tendency' (1956); namely, that the antisocial acting out is an attempt by the patient, however misguided, to elicit a different experience from that which he or she obtained in the past. Because of the dysfunctional way in which the individual attempts to obtain this new experience, the likelihood is that it will be unsuccessful, thereby re-affirming his or her view of the world.

STAFF SUPERVISION

As this example of the interaction between staff and the antisocial personality disordered adult makes clear, it is not easy for the patient to break out of this interpersonal self-confirmatory cycle. If it were, patients would have refuted their belief about themselves and their world long ago. Therefore one explanation for the persistence of the personality disorder, despite its clear-cut disadvantages to the subject, is that others with whom the individual interacts become the unwitting players in an interpersonal encounter that reinforces the disorder. As many of these exchanges are covert, it is difficult for the therapist to be aware of them while interacting with the patient. The response to this is to provide supervision for the therapist, as this is considered one way in which covert exchanges can be managed and processed. This is based on the belief that the supervisor, being a distant observer (and usually more experienced) is more likely to avoid being 'pulled in' by the projections of the patient.

Again, interpersonal theory has something useful to say about the process of supervision, for just as there are impasses between the therapist and the patient, there are also impasses between the therapist and the supervisor, and these are often related to one another. Kiesler (1996) gives an interpersonal analysis of this process as follows. When the therapy begins, the therapist is manoeuvred or pulled by the patient to provide a complementary response. As this continues, the therapist becomes increasingly anxious and this is expressed in supervision by the therapist adopting a pattern of behaviour identical to that of the patient. This re-enactment in turn pulls a response from the supervisor, which is similar to that evoked from the therapist by the patient. Thus the same impasse may occur in supervision that is occurring in the therapy and needs to be resolved if the therapy is to succeed. Kiesler (1996) also makes the point that rigidity on the part of the supervisor may create anxiety in the therapist, which in turn will be transmitted to the patient. It is important to stress that there are similarities between the relationship of the patient and therapist and the therapist and his/her supervisor. Thus, just as the patient/therapist problem may be transmitted upward to the therapist/supervision dyad, a problem between the supervisor and therapist may be transmitted downward to the therapist/patient dyad. All of this needs attention if therapy is to succeed. No one doubts the influence of supervision, which is powerful perhaps because of its detachment and the inequality of power between the therapist and supervisor. We have to recognize, however, that supervision introduces another dyad into the process: not only is there a relationship between the patient and therapist, but there is also a relationship between the therapist and supervisor or – perhaps more correctly – a triadic relationship (i.e. between patient, therapist and supervisor). If this re-enactment between therapist and supervisor were shown to be common, it would provide us with a second great opportunity for re-alignment of the personality disordered individual dysfunctional schema. This, however, remains to be demonstrated.

JUDGEMENT OF EGO STRENGTH

It is argued above that a dynamic understanding is especially helpful for staff who have to work with and survive those with personality disorder; but what about offering such treatment directly to those with severe personality difficulties? Or, to put it another way, are there individuals for whom dynamic therapy (or any other form of psychotherapy) is specifically contraindicated? This is a matter of particular concern given that treatability is one of the criteria for detaining those with the legal category of 'psychopathic disorder' under the 1983 Mental Health Act.

There are at least two reasons why one should take this question seriously. First, if the individual selected for the treatment is unlikely to benefit from it, one may be depriving

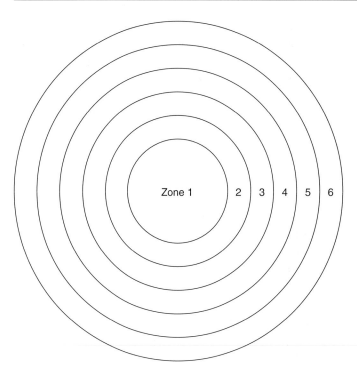

Fig. 12.2 Personality disturbances amenable and non-amenable to psychotherapy (from Stone (1993) reproduced by kind permission of the publisher)

someone else who might achieve something positive from a scarce resource. Second, there is evidence that for some antisocial individuals, treatment within the mental health system is not only of no benefit, but actually makes them worse. Each of these areas is now considered in turn.

First, there is the importance of the selection of personality disordered patients for treatment with dynamic therapy. Michael Stone has made a useful contribution to this debate in his book *Personality Abnormalities – Within and Beyond the Realm of Treatment* (Stone, 1993). He portrays the psychotherapeutic treatment of personality disorder within a series of concentric circles (Fig. 12.2) in which there is a gradual increase in the severity of the personality abnormality between the different zones from inside outwards. Thus individuals in zone 1 require no treatment as they have essentially an adaptive personality. Those in zone 2 require minimal intervention from someone with minimal training and experience. Those in zones 3 and 4 require substantial

intervention from skilled practitioners; these are the individuals who ought to be treated in specialized units. Those in zone 5 are untreatable except by some exceptional intervention, luck or the passage of time. Zone 6 consists of individuals with such serious pathology that they are not treatable with our present armamentarium; according to Stone (1993), the presence of sadistic traits characterizes individuals in this outermost group. This notion of a treatment continuum is useful, and would be of even greater value if one could in some way operationalize the criteria that separate one zone from another.

One of the measures that has been used to determine treatability is the Hare Psychopathy Check List – Revised (PCL-R; Hare, 1991). From a semi-structured interview and detailed chart review, an individual is given a score from 0 to 40, with scores of 30 and above considered to be indicative of psychopathy. The PCL-R has a two-factor structure, with factor 1 comprising many of the classical Clecklian features of psychopathy such as manipulativness, callousness, egocentricity etc., while factor 2 is largely concerned with antisocial behaviour.

The importance of the PCL-R lies in its prognostic validity. Those who load heavily on factor 1 have been shown to use instrumental violence, to retain their psychopathic characteristics over time and to re-offend after discharge. There is also some evidence (Rice et al., 1992) that those with high PCL-R scores who were treated in a therapeutic community were more likely to be convicted of violent recidivism after discharge compared with a matched group who were not treated. This is a counter-intuitive finding, but is believed to represent the true psychopath learning to be more exploitative within a group setting. A long-term follow-up of the Cambridge–Sommerville youth study (McCord, 1978) also showed that the assignment of delinquents to treatment made very little difference to their future re-offending. Indeed, the only significant difference between the groups was that, of the men with criminal records, more of those in the treatment group had committed at least two crimes compared with the controls. One does not want to labour the point, but we have to be aware that doing something (as with any intervention) may be worse than doing nothing. As an aside, dynamic theory has something important to say about the dangers of the omnipotence of therapists.

Another distinction that is of relevance is that between primary and secondary psychopathy (Mealey, 1995). Primary psychopaths are similar to those with a high loading on factor 1 of the PCL-R. That is to say, they have a high genetic loading, are not psychosocially disadvantaged, have a limited capacity to experience emotions, and their antisocial behaviour does not attenuate with age (Duggan, 2000). Conversely, secondary psychopaths are more psychosocially disadvantaged, are not impaired in their capacity to experience emotions (indeed, this capacity may be exaggerated), and their antisocial behaviour is likely to decrease with age. The importance of this distinction is that primary psychopaths do poorly with treatment, whereas the reverse may be true of secondary psychopaths. Following on from this, Mealey (1995), in an interesting contribution from an evolutionary perspective, proposes that primary psychopaths are best served when their misdeeds are promptly discovered and punished, rather than by attempts to manage them within a health service setting. She suggests that secondary psychopaths, conversely, may benefit from a psychotherapeutic intervention – especially some form of parenting skills programme for the parents of such antisocial individuals while they are growing up. Whether one agrees or disagrees with Mealey's proposal, it is produced with sufficient clarity for it to be testable.

Having an instrument with demonstrable prognostic utility such as the PCL-R is a mixed blessing, for, like the Sorcerer's Apprentice, we have at our disposal a powerful tool whose consequences we may not be able to control. Not only are we in a position to determine the long-term incarceration of *individuals* on the basis of data derived from *groups*, but, in addition, we now have an instrument that may also identify individuals who may be precluded from treatment as the indications may be, again on the basis of group data, that they are unlikely to benefit from it. Therefore such individuals may be doubly disadvantaged, i.e. they have a poor prognosis and are deprived of treatment that might improve their long-term course. Thus the PCL-R is a very powerful tool that requires careful application, and the implications of this have not been lost on the instrument's creator, who has written about its potential misuse (Hare, 1998).

There are therefore two major issues facing those who have to provide dynamic therapy for this group of individuals. First, there is at least the theoretical possibility that some may not benefit from, or may even be made worse by, dynamic therapy (or any other interventions). Second, this is a scarce resource and therefore careful attention has to be given to selecting those who might be most likely to benefit from it.

An important aspect of judging which type of intervention is most appropriate is to examine the maturity of the psychological structure of the individual being assessed. Psychodynamics views psychopathology as a product of intrapsychic conflict. This presupposes that there is a clear differentiation between self and object representation, that psychic structures are stable and, finally, that repression has replaced splitting as a main mechanism of defence (Akhtar, 1995). A conflict model requires the development of a strong ego together with mature ego defences.

This maturational model of ego defences has an impressive lineage within classical psychodynamics. For instance, Anna Freud wrote that 'each defense mechanism is first evolved in order to master some specific instinctual urge and so is associated with a particular phase of infantile development' (Freud A, 1976). A similar view has also been developed independently by Vaillant (1987) when writing about personality disorder. He suggested that there is a hierarchy of defensive processes, with some being primitive (e.g. splitting, denial, projective identification, idealization and omnipotence), whereas repression, rationalization and sublimation are more mature. An especially important primitive defence is that of projective identification, in which, according to Kernberg (1992), the individual:

… projects an intolerable intrapsychic experience onto an object, maintains empathy (in the sense of emotional awareness) with what he projects, tries to control the object in the continuing effort to defend against intolerable experience, and unconsciously, in actual interaction with the object, leads the object to experience what has been projected onto him.

This seems an extreme variant of describing the 'pull' that one individual has on another

using interpersonal language. Thus this is another example of the confluence between interpersonal theory and classical psychodynamics. It is important in understanding counter-transference experiences when, say, borderline patients deposit dissociated aspects of themselves onto their therapist and then pressurize the therapist to act them out. Similarly, one could interpret the antisocial personality disordered disavowing their desire for control by projecting this into the system that controls them.

Although this provides a method of understanding the process of working with individuals with severe personality disorder, it does not guarantee that, as a direct treatment, it will be appropriate. This means that for some individuals with severe personality disorder, their psychopathology is based on a deficit rather than on a conflict model. Thus, instead of a mature psychological structure described above, there is defective object consistency, ego weakness, and the employment of primitive defensive mechanisms. Central to this distinction is that conflict-related psychopathology implies intentionality (i.e. that one is the agent of one's thoughts, desires and actions and hence the need is to disguise one's unacceptable wishes) (Akhtar, 1995). For a pathology based on deficit, however:

… it is not a matter of defending oneself against anxiety connected with bad intentions, e.g., forbidden object-directed needs, fantasies, and feelings, as in the case in conflict. What is defended against is primarily anxiety of fragmentation, i.e., losing one's own feeling of identity.

(Killingmo, 1989)

This distinction has implications for technique, for an individual with a deficit-type disorder requires the kind of affirmation and support that accepts his or her experience, rather than the uncovering, interpretative kind. Those who work with mentally disordered offenders will be very aware of the salience of this fear of fragmentation in those with severe personality disorder. This may explain some of the positive findings for supportive psychotherapy in the Menninger Study. One other important consideration that makes this work difficult, particularly with those having an antisocial tendency, is the history of persistent lying that undermines the therapeutic alliance.

As a consequence of this deficit model, one is likely to find few candidates among those with a severe personality disorder who are suitable for dynamic therapy within a forensic setting; that is to say, individuals who are psychologically stable, are of reasonable intelligence, have not misused substances, have motivation, psychological mindedness and honesty – these are unusual attributes among such offender patients. As a consequence of a failure to develop a strong ego, there is an inability to tolerate anxiety, with poor impulse control and severe acting out when under pressure.

Although there may well be individual practitioners who report satisfactory outcomes in treating such patients with dynamic therapy, these are either exceptional practitioners or they have exceptional patients; they cannot be said to represent the mainstream. There is therefore insufficient evidence to make a general recommendation for this approach, especially when resources are so scarce. What would seem more sensible is to reserve a dynamic input as a consultation service for frontline staff so that they are provided with a dynamic understanding that would allow them to carry out their work more satisfactorily. After all, it is they who must bear the brunt of the projections from those who are so disordered. Successful implementation of this approach might very well enable staff to remedy the deficits pointed out above, so that, in time, the patient matures and is able to use dynamic therapy directly in the future. The author believes that this is akin to what

Winnicott (1958) referred to as 'placement' when, in his paper 'The antisocial tendency', he described his failure in dealing with his first patient, who was a delinquent, and gave the following realistic recommendation.

It can be easily seen that the treatment of this boy should have been not psychoanalysis but placement. Psychoanalysis only made sense if added after placement. Since this time I have watched analysts of all kinds fail in the psychoanalysis of antisocial children.

HOW WE FIND THE EVIDENCE FOR 'WHAT WORKS FOR WHOM'

The earlier review highlighted the absence of evidence from randomized controlled trials to support the use of dynamic therapy for individuals with severe personality disorder. This is an important omission, for these multiply disadvantaged individuals are unlikely to obtain the help they require unless it is provided from public funds. Also, those in charge of such funds have an obligation to use the limited resources to the best effect. It is essential, therefore, that we give serious consideration to how we might find the evidence to support this type of approach. Although there are formidable problems in assessing the efficacy of this form of therapy by randomized controlled trials, this nettle has to be grasped and such trials instituted. However, as the following example makes clear, even very well conducted trials can rarely provide a definitive answer to the question of how to establish efficacy for these types of disorders.

The following argument has been adapted from an excellent review of the treatment of sex offenders by Hanson (1997), who pointed out the limitations of relying solely on evidence from randomized controlled trials. He takes, as an example, the Sex Offender Treatment Evaluation Program (SOTEP) that has taken place in the State of California (Marques et al., 1994). This was a well-designed trial that included the random assignment of carefully assessed subjects, the use of state-of-the-art treatment (relapse prevention), thorough evaluations of the offenders' pre-treatment and post-treatment, and the collection of detailed follow-up information during a minimum 5-year follow-up period. This long follow-up period is necessary to draw any valid conclusions concerning the effectiveness of the treatment, as further sex offending may occur at any time after release; however, 5 years was judged to give an adequate time at risk. In passing, it should be pointed out that evaluating an intervention of personality disorder would also require at least an equal period of follow-up, as, again, it is a long-term disturbance.

Hanson (1997) cites a number of problems in interpreting the findings from this study. First, as studies of this type are not only very costly to mount but also require an enormous amount of time and effort to implement, they are unlikely to be replicated. There is a danger, therefore, that too great a reliance may be placed on the findings from any one study. Second, as it often takes a long time to conduct and report on their findings, the intervention employed may be superseded by further developments and hence the findings may no longer be relevant. This, in fact, was what happened in the SOETP trial, in which relapse prevention has fallen into disfavour for the treatment of sex offenders (Hanson, 1997). Third, if no treatment effect is found, defenders of the therapy may point out the highly skewed nature of the sample, the incompetence and poor training of the therapists etc. Conversely, if a treatment effect is found, sceptics may claim that it is a function of the careful selection both of patients and therapists, excessive training etc., and that the results are not therefore generalizable. Large randomized controlled trials are important, but, by themselves, are unlikely to provide an answer to the question of what works for the personality disordered.

Hanson (1997) therefore argues that it is more realistic to supplement the results from such studies with data from two other types of designs. First, we might be able to combine the results from several small studies in a meta-analysis so that, although the results of any one may be inconclusive, their aggregation may show some significant effects. Second, we should examine changes with treatment in dynamic factors (or proxy factors) that are thought to be linked theoretically to the disorder in question. The focus within the treatment would then be on changes in these proxy measures, and the immediate success of the intervention would be judged on whether or not the intervention effected a change in such factors. Whether such a change was linked with a change in the relevant outcome variable could then be judged by conducting a long-term follow-up. To give an example from the treatment of sex offenders, an investigator might hypothesize that low victim empathy is associated with violent sexual behaviour. Thus, increasing victim empathy becomes the focus of treatment (and a proxy measure for reduced future sexual offending). If this formulation is correct, sex offenders whose victim empathy increased ought to be at reduced risk for future violent offending. This can then be tested when participants in the sex offending programme are followed up in the community. A similar approach could be used to evaluate the impact of an intervention on different aspects of personality disorder. For instance, one might link traits of passivity to an increased likelihood of that individual committing arson. Consequently, a reduction in the individual's passivity ought to be associated with a reduction in further arson. This is a conjecture that could be tested.

CONCLUSION

It is currently fashionable to dismiss the value of dynamic therapy as an effective intervention for the treatment of personality disorder of an anti-social type. I believe that this view is mistaken and that a dynamic approach is of value, not only in the assessment of the maturity of the individual's psychological structure, but also because it provides those who are engaged with such individuals in an intimate way with an understanding of their interpersonal encounters. The latter is essential in sustaining staff who work with very difficult individuals, as well as in diminishing retaliatory attacks on vulnerable individuals. As resources are scarce and as the majority of patients do not have a psychological profile that suggests they might benefit from such an approach directly, dynamic therapy ought to be a resource for the staff, rather than for the patient, in the first instance. As with any therapy, future developments in technique may well alter this judgement.

One problem that remains is that it is difficult to underpin this intuitive appreciation of the value of a dynamic approach with empirical evidence; yet, without such evidence, it seems likely that the approach will be dismissed. The author has suggested that evidence for the effectiveness of this approach may be obtained through a process type of research in which interpersonal theory provides the necessary theoretical structure. In his celebrated article 'The antisocial tendency', Winnicott (1956) took an optimistic view of antisocial behaviour, suggesting that, despite its maladaptive nature, such behaviour implied hope, as it was an attempt by the subject to elicit from important others something that was denied him or her as a child. But he also was careful to make the point that '… over and over again one sees the moment of hope wasted or withered'. If we are to make sure that this hope is not wasted, we need to be realistic about what we can achieve with dynamic therapy and to have an approach by which it can be rigorously evaluated.

REFERENCES

Akhtar S (1995). *Quest for Answers: A Primer of Understanding and Treating Severe Personality Disorders.* North Vale, NJ: Jason Aronson.

Benjamin LS (1993). *Interpersonal Diagnosis and Treatment of Personality Disorders.* New York: Guilford Press.

Blackburn R (1998). Psychopathy and personality disorder: implications of interpersonal theory. In: Cooke DJ, Forth AE and Hare RD (eds), *Psychopathy: Theory, Research and Implications for Society.* Dordrecht: Kluwer Academic Publishers, 269–301.

Duggan CF (2000). Personality disorder: what role for mental health services? In: Gregoire A (ed.), *Adult Severe Mental Illness.* Greenwich: Medical Media, 155–76.

Freud A (1976). *The Ego and the Mechanisms of Defence.* The International Psycho-analytical Library No. 30. London: Hogarth Press. (Originally published in German 1936.)

Gabbard GO (1997). Psychotherapy of personality disorders. *Journal of Practical Psychiatry and Behavioural Health* **3**:327–33.

Hanson KD (1997). How to know what works with sexual offenders. *Sexual Abuse: A Journal of Research and Treatment* **9**:129–45.

Hare RD (1991). *The Hare Psychopathy Checklist – Revised.* Toronto: Multi-Health Systems.

Hare RD (1998). The Hare PCL-R: some issues concerning its use and misuse. *Legal and Criminological Psychology* **3**:99–119.

Horwitz L (1974). *Clinical Prediction in Psychotherapy.* New York: Jason Aronson.

Howard KI, Kopta SM, Krause MS and Orlinsky DE (1986). The dose–effect relationship in psychotherapy. *American Psychologist* Special Issue: *Psychotherapy Research* **41**:357–77.

Kernberg OF (1972). Psychotherapy research project. Summary and conclusions. *Bulletin of the Menninger Clinic* **36**:179–276.

Kernberg OF (1992). Projection and projective identification: developmental and clinical aspects. In: *Aggression in Personality Disorders and Perversions.* New Haven, CT: Yale University Press, 159–72.

Kernberg OF, Selzer, MA, Koenigsberg HW, Carr AC and Applebaum AH (1997). *Psychodynamic Therapy for Borderline Patients.* New York: Basic Books.

Kiesler DJ (1996). *Contemporary Interpersonal Theory and Research.* New York: John Wiley & Sons.

Killingmo B (1989). Conflict and deficit: implications for technique. *International Journal of Psycho-Analysis* **70**:65–79.

McCord J (1978). A thirty-year follow-up of treatment effects. American Psychologist **33**:284–9.

Marques JK, Day DM, Nelson C and West MA (1994). Effects of cognitive/behavioral treatment on sex offenders' recidivism: preliminary results of a longitudinal study. *Criminal Justice and Behavior* **21**:28–54.

McGuire J (ed.) (1995). Reviewing what works. In: *Reducing Re-Offending: Guidelines from Research and Practice.* Chichester: John Wiley & Sons.

Mealey L (1995). The sociobiology of sociopathy: an integrated evolutionary model. *Behavioral and Brain Science* **18**:523–41.

Monsen J, Odland T, Faugli A, Daae E and Eilertsen DE (1995a). Personality disorders and psychosocial changes after intensive psychotherapy: a prospective follow-up study of an outpatient psychotherapy project, 5 years after the end of treatment. *Scandinavian Journal of Psychology* **36**:256–68.

Monsen J, Odland T, Faugli A, Daae E and Eilertsen DE (1995b). Personality disorders: changes and stability after intensive psychotherapy focusing on affect consciousness. *Psychotherapy Research* **5**:33–48.

Murrell SA (1971). An open system model for psychotherapy evaluation. *Community Mental Health Journal* **7**:209–17.

Rice ME, Harris GT and Cormier CA (1992). An evaluation of a maximum security therapeutic community for psychopaths and other mentally disordered offenders. *Law and Human Behaviour* **16**:399–412.

Stevenson J and Meares R (1992). An outcome study of psychotherapy for patients with borderline personality disorder. *American Journal of Psychiatry* **149**:358–62.

Stevenson J and Meares R (1995). Borderline patients at 5-year follow-up. Presented at the Annual Congress of the Royal Australia–New Zealand College of Psychiatrists, Cairns, Australia, May 1995.

Stone MH (1993). *Abnormalities of Personality – Within and Beyond the Realm of Treatment.* New York: Guilford Press.

Strachey J (1969). Nature of the therapeutic action of psychoanalysis *Journal of Psychoanalysis* **50**:275–91.

Sullivan HS (1953). *The Interpersonal Theory of Psychiatry.* New York: Norton.

Vaillant GE (1987). A developmental view of old and new perspectives of personality disorders. *Journal of Personality Disorder* **1**:146–56.

Wallerstein RS (1986). *Forty-two Lives in Treatment: A Study of Psychoanalysis and Psychotherapy.* New York: Guilford Press.

Watzlawick P (1978). *The Language of Change.* New York: Basic Books.

Wiggins JS (1985). Interpersonal circumplex models: 1948–1983. *Journal of Personality Assessment* **49**:626–31.

Winnicott DW (1958). The antisocial tendency. In: *Through Paediatrics to Psychoanalysis.* London: Tavistock, 306–15.

Winston A, Laikin M, Pollack J, Samstag LG, McCullough L and Muran JC (1994). Short-term psychotherapy of personality disorders. *American Journal of Psychiatry* **151**:190–4.

Woody GE, McLellan T, Luborsky L and O'Brian CP (1985). Sociopathy and psychotherapy outcome. *Archives of General Psychiatry* **42**:1081–6.

Chapter 13

ACTION AND THOUGHT: IN-PATIENT TREATMENT OF SEVERE PERSONALITY DISORDERS WITHIN A PSYCHOTHERAPEUTIC MILIEU

Wilhelm Skogstad

INTRODUCTION

This chapter looks at the in-patient treatment of patients with severe personality disorder in a psychoanalytically oriented therapeutic community such as the Cassel Hospital in London, which is a non-secure hospital. It takes as a starting point the propensity of such patients for action and argues that in an in-patient setting a mixture of interpretative work and therapeutic action is necessary to help them towards more integration. In addition to staff, fellow patients are also involved in some of the therapeutic work.

The setting presented in this chapter differs in some respects from the more traditional therapeutic community setting described elsewhere (e.g. Rapoport, 1960; Hinshelwood and Manning, 1979; Norton, 1996).

ACTING INSTEAD OF THINKING

Although severe personality disorders are characterized in various ways from a psychoanalytic perspective (e.g. Kernberg, 1984; Bateman, 1991; Higgitt and Fonagy, 1993), one important characteristic is the extent to which these patients use action instead of thought. What could be a feeling, phantasy, dream or thought within the mind is turned into something concrete – an action. The mind is actively being rid of thoughts or feelings that, if kept inside it, are experienced as too painful and intolerable. More often than not, these actions are of an aggressive and destructive kind. Many patients turn their destructiveness towards themselves and their own bodies, which they cut, burn, bleed, starve or overdose. Others turn their destructive action towards other people and become, as offenders, abusive, sadistic or violent. Some do both. Mothers may use also their own offspring for destructive and perverse purposes and attack the bodies of their infants, which they treat as extensions of themselves (Welldon, 1988).

Apart from these very concrete actions towards themselves or others, there is another, more subtle, form of action that is commonly resorted to by patients with severe personality disorder, and that is projective identification of a particularly violent kind. This mechanism involves not only the defensive phantasy that feelings are lodged in another person's mind rather than one's own, but also real actions whose unconscious aim it is to push disturbing thoughts and feelings into other people. These people are used as receptacles for the disturbing contents of the patient's mind. Violent projective identification leads to serious difficulties in relationships and to strong and often disturbing feelings in the professionals. The deep splits in patients' minds often create severe splits between the professionals who care for them, leading to impasses or breakdowns in their management.

The strong tendency to act instead of using thought to deal with painful feelings is often linked with a history of deprivation and trauma. These patients' primary carers were usually not sufficiently able to contain and think about their children's feelings and to enable them to develop the capacity to contain feelings in themselves (Bion, 1962). Instead, as children, most of these patients experienced massive, uncontained feelings being pushed into them and were subjected to destructive actions such as physical or sexual abuse. Thus, in their early development, actions frequently took the place of thoughts or feelings and they had to deal with deeply disturbing experiences while having little chance to learn to think about them.

It is the strong tendency to use action and violent projective identification that often makes it necessary to treat such patients as in-patients rather than out-patients. In the treatment of patients who are less prone to action, serious acting-out may occur only in periods of severe regression (e.g. Bateman, 1998). However, the more pervasive and often addictive tendency towards action, reflecting a deeper weakness of the ego (Wood, 1968), requires a high degree of containment. Although it may sometimes be possible to contain even violent patients in intensive psychoanalysis (e.g. Fonagy and Target, 1995), the once-a-week therapy usually offered in the National Health Service (NHS) is inadequate in most cases. In-patient treatment, or sometimes day-patient treatment (Bateman, 1995), is usually more appropriate for containing the dangerous tendency to act destructively towards self or others.

THOUGHT AND ACTION IN PSYCHOTHERAPEUTIC IN-PATIENT TREATMENT

A requirement of the treatment of severe personality disorder patients is to help them become 'thinkers and feelers' instead of 'actors' (Masterson, 1972). In working towards this aim, the psychoanalytically oriented therapeutic community combines various approaches, which need to be linked together by psychodynamic understanding. The setting at the Cassel Hospital contains formal individual psychoanalytic psychotherapy on the one hand and an application of psychoanalytical ideas to all other areas of work on the other. This chapter focuses mainly on the latter.

Given the tendency of these patients to act, careful translation of action into thought and interpretation needs to be an essential part of the work, in addition to the more familiar work on thoughts and feelings in psychotherapy. This setting also derives great potential from a 'language of action' (Hinshelwood, 1987), i.e. from the use of thoughtful action, as well as interpretation, as therapeutic tools. Such therapeutic action is an integral part of nursing in the therapeutic community setting (Griffiths and Pringle, 1997; Skogstad, 2001, 2003) and is also employed in the crisis management of patients. To be helpful, this kind of action needs to be based on thought and understanding, otherwise it is always at risk of becoming an acting-out in the countertransference, driven mainly by one's own, often unconscious, emotional impulses rather than by understanding. If it is guided by thought, however, action may even 'speak louder than words' (Griffiths and Hinshelwood, 1997; McGauley, 1997).

Working with patients with severe personality disorders at the Cassel Hospital therefore involves four different layers of thought and action.

1. The thoughtful, empathic understanding of patients' feelings and phantasies, as

expressed by them in words. This is attempted in all settings, but particularly so in individual psychoanalytic psychotherapy, which is fairly similar to such work in other settings.

Even though important, this point will not be elaborated on here, the focus instead being on the following three layers, which are particularly relevant for the treatment of severe personality disorder patients.

2. The translation and integration of different fragments that are projected into various people within the hospital by acting on them. This involves work between the minds of different team members, in particular the therapist and primary nurse, and sometimes the whole team.

3. The translation of patients' actions into thought and interpretation derived from an attempt to understand the meaning of these acts. This takes place first of all in the minds of staff, but the patient's peer group may equally be involved in this work of translation.

4. The use of therapeutic action based on a thoughtful understanding of the patient's difficulties and needs. This happens particularly in the psychosocial work of nurses with their patients and in the active relationship between patients in the therapeutic community.

INTEGRATING PROJECTED PARTS

The strong tendency of severe personality disorder patients to project different parts of their internal world into those around them can lead, in any setting, to severe splits between the professionals involved (Main, 1957). One professional may only see the patient as a victim, another only as a perpetrator (Norton and Hinshelwood, 1996), and a whole drama can be created between the professionals involved (Davies, 1996), which, if not brought together sufficiently, can end up in a destructive rather than helpful situation. In-patient

psychotherapy offers a stage for these dramas and the opportunity of integrating the various fragments enacted there. This can help professionals understand the internal drama instead of being caught up in an external one (Hinshelwood and Skogstad, 1998). At the Cassel Hospital, this work of integration is done in daily team meetings and, more specifically, in nurse/therapist supervision, in which a supervisory couple meets the 'therapeutic couple' (the patient's primary nurse and therapist) to try to understand the dynamics that have developed around him or her (James, 1986; Tischler, 1986; Santos and Hinshelwood, 1998).

This can be illustrated with the following Case example (13.1).

CASE EXAMPLE 13.1

Mary, 30 years old, shows severe symptoms that involve destructive actions. As an adolescent, she took to shoplifting; now she frequently cuts herself and often masturbates compulsively to rid her mind of unbearable tension. She has often considered violent suicide and actually made two very serious suicide attempts. Her father was an alcoholic and was often violent towards her mother, who apparently killed her father when Mary was 5. Mary's mother remarried and her stepfather sexually abused her until puberty.

In nurse/therapist supervision we hear of the primary nurse's distress in working with this patient. The patient attacks her angrily for not having enough time, and when she has, turns away or tells her arrogantly how useless she is. The nurse has lost any sense of having something to give to this patient. She is so ashamed of her uselessness that she hasn't been able to approach the patient's therapist or the senior nurse of the unit, who seems liked by Mary and able to get on with her. In her individual sessions, the therapist is often presented with serious suicidal ideas, in a way that feels cruel and sadistic and leaves the therapist deeply anxious. Although Mary often wonders what the therapist has communicated to the nurse about her, the nurse and therapist have actually had hardly any contact.

These different elements were brought together in supervision. What the primary nurse was made to feel became understood as the utter despair, uselessness and shame of the patient as an abused child who had lost any hope of getting help from anyone. The therapist's experience seemed to reflect the patient's terror as a child of her cruel and murderously violent parents. The senior nurse seemed linked with the image of an idealized father, which the patient had resorted to in order to help her deal with painful reality. Following supervision, the nurse was able to regain confidence and sympathy for her patient, and this helped the patient gain a more balanced relationship with both her and the senior nurse. What emerged in therapy afterwards (and made sense of the striking lack of contact between nurse and therapist) was the patient's terror of staff getting together. They were experienced as a parental couple who, if together, would join up to mock her contemptuously or become violent with each other.

In this way, different aspects of a patient's internal world, which had been actively projected into various people and thus kept separate from each other, could be brought together in the staff's minds and this helped the patient towards more integration.

TRANSLATING ACTION INTO THOUGHT

The destructive acts of patients in in-patient psychotherapy, whether they harm themselves, attack others or damage objects, as well as apparently positive acts like giving a present, usually have a complex meaning, which staff and patients need to try to understand (Chiesa, 1989). This can be illustrated with a vignette from the same patient (Case example 13.2).

Although Mary did not actually make a suicide attempt, writing the suicide note and

CASE EXAMPLE 13.2

Mary has a daughter from a failed marriage. She already hated the child while pregnant with her, partly because the pregnancy suddenly brought back all the memories of her sexual abuse. Later, she became physically and emotionally abusive towards her daughter, who was eventually taken into care and Mary had no access to her. Now she asks for support to regain access to her child. Some work has been done in her psychotherapy about her ambivalence towards her daughter, and so the consultant agrees to write a supporting letter. Two days later, just before her daughter's birthday, for which she wanted to buy a present, Mary writes a suicide note to her daughter saying that she will kill herself and that she loves her. The following day she buys a rope to hang herself with, but eventually tells another patient.

buying the rope were powerful actions, whose meaning needed to be understood. In the team discussion they were linked with the most recent developments: the possibility of having contact with her daughter stirred up painful feelings of guilt for having abused her, but, more importantly, brought up her deep hatred and envy of her daughter and her terror of these feelings. By her actions, she seemed to communicate that these feelings of guilt, hatred and envy were uncontainable for her. More specifically, the suicide note conveyed what it was she would give to her child: not love, but something hateful and destructive. It was put to Mary that direct contact with her daughter seemed intolerable for her at this stage. This enraged her initially, but then led to a much more meaningful exploration of her hatred and envy of her daughter.

In a therapeutic community it is not only staff who are involved in translating the meaning of acts to patients. In the intense shared experience of living together, fellow patients may pick up and understand intuitively some of the messages patients give

CASE EXAMPLE 13.3

Mary is confronted about her suicidal action and talks in a cold, detached way about her suicide plans and her view that the suicide note was telling her daughter that she cared about her. Another patient, whose father committed suicide when she was an adolescent, bursts out angrily. She says that is rubbish, she knows what a parent does to a child by killing himself; she has to carry the burden and guilt all her life. Mary brushes that aside, but afterwards thinks again about this comment and then wonders more seriously about her own, deeply ambivalent, feelings towards her daughter.

through their actions. Mary experienced this in a firm meeting[1] following this incident (Case example 13.3).

Fellow patients can also be quite important when patients actually harm themselves. Different patients may react in different ways to the self-harm, thereby responding to different conscious and unconscious aspects in the mind of the self-harming patient. Some may empathize with the patient's distress leading up to the self-harm; others may express horror about the cruel way the patient treats himself/herself; and still others may show anger, thus responding to the furious attack on other people contained in the act of self-harm. If the horror and anger can be expressed in a generally sympathetic way, this may enable the patient to get in touch with otherwise split-off aspects of his or her mind. However, staff have to be watchful, because instead of giving thoughtful understanding,

---

[1]The Cassel Hospital is divided into three, open, in-patient units: adult, adolescent and families unit. Patients belong to one of these units and meet daily in 'firm meetings' with fellow patients and nurses from the unit and, on some days, their unit consultant. All patients live and work together within the whole patients' community and they all meet three times a week in 'community meetings' together with nurses from the units, the community nurses and doctor and, on one day, the hospital director.

patients (or staff) may, in the way they talk, act-out an aspect of the patient's inner world such as a cruel, punitive superego.

THERAPEUTIC ACTIONS IN MANAGING PATIENTS

Acting-out as part of a regression in psychoanalysis or psychotherapy is most helpfully dealt with by interpretation alone. However, with the general tendency towards action as part of the personality, one needs to work with a more active setting of boundaries, particularly in an in-patient setting (Wood, 1968; Kernberg, 1984). Staff have to be aware, though, that, if not sufficiently based on understanding, their own action may reflect an acting-out in the countertransference in which they enact the role of an object in the patient's inner world. For action to be therapeutic, it needs space for thinking.

A certain degree of active pressure through rules and other means can, if used thoughtfully rather than punitively, be helpful for patients who can hardly resist the urge to act. One therapeutic community, for example, has a clear rule that any self-harm or violence leads to automatic discharge. Patients can, however, ask the community for reinstatement, which is usually granted if they show a willingness to talk and think about what has been happening. In this way, pressure to think and talk rather than act is put on the patients (Norton and Dolan, 1995).

At the Cassel Hospital there is not a definite rule, but the constantly reiterated expectation that patients do not self-harm, become violent or abuse drugs or alcohol, and that instead they talk and express their thoughts and feelings verbally in the structured settings. If patients do act destructively, this is brought up in firm or community meetings and explored with patients and staff. Staff constantly work hard to maintain or re-establish a 'culture of enquiry' (Main, 1983; see also Norton, 1992; Levinson, 1996; Day and Pringle, 2001;

Skogstad, 2001, 2003), a climate of mutual enquiry into the meaning of individual symptoms and actions as well as group dynamics. If there is a general deterioration into a culture of destructive action, the reasons within the patient group as well as the staff group need to be explored.

However, there is, in response to destructive acting, also a range of therapeutic actions that attempt to combine active boundary setting with thoughtful help. Patients who have acted destructively may be seen by patients with a senior role of responsibility in the community, together with a nurse, to reiterate the boundary and to think together how they might manage things. A patient may also be met in a 'management meeting' by the consultant (or a therapist other than their own) and a nurse. These meetings combine an exploration of the more immediate reasons for the act, active thinking about alternative ways of managing their distress, and an explicit stressing of the boundaries. This may be sufficient, or may lead to plans of actions such as handing in razor blades, staying in the building or even, in serious cases, forming a rota of fellow patients to help keep him or her safe. If these measures are not sufficient, a patient may be sent home for a period of short-leave and seen again in a meeting on return to explore how he or she has used this 'time-out'. In extreme cases, a patient may have to be discharged, and continuous destructive acting may be the only way some patients can communicate their inability to manage the intensity of treatment.

A particular therapeutic action is illustrated with a vignette from a different patient (Case example 13.4).

Handing in a lethal dose or weapon a patient has stored can be an important step in treatment if it signifies an internal step towards life and away from the ever-available deadly way out, as it did with Jane. Asking a patient to do this has to be done thoughtfully. The request may be felt only to reflect staff's anxiety, which the patient can then be scornful

> **CASE EXAMPLE 13.4**
> Jane, a patient who had made two near-fatal suicide attempts, tended to be quite cut off from any feelings. When she appeared more withdrawn from the other patients and highly intellectual and unreachable in her therapy, some staff became deeply worried about her suicidal impulses. Contact with her referrer revealed that she had a lethal mix of anaesthetic drugs at home, which her referrer knew about but had not mentioned to us. The consultant at the Cassel Hospital had a meeting with her and found her deeply suicidal; he asked her to hand in these drugs when she returned from the weekend. She was furious that we had made contact with the referrer, but, after further work with her nurse, other patients and by herself over the weekend, she handed them in. This led to a process of considerable change in her.

about, particularly if it is accompanied by pressure and without giving the patient space to think it through and come to his or her own decision. However, if staff knowingly leave a patient with the means to kill him/herself, they may be perceived as colluding with the murderous part of the patient; this may actually contribute to a fatal suicide.

THERAPEUTIC ACTION IN PSYCHOSOCIAL NURSING

The most important therapeutic actions used at the Cassel Hospital are the active work of nurses in their specific approach called 'psychosocial nursing' (Barnes, 1968; Chapman, 1984; Griffiths and Pringle, 1997; Barnes et al., 1998) and the active work of patients with each other in running the therapeutic community. Unlike traditional nursing, where an *active* nurse cares for a *passive* patient, nurses work *alongside* patients to help them do the practical and emotional 'work of the day' (Kennedy, 1986) actively and jointly.

The therapeutic community forms a living environment of adults, adolescents and children in which patients, together with nurses, have normal, everyday responsibilities and enjoy leisure activities. Patients take on designated responsibilities as members of work groups, in elected posts as managers of these groups, and in posts of greater responsibility such as chairpersons of the whole patient community. Patients clean and maintain certain areas of the hospital and manage household budgets for those areas; they are responsible for planning and cooking breakfast and supper as well as for ordering and storing food. They also help baby-sit the children of the hospital's families unit and may volunteer as night contacts or members of a rota for a patient in crisis. The 'chairpersons' have an important role in thinking about disturbance in individual patients or the whole group, and chair the firm or community meetings. Patients also organize leisure activities in collaboration with nurses, such as badminton, poetry, cinema visits and sometimes bigger events such as a public garden party or a bonfire night.

It is essential that patients are given *real* responsibilities and not just contrived ones. This approach is based on the conviction that even seriously disturbed patients have sane and functioning sides that need to be mobilized and fostered rather than, as often in hospital care, discouraged and blocked by a regressive culture that helps avoid the demands of real life (Main, 1946). It is in the areas of everyday tasks and ordinary relationships that patients' emotional conflicts and disturbances show and have an immediate effect. Usually these areas have seriously broken down in their lives before they were admitted. In the practical arena of the hospital life, feelings and conflicts can be experienced and sometimes discovered for the first time; here, they can also be worked on in a thoughtfully active way, alongside the work on a deeper understanding of their difficulties within the transference setting of individual psychotherapy (Skogstad, 2001, 2003).

Actions or the failure to act have real consequences for others: a meal is only there for patients if it is actually prepared, and failing to wash the dishes leaves other people with a mess. This, therefore, becomes an arena in which responsibility, guilt and concern can be experienced and explored. Narcissistic omnipotence or the conviction of total failure can be challenged through tasks that need real work and may bring with them a sense of real achievement or limited failure. The hatred many patients feel for dependence and the excessive control they exert over others can be challenged in this culture of practical and emotional interdependence.

Nurses play a crucial part in this culture by working 'alongside' patients: they participate 'hands on' in all the tasks, but they also use their knowledge of the patients' problems and their own emotional experience of being with them to challenge and think with them about the difficulties they encounter and how they might deal with them (Case example 13.5; Flynn, 1993; Irwin, 1995; McCaffrey, 1997; Skogstad, 2001, 2003).

Nurses are often experienced as 'representatives of the reality principle' and, as such, resented by patients who wish to regress or withdraw. They may come under great

CASE EXAMPLE 13.5

When Mary took on jobs in the community, she filled herself up with responsible tasks and then became very controlling of other people, but also exhausted. She was challenged by patients, who felt increasingly angry with her. The discussion highlighted Mary's deep insecurity, mistrust and terror of losing control. The patients' group as a whole initially scapegoated her, and staff needed to intervene to point out the split that had occurred; they showed them that Mary's dilemma reflected a problem many of them had. Following this, she was actively helped by her nurse to take on a more appropriate amount of work, share responsibilities and deal with her relationships in a less controlling way. Once she had made this attempt, she was then challenged more sympathetically by fellow patients.

pressure to take over from patients. Nurses need considerable support to contain their own despair, anxiety and fury, and require thinking space to enable them to stand back where appropriate. Griffiths and Hinshelwood (1997) describe this way of nursing as 'a set of cycles, moving from actions, to reflection and understanding, and then back to actions – a form of psychodynamically informed action learning'. This cycle may gradually help patients towards more integration and a greater ability to reflect on themselves.

CONCLUSION

Patients with severe personality disorder show a serious lack of ability to contain their feelings, conflicts and impulses in their own minds. Instead of thinking about them, they often rid their minds of such feelings and conflicts by action or projective identification. In-patient treatment in a psychoanalytically oriented therapeutic community provides not only a space for thinking, but also a whole stage on which to act and enact. Therefore this setting has other approaches as essential tools in addition to psychodynamic interpretation in psychoanalytic psychotherapy. These include integrating projected aspects within the team, translating actions into meaningful thought, and therapeutic actions based on psychodynamic understanding. By integrating these approaches to contain the fragmented aspects of the personality within the institution, an attempt is made to help the patient towards more integration and self-containment.

REFERENCES

Barnes E (ed.) (1968). *Psychosocial Nursing: Studies from the Cassel Hospital*. London: Tavistock.

Barnes E, Griffiths P, Ord J and Wells D (1998). *Face to Face with Distress*. London: Butterworth-Heinemann.

Bateman A (1991). Borderline personality disorder. In: Holmes J (ed.), *Textbook of Psychotherapy in Psychiatric Practice*. London: Churchill Livingstone, 335–57.

Bateman A (1995). The treatment of borderline patients in a day hospital setting. *Psychoanalytic Psychotherapy* **9**:3–16.

Bateman A (1998). Thick- and thin-skinned organisations and enactment in borderline and narcissistic disorders. *International Journal of Psycho-Analysis* **79**:13–25.

Bion WR (1962). A theory of thinking. In: Bion WR (ed.), *Second Thoughts*. London: Maresfield Reprints (1984), 110–19.

Chapman GE (1984). A therapeutic community, psychosocial nursing and the nursing process. *International Journal of Therapeutic Communities* **5**:68–76.

Chiesa M (1989). Different origins and meanings of acute acting-out in an in-patient psychotherapeutic setting. *Psychoanalytic Psychotherapy* **4**:155–68.

Davies R (1996). The inter-disciplinary network and the internal world of the offender. In: Cordess C and Cox M (eds), *Forensic Psychotherapy*, Vol. 2. London: Jessica Kingsley, 133–44.

Day L and Pringle P (eds) (2001). *Reflective Enquiry into Therapeutic Institutions*. London: Karnac Books.

Flynn C (1993). The patients' pantry: the nature of the nursing task. *Therapeutic Communities* **14**:227–36. (Also in Griffiths P and Pringle P (eds) (2001). *Psychosocial Practice in a Residential Setting*. London: Karnac Books, 37–49.)

Fonagy P and Target M (1995). Understanding the violent patient: the use of the body and the role of the father. *International Journal of Psycho-Analysis* **76**:487–501.

Griffiths P and Hinshelwood RD (1997). Actions speak louder than words. In: Griffiths P and Pringle P (eds), *Psychosocial Practice in a Residential Setting*. London: Karnac Books, 1–17.

Griffiths P and Pringle P (1997). *Psychosocial Practice within a Residential Setting*. London: Karnac Books.

Higgitt A and Fonagy P (1993). Psychotherapy in borderline and narcissistic personality disorder. In: Tyrer P and Stein G (eds), *Personality Disorders Reviewed*. London: Gaskell, 225–61.

Hinshelwood RD (1987). Social dynamics and individual symptoms. *International Journal of Therapeutic Communities* **8**:265–72.

Hinshelwood RD and Manning N (1979). *Therapeutic Communities: Reflections and Progress*. London: Routledge.

Hinshelwood RD and Skogstad W (1998). The hospital in the mind: the setting and the internal world. In: Pestalozzi J (ed.), *Psychoanalytic Psychotherapy in Institutional Settings.* London: Karnac Books, 59–73.

Irwin F (1995). The therapeutic ingredients of baking a cake. *Therapeutic Communities* **16**:263–8. (Also in Griffiths P and Pringle P (eds) (1997). *Psychosocial Practice in a Residential Setting.* London: Karnac Books, 65–72.)

James O (1986). The role of the nurse/therapist relationship in the therapeutic community. In: Kennedy R, Heymans A and Tischler L (eds), *The Family as In-Patient: Working with Families and Adolescents at the Cassel Hospital.* London: Free Associations, 78–94.

Kennedy R (1986). Work of the day: aspects of work with families at the Cassel Hospital. In: Kennedy R, Heymans A and Tischler L (eds), *The Family as In-Patient: Working with Families and Adolescents at the Cassel Hospital.* London: Free Associations, 27–48. Reprinted in 1997 under the title: Working with the work of the day: the use of everyday activities as agents for treatment, change and transformation. In: Griffiths P and Pringle P (eds), *Psychosocial Practice in a Residential Setting.* London: Karnac Books, 19–36.

Kernberg O (1984). *Severe Personality Disorders: Psychotherapeutic Strategies.* New Haven, CT: Yale University Press.

Levinson A (1996). The struggle to keep a culture of enquiry alive at the Cassel Hospital. *Therapeutic Communities* **17**:47–57.

Main T (1946). The hospital as a therapeutic institution. In: *The Ailment and Other Psychoanalytic Essays.* London: Free Associations Books (1989), 7–11.

Main T (1957). The ailment. In: *The Ailment and Other Psychoanalytic Essays.* London: Free Associations Books (1989), 12–35.

Main T (1983). The concept of the therapeutic community: variations and vicissitudes. In: *The Ailment and Other Psychoanalytic Essays.* London: Free Associations Books (1989), 123–41.

Masterson JF (1972). *Treatment of the Borderline Adolescent: A Developmental Approach.* New York: John Wiley & Sons.

McCaffrey G (1997). The use of leisure activities in psychosocial practice. In: Griffiths P and Pringle P (eds), *Psychosocial Practice in a Residential Setting.* London: Karnac Books, 51–63.

McGauley G (1997). A delinquent in the therapeutic community: actions speak louder than words. In: Welldon E and van Velsen C (eds), *A Practical Guide to Forensic Psychotherapy.* London: Jessica Kingsley, 216–22.

Norton K (1992). A culture of enquiry – its preservation and loss. *Therapeutic Communities* **15**:173–81.

Norton K (1996). The personality-disordered forensic patient and the therapeutic community. In: Cordess C and Cox M (eds), *Forensic Psychotherapy. Crime, Psychodynamics and the Offender Patient*, Vol. 2. London: Jessica Kingsley, 393–9.

Norton K and Dolan B (1995). Acting out and the institutional response. *Journal of Forensic Psychiatry* **6**:317–32.

Norton K and Hinshelwood RD (1996). Severe personality disorder. Treatment issues and selection for in-patient psychotherapy. *British Journal of Psychiatry* **168**:723–31.

Rapoport R (1960). *The Community as Doctor.* London: Tavistock.

Santos A and Hinshelwood RD (1998). The use at the Cassel Hospital of the organisational dynamics to enhance the therapeutic work. *Therapeutic Communities* **19**:29–39.

Skogstad W (2001). Internal and external reality – enquiring into their interplay in an in-patient setting. In: Day L and Pringle P (eds), *Reflective Enquiry into Therapeutic Institutions.* Cassel Monographs, Vol. 2. London: Karnac Books, 45–65.

Skogstad W (2003) Internal and external reality in in-patient psychotherapy: working with severely disturbed patients at the Cassel Hospital. *Psychoanalytic Psychotherapy* **17**(2):97–118.

Tischler L (1986). Nurse/therapist supervision. In: Kennedy R, Heymans A and Tischler L (eds), *The Family as In-Patient: Working with Families and Adolescents at the Cassel Hospital.* London: Free Associations, 95–107.

Welldon E (1988). *Mother, Madonna, Whore.* New York: Guilford Press.

Wood EC (1968). Acting out viewed in the context of the psychotherapeutic hospital. *International Journal of Psycho-Analysis* **49**:438–42.

Chapter 14

CO-MORBIDITY AND PERSONALITY DISORDER: THE CONCEPT AND IMPLICATIONS FOR TREATMENT OF PERSONALITY DISORDER CO-MORBID WITH PSYCHOSIS

Pamela J. Taylor

CO-MORBIDITY

The principle of medical diagnosis is that all disease-phenomena should be characterised within a single diagnosis. Where a number of different phenomena coexist the question arises which of them should be preferred for diagnostic purposes so that the remaining phenomena can be considered secondary or accidental.
Jaspers (1923; English translation, 1963)

Before the American *Diagnostic and Statistical Manual of Mental Disorders*, now into its fourth edition (DSM-IV; American Psychiatric Association, 1994), Jaspers offered a multi-axial system for the classification of mental disorder. His group one (now Axis III) was 'known somatic illnesses with psychic disturbances'; his group two consisted of the three major psychoses, which seems a more clinically and aetiologically defensible 'plane' (his term) than the hotchpotch that is the DSM Axis I of 'clinical disorders and other conditions that may be a focus of clinical attention'; his third and last group was of the personality disorders, in which he included isolated abnormal reactions and neuroses and neurotic syndromes as well as abnormal personalities. The DSM-IV combines the personality disorders with mental retardation in Axis II.

The underlying tension between a hierarchical system, favoured through the twentieth century, in which a single diagnosis is 'forced', and a system that acknowledges the reality of a rich complexity of presentation in many people is explicit in both accounts.

For example, Jaspers says:

Thus neuroses commonly occur in organic illnesses; sometimes the initial feature of schizophrenia or manic–depressive illnesses appears as purely neurotic …

and

Thus in diagnosis the *previous group always has preference* over the latter.

But concedes:

This hierarchy in the diagnostic value of symptoms coincides with a narrowing down in significance of what is diagnosed. In

Group I this is just one element in a whole life, a somatic illness, which represents only a single circumscribed fact among all that embraces the total personality ...

In principle we cannot deny that a process [essentially schizophrenia] may combine with a manic–depressive disorder or that an encephalitis may combine with a schizophrenia.

Both Jaspers and the DSM imply or suggest that it is the limitations to a categorical approach, or at least to the clinical ability to define the categories, that make dual or even multiple diagnoses almost inevitable. The DSM-IV acknowledges that a dimensional approach, based on quantification of attributes rather than assignment to categories, could increase reliability and convey more clinical information, but argues that dimensional descriptions are less familiar to clinicians and there is no agreement on the choice of optimal dimensions for classification. Both sources make it clear that their classificatory systems must be regarded as temporary, and evolving. Jaspers further asserts 'the diagnostic scheme has the most scientific interest where it shows discrepancies'. For him 'co-morbidity' was one such 'discrepancy'.

The idea of the value of co-morbidity for research has been carried forward for both psychiatric practice (e.g. Rutter, 1997) and criminological research (Maughan and Farrington, 1997). Thus, the concept of co-morbidity has taken on a range of applications. Feinstein (1970) appears to be credited with coining the term, to mean the presence of an 'additional clinical entity that has existed or that may occur during the clinical course of a patient who has the index disease under study'. Clarkin and Kendall (1992) took a narrow, operational view that co-morbidity is the occurrence at one point in time of two or more DSM-III-R disorders (American Psychiatric Association, 1987). Researchers such as McCord and Enslinger (1997) and Slomkowski et al. (1997)

have used the term to include violence and anti-social behaviours as well as recognized psychological characteristics.

UNDER-ESTIMATION AND OVER-ESTIMATION OF CO-MORBIDITY: A CLASSIFICATION OR ARITHMETIC PROBLEM?

The nature of a categorical classification system is such as to increase artificially estimates of co-morbidity between certain disorders, and to decrease or dismiss estimates of co-morbidity in others. Definitions of mental disorder are rarely driven by theory, and some exclude co-morbidity by, in essence, dual conceptualization, others by exclusion. The tenth edition of the *International Classification of Diseases,* tenth revision (ICD-10; World Health Organization, 1992) gives an example of the former in the definition of schizophrenia, which includes: 'The disturbance involves the more basic functions that give the normal person a feeling of individuality, uniqueness and self-direction'.

Is this to say that schizophrenia is a personality disorder? The ICD-9 (World Health Organization, 1978) more explicitly did so, thus limiting, by definition, the potential for co-morbidity. Conversely, when the operational requirements for diagnosis specifically exclude schizophrenia, as do some for the personality disorders in the ICD-10 classification, is this artificial denial of co-morbidity? The DSM-IV suggests that schizophrenia alone may not be diagnosed simultaneously with personality disorders.

One major problem that may lead to over-counting of disorders is that, for mental disorders, no symptom is absolutely pathognomonic (characteristic) of, or specific to, any one condition. Some symptoms, such as hallucinations, are much more likely to occur in some conditions than in others; increasing the specificity of the description, for example to hearing voices discussing the sufferer in the third person, tends in many cases to increase the probability of one disorder over another, but it does not make it certain. Then, too, many symptoms, or symptom clusters, such as anxiety features, are, by definition, common to a number of disorders, and it is hardly surprising that, where this occurs, the disorders may be cited as co-morbid.

Another fundamental problem is that the definition of symptoms, signs or 'characteristics', or the threshold at which they should be regarded as abnormal, may show little interrater or test/re-test reliability. This is particularly likely to arise in conditions such as the personality disorders, for which there is relatively less agreement both on individual features and on the meaning of clusters of them than for, say, the psychotic illnesses. Indeed, Westen (1997) demonstrates convincingly that clinicians of widely differing orientations, from the 'biological' to the psychodynamic, consistently place most reliance on narrative and observed behaviour when diagnosing personality disorder and least on direct questions about 'symptoms' or self-report instruments based on DSM-IV criteria.

A combination of the effect of arbitrary and artificial exclusions and inclusions in a 'Linnean approach' to disorders of health, of double counting of some characteristics and of attempting to add dimensional descriptions, together provide for claims of co-morbidity between personality disorders. Coid (e.g. 1992) and Pfohl et al. (1986) are among the proponents of the latter. Tyrer (e.g. Tyrer and Stein, 1993) is among those who highlight the absurdity of treating the overlap between notional disorders of personality as 'co-morbidity'. It is suggested that a 'co-occurrence' of 46 per cent between borderline and histrionic personality disorder is not strongly indicative of the case for recognizing these disorders as independent in the first place, and a finding that among 180 in-patients with borderline personality disorder only 8 per cent had 'pure' borderline personality disorder (Fyer et al., 1988) seems to weigh

against it. This chapter does not pursue that argument further. In terms of service and treatment delivery, even the more modest division of personality disorders into three major clusters – the flamboyant (borderline, antisocial, narcissistic and histrionic), the eccentric (schizoid, schizotypal, paranoid) and the fearful (avoidant, obsessive–compulsive, passive–aggressive, dependent) – is often not feasible. A thoroughly mixed picture is common, and co-morbidity in this sense is not a useful concept for practice. Westen (1997) argues that multiple diagnoses of personality disorder are artefacts of the Axis I style of assessment instruments being applied to Axis II disorders, and a feature of research employing them rather than any recognizable reality. Furthermore, he noted that 3000 psychiatrists and 4000 psychotherapists he surveyed reported treating high rates of disorders that have been removed from Axis II, the latter on the basis only of research findings derived from such instruments, most without good test/retest reliability, let alone validity measures.

While Jaspers' recognition of time-limited or independent conditions, for example reversible cerebral damage or disease with mental symptoms arising in the context of a personality disorder, may be more likely than not to indicate true co-morbidity, it may be yet another source of error. The 'two conditions' may, in fact, be different manifestations of the same disorder. No one, for example, would suggest that a presentation with hypomania at one time and depression at another should lead to the diagnosis of two distinct disorders, even though the implications for treatment of each extreme of presentation are likely to be different. Different presentations over time may be more reflective of progress of a disease than two or more independent conditions. Another example might be a shift from predominantly phobic and paranoid anxiety features, through frank hallucinations and delusions, to an absence of such 'positive' features but emergence of withdrawal, apathy and irritability if approached – all of which, for some people, may be phases in a schizophrenic process.

If co-morbidity does occur, research estimates of its incidence or prevalence may be distorted by sampling. Thus, excessive estimates of the overall prevalence of co-morbidity would follow from extrapolation from samples defined by specialist treatment needs, antisocial behaviour or high scores on screening devices. A different problem may arise in relation to conditions that are in any case common. Insofar as violence can be regarded as 'morbid', it is a common problem. So are many disorders of mental state, so inevitably the two will occur together from time to time just by chance. 'Co-morbidity' here arises in any meaningful sense only if it can be shown either that the co-occurrence significantly exceeds chance expectations in the sample but is not invariable or that there is evidence of the conditions having arisen independently.

THE CLINICAL IMPORTANCE OF RECOGNITION OF CO-MORBIDITY

The attribution of a series of problems to a single condition, or the construing of a series of symptoms or signs as a single 'diagnosis', implies that this confers some understanding of cause, likely course and recognized treatment that will interfere beneficially with that course. There may be some secondary rehabilitative tasks to be undertaken; for instance, once a broken bone has been aligned and fixed, a programme of strengthening muscles is generally necessary, but in an otherwise healthy individual, the treatment of the break itself is determined by the nature of the break and nothing else. Where more than one diagnosis is made, not only may both conditions need treatment, but also the treatment of the principal presenting problem may have to be modified accordingly. The treatment of one condition may affect the other, but also the conditions may interact so that neither is adequately

helped by treatment of one alone. To extend the analogy, the treatment of a fractured femur (thigh bone) suffered by an old woman with concurrent bone disease will usually differ from that for a young, healthy man who falls from a motorbike and fractures his. For the man, only treatment of the fracture is likely to be necessary; for the woman, treatment of the bone disease as well as the fracture will be essential. She may have other co-morbid conditions too needing attention to ensure a good outcome, such as heart disease.

For mental health services, similar issues arise. The capacity for the putative patient with two or more disorders to seek or engage in the treatment of either may be influenced by the presence of the other. The capacity of staff to recognize disorder or to engage in assessment or to deliver treatment may similarly be affected. Any of these factors may contribute to failures in the effectiveness of treatment, but not necessarily fully account for them. The risks of other failures, and, indeed, of further co-morbidity and even mortality may be increased when more than one disorder is present. These issues appear to come into particularly sharp focus for people with a personality disorder. The literature is biased towards reference to the impact of personality disorder on the recognition and management of other conditions, but the converse is also important.

CONDITIONS IDENTIFIED AS CO-MORBID WITH PERSONALITY DISORDER

It is not only other psychiatric conditions that may be over-represented among people with personality disorder. While there is a fairly extensive literature showing higher than average mortality rates for many mental disorders, there is a tendency to focus on suicide; personality disorder appears to be less researched in this respect than the functional psychoses, although substance abuse disorders (most commonly co-morbid with personality disorders) would appear to be particularly strongly associated with both 'natural' and 'unnatural' causes of death. Felker et al. (1996) extended a review of studies of mortality among psychiatric patients to their non-fatal co-morbid medical problems. They observed that these physical illnesses even, though uncommonly, produced further psychiatric symptoms.

In exploring possible barriers to adequate general medical care, Sternberg (1986) described three recognizable categories.

1. Disease related – principally following from atypical presentations consequent upon co-morbidity, perhaps modified by the disorder itself, or its official treatment, or illicit substance use.
2. Staff related – in that mental healthcare staff may have insufficient competencies, and sometimes notional theoretical objections to physical examination on the grounds that it may interfere with the therapeutic relationship. Properly conducted, there is no evidence that it does (e.g. Farmer, 1987).
3. Patient-centred problems – including difficulties in communication.

Those patients in denial, or with problems of devious communication patterns, and/or failure to follow advice may be at exceptional risk (e.g. Goodwin et al., 1979). Although problems arising from organic brain deficits are most commonly cited in this area, at least these may not be the most difficult to recognize and manage. Ringbäck Weitoft et al. (1998) studied 'avoidable mortality' among more than 30 000 psychiatric patients. Apart from suicide, the major causes of death that they regarded as amenable to prevention strategies were cirrhosis of the liver and lung cancer. Other respiratory diseases were common. Although there are few direct data on personality disorder, in their study substance misuse (which is particularly likely to complicate personality disorder) was one of the highest correlates of

ill-health. In our experience at Broadmoor Hospital with people with personality disorder, physical injury is another major area for attention, albeit rarely affecting mortality figures in hospital, where these are generally sports injuries for men, but also both acceptable (body piercing) and deliberately self-harming mutilations for both sexes. Outside hospital, accidents and interpersonal violence may account for more injuries. Further, such accidents and injuries may be more serious. Services for people with personality disorder will therefore need to incorporate ready access to both emergency and regular general health services, and also health education and promotion activities.

Many of the mental disorders that may be co-morbid with personality disorder and that may call for variations in models of treatment are dealt with elsewhere in this volume (the attention deficit disorders in Chapter 16, substance misuse in Chapter 20, and learning disability in Chapter 22). It is less clear how chronic post-traumatic stress disorder (PSTD) should be treated in these terms. So many people presenting with personality disorder have faced extreme trauma in childhood that chronic PTSD may, in effect, be another name for a cluster of personality disorders, particularly in the borderline/flamboyant group (see Chapter 15). Certainly, treatment commonly needs to take explicit account of this aspect of early experience and its impact.

PSYCHOSIS AND PERSONALITY DISORDER

An established research position of first excluding schizophrenia before recognizing personality disorder (e.g. Hare and Cox, 1978) is to some extent understandable: mental disorders present complex problems, and research becomes more feasible the more homogeneity can be introduced into populations. It does not, however, make much sense in clinical practice to operate such exclusions, as both treatment efforts and therapeutic research may have to recognize that reality.

Although English special hospital patients make uncommon cases, they are not unique to England or to high-security hospital services. They have almost invariably been in general psychiatric services first. A case record survey of all residents in the first half of 1993 showed that nearly one-third of those diagnosed with a personality disorder (in ICD-10 terms), which had been continuous with conduct or emotional disorder in childhood and clearly preceded illness, also had a psychosis (Taylor et al., 1998). This co-morbidity was less common among people with schizophrenia (120 of 818 [15 per cent]) than among those with other psychosis, including schizoaffective and delusional disorders (87 of 197 [44 per cent]). There was a hierarchy of further co-morbidity (generally substance misuse) between psychoses without personality disorder (lowest), personality disorder without any evidence of psychosis (yielding an intermediate proportion of people affected) and psychoses with personality disorder (highest). In a later interview study conducted with all homicidal patients in a Finnish state psychiatric hospital, Putkonen et al. (2004) found a much higher rate of 'triple diagnosis'. Fifty-one per cent of all 90 cases had psychosis, personality disorder and substance misuse disorders.

Moran and colleagues (2003) subsequently estimated personality disorder co-morbidity with psychosis in the UK700 study, using Tyrer's Personality Assessment Schedule, Rapid Version (PAS-R) (Tyrer and Cicchetti, 2000). The UK700 study comprised 708 subjects with psychosis from four English, inner-city, general mental health services recruited in the community or at the point of discharge. In fact, a rather higher proportion of these patients (28 per cent) were rated as having a co-morbid personality disorder than amongst the English special hospital group (20 per cent overall), which would be compatible with the higher proportion of non-schizophrenia psychosis in the UK700 study (Walsh et al., 2002). Notwithstanding the link between personality disorder co-morbidity and violence shown in the UK700 sample, this does confirm that such co-morbidity is not unique to offender patients.

Further confirmation of the clinical usefulness of treating people with psychosis and such personality disorder as a distinct group with more extensive needs came from more detailed study of one high-security hospital group. A subgroup of 102 patients with schizophrenia resident in Broadmoor Hospital were interviewed as well as studied through their extensive records (Heads et al., 1997). Although about 40 per cent of them had been unremarkable childhoods, about 20 per cent had shown a collection of features such as withdrawal and phobic symptoms prior to the documented onset of psychosis. Many clinicians would construe this as a variant of developmental progression into schizophrenia, and McGlashan's (1983) report of the 15-year follow-up of the subgroup of people in the Chestnut Lodge study with schizotypal personality disorder would tend to support this. When, however, some personality disorder clusters precede onset of psychosis and persist with it, a construction of co-morbidity between personality disorder and psychosis may be valid, and useful in devising treatment strategies. Forty per cent of the Broadmoor group appeared unequivocally co-morbid. Before developing psychosis, they had shown early evidence of conduct disorders, persisting into adult life, half with situational correlates of harsh or abusive environments, and half without.

Blackburn, who has been among those who are particularly critical of categorical approaches to defining personality disorder (e.g. Blackburn, 1988), applied a dimensional approach to the study of earlier groups of special hospital patients. In the first study (Blackburn 1968), the Minnesota Multiphasic Personality Inventory (MMPI) was completed and scored for three personality scales and two hostility measures among 24 men with paranoid schizophrenia. The paranoid group showed a significantly greater tendency to extraversion (scales R and Ex) as a personality trait, which correlated with a higher incidence of previous aggression and was consistent with concepts of higher levels of arousal.

Blackburn's 1970 study was of a 28-month consecutive series of 62 homicides, nine of whom had attracted a legal classification of psychopathic disorder and the rest mental illness. Again using the MMPI, four principal groups were identified. The largest (30 per cent) was, in essence, an over-controlled represser type (high scores on defensiveness [L, K, Dn] and impulse control [R, Ma]; low scores on anxiety [a] and hostility [h]). The second type was best characterized as paranoid – aggressive, with a scatter of psychotic, anxiety, hostility, impulsive features but relative social anxiety and introversion. The smallest groups had profiles connected with being depressive – inhibited type (8) and psychopathic type (7).

In another study, Blackburn (1974) evaluated 175 consecutive male admissions to Broadmoor who were more heterogeneous for offending, with similar results. Notwithstanding the fact that 75 per cent of the subjects were legally classified under the mental illness category, indicators of abnormal personality traits, or traits to abnormal degrees, were established. Conversely, among 79 such men all detained under the category of psychopathic disorder, 21 (27 per cent) showed an MMPI profile suggestive of paranoid and psychotic disorder, but none was regarded by psychiatrists as having a psychotic illness.

Blackburn has now extended his work to incorporate high-security hospital patients from both sides of the English/Scottish border (Blackburn et al., 2003). This is important, because it provides an opportunity to test the consistency of personality pathology and psychosis co-morbidity between cultures where there are differences in serious offending patterns (Soothill et al., 2001) that do not appear to be reflected in the high-security hospitals and some relevant aspects of culture, such as use of alcohol and/or illicit drugs, which do (Taylor et al., submitted). Blackburn and colleagues used a variety of personality measures, including the International Personality Disorder Examination (IPDE) (World Health Organization, 1995), the Personality Disorder Questionnaire (PDQ-4) (Hyler, 1994), the Millon Clinical Multi-axial Inventory (MCMI-II) (Millon, 1987) and the Psychopathy Checklist – Revised (PCL-R) (Hare, 1991). For England and Wales, patients in the mental illness and psychopathic disorder legal categories (broadly equating to psychosis and personality disorder) were not differentiated by any of the personality measures. In Scotland, it is unusual for patients to be detained in hospital if they have a personality disorder alone, so almost everyone in the Scottish State Hospital has a mental illness (psychosis). Nevertheless, these measures of personality suggested that the majority were co-morbid for personality disorder. On the basis of these results, Blackburn questions, wisely I think, the rationale for setting up separate units for offenders with mental illness and offenders with personality disorder, a current feature of English health and custodial policies.

The national survey of psychiatric morbidity among prisoners in England and Wales (Singleton et al., 1998) is the other principal source of data linking psychosis and personality disorder, and potentially a potent indicator of need for specialist services in the UK. All 131 prison establishments open in October 1997 were included in the survey. Approximately one in 34 male sentenced prisoners, one in eight male pre-trial prisoners and one in three female prisoners, all aged between 16 and 64, were randomly selected for interview. Standard research schedules were used. Eighty-eight per cent complied fully, yielding 1250 pre-trial men, 1121 sentenced men, and 187 and 584 women prisoners, respectively. People with evidence of personality disorder other than antisocial personality disorder alone were three times more likely to show evidence of a functional psychosis than those with no personality disorder or antisocial personality disorder alone, whereas, conversely, evidence of functional psychosis doubled the odds of having a personality disorder. These findings were robust across the different sex, ethnic and prisoner types, although rates and numbers were highest in the male pre-trial group. Of the 112 such men with probable psychosis, lay interviewers estimated that 89 per cent had 'antisocial or other' or 'other only' types of personality disorder. Of the subgroup of 44 prisoners drawn from all groups who completed clinician-administered interviews, 86 per cent were confirmed on the Structured Interview for DSM-III-R Personality Disorders (SCID-II) (Spitzer et al., 1989) to have such personality disorders. Extrapolated numbers from relatively small subgroups (in this case approximately 120 male pre-trial prisoners with psychosis) must be viewed with caution, but these figures would yield a working estimate of up to 1200 men nationally from the pre-trial group likely to need services for psychosis *and* personality disorder.

Outside offender groups, the UK700 study apart, interest in co-morbidity with personality disorder has focused almost exclusively on neurotic and substance misuse disorders. However, Jorgensen and colleagues (1996) described a series of 39 women and 12 men admitted to a university hospital in Denmark with acute and transient psychotic disorder. About two-thirds were assessed as having a personality disorder in DSM-IV terms once the psychosis had resolved, generally in response to neuroleptics. No subtype of personality disorder was more likely than others.

Hogg et al. (1990) focused on eight women and 32 men with recent-onset schizophrenia (mean duration 2.5 years). More than half of their series met the criteria for a personality disorder, with schizotypal, borderline and antisocial types predominating according to one

instrument, and dependent, narcissistic and avoidant according to another. Jackson et al. (1991) re-analysed most of these data, adding material from patients with affective psychosis and mixed disorders, and found co-morbidity in less than one-third of those with schizophrenia. In the USA, the Epidemiologic Catchment Area study of over 20 000 community residents and others suggested a relationship between antisocial personality disorder and psychosis (Regier et al., 1990).

IMPLICATIONS FOR TREATMENT OF PSYCHOSIS–PERSONALITY DISORDER CO-MORBIDITY

As this combination of problems is so little recognized in practice, observations on its management and treatment are rare. Much has to be inferred from literature relating to other disorders co-morbid with personality disorder, which is only slightly less sparse.

Such published material as there is generally starts from a position of exploring the effect of personality disorders on the outcome of treatment for other disorders, often expressed as the 'interference' of personality disorder with the treatment of other states. There seems to be little or no concept of the possibility that psychosis, or depression, or substance misuse, may 'interfere' with the treatment of personality disorder.

Reich and Green (1991) identified 21 studies published between 1970 and 1990 mainly relating to the treatment of a range of depressive, anxiety or substance misuse disorders. They found only one study reporting improved outcome for patients with a personality pathology. Griggs and Tyrer (1981) reported that the subgroup of four people with schizoid personality disorder within a larger group of 27 engaging in group therapy for alcoholism did well, while those without personality disorder or with sociopathic personality disorder had a worse outcome. Alnaes and Torgersen (1997) added to the gloom with respect to depression, but Mulder (2002) conducted a systematic review of the literature on personality pathology and the treatment of major depression and found more grounds for optimism. Confining himself only to those studies that included measures of depression, standardized personality assessment, a clear report of the treatment and some measure of treatment outcome, he identified a short list of just over 50, although only 27 related to DSM categories of personality disorder. The best-designed studies reported the least effect of personality pathology on treatment outcome. Confounders included failure to control for the chronicity or severity of the depression, but also the amount of treatment. In some uncontrolled studies, depressed patients with personality problems were less likely to receive adequate treatment.

With respect to schizophrenia, McGlashan (1983), in the Chestnut Lodge follow-up programme, established evidence that schizotypal personality disorder may be a variant of schizophrenia, but that borderline personality disorder is not. He found that people with schizophrenia and co-morbid borderline personality disorder had a better outcome in the long-term compared with those with schizophrenia alone.

It is not evident in any of these studies that any effort was expended on the treatment of the co-morbid personality disorder, notwithstanding the apparent belief that this was probably the more limiting disorder. I could find only one study that acknowledged the possible relevance of co-morbid psychosis for the treatment of personality disorder (Reiss et al., 1996). Eight patients (16 per cent) of 49 had psychotic and/or affective illnesses, but there is no specific description of the effect of psychosis on treatment. Numbers in the co-morbid subgroup were too small for confident inferences, but only one of the eight had been discharged to the community by the end of the study compared with 29 (71 per cent) of the remaining 41 without psychosis.

FORMULATING A COMPREHENSIVE TREATMENT PLAN

It is arguable that categories or diagnostic approaches in this field are less helpful than the generation of accurate problem lists that would lead to acknowledgement of how problems may interact. While it is always possible that solving one problem may also banish its fellows, it is not uncommon that problems interact in a way that can be disruptive to assessment and treatment without recognition and management of the interaction.

Primary personality disorders, schizophrenia and other psychoses have in common that interpersonal communication is generally profoundly damaged, and yet so much of the assessment of each is dependent on the capacity to communicate. Frank and Gunderson (1990) showed that, among those being treated primarily for schizophrenia, a good therapeutic alliance predicted better treatment compliance and outcome at 2 years, but found clinical report evidence that this was harder to achieve for those who also had a personality disorder. My experience would equally suggest that an alliance sufficient for the treatment of personality disorder is challenged by the presence of active and intrusive psychotic symptoms. A further complication, as already noted, is that psychosis–personality disorder co-morbidity is likely to increase the chances of additional health problems, often amounting to a clinical diagnosis, most commonly abuse of alcohol or other drugs (Taylor et al., 1998). Such problems may persist even within an in-patient or other institutional setting, and can be used as a defence against engagement, as staff may become increasingly despairing or angry about breach of rules and challenge to their authority. Invariably, for the longer term, these problems will need separate and additional strategies for assessment, management and treatment (see Chapter 20).

Acknowledgement of personality disorder–psychosis co-morbidity should thus not only lead to a holistic programme, which will take account of multiple therapeutic need, but also allow for the temporal ordering of treatments. This generally means that medication will be used in conjunction with psychological treatments and a range of social, educational and occupational approaches. The effects of some psychotic symptoms, for example the fear or depression invoked by some delusions, must generally be relieved before a significant personal alliance can be established with anyone – peer or professional. This affective impact of symptoms can often be relieved, even when the symptoms themselves prove more resistant. Neither the extent to which psychotic symptoms must then be resolved before patients can work effectively on aspects of personality disorder nor the extent to which work on personality pathology may at least enable improved response of the psychotic symptomatology is sufficiently clear for offering general guidance. There are perhaps some hints about a possible differential effect of symptoms from the nature of the social networks adopted by symptomatic patients within an institutional setting. Those people with schizophrenic thought-disorder or negative symptoms prominent in their presentation have significantly smaller numbers of people they would rate as significant contacts or confidants than those with a predominantly delusional presentation (Heads et al., submitted). The latter may be disproportionately likely to include 'upsetting' relationships within their network, but these were not significantly correlated with violent actions, even in the high-security hospital under study. In themselves, therefore, delusions need not be a bar to, say, group psychotherapeutic approaches.

A number of studies have confirmed that psychotherapy is possible among those who have active psychotic symptoms, although on its own it is no better than a supportive milieu (May, 1968). There appears to be a complex interaction between psychotherapy and the domain of psychopathology affected when used in conjunction with medication (Gunderson et al., 1984). However, Gunderson's work, while including individuals with both personality disorder and psychosis, did not attempt to mix psychotic patients, with or without personality disorder, with those with evidence of personality disorder alone. Much anxiety has been expressed about doing this, with fears that the people with psychosis will be more vulnerable and therefore exploited by the 'more competent' patients with personality disorder. There is evidence only that some such mixing can be achieved safely, and with some therapeutic advantage to both subgroups, but again no systematic testing of optimal case mixes or information as to whether some groupings might be contraindicated. Quayle and Moore (1998), however, showed that effective group work can be achieved without equality of representation by diagnostic mix. For an interpersonal relationships group, the men with prominent mental illness, usually schizophrenia, out-numbered those with 'pure' personality disorder by five to three, whereas in the anger management group reported, the balance was reversed, with the 'pure' personality disordered men predominating by eight to two. In both groups, satisfactory therapeutic work was possible.

CONCLUSIONS

Literature, then, makes scant reference to the treatment of personality disorder and psychosis together. Further, in services that are poorly resourced, both materially and in terms of knowledge and skills for treating personality disorder, it is often convenient to ignore the disability of personality disorder. Almost all forensic psychiatrists can cite cases of patients being accepted briefly for treatment of an acute episode of psychosis, even unequivocally documented as having schizophrenia – or manic–depressive psychosis – but rejected or re-diagnosed as some of the acute psychotic symptoms resolve (or even sometimes when they do not) and the much longer standing interpersonal and antisocial difficulties are uncovered. Service development would benefit from research into the size and nature of the problem in wider practice. What appears to be happening to these patients is a form of the malignant alienation well described by Watts and Morgan (1994). While Watts and Morgan were principally concerned with malignant alienation leading to elevated suicide risk, the process may be just as pertinent for serious violence directed against others. They classified the components of malignant alienation according to patient factors, staff factors, staff–patient interaction, and hospital environment. The patient and staff–patient interaction factors appear to be, essentially, personality disorder by another, perhaps more constructive, name. The high-risk group (in this case for suicide) they described as showing longstanding interpersonal incapacity (inclusive of lifelong inability to form warm, mutually independent relationships), marital isolation, distorted communication of dependency wishes, and help negation (persistent withdrawals from or denial of helpful relationships, including professional ones). Inevitably, such characteristics invoke a response in staff. One of the most powerful, yet disempowered, subgroups they suggest is of patients who are unable to contain their own hate. This is projected into carers who, being compassionate and non-judgemental in principle, reject conscious awareness of the counter-transference. Management strategies are proposed that might prevent alienation and promote a therapeutic alliance sufficient to contain and allow a fuller assessment of the range of problems and disorder, and more accurately inform management therapy. First on the list is the capacity on the part of staff to equate challenging, even rejecting behaviours with an inability to seek help in other ways, and to acknowledge the patient's possible inner distress. This kind of empowerment of staff will almost inevitably mean the provision of appropriate supervision and advice, whatever their seniority. Armed with the resultant skills, clinicians are likely to have access to effective work with more of their patients, and in particular those with the mix of illness and personality disorder.

REFERENCES

Alnaes R and Torgersen S (1997). Personality and personality disorders predict development and relapses of major depression. *Acta Psychiatrica Scandinavica* **95**:336–42.

American Psychiatric Association (1987). *Diagnostic and Statistical Manual of Mental Disorders,* third edition, Revised. Washington, DC: American Psychiatric Association.

American Psychiatric Association (1994). *Diagnostic and Statistical Manual of Mental Disorders,* fourth edition. Washington, DC: American Psychiatric Association.

Blackburn R (1968). Emotionality, extraversion and aggression in paranoid and non-paranoid schizophrenic offenders. *British Journal of Psychiatry* **115**:1301–2.

Blackburn R (1970). Personality types among abnormal homicides. Special Hospitals Research Report No. I. Originally circulated by Special Hospitals' Research Unit (SHRU). Now available from Case Register Office, Broadmoor Hospital, Berks, RG45 7EG, UK.

Blackburn R (1974). Personality and the classification of psychopathic disorders. SHRU Report No. I0. Broadmoor Hospital, Berks, RG45 7EG, UK.

Blackburn R (1988). On moral judgments and personality disorders. *British Journal of Psychiatry* **152**:505–12.

Blackburn R, Logan C, Donnell J and Renwick S (2003). Personality disorders, psychopathy and other mental disorders: co-morbidity among patients at English and Scottish high security hospitals. *The Journal of Forensic Psychiatry and Psychology* **14**:111–37.

Clarkin JF and Kendall PC (1992). Comorbidity and treatment planning: summary and future directions. *Journal of Consulting Clinical Psychology* **60**:904–8.

Coid J (1992). DSM-III diagnosis in criminal psychopaths: a way forward. *Criminal Behaviour and Mental Health* **2**:78–94.

Farmer S (1987). Medical problems of chronic patients in a community support program. *Hospital and Community Psychiatry* **38**:745–9.

Feinstein AR (1970). The pre-therapeutic classification of comorbidity in chronic disease. *Journal of Chronic Disease* **23**:455–68.

Felker B, Yazel JJ and Short D (1996). Mortality and medical comorbidity among psychiatric patients: a review. *Psychiatric Services* **47**:1356–63.

Frank AF and Gunderson JG (1990). The role of the therapeutic alliance in the treatment of schizophrenia: relationship to course and outcome. *Archives of General Psychiatry* **47**:228–36.

Fyer MR, Frances AJ, Sullivan T et al. (1988). Co-morbidity of borderline personality disorder. *Archives of General Psychiatry* **45**:348–52.

Goodwin JM, Goodwin JS and Keller R (1979). Psychiatric symptoms in disliked medical patients. *Journal of the American Medical Association* **241**:1117–20.

Griggs SM and Tyrer PJ (1981). Personality disorder, social adjustment and treatment outcome in alcoholics. *Journal of Studies on Alcohol* **42**:802–5.

Gunderson JG, Frank AF, Katz HM, Vannicelli ML, Frosch JP and Knapp PH (1984). Effects of psychotherapy in schizophrenia: II. Comparative outcome of two forms of treatment. *Schizophrenia Bulletin* **10**:564–98.

Hare RD (1991). *The Hare Psychopathy Checklist – Revised*. Toronto: Multi-Health Systems.

Hare RD and Cox DN (1978). Clinical and empirical conceptions of psychopathy, and the selection of subjects for research. In: Hare RD and Schalling D (eds) *Psychopathic Behaviour: Approaches to Research*. Chichester: Wiley.

Heads TC, Leese M, Taylor PJ and Phillips S (submitted). Schizophrenia and serious violence: an exploration of interaction between social context, symptoms and violence.

Heads T, Taylor PJ and Leese M (1997). Childhood experiences of patients with schizophrenia and a history of violence: a special hospital sample. *Criminal Behaviour and Mental Health* **7**:117–30.

Hogg B, Jackson HJ, Rudd RP et al. (1990). Diagnosing personality disorders in recent-onset schizophrenia. *Journal of Nervous and Mental Disease* **178**:194–9.

Hyler SE (1994). *Personality Diagnostic Questionnaire – IV (PDQ-IV)*. New York: New York State Psychiatric Institute.

Jackson HJ, Whiteside HL, Bates GW et al. (1991). Diagnosing personality disorders in psychiatric in-patients. *Acta Psychiatrica Scandinavica* **83**:206–13.

Jaspers K (1923). *General Psychopathology*. Chicago, IL: University of Chicago Press English translation (1963), Manchester: Manchester University Press.

Jorgensen P, Bennedsen B, Christensen J and Hyllested A (1996). Acute and transient psychotic disorder: comorbidity with personality disorder. *Acta Psychiatrica Scandinavica* **94**:460–4.

Maughan B and Farrington DP (1997). Editorial. *Criminal Behaviour and Mental Health* **7**:261–4.

May PRA (1968). *Treatment of Schizophrenia: A Comparative Study of Five Treatment Methods*. New York: Science House.

McCord J and Enslinger ME (1997). Multiple risks and comorbidity in an African-American population. *Criminal Behaviour and Mental Health* **7**:339–52.

McGlashan TH (1983). The borderline syndrome: is it a variant of schizophrenia or affective disorder? *Archives of General Psychiatry* **40**:1319–24.

Millon T (1987). *Manual for the MCMI-II*. Minneapolis, MN: National Computer Systems.

Moran P, Walsh E, Tyrer P, Burns T, Creed F and Fahy T (2003). Impact of comorbid personality disorder on violence in psychosis. *British Journal of Psychiatry* **182**:129–34.

Mulder RT (2002). Personality pathology and treatment outcome in major depression: a review. *American Journal of Psychiatry* **159**:359–71.

Pfohl B, Coryell W, Zimmerman M and Stangl D (1986). DSM-III personality disorders: diagnostic overlap and internal consistency of individual DSM-III criteria. *Comprehensive Psychiatry* **27**:21–34.

Putkonen A, Kotilainen I, Joyal CC and Tiihonen J (2004). Comorbid personality disorders and substance use disorders of mentally ill homicide offenders: a structural clinical study on dual and triple diagnoses. *Schizophrenia Bulletin* **30**:39–72.

Quayle M and Moore E (1998). Evaluating the impact of structured groupwork with men in a high security hospital. *Criminal Behaviour and Mental Health* **8**:77–92.

Regier DA, Farmer ME, Ral DS et al. (1990). Comorbidity of mental disorders with alcohol and other drug abuse. Results from the Epidemiologic

Catchment Area (ECA) Study. *Journal of the American Medical Association* **264**:2511–18.

Reich JH and Green AI (1991). Effect of personality disorders on outcome of treatment. *Journal of Nervous and Mental Disease* **179**:74–82.

Reiss D, Grubin D and Meux C (1996). Young 'psychopaths' in special hospital: treatment and outcome. *British Journal of Psychiatry* **168**:99–104.

Ringbäck Weitoft G, Gullberg A and Rosen M (1998). Avoidable mortality among psychiatric patients. *Social Psychiatry and Psychiatric Epidemiology* **33**:430–7.

Rutter M (1997). Comorbidity: concepts, claims and choices. *Criminal Behaviour and Mental Health* **7**:265–85.

Singleton N, Meltzer H, Gatward R et al. (1998). *Psychiatric Morbidity Among Prisoners in England and Wales.* London: Office for National Statistics, The Stationery Office.

Slomkowski C, Cohen P and Brook J (1997). Sibling relationships of adolescents with antisocial and comorbid mental disorders: an epidemiological investigation. *Criminal Behaviour and Mental Health* **7**:353–68.

Soothill K, Francis B, Ackerley E and Collett S (2001). *Homicide in Britain: A Comparative Study of Rates in Scotland and England and Wales.* Edinburgh: Scottish Executive Central Research Unit.

Spitzer RL, Williams JBW, Gibbon M and First MB (1989). *Structured Interview for DSM-III-R Personality Disorders (SCID-II).* New York: New York State Psychiatric Institute Biometrics Research.

Sternberg D (1986). Testing for physical illness in psychiatric patients. *Journal of Clinical Psychiatry* **47**(Suppl. I):3–9.

Taylor PJ, Leese M, Williams D, Butwell M, Daly R and Larkin E (1998). Mental disorder and violence – a special (high security) hospital study. *British Journal of Psychiatry* **172**:218–26.

Tyrer P and Cicchetti D (2000). Personality Assessment Schedule. In: Tyrer P (ed.), *Personality Disorders: Diagnosis, Management and Course.* Oxford: Butterworth-Heinemann, 51–71.

Tyrer P and Stein G (1993). *Personality Disorder Reviewed.* London: Gaskell.

Walsh E, Leese M, Taylor PJ et al. (2002). Psychosis in high-security and general psychiatric services. *British Journal of Psychiatry* **180**:351–7.

Watts D and Morgan G (1994). Malignant alienation. Dangers for patients who are hard to like. *British Journal of Psychiatry* **164**:11–15.

Westen D (1997). Divergences between clinical and research methods for assessing personality disorders: implications for research and the evolution of Axis II. *American Journal of Psychiatry* **154**:895–903.

World Health Organization (1978). *Mental Disorders: Glossary and Guide to their Classification in Accordance with the Ninth Revision of the International Classification of Diseases.* Geneva: WHO.

World Health Organization (1992). *The ICD-10 Classification of Mental and Behavioural Disorders.* Geneva: WHO.

World Health Organizsation (1995). *International Personality Disorder Examination (IPDE) Manual.* Geneva: WHO.

Chapter 15

CHRONIC POST-TRAUMATIC STRESS DISORDER AND PERSONALITY DISORDER

David Reiss

PSYCHOLOGICAL RESPONSES TO TRAUMA

It has long been recognized that a proportion of those people who have been victims of stressful, traumatic events develop disabling and prolonged psychological reactions even if they have suffered no severe or lasting physical injury. Such conditions were first described as a consequence of combat, and the current psychiatric formulation of post-traumatic stress disorder (PTSD) had its origins in Kardiner's 1941 book *The Traumatic Neuroses of War*. Even today, Western society tends not to recognize fully the psychological harm caused to soldiers exposed to violence or to other victims who have, for example, experienced violent or sexual assault or natural disaster.

Post-traumatic stress disorder was only formally incorporated into the international psychiatric classification systems about 25 years ago. An increasing awareness of the plight of victims of adult trauma, such as Vietnam veterans, led to the incorporation and definition of the syndrome in the third edition of the *Diagnostic and Statistical Manual of Mental Disorders* (DSM-III; American Psychiatric Association, 1980), now revised in the DSM-IV (American Psychiatric Association, 1994)

and also included in the current *International Classification of Diseases*, tenth revision (ICD-10; World Health Organization, 1992). These manuals describe the core symptoms of PTSD within three descriptive clusters: re-experiencing, which includes episodes of repeated reliving of the trauma in intrusive memories, flashbacks or dreams; avoidance and emotional numbing; and hyperarousal, which may be associated with excessive irritability and pathological anger.

The majority of people who have experienced traumatic events do not suffer long-lasting psychological sequelae. The development of post-traumatic psychopathology depends on individual vulnerability, both genetic and acquired, the nature and severity of the traumatic event, and the quality of the post-traumatic environment. Children who are the victims of abuse or neglect may be particularly profoundly affected by their experience. Even if the stress is only relatively small, if the trauma occurs at a sensitive or critical period of psychological development, a child's cognitive or emotional functioning may not progress normally. The psychopathology of severe personality disorder may thus originate at an early age. Adults who have previously experienced such traumatic events and who are then involved in later traumatic incidents may be particularly susceptible subsequently to manifest severe psychological disorder. However, even if there is no pre-existing vulnerability, severe trauma can lead to the development of the full range of abnormal psychological symptoms in someone who was previously healthy.

A variety of psychological disorders may be manifested by those people who develop symptoms after stressful incidents. Although PTSD is the only psychiatric condition that, by definition, requires a traumatic event to have occurred, it has substantial co-morbidity and only rarely occurs in isolation (Kessler et al., 1995). Other post-traumatic syndromes include generalized and phobic anxiety, depression, substance abuse, somatization, and dissociation, all of which may develop independently of PTSD, but frequently occur in association with it.

Even allowing for co-morbidity with other psychiatric disorders, the basic concept of PTSD has proven too limited and inadequate to be a satisfactory description of the complexity and depth of the psychological problems of many victims, particularly those who have experienced prolonged and repeated trauma (Herman, 1992). A high proportion of the lasting and profound difficulties experienced by those who suffer from personality disorders, such as problems in interpersonal relationships, an unstable sense of the self, impulsivity, aggression, re-enactment and revictimization, as well as self-mutilation and suicidal behaviour, may be related to chronic PTSD symptoms. This may be particularly true for those that develop following childhood abuse or neglect, although similar difficulties may also arise subsequent to adult trauma.

SYMPTOM DEVELOPMENT

A central component of the core syndrome of PTSD is an underlying difficulty with the regulation of a variety of affects such as anger, anxiety and sadness (Chemtob et al., 1994;

van der Kolk, 1996). Adults with PTSD who are exposed to reminders of their trauma demonstrate increased activity in brain areas associated with emotions and arousal, and simultaneously decreased activity in the region responsible for verbalization of their thoughts and feelings (Rausch et al., 1996). Traumatized victims of any age may also have a significant impairment in their ability to assess external stimuli and, particularly when aroused and excited, can be unable to make informed and appropriate judgements about the meaning and significance of what is happening around them. Due to their impaired ability to assess external information, they are unable to use their feelings as a sensitive and accurate guide to the timing and nature of appropriate action. They may thus appear to act impulsively with a response following a stimulus, because they are unable to make the appropriate, necessary psychological assessment of what is going on around them (Krystal, 1978; van der Kolk and Ducey, 1989).

Traumatized adults with PTSD are often very obviously unable to advance their lives beyond the time at which the trauma occurred. Trauma-related symptoms such as repetitive intrusive thoughts, frequent flashbacks, severe hypervigilance and an excessive startle response keep the victim focused on the past and interfere with social and occupational functioning. Although such people can respond to reminders of their trauma with a high level of uncontrolled emotion, in many cases such a response is protected against by the development of avoidance and emotional numbing. Victims with these symptoms tend to avoid stimuli that remind them of their trauma, and they may also suffer from a persistent tendency towards emotional unresponsiveness, which, although successful in protecting themselves from their own affective reactions, can in itself be extremely uncomfortable and distressing (Litz and Keane, 1989).

Other symptoms that are frequently associated with PTSD and that may lead to difficulties in daily functioning may be caused by psychological mechanisms which, although protective in the acute trauma situation, become maladaptive when they persist after the stress has gone. It is common for victims to report that during their traumatic experience they were able to detach themselves from it by observing themselves being traumatized from a distance, perceiving it as though it was happening to someone else (Rose, 1986; Spiegel et al., 1988). Such dissociation, with the separation of different aspects of mental functioning, may be helpful at first, in that it protects the victim from full mental and physical awareness of the event, thereby reducing pain and acute suffering (Noyes and Kletti, 1977; Gelinas, 1983). However, if this psychological process persists when there is no trauma in progress, it may then become an integral, symptomatic part of PTSD (Marmar et al., 1994). Within its subsequent pathological context, dissociation prevents incorporation of the trauma into the normal continuity of memory and experience, interferes with full integration of the self, and reduces social functioning, thus being associated with a variety of psychological symptoms including nightmares and flashbacks, physical symptoms for which no cause can be found, and a lack of interpersonal connection with others (Pribor et al., 1993; Saxe et al., 1993, 1994). The victims' disturbed sense of their own being may lead to a view of themselves as helpless and ineffective, body-image disturbances and a loss of their autobiographical memories (Cole and Putnam, 1992). Such people may develop paranoid attributions, as they have difficulty in appreciating their own contributions to their problems (van der Kolk, 1996).

Violence towards others may be facilitated by the combination of lack of stimulus discrimination and inability to attribute correctly the cause of external events, which together promote a heightened sensitivity to threat within the immediate environment. An extreme vulnerability to current stressors, originating in the traumatic experience, means that victims may be exquisitely sensitive to reminders of the past, resulting in normally insignificant stimuli being interpreted as threatening and causing significant distress. As traumatic memories are often not properly integrated, such victims are usually unaware of how their past trauma can influence their current emotions.

PERSONALITY DEVELOPMENT

Children who are abused may, as a consequence, have seriously adversely affected personality development. If it happens at the critical stage when they should be learning how to interact with others through play, the traumatic experience may impair their social development. They may then be unable to learn how to socialize appropriately and cannot either form or gain fulfillment from relationships within their peer group. Their consequent lack of social integration may lead to further difficulties with issues around safety, security, trust, intimacy and self-assertion. A deficiency of the skills necessary to resolve interpersonal conflicts appropriately may result in angry, threatening and bullying behaviours, which draw attention to the individual, or, alternatively, the victim may appear shy, submissive and fearful, and tend to withdraw from social interactions (Cicchetti and White, 1990).

The interpersonal nature of the trauma suffered by children who are abused or neglected may also be responsible for the development of profound deficits in social functioning. Childhood trauma frequently occurs within a family environment from which the victim is unable to escape; the child is effectively a captive under the control of the perpetrator. Trauma that is inflicted by those responsible for the care of young victims may severely impair their ability to trust others and form intimate relationships, resulting in an increase in their level of aggression (Burgess et al., 1987).

Underlying assumptions held by adults about how they interact with their external environment, which determine their view of the world, may also be adversely affected in those who were traumatized as children, strongly influencing their subsequent expectations and behaviour (van der Kolk and Ducey, 1989). For example, if victims have felt helpless while being abused by powerful aggressors, they may tend to conceptualize their relationships in terms of dominance and submission. Being terrified of both being abandoned and being dominated, they may form intense, unstable relationships, within which their behaviour may change rapidly between the extremes of passive acquiescence and rebellion (Melges and Swartz, 1989).

In terms of their development, adults and adolescents who have been traumatized as children are often stuck at the emotional and cognitive level they were at when the stressful event(s) occurred. As a consequence, their view of their place in the world may be profoundly distorted. For example, people who have been abused at a stage when they believed that everything that happened was caused either by their own magical thoughts or their behaviour may suffer from a continuing and inappropriate tendency to self-reproach, with consequent persistent feelings of guilt and shame. Such victims suffer from chronically low self-esteem, and may blame themselves not only for their own abuse, but also for subsequent problems and traumas that may be entirely out of their control (Ogata et al., 1990).

Personality development may be particularly seriously adversely affected in symptomatic abused children who develop a combination of chronic dissociation and a lack of ability to self-regulate. A reduced capacity to focus attention on appropriate aspects of the environment, together with an inability to control unstable internal emotions and a high level of impulsivity, when combined with low-self esteem, lack of trust in others and excess aggression, may make people more likely eventually to cause harm to themselves or others (Cole and Putnam, 1992). Such children may therefore be particularly at risk of antisocial behaviour in later

life. As they grow up, attempts to change their abnormal functioning, even if their environment becomes less stressful, may be hampered by the fact that they have known no other way of interacting and behaving. However, adults who have lost their ability to self-regulate and may be unable to control many of their moods and actions will usually have some insight into the fact that they have changed. The maintenance of such a tenuous but significant link with their previous lives can allow them to impose upon themselves a degree of behavioural inhibition.

SUBSTANCE ABUSE

Alcohol and substance abuse are common complications of personality disorder, and significant associations have also been found between substance abuse and being a victim of violent or sexual trauma, during both childhood and adulthood (Dembo et al., 1988; Hernandez and DiClemente, 1992; Lisak, 1993; Fullilove et al., 1993). Within the context of PTSD, alcohol is probably effective as a short-term treatment for distressing intrusive symptoms such as flashbacks, and it may also help with sleep disturbance and nightmares. Other drugs may have similar effects. It is therefore perhaps not surprising that high rates of alcohol and drug abuse have been reported in traumatized adults (Keane et al., 1988; Keane and Wolfe, 1990; Kulka et al., 1990), perhaps arising from initial attempts at self-medication.

REPETITION OF THE TRAUMA AND RE-TRAUMATIZATION

Without consciously realizing what they are doing, traumatized people who have been victims of earlier abuse may repeat certain aspects of their lives. For example, they can recreate interpersonal social situations that resemble the environment in which they themselves were traumatized (although in the replay they may take the role of perpetrator), and thus may cause themselves and/or others considerable distress.

People who have been traumatized on one occasion are subsequently particularly vulnerable to being victimized again: rape victims are more likely to suffer another rape, and women who were physically or sexually abused as children are more likely to be abused or assaulted again, often by forming a relationship with an abusive partner (Hilberman, 1980; Russell, 1986; Mezey and Taylor, 1988). An association has also been found between having suffered the experience of childhood physical and/or sexual abuse and the commission of crimes, often involving the victimization of others, in later life (Groth, 1979; Burgess et al., 1987).

The experience of chronic victimization may lead not only to the repetition of trauma, but also to behaviour that perpetuates long-term abuse. Children and adults who are frightened seek increased protection (van der Kolk, 1989). Victims often have no alternative but to turn towards the source of their fear for comfort, with the consequence that the abused often resist being removed from their abusers (Dutton and Painter, 1981). Similarly, battered spouses may be subsequently prevented from exiting relationships because of the strong attachments they have formed to their violent partners (Walker, 1979).

PROTECTIVE FACTORS

An individual may be protected against the development of character pathology even when significant trauma occurs. Secure attachment bonds are probably the best defence against trauma-induced psychopathology in both children and adults (Finkelhor and Browne, 1984). In children who have been exposed to severe stressors, the quality of the parental bond is probably the single most important determinant of long-term damage (McFarlane, 1988). Traumatized adults with childhood histories of

severe neglect have a particularly poor long-term prognosis, compared with traumatized individuals who have had more secure attachment bonds as children (van der Kolk and Fisler, 1994).

CO-MORBIDITY

In those who have been traumatized as adults, co-morbidity of personality disorder with PTSD is common. Male Vietnam war veterans with PTSD have been diagnosed with high levels of both antisocial personality disorder (Sierles et al., 1983, 1986; Kulka et al., 1988; Keane and Wolfe, 1990; Keane et al., 1996) and borderline personality disorder (Southwick et al., 1993; Keane et al., 1996). High rates of paranoid personality disorder have been found in recently sexually or non-sexually assaulted female subjects suffering from both acute and chronic forms of PTSD, with chronic cases also showing high rates of borderline personality disorder and avoidant personality disorder (Cashman et al., 1995).

In those people with both personality disorder and PTSD, the nature of the temporal and causal relationships between the two syndromes is frequently uncertain. Personality disorder may render victims vulnerable to the development of PTSD, and may also be a manifestation of the post-traumatic syndrome (Gunderson and Sabo, 1993). In those who offend, symptoms such as anger and compulsion to repeat the trauma may contribute to their criminal behaviour, and offenders, particularly psychologically vulnerable ones, may be traumatized by their own deeds (Thomas et al., 1994; Kruppa et al., 1995).

As discussed above, victims of physical and sexual abuse whose abuse occurred during a vulnerable period of their development in childhood may be especially likely to suffer from chronic and enduring changes in character. Although many psychiatric patients have histories of trauma, it is childhood abuse and neglect that have been found to be particularly associated with subsequent borderline person-ality disorder (Gunderson and Zanarini, 1989) and antisocial personality disorder (Pollock et al., 1990; Luntz and Widom, 1994).

Borderline personality disorder may arise out of chronic fear experienced during childhood, and a particular association has been found between the borderline syndrome and child-hood sexual abuse (Herman et al., 1989). The long-term effects of childhood sexual abuse include a number of psychopathological fea-tures that are characteristic of patients with borderline personality disorder, for example a variety of forms of self-harm in later life, espe-cially self-cutting and self-starving (van der Kolk et al., 1991). This finding supports the hypoth-esis that childhood sexual abuse may be an aetiological factor for the syndrome (Browne and Finkelhor, 1986). In addition to sexual abuse, significantly higher frequencies of intra-familial physical abuse (Links et al., 1988; Herman et al., 1989; Westen et al., 1990; Paris et al., 1994a), separation from or loss of parents early in life (Bradley, 1979; Links et al., 1988; Paris et al., 1988, 1994b; Zanarini et al., 1989) and abnormal parental bonding (Gold-berg et al., 1985; Zweig-Frank and Paris, 1991; Torgersen and Alnaes, 1992; Paris et al., 1994b) have also been found in patients with borderline personality disorder.

However, the correspondence between child-hood sexual abuse and the borderline syndrome is variable. Many borderline patients have no history of childhood sexual abuse, whereas many non-borderlines do. So although child-hood abuse is probably an important factor in the development of borderline personality dis-order, it is not in itself sufficient to account for its presence in any individual. The experience of trauma may be most pathogenic for chil-dren with vulnerable temperaments or for those without protective factors.

Antisocial personality disorder is more com-mon in males, but has a marked overlap with borderline personality disorder in its symp-toms (personality characteristics, particularly impulsivity), community prevalence, risk fac-tors, outcome and response to treatment. However, borderline personality disorder is more prevalent in females. Antisocial person-ality disorder and borderline personality dis-order could therefore be conceptualized as being different but related manifestations aris-ing out of similar underlying psychopathology and traumatic aetiology, but with the former manifesting predominantly in males with more outwardly directed hostility, and the latter in females with greater inwardly directed anger (Stone, 1990; Paris, 1997).

CONCLUSION

The basic symptoms of PTSD are inadequate as a summary of post-traumatic psychopath-ology, which may take many different forms. Children may be particularly adversely affected by traumatic experiences, especially if their abuse or neglect occurs at a vulnerable or crit-ical period in their development and is inflicted by a caregiver. Long-lasting and profound dysregulation of affect in combination with other post-traumatic symptoms may give rise to the psychopathology of personality dis-order. Borderline and antisocial personality disorders are the two syndromes that are most likely to have underlying traumatic aetiology.

REFERENCES

American Psychiatric Association (1980). *Diagnostic and Statistical Manual of Mental Disorders*, third edition. Washington, DC: American Psychiatric Association.

American Psychiatric Association (1994). *Diagnostic and Statistical Manual of Mental Disorders*, fourth edition. Washington, DC: American Psychiatric Association.

Bradley SJ (1979). The relationship of early maternal separation to borderline personality disorder in chil-dren and adolescents. *American Journal of Psychiatry* **136**:424–6.

Browne A and Finkelhor D (1986). Impact of child sex-ual abuse: a review of the research. *Psychological Bulletin* **99**:66–77.

Burgess AW, Hartman CR and McCormick A (1987). Abused to abuser: antecedents of socially deviant behavior. *American Journal of Psychiatry* **144**:1431–6.

Cashman L, Molnar C and Foa EB (1995). Comorbidity of DSM-III-R Axis I and II disorders with acute and chronic post-traumatic stress disorder. Paper presented at the 29th annual convention of the Association for the Advancement of Behavior Therapy, Washington, DC. Reported in Keane TM and Kaloupek DG (1997). Comorbid psychiatric disorders in PTSD: implications for research. *Annals of the New York Academy of Sciences* **821**:24–34.

Chemtob CM, Hamada RS, Roitblat HL and Muraoka MY (1994). Anger, impulsivity, and anger control in combat-related posttraumatic stress disorder. *Journal of Consulting and Clinical Psychology* **62**:827–32.

Cicchetti D and White J (1990). Emotion and developmental psychopathology. In: Stein N, Leventhal B and Trebasso T (eds), *Psychological and Biological Approaches to Emotion*. Hillsdale, NJ: Erlbaum, 359–82.

Cole P and Putnam FW (1992). Effect of incest on self and social functioning: a developmental psychopathology perspective. *Journal of Consulting and Clinical Psychology* **60**:174–84.

Dembo R, Williams L, Wish ED et al. (1988). The relationship between physical and sexual abuse and illicit drug use: a replication among a new sample of youths entering a juvenile detention center. *International Journal of Addiction* **23**:1101–23.

Dutton D and Painter SL (1981). Traumatic bonding: the development of emotional attachments in battered women and other relationships of intermittent abuse. *Victimology* **6**:139–68.

Finkelhor D and Browne A (1984). The traumatic impact of child sexual abuse: a conceptualization. *American Journal of Orthopsychiatry* **55**:530–41.

Fullilove MT, Fullilove RE, Smith M et al. (1993). Violence, trauma and post-traumatic stress disorder among women drug users. *Journal of Traumatic Stress* **6**:533–43.

Gelinas DJ (1983). The persistent negative effects of incest. *Psychiatry* **46**:312–32.

Goldberg RL, Mann LS and Sie TN (1985). Parental qualities as perceived by borderline personality disorders. *Hillside Journal of Clinical Psychiatry* **7**:134–40.

Groth AN (1979). Sexual trauma in the life histories of sex offenders. *Victimology* **4**:6–10.

Gunderson JG and Sabo AN (1993). The phenomenological and conceptual interface between borderline personality disorder and PTSD. *American Journal of Psychiatry* **150**:19–27.

Gunderson JG and Zanarini ME (1989). Pathogenesis of borderline personality. In: Tasman A, Hales RE and Frances AJ (eds), *Psychiatry Annual Review*. Washington, DC: American Psychiatric Association, 25–50.

Herman JL (1992). Complex PTSD: a syndrome in survivors of prolonged and repeated trauma. *Journal of Traumatic Stress* **5**:377–91.

Herman JL, Perry JC and van der Kolk BA (1989). Childhood trauma in borderline personality disorder. *American Journal of Psychiatry* **146**:490–5.

Hernandez JT and DiClemente RJ (1992). Emotional and behavioral correlates of sexual abuse among adolescents: is there a difference according to gender? *Journal of Adolescent Health* **13**:658–62.

Hilberman E (1980). Overview: the wife-beater's wife reconsidered. *American Journal of Psychiatry* **137**:974–5.

Kardiner A (1941). *The Traumatic Neuroses of War*. New York: Hoeber.

Keane TM, Colb L, Kaloupek D et al. (1996). A psychophysiological study of chronic combat-related PTSD: results from a Department of Veteran Affairs cooperative study. Unpublished manuscript. Reported in Keane TM and Kaloupek DG (1997). Comorbid psychiatric disorders in PTSD: implications for research. *Annals of the New York Academy of Sciences* **821**:24–34.

Keane TM, Gerardi RJ, Lyons JA and Wolfe J (1988). The interrelationship of substance abuse and posttraumatic stress disorder: epidemiological and clinical considerations. In: Galanter M (ed.), *Recent Developments in Alcoholism*, Vol. 6. New York: Plenum Press, 27–48.

Keane TM and Wolfe J (1990). Comorbidity in posttraumatic stress disorder: an analysis of community and clinical studies. *Journal of Applied Social Psychology* **20**:1776–88.

Kessler R, Sonnega A, Bromet E and Nelson CB (1995). Posttraumatic stress disorder in the National

Comorbidity Survey. *Archives of General Psychiatry* **52**:1048–60.

Kruppa I, Hickey N and Hubbard C (1995). The prevalence of post traumatic stress disorder in a special hospital population of legal psychopaths. *Psychology, Crime and Law* **2**:131–41.

Krystal H (1978). Trauma and affects. *Psychoanalytic Study of the Child* **33**:81–116.

Kulka RA, Schlenger WE, Fairbank JA et al. (1988). *National Vietnam Veterans Readjustment Study (NVVRS): Description, Current Status, and Initial PTSD Prevalence Estimates. Final Report.* Washington, DC: Veterans Administration.

Kulka RA, Schlenger WE, Fairbank JA, Hough RL, Jordan BK and Marmar CR (1990). *Trauma and the Vietnam War Generation: Report of Findings from the National Vietnam Veterans' Readjustment Study.* New York: Brunner/Mazel.

Links PS, Steiner M and Offord DR (1988). Characteristics of borderline personality disorder: a Canadian study. *Canadian Journal of Psychiatry* **33**:336–40.

Lisak D (1993). Men as victims: challenging cultural myths. *Journal of Traumatic Stress* **6**:577–80.

Litz BT and Keane TM (1989). Information processing in anxiety disorders: application to the understanding of post-traumatic stress disorder. *Clinical Psychology Review* **9**:243–57.

Luntz BK and Widom CS (1994). Antisocial personality disorder in abused and neglected children grown up. *American Journal of Psychiatry* **151**:670–4.

Marmar CR, Weiss, DS, Schlenger WE et al. (1994). Peritraumatic dissociation and posttraumatic stress in male Vietnam theater veterans. *American Journal of Psychiatry* **151**:902–7.

McFarlane AC (1988). Recent life events and psychiatric disorder in children: the interaction with preceding extreme adversity. *Journal of Clinical Psychiatry* **29**(5):677–90.

Melges FT and Swartz MS (1989). Oscillations of attachment in borderline personality disorder. *American Journal of Psychiatry* **146**:1115–20.

Mezey GC and Taylor PJ (1988). Psychological reactions of women who have been raped. *British Journal of Psychiatry* **152**:330–9.

Noyes R and Kletti R (1977). Depersonalization in response to life threatening danger. *Comprehensive Psychiatry* **18**:375–84.

Ogata SN, Silk KR, Goodrich S, Lohr NE, Westen D and Hill EM (1990). Childhood sexual and physical abuse in adult patients with borderline personality disorder. *American Journal of Psychiatry* **147**: 1008–13.

Paris J (1997). Antisocial and borderline personality disorders: two separate diagnoses or two aspects of the same psychopathology. *Comprehensive Psychiatry* **38**:237–42.

Paris J, Nowlis D and Brown R (1988). Developmental factors in the outcome of borderline personality disorder. *Comprehensive Psychiatry* **29**:147–51.

Paris J, Zweig-Frank H and Guzder J (1994a). Psychological risk factors for borderline personality disorder in female patients. *Comprehensive Psychiatry* **35**:301–5.

Paris J, Zweig-Frank H and Guzder J (1994b). Risk factors for borderline personality in male outpatients. *Journal of Nervous and Mental Disease* **182**:375–80.

Pollock VE, Briere J, Schneider L, Knop J, Mednick SA and Goodwin DW (1990). Childhood antecedents of antisocial behavior: parental alcoholism and physical abusiveness. *American Journal of Psychiatry* **147**:1290–3.

Pribor EF, Yutzy SH, Dean T and Wetzel RD (1993). Briquet's syndrome, dissociation and abuse. *American Journal of Psychiatry* **150**:1507–11.

Rausch SL, van der Kolk BA, Fisler RE et al. (1996). A symptom provocation study of posttraumatic stress disorder using positron emission tomography and script-driven imagery. *Archives of General Psychiatry* **53**:380–7.

Rose DS (1986). 'Worse than death': psychodynamics of rape victims and the need for psychotherapy. *American Journal of Psychiatry* **143**:817–24.

Russell D (1986). *The Secret Trauma.* New York: Basic Books.

Saxe GN, Chinman G, Berkowitz R et al. (1994). Somatization in patients with dissociative disorders. *American Journal of Psychiatry* **151**:1329–35.

Saxe G, van der Kolk BA, Hall K et al. (1993). Dissociative disorders in psychiatric inpatients. *American Journal of Psychiatry* **150**:1037–42.

Sierles FS, Chen J, McFarland RE and Taylor MA (1983). Post-traumatic stress disorder and concurrent psychiatric illness. *American Journal of Psychiatry* **140**:1177–9.

Sierles FS, Chen J, Messing ML, Besyner JK and Taylor MA (1986). Concurrent psychiatric illness in non-Hispanic outpatients diagnosed as having post-traumatic stress disorder. *Journal of Nervous and Mental Disease* **174**:171–3.

Southwick SM, Yehuda R and Giller EL (1993). Personality disorders in treatment-seeking combat veterans with posttraumatic stress disorder. *American Journal of Psychiatry* **150**:1020–3.

Spiegel D, Hunt T and Dondershine HE (1988). Dissociation and hypnotizability in posttraumatic stress disorder. *American Journal of Psychiatry* **145**:301–5.

Stone MH (1990). *The Fate of Borderline Patients.* New York: Guilford Press.

Thomas C, Adshead G and Mezey G (1994). Case report: traumatic responses to child murder. *Journal of Forensic Psychiatry* **5**:168–76.

Torgersen S and Alnaes R (1992). Differential perception of parental bonding in schizotypal and borderline personality disorders. *Comprehensive Psychiatry* **33**:34–8.

Van der Kolk BA (1989). The compulsion to repeat the trauma. *Psychiatric Clinics of North America* **12**:389–411.

Van der Kolk BA (1996). The complexity of adaptation to trauma: self-regulation, stimulus discrimination, and characterological development. In: Van der Kolk BA, McFarlane AC and Weisaeth L (eds), *Traumatic Stress.* New York: Guilford Press, 182–213.

Van der Kolk BA and Ducey C (1989). The psychological processing of traumatic experience: Rorschach patterns in PTSD. *Journal of Traumatic Stress* **2**:259–74.

Van der Kolk BA and Fisler R (1994). Childhood abuse and neglect and loss of self-regulation. *Bulletin of the Menninger Clinic* **58**:145–68.

Van der Kolk BA, Perry C and Herman JL (1991). Childhood origins of self-destructive behavior. *American Journal of Psychiatry* **148**:1665–71.

Walker L (1979). *The Battered Women.* New York: Harper and Row.

Westen D, Ludolph P, Misle B et al. (1990). Physical and sexual abuse in adolescent girls with borderline personality disorder. *American Journal of Orthopsychiatry* **60**:55–66.

World Health Organization (1992). *International Classification of Diseases,* tenth revision. Geneva: World Health Organization.

Zanarini ME, Gunderson JG, Marino MF, Schwartz EO and Frankenburg FR (1989). Childhood experiences of borderline patients. *Comprehensive Psychiatry* **30**:18–25.

Zweig-Frank H and Paris J (1991). Parents' emotional neglect and overprotection according to the recollections of patients with borderline personality disorder. *American Journal of Psychiatry* **148**:648–51.

Chapter 16

TREATMENT OF ATTENTION DEFICIT HYPERACTIVITY DISORDER

Susan Young and Brian Toone

INTRODUCTION

Attention deficit hyperactivity disorder (ADHD) is a common disorder of childhood. It is estimated that approximately 0.5–1 per cent of the young adult population in the UK continues to have symptoms associated with ADHD (Toone and van der Linden, 1997). The criteria of the *Diagnostic and Statistical Manual of Mental Disorders,* fourth edition (DSM-IV, American Psychiatric Association, 1994), for diagnosis suggest inattentive, impulsive and hyperactive behaviours must be pervasive across two or more settings before the age of 7. There must be clear evidence of clinically significant impairment in social, academic or occupational functioning. Exclusions include symptoms that occur exclusively during the course of a pervasive developmental disorder, schizophrenia or other psychotic disorder. The aetiology of ADHD remains uncertain; studies evidence the importance of genetic factors (Goodman and Stevenson, 1989), alterations in brain function (Lou et al., 1989; Zametkin et al., 1990), alterations in brain structure (Castellanos et al., 1994; Giedd et al., 1994) and neurochemical change (Shen and Wang, 1984; Zametkin et al., 1984; Bowden et al., 1988).

Early research suggested that many children grow out of their symptoms as they mature, and this seems to be the case for many young adults, but long-term prospective studies show that others continue to be impaired by the core symptoms of inattention, impulsiveness and restless behaviour, as well as experiencing significant problems with the negative features associated with the disorder. Executive deficits have also been reported in adults (Aman et al., 1998; MacLean et al., 2004) and it is thought their neuropsychological basis involves dysfunction in working memory, self-regulation of cognition and future-directed behaviour (Barkley, 2001). In particular, a planning impairment has been linked to impulsive responding for ADHD adults, shown by shorter thinking times and increased errors with more complex problems in an experimental task. Problem-solving and planning are essential skills required for daily living activities and these impairments may translate into deficits in everyday planning ability (Young et al., submitted). Associated factors include antisocial and criminal behaviour, interpersonal difficulties, low self-esteem, educational failure and occupational problems (for review, see Young, 2000). Up to 40 per cent of children will develop conduct problems, and by early adulthood, it has been associated with criminal behaviour, substance abuse and personality disorder (Weiss and Hechtman, 1986; Mannuzza et al., 1989, 1993; Satterfield et al., 1994; van der Linden et al., 2000; Young et al., 2003; Young and Gudjonsson, in press). Attention deficit hyperactivity disorder in adults is now more frequently diagnosed in the UK in adult psychiatric services, but in forensic psychiatry there is a failure to diagnose and treat people with this disorder (Collins and White, 2002). Impulsivity rather than inattention is the component of ADHD that is most likely to be associated with antisocial behaviour (Colledge and Blair, 2001; Young and Gudjonsson, 2005). However, ADHD adults may under-report impulsive behaviour (Young, 2004; Young and Gudjonsson, 2005).

The outcome of personality disorder has been studied in three centres investigating the long-term outcome of hyperactive children, in Montreal by Weiss et al. (1985), in New York by Mannuzza et al. (1993), and in London by Taylor et al. (1996). All studies found hyperactivity to be a risk for personality disorder. Mannuzza and colleagues followed up a cohort of hyperactive 6–12-year-old boys and found that, compared with controls, the index group was nearly ten times more likely to have antisocial personality disorder at follow-up. At 23–30 years of age, 18 per cent met DSM-IIIR criteria for antisocial personality disorder, compared with 2 per cent of controls. The Montreal group reported antisocial personality disorder to be the only DSM-III diagnosis that was more common to the former hyperactive group than to controls (23 per cent vs. 2 per cent) at 21–33 years of age. The authors caution, nevertheless, that one-third of cases were mild. In a smaller, rural study in Iowa, Loney et al. (1983) compared 22 hyperactive boys with their brothers and found antisocial personality disorder to be more prevalent at age 21–33 years (45 per cent and 18 per cent respectively). The London study controlled the risk for hyperactivity with conduct problems and found only individuals in the hyperactivity group (four young men, or 13 per cent) met *International Classification of Diseases*, tenth revision (ICD-10, World Health Organization, 1992) criteria for personality disorder (Taylor et al., 1996).

Our own research on a clinically referred group found that more patients with ADHD met ICD-10 criteria for a personality disorder, especially dissocial (van der Linden et al., 2000; Young et al., 2003). Antisocial behaviour has consistently been reported, and prison studies using screening measures suggest up to 67 per cent of inmates had childhood ADHD and 30 per cent continue to be symptomatic (Eyestone and Howell, 1994; Vitelli, 1995; Dalteg et al., 1999; Rasmussen et al., 2001). High rates of recidivism have been reported (Satterfield et al., 1982, 1994; Hechtman and Weiss, 1986; Lambert, 1988; Mannuzza et al., 1989) and crimes are likely to be opportunistic and unplanned. Young et al. (2003) investigated ADHD in personality disordered offenders detained in medium-security and maximum-security hospitals. Using screening measures on a sample of 69 males, they found that 78 per cent obtained scores consistent with childhood ADHD, but only three people were likely to meet adult criteria. However, approximately 29 per cent were classified as 'in partial remission'. They found the symptomatic group (consisting primarily of individuals in partial remission) had a significantly greater number of critical incidents of aggressive behaviour recorded in their patient notes. The study highlights the risk presented by personality disordered patients who may have at least residual ADHD symptoms. The lower than expected percentage of patients likely to meet full criteria may be due to uncooperative and more disruptive patients refusing to participate in the research. Interestingly, primary nurses did not rate a significant difference between groups on a measure of disruptive behaviour, highlighting the potential problem with relying on subjective impressions that may be influenced by personal feelings about individual patients in this population based on their disruptive behaviour.

In this population, ADHD may be unrecognized because of co-morbid problems of personality, mood, anxiety and/or substance misuse (Young and Harty, 2001). Not one person in the study had been assessed for ADHD, and the study illustrates how a straightforward screening process may usefully identify appropriate individuals for multidisciplinary assessment. (For information about assessment, see Young and Toone, 2000.) Personality disordered individuals are acknowledged to be difficult and challenging to treat and their complex presentation may result in them being considered 'untreatable'. Personality disordered patients with ADHD are likely to be particularly disruptive, provocative and challenging to manage. Yet treatment with stimulant medication has been shown to be efficacious in the treatment of ADHD adults, and improvement in underlying symptoms may predispose individuals to engage in psychological therapy, occupational therapy and educational programmes. This may result in a reduction of risk and an accelerated move into lower security and rehabilitation in the community.

CLINICAL MANAGEMENT

As in the management of ADHD in childhood, pharmacotherapy has the major role. In childhood ADHD, management comprising psychological and social treatments alone is less effective than that comprising pharmacological treatments alone, but a combination of both approaches is more efficacious than either alone (Multimodel Treatment of Children with ADHD (MPA) Study – Jensen et al., 1999). It is very likely that the same will be true of ADHD in adulthood, but as yet the psychosocial approach has received little attention. This section therefore deals with pharmacological and psychological management.

PHARMACOLOGICAL MANAGEMENT

The mainstay of the pharmacological treatment of ADHD has been the class of drugs referred to as cerebral stimulants. Only in this group has a sufficient number of randomized controlled trials (RCTs) been conducted to provide evidence-based support for prescribing habits, and even this hardly compares with the extent to which such drugs have been studied in children. Other drugs, notably the tricyclic antidepressant desipramine and, more recently, venlafaxine and tomoxetine, have been studied, but more is known about the cerebral stimulants and they remain the drug treatment of first choice.

The cerebral stimulants, of which methylphenidate and dexamphetamine are representative members, have an effect on monoaminergic neurotransmission pathways, principally through their action on pre-synaptic re-uptake sites. The overall effect is to increase the synaptic concentrations of dopamine and noradrenaline (norepinephrine), although the two drugs differ in their precise locus of action. The effectiveness of the cerebral stimulants has drawn attention to the putative role of noradrenaline and, in particular, dopamine transmission in the genesis of ADHD, but there is as yet only limited understanding of ADHD pathogenesis, to the extent that there is continuing uncertainty whether untreated ADHD reflects a hypo-dopaminergic or hyper-dopaminergic state. A consideration of cerebral stimulant action does little to resolve that uncertainty: an increase in synaptic cleft monoamines may increase or decrease transmission depending on the balance of post-synaptic and pre-synaptic autoreceptor activation.

The efficacy of cerebral stimulants in the treatment of ADHD has received far less attention in adults than in children. In nine controlled studies, the majority involving methylphenidate, the response rate varied between 25 per cent and 73 per cent, with a mean of 60 per cent, compared with a response rate of 60–70 per cent in children aged 6–12 years and 75 per cent in adolescents (Wilens and Spencer, 2000). The relatively low response rate may reflect the greater difficulties in making the diagnosis in adulthood, poor compliance, and lack of adequate outcome measures. It may also be due to inadequate dosage. In the first four controlled studies of methylphenidate, the average drug dose was 0.6 mg/kg and the average response rate 50 per cent. In the fifth study (Spencer et al., 1995), a dose of 1 mg/kg yielded a response rate of 78 per cent.

Methylphenidate and dexamphetamine are the most widely prescribed cerebral stimulants. Both are available in immediate release and sustained release forms, but doubts have been expressed about the efficacy of the latter. A more effective sustained release form of methylphenidate (Concerta) has recently become available. Pemoline, a cerebral stimulant with a longer half-life, has recently been withdrawn due to hepatotoxicity. Adderall, a combination of d-l-amphetamine, also has a very long half-life; it is widely prescribed in the USA, but its availability in the UK is limited.

The therapeutic actions of methylphenidate and dexamphetamine are very similar. Both are controlled drugs; neither is licensed for use in adults with ADHD, and prescribing is conducted on a 'named' basis. Methylphenidate is the most prescribed cerebral stimulant and its actions will be described in more detail. The immediate release form is marketed as a 10 mg preparation (Ritalin) and a 5 mg preparation (Equasym). It has a half-life of approximately 3 hours and is excreted within 12 hours. It is rapidly absorbed, reaching a peak plasma concentration at between 1 and 1.4 hours. The behavioural effects are experienced within 20–30 minutes, reaching a peak between 1 and 2 hours. They wear off between 3 and 4 hours post-ingestion, so that repeat doses during the course of the day are necessary. The introduction of Concerta, the sustained release preparation of methylphenidate, marked a distinct advance. Its duration of action of 12 hours permits once-daily dosing. The smooth, sustained action is preferable to the intermittent action of the immediate release preparations. However, a 'rebound' effect may still appear as the dose wears off.

Cerebral stimulants should be prescribed as a first-line treatment choice in adults who meet DSM-IV criteria for ADHD. They may also be used in subjects who have symptoms that persist and are distressing and/or disabling, but who do not meet full criteria. There are few absolute contraindications. It is not possible to treat effectively patients who are currently abusing drugs, particularly amphetamines and cocaine. Psychotic symptoms may be aggravated by cerebral stimulants. As a general principle, it is better to treat co-morbid psychiatric disorders and then to reassess: the diagnostic picture will become clearer and if cerebral stimulant drugs are still indicated, they are likely to be more effective and their actions more readily evaluated.

Other contraindications, such as a history of drug misuse, no longer current, or a past, resolved psychotic episode, are relative and indicate a need for caution rather than inaction. The risk of exacerbating a pre-existing tic disorder is much smaller in adults.

The cerebral stimulants are well tolerated. The principal side effects, in order of frequency of presentation, are insomnia, edginess, diminished appetite, dysphoria and headaches (Wilens and Spencer, 2000). They are most prominent immediately after the introduction of treatment or after an increase in dosage. They usually remit over time or following a reduction in dosage. Appetite suppression may persist and lead to weight loss; this is not always unwelcome, but can be avoided by taking the drug with or after meals. Cerebral stimulant-induced psychosis has been reported anecdotally in children, but not in adults. The potential for iatrogenic drug abuse clearly exists, but has yet to be reported. The effects of cerebral stimulants on heart rate and blood pressure appear to be less important in adults.

The action of dexamphetamine is similar to that of methylphenidate, but the half-life is a little longer. Many patients who fail to respond to one cerebral stimulant will respond to the other, and when the drugs are used sequentially, less than 4 per cent will fail to respond to one or the other (Elia et al., 1991).

The initial starting dose of methylphenidate is 18 mg daily if Concerta is used, or 5 mg two to four times a day, according to requirements, if Equasym is used. The advantage of the sustained release form has been considered, but the immediate release forms do provide greater flexibility. An equivalent starting dose of dexamphetamine would be 5 mg three times a day. The therapeutic effect of a cerebral stimulant at any given dose is immediately apparent. Consequently the dose could be increased incrementally at short time intervals, e.g. weekly, until the optimal dose is determined according to the usual criteria: a failure to show a further response to a further increase in dose or unacceptable and unresolvable side effects. Whether or not tolerance develops has been hotly debated. Certain effects, e.g. appetite suppression and cardiovascular changes, do subside within weeks of starting treatment, but whether this also applies to the therapeutic benefits remains unresolved. Sensitization does not appear to occur in a clinical setting. In many adults, ADHD symptoms will diminish with the passage of time. Periodic drug withdrawal is advisable to determine whether treatment is still needed. There are no clearly established guidelines, but withdrawal for a period of a month once every 2 years would seem reasonable.

Experience with drugs other than cerebral stimulants is limited. Desipramine and, more recently, venlafaxine and tomoxetine, have been shown to be more effective than placebo but have not been compared directly with cerebral stimulants. Desipramine and venlafaxine have an antidepressant as well as an anti-ADHD action and may be useful in the management of co-morbid mood disturbance. Tomoxetine is well tolerated, but its precise role in ADHD management remains to be determined.

PSYCHOLOGICAL MANAGEMENT

Adults with ADHD have different types of problems from those of children and they have lived with their symptoms and associated problems for a long time. Personality disorder and criminal behaviour are common outcomes. As individuals mature, their symptoms decrease; however, ADHD is a heterogeneous disorder and reduction of symptoms will occur at different rates. Even when the symptoms have remitted, feelings of internalized failure and learned helplessness may be retained. The misattribution of the intent and behaviour of others and their own maladaptive behaviour may become part of a cycle that is difficult to break. Personality disordered offenders who are in partial remission of their ADHD symptoms may be more aggressive than their personality disordered peers (Young et al., 2003). They may cope poorly in an environment that limits their opportunity for high stimulus. Stimulant medication will help alleviate core symptoms, but co-morbid problems and low self-esteem will be usefully addressed by psychological interventions. Childhood ADHD is frequently undiagnosed and, by adulthood, individuals often present with a long history of under-performance resulting in repeated failure. By adulthood, many individuals have had multiple presentations to different education and mental health services (Young et al., 2003) but, despite this, the diagnosis of ADHD is often only made after repeated service contact. Individuals diagnosed for the first time in adulthood may feel they have been unfairly treated by a system that has failed to identify their problems. They may feel angry and bitter and lack trust in service providers. It is important that they develop confidence in yet another clinician before them. Once individuals are diagnosed with ADHD for the first time in adulthood, they may go through a psychological process of adjustment as they come to terms with the diagnosis and what this means. They may look back on past experiences and ruminate on these from a different perspective. For individuals with a particularly negative outcome, there is a risk of depression as they imagine how different their lives might have been.

Structured cognitive–behavioural and skills training techniques are likely to be the most effective psychological treatments for ADHD adults. Borderline as well as antisocial personality problems may be present in adults with ADHD, and such individuals are particularly likely to present with rigidity and inflexibility in thought and behaviour as well as long-term interpersonal problems. Psychological treatment should include a psychoeducational component in order to inform the individual about ADHD and dispel lay beliefs. Education about the disorder and open discussion may facilitate understanding, for example of the fact that it is a neurodevelopmental disorder.

There is a need for future work to examine the value of psychological therapy in comparative outcome studies in ADHD adults. Psychological therapy may be of value on an individual or group basis. Adults with ADHD may feel socially isolated and misunderstood by others, and a group forum provides the opportunity to meet people with similar problems and to learn how others cope with their difficulties. It provides a supportive environment for acquiring and rehearsing key skills such as communication skills and anger and stress management. At the adult ADHD clinic in the Neuropsychiatry Department of the Maudsley Hospital, London, group workshops provide the opportunity for individuals to meet others who share common experiences and problems. We have found that running stand-alone group workshops has been very successful, as they represent short, focused, brief interventions. The workshops have also been adapted and run in forensic settings with success.

A series of one-day workshops, held monthly, provides intensive treatment based on a cognitive–behavioural model of intervention. The workshops include techniques drawing on motivational interviewing to encourage change and address ambivalence. Their objectives are to teach skills, to enable individuals to build on what they learned and to apply their skills.

In traditional group therapy, patients meet weekly for 1–2 hours over a set period, but we have found that the one-day workshop paradigm appeals more to ADHD individuals, who have difficulty with delayed gratification. They respond positively to the 'immediacy' of one-day workshops and are not expected to commit to weeks of treatment. In the workshops, attention and interest are maintained by introducing a variety of techniques, e.g. playing videos, didactic teaching, overheads and PowerPoint presentation, group discussion, individual work using exercise books, brainstorming, role-play and modelling. There are frequent breaks in the programme (e.g. 10 minutes every 1.5–2 hours) and participants are provided with detailed handouts or 'workbooks', which contain exercises to complete within the workshop and/or later in private, to reinforce the techniques presented. The aim of the workshops is threefold: (1) to provide information about ADHD, (2) to discuss psychological strategies for dealing with symptoms and associated problems, and (3) to meet others with similar difficulties and experiences. Thus the workshops provide an integrated framework for understanding ADHD, adjusting to the diagnosis, and developing techniques to cope with symptomatology through the provision of psychoeducational information, cognitive–behavioural therapy and peer support. Topics include coping with feelings of anxiety; depression; anger; emotional lability; the development of prosocial skills; problem-solving skills; time-management skills; learning techniques to develop impulse control; substance misuse; and sleep hygiene. By focusing on the positive aspects of ADHD within a group setting, participants often identify personal 'islands of excellence', representing areas in which they have enjoyed success and often involving some form of creativity and originality.

We are in the process of evaluating the groups, and the numbers are relatively small at present. However, preliminary data show promise in terms of the achievement of their three aims. In terms of their understanding and knowledge of the disorder, the individuals involved in these groups are demonstrating a change in their concept of ADHD, i.e. they have greater understanding that the disorder has a neurodevelopmental aetiology and is associated with neuropsychological deficits. Measures show improvement in anxiety, depression, anger, self-efficacy and self-esteem. According to evaluation sheets, the most useful aspect has been sharing experiences in a group, and participants have wanted more sessions to do so.

Psychological therapy can help people make sense of their difficulties, lessen their feelings of self-blame, increase self-efficacy and enhance self-esteem. Applying motivational interviewing techniques will overcome ambivalence. Individual sessions may need to be adapted according to the ability of the individual, e.g. more frequent shorter sessions such as 30-minute sessions twice per week. Success and achievement need to be reinforced by the introduction of small immediate rewards, e.g. by applying a token economy system and/or by introducing periods of high stimulation/ activity as a reward for accomplishing mundane and challenging tasks. Treatment should focus on self-management strategies, and important topics to include are impulse control, organizational skills, emotional lability, problem-solving skills and interpersonal skills.

Impulse control

Adults with ADHD have difficulty inhibiting the impulse to avoid aversive tasks and/or situations. They may feel overwhelmed by everyday tasks, anticipated failure and anxiety. Therapy should focus on the development of strategies to help them concentrate on and complete tasks by implementing a reward system. Decision-making processes may be impulse driven, with an individual making important choices rapidly and without planning. Behavioural strategies can be applied to

teach the individual self-regulation and the ability to curb impulses, e.g. to 'stop and think' and to consider alternatives and the consequences of action.

Organizational skills

For difficulties relating to forgetfulness and organizing tasks, time-management and self-organization skills can be taught by introducing the use of a diary and appointment book. A notebook or Dictaphone allows a person to make an immediate note of an idea before being distracted by a new stimulus. Individuals should be taught to prioritize tasks, in terms of their urgency and importance, and to make lists of tasks for the day/week and break them down into small, achievable steps. Individuals should be encouraged to timetable their daily schedule, with regular periods of high stimulation, e.g. physical activity, in order to avoid boredom and distractibility.

Emotional lability

Adults with ADHD may present as hyperaroused individuals with a tendency to temper or violent outbursts, anxiety and depression. Emotional lability may be the key difficulty, and fluctuating moods are likely to activate negative schemata and faulty information processing. By using a cognitive–behavioural approach, the therapist can challenge negative automatic thoughts and help the individual to self-monitor performance, by recognizing errors in thinking, and to evaluate cognitive distortions and misattributions. This can be achieved through graded task assignments, modelling and role-play. Progressive relaxation techniques may help reduce feelings of anxiety and anger, and anger-management techniques will be important in learning to cope with feelings of anger and aggression.

Problem-solving skills

An impulsive nature and cognitive deficits may result in adults with ADHD having inadequate problem-solving skills. For example, individuals may have difficulty logically following through a train of thought rather than making snap decisions. They may tend to make swift decisions, based on inadequate or inappropriate information, resulting in fundamental errors of attribution and judgement. Problem-solving therapy may help them recognize the resources they possess, teach systematic methods of overcoming current problems by breaking them down into smaller steps, and enhance their sense of control, as well as preparing them for coping with future problems. Thus individuals can be helped to define the problems they are facing, generate solutions to these problems, and apply these skills to anticipate future problems (relapse prevention). The difficulties they may have in putting appropriate solutions into action (both cognitive and practical) should be discussed to circumvent any potential problems and anxieties.

Interpersonal skills

Adults with ADHD often report difficulties interacting with others and forming long-term relationships, and this may stem from an underlying problem in communication skills. Inattention and distractibility may be perceived as an inability to listen or a lack of interest. Impulsivity may be interpreted as rudeness if a person makes untimely and inappropriate interruptions to conversations. Failure to follow instructions coupled with an argumentative nature and/or low self-esteem may be perceived as an inability to be a 'team player' or to act appropriately with authority figures. Social-skills training teaches the behavioural responses necessary for successful outcomes in social situations. This may range from micro-skills (e.g. maintaining eye contact, appropriate voice volume and tone) to macro-skills (e.g. giving compliments and constructive feedback, turn-taking and listening skills). Social-perception training will help resolve errors in perception or the misinterpretation of social cues. This can be achieved through role-play demonstrating how to respond appropriately to others, especially in situations that demand rapid shifts in style or topic of conversation.

CONCLUSION

Childhood ADHD is a risk for multiple problems in adulthood, including abnormal personality traits and disorder. When treated with stimulant medication, ADHD adults report amelioration in attentional and impulse control. Adult prognosis may be considerably improved by psychological interventions that aim to increase self-esteem and self-efficacy. Adults with ADHD detained in secure settings may cope poorly living in an environment that limits their opportunity to seek high stimulation and to satisfy feelings of restlessness. However, once identified and treated with stimulant medication, and once their core symptoms have been alleviated, they are in a position to access further education facilities and psychological and occupational therapies. They may be better able to cope with individual and group treatments in these settings. Also, from a clinical management perspective, individuals who are more focused and successful in tasks may experience less frustration, behave with less aggression towards others, and break a cycle of negativity and perception of hopelessness for the future. Thus individuals may become less aroused and interact more positively with peers and staff. This is likely to impact positively on their risk assessment and may mean earlier discharge from hospital or prison.

REFERENCES

Aman C, Roberts RJ Jr and Pennington BF (1998). A neuropsychological examination of the underlying deficit in attention deficit hyperactivity disorder: frontal lobe versus right parietal lobe theories. *Developmental Psychology* **34**(5):956–69.

American Psychiatric Association (1994). *Diagnostic and Statistical Manual of Mental Disorders*, fourth edition. Washington, DC: American Psychiatric Association.

Barkley RA (2001). Executive functioning and self-regulation: an evolutionary neuropsychological perspective. *Neuropsychology Review* **11**(1):1–29.

Bowden CL, Deutsch CK and Swanson JM (1988). Plasma dopamine-β-hydroxylase and platelet monoamine oxidase in attention deficit disorder and conduct disorder. *Journal of the American Academy of Child and Adolescent Psychiatry* **27**:171–4.

Castellanos FX, Giedd JN, Eckburg P et al. (1994). Quantitative morphology of the caudate nucleus in attention deficit hyperactivity disorder. *American Journal of Psychiatry* **151**:1791–6.

Colledge E and Blair RJR (2001). The relationship in children between the inattention and impulsivity components of attention deficit and hyperactivity disorder and psychopathic tendencies. *Personality and Individual Differences* **30**:1175–87.

Collins P and White T (2002). Forensic applications of attention deficit hyperactivity disorder (ADHD) in adulthood. *Journal of Forensic Psychiatry* **13**:263–84.

Dalteg A, Lindgren M and Levander S (1999). Retrospectively rated ADHD is linked to specific personality characteristics and deviant alcohol reaction. *Journal of Forensic Psychiatry* **10**(3):623–34.

Elia J, Borcherding B, Rapoport J and Keysor C (1991). Methylphenidate and dextroamphetamine treatments of hyperactivity: are there true non-responders? *Psychiatry Research* **36**:141–55.

Eyestone LL and Howell RJ (1994). An epidemiological study of attention-deficit hyperactivity disorder and major depression in a male prison population. *Bulletin of the American Academy of Psychiatry and the Law* **22**(2):181–93.

Giedd JN, Castellanos FX, Casey BJ et al. (1994). Quantitative morphology of the corpus callosum in attention deficit hyperactivity disorder. *American Journal of Psychiatry* **151**:665–9.

Goodman R and Stevenson J (1989). A twin study of hyperactivity. II: The aetiological role of genes, family relationships, and peri-natal adversity. *Journal of Child Psychology and Psychiatry* **30**:691–709.

Hechtman L and Weiss G (1986). Controlled prospective fifteen-year follow-up of hyperactives as adults: non-medical drug and alcohol use and anti-social behavior. *American Journal of Orthopsychiatry* **54**(1):415–25.

Jensen PS, Arnold LE, Richters JE, Severe JB, Vereen D and Vitiello B (1999). A fourteen month randomised clinical trial of treatment strategies for attention-deficit/hyperactivity disorder. *Archives of General Psychiatry* **56**:1073–86.

Lambert NM (1988). Adolescent outcomes for hyperactive children. Perspectives on general and specific patterns of childhood risk for adolescent educational, social and mental health problems. *American Psychologist* **43**:786–99.

Loney J, Whaley-Klahn MA, Kosier T and Conboy H (1983). Hyperactive boys and their brothers at 21: predictors of aggressive and antisocial outcomes. In: Van Dusen KT and Mednick SA (eds), *Prospective Studies of Crime and Delinquency.* Boston, MA: Kluwer-Nijhoff, 181–206.

Lou HC, Henriksen L, Bruhn PI, Borner H and Nielsen JB (1989). Striatal dysfunction in attention deficit and hyperkinetic disorder. *Archives of Neurology* **46**:48–52.

MacLean A, Dowson JH, Toone BK, Young SJ, Bazanis E, Robbins TW and Sahakian B (2004). Characteristic neurocognitive profile associated with adult attention-deficit/hyperactivity disorder. *Psychological Medicine* **34**:681–92.

Mannuzza S, Klein RG, Bessler A, Malloy P and LaPadula M (1993). Adult outcome of hyperactive boys: educational achievement, occupational rank and psychiatric status. *Archives of General Psychiatry* **50**:565–76.

Mannuzza S, Klein RG, Konig PH and Giampino TL (1989). Hyperactive boys almost grown up. IV. Criminality and its relationship to psychiatric status. *Archives of General Psychiatry* **46**:1073–9.

Rasmussen K, Almik R and Levander S (2001). Attention deficit hyperactivity disorder, reading disability and personality disorders in a prison population. *Journal of the American Academy of Psychiatry and Law* **296**:186–93.

Satterfield JH, Hoppe CM and Schell AM (1982). A prospective study of delinquency in 110 adolescent boys with attention deficit disorder and 88 normal adolescent boys. *American Journal of Psychiatry* **139**(6):795–8.

Satterfield T, Swanson J, Schell A and Lee F (1994). Prediction of anti-social behaviour in attention-deficit hyperactivity disorder boys from aggression/defiance scores. *Journal of American Academy of Child and Adolescent Psychiatry* **33**:185–90.

Shen Y and Wang Y (1984). Urinary 3-methoxy-4-hydroxyphenylglycol sulfate excretion in seventy-three school children with minimal brain dysfunction syndrome. *Biological Psychiatry* **19**:861–77.

Spencer T, Wilens D, Biederman J, Faraone SV, Ablon JS and Lapey K (1995). A double blind crossover comparison of methylphenidate and placebo in adults of childhood-onset attention deficit hyperactivity disorder. *Archives of General Psychiatry* **52**:434–43.

Taylor E, Chadwick O, Heptinstall E and Danckaerts M (1996). Hyperactivity and conduct problems as risk factors for adolescent development. *Journal of the American Academy of Child and Adolescent Psychiatry* **39**(9):1213–26.

Toone BK and van der Linden GJH (1997). Attention deficit hyperactivity disorder or hyperkinetic disorder in adults. *British Journal of Psychiatry* **170**: 489–91.

Van der Linden GJH, Young SJ, Ryan P and Toone BK (2000). Attention deficit hyperactivity disorder in adults – experience of the first National Health Service clinic in the United Kingdom. *Journal of Mental Health* **9**(5):527–35.

Vitelli R (1995). Prevalence of childhood conduct and attention-deficit hyperactivity disorders in adult maximum-security inmates. *International Journal of Offender Therapy and Comparative Criminology* **40**(4):263–71.

Weiss G and Hechtman L (1986). *Hyperactive Children Grown Up: Empirical Findings and Theoretical Considerations.* New York: Guilford Press.

Weiss G, Hechtman L, Milroy T and Perlman T (1985). Psychiatric status of hyperactives as adults: a controlled prospective 15-year follow-up of 63 hyperactive children. *Journal of the American Academy of Child Psychiatry* **24**(2):211–20.

Wilens TE and Spencer TJ (2000). The stimulants revisited. *Child and Adolescent Psychiatric Clinics of North America* **9**:573–603.

World Health Organization (1992). *International Classification of Diseases,* tenth revision. Geneva: WHO.

Young SJ (2000). ADHD children grown up: a review of the literature. *Counselling Psychology Quarterly* **13**(2):1–10.

Young S (2004). The YAQ-S AND YAQ-I: the development of self and informant questionnaires reporting on current adult ADHD symptomatology, comorbid and associated problems. *Personality and Individual Differences* **36**:1211–24.

Young S and Gudjonsson G (2005). Neuropsychological correlates of the YAQ-S self-reported ADHD symptomatology, emotional and social problems, and delinquent behaviour. *British Journal of Clinical Psychology* **44**:47–57.

Young S and Gudjonsson G (in press). ADHD symptomatology and its relationship with emotional, social and delinquency problems. *Psychology, Crime and Law.*

Young SJ, Gudjonsson GH, Ball S and Lam J (2003). Attention deficit hyperactivity disorder in personality disordered offenders and the association with disruptive behavioural problems. *Journal of Forensic Psychiatry and Psychology* **14**:491–505.

Young SJ and Harty MA (2001). Treatment issues in a personality disordered offender: a case of attention deficit hyperactivity disorder in secure psychiatric services. *Journal of Forensic Psychiatry* **12**:158–67.

Young S, Morris RG, Toone BK and Tyson C (submitted). Planning ability in adults with attention-deficit/hyperactivity disorder.

Young SJ and Toone B (2000). The assessment of ADHD in adults: clinical issues. A report from the first NHS clinic in the UK. *Counselling Psychology Quarterly* **13**(3):313–19.

Young S, Toone B and Tyson C (2003). Comorbidity and psychosocial profile of adults with attention deficit hyperactivity disorder. *Personality and Individual Differences* **35**(4):743–55.

Zametkin AJ, Karoum G, Rapoport JL, Brown GL and Wyatt RJ (1984). Phenylethylamine excretion in attention deficit disorder. *Journal of the American Academy of Child Psychiatry* **23**:310–14.

Zametkin AJ, Nordahl TE, Gross M et al. (1990). Cerebral glucose metabolism in adults with hyperactivity of childhood onset. *New England Journal of Medicine* **323**:1361–6.

Part 3

THE WOODSTOCK MODEL:
APPLICATIONS AND VARIATIONS

Chapter 17

SETTINGS FOR THE TREATMENT OF PERSONALITY DISORDER

Clive Meux and Pamela J. Taylor

INTRODUCTION

It is important for any person embarking on any treatment to receive that treatment in an appropriate environment. Effective delivery of complex treatments is almost impossible if the environment is inappropriate. The environment itself can be therapeutic but, conversely, certain qualities in it could reinforce pathological behaviours. In effect, it is necessary to make sure that the right person is in the right place at the right time. Theoretical issues in formulating and deciding on appropriate assessment and treatment for people with personality disorder have been discussed in previous chapters. This section explores the characteristics of places where treatment is delivered – the therapeutic milieu. In the UK, and in many other countries too, the majority of institutionalized people with personality disorder who also offend seriously are held in prison; a few are in hospitals, generally secure hospitals. This chapter specifically considers the effects of a prison environment on therapeutic prospects and of physical security on treatment in a hospital.

In many countries, specialist environments for the assessment and treatment of personality disordered offenders are under-developed.

Exceptionally, a nation, such as Holland, has a dedicated system (McInerny, 2000; see also Appendix 1 of this book). In Britain, there are few specialist services, but, for serious offenders, they exist both in prisons and hospitals. Neither has an exclusively successful record, but each can offer models of good practice. The core question is whether basic environmental prerequisites for treatment can be defined. Another important issue is whether the relative strengths and weaknesses of hospitals and prisons can be elucidated in order to assist in the identification of best fit between any given serious offender with personality disorder on the one hand and the services available on the other.

ENVIRONMENTAL PREREQUISITES

Treatment for serious offenders with personality disorder requires contact with appropriately skilled and experienced staff, who are well managed and operating within a clearly formulated and explicit philosophy and legal framework. A range of specific therapies will be required within a physical environment that is safe, secure and satisfactorily resourced. Qualities in the environment should be congruent with the specific treatments and reinforce positive change. Maintenance of the therapeutic potential of an environment requires strategies for the recognition and management of the kind of adverse relationship developments between residents or between residents and staff that can emerge as repetitions of past maladaptive behaviours.

A core element in facilitating treatment for offenders with personality disorder is the establishment of boundaries, both physical and psychological. For some, treatment can only be satisfactorily established in an appropriately physically secure environment. A full multidisciplinary clinical team of medical, psychological, nursing, social work, occupational and educational staff, who meet regularly, share information and communicate clearly, is in a good position to establish, implement and maintain boundaries when lines of responsibility and leadership are also explicit. It is often helpful, particularly with more challenging residents, prisoners or patients, to formulate a written treatment and care contract, which all parties, including the resident, patient or prisoner, formally sign.

It is essential, too, that the therapeutic teams have a clear understanding with service managers and purchasers about what is and is not achievable. It is inevitable that things will go wrong from time to time, and it helps if this is as explicit as possible. Wise therapists and managers in secure institutions will, for example, have an 'escape delivery plan'. This may sound alarming, but it enables a distinction to be made between the unacceptable and the undesirable, and provides a standard that is simultaneously permissive and limiting. It may be regarded, for example, as completely unacceptable for any resident of a secure institution to leave the secure perimeter without permission. Insofar as any such escape takes place, it would automatically lead to inquiry, and could lead to disciplinary action. If residents are allowed periods outside the secure perimeter as part of their rehabilitation programme, perhaps testing their ability to be in

the community, certain calculated risks must be taken. It would be unacceptable if during such a period an individual committed a further offence; it might be regarded as undesirable, but not necessarily unacceptable, if he or she failed to return to the institution on time. Indeed, it is arguable that therapists are not doing their job effectively if every person in such a testing situation always returns promptly to the institution. Therefore, some sort of guiding standard, often arbitrary, may be set. Management would continue to show confidence in a unit if, say, 5 in 100 residents returned late from rehabilitation visits, would hold informal discussions with clinicians if 10 per cent of such visits ran into such problems, but would consider more stringent intervention if such failures occurred at a higher rate. If the local community can also be engaged in setting standards along these lines, so much the better.

Therapists and managers alike must have a good enough relationship to be able to hold a frank inquiry about things that do go wrong. Managers have a responsibility to be informed enough of the challenges of such work to make sense of the issues, to ensure that the service is adequately resourced, and to support their staff; staff have a responsibility to keep management satisfactorily informed. On those occasions when staff have done something wrong, or a member of staff is found to be unsuitable for the work, management still have a responsibility to ensure that that person has access to appropriate advice to work through the problems, even if, at one extreme, this may mean termination of employment or disciplinary action. When staff are doing well, it would be good if that were acknowledged from time to time. All staff, of whatever seniority, will require access to professional clinical supervision *and* the time and opportunity to take it up in order to remain effective. Policies, procedures and practice need regular review and, indeed, in the public health sector within the UK, practice reviews of various kinds are now prescribed by government.

HOSPITAL AND CRIMINAL JUSTICE SETTINGS: SOME CHARACTERISTICS, BENEFITS AND DISADVANTAGES

The philosophies adopted in hospitals will, by definition, be dominated by treatment matters. In principle, their main focus is on care and support and bringing about positive changes in mental state and behaviour. In theory, hospitals will not contain the elements of punishment and retribution present in prisons, but practice can differ, or appear to differ, from this theory. For patients who have offended seriously, the hospital may have to be one that is physically secure. Furthermore, the person may be detained there, in the legal jargon, 'without limit of time'. For a patient/resident, the lack of certainty about when he or she may leave can, in itself, be perceived as punitive.

Although the main aim of treatment for personality disorder may be to bring about fundamental personal change, other aims include reduction of personal distress and increase in personal safety. Public safety issues are important, but taken as an integral part of addressing the individual's needs. After all, the individual with personality disorder is hardly helped by being allowed the freedom to go out if they then repeat a homicide or another serious offence. However, prison work tends to be offence and penalty centred. There is concern about public safety, but the majority of people in prison will be serving a fixed-term sentence and, with respect to detention, neither individual nor public safety needs can take priority over final tariff. This has an important influence on any treatment, which must fit the time available. Differences between an English security hospital unit and prison therapeutic community in terms of the focus of treatment and the extent to which it is anchored in a wider social context have been observed by an independent researcher (Rawlings, 2003).

By definition, hospitals contain a wide range of clinically trained and qualified staff and

there is a broader availability of, and importance attached to, multidisciplinary working. However, many more of the people who have personality disorder in association with offending are in prison. Surveys of mental disorder among prisoners in England and Wales in the early 1990s (Gunn et al., 1991; Maden et al., 1996) found quite a low prevalence of personality disorder, little different from that in the wider community, partly because they focused on clinical need. The later survey for the Office of National Statistics (Singleton et al., 1998) gave much higher figures – suggesting that most people in the prison population had a personality disorder, but there was less clarity about the clinical importance of this. The relative distribution of expert staff and potential treatment candidates with personality disorder between the settings – more experts and fewer candidates in hospital, fewer experts and more candidates in prison – is, however, unlikely to be disputed and is probably representative of the pattern in many other countries too. This relative balance is another factor influencing differences in milieu and framework for treatment. The higher staff-to-patient ratio in hospitals allows for more individualization of the treatment package, but the smaller numbers of people available for treatment may make truly appropriate selection for groups a challenge.

Criminal justice services, and perhaps particularly those in prisons, place less emphasis on the individual person than hospital services. Treatment packages in the criminal justice system tend to be régime based and offence focused. There are advantages to this. The psychological/educational treatments can be clearly defined, delivered with consistency, and readily monitored for the maintenance of acceptable standards. The evidence base for the effectiveness of some of the cognitive–behaviourally based programmes is good for a range of offenders (e.g. McGuire, 1995). In the UK, such régimes for sex offenders, such as the Sex Offender Treatment Programme (Mann and Thornton, 1998; Launay, 2001), are more likely to be available in custodial settings, although there are similar hospital programmes, such as those available on the Addictive Behaviours Unit at Broadmoor High Security Hospital (McKeown et al., 1996). (The specific issues relating to sex offenders are discussed in more detail in Chapter 21.) An important issue for the research community is the establishment of evidence-based guidance on best fit between the characteristics of the person with personality disorder and the choice of more individualized hospital work or strict régime work.

In a hospital setting, including secure hospital settings, where, at least in theory, the presenting patient's needs and rights are paramount, there is an established practice of openness with the individuals who are resident. This has grown over the years in the UK, such that patients' rights – of access to their records, to have and hold copies of them and to request other information – are enshrined in legislation. The various rights in this regard have been brought together under the Data Protection Act 1998. Patients may also participate in detailed, formal, independent reviews of their treatment and continuing need for detention, mainly under mental health legislation. In relation to this, they are entitled to legal representation. In prisons, the prisoner still has fewer rights in these respects, and usually has fewer opportunities to understand management or make a case for parole or challenge continued detention.

From the perspective of a therapist, the rights available to patients do not invariably appear to be to their advantage. The scope for review of detention in secure hospitals can be used as a defence against engaging in treatment. The Mental Health Act 1983, which is still the principal legislation in England and Wales for mentally disordered offenders, requires evidence in respect of personality disorder (in legal terms, psychopathic disorder) not only that it is of a nature and degree that would warrant detention on the grounds of the

individual's health or safety and/or the safety of others, *but also* that it is treatable. The criteria for treatability are broad, but many patients live in hope that in refusing treatment they can be established as untreatable, and thus their detention order may be discharged. This is not compatible with the spirit of the Act, but occasionally a patient who has sustained resistance for a long period may persuade a tribunal that he or she is untreatable.

There are paradoxes in the degree to which coercion applies, with hospitals potentially having much greater internally coercive powers than prisons, as long as the detention order is sustained. Whereas prisoners may not leave the prison until they have completed the minimum period for detention specified in their sentence, their choice to opt out of any treatment is almost invariably quickly acted upon, with little persuasion otherwise or confrontation, even though that may mean they have to move to another prison and/or the decision may have adverse consequences for early release. Within a UK hospital setting, attempts to opt out of treatment are managed, even in law, with counter-efforts to encourage and enforce it.

There are certainly aspects of the criminal justice system, and prisons in particular, that may tend to maintain the pathological personality traits of a person with personality disorder. Prisons are explicitly for punishment, and are generally harsh. Many offenders with personality disorder have had punitive backgrounds: prison, therefore, often fits with their expectations and experience and simply reinforces adverse reactions. As indicated above, prison also tends to emphasize the offence, or offending, at the expense of 'ordinary life'. Some offenders may enjoy (or otherwise) a place in a hierarchy according to their offence. Whereas sex offenders may be universally despised, and need special visits and special protection, people who have killed, or attracted long or life sentences, may often have a higher status than other prisoners.

The care programme approach (see Chapter 25) sets principles and standards for the continuity of care between health services, generally in-patient and out-patient services. It applies to all service users, regardless of severity of disorder or of any associated offending. Although its use with mentally disordered prisoners receiving in-reach psychiatric care is increasing, other models of approach in the criminal justice system, for example through-care, tend to be reserved for more serious offenders and to be uni-disciplinary.

ISSUES IN DEVELOPING TREATMENT SETTINGS

SAFETY AND SECURITY

In both prisons and hospitals, physical security is generally provided by a secure perimeter and varying degrees of internal locking and specialist design. At the highest level of prison security, the building may be designed as much to prevent break-in by professional criminals or politically motivated groups (to 'rescue' their colleagues) as to prevent escape. Individual cells may be made of reinforced concrete. The durability of materials for security is important, and sometimes not recognized by builders.

Within the hospital system in the UK, the distinctions are mainly between high, medium and low security. The highest is probably about equivalent to middle-ranking prison security in terms of physical provision, but offers much more relational security. The three high-security hospitals have high perimeter walls, further reinforced with extra internal and external fences since 2000. Within the walls, the multiple blocks or villas are similar to medium-security units. The walls of the blocks or units provide security; for medium security units, they generally provide the main perimeter security, complemented with fences. Windows are reinforced and specially constructed, and there is a system of inner and outer doors with different locks. In hospitals, even high-security hospitals in the UK, people are not locked in their rooms at any time, although most may lock their own doors subject to staff override. The new units for people with 'dangerous and severe personality disorder', even when within a high-security hospital, will constitute exceptions to this rule and, thus, even in their high-security *hospital* incarnations, be more like prisons. In these units, people tend to spend more time locked in their cells than in association with others. Low-security units generally have only a locked or lockable entrance/exit door as their distinguishing physical security attribute. Most hospital units, whether high, medium or low security, provide a special room in which one patient may be secluded (locked away) from the others in the event of acute disturbance. Such a procedure is under very strict controls and monitoring. On Woodstock, the unit at the centre of this book, seclusion would also commonly trigger an emergency community meeting.

Procedural security is that aspect of security that requires staff and patients/residents/prisoners to follow a set of checks in relation to a number of activities. These include searching for potential weapons or substances of misuse on entry to or exit from the hospital/prison, and often also before and after movement between units within the institution. In high-security hospitals and prisons, both patients/prisoners and staff may be subject to searches. Rooms may be searched – randomly or for specific reason. Random urine screening for substance misuse is another important area of procedural security. Although there are many aspects of such work that can become irritating to staff and residents alike, in practice, if the procedures are explained properly and carried through with sensitivity, they can be appreciated as much by residents as by staff. Ultimately, it is the offenders who have to live with each other, and most are explicit about endorsing measures that will keep them safe.

Relational security is the most sophisticated of the three main categories of security and the most at risk of subversion. Regular monitoring of the process is essential. At best, it is founded in detailed staff knowledge of the individual in question, and of his or her relationships and activities. Proportionately more emphasis is placed on this kind of security in hospitals than in prisons, not least because it is crucial to the process of monitoring the effects of treatment. In an institution, relational security is founded on observing and reflecting on qualities in the staff–resident relationships, and encouraging mutual trust, while retaining objectivity. A real problem with relational security within institutions, however, is that it tends to render people fit for living in the institutions. Neither hospitals nor prisons have yet mastered consistently good strategies for certain aspects of relational security – especially romantic/sexual attachments. In both hospitals and prisons, the focus tends also to be too short term. Safety may be established within the institution, but this can be at the expense of exposure to more ordinary community risks. When the consequently naïve individual moves on to a less regulated community, this can create real, if generally temporary, problems: the individual may prove to have become too dependent on others regulating his or her behaviour.

STAFFING

Both recruitment and retention of staff to look after offenders with personality disorder are difficult. It is arguable that staff for a therapeutic setting should always have chosen to be there, rather than having been allocated by a central management. There must be structures for personal and career development, including supervision and training. Although a core of staff must provide consistency, consideration should also be given to rotating staff through different assessment and treatment settings. This, combined with the appointment of individuals to posts with more than one centre, the

use of secondment and good continuing professional development and training, can help to avoid stagnation and 'burn out' as well as increasing the breadth of staff skills.

In order to avoid splitting within the team, the acceptance of mechanisms for staff supervision and regular team meetings must be expected rather than merely optional. The growing 'super-specialty' of forensic psychotherapy is particularly valuable here. All staff need to know how to cope with challenging and possibly treatment-resistant patients, often while working in an environment that is in a media and/or professional spotlight. In both prison and hospital settings, many of the staff have no professional qualifications, although they are often the people who have most contact with the institution's residents. It is particularly important to ensure that they are included in supervision and skills development, and yet it is the needs of this group that are most often neglected, at least within hospital systems. In the absence of a professional code, such staff may be helped by the inclusion in their job plan of details relating to such issues as personal privacy or limits to confidentiality.

Each member of the multidisciplinary team should have a particularly robust sense of his or her own skills, strengths and weaknesses to be able to work effectively with people with personality disorder. Providing that is the case, most people are able to work comfortably across disciplines when the need arises. The wide range of need on the part of treatment candidates suggests that the recruitment of people across a wide range of disciplines will be important. In addition to a core group of psychiatrists, psychotherapists, nurses and social workers, others, such as educational staff, specialist rehabilitation staff and occupational therapists, social therapists, probation officers and creative therapists, will all be important. Staff should include individuals from varying ethnic and cultural backgrounds, of both genders and a mix of the younger and more mature. This should hold true even if a particular unit's selection criteria result in patients being gender or age segregated. Staff members should be psychologically minded, intelligent, verbally and interpersonally skilled, empathic, questioning, reflectively self-aware and appropriately assertive. Their communication should be clear and unambiguous. They should be able to engender trust and respect in others. As people in their care may well model on them, and internalize issues learnt in therapy, the overall behaviour of each member of staff is vitally important.

The numbers of staff required for a particular therapeutic unit will depend to some extent on the physical structure of the unit, the dependency and lability of the personality disordered offenders residing there, the model and intensity of the therapy being offered, and the personal qualities of the staff members. A basic core number of staff is required so that flexibility can be maintained to ensure sickness and leave are adequately covered by regular staff and that dependency on temporary or locum staff does not occur. Experiences of inconsistent, varying and multiple carers have often already been negative features in the past of personality disordered offenders, and should not be re-enacted. However, in order to have staff in training on a therapeutic unit, which is important for service development as well as for local morale, some movement of perceived carers will regularly occur. This must be safely and satisfactorily managed, and a method of complementing long-term core therapists with co-therapists, who may be more transient trainees, can assist with this. Staff often find it difficult to be explicit with residents or patients about their own imminent departure, with the risk that the resident or patient merely experiences another episode of abandonment. Properly managed, high turnover among a subgroup of staff can even promote the therapeutic exploration of issues of loss, change and anger.

Qualities in leadership of the clinical team are important. In Britain, the psychiatrist has legal responsibility for detained patients in hospital and therefore, in those settings, usually leads the clinical team. This is generally not compatible with being the primary therapist and therefore treatment is more often administered in most units by individuals of other disciplines, such as psychologists or nurse therapists. Specific training and/or supervision in the therapies used are generally more important here than professional discipline of origin. Given such distribution of duties, the clinical team leader can remain objective and 'tough', freeing the therapists to a large extent to be able to respect confidentiality, as consistent with wider clinical practice. Negotiation between therapist, patient and clinical team over what may and may not remain confidential to the therapy is an important early phase in establishing the psychological milieu of treatment.

Working under therapeutic community principles with personality disordered offenders can be useful (see Chapter 15). People with personality disorder often have little sense of community, so some development of this can be indicative of real progress. Further, people tend to be more likely to respect rules if they feel some ownership of them. Therapeutic communities encourage people to achieve this. However, the flattened hierarchies of such communities can be perceived by staff in day-to-day contact with the residents as putting them (the staff) under too much pressure. The unit must therefore have written policies that set clear boundaries, while stimulating debate and negotiation, and encouraging self-determination and responsibility. Policies can and should be written in consultation with service users, even in a secure setting, and all on a unit must have access to them and adhere to them. Prisons can achieve such an approach as well, perhaps even better than most hospital units. In the UK, Grendon Underwood Psychiatric Prison is well documented and researched (Gunn et al., 1978; Genders and Player, 1995).

A research programme investigating important aspects of the assessment, treatment and outcome of the service users is a vital investment for the future. Robust clinical audit within the service should also be applied.

MANAGEMENT

The management of such settings, whether in hospital or prison, is a highly skilled task. It must not just ensure quality of care, but also actively facilitate its provision and not inadvertently handicap it. For staff to function satisfactorily with personality disordered offenders, they must feel safe and confident in their environment. Management policies and style must allow this, not least by being open and sharing responsibility for care (and difficulties when they arise) rather than adopting a closed 'blame culture'. The facilitation of openness to outside scrutiny is helpful, and also probably inevitable. For their part, staff working with people with personality disorder, perhaps especially on a dedicated unit, must acknowledge that they are part of the wider institution, with responsibility to that wider community.

Another delicate balance is between openness to development and change and the maintenance of enough consistency in approach that the unit is stable and safe. Further, multiple reorganizations can reflect the background of many residents, patients and prisoners in an unhelpful way. They have commonly already experienced much change, inconsistent care and loss. In a recent commentary by Quinsey (1999) on an inquiry into a malfunctioning personality disorder unit at Ashworth high-security hospital in England, he pertinently quotes Petronius from the first century CE:

We trained hard but it seemed that every time we were beginning to form teams we would be reorganised. I was to learn later in life that we tend to meet every situation in life by reorganising, and a wonderful method it can be for creating the illusion of progress while producing confusion, inefficiency and demoralisation.

There is often much talk of management training for clinicians, but improvement in awareness of clinical issues for managers in challenging treatment environments, such as those involving personality disordered offenders, is just as relevant. These issues apply no less in prisons than in hospitals.

ECONOMIC ISSUES

The cost of providing significantly effective (or even adequate) treatment for personality disordered offenders is high because it mainly consists of skilled interventions by professional and suitably trained allied staff over long periods of time. In 2003, the average treatment cost of the average stay of an offender patient with personality disorder in an English high-security hospital was about £750,000. The costs for less therapeutic containment in prison were significantly lower. How, though, can the cost effectiveness of the treatment be measured?

There is remarkably little precedent for doing this. Cohen et al. (1994) provide one model. Calculation of the costs of treatment is relatively straightforward, but how can the costs relating to prevention, or failure of prevention, of further violence or offending be calculated? If a man or woman with personality disorder re-offends, police and criminal justice service time can be very expensive, and the 'costs' to victims and their families, for example, of injury, suffering, time off work etc., can be very high. Further, people with personality disorder not uncommonly have their own children, who, without treatment of the parent's disorder, will also grow up in the shadow of that disorder. In turn, victims of the violence or sex offending may themselves embark on a pattern of aggressive or antisocial acting-out.

A measure of cost effectiveness requires a measurement of successful treatment outcome, but this is difficult to achieve. Measuring outcome by recidivism may be popular with the public and politicians. This measure alone, however, may actually be measuring the effectiveness of maintenance care rather than of the primary treatment, or perhaps it measures the ability of the police to detect offences, or the offender's inability to avoid capture. Fortuitous events in the offender patient's life may bring about a sudden change of course, for good or ill. For example, the establishment of a healthy emotional partnership is generally positive, but if it breaks down, relapse to old styles of relating may occur.

One of the key issues for service development for people with personality disorder who also seriously offend is that politicians tend to take a keen interest. This may be a clear positive in relation to funding. It may mean, however, that heavy controls on service development and delivery are required in exchange. In the UK at least, if a major problem emerges, politicians will want to distance themselves from the service. One technique for doing this is to call for an independent inquiry, often, perhaps unconsciously, seeking to ensure that 'blame' falls elsewhere. There is little difference between hospitals and prisons in these respects. However, prison staff are commonly dealing with fixed-term prisoners who will return to the community whatever the staff views. In addition, insofar as they offer treatment, it tends to be within highly prescribed regimes, so prison staff may be less vulnerable to criticism than health service staff, who still have a significant role in decision making in relation to this patient group.

TENSIONS BETWEEN SECURITY, COERCION AND TREATMENT

There is a view that if psychotherapy and/or other psychological treatments are to be successful, they must be undertaken voluntarily. There are at least three major considerations behind this idea. The first is the general principle of autonomy that – except in the rarest of life-saving, bona fide emergencies when a person to be treated may be unconscious, or in a situation clearly prescribed in law – individuals may not have things done to them without their consent. The second is that there is a belief that, in any case, psychological treatments are less effective without the full and voluntary participation of the treated person. The third lies in remaining doubts about the effectiveness of treatment. If freedom of choice is to be overridden, it may be acceptable to confine a person in order for him or her to receive a treatment of proven value, but it is another matter to do so if there is a no better than evens chance of benefit. The first of these principles is an ethical concept and, as such, is for the mores of the wider national and international community rather than a traditional evidence base. The other two are more susceptible to scientific inquiry. The evidence base for the effectiveness of treatment is considered elsewhere (see Chapter 30), and would bear further development.

The issue of 'voluntariness' has been little researched with specific reference to personality disorder, but work in related fields with related problems or disorders suggests that elements of coercion may be helpful to engagement in the 'treatment' process. Offenders whose mental condition is generally undefined, but most of whom, on the evidence in England and Wales of the Office of National Statistics Summary of Mental Disorder in Prisons (Singleton et al., 1998), are likely to have personality disorder, have been engaged with much reported success in cognitive–behaviourally based training packages. Lösel (1998) has even begun to translate this sort of work into the language of 'treatment for psychopaths'. Elements of coercion include the fact that participants are in prison, often with an implicit or explicit indication that early release might follow from co-operation, or they are in the community, but with participation a condition of remaining there on one of the community orders available for imposition by the courts. It may be that containment and/or the framework of a legal structure for holding a person in therapy provide a necessary counter-weight to the chaos and distractions of his or her regular lifestyle as much as coercion per se. For individuals who have spent much of their lives running away from emotional pain and distress, often literally, containment may be an essential prerequisite to treatment. More passively avoidant behaviours, or retreat into substance misuse, may similarly require it on occasion.

Sowers and Daley (1993) reviewed treatments for addictions and their implementation and found that people who had an initial period of coercion were more likely to remain in the programmes and do well, even after the coercive elements had been lifted, than those who had remained entirely 'free' to choose from the outset. The nature of such disorders may itself limit that freedom, and such coercion, in practice, may provide some release from the constraints of the untreated disorder. They further argued that to reserve such coercion as a 'last resort' might be to leave a person untreated until he or she were too damaged or disabled to be able to participate or gain significant advantages. More evidence on the relative benefits and drawbacks of coerced treatment in these areas would assist what must be a continuing debate about the role of coercion.

Murray Cox (1976, 1986, 1996a,b), who offered psychotherapy in a high-security hospital for many years, has perhaps most eloquently described the intimate relationship between the physical security of the building, the procedural security and the holding function supplied by the psychotherapy itself. The wealth of experience that led him to such description is important evidence that security, elements of coercion and psychotherapy can sit together with benefit. However, it will only partially satisfy people who prefer their evidence to emerge from traditional treatment trial designs.

CONCLUSION

There is already an infrastructure in both the health and criminal justice systems, with strengths and weaknesses in both, for managing and treating offenders with personality disorders. It is possible to clarify some basic requirements for the physical and social milieu for treatment, but research is needed to establish evidence-based guidance for the choice of optimal setting to facilitate engagement in appropriate treatment. Coercion and security may have an important role to play. Treatment, coercion and secure hospital placement need not be a contradiction in terms for these individuals. The 'Woodstock model' described in the next chapter is a practical example of how we work constantly to resolve such tensions and to establish treatment that will benefit the young men who are accepted there.

REFERENCES

Cohen MA, Miller TR and Rossman SB (1994). The costs and consequences of violent behavior in the United States. In: Reiss AJ and Roth JA (eds), *Understanding and Preventing Violence. Consequences and Control*, Vol. 4. Washington, DC: National Academy Press, 67–166.

Cox M (1976). Group psychotherapy in a secure setting. *Proceedings of the Royal Society of Medicine* **69**:215–20.

Cox M (1986). The 'holding function' of dynamic psychotherapy in a custodial setting: a review. *Journal of the Royal Society of Medicine* **79**:162–4.

Cox M (1996a). Psychodynamics and the special hospital. 'Road blocks and thought blocks'. In: Cordess C and Cox C (eds), *Forensic Psychotherapy*. London: Jessica Kingsley, 433–48.

Cox M (1996b). Supportive and interpretive psychotherapy in diverse context. In: Cordess C and Cox C (eds), *Forensic Psychotherapy*. London: Jessica Kingsley, 83–93.

Genders E and Player E (1995). *Grendon. A Study of a Therapeutic Prison*. Oxford: Clarendon Press.

Gunn J, Maden A and Swinton M (1991). Treatment needs of prisoners with psychiatric disorders. *British Medical Journal* **303**:338–41.

Gunn J, Robertson G and Dell S (1978). *Psychiatric Aspects of Imprisonment*. London: Academic Press.

Launay G (2001). Relapse prevention with sex offenders: practice, theory and research. *Criminal Behaviour and Mental Health* **11**:38–54.

Lösel F (1998). Treatment and management of psychopaths. In: Cooke DJ, Forth AE and Hare RD (eds), *Psychopathy: Theory, Research and Implications for Society.* Dordrecht: Kluwer, 303–84.

Maden A, Taylor CJA, Brooke D and Gunn J (1996). *Mental Disorder in Remand Prisons.* London: Home Office.

Mann RE and Thornton D (1998). The evolution of a multi-site offender treatment program. In: Marshall WL, Fernandez YM, Hudson SM and Ward T (eds), *Sourcebook of Treatment Programs for Sexual Offenders.* New York: Plenum Press, 47–58.

McGuire J (1995). *What Works: Reducing Reoffending.* Chichester: John Wiley & Sons.

McInerny T (2000). Dutch TBS forensic services: a personal view. *Criminal Behaviour and Mental Health* **10**:213–28.

McKeown M, Forshaw D, McGauley G, Fitzpatrick J and Roscoe J (1996). A forensic addictive behaviours unit: a case study (part 1). *Journal of Substance Misuse* **1**:27–31.

Quinsey V (1999). Report of the Committee of Inquiry into the Personality Disorder Unit, Ashworth Special Hospital, Vol. 1. *Journal of Forensic Psychiatry* **10**:635–48.

Rawlings B (2003). Presentation to Broadmoor Quarterly Seminar. Real Life in the Communities: Preliminary Results of Qualitative Study. ATC/NLCB Therapeutic Communities Project, Nottingham, UK.

Reiss D, Grubin D and Meux C (1996). Young 'psychopaths' in special hospital: treatment and outcome. *British Journal of Psychiatry* **168**:99–104.

Reiss D, Meux C and Grubin D (2000). The effect of psychopathy on outcome in high security patients. *The Journal of the American Academy of Psychiatry and the Law* **28**:309–14.

Singleton N, Meltzer H, Gatward R, Coid J and Deasy D (1998). *Psychiatric Morbidity among Prisoners in England and Wales.* Survey by Social Survey Division of ONS. London: Stationery Office.

Sowers W and Daley D (1993). Compulsory treatment of substance use disorders. *Criminal Behaviour and Mental Health* **3**:403–15.

Chapter 18

WOODSTOCK: AN ECLECTIC MODEL FOR TREATMENT OF YOUNG MEN WITH PERSONALITY DISORDER

Chris Newrith, Pamela J. Taylor and Tim McInerny

INTRODUCTION

Woodstock is a ward within an English high-security hospital. The staff aim to work with the young men who become resident there to create a community that is safe and therapeutic. They try to do this in the context of the special security requirements that apply everywhere in the hospital, including Woodstock, and the fact that the men are compulsorily detained and often ambivalent about treatment. Most of the men have a complex mix of mental and physical disorders, some of which may require treatment with medication to enable progression into psychotherapeutic work. The young men who are there for treatment generally come from difficult and sometimes chaotic social settings, where any sense of, or commitment to, community is minimal.

Woodstock differs from other areas of the hospital because of the emphasis on community and elements of democracy. The residents are encouraged to debate the unit's policy, are given the role of running the community meeting, and are invited to work with staff on setting internal rules which will be for the common good. It is the same as the rest of the hospital in being subject to stringent security policies; these cannot be significantly influenced by patients or staff working in the hospital, and

include requirements for personal searches, room searches, restrictions on property and on movement both within and outside the hospital. These issues are contrary to most of the principles of therapeutic communities, but, in the way they are imposed, they tend to have a positive side effect in bonding staff and residents. Staff and residents share common ground because of the need for safety in a community where the residents have a propensity for serious violence, including homicide, to others – often others in their social circle. There is also often entirely mutual irritation at some of the more arbitrary restrictions, such as the maximum number of socks or books an individual may have in his own room, regardless of his state of health, behavioural profile or specific personal need.

Woodstock is a unit in development, and likely to remain so. Research, audit, training experiences and the community meeting are among the influences that can bring about change in the unit. Change is kept in check, however, by recognition that measurable, consistent standards in service delivery and treatment are important, both for further evaluation of outcome and for the provision of stable boundaries and clear limits for people whose problems include poor awareness of boundaries and challenging behaviour.

THE PHYSICAL SETTING

Woodstock was built as a 25-bedded ward in Broadmoor Special Hospital.* Annual occupancy of the hospital was 412 in 1999/2000, with a ratio of 4 men:1 woman. Occupancy is ever changing, however, with 2005 targets to relocate all women's services away from the hospital and to open an independent, 90-bedded, personality disorder unit the 'DSPD' programme. Woodstock was not designed for its purpose; its occupancy is also reducing. Patients can find it both oppressive ('How would you like to be living in this space with 24 other young psychopaths?', said one), but also dependency inducing. It is often the first consistent, caring environment that young men have experienced since adolescence, and in some cases the first ever.

Each man has his own room, with integral toilet and washing facilities. He may lock his door, whether in or out of his room, although there is a staff over-ride facility. The men are not allowed in each other's rooms. There are four communal areas – a day room, a television room, a 'quiet' room and a dining room with kitchen. Staff have a single, small 'goldfish bowl' office, so they can see and be seen at all times. They also have a small rest room, which is supposed to be private. There is a single small interview room, and a treatment room for medical examinations. Group work requires negotiation for one of the patients' communal spaces.

The unit is home for most of the young men for 4–5 years. Despite this, they are limited by hospital policies in what they can do at any stage. Each is allowed to keep some personal belongings in his room, such as books and electronic equipment, but they are explicitly forbidden to have personal computers. Their communications with people outside the unit

*In July 2005, Woodstock was relocated as a 12-bedded unit with slightly different physical characteristics, and one consultant forensic psychiatrist.

are strictly limited, and monitored. For example, the list of people each man may phone has to be formally checked and agreed, and each may phone only from the single designated phone on the unit. Phone calls may be monitored. There are opportunities for more extensive recreational and occupational opportunities off-ward, and these are utilized on a daily basis by most of the patients as part of their daily programme, which each man helps to devise in collaboration with his primary nurse and others in the clinical team.

THE RESIDENT GROUP

Woodstock residents are all male, and generally between 18 and 25 years old at the time of admission. Few are over 30, although most leave the unit when they are ready to leave the hospital; departure is always on clinical rather than arbitrary age grounds. Many of the staff are women, although there is generally a majority of men in the nursing group. A typical patient group is illustrated in Table 18.1.

The offending profiles of the Woodstock men are broadly similar to those of the other men in the hospital in that most have committed serious violent crimes, including murder, attempted murder and sexual offences. A few of them, however, have committed index crimes or acts that are generally perceived to be less serious. It is the man's psychopathology at the time of assessment rather than his index offence per se that qualifies him to be considered for treatment on the unit, although the disorder was almost invariably relevant to the index offence. Most are detained under the legal classification of psychopathic disorder under the Mental Health Act 1983, although a number also have classifications of mental illness in addition. One or two have mental illness classifications only. However, to some extent, such legal classifications make an artificial distinction in that patients within a category of mental illness often display personality traits that are highly dysfunctional, while the psychic

Table 18.1 A typical resident population of Woodstock (all are men)

Resident[a]	Age (years)	Length of stay on Woodstock	Diagnoses additional to PD (ICD-10)	Principal offence(s)/reason for admission
1	30	2 years	Schizoaffective psychosis (F25); borderline PD (F60.3); alcohol and multi-drug use (F10.1; F19.1)	Theft
2	36	8.5 years	Factitious disorder (F68.1); possible Asperger's syndrome (F84.5)	Manslaughter
3	24	3.5 years	ADHD (F90.1); harmful use of alcohol (F10.21); multiple drug use (F19.1)	Arson × 2; burglary
4	23	2.75 years	Mixed PD (F61.0) with schizoid, borderline and dissocial traits; harmful use of alcohol (F10.1); Asperger's syndrome (F84.5)	Arson
5	24	2.75 years	Mixed PD (F61.0); substance misuse, alcohol abuse (F19.1, F10.1)	Manslaughter
6	21	1 month	Unspecified PD; alcohol and drug problems (under assessment)	Wounding with intent; burglary × 3; threatening behaviour; criminal damage
7	29	3 years	Paranoid schizophrenia (F20.0); alcohol and illegal drug abuse (F10.1, F19.1)	Murder; rape
8	29	4.5 years	PD, with paranoid and antisocial traits (F60); bipolar affective disorder (F31.0)	Wounding with intent; ABH
9	24	3.75 years	Paranoid schizophrenia (F20.0); harmful use of alcohol and illegal drugs (F10.1, F19.1)	Manslaughter
10	23	2 months	Unspecified PD	Violence against person
11	22	2.75 years	Borderline PD (F60.31); alcohol and drug misuse (F10.1, F19.8); schizoaffective psychosis (F25)	Arson
12	25	2.5 years	Mild mental retardation (F70); mixed PD with paranoid and dissocial traits (F60.0, F60.2)	ABH; GBH
13	32	5 years	Paranoid schizophrenia (F20.0); independent borderline PD (F60.31, F60.7)	Manslaughter
14	21	2 years	Paranoid schizophrenia (F20.0)	Rape; attempted murder
15	21	2 years	Mixed PD with borderline and dissocial traits (F60.31, F60.2); paranoid schizophrenia (F20.0); sadism (F65.5)	Threats to kill
16	20	10 months	Unspecified psychosis (F29); mixed PD (F61) with paranoid, narcissistic and antisocial traits	ABH

(Continued)

Table 18.1 (*Continued*)

Resident[a]	Age (years)	Length of stay on Woodstock	Diagnoses additional to PD (ICD-10)	Principal offence(s)/ reason for admission
17	24	7 years	Mixed PD (F61.0); harmful use of alcohol (F10.01)	Murder
18	21	1.5 years	Mixed PD with histrionic and dissocial features (F61.0); drug-induced psychosis	Robbery; false imprisonment × 2; common assault × 4 and GBH × 4
19	24	2.5 years	Schizoaffective disorder mixed type (F25.2); borderline (F60.30); disorders due to alcohol abuse and multiple drug use (F10.71 F19.1)	ABH
20	20	1.3 years	Borderline PD (F60.31); disorder due to drug abuse and psychoactive substances (F19.1)	GBH with intent
21	31	5 years	Mixed PD (F61.0) with schizoid, avoidant, passive aggression, paranoid, sadistic and dissocial features and drug misuse (F19.21)	Manslaughter
22	30	7.25 years	Mixed PD (F61.0)	Attempted rape; unlawful wounding
23	20	1.75 years	Mixed PD (F61.0) with paranoid obsessional and dissocial traits	Attempted murder
24	27	6.25 years	Borderline PD (F60.31)	Damaging property; robbery × 2; attempted robbery
25	23	2.75 years	Mixed PD (F61.0) with dissocial, paranoid and emotionally unstable traits	Indecent assault; breach of licence
26	29	6 years	Mixed PD (F61.0) with histrionic, borderline traits; misuse of alcohol (F10.21)	Attempted rape; indecent assault; robbery

[a]The number always exceeds the bed number count because, in the early stages of transfer from the hospital, the men generally remain the responsibility of the Woodstock team for up to 12 months, and very occasionally longer. The new team takes the active role in management and treatment, but major decisions, for example on change of direction of treatment, would be referred back to the Woodstock team, and the man could be sent back to Broadmoor immediately if the placement was breaking down for any reason.

PD, personality disorder; ABH, actual bodily harm; GBH, grievous bodily harm.

architecture of people with severe personality disorder may be psychotic in its organization.

The length of stay on the unit is conditioned by suitability for continuing treatment in lower security or, occasionally, the wider community. Most of the men are under court-imposed Home Office restrictions on discharge on grounds of public protection, so their stay on Woodstock may not be solely determined by clinical team opinion. The Home Office has to approve the transfer decision *and* a bed has to be available in one of the over-subscribed specialist units of lesser security. Reiss et al. (1996) carried out a retrospective study of 49 patients treated on the unit and found the mean length of stay to be 4.6 years.

THE STAFF

Nurses form the largest group of mental health-care professionals working on the unit, with a line management structure of three on-ward team leaders and one ward manager, who is answerable to higher service managers in the wider hospital hierarchy. About half of the nursing team are qualified psychiatric nurses, and half are unqualified nursing assistants from various backgrounds. In both groups, many have long experience of the provision of nursing care in a secure hospital setting. The nursing assistants work under the supervision of the qualified staff. All nursing staff who work on the ward choose to do so, which brings a high degree of motivation to the team. Some of the nurses still wear uniform, which is simply a white shirt and dark trousers for men and a blue dress for women, but increasingly they take up the option of not doing so.

There are two half-time consultant forensic psychiatrists, who also act as the Responsible Medical Officers (RMOs) for legal purposes, each having responsibility for about half of the patients.* All representations to outside bodies (such as the Home Office or other forensic settings) are made through one of these doctors. Trainee psychiatrists, at both senior specialist forensic psychiatry and more junior general psychiatry levels, also carry out placements on the ward as part of their rotational training schemes. Medical students frequently attend as observers.

The specialized demands of this model of care require strong psychology and psychotherapy services. The hospital has a department of

psychology, a medical psychotherapy department, and also speech and language therapists, creative arts therapists, and nurse therapists. The multidisciplinary team also comprises staff from the educational services and social work services.

The extensive baseline psychometric testing and functional analysis of offending behaviour is mainly provided by the lead clinical psychologist, with supplementary expert input or assistance (see Chapter 4). The lead clinical psychologist also designs and guides the structured, task-oriented group work as well as delivering substantial elements of group and individual therapy. Basic communication skills are often subtly impaired among the young men, and speech and language therapists provide a specialist resource for assessment, and specific treatment as necessary. Creative arts therapists provide therapeutic input, particularly for those men who may respond better to non-verbal means of exploration and communication.

The rehabilitation therapy service (RTS) staff have responsibility for the provision of vocational and recreational activities to facilitate social and practical skill development, but in addition can thereby assess each man's needs and strengths in these areas. A wide variety of activities are offered, which both improve life skills and have a social therapy role. These include woodwork, bricklaying and printing as well as ceramics, cookery and textile work. The young men can, and often do, obtain national vocational qualifications (NVQs).

Education staff determine the academic capabilities of the men, as well as providing educational, academic and information technology input; for many, basic schooling suffered through truancy or poor conditions. Education here serves not only to improve employment prospects later, but also to raise self-esteem.

Two social workers are attached to Woodstock, each for about half of their time, working elsewhere in the hospital for the rest. They fulfil a variety of functions, initially playing a valuable role in clarifying details of the life stories of each young man through interview with relatives, survivors and local services. They also provide links with relatives and with outside local authority social services, and may have a key role in clarifying the current status and views of surviving victims of a patient. With the Domestic Violence, Crime and Victims Act 2004, a statutory requirement to inform victims about review dates and to seek their views on release conditions will apply to all offenders, including offender patients. This function becomes particularly important as a patient nears discharge. A few will not be able to return to their home community because of victim issues. In addition, many of the young men have children; some were the result of casual relationships. Team members are always reluctant to make the first move to establish contact if a man has not previously met his child. The over-arching principle of the Children Act 1989 is that a child's best interests are paramount. Other men have had relationships with their child/children, but these are often fragile and shattered by the index offence and its aftermath. Contact and steady rebuilding of a relationship can then certainly be in the child's interests as well as the man's. Assessment, supervision monitoring and support for such relationships are a growing part of the work, so some nurses as well as the social workers must receive training in child protection.

Psychodynamic psychotherapists provide assessments to determine suitability for psychotherapy, but also for the purposes of formulation and advice. They provide individual and group therapy, but more usually supervision for such work. They further provide specialist advice on the dynamics within the staff team. This is an important function for staff treating people with personality disorder where there is a high risk of team splitting and other forms of acting-out.

These different professionals come together on a weekly basis for the unit clinical team meetings, allowing discussion of observations and findings and for review of the progress of each man and any fine tuning of treatment programmes. Full individual case review and care planning, together with relevant outside agencies where possible, occurs about every 6 months. Not only are the individuals subject to review, but the therapy programme itself is also reviewed on a quarterly basis, and new groups are decided according to resident mix and needs. Also quarterly, there is a 4-hour session for staff outside the hospital to review team functioning. In the safety of these 'away days', staff can and do tackle their own conflicts and emotions as well as more academic matters of service development.

THE THERAPEUTIC PROGRAMME

REFERRAL AND SELECTION PROCEDURES

Men admitted to Broadmoor Hospital generally spend their first 6 months on a single general assessment unit. Referral to Woodstock is generally from the men's admission unit, where a preliminary face-to-face assessment is made by at least two members of the Woodstock team, usually a psychiatrist and a member of the nursing staff. The case notes will be reviewed and a standard assessment checklist completed. The patient's case is then presented to the multidisciplinary team at the next available opportunity, usually within a week, and a team decision is made on whether to offer a place on Woodstock. Woodstock residents do not at present participate formally in this decision-making process. Preliminary discussion has taken place about introducing such participation, but the men themselves are reluctant on grounds of confidentiality of sensitive material. Staff also have similar concerns, but many of the men openly make known their views at the staff–resident community meeting. Although these views are taken into account, staff are aware that, as patients from the different units in the hospital do mix, a certain amount of covert patient activity goes on encouraging or discouraging putative candidates for the ward. This area is likely to be reviewed again from time to time.

Several factors are considered in assessing suitability. Clear evidence of an *International Classification of Diseases,* tenth revision (ICD-10; World Health Organization, 1992) diagnosis of personality disorder is the main indication, whether or not there is mental illness present. If mental illness is present, symptoms should be relatively stable with medication and should interfere minimally with communication. The man must be under 30 at the time of referral, and should display a reasonable competence with language in order to utilize the ward therapies to the full. The principal requirement, however, is a willingness – even readiness – to change, even if this fluctuates. For the purposes of assessment, readiness for change is considered to exist in four stages (from Prochaska and DiClemente, 1983):

1. 'pre-contemplative', where he feels pressured to change but does not believe he has a problem;
2. 'contemplative', where he has a subjective sense of having some type of problem and may want to discover more about it, though showing no definite commitment to change;
3. 'action', where a commitment to change has taken place and he is ready to take responsibility, although has not yet achieved change;
4. 'maintenance', where significant change has already occurred but this needs to be actively maintained and relapse actively avoided.

The 'contemplative', 'action' and 'maintenance' stages are seen as evidence of adequate readiness for change and are a positive indication for acceptance, but this is always considered in the context of the wider clinical picture. Pressures from the wider hospital have sometimes mitigated against accurate implementation of the admissions process.

As soon as is practicable after the acceptance of a referral, the potential resident will be allocated a 'primary nurse', who will start liaison with the primary nurse on his current ward, and a preliminary care plan will be drawn up in anticipation of his starting on Woodstock Ward. Some men may be invited to attend a preliminary group before residence as further assessment and preparation for admission.

PSYCHOLOGICAL TREATMENTS

Psychological treatments form the mainstay of the therapeutic programme; all other interventions support the man's ability to undergo psychological treatment. The exact composition of an individual programme of therapy is devised by the multidisciplinary team in conjunction with the man himself. In general, each man is expected to be in each of two strands of group psychotherapy – one of structured, task-oriented groups and the other of unstructured, more dynamically orientated groups; in addition he will be in some form of individual psychotherapy. The lines of group work are hierarchical in terms of difficulty or challenge. Reasons for not being engaged in any line of work may include a need for special preparation work, for example speech and language therapy, or relapse into an acute psychotic or aggressive episode.

GROUP THERAPIES

Unstructured, interpretative groups

The unstructured psychodynamic groups start at a level of clarifying group rules and emphasize supportive work; the intermediate and senior groups become more interpretive and challenging in turn. Both types are 'slow–open' groups, with members moving on to other groups as determined at quarterly review. Although from time to time a resident may opt out, or have to be withdrawn abruptly, in general only a decision at the quarterly review would result in termination of work in one group and commencement in another. It is anticipated that termination will take 6 weeks and that, where the aim is progression to a higher level group, not only will the prospective new member have preparation to do, but so also will the group receiving its new member.

The supportive group is intended for new arrivals to the ward, who will almost invariably be psychologically naive and relatively new to group processes, at least in a hospital setting. It allows its members the experience of being in a group and uses discussion of general topics and of group rules, such as confidentiality. Direct confrontation and challenges are generally avoided. As the members grow in this experience and become more confident of their and the group's ability to tolerate the anxiety that is generated in a group setting, so a man can 'graduate' to one of the more confrontative groups. There are two levels of these, as indicated. Here, past behaviours and personal histories are discussed and explored. The highest level group requires a sound ability to be reflective and to tolerate the anxieties of challenge and interpretation.

These groups are run by a trained dynamic psychotherapist, or someone in formal psychotherapy training, together with a Woodstock nurse. As far as possible, the same staff always act as facilitators, although this can be difficult for nursing staff working on shifts. The nurse co-therapist is generally from a pool of two or three available to the group by virtue of shift requirements.

Structured, cognitive–behavioural groups

Closed, structured groups that deal with specific issues or behaviours are also run on the ward. The timing of such groups depends on resident mix and experience. There is an expectation, for example, that residents will have participated in a number of these closed groups, from a number of different strands, before attending a group on 'victim empathy'.

These structured groups run on a modular basis and deal with three major themes, or 'strands': social, sexual and awareness/insight (Quayle et al., 1996). In the social strand, there are groups covering social skills, attitudes, assertiveness and anger management. The sexual strand of the programme includes groups on sex education, sexual matters and interpersonal relationships. The awareness/insight strand deals with self-awareness and sensory awareness, family awareness, moral awareness and victim empathy. This last group deals with exploration of the index offence from the victim's viewpoint, and works by engaging the patient in exploration of the offence from, to him, novel positions. Drama is an important module in this work. The man is given tasks by the group, tailored to what the group perceives to be his individual needs. In a recent situation, for example, a key task was to draft a letter to the victim. The group accurately perceived that one individual regarded this as straightforward because his victim was a complete stranger who had died in the attack. For him, the task was changed to writing a letter to a person close to the victim. He began to recognize a personal impact of his crime that had formally eluded him.

It may be helpful to describe one of the task-orientated groups – a family awareness group – in more detail. Each potential member completes a baseline assessment of family attitudes and perspectives, in part to judge his readiness for the group. Some may recognize for themselves that they are not ready when they see the tasks involved in the assessment, but for most this is the standard by which their own progress will be measured. Such a group would ordinarily have six to eight Woodstock resident members, at least one staff facilitator (the same person throughout), at least one nurse from the unit, who may or may not be the same one throughout, and additional therapists for sessions as relevant to the therapy (e.g. a

Table 18.2 Family awareness – the sessional task

1. Family tree presentations	Introduces collaborative work Establishes group norms and safe context
2. Understanding relationships over time	Construct biographies, interview each other about family influences Listening and sharing skills Enhance perspective taking by telling through another
3. Using another creative medium to symbolize self within family	Another method of self-disclosure Links between family and current roles Midway reports and feedback
4. Stages of development and generational patters	Reflecting on parent–child dyads Preparing for disengagement
5. Presentations of important relations – past, present, future	Practical collaboration, use of drama therapy techniques Endings and new beginnings
6. Individual review and assessment and final group review	

drama therapist). Any staff variation is explicit in advance, and therefore this is, in effect, a closed group with a time-limited task.

The first session, as indicated in Table 18.2, begins by establishing the rules and working pattern of the group, the concept of family and the significant family members in each patient's mind. These may or may not be blood relations. The second session develops this process, and the third generally employs drama therapy to enable enactment of some of the issues. The midway reports and feedback are essential elements of the group process. Work then continues, with the final session being principally a matter of group feedback. Each group member also comments on his own feedback. The quantity as well as the quality of feedback varies according to the member being discussed, and is noted. Overall evaluation of the group work includes a note of attendance and more objective evaluations specific to the work, including the Family Relations Test and a card sort test in which emotional themes, such as affectionate, neglectful, understanding, angry, jealous or strong, were given, but the people to whom they were to be related were chosen by each group member for himself. The choice of people is often revealing in itself, but the key interest is in any shift in the descriptors of the chosen people before and after the group. The Family Relations Test compares the participant's feelings about others with his perception of their feelings about him within the group he has chosen as family. Again, the main interest is on change from before to after the group.

For a more detailed account of the structured group modules, including the approach taken within each structured group, see Quayle et al. (1996).

INDIVIDUAL THERAPY

As a minimum, each resident works with his primary nurse on day-to-day issues, taking up matters emerging from therapies and problem solving. Most residents do additional individual work – with specialist therapists for specific problems, dynamic work or both. Residents receive assessments for suitability by trained psychotherapists, and will receive their therapy on the ward. There is a particular issue of confidentiality in this situation, because of the potential amongst these men of the risk of serious harm to themselves or others, and yet privacy is important to effective and ethical psychotherapy. Discussion of process (the dynamics of the therapeutic relationship) with other staff is possible, and occasional reports are prepared with the resident's co-operation and knowledge. Disclosure of any that indicates imminent risk of harm to self or others is explicitly excluded from the confidentiality contract.

OTHER THERAPIES

There is a growing body of expertise in the humanistic therapies in the hospital. The men may, as appropriate and if selected, participate in art therapy, music therapy or other creative therapies. These would principally be indicated for those with problems that are best explored using experiential and non-verbal means of communication. These therapies are used to complement rather than replace the Woodstock programme. Towards the end of their residency, access may be negotiated for some men to repeat certain specific aspects of their work (for example anger management) on a hospital-wide basis. This allows for a certain amount of testing of generalizability of new skills.

TRANSITIONARY THERAPIES

Those men who engage best in the psychotherapies and make most effective use of them, and who develop the most responsible sense of community, may, paradoxically, face a most daunting side effect. They may develop a dependency on the therapies and the community that can leave them vulnerable as they move on. To compound this, separation anxiety (or related difficulties) may have been an important factor in the index offence. The unit offers a leavers' group to all of the men once the Woodstock and receiving clinical teams have agreed readiness for departure. Men who have left the unit and the hospital return from time to time to report their experiences and advise. Visits to the new placement are encouraged, and supported by both clinical teams, so that the man can begin to build his new clinical relationships before departure. For those in individual psychodynamic psychotherapy, arrangements are now made, whenever possible, to continue that therapy through the transition into their new placement. This is made

easier by the fact that the psychotherapists generally hold part-time appointments with the hospital and part-time appointments with community-based health care trusts. Occasionally, this principle has been challenged by receiving teams, concerned that the man will not make new therapeutic alliances while retaining such a key therapeutic relationship. On the one occasion when a receiving team refused to support maintenance of the individual psychotherapy, the placement broke down. Its reinstatement in a unit receptive to maintenance of the resumed individual work was successful. While it can be unwise to generalize, the fact that in a number of cases individual psychotherapy was maintained and good therapeutic relationships established with a new team tends to confirm that such psychotherapy does not, at least, restrict development of new team relationships.

THE ROLE OF MEDICATION

Stabilization

For those residents suffering from a mental illness, the admission unit will generally have identified its nature and implemented a regime of antipsychotic or antidepressant medication, as relevant and necessary, to stabilize their state sufficiently to allow them to benefit from the more psychotherapeutic interventions. Some men, however, have relapsing–recurring disorders, or relatively unusual disorders such as adult hyperactivity or impulsivity disorders, which are only confirmed after prolonged specialist assessment. In these circumstances, treatment may be first started on Woodstock. (See also Chapters 14 and 30.)

Supportive prescribing

Many of the men frequently request medication for the relief of psychological and somatic symptoms. These are most commonly depressive or anxiety symptoms, which often arise in connection with material being worked through as part of the psychotherapeutic programme. In the context of the common potential for the abuse of drugs, this puts a specific responsibility on the nursing staff and the pre-scribing psychiatrist for special care in the evaluation of the level of need for medication, as opposed to the need for understanding and containment. This can only be achieved through discussion with the individual concerned and members of the staff team. It may be important to challenge the desire for a 'quick fix' or the immediate suppression of emotion that may be painful but appropriate. There are times, how-ever, when a compromise may be helpful, for example by agreeing a certain dosage of a mild sedative for a clearly defined length of time. As with all people with personality disorder, these boundaries may be tested and attempts made to split the team. Demands or apparent need to breach the boundaries of agreements on medication should be referred back to the clinical team for decision.

Risks of inappropriate prescribing

Medication can acquire considerable 'cur-rency', which may take the form of a misplaced hope of 'cure' by either the staff or a patient. The old maxim that asks whether the medica-tion is being used to treat the patient's or the doctor's anxiety should be borne in mind, especially if some type of inappropriate behav-iour is being threatened by the patient if the desired medication is not forthcoming. In add-ition, there is the ever-present problem of certain prescribed medications being used as recreational drugs. For people determined in their perceived need for sedative medications, and who may become violent to themselves or others in that context, there is a real risk of reinforcing violence if sedative medication is a common or apparently necessary part of the response to that.

SOCIAL DEVELOPMENT

For people with personality disorder, the capac-ity for healthy, lasting and creative social rela-tionships is, by definition, impaired to varying degrees. Therefore, the provision of adequate resources to allow them to explore ways of socializing is important. At an everyday level, the unit environment does this with communal rest and dining areas, and nursing staff acting as both models and moderators as the resi-dents learn mutual respect and tolerance for each other through community living.

Wider social opportunities are also available in the form of the rehabilitation therapy ser-vices, sport and work activities, which foster social cooperation in addition to practical skills. There are also increasingly limited off-ward social functions. In the past, theatre pro-ductions were an added bonus in this respect. Until 2002, there were valuable opportunities for social contact with members of the oppo-site sex. Relationships that were significant for both parties could and did develop. After all, these men and many of the women are in the peak age range for forming romantic and sexual partnerships. Although sexual activity was and is not permitted at Broadmoor, many of the men had girlfriends in the hospital, and some had boyfriends. Very few either main-tained or established such relationships outside the hospital. Staff are properly concerned about such relationships and their risks. One of the risks is of adverse public interest. Some of the most troubling relationships have involved vol-unteers from outside the hospital. Although many relationships formed by the men had the potential to be positive and stabilizing experi-ences for both parties, it had to be recognized, too, that as so many patients come from dys-functional and abusive backgrounds, each part-ner could bring substantial problems to the relationship. The newly formed relationships could, in turn, become dysfunctional and abu-sive. Resultant risks include, at best, damage to progress through therapy and, at worst, dam-age to the emotional, sexual and physical health of one or both parties. Recognition of the full range of positive and negative poten-tial, the need for careful and sensitive moni-toring and, as appropriate, management of or specific therapies for such relationships as they emerge is an important aspect of a holistic service (Taylor and Swan, 1999).

THE COMMUNITY MEETING

An essential part of a community is the community meeting. Routine community meetings on Woodstock occur weekly, and have a potential membership that changes so slowly as to be relatively fixed – all ward staff and all residents. In practice, there is a considerably varying membership. Half to two-thirds of residents attend any given meeting, with about half of these being consistent attenders. Some sit in the circle, some prefer to hover in the background. A few move in and out of the meeting. There is always at least one nurse and one medical member, but extended medical and nursing representation is variable, as is that from other disciplines, such as social work or psychology, where there is in any case only one (occasionally two) potential representative(s). Visitors may attend by agreement of senior staff and the residents' chairman. Crisis meetings generally call for mandatory attendance of all residents and as many ward staff as are in the hospital on the day. Precipitating crises may be a violent incident or an unexplained threat to the community, such as contamination of food in the unit's fridge.

Staff or the men bring forward matters for discussion – which range from the practical frustration of malfunctioning equipment and the slow response of hospital support services, through expenditure of the small unit recreational budget, to policy review or interpersonal crises. There is a booklet setting out rules for living on Woodstock, and sanctions for breach of such rules. From time to time these rules are reviewed by the community – variously as routine or in the light of a crisis. The residents can and do influence rules and sanctions, although the latter rarely, if ever, in an individual case. The meeting is also a forum for discussing wider hospital and, effectively, national policy and its impact. Sometimes this is a bonding experience for staff and patients,

mutually affected by some new piece of bureaucracy. Sometimes delicate management of the potential for splitting is needed, as staff recognize that one or more of their members may be inconsistent or deficient in certain of their approaches. It can even happen that one staff member is not popular with other staff, but he or she is nonetheless an integral part of the team, and this tension must be dealt with.

MONITORING PROGRESS

The weekly clinical team meeting is used for monitoring progress, but there is always space too for crisis management review. An alternating format is used: on one week there will be a meeting in which each man is briefly reviewed and discussed, and, generally, on alternate weeks there will be a case conference and care planning meeting in which one resident is discussed in depth. Alternation is not rigid, because of the need to fit in therapy reviews and away days. For the general team meetings, all psychiatric staff attend, and representatives from the other departments involved try to attend with as many nursing staff as practicable.

At the case conference and care programme planning meetings, the team composition is different. Only those in the Woodstock clinical team with a close interest attend, but, in addition, other relevant parties are also invited, usually psychiatric staff (or deputies) from the Regional Secure Unit (RSU), even if the transfer seems some way off. The Woodstock team can learn a lot from the home base team's experience of the resident, while all parties need regular reminding that treatment in Broadmoor is just a phase in a longer term treatment plan. The resident is also invited to attend for most of his treatment planning conference. Most take up this opportunity to hear and discuss progress reports and share in planning for the next stage. Some even prepare their own, formal reports. Evaluation of treatment effects in relation to specific pieces of work, especially the structured groups, is conducted using specific relevant tests (see also Chapter 4) and reported at these meetings.

Both general and case conferences are fully documented and, in relation to the latter, documentation is also completed for the 'Care Programme Approach' required nationally. The man is entitled to read and comment on his report, sometimes leading to factual corrections. He may keep a copy of the final report and the resulting treatment plan. Furthermore, under British legislation, patients are entitled to see and have a copy of any part of their record unless disclosure is likely to cause harm to the physical or mental state of the patient or anyone else, or if disclosing a record or part of a record identifies a third party (not a health professional) who has not consented to this or cannot be anonymised. All this, however, raises a real security issue for the patients. In holding their own copies of their records, with often only a limited idea of how to protect their security as well as limited resources for doing so, they increase the risk of often very sensitive material no longer being confidential. A secure filing cabinet is provided for the men to store their own copies of records, although it has to be accessed through staff; immediate access can be obtained by making a simple request, although such requests are not often made.

In addition to the above meetings, there is an informal weekly 'business' round at the beginning of the week when a staff nurse and one of the junior medical staff briefly review the patients. This acts as a 'caretaking meeting', and also highlights issues that may need to be discussed more fully in the team meeting later in the week. Medical staff and nurse managers are invariably available on call. Certain interventions, particularly seclusion, which is occasionally used, require formal monitoring and central record keeping.

In addition to the in-house evaluation of treatment effect, the ward is included in hospital-wide audits, statutory audits and research. The hospital-wide audits so far have centred on compliance with policy, such as the care programme approach, drug prescription charts, incident rates and complaints. Statutory audit occurs when government-appointed bodies such as the Mental Health Act Commission (MHAC) – the special mental health authority for detained patients, set up under the Mental Health Act 1983, which is an entirely independent of the hospital – attend for both planned and unannounced visits. The MHAC audits documentation of detention papers and legal aspects of treatment, and also holds confidential visits with patients who request to see them. Since 2003, representatives of a succession of bodies under the auspices of the government Department of Health, currently (2005) the Healthcare Commission, also visit. Research projects are many and various, conducted by both staff internal to the hospital and external researchers. Some of the research completed specifically in relation to the ward (e.g. Reiss et al., 1996) is reported more fully elsewhere (Chapter 30). Finally, as an informal sort of audit, the unit status as a teaching unit means that students from all disciplines regularly attend or are involved in the work in some way. Some are on placement, some visit as observers. The unit also hosts a number of national and international visitors. All ask challenging questions. Patients generally welcome these visitors and, indeed, include many of them in the community meetings.

MAINTAINING A HEALTHY AND FUNCTIONAL STAFF

SUPPORT AND SUPERVISION

Staff spending prolonged periods (up to 12 hours) in close contact with extremely disturbed and disorganized men face constant exposure to pathologically high levels of projections and projective identification. They often find themselves being 'recruited' to particular roles in the long-standing relationship patterns of the men (Adshead, 1998). As a result, nursing staff, in particular, are at risk of slipping into states of collusion, identification and acting-out, as well as splitting of the team consensus (Main, 1957; Gabbard and Wilkinson, 1994). Supervision (which can be carried out in groups or on an individual basis) is the process whereby time and space are scheduled into the working day for all staff members to explore and understand their reactions to the people under treatment. It is essential. As the relationship with the supervisor develops, it usually becomes increasingly possible for staff members to acknowledge the feelings of frustration and impotence they experience working with this difficult and demanding group (Hinshelwood, 1999). As insight is gained into the nature of their responses, and their origins, staff members become increasingly able to tolerate these experiences. With this growing awareness, they are increasingly able to control their reactions, thereby lowering stress levels and reducing the risk of the various types of counter-therapeutic or risky activity described above. This type of supervision does, however, rely on mutual trust and respect between supervisor and supervisee, to enable the supervisee to discuss his or her experiences freely. It also requires a commitment by the staff team to support the provision of supervision – this may be difficult in a busy ward, where acute demands might threaten to take priority over the supervision session. Careful scheduling of work patterns is required to safeguard the supervision process and to ensure that the staff team understands and respects its importance.

Each professional group has its own system of clinical supervision and mentoring to provide support, and each needs constant safeguarding against erosion by other commitments. Specific psychotherapy supervision is interdisciplinary.

The quarterly 'away day' – about 4 hours for the team together outside the hospital – provides an opportunity for laying bare some of the frustrations and anxieties in a safe setting, as well as allowing for creativity in developing policy and considering change.

Supervision can help guard against destructive and harmful unconscious responses, and education is used to reduce this risk by working at the cognitive level. All staff members are encouraged to visit similar units in other security settings, open hospitals and prisons, and to make reciprocal arrangements.

TRAINING AND EDUCATION

Staff from various professions, including trainee psychiatrists and nursing students, work on the ward as part of their training. All have to attend a general induction course of several days for the main hospital, training particularly in security issues. Induction to the ward per se is brief, but each trainee has regular personal supervision and mentorship as well as attending group therapy or educational training sessions. Trainees with little previous experience of patients suffering from this degree of personality disorder are potentially particularly vulnerable, not least because some of the men will knowingly try to exploit their lack of experience. Clear explanation of the potential risks, together with full involvement in team discussions, in conjunction with individual supervision, should keep these risks to a minimum. Indeed, feedback shows that trainees enjoy their placement, find it a valuable educational experience and in turn are valued by regular staff and patients. Several have, in fact, been recruited to one of the clinical specialties. There are also opportunities for other professionals such as visiting specialist registrars and overseas forensic psychiatry diploma students to carry out ward placements.

As these trainees go on to practise professionally, they will do so with the experience of the potential for treatment of this type of patient and the problems involved, thus challenging the 'traditional' view of personality disorder patients being untreatable.

CONCLUSION

Woodstock is a unit for a group of young, male, serious offenders who suffer from personality disorder, with or without co-morbid conditions. Those who participate in this programme of treatment have all been assessed and generally selected for their potential to change and/or stated willingness to try to do so. The staff all have a particular interest in this type of work and have all made an active choice to work on the ward, but have varying levels of training and experience. The unit has evolved over the 20 years or so since the early concept of a 'young person's unit', as review of the descriptions of it over the years shows (Grounds et al., 1987; Quayle et al., 1996; Brett, 1992). As long as it remains a healthy unit, further change will undoubtedly follow.

The staff team is multidisciplinary, and particular attention is paid to involving all members of the team to the highest degree possible in clinical planning. Each resident actively participates as far as he can in setting up a therapeutic programme. This makes use of elements available on and off the ward, but is tailored to his specific needs as formulated by the multidisciplinary team, and places emphasis on membership of a community – Woodstock.

Progress is monitored continuously, but formally assessed at clinical team meetings, sometimes before and after specific pieces of therapeutic work, and with support from standard assessment schedules as well as clinical judgement. However, many of the most serious risks are highly individual, and standardized approaches are of little help. Attention is paid to liaison with those local services into whose care the man will eventually pass. Transitionary psychotherapy arrangements may be vital to the maintenance of progress.

For all staff working in this type of setting, personal supervision and/or monitoring are essential; further training in specific skills and general progressive development through education are not only valuable, but also safeguard against potentially counter-therapeutic or unsafe collusion with some of the patterns of behaviour encountered among the young men.

REFERENCES

Adshead G (1998). Psychiatric staff as attachment figures. *British Journal of Psychiatry* **172**:64–9.

Brett T (1992). The Woodstock approach: one ward in Broadmoor Hospital for the treatment of personality disorder. *Criminal Behaviour and Mental Health* **2**:152–8.

Gabbard GO and Wilkinson SM (1994). *Management of Countertransference with Borderline Patients.* Washington, DC: American Psychiatric Press.

Grounds AT, Quayle MT, France J, Brett T, Cox M and Hamilton JR (1987). 'A unit for psychopathic disorder patients in Broadmoor Hospital. *Medicine, Science and the Law* **27**:21–31.

Hinshelwood RD (1999). The difficult patient. The role of 'scientific psychiatry' in understanding patients with chronic schizophrenia or severe personality disorder. *British Journal of Psychiatry* **174**:187–91.

Main TF (1957). The ailment. *British Journal of Medical Psychology* **30**:129–45.

Prochaska JO and DiClemente CC (1983). Stages and processes of self-change of smoking: toward an integrative model of change. *Journal of Consulting and Clinical Psychology* **51**:390–5.

Quayle M, France J and Wilkinson E (1996). An integrated modular approach to therapy in a special hospital young men's unit. In: Cordess C and Cox M (eds), *Forensic Psychotherapy*, Vol., II. London: Jessica Kingsley, 449–63.

Reiss D, Grubin D and Meux C (1996). Young 'psychopaths' in special hospital: treatment and outcome? *British Journal of Psychiatry* **168**:99–104.

Taylor PJ and Swan T (eds) (1999). *Couples in Care and Custody.* Oxford: Butterworth-Heinemann.

World Health Organization (1992). *International Classification of Diseases,* tenth revision. Geneva: World Health Organization.

Chapter 19

SERVICES FOR WOMEN OFFENDERS WITH PERSONALITY DISORDER: FOCUS ON A TRAUMA-BASED APPROACH TO TREATMENT

Fiona L. Mason

INTRODUCTION

Women who offend in the context of personality disorder have tended to suffer for being a small group. In the whole of the prison service for England and Wales in 1988, it was suggested that just over 8 per cent of sentenced women had a personality disorder (Gunn et al., 1991) and 15.5 per cent of pre-trial women in 1993/4 (Maden et al., 1996). In both of these studies, the estimates were based on clinical assessment. In 1997, when the assessment was made by trained lay interviewers using a standard interview schedule – the Structured Clinical Interview for DSM-IV* (SCID) – 64 per cent of sentenced and 53 per cent of pre-trial women were found to be so disordered (Singleton et al., 1998). It is probable that some of this difference is accounted for by differences in methodology, but the latter study was done at a time when the number of women being imprisoned was rising at an even steeper rate than the number of men. There may be some real increase in need. At the end of March 2000, 3391 prisoners in

England and Wales were women, out of a total of about 65 000. The trend continues: on 7th January 2005, there were 73 085 people in prison, of whom 4109 (approximately 6 per cent) were women.

The relative proportions of women and men in prison and secure psychiatric settings differ little in different countries, with women always constituting a small minority. It is this disproportion that makes it difficult to provide for them adequately on cost and supply grounds. The argument for reciprocity, however, is at least as important for women as for men. If women with recognized mental disorder are to be deprived of their liberty, whether in prison or hospital, some proper provision must be made, at the least, for their habilitation or rehabilitation. There are powerful arguments that many of them should not be in custody at all (Howard League for Penal Reform, 2000), although such arguments are not against consideration of need. The Home Office and Department of Health (1999), in advancing their proposals for service development for people with 'dangerous severe personality disorder', barely mentioned women, although, by implication, the citizens of England and Wales can expect to be harbouring about 40 such women. As across the rest of the spectrum, there seems little idea of what

---

Diagnostic and Statistical Manual of Mental Disorders, fourth edition (American Psychiatric Association, 1994).

should be offered. In the criminal justice system, treatment regimes according to the 'what works' approach (McGuire, 1995) have been almost exclusively directed at men, whether in the UK or elsewhere.

While it might be expected that there would be some similarities in treatment, educational, occupational and social needs of such men and women, they are likely also to have needs influenced, if not dictated, by their gender, particularly given the markedly different offending and social profiles of incarcerated men and women. In 2002, the Department of Health issued a consultation document that provided a review and radical proposals for changes in mental health services for women. This emphasizes recommendations for the provision of gender-specific services – which in many sub-specialty areas would be contentious – and gender-sensitive services – which would be uniformly welcomed. There are three short paragraphs specific to the women with a diagnosis of personality disorder, indeed specifically borderline personality disorder.

Until the 1990s, the high-security hospitals for England and Wales and in Scotland had long differed from most prisons in that men and women shared the site, had separate living accommodation, but had access to most of the facilities. As was considered appropriate, many of the women would share educational, work and social sessions with the men. Their minority status (1:4), nevertheless, meant that at least until the 1990s, provision had never been determined by specific needs assessment of women. Nor, prior to that time, had much thought been given to the pros and cons of the partial integration of these women with these men. In the smaller regional units of lesser security, such difficulties came into sharper focus much more quickly, because even living accommodation tended to be gender integrated, and the women not uncommonly in a minority of one or two women to ten men. In the late 1990s, there was further separation of the men and women in high-security hospitals,

with previously integrated activities being ended. At the medium-secure level, a number of women-only units have been opened, and more are currently in development, with the hope that even smaller numbers of women will need high security. The additional development of enhanced medium-secure services would reduce these numbers even further. Such developments are in themselves of great interest; however, they will not be considered further here, given that the focus in this chapter is on therapeutic approaches rather than political and organizational developments.

A DEDICATED PERSONALITY DISORDER SERVICE FOR WOMEN IN A HIGH-SECURITY HOSPITAL

The service described was developed in an English high-security hospital at a time (1996) when about 90 of the 450 patients were women. In September 2005, there were 254 men, of whom 22 were on leave, and 44 women, of whom 2 were on leave. Services for women are now being phased out of two high-security hospitals, but the principles and practice in the development described could be applied for women elsewhere. Nearly half of those on the unit being discussed had personality disorder as their primary diagnosis, the main subgroup being borderline personality disorder. Many of this group, and, indeed, some of the women with psychosis, presented with numerous other problems related to previous experience of traumatization. A broad range of psychopathology resulted, including affective disorders, substance misuse disorders, eating disorders and post-traumatic stress disorder (PTSD). The service that was run between 1996 and 2001 was a dedicated service for such women, but those with a primary diagnosis of schizophrenia or other psychotic illness could be admitted if they required the treatment approach offered and their psychosis was well controlled.

The principle underlying the work on the ward was that, for the majority of women, early repeated trauma had played a key role in the pathway to their adult clinical presentation and offending behaviour. Thus all staff needed to have an awareness and understanding of trauma-related issues if they were to work successfully with these patients. Bloom (1997) has written of the need to 'create sanctuary', and refers to the shared experience of creating and maintaining safety within a social environment. At all times it was important for the staff and resident women that this unit created such an environment. A lot was asked of the patients, who were expecting to work on the most damaged part of themselves. Such work could not take place unless safety was maintained, and felt to be maintained.

The size of the ward was carefully considered. It was recognized that the initial number of 23 beds was far too high, but practical considerations meant that a reduction to 18 beds was all that could be achieved. This was also considered too high, as it was recognized that the dynamics within the patient group and between patients and staff were harder to manage the larger the number and greater the diversity of the patients. In addition, the physical environment did not lend itself to ensuring the safety and comfort of the women, who were likely to remain on the ward for some years. Plans were therefore put in place to reduce the number, and to move the ward to a more suitable, refurbished unit, where the team, informed by their knowledge of the patient group, influenced the design and layout as far as was possible. It was acknowledged, however, that even with these changes, the environment was far from ideal, given the constraints of working in buildings constructed in the nineteenth century.

The service aimed to offer a multi-modal therapeutic programme for the women. The importance of providing high-quality physical healthcare services was acknowledged, given the complex multiple physical health problems from which this patient population suffered. It also emerged that food-related issues were significant, with high levels of obesity amongst the patients creating significant difficulties. A wide range of psychological treatments, including dialectical behaviour therapy, psychodynamic psychotherapy, cognitive–behavioural therapy, and specific problem-solving groups, such as social skills, anger management, assertiveness training and relaxation, were utilized. All patients were expected to participate in regular meetings involving the whole community. Psychoeducation was seen as a core need, most of this work being carried out in time-limited groups. It was hoped, as services within the wider hospital expanded, that it would prove possible to introduce other relevant therapies, for example art, music and drama therapies. Given that the patients had multiple diagnoses, flexibility in programme planning was considered vital, and emphasis was placed on one-to-one support to supplement all other work. Each patient's underlying mental disorder and dangerousness needed concurrent treatment and management in a manner complementary to the over-arching unit programme.

Little is known of the outcome of these therapeutic interventions in women presenting with such disorders. The unit aimed to ensure, nevertheless, that clinical practice was shaped and led by audit and research. Assessments of outcome of the overall programme, and of specific interventions within the programme, were based on standardized or semi-standardized questionnaires, interviews and investigations wherever possible. It was recognized that detailed assessment packages needed to be developed, and that a clinical steering group and a research steering group, with multidisciplinary memberships, should jointly oversee the development process as the unit moved closer to realizing the vision. Subsequent political, personal and organizational decisions impacted on the development of the unit; however, the service model developed, and the journey taken by staff and patients alike is presented, given the value in learning from previous experience in this widely unexplored area of work.

THE BACKGROUND AND EVOLUTION OF THE UNIT

A large unit with a broad mix of patients, both in terms of age and diagnosis, presents an enormous challenge to all those working within it. In the case of the 'parent' high-security hospital unit under consideration, this was partly a simple function of the then higher patient-to-staff ratio (23 patients with 4 or 5 staff per shift), but it was partly also because of the level and nature of the psychopathology and disturbed behaviour presented by the patients. Incident levels were high, as were the frequency and severity of self-harming behaviours. Staff sickness was also an important problem. Further, the patient mix meant that approaches on the ward had to be so varied that no over-arching philosophy and little structure were possible. In part, too, this was a reflection of the lack of evidenced-based research into the treatment of personality disorder among women. After review, reflection and consultation, it was considered that a number of changes were essential if the ward was to become 'fit for purpose'. The ideal that the ward should be divided into two, ten-bedded units was not achieved, but a two-stage reduction in numbers was accepted. A maximum of 12 women within one ward space was planned for the refurbished unit. A radical shift in patient mix enabled staff to draw up and implement a treatment philosophy, which was clear for patients and staff alike. However, continuing turnover in staffing remained a problem, thus rendering consistent implementation difficult. Periods of such instability are not unusual in this type of unit, so understanding them, and the causes for them, is important.

DEVELOPMENT OF THE PHILOSOPHY OF CARE

In 1992, Blackburn (see also Chapter 3 in this book) highlighted the stages of assessment of treatability for people suffering with personality disorder. He proposed first the assessment of the nature of the disorder, second the identification of targets for therapeutic change, and third knowing and balancing the nature of interventions available to achieve these targets. A subsequent Special Hospitals' Service Authority (SHSA) Advisory Group (1994) then identified six principal goals for the assessment of people with personality disorder.

1. To identify and describe the enduring cognitive, emotional and actional strengths and weaknesses of the patient.
2. To identify those aspects of the patient's environment, and especially his social environment, including his family, which have reinforced the patient's strengths and challenged the weaknesses.
3. To determine appropriate treatment.
4. To predict likely course with treatment and likely course without.
5. To demonstrate change, or lack of it, and plot the real progress against predicted course.
6. To identify those factors in therapy and in the environment which diminish pathology in the patient and those (not necessarily different) which promote health and enhance adaptive functioning, particularly where those factors are likely to be replicable outside special hospital. To note any damaging effects of therapy.

At about the same time, also from the SHSA, the particular characteristics of women in special hospitals were documented (Kaye, 1994) and the following six characteristics emphasized.

1. Experience of physical, sexual and psychological abuse.
2. High prevalence of eating disorders.
3. High incidence of suicidal thought, depression and self-harm.
4. High prevalence of feelings of worthlessness and low self-esteem, guilt and anger.
5. Treatment to date has predominantly been dependent on medication to treat symptoms.
6. Misdiagnosis is common and many are suffering from borderline personality disorder.

The last point is one that is of particular interest, given the postulated link between borderline personality disorder and experience of early trauma (Herman et al., 1989) and the belief in recovery (Herman, 1992a). Herman (1992b) subsequently described a disorder not included in the American DSM-IV (American Psychiatric Association, 1994), but, in the author's opinion, of great value when assessing and treating the particular group of women for whom this specialist unit was developed. Herman called this disorder 'complex PTSD' and described the following core features.

A history of subjection to totalitarian control over a prolonged period (months to years), e.g. hostages, prisoners of war, concentration-camp survivors, survivors of domestic battering, childhood physical or sexual abuse, and organised sexual exploitation. In addition the following features are seen:

1. alterations in affect regulation
2. alterations in consciousness
3. alterations in self-perception
4. alterations in perception of perpetrator (it should be noted that subsequently this item has been removed)
5. alterations in relations with others
6. alterations in systems of meaning.

Comparison with the diagnostic criteria for borderline personality disorder will reveal many similarities, particularly in the area of relationship disruption and attachment to others. There is also a considerable amount of work examining the ability of these patients to manage emotion and affect, and the links between these difficulties and early trauma (van der Kolk et al., 1996). It is postulated that the effect of the abuse depends, to a certain extent, on the stage of development at which it takes place, and that sustained early-onset traumatic events, as reported by our patients, have a very profound effect. Clinically, some of these women, with similar presentations, will be diagnosed as suffering from a personality disorder, whilst others will be diagnosed as having a mental illness. All, however, present with varying, but similar, symptom patterns and behaviours, which can be understood in terms of the trauma-based model. It is postulated that this model will allow more effective and successful work with some of the most difficult and damaged individuals. There are, in essence, two areas that need to be considered in relation to this work: namely, the treatment methods utilized in direct work with patients, and the attitude adopted when caring for those being treated. It is this latter area that so often inhibits the treatment being offered to the patient, and undermines recovery.

TREATMENT

In establishing the treatment regimes on the unit, it was necessary to consider a number of areas of research and writing. The following areas are considered to be particularly relevant.

- The effects of trauma on the mind, and the links between trauma and offending.
- The assessment and treatment of personality disordered patients (and, in particular, borderline personality disorder).

- The development of therapeutic communities.
- Research into and evaluation of services developed to work with this patient group.
- Women and mental health.
- Specific clinical conditions and behaviours, including addictive behaviours, eating disorders, anxiety states, mood disorders and self-harming behaviours.
- Attachment theory.
- Trauma-based approaches to treatment.

It is not possible to expand on all of these here; however, the last was central to our work. The theoretical base we tried to adopt, with some modification, was essentially drawn from Sandra Bloom's experiences working with traumatized individuals in 'The Sanctuary', a trauma-based treatment service in the USA (Bloom, 1997). Given the importance of these concepts to the work, they are outlined in some detail below.

In Bloom's (1997) model, traditional assumptions made about patients are challenged to some extent. The patients – here, the women – rather than what may have happened to them, or their environment, are often seen as the problem and there is generally no shared theoretical basis on which they are considered. Very often, there is little communication between the personnel involved in the different treatment settings. Given this fragmentation, staff well-being is also often overlooked, and yet the anger commonly associated with trauma may be projected on to them. Trauma is not necessarily seen as an acceptable reason for a patient's problems and, if it is, as the fact of the trauma is fixed, so it may be perceived that its consequences are too. The template for risk assessment generated by Steadman et al. (1994) presents such a view. This is of renewed importance given the status accorded to a self-reported history of child abuse for the prediction of violence in a general psychiatric hospital sample in the USA

(Monahan et al., 2000). In a related paper, Monahan and Appelbaum (2000) include a rather disturbing sentence that implies that belief in the veracity of the experience of such patients is even often doubted:

Even if one took the view that these self-reports are often merely a reflection of psychopathic lack of responsibility-taking, the predictive fact would remain that a self-report of having been abused was significantly and prospectively correlated with violence.

Commonly, these people are not expected to get better. The goals of treatment are therefore often unclear. Patient input is generally discouraged, as is emotional expression. Very often the patients will be offered crisis management, for example after self-harming behaviour; however, they are rarely engaged in on-going individual therapy. Violence is accepted as inevitable, and responses to violence often involve seclusion, restraint and medication.

Given this traditional pattern of working, it is important for shared assumptions to be held by the team attempting to do things differently. Bloom believes the key assumptions to be that the patients originally came from normal beginnings, but that traumas they experienced affected their development, and have biological, psychological, social and moral effects. Such individuals, she suggests, then go on to develop adaptive coping to maladaptive symptoms, and become trapped within such cycles. Experiences become fragmented and are repeated through repetitive, intrusive thoughts, emotions, flashbacks and dreams. The affect that accompanies these experiences is overwhelming and poorly modulated, and dissociation and repression are commonly seen. Helplessness and lack of control are common themes, and relationships in the present are adversely affected by the disrupted attachment of the past. Addictions are commonly seen, and serve to numb. Individuals can also become addicted to trauma itself, leading to re-traumatization. Guilt, depression, anxiety, low self-esteem, helplessness, difficulty managing aggression, perpetration, and inappropriate attachment to others as buffers against trauma are also frequently seen.

Successful working necessitates adopting shared goals, such as the substitution of healthy relationship for self-destructive behaviours, the promotion of a coherent and meaningful narrative, and the creation of a desire to 'build' a different, non-violent, normative environment in which violent perpetration ends. In addition to these goals, Bloom argues for the importance of shared practice, in which norms are established, emotions are managed, boundaries protected, unconscious conflicts resolved and violence dealt with using consistent approaches. She believes that the group consciousness cannot be ignored, and that the whole should become a living–learning environment.

The adoption of these philosophies was seen as a way of understanding patients struggling with such difficulties, and enabling safety to be maintained whilst active treatment proceeded. A variety of specific treatment approaches were adopted on Leeds Ward (the unit at Broadmoor Hospital), marrying Bloom's principles with those of Ochberg (1991), who proposed that therapy with those who had been traumatized should encompass:

- normalization,
- collaborative treatment with the therapist,
- remembering the uniqueness of the individual.

Ochberg also proposed that a variety of techniques should be used, including:

– a holistic approach,
– education,
– social support and integration,
– therapy to include:
    telling the trauma story

    symptom suppression
    individualized search for meaning,
– treatment for any co-existing problems.

Detailed description of all the treatment modalities lies outside the scope of this chapter; however, some of the core treatment approaches are listed below, and the general principle of treatment was that a phased, stage approach was utilized.

- Dialectical behaviour therapy.
- Cognitive–behavioural approaches.
- Dynamic psychotherapy.
- Supportive psychotherapy.
- Medication.
- Psychoeducation.
- Skills-based group work.

STAFF RECRUITMENT AND RETENTION

As noted above, one of the key difficulties in establishing the programme for this team was achieving a stable composition of the staff. We doubt if this was a unique experience. The problem was particularly noticeable within the nursing team, in the longest and most direct contact with the patients. For the nurses, turnover and staff sickness were high. In part, these difficulties appeared to relate to inherent problems with methods of recruitment. This was at a time, for example, when it was not possible to recruit specifically for the ward, or even specifically for Women's Services. Staff had rarely chosen to work on the unit; most had been directed there from the hospital's general pool of staff. The problem also related to the low staffing numbers and skill mix allocated as establishment to the ward. Both of these factors were changed, and a more specifically targeted recruitment for staff with relevant qualifications began to bear fruit. Staff support and supervision (in the psychotherapeutic sense) were increased, and time was made to ensure that appropriate training was delivered. It may be of importance that an audit suggested that the preliminary process of revision, circulation and discussion of protocols reflecting an understanding of links between childhood trauma and adult behaviour was associated with substantial reduction in incident levels on the ward. Staff sickness levels also improved. It could be useful to set up a formal evaluation of the impact on staff of presentation of the evidence base for service review or re-development. Preparation of such a process could be a highly cost-effective way of safeguarding the interests of patients and protecting the well-being of staff.

CONCLUSION

The developments outlined raise as many questions as solutions, but questions that, if adequately formulated for research, could have far-reaching implications. The trauma-based approach to treatment for women who have personality disorder and who have offended is based on theoretical arguments, but untested for its effectiveness in ameliorating distress or reducing violence and the risk of violence. While presented as something of a departure from models set up for men, it may be that as the model is refined, and tested and proven for such women, applications may also prove relevant for some men. Certainly many men also describe childhoods filled with prolonged and severe abuse. It is essential that the integrity of the programme be maintained, so as to enable evaluation of the impact on individual women and on the service for both the short and longer term. Only then will it be possible to expand the programme, if appropriate, to other, similar populations.

REFERENCES

American Psychiatric Association (1994). *Diagnostic and Statistical Manual of Mental Disorders,* fourth edition. Washington, DC: American Psychiatric Association.

Blackburn R (1992). Clinical programmes with psychopaths. In: Howells K and Hollis C (eds), *Clinical Approaches to the Mentally Disordered Offender.* Chichester: John Wiley & Sons.

Bloom S (1997). *Creating Sanctuary. Towards an Evolution of Sane Societies.* New York/London: Routledge.

Department of Health (2002). *Women's Mental Health: Into the Mainstream. Strategic Development of Mental Health Care for Women.* London: Department of Health.

Gunn J, Maden A and Swinton M (1991). Treatment needs of prisoners with psychiatric disorders. *British Medical Journal* **303**:338–41.

Herman J (1992a). *Trauma and Recovery.* New York: Basic Books.

Herman J (1992b). Complex PTSD: a syndrome in survivors of prolonged and repeated trauma. *Journal of Traumatic Stress* **5**:377–91.

Herman J, Perry C and van der Kolk B (1989). Childhood trauma in borderline personality disorder. *American Journal of Psychiatry* **146**:490–5.

Home Office and Department of Health (1999). *Managing Dangerous People with Severe Personality Disorder Proposals for Policy Development.* London: Home Office.

Howard League for Penal Reform (2000). Women in Prison. Fact Sheet. Available from 1 Ardleigh Road, London, N1 4HS, UK.

Kaye C (1994). Prurience and public interest. *Health Service Journal* Open Space, 7 April, p. 15.

Maden A, Taylor CJA, Brooke D and Gunn J (1996). *Mental Disorder in Remand Prisons.* London: Home Office.

McGuire J (ed.) (1995). *What Works: Reducing Reoffending.* Chichester: John Wiley & Sons.

Monahan J and Appelbaum PS (2000). Reducing violence risk. In: Hodgins S (ed.), *Violence among the Mentally Ill.* NATO. Dordrecht: Kluwer Academic Publishers, 19–34.

Monahan J, Steadman H, Appelbaum PS et al. (2000). Developing a clinically useful actuarial tool for assessing violence risk. *British Journal of Psychiatry* **176**:312–18.

National Institute for Mental Health in England (2003). *Personality Disorder: No Longer a Diagnosis of*

Exclusion. Leeds: The National Institute for Mental Health in England.

Ochberg F (1991). Post-traumatic therapy. *Psychotherapy* **25**:5–16.

Singleton N, Meltzer H and Gatward R (1998). *Office of National Statistics Survey of Psychiatric Morbidity among Prisoners in England and Wales.* London: The Stationery Office.

Special Hospitals' Service Authority (1994). Preliminary Report of SHSA Advisory Group on the Management of People with Personality Disorder Referred for a Special Hospital Opinion and Already within the Hospitals. Available from Research Unit, Broadmoor Hospital, Crowthorne, Berks RG45 7EG, UK.

Steadman HJ, Monahan J, Appelbaum PS et al. (1994). Designing a new generation of risk assessment research. In: Monahan J and Steadman HJ (eds), *Violence and Mental Disorder: Developments in Risk Assessment.* Chicago, IL: Chicago University Press, 297–318.

Van der Kolk B (1989). The compulsion to repeat the trauma: re-enactment, revictimisation and masochism. *Psychiatric Clinics of North America* **12**:389–411.

Van der Kolk B, Pelcovitz D, Roth S, Mandel F, McFarlane A and Herman JL (1996). Dissociation, somatization, and affect dysregulation: the complexity of adaptation of trauma. *American Journal of Psychiatry* **153**(Suppl.):83–93.

Chapter 20

THE IMPLICATIONS FOR SERVICES OF PSYCHOACTIVE SUBSTANCE ABUSE DISORDERS CO-MORBID WITH PERSONALITY DISORDER

Tracey Heads

PERSONALITY DISORDER AND SUBSTANCE USE DISORDERS: THE EPIDEMIOLOGY OF ASSOCIATION

Abuse of alcohol and/or illicit drugs is extremely common among people with personality disorder (Chiles et al., 1990; Regier et al., 1990). Based on Epidemiologic Catchment Area data drawn from five sites in the USA between 1981 and 1985, Robins et al. (1991) estimated that, while the average odds ratio for co-occurrence of one disorder and another was 2, the odds ratio for the co-occurrence of anti-social personality disorder (ASPD) and alcohol disorder in the year of interview was 29. By the same sort of calculation, it was 12 times more likely that someone with ASPD would have some other form of drug dependency or abuse than someone without this disorder.

Verheul et al. (1995) included European figures in their review of 50 studies, and endorsed the evidence of substantial overlap between the conditions. Some authors have drawn attention to further co-morbidities, particularly with depression and/or other mood disorders (Flynn et al., 1996; Kokkevi et al., 1998). These may be especially important with respect to treatment engagement and maintenance.

Among offenders specifically, co-morbidities between personality disorder and substance misuse may be even higher (e.g. Teplin, 1994 [male prisoners]; Teplin et al., 1996 [female prisoners], Teplin et al., 2003 [youths]). Figures for substance misuse have almost certainly been higher in urban USA than in the UK, but among people admitted to the English high-security hospitals, trends for regular harmful use of alcohol or other drugs in the year prior to admission to the hospitals show an increase in the proportion of patients across all categories of substance use over the 25 years to 1999 (McMahon et al., 2003, in preparation).

Substance misuse disorders and personality disorders are acknowledged as different but strongly associated, so questions arise about the nature of the relationship. Does one cause the other? Is their association entirely explained by overlapping symptoms or shared risk factors? Is it even possible that two disorders treated as separate are different expressions of the same disorder? Robins (1998) reviewed the evidence for each of these possibilities for this combination, and demonstrated the difficulties in interpretation. She relied on Susser (1991) for models of use of epidemiological data – testing temporal order, coherence with existing beliefs, dose-related liability and understandable mechanisms. These are complicated here, though, because, in operational terms, personality disorder may not be diagnosed before the age of 18, and the reality of features of conduct disorder is that many may be present before they are recorded. Below a certain age, such features might be regarded as unremarkable and only abnormal when they persist. Perceived age of onset of substance misuse may be fixed in part by culturally determined conventions. She concludes that the case that conduct/personality disorder causes substance misuse is easier to make than the reverse, but prefers a more practical approach of considering how one disorder affects the course of another.

Mueser et al. (1998b) and Tiihonen and Swartz (2000) considered the problem of substance misuse in the context of psychotic illness, but the models they reviewed largely apply to, and complement and extend, Robins' review of personality disorder. Tiihonen and Swartz focus in particular on understanding pathways to antisocial acts. Setting aside the more illness-specific issues (e.g. medication substitution) and the concept of substance abuse in this context as a proxy for personality disorder, hypotheses relevant to clinical practice include one that substance abuse reduces impulse control, that exposure to adverse environments leads to substance abuse and that aggressive behaviour, boredom and lack of structure lead to substance abuse.

THE RISKS OF FAILURE TO TREAT

Thus substance abuse commonly occurs in the context of a wide range of other difficulties, including childhood experiences of deprivation and/or abuse, low self-esteem, difficulties coping with emotions such as anger, anxiety and dysphoria, social difficulties, poverty, unemployment etc., many of which are features common to personality disorder. Further, abuse of or dependency on alcohol or other drugs is associated with a range of secondary problems, including serious damage to physical and mental health, relationships, work performance, financial management and offending and/or violent behaviour. Although the sort of computations for increased risk of violence when people with psychosis use substances appear not to have been done for people with personality disorder, it is likely that the risks of violence problems of each disorder are compounded when they occur together. Certainly structured tools for assessing risk of violence would incorporate both estimates of personality disorder and substance misuse in the ratings (e.g. Webster et al., 1997). People with both sets of disorder are likely to have multiple and pervasive difficulties that call for a broad range of services and staff skills – not only to help the individual, but also to offer support for the family, and to enable many practical interventions, including safe accommodation and constructive occupational, social and recreational activities. Robins' insistence on considering how the course of each disorder affects the other makes sense.

ADVERSE ATTITUDES TO TREATMENT AND EVIDENTIAL REALITY

The damage caused to the individual by substance abuse, the probable exacerbation of features of personality disorder and the contribution to offending and/or violent behaviour indicate the need for substance abuse itself to be managed, and preferably treated. People with both personality and substance use disorders are, however, particularly likely to be perceived in negative, even hostile, terms by professionals, and rejection by services is common. Many forensic clinicians express a nihilistic attitude towards therapeutic interventions in relation to substance abuse, a commonly held view being that 'as alcohol and drugs are readily available in society, there is nothing that can be done'. This can extend to a sense of helplessness in institutional settings. The availability of substances might be controlled, but the susceptibility of individuals is thus 'untestable', or subject to denial, and 'untreatable'. There is certainly evidence that in the English high-security hospitals, access to illicit substances per se has been controlled. However, patients in these circumstances are creative, and some shift to prescribed medications that might mimic the effect of stimulants or demand codeine-containing analgesics (Kendrick et al., 2002).

In common with personality disorder, substance misuse seems to be preferentially construed by professional clinicians as well as the lay public as some sort of 'moral defect', albeit on less well tested and certainly less technical or theoretical grounds. These failures in moral development appear to be construed as more worthy of punishment than therapeutic assistance. These attitudes and responses are surprising given the significant advances made in the development of treatment interventions for patients with addiction disorders, including, for example, motivational interviewing (Miller and Rollnick, 1991), relapse prevention (Marlatt and Gordon, 1985), therapeutic communities (Rosenthal, 1991) and the development of treatment approaches for dual diagnosis patients (Solomon et al., 1993). In the light of these developments, and given the chaotic lifestyle characteristic of this group, a remand period, custodial sentence or compulsory hospital admission can (perhaps should) be viewed as a therapeutic opportunity.

Those with personality and substance disorders vary widely in terms of type and severity of abuse/dependence, range of personality difficulties, and seriousness of offending/violent behaviour. Also, individuals vary in their treatment and security needs at different stages in the courses of the disorders. In general, progress is likely to be slow, and many relapses may occur before sustained progress is made. A long-term perspective towards service provision that ensures that interventions are optimally timed to fit a patient's current motivational state is therefore required.

SOME SERVICES OFFERED

Although substantial numbers of individuals with personality and substance disorders are able, in Britain, to receive treatment within National Health Service (NHS) facilities, many are in prison, either awaiting trial under remand after conviction or under sentence. Although there may be considerable difficulties in establishing services within the prison environment (Jones, 1997), prison survey data for England and Wales at different times confirm the extent of these dual diagnoses (Gunn et al., 1991; Maden et al., 1995; Singleton et al., 1998). In the prison environment, as in all settings for these groups, treatment must be co-ordinated with security and safety issues.

On entering the twenty-first century, services in the UK for this group of patients are extremely limited, and a Royal College of Psychiatrists Report (2005) highlights this for specialist medium security services. A forensic addictive behaviours unit was opened at Broadmoor Hospital, post-dating Woodstock (described in Chapter 18), by nearly 20 years, and has since closed. The addictive behaviours unit admitted men with major mental illness (generally schizophrenia) as well as men with personality disorder who also had addictive behaviours (McKeown et al., 1996). There is a somewhat comparable unit in the prison service, The Max Glatt Centre, a therapeutic community at HMP Wormwood Scrubbs, which accepts male prisoners with a variety of problems, including addiction and personality disorders (Jones, 1997).

The American penal service, in contrast, has many well-developed and successful therapeutic community programmes for inmates with substance abuse problems, many of whom also have personality disorder (Wexler, 1997).

SERVICE MODELS

In all settings, custodial as well as hospital, a major service issue is to overcome resistance to working therapeutically with this group. Because they are unlikely to make major changes in the short term, the engagement and motivating of staff may need as much attention as the engagement and motivating of the patient. At least the former process may prevent patient difficulties with motivation or engagement being taken as criteria for exclusion from services. Mueser and colleagues (1998a) outline four stages in treatment engagement:

1. the establishment of a working alliance,
2. persuasion, when regular contact is established but the patient does not want to work on reducing substance abuse and the goal is to develop awareness and motivation,
3. active treatment,
4. relapse prevention.

The parallels with the Prochaska and DiClemente (1983) pre-contemplative, contemplative, action and maintenance stages, which have been adopted in conceptualization of course of progress in treatment on Woodstock Ward are considerable (see also Chapter 18).

A comprehensive service would provide treatment of varying degrees of intensity, ranging from intensive in-patient/residential programmes to out-patient care, across different levels of security, and with the facility for ready transfer with improvement or deterioration. The possibility of transfer from custodial to hospital settings may also be required at times, for example in association with deterioration in mental state. Any transfer from greater to lesser security is likely to be associated with exposure to greater risk factors for relapse, such as the ready availability of alcohol or drugs, increased social pressures, greater exposure to a drug-using or criminal subculture, and increased opportunities for offending. Ongoing close monitoring, support and therapeutic input, particularly when moving from a custodial or hospital setting to the community, are essential (Wexler, 1997). Establishing links with other services,

such as specialist community drug and alcohol teams, and Alcoholics and/or Narcotics Anonymous, would aid in co-ordinating the transition of care. At all times, ready access to hospital medical care is essential, as serious medical conditions may be associated with alcohol and other drug use and its withdrawal. Some, on entering prison or hospital, will require medically monitored detoxification. The extent to which other drug treatments for the longer term (for example mood stabilization) may be helpful will also need evaluation.

Treatment of this group is therefore best provided by an integrated programme incorporating and adapting treatment interventions from general and forensic psychiatric and addiction fields. Mueser and colleagues (1998a) define an integrated treatment programme as one in which the same clinician or team of clinicians provides treatment for both the mental illness – or, here, personality disorder – and the substance use disorder at the same time. The clinician assumes responsibility for integrating the mental health and substance abuse treatment so that the interventions are selected, modified, combined and tailored for the specific patient. Integrated treatment, they emphasize, does not merely mean that two agencies or programmes agree on collaboration. Effective integration is likely to follow from training in addictions work as well as work with personality disorder and offending. They view essential components as comprehensiveness, shared decision making, long-term commitment and stage-wise treatment, to which would be added assertive outreach for the out-patient and pharmacotherapy for those with major mental illness.

A comprehensive treatment programme involves many elements, including attention to physical health (e.g. National Institute on Drug Abuse, 1999). In the acute stage, treatment may include management of alcohol or drug withdrawal in a safe and supportive environment, stabilization, and encouragement to engage with services and work on motivation to change. Establishing residence in a drug-free environment, or at least in an environment more supportive of change, for example moving to a drug-free wing in prison or moving out of a drug/offending subculture in the community, provides a basis for further work on rehabilitation. There is evidence that therapeutic community approaches are beneficial for this group (Wexler, 1997). Indeed, the so-called 'concept' therapeutic communities emerge as consistently effective in randomized controlled trials (Lees et al., 1999; see also Chapter 30). Group therapy is a core treatment, and may include:

- education groups, on such topics as basic drug information, dependency and problem use, harm reduction and human immunodeficiency virus (HIV);
- relapse prevention groups, on the identification of risks factors for relapse and the development of appropriate coping strategies;
- specific problem groups, using cognitive–behavioural approaches, for example addressing social skills, assertiveness, anger management, relaxation techniques, problem solving;
- psychodynamic group work.

CONCLUSION

The common ground between substance misuse disorders and personality disorders in presentation and background makes it inevitable that a comprehensive and integrated treatment programme for one will largely cover the needs of the other, and models will have more similarities than differences. Such co-morbidity is not grounds for despair, but long-term vigilance and commitment are essential. McMurran (2002) sets out some of the key research questions and strategies for progress.

REFERENCES

Chiles JA, Von Cleve E, Jemelka RP and Trupin EW (1990). Substance abuse and psychiatric disorder in prison inmates. *Hospital and Community Psychiatry* **41**:1132–4.

Flynn PM, Craddock SG, Luckey JW, Hubbard RL and Dunteman GH (1996). Co-morbidity of antisocial personality and mood disorders among psychoactive substance-dependent treatment clients. *Journal of Personality Disorders* **10**:56–67.

Gunn J, Maden A and Swinton M (1991). Treatment needs of prisoners with psychiatric disorders. *British Medical Journal* **303**:338–341.

Jones L (1997). Developing models for managing treatment integrity and efficacy in a prison-based TC: the Max Glatt Centre. In: Cullen E, Jones L and Woodward R (eds), *Therapeutic Communities for Offenders*. Chichester: John Wiley & Sons, 121–57.

Kendrick C, Basson J and Taylor PJ (2002). Substance misuse in a high security hospital: period prevalence and an evaluation of screening. *Criminal Behaviour and Mental Health* **12**:123–4.

Kokkevi A, Stefanis N, Anastasopoulou E and Kastogianni C (1998). Personality disorders in drug abusers: prevalence and their association with Axis 1 disorders as predictors of treatment retention. *Addictive Behaviours* **23**:841–53.

Lees J, Rawlings B, George K, Manning N and Rawlings B (1999). *Therapeutic Community Effectiveness: A Systematic International Review of Therapeutic Community Treatment for People with Personality Disorders and Mentally Disordered Offenders*. York: York Publishing Services.

Maden A, Taylor CJA, Brooke D and Gunn J (1995). *Mental Disorder in Remand Prisons*. London: Home Office.

Marlatt G and Gordon J (1985). *Relapse Prevention*. New York: Guilford Press.

McKeown M, Forshaw DM, McGauley G, Fitzpatrick J and Roscoe J (1996). A forensic addictive behaviours unit: a case study (Part 1). *Journal of Substance Misuse* **1**:27–31.

McMahon C, Butwell M, Nikolaou V and Taylor PJ (in preparation). Trends in illicit substance misuse by people with mental disorder committing serious offences.

McMahon C, Butwell M and Taylor PJ (2003). Changes in patterns of excessive alcohol consumption in 25 years of high security hospital admissions from England and Wales. *Criminal Behaviour and Mental Health* **13**:17–31.

McMurran M (2002). *Dual Diagnosis of Mental Disorder and Substance Misuse*. London: National Programme on Forensic Mental Health Research and Development (www.nfmhp.org.uk).

Miller WR and Rollnick S (1991). *Motivational Interviewing. Preparing People to Change Addictive Behaviour*. New York: Guilford Press.

Mueser KT, Drake RE and Noordsy DL (1998a). Integrated mental health and substance abuse treatment for severe psychiatric disorders. *Journal of Practical Psychiatry and Behavioral Health* **4**:129–39.

Mueser KT, Drake RE and Wallach MA (1998b). Dual diagnosis: a review of etiological theories. *Addictive Behaviors* **23**:717–34.

National Institute on Drug Abuse (1999). *Principles of Drug Addiction Treatment: A Research-based Guide*. Rockville, MD: National Institute on Drug Abuse. NIH Publication. No. 99–4180.

Prochaska JO and DiClemente CC (1983). Stages and processes of self-change of smoking: toward an integrative model of change. *Journal of Consulting and Clinical Psychology* **51**:390–5.

Regier DA, Farmer ME, Rae DS et al. (1990). Co-morbidity of mental disorders with alcohol and other drug abuse. Results from the Epidemiological Catchment Area (ECA). Study. *Journal of the American Medical Association* **264**:2511–18.

Robins LN (1998). The intimate connection between antisocial personality and substance abuse. *Social Psychiatry and Psychiatric Epidemiology* **33**:393–9.

Robins LN, Locke B and Regier D (1991). An overview of psychiatric disorders in America. In: Robins LN and Regier D (eds), *Psychiatric Disorders in America*. New York: Free Press, 328–36.

Rosenthal MS (1991). Therapeutic communities. In: Glass IB (ed.), *The International Handbook of Addiction Behaviour*. London: Routledge, 258–63.

Royal College of Psychiatrists (2005). *The Availability of Treatment for Addictions in Middle-secure Psychiatric In-patient Services*. London: Royal College of Psychiatrists Research Unit.

Singleton N, Meltzer H and Gatward R (1998). *Office of National Statistics Survey of Psychiatric Morbidity Among Prisoners in England and Wales*. London: The Stationery Office.

Solomon J, Zimberg S and Shollar E (1993). *Dual Diagnosis. Evaluation, Treatment, Training, and Program Development*. New York: Plenum Medical Book Co.

Susser M (1991). What is a cause and how do we know one? A grammar for pragmatic epidemiology. *American Journal of Epidemiology* **133**:635–48.

Teplin LA (1990). The prevalence of severe mental health disorder among male urban jail detainees: comparison with the Epidemiologic Catchment Area Program. *American Journal of Public Health* **80**:663–9.

Teplin LA (1994). Psychiatric and substance abuse disorders among male urban jail detainees: comparison with the Epidemiologic Catchment Area Program. *American Journal of Public Health* **84**:290–3.

Teplin LA (2003). Co-morbid psychiatric disorders in youth in detention. *Archives of General Psychiatry* **60**:1097–108.

Teplin LA, Abram KM and McClelland GM (1996). Prevalence of psychiatric disorders among incarcerated women. I. Pretrial jail detainees. *Archives of General Psychiatry* **53**:505–12. Erratum in *Archives of General Psychiatry* 1996; **53**:664.

Tiihonen J and Swartz MS (2000). Pharmacological intervention for preventing violence among the mentally ill with secondary alcohol- and drug-use disorders. In: Hodgins S (ed.), *Violence among the Mentally Ill*. Dordrecht: Kluwer Academic Publishers, 193–212.

Verheul R, van den Brink W and Hartgers C (1995). Prevalence of personality disorders among alcoholics and drug addicts: an overview. *European Addiction Research* 1995; **1**:166–177.

Wexler H (1997). Therapeutic communities in American prisons. In: Cullen E, Jones L and Woodward R (eds), *Therapeutic Communities for Offenders*. Chichester: John Wiley & Sons, 161–81.

Webster CD, Douglas KS, Eaves D and Hart SD (1997). *HCR-20 Assessing Risk for Violence*, Version 2. Vancouver: Mental Health, Law and Policy Institute, Simon Fraser University.

Chapter 21

VARYING THE MODEL FOR SEX OFFENDERS

Don Grubin

INTRODUCTION

The principles underlying the treatment of sex offenders apply to most such men, for they usually are men, whether in the criminal justice system, as is more usual, or in mental health services; whether in secure environments or in the community. The special characteristics of a secure environment carry with them a number of advantages for the treatment process, but they are also the source of a variety of potential pitfalls. In many ways, the two are closely related to each other.

PRINCIPLES OF TREATMENT

Until recently, the question of whether re-offending by sex offenders could be reduced by treatment was difficult to answer. At the end of the 1980s, for example, a comprehensive and often quoted review by Furby et al. (1989) concluded that the research published up to then had abjectly failed to demonstrate that treatment had any beneficial impact whatsoever on sex offender recidivism. However, many of the programmes reviewed by Furby et al. were of poor quality, often based on treatment models now known to be ineffective, or even counterproductive. Since that review was published, there has been a gradual accumulation of evidence to suggest that well-designed

programmes, aimed at higher risk men and targeting specific 'criminogenic' factors, can in fact reduce recidivism; indeed, a meta-analysis of outcomes from a number of such programmes found that re-offending rates were reduced by about a third (Nagayama Hall, 1995). More recent reviews have also come to more optimistic conclusions than Furby (Alexander, 1999; Lösel and Schmucker, 2005).

Psychiatrists with an interest in the treatment of sex offenders have tended to work within a psychodynamic framework, and hence treatment programmes in psychiatric hospitals have often been based on psychodynamic concepts of sex offending and insight-oriented treatment approaches. Although these may contribute to an understanding of the psychic mechanisms underlying sexual aggression, such an understanding does not appear sufficient to modify sexually aggressive behaviour. For example, in a rare random allocation study in which sex offenders received either psychodynamic group psychotherapy or intensive probation supervision, the re-arrest rate for those in the psychotherapy group was twice that of those receiving probation supervision (Romero and Williams, 1983). Similarly, in an outcome study of personality disordered patients treated within the therapeutic community model just described, in Broadmoor Hospital, sexual re-offending was notable for its prominence (Reiss et al., 1996).

Successful modern sex offender programmes tend to be cognitive–behavioural in their format, run on a group basis, and target four main areas:

- the cognitive distortions often found in sex offenders that are supportive of sexual aggression;
- deficits in the self-regulation of negative emotional states, anger and impulsivity;
- victim empathy;
- sexual deviance.

In addition, effective treatment programmes provide offenders with relapse prevention 'skills' that enable them to identify when they are at increased risk of re-offending, and to develop strategies to manage that risk. Laws et al. (2000) consider in depth the applications of the principles specifically to sex offenders.

More generally, sex offender programmes share with offender behaviour programmes as a whole the need to ensure that the amount, intensity and sequencing of treatment 'dose' are appropriate, and that treatment integrity is monitored closely. When treatment is followed by release, the issue of aftercare must also be considered.

These principles apply regardless of whether treatment takes place in hospital, prison or the community. What, then, is different about treatment in a secure setting?

ADVANTAGES OF TREATMENT IN A SECURE SETTING

SECURITY

The most obvious advantage of providing treatment in a secure setting is that the risk of re-offending during treatment is low. Because the individual is contained and monitored, destabilization during treatment can be identified and managed, and although it may result in dysfunctional behaviour, the potential harm caused to others is limited. Treatment can therefore be more intense and challenging than might otherwise be the case.

MODELLING

In the community, few programmes involve more than about 8 hours of treatment a week. This means that for the remaining 160 hours of the week, those on the programme are doing other things, in other places, about which those providing treatment know little and therefore can do little about. In a secure setting, however, individuals live in the same place as they are receiving treatment, and it is therefore possible to have some influence on their environment. In particular, behaviour modelling by nurses and other staff can have an important effect on behaviour, while problematic behaviours can be identified and addressed.

TREATMENT 'DOSAGE' FLEXIBILITY

Because offenders' other commitments are limited, the sequencing and spacing of treatment can be designed to meet the requirements of the programme rather than the pragmatic demands of individuals living in the community. Although difficult even in secure settings, it is also possible to design the treatment schedule to reflect the needs of the group.

ADDITIONAL TREATMENT MODALITIES

Additional treatment needs for individuals within the group are often identified, but in the community it can be difficult to ensure these are met. In a secure setting, however, further assessment and treatment are both more readily available. This is especially relevant when issues relating to sexual fantasy, subjectively high sexual drive, or the offender's own victimization history emerge, none of which is easily dealt with in a group setting.

The containment and control inherent within a secure setting can clearly be used constructively in developing and delivering a treatment programme. However, if care is not taken, secure settings also contain within them the potential to undermine even the most well-designed treatment strategy.

DISADVANTAGES OF TREATMENT IN A SECURE SETTING

INABILITY TO TEST BEHAVIOUR

While secure settings mean that offenders are kept safe during treatment, this carries with it the problem that it is difficult to measure improvement (or deterioration) in them, or to monitor relevant behaviour. Risk management strategies may be over-optimistic and, in the absence of risk factors or other stressors, progress in treatment may be illusionary. This problem can be overcome to some extent, however, by careful observation of behaviour within the institution, particularly in respect of an individual's interactions with others. In addition, the use of psychometric measures can provide an indication of whether improvement is real or apparent.

LACK OF CONTROL OVER DISCHARGE

Treatment completion is often out of step with the release timetable, and discharge may be delayed for months or years. Treatment effects, of course, diminish with time, exacerbated by the lack of 'practice' associated with continued detention. Many programmes deal with this by providing 'booster' treatment periodically, and before release.

NETWORKS

Community programmes often insist that participants leave at the end of treatment sessions, and do not associate with each other in between. This is clearly not possible in a secure setting, and there is thus ample opportunity for sex offenders to form networks amongst themselves, both undoing the treatment work and increasing future risk. Sex offenders whose peers are sex offenders are known to have a higher rate of re-offending, probably because of the reinforcement and moral support they provide for each other, as well as through the exchange of information about where and how to obtain victims (Hanson and Scott, 1996).

THE INSTITUTION ITSELF

Unless the treatment programme is accepted throughout the institution, from the highest level down, and vice versa, the programme can be threatened by indifference as well as by outright hostility. Appropriate treatment facilities need to be made available, treatment staff need to be given time to prepare before sessions and to debrief afterwards, and treatment provision needs to be maintained in spite of competing demands for time and resources elsewhere in the institution. In addition, those receiving treatment as well as those providing it need to be protected from others in the institution who view sex offender treatment as a waste of time, or something to be mocked. Although staff can model prosocial behaviour, they are just as capable of modelling the reverse.

HEALTH AND CRIMINAL JUSTICE SYSTEMS: THE RELATIVE MERITS

A universal difficulty in treating sex offenders is that any system with a hierarchy tends to place them at the lowest end. Treatment providers often regard them as the least deserving of services, other service users may regard them with hostility, and the general public just want them locked away indefinitely, sometimes organizing vigilante groups when this is not done. Even sex offenders themselves may follow this pattern. Within the group, rape may be construed as a higher order behaviour compared with offences against children. Such attitudes mean that any service should have explicit strategies for ensuring not only the assessment of need and delivery of resultant action to meet it, but also the safety of the individual sex offenders. From within and outside the group, individuals may be subject to bullying or actual physical attack.

The criminal justice system, particularly in its custodial services, often seeks to protect the safety of individuals by making segregated services available. Such offenders are generally not required to live apart from their murderous, assaultive or thieving peers, but may choose to do so. Some prisons have specialist sex offender units. Hospitals, by contrast, insofar as they accept sex offenders at all, place emphasis on integration. For a small subgroup of such offenders, those with psychotic illnesses, this may be relatively straightforward, particularly when symptoms of that illness are clearly relevant to the offending behaviour, as is commonly the case in these circumstances (Smith and Taylor, 1999a).

For others, the process of integration can be almost as risky in hospital as it is in prison. Even in secure hospitals, observations of all patients cannot be constant, and safety is thus to an extent dependent on a sophistication of understanding commonly lacking in the healthy peers of the other patients, let alone in the patients themselves with their added psychopathology. Nevertheless, it is arguable, if unproven, that the greater potential in hospital for the safe integration of sex offenders with other offenders than can be achieved in prison offers possible advantages. Reinforcement of sexual deviancy is less likely, and appropriate peer group as well as professional challenges to it perhaps more likely.

Sex offending may be an unusual complication of psychotic illnesses (Phillips et al., 1999; Smith and Taylor, 1999b). In these circumstances, there seems little doubt that a hospital placement is likely to be more appropriate than prison. The question is whether, in the absence of such clear-cut illness, hospitals, secure or otherwise, offer any further advantage. There is a theoretical point – which clinicians would advance – that prison models of treatment tend to be régime centred, and time-limited régimes at that. Thus, they are dependent on the principle that sex offenders within the class for which a particular programme is designed are homogeneous and potentially 'curable'. Hospital models would invariably place emphasis on individual differences, and devise individual treatment programmes. These would certainly include group work and an understanding that while pathology tends to reduce individual differences, individual variation must still be taken into account. Further, the need to continue working in transition from institution back to the wider community is accepted and generally taken into account in the care programme approach.

What seem like fine principles in the health service, however, carry the risk of an inadvertent lapse into poor practice. Audits, even of the more rigorously tested treatments in psychiatry such as the use of mediation, suggest widespread deviation from recommended practice (e.g. Taylor et al., 1997; Royal College of Psychiatrists (1999), unpublished document). The comparable concept for criminal justice is the 'what works' principle (Maguire, 1995). Founded in meta-analysis, generally based on a number of small, previously published studies rather than arguably more robust randomized controlled trials, has led to the construction of the programmes referred to above, which thus have some evidential foundation. The emphasis, even for offenders with psychotic symptoms driving their offences (Maguire, 1995, p. 19), is on cognitive–behavioural models, which means that the resulting regimes can be tightly defined and standardized, allowing them to be evaluated in a way that can be difficult for more eclectic medical models. Accreditation of such programmes in the criminal justice system depends on the demonstrable establishment and maintenance of their integrity.

CONCLUSION

Effective treatment of sex offenders depends as much on treatment delivery as it does on the content of the programme itself. The design of programmes in any setting, therefore, needs to take account of special characteristics of the clientele as well as the unique properties of that setting if they are to be successful. Unless programme integrity can be maintained, however, the chances of successful treatment outcome seem slight. Perhaps the most important question for the next wave of research concerns the goodness of fit between subgroups of offenders and approaches. Despite the momentum of 'what works' and the accreditation of tight, unwavering régimes, it seems unlikely that one strategy will suit all in a heterogeneous clientele. Mental health and criminal justice system collaboration raises the possibility of establishing evidence not just for what works, but also for the more satisfactory 'what works, for whom, when and under what circumstances'.

REFERENCES

Alexander MA (1999). Sexual offenders' treatment efficacy revisited. *Sexual Abuse: A Journal of Research and Treatment* **11**:101–16.

Furby L, Weinrott MR and Blackshaw L (1989). Sex offender recidivism: a review. *Psychological Bulletin* **105**:3–30.

Hanson RK and Scott H (1996). Social networks of sexual offenders. *Psychology, Crime and Law* **2**:249–58.

Laws RD, Herdson SM and Ward T (2000). *Remaking Relapse Prevention with Sex Offenders*. Thousand Oaks, CA: Sage.

Lösel F and Schmucker M (2005). The effectiveness of treatment for sexual offenders: a comprehensive meta-analysis. *Journal of Experimental Criminology* **1**:117–46.

Maguire J (ed.) (1995). *What Works: Reducing Re-offending*. Chichester: John Wiley & Sons.

Nagayama Hall GC (1995). Sex offender recidivism revisited: a meta-analysis of recent treatment studies. *Journal of Consulting and Clinical Psychology* **63**:802–9.

Phillips SL, Heads TC, Taylor PJ and Hill GM (1999). Sexual offending and antisocial sexual behavior among patients with schizophrenia. *Journal of Clinical Psychiatry* **60**:170–5.

Reiss D, Grubin D and Meux C (1996). Young psychopaths in special hospital: treatment and outcome. *British Journal of Psychiatry* **168**:99–104.

Romero J and Williams L (1983). Group psychotherapy and intensive probation supervision with sex offenders: a comparative study. *Federal Probation* **47**:36–42.

Royal College of Psychiatrists (1999). The national audit of the prescribing of anti-psychotic medication. Module 2 Group 'B' Patients. National results. Unpublished document, available from the College Research Unit.

Smith AD and Taylor PJ (1999a). Serious sex offending against women by men with schizophrenia. Relationship of illness and psychotic symptoms to offending. *British Journal of Psychiatry* **174**:233–7.

Smith A and Taylor PJ (1999b). Social and sexual functioning in schizophrenic men who commit serious sex offences against women. *Criminal Behaviour and Mental Health* **9**:156–67.

Taylor D, Holmes R, Hilton T and Paton C (1997). Evaluating and improving the quality of risperidone prescribing. *Psychiatric Bulletin* **21**:680–3.

Chapter 22

LEARNING DISABILITY, PERSONALITY DISORDER AND OFFENDING: TREATMENT APPROACHES

Stephen Tyrer and Tim Howard

INTRODUCTION

It is notoriously difficult to diagnose personality disorder in a population whose behaviour is frequently socially inappropriate. This accounts for the very wide range of the prevalence of personality disorder (1–92 per cent) in learning disability (Alexander and Cooray, 2003). Personality disorder can be better diagnosed in one in five of psychiatric patients with mild/moderate learning disability (Corbett, 1979; Reid and Ballinger, 1987) and is particularly common in institutionalized populations (Deb and Hunter, 1991). The entire range of personality disorders is represented, with an excess of dependent and avoidant types occurring in community samples (Goldberg et al., 1995; Khan et al., 1997) and an excess of aggressive and explosive types occurring in institutional populations (Reid and Ballinger, 1987).

The diagnosis of personality disorder in those who have severe or profound learning disability is difficult. This has been recognized by the Royal College of Psychiatrists (2001) who have recommended, in *Diagnostic Criteria in Learning Disability*, that the diagnosis of personality disorders in this group is inappropriate.

The prevalence of personality disorder among learning disabled offenders has not received systematic study but is likely to be high. Lund (1990), in a study of learning disabled offenders on community treatment orders in Denmark, estimated 87.5 per cent to be suffering from 'behaviour disorder', a diagnostic construct, which, when closely examined, is not dissimilar from antisocial personality disorder. Day (1994), in a study of male mentally handicapped sex offenders, diagnosed personality disorder in 47 per cent of the sample. In his follow-up study of 20 learning disabled offenders previously detained on hospital orders (Day, 1988), he considered that all were suffering from personality disorder, the antisocial type predominating.

The study of personality disorder in learning disability has been somewhat neglected.

Researchers in learning disability have traditionally focused on cognitive and behavioural aspects of psychopathology rather than on the study of individual difference (Zigler and Burack, 1989). Many learning disability psychiatrists continue to question the usefulness of the concept of personality disorder, particularly of the antisocial type, and are reluctant to diagnose it (Goldberg et al., 1995, Hurley and Sovner, 1995). Many personality traits, such as dependency, lack of ambition and difficulties in interpersonal problem solving, are so common among the learning disabled that they are unreliable as diagnostic criteria for personality disorder. Issues of diagnostic overshadowing (Reiss et al., 1982), the lack of a fully validated, developmentally dependent assessment of personality for people with learning disability (Wagner, 1991), the paucity of personality inventories applicable to learning disabled people (Sturmey et al., 1991), and the problems encountered by learning disabled people in dealing with self-report measures (Reid, 1997), have ensured that the effectiveness of treatment in modifying core features of personality in learning disabled people remains unexplored.

PSYCHOLOGICAL AND PSYCHOTHERAPEUTIC TREATMENTS

Many learning disabled offenders with unequivocal personality disorder require specialist in-patient treatment. In most cases, they are detained under the provisions of the Mental Health Act 1983, classified under the rubric of either 'mental impairment' or 'psychopathic disorder', or both, depending upon the relative roles of cognitive dysfunction and personality factors in the genesis of their offending behaviour (Clarke et al., 1992).

For those who have committed a serious offence, or proved too challenging for regular services, treatment is likely to commence in conditions of either high or medium security. An important, although perhaps artificial, line needs to be drawn between the treatment of *pervasive developmental learning and related cognitive disabilities* and the treatment of *developmental disorders of emotional and social behaviour.*

Any treatment plan with an aim of modifying personality in people with learning disability should include a socialization programme aimed at improving independence, problem-solving skills and personal responsibility taking by enhancing existing intellectual and interpersonal skills. This approach is emphasized by Day (1988) in his description of an in-patient unit for the treatment of learning disabled offenders. He illustrates the way in which educational and occupational training can help the learning disabled offender to develop a sense of personal responsibility, self-confidence and social awareness, and an understanding of the social rules underpinning civil behaviour. This process is supported by formal social skills and self-awareness training in small group settings. These therapeutic measures are underpinned by a highly structured daily programme and a weekly incentive scheme based on token economy principles. The scheme involves five grades, the highest grade carrying the highest financial and social reward. Dependent upon behaviour, patients may move either up or down the grades, such moves being decided at weekly meetings of the multidisciplinary team. Most people with mild learning disability are able to understand this scheme, although people with a moderate learning disability may require a scheme based upon daily reward. Incentive schemes can have a powerful effect in raising consequence awareness and foresight as well as self-esteem.

Whilst measures aimed at improving socialization remain the bedrock of treatment (Day, 1997), specific therapeutic strategies may be required for personality difficulties. The management of severe personality disorder in learning disability requires a flexible, pragmatic approach utilizing a broad range of cognitive–behavioural, psychodynamic and psychopharmacological treatments. It is underpinned by certain basic principles, including the need to gain some measure of control over the patient's behaviour by obtaining a positive response to direction from staff, the need to establish a pattern of prosocial behaviour, and the need to establish a control stimulus in the form of a key worker through whom the therapeutic efforts of the team are channelled (Dana, 1993).

Cognitive behavioural therapy is mainly applicable in those with a mild degree of learning disability. Lindsay et al. (1998) have shown benefits with this technique in the treatment of sex offenders. Improvement was also shown using similar methodology by Taylor et al. (2002) in arsonists. Both these techniques require a longer period of therapy than in those of normal intelligence and in-patient treatment time may need to be correspondingly extended (Mayor et al. 1990).

Where patients with learning disability and severe personality disorder detained for treatment in hospital are offenders, offence-specific treatment in the form of debriefing is invariably necessary. A full exploration of the cognitive and emotional aspects of the learning disabled person's offending behaviour is not only important for the process of continuing risk assessment, but also forms the first step in assisting the offender towards recognizing issues of victim awareness and may be vital in securing a full understanding of his or her own predicament. Many learning disabled offenders deny the seriousness of their offending, and sometimes even their guilt. Patience and perseverance are required to deal with this.

Individual psychodynamic psychotherapy has an established place in the psychiatry of learning disability because of the importance of 'emotional' as opposed to cognitive intelligence in the psychotherapeutic process (Stokes and Sinason, 1992). It is now believed by psychotherapists working with the learning disabled that there is no level of handicap that makes someone unsuitable for psychodynamically based treatment (Hollins et al., 1994). The basic principles of treatment are no different from those described for people of normal intelligence, but in the case of learning disabled people, a more directive approach on the part of the therapist is required, with greater reliance placed on non-verbal material. Similarly, the therapist may have to work through specific examples rather than giving abstract interpretations, and at other times function as an auxiliary intellect, putting into words that which the patient is thinking and feeling (Hollins et al., 1994). More use of repetition may also be helpful and, if agreed with the patient, key issues or interpretations in the work may be shared between the primary therapists and others in the team so that they can appropriately reinforce the work, especially if the individual seeks clarification. Greater extremes of emotion, such as anger, may have to be tolerated in the therapeutic setting, and care needs to be taken with negative transference interpretations lest they be construed as criticism. The best approach is flexible and eclectic, rather than adhering to a strict theoretical model (Monfils and Menolascino, 1984). Individual therapy has been reported as useful in the management of borderline personality disorder in mild learning disability (Gravestock and Puffett, 1995).

Group processes in learning disability are well understood (MacDonald et al., 2003) and psychodynamic principles are often applied in the group setting with learning disabled patients (Gravestock and McGauley, 1994). Because treatment takes longer in people with learning disability, slow-open groups tend to be favoured (Hollins et al., 1994), although closed groups are not ruled out. Most group approaches taken with learning disabled offenders are either psychoeducational (Charman and Clare, 1992) or cognitive–behavioural in form, concentrating on the patient's habilitative needs (Monfils and Menolascino, 1984). These groups are structured in their approach and aim at a particular area of handicap such as inappropriate anger (Benson et al., 1986), sexual offending (Swanson and Garwick, 1990) and social skills impairment (Perry and Cerreto, 1977). Psychological treatment tends to take longer in the presence of learning disability, and account must be taken of this in other aspects of group design too, as must the need for properly trained group facilitators (Day, 1997).

The use of illicit substances, solvents and alcohol is increasing in the mildly learning disabled population, and psychiatrists are now seeing increasing numbers of such people who have offended whilst under the influence of drugs and/or alcohol. Whilst substance abuse in learning disabled people with or without personality disorder appears to be a consequence of lack of structure and cultural factors as opposed to a direct consequence of psychopathology, it is important to address this issue vigorously. Close liaison with generic drug and alcohol services is important for those patients treated in the community and in devising aftercare programmes for inpatients. A group approach utilizing 'team quizzing' and role-play, and aimed at enhancing knowledge of the effects of alcohol and encouraging sensible use, has proved effective (McGillicuddy and Blane, 1999), particularly so when combined with individual therapy aimed at defining the effects of alcohol/substance abuse in the genesis of offending.

PSYCHOPHARMACOLOGICAL TREATMENT

The evidence for the value of psychotropic drugs in the treatment of personality disorder in those with learning disability is, as for those without (Stein, 1992), not strong. The number of randomized controlled trials that have been carried out on adequate numbers of individuals with learning disability does not reach double figures. The evidence for benefit is strongest for lithium and the newer neuroleptic drugs. Whilst the older antipsychotic drugs, anticonvulsants or mood stabilizers such as carbamazepine and sodium valproate, beta-adrenergic blocking drugs, the selective serotonin reuptake inhibitor (SSRI) drugs and buspirone have been used in this population, they have not received sufficiently close scrutiny for their roles to be precisely defined (Tyrer and Hill, 2001).

Lithium has been evaluated in three double-blind controlled trials against placebo in people with learning disability who exhibited aggressive or self-injurious behaviour and was found significantly to reduce aggression in all three studies (Worrall et al., 1975; Tyrer et al., 1984; Craft et al., 1987). Behaviours that were significantly improved by lithium included both physical aggression towards others and social behaviour (Tyrer et al., 1993). However, the majority of patients involved in these studies were not offenders and the extent of personality disorder was not ascertained. Lithium has been shown to be significantly superior to placebo in reducing major infractions of behaviour in a naturalistic study of a young offenders institution in Connecticut, USA (Sheard et al., 1976), and there are reasons for supposing that this drug may be valuable in this population.

The benzisoxazole derivative risperidone was more effective than placebo when given as add-on therapy to people with learning disability who had a behaviour disorder (Van Den Borre et al., 1993), but again this was not in a population of personality disordered offenders. A major UK trial of risperidone, termed NACHBID, is being conducted in the UK at present. In patients with borderline personality disorder, some of whom are represented in offending populations, haloperidol has been found to be a better drug than amytriptyline (Soloff et al., 1989). Buspirone (Ratey et al., 1991) and the SSRI group of drugs (Stein, 1992) have been shown in non-double-blind studies to have beneficial effects in those with persistent behaviour disorder and learning disability.

Anti-libidinal medication may be required for those serious and persistent sex offenders who fail to respond adequately to psychotherapeutic and self-management treatments (Clarke, 1989). Both the oral anti-androgenic drug, cyproterone acetate, and the depot gonadotrophin-releasing hormone antagonist goserelin acetate have been shown to reduce not only sexual drive in people with learning disability but also deviant sexual fantasy and behaviour (Myers, 1991; Delle Chiaie and Picardi (1994); Thibaut et al., 1998). However, there remains a need for systematic evaluation of these treatments in the form of controlled trials incorporating adequate patient numbers, clearly defined inclusion criteria and reliable measures of outcome (Clarke, 1989; Cooper, 1995). Cyproterone is probably the drug of choice, as it is specifically anti-androgenic in action and has fewer side effects (Clarke, 1989). Pre-prescription screening of individuals for blood count, liver function tests, blood sugar and adrenocortical function should be performed and repeated at regular intervals. It is also important to check testosterone levels before and after starting the drugs. Consent to such treatment will need particular care given the risk, albeit usually manageable, of breast enlargement and infertility.

The problems of carrying out trials in those with personality disorder and learning difficulties should not be underestimated (Tyrer and Cooray, 2004). The problems of obtaining consent in such trials, particularly involving patients who are detained under mental health legislation, are considerable. In the UK, there is no allowance for surrogate consent, although incapacity legislation is pending. Even when trials show that drugs are valuable under controlled conditions, the motivation for patients to take such agents if they are unsupervised is often not sufficiently strong for them to maintain treatment, even when this has been shown to be of help.

Whatever the determinant of outcome used, the most important factor in determining prognosis is the quality of aftercare provided on discharge (Day, 1988).

AFTERCARE

A full and comprehensive system of community support, including occupational, residential and therapeutic components, based on multi-agency cooperation and a detailed risk assessment, is required if further offending is to be prevented (Craft, 1984; Day, 1997). Multi-agency cooperation at discharge is facilitated by ensuring good communication between the different agencies likely to be involved in the offender's aftercare whilst he or she is undergoing treatment. Self-management strategies, particularly in the case of sex offenders, will require monitoring and modification, necessitating regular psychiatric and psychological review. A key worker is essential to monitor the implementation of the aftercare plan, coordinate the activities of the various agencies involved and act as a point of contact for the patient in the event of crisis.

CONCLUSION

There are more similarities than differences between the treatment of personality disorder within the different categories of learning disability. Both groups may be helped by pharmacological approaches to specific problems, and both will benefit from individual and group psychological approaches, particularly the latter. The difference lies principally in the degree of preparation staff must make to prepare the more learning disabled clientele for the work. Structured, task-orientated work is more likely to bear results, but elements of more dynamic approaches should not be eschewed, if necessary. It is vital that the pace of work is adjusted to the speed at which any given individual can realistically work.

REFERENCES

Alexander R and Cooray S (2003). Diagnosis of personality disorders in learning disability. *British Journal of Psychiatry* **182**(Suppl 44): S28–31.

Benson BA, Rice CJ and Miranti SV (1986). Effects of anger management training with mentally retarded adults in group treatment. *Journal of Consulting Clinical Psychology* **54**:728–79.

Charman T and Clare IHC (1992). Education about the laws and social rules relating to sexual behaviour. *Mental Handicap* **20**:74–80.

Clarke D, Beasley J, Corbett JA, Krishnan VHR and Cumella S (1992). Mental impairment in the West Midlands. *Medicine, Science & the Law* **32**:225–32.

Clarke DJ (1989). Antilibidinal drugs and mental retardation: a review. *Medical Science and the Law* **29**: 136–46.

Cooper AJ (1995). Review of the role of two antilibidinal drugs in the treatment of sex offenders with mental retardation. *Canadian Journal of Psychiatry* **33**:42–8.

Corbett JA (1979). Psychiatric morbidity and mental retardation. In: James FE and Snaith RP (eds), *Psychiatric Illness and Mental Handicap.* London: Gaskell Press, 11–25.

Craft M (1984). Should one treat or gaol psychopaths? In: Craft M and Craft A (eds), *Mentally Abnormal Offenders.* London: Baillière Tindall, 384–96.

Craft M, Ismail IA, Krishnamurty D et al. (1987). Lithium in the treatment of aggression in mentally handicapped patients: a double blind trial. *British Journal of Psychiatry* **150**:685–9.

Dana L (1993). Personality disorder in persons with mental retardation: assessment and diagnosis. In: Fletcher RJ and Dosen A (eds), *Mental Health Aspects of Mental Retardation.* New York: Lexington Books, 130–40.

Day K (1988). A hospital based treatment programme for male mentally handicapped offenders. *British Journal of Psychiatry* **153**:635–44.

Day K (1994). Male mentally handicapped sex offenders. *British Journal of Psychiatry* **165**:630–9.

Day K (1997). Sex offenders with learning disabilities. In: Read SG (ed.), *Psychiatry in Learning Disability.* London: Saunders, 278–306.

Deb S and Hunter D (1991). Psychopathology of people with mental handicap and epilepsy. III: Personality disorder. *British Journal of Psychiatry* **159**:830–4.

Delle Chiaie R and Picardi A (1994). Supra-hypophyseal block in gonadal function in the treatment of paraphilia. Administration of goserelin in five case reports. *Rivista di Psichiatria* **29**(1 suppl.):39–46.

Goldberg B, Gitta BM and Puddephatt A (1995). Personality and trait disturbances in an adult mental retardation population: significance for psychiatric management. *Journal of Intellectual Disability Research* **39**:284–94.

Gravestock S and McGauley G (1994). Connecting confusions with painful realities: Group Analytic Psychotherapy for adults with learning disabilities. *Psychoanalytic Psychotherapy* **8**:153–67.

Gravestock S and Puffett A (1995). Learning disabilities and borderline personality disorder. *Journal of Intellectual Disability Research* **47**(Suppl 1):13–18.

Hollins S, Sinason V and Thompson S (1994). Individual, group and family therapy. In: Bouras N (ed.), *Mental Health and Mental Retardation.* Cambridge: Cambridge University Press.

Hurley AD and Sovner R (1995). Six cases of patients with mental retardation who have antisocial personality disorder. *Psychiatric Services* **46**:828–31.

Khan A, Cowan C and Roy A (1997). Personality disorders in people with learning disabilities: a community survey. *Journal of Intellectual Disability Research* **41**:324–30.

Lindsay WR, Neilson CQ, Morrison F et al. (1998). The treatment of six men with a learning disability convicted of sex offences with children. *British Journal of Clinical Psychology* **37**:83–98.

Lund J (1990). Mentally retarded criminal offenders in Denmark. *British Journal of Psychiatry* **156**:726–31.

MacDonald J, Sinason V and Hollins S (2003). An interview study of people with learning disabilities' experience of, and satisfaction with, group analytic therapy. *Psychology & Psychotherapy: Theory, Research & Practice* **76**:433–53.

Mayor J, Bhate M, Firth H, Graham A, Knox P and Tyrer S (1990). Facilities for mentally impaired patients: three years experience of a semi-secure unit. *Psychiatric Bulletin* **14**:333–5.

McGillicuddy N and Blane HT (1999). Substance use in individuals with mental retardation. *Addictive Behaviors* **24**:869–78.

Monfils M and Menolascino F (1984). Modified individual and group treatment approaches. In: Menolascino FJ and Stark J (eds), *Handbook of Mental Illness in the Mentally Retarded.* New York: Plenum Press.

Perry MA and Cerreto MC (1977). Structured learning training of social skills for the retarded. *Mental Retardation* **15**:31–4.

Myers BA (1991). Treatment of sexual offenses by persons with developmental disabilities. *American Journal on Mental Retardation* **95**:563–9.

Ratey JJ, Sovner R, Park A et al. (1991). Buspirone treatment of aggression and anxiety in mentally retarded patients: a multiple baseline, placebo lead-in study. *Journal of Clinical Psychiatry* **52**:159–62.

Reid AH (1997). Personality disorders. In Read SG (ed.), *Psychiatry in Learning Disability*. London: Saunders, 117–28.

Reid AH and Ballinger BR (1987). Personality disorder in mental handicap. *Psychological Medicine* **17**:983–7.

Reiss S, Levitan GW and Szyszko J (1982). Emotional disturbance and mental retardation: diagnostic overshadowing. *American Journal of Mental Deficiency* **86**:567–74.

Royal College of Psychiatrists (2001). *Diagnostic Criteria In Learning Disability (DC-LD)*. London: Gaskell.

Sheard MH, Marini JL and Bridges CI (1976). The effect of lithium on impulsive aggressive behavior in man. *American Journal of Psychiarty* **133**:1409–13.

Sinason V (1992). *Mental Handicap and the Human Condition – New Approaches from the Tavistock*. London: Free Association.

Soloff PH (1981). Pharmacotherapy of borderline disorders. *Comprehensive Psychiatry* **22**:535–43.

Stein G (1992). Drug treatment of the personality disorders. *British Journal of Psychiatry* **161**:167–84.

Stokes J and Sinason V (1992). Secondary mental handicap as a defence. In: Waitman A and Conboy-Hill S (eds), *Psychotherapy and Mental Handicap*. London: Sage Publications, 46–58.

Sturmey P, Reed J and Corbett J (1991). Psychometric assessment of psychiatric disorders in people with learning difficulties (mental handicap): a review of measures. *Psychological Medicine* **21**:143–55.

Swanson CK and Garwick GB (1990). Treatment for low functioning sex offenders: group therapy and interagency co-ordination. *Mental Retardation* **28**:155–61.

Taylor, J, Thorne I, Robertson A and Avery G (2002). Evaluation of a group intervention for convicted arsonists with mild and borderline intellectual disabilities. *Criminal Behaviour & Mental Health* **12**: 282–93.

Thibaut F, Kuhn JM, Cordier B et al. (1998). Hormone treatment of sex offenses. *Encephale* **24**:132–7.

Tyrer P and Cooray S (2004). Put knowledge before ignorance. *Community Care* July 15.

Tyrer S and Hill S (2001), Psychopharmacological approaches. In: Dosen A and Day K (eds), *Treating Mental Illness and Behavior Disorders in Children and Adults with Mental Retardation*. Washington, DC: American Psychiatric Press, Inc., 45–67.

Tyrer SP, Aronson ME and Lauder J (1993). Effect of lithium on behavioural factors in aggressive mentally handicapped subjects. In: Birch NJ, Padgham C and Hughes MS (eds), *Lithium in Medicine and Biology*. Carnforth: Marius Press, 119–25.

Tyrer SP, Walsh A, Edwards DE, Berney TP and Stephens A (1984). Factors associated with a good response to lithium in aggressive mentally handicapped subjects. *Progress in Neuro-psychopharmacology and Biological Psychiatry* **8**:751–5.

Van den Borre R, Vermote R and Butiens M (1993). Risperidone as add-on therapy in behavioral disturbances in mental retardation: a double-blind placebo-controlled cross-over study. *Acta Psychiatrica Scandinavica* **87**:167–71.

Wagner P (1991). Developmentally based personality assessment of adults with mental retardation. *Mental Retardation* **29**:87–92.

Worrall EP, Moody JP and Naylor GJ (1975). Lithium in non-manic-depressives: antiaggressive effect and red blood cell lithium values. *British Journal of Psychiatry* **126**:464–8.

Zigler E and Burack JA (1989). Personality development and the dually diagnosed person. *Research in Developmental Disabilities* **10**:225–40.

Chapter 23

THE APPLICATION OF HIGH-SECURITY MODELS OF CARE TO OTHER LESS SECURE SETTINGS

Christopher Cordess

INTRODUCTION

Readers may be excused for wondering whether they have read the title of this chapter correctly – for, indeed, high-security models of care have not traditionally been held in the highest regard. For England and Wales, the most recent of what has become something of a spate of inquiries – The Report of the Committee of Inquiry into the Personality Disorder Unit at Ashworth Hospital (Fallon et al., 1999, the so-called 'Fallon Report') – has pronounced, first, on what it thinks should be changed and improved in the assessment and treatment of personality disordered offenders in high-security establishments, and second, how it thinks this would be better achieved. This is but one review with recommendations amongst many – including reports of inquiries into aspects of care at Rampton Hospital (1989), Ashworth Hospital (1992) and Broadmoor Hospital (1993) – and by design largely concerns itself with matters of management and the safety of third parties rather than more strictly clinical concerns, with the exception of a preoccupation with 'outcome' in terms of re-offending rates. Many countries have some sort of high-security treatment options and few have been without scandal (Taylor et al., 1993).

The point, however, is that the perception of the outsider and, most importantly, of the politician is that there is something (chronically) rotten in the state of the high-security hospitals as institutions in general, and in their treatment and management of the personality disordered offender in particular. Whatever the complaints, in England and Wales, it is the high-security hospitals that have taken on the challenge of the severely personality disordered offender patient, and the prisons that have to manage the majority who are considered not to be treatable. There has not been a rush from clinicians generally, and those working in regional secure units specifically, to get in on the act. In Scotland, the most recent public inquiry into the matter was over extrusion from services at the State (Security) Hospital, and reflects perhaps an even greater reluctance to treat people with personality disorder in health settings there (Mental Welfare Commission for Scotland, 2000).

There is a particular difficulty in writing about the *clinical* aspects of dissocial (psychopathic or antisocial personality disorder) or, perhaps better, personality disorder complicated by offending, at this time, during the politically driven furore surrounding the publication of the joint Department of Health and Home Office (1999) consultation document

Managing Dangerous People with Severe Personality Disorder. It is clear that this is only secondarily a clinical initiative and primarily one of social control and public protection. The label 'dangerous severe personality disorder' (DSPD) is an administrative creation and is not defined. The document is radical. It not only challenges assumptions of civil rights law (preventative detention for non-offenders), but also clearly seeks to implicate the clinical professions (and primarily psychiatry and forensic psychiatry) in achieving its aims. At best, this newly discovered and ulterior enthusiasm for the hitherto neglected conditions that go under the name personality disorder will be a spur to improved ways of conceptualizing and to greater research into these heterogeneous groupings. At worst, there will be another administrative, therapeutic and ethical disaster (see Mullen, 1999).

In *Modernising Mental Health Services* (Department of Health, 1998), too, the public protection emphasis is depressingly clear: 'Community care has failed', it declares, and offers a strategy for providing a service 'in which patients, carers and the public are safe and where security and support are provided to all'. The strategy has 'two key elements: increased investment and increased control (over patients and clinicians)' (Marshall, 1999). The relatively small increased investment for the job in hand is largely to be spent on beds in hostels and secure units, and increased control of patients will be achieved by 'modernising' mental health legislation to 'ensure compliance with appropriate treatment'. This modernization will include the introduction of community treatment orders, which the profession has widely rejected as stigmatizing and anti-therapeutic, and will permit 'a new form of reviewable detention for those people with severe personality disorder' (Marshall, 1999). 'Security', 'control' and 'compliance' are the leitmotif and the watchwords.

This is the context in which an attempt will be made here to extract some sparks of clinical

optimism for the treatment (as opposed to containment or warehousing) of this extremely challenging and demonstrably needy group of people. It is one of professional foreboding for the immediate future.

Specialist institutions have had success with their own particular populations, for example the Henderson Hospital (Norton, 1997; Norton and Dolan, 1995), which provides therapeutic community care for people with personality disorder, and, differently, Grendon Underwood, a therapeutic prison to which prisoners within the general prison population can request transfer in the last 2 years or so of their sentences (Gunn et al., 1978; Genders and Player, 1995). To take a more optimistic view, it is perhaps a measure of the political will to do something about the troublesome individuals with personality disorder that both these institutions are currently in the process of gestating clones outside of the Home Counties. Whether any initiatives will be forthcoming to invest resources in the *suffering* of the estimated 10 per cent of the general population who fulfil the criteria for one type of personality disorder or another – and the indirect suffering they cause – remains to be seen. Mental health services (especially those providing community services), whilst said to be prioritized, have not been overwhelmed by resource support. As for *preventative* social and health initiatives, especially those aimed at primary prevention of the emotional and developmental aspects of personality disorder, they remain as yet unexplored.

This introduction aims to contextualize the problem of the specific healthcare task of offering models of care developed in high security to less secure settings. Increasing the custodial role of clinicians and the physical security of institutions, whilst not always necessarily and linearly anti-therapeutic, nevertheless has major effects on institutional culture and tends to reduce the therapeutic enthusiasm of individuals and the therapeutic ethos of the places in which they work. It may further the haemorrhage of staff from psychiatric services and discourage the skilled and enthusiastic, leaving only a custodial, and frequently institutionalized, core.

That balance, specifically for the forensic psychiatrist – but shared by other clinicians – of the 'dual role' or 'dual agency', between that of doctorly responsibility to individual patients on the one hand, and responsibility to the wider society, potential victims and criminal justice on the other, is a fine one. It cannot be radically changed in this way without risking destruction of the already thin clinical base.

It would take a bold, and possibly a stupid, person to argue that our high-security hospitals are models of perfection. Nevertheless, the core group of seriously personality disordered offenders is not going to go away – whatever the new structures. This chapter attempts to extract the core of the best elements – and some of the downside – of the high-security models of care and treatment for the personality disordered offender with a view to informing those who conceivably *may* take on the care and treatment of similarly personality disordered people in lesser degrees of security. In the future, in England and Wales, this may include the proposed new 'third service' (third way) units for those with a primary diagnosis of personality disorder who fulfil the many and diverse criteria for the label 'severe' and who are judged by whatever means to be 'dangerous' – and are therefore presently described as manifesting 'dangerous severe personality disorder'.

The clinical and research field at present is motley and much in need of fertilization. With a handful of notable exceptions, treatment for the dangerous personality disordered offender has become increasingly a minority activity for individual clinicians, as well as for institutions, for a number of reasons: because of the difficulties and dangers of demoralization, burnout and emotional suffering of staff; because of the unacceptable professional dangers involved in treating the high-risk and ultimately unpredictable patient within a predominantly

blame culture (Coid and Cordess, 1993); and because of a culture of antipathy to personality disordered offenders, including within the profession and within the forensic psychiatry specialty – perhaps, by association, one is identified with the patients one treats. Regional secure units (RSUs) – again with notable exceptions – have eschewed the necessarily sophisticated, highly specialized, highly trained clinical teams and interventions that the personality disordered, even more than the mentally ill, patient demands. This contrasts with their original aims. When the small cadre of forensic psychiatrists at that time were advising the Butler Committee (Home Office, Department of Health and Social Security, 1975), which resulted, amongst other achievements, in the RSUs, it was largely intended to set up units for these types of disruptive personality disordered patients (Bluglass, 1996). Similarly, community and outreach services have not been active, with isolated exceptions, in the management of the forensic personality disordered offender outside of physical security.

SETTING THE SCENE

It is important to acknowledge the fact of significant change over recent decades in conceptualization and models of delivery of care in the high-security hospitals – although patients are probably similar now to then. Thus, for example, Udwin (1963) reports on the methods of the 1950s of treating a group of 'aggressive psychopaths' in Broadmoor Hospital. He describes how mixed diagnostic states were so usual that a straightforward diagnosis was seldom possible. Common to all was violence and anti-authority behaviour. 'Sexual psychopaths' were said to be a group apart. Patients could be divided into two broad groups – those with psychotic episodes and those without (i.e. the rarer, 'pure', personality disorder group). He writes:

These men could only be handled under the highest security, and the hierarchy of the institution was somewhat rigid. ... The nurses readily distinguished between the 'mad' and the 'bad', and allowed the impulsive schizophrenic considerably more latitude than the acting out psychopath. ... *Nurses used to be forbidden to speak to patients.*

Of the early 1960s, Udwin writes:

Nowadays administration has become less rigid, though security precautions still interfere with what is otherwise a fairly normal hospital regime. The nurses are often the second or third generation of a family to work at Broadmoor; and they tend to be suspicious of outside doctors and newfangled ideas. ... Among the doctors there is a tendency towards a more permissive regime with more use of occupational therapy and discussion groups. *This is not always welcomed by the psychopaths, who tend to be rigid, conservative and punitive. One has said that he would rather do nine months solitary than spend his time arguing about why he had hit someone.*

Group sessions tend to produce 'jealousy and disruption, perhaps because of the large proportion of homosexuals. On the whole, however, the men are not highly sexed and are little upset by prolonged deprivation'. Dr Udwin went on to express the further opinion that 'under the traditional reward–punishment regime the patient probably leaves hospital unchanged, unless he happens to mature during his stay' (Udwin, 1963).

It would be too easy to criticize this account, first, for its failure to make clear diagnostic distinctions, using instead the catch-all term 'psychopath'. This criticism possibly holds limited weight, as the mishmash term 'dangerous severe personality disorder' seems set to replace the discredited term 'psychopath'. It might also be criticized for its apparent complacency and – from our contemporary perspective – lack of clinical sophistication, particularly in regard to the homosexual reference. However, it is quoted as an interesting 'historical' document, written in uncompromising language, which makes some astute clinical observations, by one of the liberal medical superintendents of his era. We now have good evidence, for example, that the majority of patients detained in special hospitals under the legal category of 'psychopathic disorder' suffer from some form of other psychiatric disorder at some time, including depressive disorder, hypomania, substance abuse disorders, brief psychiatric episodes, schizophrenia, as well as phobias, panic attacks and obsessive–compulsive disorder – in Coid's sample, some 80 per cent overall (Coid, 1992). This co-morbidity is one of the many 'complications' that have been glossed over by the current, politically driven, proposals. With regard, more optimistically, to achieving a change of institutional culture, the reference to nurses being forbidden to speak to patients puts the present-day situation in quite a favourable light.

Contrast this with the contemporary regimes of milieu therapy at, for example, Broadmoor Hospital as described by Grounds et al. (1987), Quayle et al. (1996) and in chapters in this volume. One aspect is that of the increasing recognition of the place for a psychodynamic attitude, and for group and individual psychotherapies within the multidisciplinary delivery of care. Murray Cox, psychotherapist at Broadmoor for more than 20 years, must take some of the credit for this cultural shift (Cordess and Cox, 1996). Within such a 'milieu', it is the relationship-based interventions, including, but not solely, the psychodynamic, along with the sociotherapeutic, which, in this author's view, are primary to the therapeutic endeavour, whilst, however, cognitive and related specifically targeted therapies, and skills-based therapeutic approaches, have a recognized place (see Chapter 12).

The repeated tendency to 'split' the whole-person offender into artificially 'clean' and convenient diagnostic categories is one to which we can all succumb. It has heuristic merit for research purposes, but is clinically damaging. Legal classifications necessarily make artificial distinctions, but it is essential that we keep in mind that patients with a category of mental illness often display personality traits which are largely psychopathic, while the psychic architecture of highly psychopathic patients is frequently psychotic in its organisation.

COMPARISON OF TWO HIGH-SECURITY HOSPITAL TREATMENT UNITS IN ENGLAND

In this section, an outline comparison is made between the published descriptive accounts of two specialist units, one in Broadmoor Hospital and one in Rampton Hospital. The personality disorder unit at Ashworth Hospital is well known (unfortunately) from a number of recent and not so recent reports (e.g. Fallon et al., 1999), but has not been written up in a professional journal, and perhaps this 'inverse relationship' is not incidental. No further comment will be made about the Ashworth unit, except that its troubles well illustrate the havoc that certain personality disordered patients can wreak in a unit in which staff may be insufficiently trained or insufficiently alert to the intensity and destructiveness of patients' psychopathology. It has to serve as a warning.

1. An account of a ward for 25 young personality disordered men (age range 18–30 years) at Broadmoor Hospital – Woodstock Ward – is given by Newrith et al. (see Chapter 18). There is one favourable preliminary study of this unit by Reiss et al. (1996) (see also Chapter 30). It is loosely based on therapeutic community concepts, but is necessarily considerably modified for the patients who, by definition, have especially longstanding and pervasive problems. It is clearly distinguished, too, by the non-voluntary and secure and coercive nature of the patients' detention (see Bermen and Segel,

1982). Some of the Woodstock characteristics may be briefly summarized as follows.

- Standardized assessment, with acceptance into the unit dependent on diagnosis and some indication of readiness to change.
- A regulated and structured culture and programme, but preserving some 'autonomy, flexibility and personal choice'.
- Patients who have committed major offences of violence and some sexual offences; the mean length of stay is approximately 4.5 years.
- An emphasis on multidisciplinary work within a balanced team, with the inclusion of speech and language therapists and creative arts therapists, as well as the usual multidisciplinary team constitution.
- Psychodynamic psychotherapy assessments, advice and, in some cases, individual and group psychotherapy by consultant psychotherapists.
- Psychological treatments, including 'unstructured, interpretive' groups; structured, task-oriented groups; the creative therapies, and individual and group psychodynamic psychotherapy – these treatments together 'form the mainstay of the ward regime'.
- Monitoring of patient progress, audit and follow-up evaluation.
- Emphasis on staff support and training.

2. A brief description and a first-stage evaluation of a smaller unit for (considerably older) men with personality disorder (mean age 41 years) at Rampton Hospital is described by Hughes et al. (1997). Some of its characteristics may be summarized as follows.

- A standardized (but similar) protocol of assessment, particularly making use of the Psychopathy Checklist – Revised

(PCL-R; Hare, 1991), but excluding patients with scores above 30.

- A highly regulated and structured regime, less consciously focusing on the autonomy of patients, and personal choice, than the Broadmoor unit.
- All patients have committed sexual offences, but also other violent offences; however, it is not a sex offender unit. The mean length of planned stay is less, at 2 years.
- An emphasis on multidisciplinary team work, without, however, the inclusion of speech and language therapists or creative arts therapists, and *no* psychodynamic assessments, advice or therapeutic intervention.
- A supportive ward milieu (consciously *not* a therapeutic community, but nevertheless a communal ethos); group work (including specific 'assertiveness', 'men talking', 'cognitive skills', 'self-esteem', 'problem-solving', and 'emotional awareness' groups); and 'individual support and treatment' as appropriate. The groups are considered to be 'the main vehicle of therapeutic change'; there is no group analytic or 'interpretive' group therapy component.
- Close monitoring of each individual patient's 'global change', and audit. Opportunity has not yet arisen for follow-up evaluation of patients after they leave the unit.
- Reference is made to: 'a development programme for all staff, including nurses, psychologists, and social workers – prior to the opening of the ward'. On-going support and training are not emphasized.

This regime at Rampton Hospital screens out patients with a high PCL-R score. The group of patients followed up from the Broadmoor unit, as described by Reiss et al. (1996), had a mean PCL-R score of 19.6, although there had been no special screening. Targeting of those with lower PCL-R scores reflects the few studies (e.g. Ogloff et al., 1990) that have shown lower levels of clinical improvement and even higher rates of recidivism after an intensive experience in a therapeutic community for those 'psychopathic' patients with scores above 25. The regime studied by Rice and colleagues (1992) was very different from the Broadmoor or Rampton model, but these suggestions are too important not to need testing in different populations and within different treatment regimes. Preliminary indications are that nihilism and indeterminate incarceration with non-intervention for high PCL-R scores may not be justified when an alternative is the kind of therapeutic régime just described (Reiss et al., 2000).

The point about this comparison is not to make judgements about obvious differences of provision and emphasis, which would be premature given the state of the art. In any case, the texts from which the comparison is made have different foci – the Broadmoor one descriptive, the Rampton one emphasizing evaluation, albeit in the unit and on psychological measures, not post-discharge.

It seems to the author that at Rampton the original aim, in about 1994, was for a smaller unit. Having started many years after the Broadmoor unit, however, it now provides 38 beds in a much better working environment, achieving an impression of small size by having separate admission, main treatment phase and rehabilitation units. While the Broadmoor unit is emphatically multidisciplinary, the Rampton unit was explicitly psychologist led, many of the medical staff at Rampton at first having been against the idea of the unit. However, the multidisciplinary ethos is now strong. It eschews psychodynamic psychotherapeutic input to either staff or patients, with a goal of shorter length of stay. Following a review of patient need across the hospital, however, this may change. Sixty patients elsewhere in the hospital were identified as not receiving services directed at their personality problems and, in proposals to extend the service, the range of treatment options is also being reconsidered. Since the unit opened, it has evolved to use a case formulation methodology that provides a mechanism for selecting, sequencing and combining interventions from a range of treatment approaches. While cognitive–behaviour therapy and, in particular, dialectical behaviour therapy primarily inform this process, elements of other models are also used, including the milieu model of Maxwell Jones, Blackburn's interpersonal model and Bowlby's attachment models. As at Broadmoor, weight is placed on the Prochaska and Diclemente (1986) concept of stages of progress and readiness for treatment. It seems likely that different patients may function better in different settings, and the elements of difference here do provide an exciting opportunity for beginning the process of testing models of best fit.

Implicit in all this is that models of care – and high-security models of care in particular – should be coherent, safe and know what they think they are doing. This could not be more important at a time when change – some of it necessary, some not – is being thrust upon services from outside. For example, the author's own experience in an RSU was one day to find that overnight, completely without consultation, a psychologically very fragile patient had been moved precipitously to another ward with strange staff, for no doubt exigent, organizational reasons 'to make the bed available'. The consequences were predictably negative, psychologically at least, unhelpful, and costly in terms of weeks (or more) of repairing the situation. Central to such action – and widespread through the National Health Service (NHS) – is a failure to recognize the healthy emotional dependencies that patients need to make. It is as if the hospital regimes are *iterative*, in the particular case of the forensic psychiatric patient, of what is the patient's own core pathology. Real emotional investment, proper acknowledgement of loss and respect

for the mourning process are just what these patients lack – and they need to find them in relationships within the system, rather than find their lifetime failures repeated.

THE MANAGEMENT OF THE INSTITUTION AND THE UNIT

Forensic psychiatric practice lives on the cusp of therapeutic encouragement of increased degrees of psychological and actual freedom, and the necessary provision of psychological and physical security, both for the individual and for public protection. It is prone to a skewing of balance, with the creation of bureaucratic constitutions (and institutions), and other forms of rigidity and ossification, as defensive manoeuvres to combat fear and anxiety. Such processes may stem from clinical staff, from management, or in response to impossible political demands. Hinshelwood (1987) has written compellingly of the dangers of working in intense institutional settings (and specifically therapeutic communities) from the point of view of clearly pathological reactions or 'acting-out' by staff in response to the institutional dynamic. For example, and possibly of particular relevance for forensic psychiatry because of its special intensity of working with acting-out and severely damaging individuals, he writes of the characteristic leaders of the institution or unit as (sometimes) behaving like 'schizoid, psychopathic, demanding, dependent and obsessionally bureaucratic individuals' – which are obvious, but potentially lethal, modes for an institution that is attempting to 'solve' its problems with disordered and dangerous individuals. This may be seen – when it occurs – as the consequence of the influence of the pathology of the patients and institution upon a vulnerable (but omniscient) leader.

It is the author's view, only apparently paradoxically, that there is less danger of massive acting-out of this process within the high-security hospitals than in individually 'champion'-led medium or other secure units, which, initially (and so far), can look 'successful'. With a notable exception, units have not been provided for severely personality disordered offender patients. The currently proposed, separate, specialist units would be in danger of falling into this implied predicament. The problem within the high-security hospitals has been more one of demoralization and neglect, but also of having to adopt the 'depressive position' (often vilified by others), rather than of charismatic (mis)leadership in which the small organization comes to reflect a composite of the dominant internal object pathology of the 'leader' and the projected pathologies of the patients and overall institution. In this scenario, the leader remains dependent upon the community (of staff and patients) over which he or she 'rules', whilst evading his or her own problems. In this dangerous and antitherapeutic situation, the reverse of the usual understanding obtains: such 'leaders' stay on and on because of their dependency (Hobson, 1979). The high-security hospitals have been freed from such dramatizing leaders, partly by the relatively rapid turnover of managers and senior clinicians who have been confronted by their own vulnerabilities, in the face of what can be an intractable task.

It may be instructive to focus on some of the questions asked in Part 5 of the *Managing Dangerous People with Severe Personality Disorder* document (Department of Health and Home Office, 1999).

3. What difficulties (if any) do you think there are in ensuring that any provisions for DPSD people meet with their security and therapeutic needs?
4. What arrangements would need to be put in place to deal with the challenge of managing this group in separate specialist units?
5. What skills would be required to provide the specialist programme needed, and where should they be drawn from?

Following from what has been said above, the author believes that this group of patients will always present enormous difficulties in whatever new structure or infrastructure (with its 'seamless' service mission statement) they are placed. That follows from the intrinsic nature of the disorder. Insofar as physical security is increased, so will enforced compliance (probably) occur; prisons – and particularly Close Supervision Centres (CRCs) – are the experts in this regard; however, these regimes have little to do with treatment, but can be very effective in 'managing' antisocial behaviour. By contrast, therapeutic goals need established and increasing degrees of freedom. There is an 'ideal form' that can be imagined, which would necessarily entail degrees of risk. These current proposals are directed at achieving the unobtainable – a risk-free combination of security (foremost) and therapeutic gain (second). I do not foresee difficulties; it is not possible.

The proposal for separate specialist units is an intriguing one at a time when high-security hospitals are joining with other NHS services to form new NHS Trusts. The thinking behind this change has been (1) to reduce the isolation of the high-security hospitals, and (2) to bring about some 'normalization' of them (rather than, an equal possibility, the 'contagion' of their future partners). By contrast, and in conflict with this, not only are mental health monies to be spent on extra new security fences (for which there is no evidence of need), but also it is proposed that any such new 'third service' specialist units would be managed 'separately from prison and health service provision'. This is logical in that (1) those detained would be held under new orders as a consequence of new legislation, (2) the 'ethos' of these units would be neither those of 'health' nor 'prison', but is yet to be determined, and (3) the staffing would similarly be quite separately structured and would be unlikely to include a major health staff complement. It is difficult to see how this would not be a prescription for isolation. For all their faults, high-security hospitals have gone some way towards demonstrating the possibilities for separate personality disorder units to be run within the overall management structure of the main secure hospital. In the case of Ashworth Hospital, the failure appears to have been in the management of the separate unit, within the overall hospital, and not in the concept of a therapeutic unit within the health system.

The skills needed to run the 'specialist programmes needed' have been discussed in the light of two units – at Broadmoor and Rampton Hospitals. They are formidable. Such therapeutic skills are a scarce resource and could not realistically 'be drawn from' any of the present facilities, wholesale, without considerable detriment. A full-scale training programme of an intense experiential and educational content, with continuing supervision, would be required – for an, as yet, undefined workforce.

The needs and risks of the woman with severe personality disorder who offends have not been addressed, since this is another, and relatively neglected, subject in itself. It does seem that for that minority of women who need to be in conditions of high and medium security, a different therapeutic regime is necessary (e.g. see Chapter 19). The psychopathology appears to be fundamentally different – and largely of a severe borderline personality type. There are massive issues of dependency that arise particularly in this group. This has relevance for staffing ratios and for a culture of even greater support for staff, if they are to survive the demands of an in-patient secure unit for women. This greater emotional dependency has actual manifestations that could be measured, but the author knows of no such work hitherto.

A unit for personality disordered patients is a crucible of psychopathology. By definition, these patients exhibit that pathology by acting on others. This can be conceptualized within psychodynamic object relations theory, or interpersonal theory (see Kiesler, 1996; and Chapter 12).

Jaques (1955) and Menzies (1959) explored the *social defence systems* of institutions and general hospitals, respectively. Hinshelwood (1993) applied some of these ideas to the defensive aspects of a prison. All of these studies follow a similar thesis (Hinshelwood, 1993):

> The work task creates specific anxieties that disturb the people engaged on the work to a greater or lesser extent. Individuals may seek to protect themselves against those anxieties – to make them unconscious – by using *psychological defences*. In the working institutions these psychological defences may be supported by collective agreements to perform the work in specific ways; and that will involve the development of certain attitudes to the work, often unrealistic, and certain work practices, called *defensive techniques*.

In the author's view, these phenomena need to be addressed centrally in the case of any current or newly proposed personality disorder units – particularly so in the case of proposals for free-standing, separate specialist units, where these mechanisms are multiplied many fold. The 'successful' running of such units requires consideration of these defences, day to day, if 'unrealistic' attitudes either of 'manic' (or omnipotent) success or detached hopelessness, and consequent individual and group lapses from vigilance, are not to occur.

Jaques (1955) writes of any persons in institutional life (i.e. including staff):

> One of the primary cohesive elements binding individuals in institutionalised human association is that of defence against psychotic anxiety. In this sense individuals may be thought of as externalising these impulses and 'internal objects' that would otherwise give rise to psychotic anxiety, and pooling them in the life of the social institution ... (This implies) that we would expect to find in group relationships manifestations

of unreality, splitting, hostility, suspicion and other forms of maladaptive behaviour.

This, according to Jaques, is the given nexus into which the patients' pathology is received. It surely needs serious attention in a 'forensic' therapeutic institution.

PSYCHODYNAMIC ASPECTS

What appears to be missing from much of the therapeutic input of forensic institutions, amidst the many separate and highly structured programmes, is a formal evaluation and understanding of the emotional life of the patients – although the Broadmoor/Woodstock Ward model is an example that does have formal psychotherapeutic provision. There is a danger that these patients, whose primary psychological deficit or defence is largely to eschew emotional life, are met with a therapeutic response which, interactively, precisely fails to help them recognize this avoidance and deal with it. There may be, for example, the necessary provision of (1) firm boundary setting and structured 'management', (2) clinical psychology input, including cognitive–behavioural and dialectical behaviour therapy, and a functional analysis of offence behaviour, and (3) a range of educational, occupational and social therapies and even, in some settings, the creative arts therapies. But any complete system, or one that aspires to achieve more than compliance and tolerable behaviour, must seek to address 'the inner state that brings such human tragedy ... the narcissism, which gives the most convincing account of human greed and rapaciousness' (and, in its extreme form, offending behaviour) (Symington, 1994).

The observation from Udwin, quoted earlier in this chapter, that 'psychopaths' 'tend to be rigid, conservative and punitive' is astute and correct. Many of those who are behaviourally seriously delinquent – as well as commonly profoundly emotionally, psychologically and behaviourally restricted and

impoverished – suffer from harsh, and sadistic, super-egos. This results in their being moralistic (rather than moral) and righteous to others (by projection), as well as harshly self-critical of themselves (by projective identification). Specifically, it is surely too easy to 'buy' the communication offered that delinquent and antisocial behaviour bespeaks 'freedom', when the opposite is predominantly the case.

Much has been written of this punitive, and frankly persecutory, super-ego of the so-called 'psychopathic' personality from Klein (1933) onwards, and of the psychological necessity, because of its harshness, for its externalization or 'projection'. The paranoid and ultra-sensitive, narcissistic personality is familiar to all who work with patients in units like those described (although clearly all differ in structure and degree). Thus, for example, do notorious offenders in prison (and especially sex offenders) mostly need protection from the punitive and violent threats from their own kind, rather than from the depredations of the 'system'.

The move – in what have become somewhat clichéd Kleinian terms – from the presented *paranoid–schizoid* 'position' to that of a stance of greater 'concern' (for self as well as others), the so-called *depressive* position, is marvellously described in Dostoievski's (1866/1991) account of the psychological maturation of the hero Raskolnikov in *Crime and Punishment*. From the position of hurt pride ('narcissistic' wounding) prevalent at the beginning of the novel, then the actual 'acting-out' of the murder of an old lady, and also her sister, Raskolnikov is capable in the end of achieving a personal, existential transformation through an acceptance of inevitable suffering, by mourning his murderous destructive acts as well as his self-destruction. This is true (in less dramatic form) for the psychological development of any human being, and especially for the (so-called) personality disordered person.

Generally speaking, those suffering from narcissistic, dissocial and borderline personality disorders, however 'macho' their demeanour, suffer from poor self-esteem and are exquisitely sensitive and vulnerable to perceived criticism. They know about humiliation, and have often suffered it from childhood onwards. Much of their apparent personality structure is a defensive manoeuvre to obscure this fact. A therapeutic regime must aim to build up the individual's sense of identity and self-worth, and never proceed by further intentional humiliation. This would be partly to repeat that state of affairs in which a harsh, self-criticizing super-ego dominates. The individual invites outside criticism (by projection), since it is more tolerable than his or her own self-criticism. There is rarely a shortage of those willing to comply, and this further confirms the person's core sense of worthlessness. So, too, with shame: Gilligan (1996, 1999) writes of the primary role that a sense of overwhelming shame plays in many violent offences, and (counter-productively) of the central role of shame and sharing in the regimes of many custodial and correctional institutions in the USA. Thereby, the criminal justice system provides precisely the iterative response – unwittingly – that encourages that very reactive and defensive behaviour it seeks to address and reform.

Although the author is a strong advocate for the forensic psychotherapeutic presence to be within the *whole* structure of the institution and the team, to inform all the day-to-day interactions with the patient – whether spoken or otherwise – there is a danger that, thereby, only lip service is paid to offers of proper psychodynamic understanding. Certainly, a psychodynamic understanding needs to be part of every full assessment, but there are just not the resources of properly trained people available. Thus, Coid, in Part 2 of the Fallon Report (Fallon et al., 1999), suggests that a proposed four-part, multiple-system protocol for the minimal baseline assessment of personality disordered offenders should include: (1) Axis II evaluation according to either the *Diagnostic and Statistical Manual of Mental Disorders,*

fourth edition (DSM-IV; American Psychiatric Association, 1994) or the *'International Classification of Diseases,* tenth revision (ICD-10; World Health Organization, 1992); (2) the Psychopathy Checklist (Hare, 1991); (3) Blackburn's typology (see Chapter 29); and also (4) a 'psychodynamic classification'. Of the last, he comments:

> The problem with this is that the diagnostician must be trained as a psychotherapist or psychoanalyst to administer it, or at least have a considerable understanding of psychodynamics. It is, therefore, irrelevant for the majority of clinicians in this country although I personally find many of the concepts of considerable use in clinical practice.

This refers to the assessment only – far greater is the shortage of sufficiently trained psychotherapists for the actual provision of psychotherapy. If there is to be proper intensive psychodynamic psychotherapy, this has to be provided and supervised from outside the multidisciplinary team. It therefore needs a commitment of resources and planning. Related to this, Coid later comments, in the context of the relative disarray of current systems for the assessment and treatment of personality disordered individuals, that 'the problem, in my opinion, is with the diagnosticians, not with the diagnosis'.

CONCLUSION

With this background, it will be clear that if there is to be any change in the psychopathology and personality structure of severely personality disordered individuals as a consequence of treatment within maximum or medium security care, a number of conditions must be met.

- A prolonged duration of care and treatment – measured in several years (minimum), to include supervision and care by way of follow-up after the period of residential treatment.

- A sufficiently (i) physically and (ii) emotionally/psychologically secure environment with clear and robust boundaries. This is in no way to argue for a *harsh* regime – indeed, following on from previous remarks, quite the opposite – but rather for one in which the rules and regulations are reliably (but flexibly) upheld, and the client/patient knows where he or she stands.

  This population of patients is invariably characterized – in addition to their offending – by failure to have had in their psychological development at least one experience of 'good enough mothering' (Winnicott, 1960) or, indeed, one 'good enough' emotional experience of being psychologically 'held' and 'contained' during their earliest or later years by anyone. Constancy and continuity are, therefore, crucially important. This has been possible in high-security hospitals, which have historically kept their staff longer than other NHS hospitals, albeit sometimes for mixed reasons, including aspects of institutionalization. In an era of rapid change in our management and clinical structures and greater turnover of clinical and management staff, constancy and continuity need to be valued more than at present.

- Working close to the patient, and working within an effective multidisciplinary team, is acknowledged as essential within high-security settings. In a community setting, working with personality disordered patients, the merits of such team working was described by Glover (1960) as one of making use of a 'distributive transference' – i.e. spreading the emotional load for individual team members. It also allows for some degree of constancy and continuity (see above), if any one member of staff is away or leaves a post. The extraordinary,

and institutionally defensive, practice of changing patients and staff around without warning or concern is counterproductive, and mirrors the history and pathology of these patients. Mourning of loss and of change is just what these patients have not been allowed, and it is necessary for creative development. Where a 'new start', with a new team, is considered necessary, because, for example, of some insurmountable difficulties, preparation for the change, over a period often of months, will minimize the institutional and impersonal message.

- The 'sensitivity' and awareness of high-security staff – by experience and training – of the aggressive and destructive spectrum of mentation and behaviour make for a more contained therapeutic milieu. It is less likely to be one of staff acting-out – either against the patient or by displacement outside of the clinical situation. Such staff readily recognize concepts of *negative transference* and *negative therapeutic reactions*, whereby one needs to be aware, with these patients, of the continual likelihood of a positive relationship or real improvement being undermined – frequently clandestinely or with a deceptive guise. This is not to predict, and certainly not to provoke, any particular negative phenomenon, but to have a general state of preparedness for destructive capacity. It is not sufficient to look *only* for the best in any patient; failure to be aware of their negative potential is potentially lethal at this level of pathology. Whilst acknowledging the possibly positive and genuinely creative aspects of the patient, one must not ignore the tendency of such self-destructive patients to undermine a sense of the positive and of hope and, thereby, to snatch, as it were, failure from the jaws of success. Such an acknowledgement is necessary for staff survival, but also offers containment to patients in that staff know something about what they find themselves repeatedly committed to re-enacting ('acting-out'). Put in other terms, the majority of these patients are 'self-defeating', and persistently shoot themselves in the foot.

- In terms of continuity of care, it would be ideal if a member of the team who is significant to the patient (i.e. has established a 'therapeutic alliance') were able to move with the patient from one level of security to another. Such a situation may be possible with the forthcoming integration of services of different levels of security, and the assumed creation, thereby, of joint appointments between different units and institutions. Recent evidence (Maden et al., 1999) concerning those patients discharged from medium-secure hospitals can be read within this light.

Overall, it is the case that care and treatment in total, or near-total, institutions are difficult to evaluate by the most rigorous methodologies. A comparison study of the effectiveness of psychoanalytically oriented *partial* hospitalization with standard psychiatric care for patients with borderline personality disorder does, however, demonstrate that it is possible to follow a randomized and controlled methodology in evaluating the psychotherapy of the personality disordered patient (Bateman and Fonagy, 1999).

Moran (1999) writes:

Doctors may not have found a way to radically alter personality structure, but they do have the ability to build supportive relationships with a group of difficult, distressed and usually isolated people who simply do not conform to society's rules. However, the current preoccupation with finding effective treatments may have distanced doctors from their other traditional roles of relieving suffering and providing comfort.

In the present climate, it would be too easy to lose sight of this predominantly clinical function.

REFERENCES

American Psychiatric Association (1994). *Diagnostic and Statistical Manual of Mental Disorders,* fourth edition. Washington, DC: American Psychiatric Association.

Appelbaum P (1997). A theory of ethics for forensic psychiatry. *Journal of the American Academy of Psychiatry and Law* **25**:233–47.

Bateman A and Fonagy P (1999). Effectiveness of partial hospitalization in the treatment of borderline personality disorder: a randomized controlled trial. *American Journal of Psychiatry* **156**:1563–9.

Bermen E and Segel R (1982). The captive client: dilemmas of psychotherapy in the psychiatric hospital. *Psychotherapy, Research and Practice* **19**:31–42.

Bluglass R (1996). Valedictory address: free use of unexpired time; my clinical career. *Criminal Behaviour and Mental Health Supplement* **6**:95–106.

Coid J (1992). DSM-III diagnosis in criminal psychopaths: way forward. *Criminal Behaviour and Mental Health* **2**:78–94.

Coid J and Cordess C (1993). Compulsory admission of dangerous psychopaths. *British Medical Journal* **304**:1581–2.

Cordess C and Cox M (eds) (1996). *Forensic Psychotherapy. Crime Psychodynamics and the Offender Patient.* London: Jessica Kingsley.

Department of Health (1998). *Modernising Mental Health Services.* London: HMSO.

Department of Health and Home Office (1999). *Managing Dangerous People with Severe Personality Disorder.* London: Home Office.

Dolan B and Coid J (1993). *Psychopathic and Antisocial Personality Disorders: Treatment and Research Issues.* London: Gaskell Books.

Dostoievski F (1866/1991). *Crime and Punishment.* Harmondsworth: Penguin Books.

Fallon P, Bluglass R, Edwards B and Daniels G (1999). *The Report of the Committee of Enquiry into the Personality Disorder Unit at Ashworth Hospital,* Vols I and II. London: HMSO.

Genders E and Player E (1995). *Grendon. A Study of a Therapeutic Prison.* Oxford: Clarendon Press.

Gilligan J (1996). Exploring shame in special settings: a psychotherapeutic study. In: Cordess C and Cox M (eds), *Forensic Psychotherapy, Crime, Psychodynamics and the Offender Patient.* London: Jessica Kingsley, 475–89.

Gilligan J (1999). *Violence.* London: Jessica Kingsley.

Glover E (1960). *The Roots of Crime.* London: Imago Publishing Co.

Grounds AT, Quayle MT, France J, Brett T, Cox M and Hamilton JR (1987). A unit for psychopathic disorder patients in Broadmoor Hospital. *Medicine, Science and the Law* **27**:21–31.

Gunn J, Robertson G and Dell S (1978). *Psychiatric Aspects of Imprisonment.* London: Academic Press.

Hare RD (1991). *The Hare Psychopathy Checklist – Revised.* Toronto: Multi-Health Systems.

Hinshelwood R (1987). *What Happens in Groups.* London: Press Association Books.

Hinshelwood R (1993). Locked in a role: a psychotherapist within the social defence system of a prison. *Journal of Forensic Psychiatry* **4**:427–40.

Hobson RF (1979). The messianic community, In: Hinshelwood RD and Manning N (eds), *Therapeutic Communities: Reflections and Progress.* London: Routledge and Kegan Paul.

Home Office, Department of Health and Social Security (1975). *Report of the Committee on Mentally Abnormal Offenders (The Butler Report).* Cmnd 6244. London: HMSO.

Hughes G, Hogue T, Hollin C and Champion H (1997). First-stage evaluation of a treatment programme for personality disordered offenders. *Journal of Forensic Psychiatry* **8**:515–17.

Jaques E (1955). Social systems as a defence against persecutory and depressive anxiety. In: Klein M, Heimann P and Money-Kyrle RE (eds), *New Directions in Psychoanalysis.* London: Tavistock Publications.

Kiesler DJ (1996). *Contemporary Interpersonal Theory and Research: Personality, Psychopathology, and Psychotherapy.* New York: John Wiley & Sons.

Klein M (1933/1985). The early development of conscience in the child. In: *The Writings of Melanie Klein*, Vol. 1: *Love, Guilt and Reparation.* London: Hogarth Press and the Institute of Psychoanalysis, 248–57.

Maden A, Friendship C, Rutter S, McClintock T and Gunn J (1999). Outcome of admission to a medium secure psychiatric unit (1. Short- and long-term outcome). *British Journal of Psychiatry* **175**:313–21.

Marshall M (1999). Modernising mental health services. Editorial. *British Medical Journal* **318**:3–4.

Mental Welfare Commission for Scotland (2000). *Report of the Inquiry into the Care and Treatment of Noel Ruddle.* Edinburgh: Scottish Parliament.

Menzies I (1959). The functioning of social systems as a defence against anxiety: a report on the study of a nursing service of a general hospital. *Human Relations* **13**:95–102.

Moran P (1999). *Should Psychiatrists Treat Personality Disorders?* Maudsley Discussion Paper No. 7. London: Institute of Psychiatry.

Mullen P (1999). Dangerous people with severe personality disorder. British proposals for managing them are glaringly wrong – and unethical. *British Medical Journal* **319**:1146–7.

Norton K (1997). In the prison of severe personality disorder. *Journal of Forensic Psychiatry* **8**:285–98.

Norton K and Dolan B (1995). Acting out and the institutional response. *The Journal of Forensic Psychiatry* **6**:317–22.

Ogloff J, Wong S and Greenwood A (1990). Treating criminal psychopaths in a therapeutic community program. *Behavioral Sciences and the Law* **8**:81–90.

Prochaska JO and Diclemente CC (1986). Towards a comprehensive model of change. In: Miller WEC and Heather N (eds), *Treating Addictive Behaviors.* New York: Plenum Press.

Quayle M, France J and Wilkinson E (1996). An integrated modular approach to therapy in a special hospital young men's unit. In: Cordess C and Cox M (eds), *Forensic Psychotherapy: Crime, Psychodynamics and the Offender Patient*, Vol. 2: *Mainly Practice.* London: Jessica Kingsley, 449–63.

Reiss D, Grubin D and Meux C (1996). Young 'psychopaths' in special hospital: treatment and outcome. *British Journal of Psychiatry* **168**:99–104.

Reiss D, Meux C and Grubin D (2000). The effect of psychopathology on outcome in high security patients. *Journal of the American Academy of Psychiatry and the Law* **28**:309–14.

Rice ME, Harris GT and Cormier CA (1992). An evaluation of a maximum security therapeutic community for psychopaths and other mentally disordered offenders. *Law and Human Behavior* **16**:399–412.

Symington N (1994). *Emotion and Spirit.* London: Cassell.

Taylor PJ, Grounds A and Snowden P (1993). Forensic psychiatry in the National Health Service of England and Wales. In: Gunn J and Taylor PJ (eds), *Forensic Psychiatry: Clinical, Legal and Ethical Issues.* Oxford: Butterworth-Heinemann, 709–10.

Udwin EL (1963). *The Aggressive Psychopath.* Royal Medico-Psychological Association, Medical Societies. *Lancet*, 1084.

Winnicott DW (1960). The theory of the parent–infant relationship. In: *The Maturational Processes and the Facilitating Environment.* London: Hogarth Press, 37–55.

World Health Organization (1992). *International Classification of Diseases.* Geneva: World Health Organization.

Part 4

SEPARATION AND FACILITATING DEPARTURE

Chapter 24

TRANSFER OF PATIENTS BETWEEN SERVICES

Tim Howard

INTRODUCTION

The circumstances surrounding the transfer of patients between services will vary according to the degree of dangerousness of the patient, the extent of change in the environment and supervision in the new facility, and the reason for transfer. More attention needs to be given to this process when the patient is being transferred to a more secure facility. Transfers include movement from hospital to community, from hospital to hospital, from general service to specialist service, and from community service to community service. Whatever the circumstances, the aims of any transfer process must always be the same: to achieve a safe and expeditious transfer of care from one service to another that is comfortable for the patient, acceptable in terms of risk and maintains therapeutic gains. Despite variations in circumstances and the obvious absence of a single process model, certain principles underpin all forms of transfer. This chapter is concerned with the most salient aspects of these.

PROCESS OF TRANSFER

COMMUNICATION OF RISK

Clear, concise communication at both inter-disciplinary and intra-disciplinary levels in both services is fundamental to safe transfer.

Each member of the receiving service must be in possession of all the information necessary to ensure accurate participation in all stages involved in the process of transfer. This places a responsibility for full and honest disclosure of all relevant information to the transferring service.

Patients with severe personality disorder may sometimes object to the passing of information, claiming that it is 'confidential'. A clear understanding of the nature of professional confidentiality is therefore necessary, especially for those professionals who lead the transfer process. The Ritchie Inquiry (Ritchie et al., 1994) opined that the communication of risk issues, particularly those involving the possibility of violence towards others, outweighed all other considerations of professional confidentiality. Disclosure and sharing of personal, health-related information is governed by a complex common law and statutory framework, which, for those working in the health-care field, is further complicated by various professional codes of conduct that are not always in precise agreement with one another. The impact of the Human Rights Act 1998 and the European Convention on Human Rights, particularly Articles 6 (right to a fair trial) and 8 (right to respect for private and family life), has been significant and will continue to exert an effect. Nonetheless it may, from time to time, be necessary to disclose information to other agencies and/or teams of professionals, and a full understanding of the circumstances in which it is lawful to do so is essential for those working with high-risk individuals.

In essence, disclosure of confidential information may be permitted or required by statute, where the person consents and where there is an overriding public interest (see W v. Egdell and Others [1990], X v. Y [1988]). Where transfer may involve risk to the life of another person, a duty of disclosure exists (see Osman v. UK [2000]; Jones, 2004). Given these complexities, professionals should always seek the patient's consent before breaching confidentiality. This should only be done after full multidisciplinary discussion, and then only to the extent, in terms of scope and purpose, that is necessary to ensure safety. If there is any doubt whatsoever, professionals should seek advice from professional bodies, independent legal sources and senior colleagues. Full documentation, particularly of the reasons for breach, is imperative. For a full review of this area see Morris (2003).

Patients with severe personality disorder frequently have difficulty in coping with stress, and any transfer process, particularly one involving discharge from hospital, is likely to pose difficulties for them. Patients often fail to tolerate change and frequently cope badly with loss, for instance the attentions of a particularly valued staff member. Transfer may involve a temporary loss of possessions or privileges and/or reduction or distortion of therapeutic and containing boundaries that may lead to violence or deliberate self-harm. Transfer is, therefore, a time of heightened risk, and its specific risks should be assessed at the time of the transfer process.

In spite of the commonly held pessimistic belief that the prediction of clinical risk has limited accuracy, there is evidence that its effectiveness is improved when carried out in a multidisciplinary setting and regularly reviewed (Snowden, 1997). It should be a structured (Maden, 2001) and monitored process that is shared between the transferring and receiving services, and should take place in an atmosphere of risk awareness that encourages honest reporting. Actuarial risk assessment tools may be useful, but their over-reliance on static, historical risk factors limits their use in the transfer process. It is as important to concentrate on the assessment of dynamic risk factors, particularly those factors that determine the patient's habitual response to stress. Regular assessment of the patient's mental state is required, paying particular attention to attitudes and intentions, emerging psychiatric symptoms, and transference issues, particularly in patients with borderline personality disorder (Dubin, 1989). Other situational risk factors that need to be considered include the behaviour of the patient during leave of absence, inappropriate use of drugs and/or alcohol, compliance with leave directions and prescribed medication (Lipsedge, 2001).

GUIDELINES FOR IMPLEMENTATION OF TRANSFER

The Care Programme Approach (CPA) is the established framework for the co-ordination of transfer between mental health services (Department of Health, 1995). The core features of the approach include:

- full needs assessment, including both health and social care needs;
- a written care plan, agreed between professional carers, lay carers and the patient;
- the allocation of a key-worker whose role is one of co-ordinator, ensuring that the care plan is delivered and that remedial action is taken when it is not;
- the empowerment of any individual member of the care team to call for a full case review, thus allowing all concerns about the patient to be discussed;
- risk management and relapse prevention planning.

There are different levels of CPA supervision dependent on the perceived need. Standard and enhanced forms of CPA have been devised, with the enhanced form being reserved for those patients requiring multi-professional support and who pose significant risks to either themselves or others. The CPA is an integral part of clinical governance in the National Health Service (NHS), where its implementation is obligatory. Its tenets have also been readily adopted by the private sector. Although subject to criticism in its application to patients in adult general psychiatry (Marshall et al., 2003), in part because of evidence for the increased cost of this process (Tyrer, 1998), others have argued for the usefulness of case management in mental health (Burns, 1996; Rosen, 2001). There may be better reasons to adopt these procedures in the forensic field, and these guidelines have been viewed as representing a standard for good practice (Harrison, 1997).

Complementary to the CPA are integrated care pathways. These are guidelines used to manage the clinical care of selected patients that have been developed to try to establish standards for pathways of care. Although procedures have not yet been universally agreed, they are being refined by continuing audit and evaluation. Although criticized as being unduly mechanistic and undermining of professional integrity (Jones, 1999), there is emerging evidence that they may lead to a perception on the part of patients of an increased quality of care with more patient participation (Anders et al., 1997).

Finally, those professionals leading the transfer process require a close knowledge of the legal structures under which transfer may take place, especially those governed by the Mental Health Act 1983. Perhaps the most important areas are Leave under Section 17, Guardianship under Section 7, Supervised Discharge under Section 25 (A), After-care under Section 117, and the Mechanisms for the Transfer of Responsibilities for Detention under Section 17. Where transfer occurs from a hospital to a community-based service and the perception of risk is high, it may be necessary to arrange a multi-agency public protection meeting (Maguire et al., 2001). Transferring and receiving services will also need to be familiar with local child protection arrangements. The requirements for registration of sex offenders under the Sex Offenders Act 1997 should not be forgotten.

REFERENCES

Anders R, Tomai J, Clute R and Olson T (1997). Development of a Scientifically Valid Co-ordinated Care Path. *Journal of Nursing Administration* **27**(5):45–52.

Burns T (1996). Case management: case management confers substantial benefits. *British Medical Journal* **312**:1540.

Department of Health (1995). *Health of the Nation. Building Bridges: A Guide to Inter-agency Working for the Care and Protection of Securely Mentally Ill People.* London: Department of Health.

Dubin WR (1989). The role of fantasies, counter transference and psychological defences in patient violence. *Hospital and Community Psychiatry* **40**:1280–3.

Harrison G (1997). Risk assessment in a climate of litigation. *British Journal of Psychiatry* **170**(Suppl. 32):37–9.

Jones A (1999). A modernised mental health service: the role of care pathways. *Journal of Nursing Management* **7**(6):331–8.

Jones R (2004). *Mental Health Act Manual*, ninth edition. London: Sweet and Maxwell, 772–3.

Lipsedge M (2001). Risk management in psychiatry. In: Vincent C (ed.), *Clinical Risk Management.* London: BMJ Books, 219–40.

Maden A (2001). Practical application of structured risk assessment. *British Journal of Psychiatry* **178**:479.

Maguire M, Kemshall H, Noaks L, Wincup E and Sharpe K (2001). *Risk Management of Sexual and Violent Offenders: The Work of Public Protection Panels.* Police Research Series Paper 139. London: Home Office.

Marshall M, Gray A, Lockwood A and Green R (2003). Case management for people with severe mental disorders. Cochrane Review. In: *The Cochrane Library*, Issue 3.

Morris F (2003). Confidentiality and the sharing of information. *Journal of Mental Health Law* **9**:38–50.

Ritchie JH, Dick D and Lingham R (1994). *Report of the Inquiry into the Care and Treatment of Christopher Clunis.* London: HMSO.

Rosen A (2001). Does case management work? The evidence and abuse of evidence-based medicine. *Australian and New Zealand Journal of Psychiatry* **35**:731–46.

Snowden P (1997). Practical aspects of clinical risk assessment and management. *British Journal of Psychiatry* **170**(Suppl. 32):32–4.

Tyrer P (1998). Cost-effective or profligate community psychiatry? *British Journal of Psychiatry* **172**:1–3.

CASE LAW

Osman v. United Kingdom (2000) 29 EHRR 245.

W v. Egdell and Others (1990) 1 All ER 835.

X v. Y (1988) 2 All ER 648.

Chapter 25

GENERAL PRINCIPLES OF DISCHARGE PLANNING

Elaine McNicholas

INTRODUCTION

Planning for discharge and liaison between services have become major issues in safely and effectively caring for mentally disordered patients in the community in England and Wales. The introduction of Section 117 (Aftercare) in the 1983 Mental Health Act and subsequently the Care Programme Approach (CPA) in 1991 underlined this (Department of Health, 1996a). The introduction of supervised discharge in 1996 (Department of Health, 1996b), which, in theory, gave extra powers to Section 117, further emphasized the importance of a systematic, planned approach to managing the care of patients leading up to and following discharge from in-patient care.

Patients suffering from personality disorders have usually suffered severe disturbance in behaviour, which is nearly always associated with considerable personal and social disruption. Added to this, they have often been involved with many different professionals, in many different settings, which may have further disrupted their lives. Therefore, it is important that any planning for aftercare is tailored to the individual needs of the patient, with every member of the care team, be they based in hospital or the community, being aware of how best the patient may be managed. This must be based on a systematic assessment of the patient's health and social care needs and the areas of risk.

A major factor in an effective approach to patients with personality disorders is consistency, and this can be problematic when several disciplines are involved in the patient's care and aftercare planning. Therefore, it is important that there are regular multidisciplinary review meetings, and a timely introduction of the community workers (long before discharge) who will continue the care of the patient following discharge, to ensure continuity and a smooth transfer from in-patient to community services. In order to assist this as part of the CPA process, one person should be named who is willing and able to co-ordinate the care by liaising with all members of the multidisciplinary team, the patient and relatives, where appropriate. This should ensure a systematic approach to the planning and also reduce any potential inter-agency conflicts.

Many say that the planning for a patient's discharge and aftercare should commence on admission. However, this is not to say that housing needs and support in the community would be necessarily considered as priority on admission, but rather that the problems and needs of the patient would be taken into consideration in relation to how he or she can be prepared for discharge and cared for afterwards. Part of this process is recognizing that the environment of a hospital is a different environment from that outside the hospital walls, in that the daily living skills required to live an independent life are, for the most part, redundant in a ward environment. For instance, patients would not have to be concerned about paying bills, buying food etc., and most of the decisions about their lives are made by other people. This could lead to the patient becoming de-skilled and disempowered or institutionalized, depending on the length of stay in hospital and how they are cared for on the ward. Therapy groups such as social and practical skills groups are essential in order to prevent any deterioration in skills of living and, as much as possible, patients should be involved in decisions about their care and living environment.

MULTIDISCIPLINARY ASSESSMENT

The CPA provides a structure for planning for discharge and then managing care in the community; the guidance for CPA looks at the wider picture of health and social care, recognizing that, although healthcare workers would play a large part in the care of someone with a mental health problem, the mental health problem cannot be seen alone and other factors may have a significant effect on the health of the patient, i.e. housing, financial circumstances. The CPA also guides us towards a systematic approach to the assessing, planning and monitoring of care for the patient in the community.

Traditionally within health services, the usual way of assessing a patient's needs or the services required has been to look at what is available to support the patient in the community. However, over the last few years this has not been considered an effective way of providing a service and, indeed, within social care, needs-led as opposed to service-led assessments are the norm. When looking at the problems and therefore the needs of the patient, it is important that the assessment is geared to the individual, in effect looking at all of the structures that must be in place in order to facilitate his or her discharge and then care in the community.

An holistic approach to the assessment of the patient's needs would look at areas beyond just the mental health problems the patient may have. In this sense, it is essential that this is a multidisciplinary approach. As well as mental health, other areas of the patient's life should be taken into consideration to ensure he or she is supported in the community and able to lead as independent a life as possible. Mental health service users, particularly those with the most complex and enduring needs, can require help with other aspects of their lives, e.g. housing, finance, employment, education and physical health needs (Department of Health, 2000). All of these areas mentioned could have a bearing on the patient's mental health and ability to cope in the community; this will be as important to the patient as it is to have support with mental health problems.

Housing is obviously an important issue in terms of discharge; therefore it is essential that a housing officer is involved in the planning process from the earliest appropriate opportunity. It is important that the housing officer is given as much relevant information as possible in terms of needs and risk assessment in order to find suitable accommodation for the patient. The recommendations of the Newby Inquiry suggested that 'housing should be regarded as an integral part of a care plan by key workers and care managers' (Davies, 1995, p. 154). This would involve taking into consideration issues of confidentiality, and information should only be given on a 'need to know' basis, after first seeking the permission of the patient. However, when there is a concern for public safety or the safety of the housing officer, it is essential that this information be shared.

Other more social aspects of the patient's life should also be taken into consideration, such as support networks; this may involve the family and friends of the patient as well as voluntary sector agencies such as MIND. It is important that family and friends are involved with the patient's care when appropriate – taking into consideration issues of confidentiality – as often they will be the main carers for the patient once he or she is discharged. However, when involving relatives and friends, part of the care plan should take into consideration the provision of support and advice for them, to enable them to be effective in the carer role, and so that it does not become detrimental to their health or safety. Carers are now entitled to an assessment of their needs and for these needs to be part of a care plan.

BALANCING NEED AND RISK

In the early to mid 1950s, an 'open door policy' for psychiatric patients began; this meant that there was a move towards unlocking doors, more occupational and recreational therapies, more respect for patients, etc. In later years this proved to be a problem when dealing with patients who were a risk to themselves or others and who perhaps required more secure settings. This meant that some patients could not be dealt with in open National Health Service (NHS) psychiatric wards. In looking at the needs of the patient with personality disorder in the community, attempts must be made to try to strike a balance between recognizing that institutionalized care can have a negative effect; however, public safety must be given a high priority.

In recent years there has been increasing public concern, fuelled by emotive media coverage, that the public is at serious risk of violence from people with mental health problems. *The National Confidential Inquiry into Suicide and Homicide by People with Mental Illness* (Royal College of Psychiatrists, 1996) produced figures that showed that, in fact, only 5 per cent of people convicted of homicide have symptoms of psychotic illness, another 12 per cent have other signs of mental disorder, including personality disorder, but 83 per cent have none. The Government has used this report to attempt to reassure the public; however, it continues to emphasize the need for

risks to be identified for patients suffering from mental disorders. No decision to discharge a patient should be agreed until the care team in charge of the patient can demonstrate that the decision to discharge has been taken after full consideration of any risk and how this can be managed (Department of Health, 1994).

The CPA guidance states that, as much as possible, the patient should be able to have some choice in the key-worker or care co-ordinator who will deal with his or her case. This is not as straightforward as it might appear, especially when dealing with personality disordered patients. Certainly, issues such as gender and good working relationships should be taken into consideration. The worker's response to those patients with personality disorders who have committed offences is important in terms of how he or she will be able to monitor and work with the patient once discharged into the community. Forming a working relationship is a large part of the community workers role, as this may be the difference between maintaining contact with the difficult patient in the community and the patient disengaging or disappearing from the service.

Again, when trying to decide who would be best placed to carry out the role of care co-ordinator, the individual needs and risks of the patient should be taken into consideration. Someone who has been subject to a Restriction Order under Section 41 of the 1983 Mental Health Act may be discharged from hospital, subject to conditions imposed by the Home Office (under Section 42) or by the Mental Health Review Tribunal (under Section 73). The conditions that can be imposed are not defined in the act, but might typically include supervision by a social supervisor (normally a local authority social worker or a probation officer), who will provide support to assist the person's resettlement in the community. The social supervisor will also alert the Home Office to any potential need for the person to be recalled to hospital or, on the other hand, to any indications that absolute discharge should be considered (Turner, 1996).

THE ROLE OF THE CARE CO-ORDINATOR

As the role of the care co-ordinator and that of the social supervisor are similar, it may be appropriate for the social supervisor to fulfil both roles. The guidance for social supervision states that the role of the supervisor is (HO/DHSS, 1987a, as cited in Vaughan and Badger, 1995):

> to assist the patient's successful integration into the community and to closely monitor the patient's progress so that in the event of subsequent deterioration in the patient's mental health or of a perceived increase in the risk of danger to the public, steps can be taken to assist the patient and protect the public.

On the other hand, the care co-ordinator could be any other member of the multidisciplinary team, including the community psychiatric nurse (CPN), who may be in a better position to liaise with other members of the care team as well as having regular contact with the patient.

It is important that the co-ordinator has the necessary skills of negotiation and liaison to enable him or her to maintain contact with all involved in the patient's care and the confidence to arrange meetings, especially in a crisis situation, when circumstances demand. Most importantly in terms of risk, the care co-ordinator should have experience in dealing with personality disordered offenders and the ability to monitor the patient in terms of risk and early indicators of relapse. Further to this, it is essential that all involved in the care recognize the role of the co-ordinator and that they support and assist him or her in this role by sharing valid information.

PLANNING AND REVIEWING CARE

The formulation of the multidisciplinary plan of care from the needs and risk assessments should describe all aspects of the care to be received by the patient. The parts of the plan should be discussed and agreed with all who are designated to deliver the planned care and this should also be agreed with service managers in terms of funding and resourcing, etc. Therefore it may be necessary to have a series of multidisciplinary meetings before the pre-discharge meeting to finalize arrangements. As well as the plan of care, contingency plans should be considered and agreed; this may be necessary in case of sickness or a missed appointment, etc. Crisis plans should also be considered, which should detail any early indicators for relapse, what would be done in times of crisis, and who is responsible for ensuring that the planned steps are taken. Obviously patients should be able to participate fully in the discussions about the plans, so that they are aware of what is expected of them and the care team once discharge takes place.

If a patient is subject to conditional discharge or Supervised Discharge, the conditions or requirements should be written within the care plan so that everybody has a clear understanding of all aspects of the plan of care. Where a patient is subject to the provisions of the Sex Offenders Act 1997, it is important that the multidisciplinary team is able to take into account in planning discharge of what, if any, impact the need to comply with registration requirements may have on the patient (Department of Health, 1997). Patients need to be fully informed of their rights and of any conditions or requirements imposed.

Finally, the frequency of review should be considered before discharge, which will obviously depend on the needs of the patient or potential risk factors. In any case, a date for CPA review should be set for no longer than

3 months following discharge, to ensure that the plan is considered and any further needs are included in it. The care co-ordinator (or, indeed, any other member of the care team) can ask for a CPA meeting to be convened at an earlier date should there be any concerns about the progress of the patient or the care plan (Department of Health, 1996a).

REFERENCES

Davies N (1995). *Report of the Inquiry into the Circumstances Leading to the Death of Jonathon Newby (a Volunteer Worker).* Oxford: Oxfordshire Health Authority.

Department of Health (1994). *Guidance on the Discharge of Mentally Disordered People and their Continuing Care in the Community.* HSG (94). 27/LASSL (94)4 DH 1994. London: Department of Health.

Department of Health (1996a). *Building Bridges: Arrangements for Inter-agency Working for the Care and Protection of Severely Mentally Ill People.* HSG(95)56/LASSL(95)12. London: Department of Health.

Department of Health (1996b). *Guidance on Supervised Discharge (Aftercare under Supervision) and Related Provisions.* HSG(96)11/LAC (96)8. London: Department of Health.

Department of Health (1997). *Guidance to Hospital Managers and Local Authority Social Services Departments on the Sex Offenders Act, 1997.* HSG(97)37/LASSL(97)17. London: Department of Health.

Department of Health (2000). *National Service Framework for Mental Health – Effective Care Co-ordination in Mental Health Services – Modernising the Care Programme Approach.* London: Department of Health.

Steering Committee of the Confidential Inquiry into Homicides and Suicides by Mentally Ill People (1996). *Report of the Confidential Inquiry into Homicides and Suicides by Mentally Ill People.* London: Royal College of Psychiatrists.

Turner N (1996). HyperGuide to the Mental Health Act (www.hyperguide.co.uk).

Vaughan P and Badger (1995). *Working with mentally disordered patients in the community.* In: *Excerpts from Guidance Notes for Social Supervisors.* HO/DHSS 1987a. London: Chapman & Hall, 154.

Chapter 26

SEPARATION FROM THE TREATMENT CENTRE: A PSYCHODYNAMIC UNDERSTANDING

Rex Haigh

ATTACHMENT DISORDERS

Life is a succession of losses: we start with being violently expelled from the only place we don't have to breathe or eat, then we are weaned off the breast (or bottle), sent out to school, made to look after ourselves, leave home, lose independence and have children, our parents die, we have more and more uncertain health, and then die ourselves. Those who can fully experience all those and survive and grow from them might be said to enjoy a healthy primary emotional development.

All individuals start their lives attached: umbilically, within the mother and with the blood of one flowing only a cell or two away from the blood of the other. At birth, this attachment is suddenly and irreversibly severed: the smooth and fairly tranquil life of swooshing around in a warm ocean that is your whole world, without ever needing to eat and breathe, is over. It is the first separation and loss, with many others to come later. The easy life is lost, and experience suddenly becomes bumpy, with good and bad parts and, for the lucky ones, with people close enough to help you through it. For the baby who is fortunate, the physical and physiological bond will be smoothly and seamlessly

replaced with an emotional and nurturant one, which will grow and develop until various features of that, too, are invariably broken, lost and changed in the inevitability of development. This secure early attachment gives the infant a coherent experience of existence, and protects against being later overwhelmed by life's vicissitudes.

It is through relationship that loss is made bearable – one attachment broken, but another containing the angst and despair and primitive anxiety that threaten to overwhelm. It is where this fails that attachment disorders arise. There are a number of reasons this early attachment can go seriously wrong, and leave the infant without a secure sense of the world. Some babies certainly seem extra needy or awkward – and some of the explanation for this may even be found at an identifiable locus on a definable chromosome one day. But many babies who are not born with any congenital impairment have a disrupted development because their parents cannot (or will not) do what is needed to provide them with an adequate environment in which to develop. Objective and subjective problems of emotional development are likely to follow.

This is the basic fault (Balint, 1968): the attachment is inadequate, containment is not good enough, the bond is insecure and so is the infant. Although this describes it as all happening in infancy, it is probably more accurate to think of it as the milieu – or the aggregate experience of the psychosocial environment – in which the whole of this primary emotional development takes place. In what can be seen as an effort to survive in the face of an environment that does not meet an individual's social needs, counterproductive patterns of thoughts, behaviours and feelings develop, which may come to be diagnosed as personality disorder in adulthood. The different tracks from the early attachment deficit have been well researched and verified by robust research since the 1960s (Holmes, 1993; see also Chapter 3).

Probably everybody who ends up seeking treatment in a therapeutic community – prison, special hospital, mental health unit, special school, or psychospiritual – suffers from some variant of this, and they are often some of the most severely affected. Those who do not want or find their way to appropriate treatment often seem to have an unquenchable thirst for 'care' – whether medical, psychiatric or penal – which is frequently quite inappropriate, causes a hostile counter-reaction by the professionals involved, and costs a great deal of money (Davies, 1998).

SECONDARY EMOTIONAL DEVELOPMENT

With loss – of contact, of relationship, of security, of hope – placed centre stage in the process of individuation, attachment must take place so that loss can happen. It is through the successful endurance of loss that we all have to survive and change to live on. This is recreated, with some intensity, in therapeutic communities.

When disturbance is as fundamental as it is in the members of a therapeutic community, the first task of treatment is to reconstruct a secure attachment, and subsequently use that to bring about changes in deeply ingrained expectations of relationships and patterns of behaviour. This invokes a model of secondary emotional development, where fundamentals like attachment, containment, communication, involvement and agency are engineered to be securely in place (Haigh, 1998). Members need to have a sense of belonging – a place where membership is valued and members themselves feel they are valued. It must feel safe, open and inclusive. It must also be somewhere one's effectiveness in relationships – personal agency and power – can be felt. This is particularly difficult for those who come with a lifelong history of unsatisfactory relationships, expecting hostility, abuse, trauma or abandonment.

In the clinical work of therapeutic communities, it often seems that the most important thing about attachment is detachment. Leaving is often a dread on members' minds as they join. It is through making a new type of attachment in full knowledge that it will end that it can be usefully internalized. This happens throughout the life cycle in normal life; in therapy, it is intensified, accelerated and scrutinized. In a sense, if all life is about managing loss, the best we can hope for is to survive these losses in a way from which we learn, and by which we develop. Through the pain of it, something active and creative can be taken in to germinate and grow.

Often, attachment is powerfully sought but strongly feared. This is the struggle between Fairbairn's (1952) libidinal and anti-libidinal egos: the one desperate and needy, and the other angry and rejecting. Not enough stable terrain has developed between them, and the demands of reality almost always meet the emotional responses of anger, shame, humiliation and pain. When this is played out as the ambivalence to attach or not, it is often the very meat of the therapeutic process: can intimacy be tolerated, perhaps even used and enjoyed, or is it just too terrifying? Many never join, or drop out, because the fear of letting others know them – of getting close and relying on them in a way they know must end – is too great.

For those who fall into membership of a therapeutic community like a warm duvet, the natural course of development demands that their intrauterine-like experience soon becomes more complex. Members of any society who stay under the duvet all day will soon start having their responsibilities to themselves and others pointed out. For some, working with this can be the main therapeutic task: facilitating disillusion from the symbiotic fusion fantasy of the early attachment, like growing up and leaving home.

Marked hostility to joining is also common: the destructive urges can operate through a wide range of primitive mental mechanisms, predominantly using denial, splitting, projection and projective identification. They can represent a deeply unconscious need to spoil, steal or envy what is good. Various elements of the community are felt as powerfully good or powerfully bad things, opening up the possibility of vigorous attack as well as the opportunity for comfort. Much work is needed to achieve a realistic expectation of relationships: a source of hope, a cause of frustration, a struggle that is never wholly won or lost.

THE PRACTICALITIES

In a therapeutic programme, this demands great heed be given to joining and leaving. The joining process is all about referral and assessment, and how prospective members of a community are dealt with. The very first contacts with people will have significant impact on how potential members feel about attaching to a community – much of this will be in a complicated interplay with their expectations of what to expect of relationships – and a successful therapeutic community does need to believe in what it is doing and present itself as a place worth belonging to. Being realistic

about difficulties and doubts is necessary, but an early alienating experience in joining a therapeutic community – perhaps complacency or being shrouded in mystery – will trigger persecutory or excluded feelings, and defensive actions.

It is rather paradoxical, but all this 'joining' must be done carefully so that the full impact of leaving – the loss – can be felt. In non-residential therapeutic community programmes in the NHS ('day TCs'), the members get a great deal of practice at endings and abandonment; they have a little every day, quite a big dose every weekend, and occasional full-scale dress rehearsals when they have a holiday, or get suspended, or for the Christmas break. This particular model would be adaptable for using in secure settings, provided that only a portion of the detained population are members of a part-time community, so that potential members could exercise choice about joining. It is also to provide effective sanctions such as suspension and discharge, and a planned ending towards which work is done.

When leaving represents the ending of such an important attachment, the negotiation of it is one of the most crucial parts of the whole process of therapy. An angry or disillusioned leaving is realistic and necessary for some, and does not necessarily indicate failure. Communities often arrange rituals and gifts, but the full sense of sadness and loss needs to be experienced, for it is by being fully aware of the pain of detachment that the intensity and meaning of the attachment before can be understood and 'taken inside'. It is usually clear when the rituals are empty and defensive, and when they are passionate (in whatever way) and heartfelt. Commonly, they involve an intense mixture of anger, desolation, yearning and hope: the end of something very important, but also the beginning of the rest of life starting in a different mental place – with different expectations of relationship and repertoires of behaviour.

When somebody leaves a day TC, the practical side of the process usually begins at their 15-month review, when a leaving date is set, a maximum of 3 months hence. Between then and the end, work is done in all sorts of ways: the attachment has to be internalized to make it safe for them to leave, and leave they must. The whole community usually does that work – it is painful for everybody when somebody ends their therapy in a state of mind in which they were not ready or suitably prepared for leaving. The process is often rocky and difficult, for example with recurrence of original symptoms and destructive relationships within the community. It never looks as neat as this description, close up. Occasionally a member is scapegoated and the community is pleased to see the back of him or her, but when this is processed later, there is often much projected hostility, splitting and guilt that emerges. Angry, unplanned leavings are different again – although communities generally develop systems of possies and deadlines and various communications that seems to make them quite contained and safe.

The last week is often full of special events for the leaver. These include community and small group gifts, having personal choice of activity sessions for the leaver to do what he or she likes with all the community members and staff, and perhaps a special meal for which everybody prepares and brings in dishes of food. 'Goodbye' itself is usually on a Friday afternoon. Although the overall pattern is fixed, members are encouraged to innovate and vary it to suit the way in which they wish to say their goodbyes – perhaps not unlike the different ways in which the bereaved bear their suffering.

Although it is arranged with rituals and gifts – to make it more bearable in some ways (perhaps like a 'good funeral' – whatever that is) – the real sense of sadness and the finality of loss need to be experienced. The staff can tell when somebody has left well: they too will feel that mixture of sadness and optimism, perhaps with the professional part of their mind able to take stock from a slight distance and be objective, although sometimes that ability only seems to come later.

In one model, leavings are managed in an absolute and edge-of-the-cliff sort of way. There is no option whatsoever to extend stay, no opportunity for follow-up, and a (generally) adhered-to guideline of 'no contact with others' for 6 months. There is a Christmas pantomime and a summer trip for all leavers from the last year – but nothing else. The staff have to grit their teeth and suffer it with the members – it would be letting the members down if the importance of negotiating that detachment was watered down in any way, perhaps by offering a bit more of something 'just to make sure they are all right'. Interestingly, one of the older NHS day TCs (Winterbourne in Reading) recently discussed whether it would help to have some sort of follow-up group afterwards, and the verdict, especially amongst the more senior members who were closest to leaving, was that it would be a 'cop-out'. It is a leap of faith and, for the staff, it is one that needs a very solid belief in what is being done in order to be able to contain it for themselves. The belief needs to be backed by evidence (of previous successes) as well as by hope. In contrast, the newer day TCs in the NHS are all planning programmes with 'softer landings' to reintegrate their members into day-to-day life.

Leaving successfully is what has not happened successfully for these people before: leaving has never been managed in such a way as to leave the individual feeling stronger, with a 'good object' inside. The most important task is to take inside, and own, qualities of relationship that make life bearable, possibly meaningful and, it is to be hoped, fulfilling.

REFERENCES

Balint M (1968). *The Basic Fault*. London: Tavistock.

Davies S (1998). Survival and growth in the marketplace: does every district need a TC? In: Haigh R and

Campling P (eds), *Therapeutic Communities, Past, Present and Future.* London: Jessica Kingsley Publishers, 223–34.

Fairbairn WDR (1952). *Psychoanalytic Studies of the Personality.* London: Routledge and Kegan Paul.

Haigh R (1998). The quintessence of a therapeutic environment. In: Haigh R and Campling P (eds), *Therapeutic Communities, Past, Present and Future.* London: Jessica Kingsley Publishers, 246–57.

Holmes J (1993). *John Bowlby and Attachment Theory.* London: Routledge.

Chapter 27

CONFIDENTIALITY

Rob Hale

All that may come to my knowledge in the exercise of my profession or outside of my profession or in daily commerce with men which ought not to be spread abroad, I will keep secret and will never reveal.

Nowhere is Hippocrates' advice more sorely tested than in the treatment of the person with severe personality disorder. The problems centre around the disclosure of information to third parties. Typically, the clinician is made aware by the patient that he or she has committed or intends to commit a serious crime, usually violent or sexual, against another person. The patient is not, in the normal sense of the word, psychotic. He or she is therefore responsible for his or her actions. Why, then, does the patient tell the clinician of his or her intentions? What courses of action are open to the clinician and what are the consequences of such actions? At the centre of these questions lies confidentiality. To whom does the clinician owe allegiance – to the patient or to the potential victim? There are many layers to these problems, with surprisingly few simple answers. A clinical example may help us to explore the area. The events took place some 20 years ago.

Mr K was a middle-aged man with a long history of offences against young girls, which gradually escalated in seriousness. Eventually, after a couple of non-custodial sentences, he was convicted of gross indecency and imprisoned for a year. On release, he was referred for out-patient psychotherapy, an offer he readily accepted. Although apparently compliant, his previous history led the therapist to hold a healthy scepticism as to whether Mr K was continuing to offend during the early months of his treatment. About 18 months into the treatment, he told the therapist that he had moved in with a divorced woman with two young girls. He described the dilemma of standing on the landing and being unsure which bedroom he should enter – the mother's or the children's. This in turn placed the therapist in a dilemma: should he break confidentiality and inform the police or social services, or should he maintain confidentiality and depend on the power of the therapeutic relationship and interpretation to contain a potentially disastrous situation. In the event, he chose the latter course. He interpreted that Mr K was communicating his intentions because he, Mr K, was aware of the damage that would be done to the children and that he was asking the therapist to stop him. The therapist went on to link the current situation to Mr K's own childhood: his father had gone missing at sea during the war; an uncle had led him to believe that if he prayed hard enough his father would return. His father never did return. Mr K felt betrayed and abandoned and in adolescence began to experience (retaliatory) paedophilic impulses. The only time in his life that he was free of these impulses was when he was doing his national service in the Navy.

The therapist interpreted that Mr K was looking for external authority to control his destructive impulses, a control that he had only found for himself when he had donned the uniform of his dead father. Could he not now exert his own authority without external coercion or a containing uniform?

The next week, much to the therapist's relief, Mr K reported that he had moved out of the house and was again living alone. He did not offend again for 13 years.

Many points can be drawn from this story, including Mr K's written permission to publish his clinical material, albeit in a disguised form. The first, and perhaps most important point, is that disclosure of confidential information is at the clinician's discretion – except when required to do so by Act of Parliament (e.g. notification of diseases) or by order of a court. A common misconception is that we are required to disclose by law when we believe one of our patients may be going to commit a serious crime (usually sexual or violent). There is, in fact, no common law obligation to disclose such information, although we are entitled to do so if we so decide. It is the anxiety generated by the responsibility of making such a decision that unwittingly promotes the belief that we have no choice.

The decision to disclose is based on the judgement that the responsibility to protect the public outweighs the duty to the patient to protect his confidentiality. In Mr K's case, the therapist would argue that the longer term objective of protecting many children was better served by maintaining confidentiality, keeping the patient in treatment, and allowing the psychic change of internalizing a super-ego. In the short term, this involved the high-risk strategy of leaving the children at risk (for a week at least) in the hope that the patient would feel himself empowered to take responsibility for his own actions.

Had things turned out differently – had Mr K molested one of the children – the therapist would have faced two forms of censure. He could have been sued in the civil courts by the injured party (the child) for damages for failing to discharge his professional duties, the judgement being based on whether there was a reasonable body of professional (medical) opinion that would have agreed with his actions. This does not imply or require unanimity within the profession. The second form of censure would be that his professional body (the General Medical Council in this case) would, using the same basis for their judgement, consider him guilty of professional misconduct and revoke his certificate of registration to practise.

It is significant that the events described above took place in the early 1980s. It is open to question as to whether the therapist would make the same judgement today – a time of virtual zero tolerance for sexual crimes. The clinician must recognize changing social values and pressures.

The fundamental psychopathology of the patient and his current state of mind will be used by the clinician in reaching a judgement as to whether the patient can or might act responsibly. So, too, the nature of the relationship (i.e. the state of the transference) between the therapist and the patient will be equally important.

In this case, the nature of the patient's personality disorder, though enduring and anti-social, was to an extent predictable. He was not in the throes of a depressive episode, which might have projected him into further acting-out, and his relationship with the therapist, although containing within it elements of duplicity, had the external skeleton of regular voluntary attendance. It is easy to imagine a scenario in which all these factors would have gone the other way and loaded the scales more clearly in the direction of disclosure.

Notwithstanding, there were many clinicians at the time the events occurred who would have disclosed, and even more now. The therapist did not follow one piece of current guidance, in that he did not discuss his decision with a colleague. He did, however, record his decision and the reasoning behind it. Whilst working within an organization, he was solely responsible for clinical decisions.

Had he been working within a multidisciplinary team, there might have been those from other professions whose code of conduct or terms of employment prevented them from signing up to such a decision – they would have been forced to disclose.

The context in which the clinician is working is obviously relevant; for example, when preparing a court report, one has a duty to the court, and thus to the public, as well as to the patient. Most clinicians warn patients of this dual responsibility – with the consequence that the patients may conceal the more crucial part of their history or their innermost fantasy, each of which may crucially inform the assessment of their future dangerousness.

The suggestion has been made that different professions – and, indeed, different divisions of a profession – should operate different thresholds for the disclosure of information, thus defining the role of each profession in relation to the patient. It is instructive that lawyers are required to maintain absolute confidentiality to their clients: it has been argued that we have a *public* responsibility to protect the patient's *individual* right to confidentiality. In the UK, the clinician must make a considered decision to infringe that right to confidentiality: statute law (e.g. notification of diseases) determines when the clinician *must* infringe that right, and case law when the clinician *may* do so. This is clearly enunciated in the guidelines on confidentiality of the General Medical Council and those of The Royal College of Psychiatrists. In other countries, particularly certain states of the USA, clinicians are statutorily required to disclose whenever there is a danger to a third party. The result is that the clinician is now dubbed 'the new informant for the state'. Difficult and painful as it is to achieve a balance between our duty to the patient and our duty to the public, we must surely seek to maintain that balance if we are to continue to enjoy the confidence of the vast majority of our patients.

So far the comments in this chapter apply to those who are at liberty in the community – perhaps real psychic change can only take place when the patient is free to act and the therapist is free to treat. However, much of this book concerns itself with those who are detained in institutions; here the parameters are very different. The general assumption is that knowledge revealed to one staff member will be shared with all other members of the clinical team. Coming from different professions, the staff will have different thresholds for disclosure from those of outside agencies and the threshold for the whole team will be that of the profession under the greatest pressure to disclose. In a sense, it is the lowest common denominator that prevails. Although the ultimate responsibility lies with the responsible medical officer, the professions of nursing, psychology, social work and psychiatry do not have any agreement, and it is therefore left to local negotiation and 'arm wrestling'. This is unsatisfactory both for the professionals and also because the patients often assume a greater sense of confidentiality than actually exists.

Although disclosure is for the most part currently covered in the UK by common law, there is a permanent pressure from the Government to reduce the professional's scope for judgement and to require them under Statute Law to disclose, particularly when the patient is detained. The clinician will have to inform the patient of such statutory obligations with the result that the patient will say nothing and the professional will not ask. It is a serious development, which leads the mental health professional further into becoming an agent of social control.

Chapter 28

PERSONALITY DISORDER, THE LAW AND INDIVIDUAL RIGHTS

Anselm Eldergill

INTRODUCTION

For some years the Home Office and the Department of Health have been considering the introduction of new laws aimed at protecting the public from individuals who have a 'dangerous and severe personality disorder' (DSPD). In July 1999, the two departments published a consultation document, setting out proposals intended to ensure 'that DSPD people are kept in detention for as long as they pose a high risk. The approach the Government has developed … involves the idea of detention based on the serious risk such people present to the public' (Home Office and Department of Health, 1999).

Option B, which the Government favoured, involved a new power of indefinite detention in criminal and civil proceedings. Following a 'DSPD direction', individuals would be detained in a specialist facility until they no longer presented a serious risk. At that point they would be released into the community, subject to supervision and recall. Those requiring detention would be kept in facilities run separately from prison and health services, in adult secure accommodation of the kind presently provided for some behaviourally disturbed children ('third units').

The Government was therefore advocating that, in addition to mental disorder and

criminal acts, risk alone may also justify detention. This is a quarantine argument, one which holds that, subject to problems of identification, the civil detention of dangerous people is justified even if they have not committed a violent offence.

The contrary argument is that the civil detention of dangerous non-offenders is never warranted, because it is a fundamental principle that citizens who obey our laws have a right to be at liberty. To imprison a person who has not yet committed the offence one fears is the criminal justice system of Alice's Wonderland: '"No, no!" said the Queen. "Sentence first – verdict afterwards".'

In the event, the 1999 proposals did not result in any 'third-unit' legislation, probably because it was realized that indefinitely detaining non-offenders in civilian accommodation risks infringing the European Convention on Human Rights. Article 5 of the Convention permits the detention of convicted persons and those of unsound mind in appropriate facilities (prisons and hospitals, respectively), but it does not in clear terms permit the detention of citizens who have not offended, merely because there is a risk they will do so in future. Detention in secure non-hospital accommodation rather rules out pleading mental disorder and a need for treatment as the justification, and nor can punishment or lawful sentence be pleaded, because the individuals are not serving a term of imprisonment.

Having seemingly abandoned the third-unit approach, the two departments published a White Paper in December 2000 (Department of Health and Home Office, 2000), setting out in general terms their proposals for reforming the existing Mental Health Act 1983 ('the 1983 Act').

Part II of the White Paper was exclusively concerned with high-risk patients, including more than 2000 'dangerous people with severe personality disorder'. The legal framework was, however, the same as that described for all patients in Part I, with emphasis being placed on the following powers: the removal of existing legal prohibitions that prevent certain kinds of behaviour from being classified as forms of mental disorder (dependence on alcohol or drugs, sexual deviancy, promiscuity, immoral conduct); the power of the police, probation and prison services to require a preliminary examination of persons thought to be at risk or a risk to others; the abolition of treatability as a statutory condition of compulsion; and the introduction of orders allowing for compulsory care and treatment in the community.

According to the White Paper, the new civil powers outlined in Part I would 'provide for the detention of dangerous people with severe personality disorder in a therapeutic environment for as long as they pose a risk ...'.

The White Paper was followed by a draft Mental Health Bill on 26 June 2002 (Department of Health, 2002). The Bill was widely condemned as unprincipled and impractical by professional bodies, carers and patients' groups. Consequently, a number of amendments were made, and a revised draft Bill was published in September 2004 (Department of Health, 2004). This revised Bill includes a number of provisions directed at managing people who are considered to have abnormal personalities and/or whose conduct is antisocial.

In contrast to the present Act, the Bill does not provide that a person may not be dealt with as mentally disordered by reason *only* of promiscuity, immoral conduct, sexual deviancy or dependence on alcohol or drugs. Thus, one is entitled to assume that the Government intends that it will be lawful compulsorily to treat individuals on the sole ground that their behaviour is of such a kind.

The term 'medical treatment' is defined so that it includes education, work training, and training in social skills, which need not be provided under medical supervision. Consequently, a person who is drug dependent, or whose behaviour is habitually antisocial and alarming, may be said to have a mental disorder that warrants providing medical treatment, in the form of work or social skills training under psychological supervision.

What constitutes 'a hospital' is also broadly defined. A private establishment, such as a converted house, is a hospital if its main purpose is to provide 'medical treatment' for 'mental disorder' to people subject to the legislation.

It can be seen that defining antisocial people as mentally disordered, supervised social interventions as medical treatments, and establishments that detain such people or provide social services as hospitals enables detention in adult secure accommodation to be dressed up for Convention purposes as hospital medical treatment for persons of unsound mind.

The 'third-unit' approach has not been abandoned at all. All that has happened is that the 1999 proposals have been translated into medical language. The Government has simply retreated to the justification that such people are mentally disordered; they require detention and treatment in 'hospital' or supervised 'medical treatment' in the community.

THE ISSUES

The Government's approach raises important issues about how society should respond to violence, 'sexual deviancy', substance abuse and other forms of antisocial behaviour.

Previous schemes of preventive detention have ended in failure, and the dilemma facing the Government is how to identify and contain dangerous individuals without endangering civil liberties.

The question 'What should the law do about this state of affairs?' may more precisely be formulated as 'What should *we*, through our parliament, do about it?'

The central questions are as follows.

- What are the purpose and limitations of legislation in this area?
- Are those persons categorized as having a 'personality disorder' mentally disordered? (If not, they have no place in a hospital, and there can be no justification for imposing compulsory medical treatment.)
- If a 'personality disorder' is a form of mental disorder, in what circumstances should the law allow detention and treatment under mental health legislation?

PURPOSE AND LIMITATIONS OF LEGISLATION

One can legislate for marriage but not for a happy marriage. Legislation is a relatively ineffective means of modifying behaviour and, although it can provide a framework for managing violence associated with mental disorder, it cannot significantly reduce the risks. That this is so is clear from recent homicide inquiry reports. Had the professional carers in these cases foreseen what was about to happen, they had power under the 1983 Act to intervene. That they did not was due, not to any lack of legal powers, but to the fact that they did not foresee what was about to happen. Yet no amount of new legislation can improve foresight. Nor, for example, can it improve insight, for 'he that complies against his will, is of his own opinion still' (Butler, 1663).

Related to this issue is the extent to which legislation and departmental directives modify medical practice and outcomes. Legislation has a standard form, and is drafted in accordance with certain conventions, so that the distinction here is analogous to that made in psychiatry between the form and content of a person's thoughts. Implicit within any discussion about the need for new laws is the assumption that modifying their content modifies medical practice and outcomes. However, the extent to which this is true has not been demonstrated.

Furthermore, even if people can be better protected from the actions of those who suffer from mental disorder or behave antisocially, this may not be a fault of our laws. It may be due to insufficient resources, poor government, poor service management, poor risk management, faulty practice, a faulty understanding of the law, or simply part of the human condition. In other words, a problem or limitation that is to a significant extent replicated across a world full of different criminal and mental health laws.

The key to progress may lie with improving government, resources, diagnostic tools, treatments and training, and, most fundamentally of all, with education.

I believe that education is the fundamental method of social progress and reform. All reforms which rest simply upon the law, or the threatening of certain penalties, or upon changes in mechanical or outward arrangements, are transitory and futile. ... But through education society can formulate its own purposes, can organize its own means and resources, and thus shape itself with definiteness and economy in the direction in which it wishes to move. ... Education thus conceived marks the most perfect and intimate union of science and art conceivable in human experience.

(Dewey, 1897, p. 234)

RISK MANAGEMENT AND LEGISLATION

These observations lead to a supplementary point, which is the need to encourage people to be realistic about risks and their management.

It is impossible for mental health services to be totally safe. Governments should be aware of the natural limits of practice before they categorize particular practices as unsatisfactory and unsafe and in need of a legislative remedy. Some of these natural limits are as follows.

- Risk cannot be avoided, and even a very low risk from time to time becomes an actuality. However careful the assessment, it is inevitable that some patients will later take their own lives or commit a serious offence.
- Any decision to detain an individual, or to compel them to have treatment, involves balancing competing risks, of which the risk that others may suffer physical harm is but one. For example, detention and compulsory treatment risk loss of employment, family contact, self-esteem and dignity, unnecessary or unjustified deprivation of liberty, institutionalization and disabling side effects.
- The purpose of compulsory powers is not to eliminate that element of risk in human life that is a consequence of being free to act, and to make choices and decisions; it is to protect the individual and others from risks that arise when a person's judgement of risk, or capacity to control behaviour associated with serious risk, is significantly impaired by mental disorder.
- Good practice relies on good morale and a feeling amongst practitioners that they will be supported if they act reasonably; it is unjust to criticize them when decisions properly made have unfortunate, even catastrophic, consequences.
- The occurrence of such tragedies does not per se demonstrate any error of judgement on the part of those who decided that allowing the patient his or her liberty did not involve unacceptable risks.
- An outcome is often the result of a complex series of events, and the choice of one particular causal factor may be arbitrary.

- Small differences in one key variable can result in vastly different behaviours and outcomes: just as a sudden change in the physical state of water into steam or ice occurs with the rise or fall of temperature beyond a critical level, so the addition of a small additional stress on an individual may have a profound effect on his or her mental state or behaviour.
- All violence takes place in the present, and the past is a past, and so unreliable, guide to present and future events.
- Understanding the situations in which a person has previously been dangerous, and avoiding their repetition, can give a false sense of security about the future. Although life is understood backwards, it must be lived forwards, and the difference between explanation and prediction is significant: explanation relies on hindsight, prediction on foresight, and the prediction of future risk involves more than an explanation of the past.
- Unless the individual's propensity for violence has a simple and readily understandable trigger, it is impossible to identify all of the relevant situations; some of them lie in the future, and will not yet have been encountered by the patient.
- Predictions are most often founded not on fact but on 'retrospective predictions' of what occurred in the past ('retrodiction').
- A risk can, in theory, be measured and is the basis of actuarial prediction – in theory because in practice all of the critical variables are never known. The risk depends on the situation, but the situations in which patients may find themselves in the future can only be speculated upon.
- Because future events can never be predicted, it is important to put in place an adequate system for supervising an individual whose own safety may potentially be at risk or who may pose a threat to the safety of others. However, this approach is not fail-safe: it is based on the

assumption that most attacks do not erupt like thunderstorms from clear skies. In reality, as with weather systems, only the pattern of events for the next 24 hours can usually be forecast with some accuracy, and contact with supervisors is less regular.

- All human beings, regardless of their skills, abilities and specialist knowledge, make fallible decisions and commit unsafe acts, and this human propensity for committing errors and violating safety procedures can be moderated but never entirely eliminated.

PRINCIPLES OF MENTAL HEALTH LEGISLATION

A pragmatic approach to law making involves considering whether the government's solution violates other important convictions. Does it show adequate regard for those principles that have been demonstrated to have value? Even if there is benefit in the proposals, what is the cost?

Some of the most important principles concerning the formulation of mental health laws may be stated here.

- There are many reasons to limit state intervention in people's lives: errors in law spread their negative effects throughout the nation, as opposed to individual errors that are limited in scope; the damage of erroneous laws affects citizens more than legislators, who are thus less inclined to repeal them; it takes longer to repair the damage done by legislation than the damage done by individuals as a result of their own private choices; because of the constant watch of critics, politicians are less inclined to admit error publicly and undo the damage done; politicians are more inclined than citizens to make decisions based on political gain and prejudice, rather than principle (Constant, 1988).
- The British constitution separates powers, the aim being to keep executive powers in check and under proper scrutiny, and so to secure good government. This is necessary because the 'whole art of government consists in the art of being honest' (Jefferson, 1774), and 'it is not by the consolidation, or concentration of powers, but by their distribution, that good government is effected' (Jefferson, 1821).
- Promoting liberty, protecting individuals from harm caused by those at liberty, and those not at liberty from abuse by those who are, alleviating suffering, and restoring to health those whose health has declined are all legitimate objectives, in that they reflect values embraced by virtually all members of our society (Eldergill, 1997).
- We are, however, 'faced with choices between ends equally ultimate, and claims equally absolute, the realisation of some of which must inevitably involve the sacrifice of others' (Berlin, 1969). Whether individuals 'should be allowed certain liberties at all depends on the priority given by society to different values, and the crucial point is the criterion by which it is decided that a particular liberty should or should not be allowed, or that its exercise is in need of restraint' (Dias, 1985).
- When enacting mental health legislation, Parliament has generally sought to erect a balanced legal structure that harmonizes three things: individual liberty, bringing treatment to bear where treatment is necessary and can be beneficial, and the protection of the public (Hansard).
- Those we describe as 'patients' are themselves members of the public, so that the law must seek to ensure that members of the public are not unnecessarily detained, and also that they are protected from those who must necessarily be detained.
- The use of compulsion has been permitted when significant harm is foreseeable if an individual remains at liberty. Its purpose is to protect the individual or others from

those risks that arise when a person's capacity to judge risks, or to control the behaviour that gives rise to them, is impaired by mental disorder.

- Other risks are, constitutionally, matters for citizens to weigh in their own minds. The purpose of compulsion is not to eliminate that element of risk in human life that is simply part of being free to act and to make choices and decisions. A person who obeys our laws is entitled to place a high premium on their liberty, even to value it more highly than their health. Subject to the stated limits, people are entitled to make what others regard as errors of judgement, and to behave in a manner that a doctor regards as not in their best interests, in the sense that it does not best promote health.

- This desire to determine one's own interests is common to human beings, and so not to be portrayed as an abuse of liberty. On the one side stands liberty, a right that Parliament and the law should always favour and guard; on the other licence, a wilful use of liberty to contravene the law, which the law must, of necessity, always punish.

- Any power given to one person over another is capable of being abused. No legislative body should be deluded by the integrity of their own purposes, and conclude that unlimited powers will never be abused because they themselves are not disposed to abuse them (Jefferson, 1782). Mankind soon learns to make interested uses of every right and power which they possess or may assume (*ibid*).

- This risk of abuse is multiplied if the individual is not free to escape abuse, is incapacitated or otherwise vulnerable, or his or her word is not given the same weight as that of others. Children and adults with mental health problems are particularly at risk, and the law has usually afforded them special protection.

- This protection involves imposing legal duties on those with power, conferring legal rights on those in their power, and independent scrutiny of how these powers and duties are exercised. The effectiveness of such schemes depends on whether, and to what extent, they are observed.

- This is a matter of constitutional importance, for the observance of legal rights and the rule of law are the cornerstones of all liberal democracies. The rule of law 'implies the subordination of all authorities, legislative, executive [and] judicial ... to certain principles which would generally be accepted as characteristic of law, such as the ideas of the fundamental principles of justice, moral principles, fairness and due process. It implies respect for the supreme value and dignity of the individual' (Walker, 1980).

- In any legal system, 'it implies limitations on legislative power, safeguards against abuse of executive power, adequate and equal opportunities of access to legal advice and assistance, ... proper protection of the individual and group rights and liberties, and equality before the law ... It means more than that the government maintains and enforces law and order, but that the government is, itself, subject to rules of law and cannot itself disregard the law or remake it to suit itself' (*ibid*).

- In framing these principles and laws, Parliament has sought to be just, justice being 'a firm and continuous desire to render to everyone that which is his due' (Justinian).

- If new laws are necessary, they should impose minimum powers, duties and rights; provide mechanisms for enforcing duties and remedies for abuse of powers; be unambiguous, just, in plain English, and as short as possible.

- Because there is a long record of experimentation in human conduct, cumulative verifications give these principles a well-earned prestige. Lightly to disregard them is the height of foolishness (Dewey, 1922).

When we contemplate extending the powers that people in authority may exercise over their fellow citizens, it is therefore prudent to realize that legislation is a relatively ineffective means of modifying behaviour, that risk cannot be avoided, that people and governments must be realistic about risks and their management, and that the rule of law and autonomy are fundamental to the liberty that we all enjoy.

One should also be suitably cautious about pleas to increase public powers of coercion that are based on expediency or necessity. As Lord Chief Justice Lane once put it, 'Loss of freedom seldom happens overnight. Oppression doesn't stand on the doorstep with toothbrush moustache and swastika armband – it creeps up insidiously … step by step, and all of a sudden the unfortunate citizen realizes that it is gone'.

ARE 'PSYCHOPATHS' MENTALLY DISORDERED?

Much of the recent debate surrounding 'DSPD' has centred on whether the National Health Service (NHS) and other agencies are resourced to provide such an extensive service. However, this assumes that such people may properly be detained on the basis that their conduct is evidence of a medical condition that requires medical intervention.

The constitutional purpose of defining 'mental disorder', and dividing disorders into different classes, is to define, as far as practicable, the group of citizens to whom the statute applies, and the circumstances in which resort may be made to compulsory powers.

More generally, it is necessary to define or describe who within a population is mentally disordered before it is possible to estimate the level of violence for which they are collectively responsible.

If people with antisocial or psychopathic personalities are categorized as being mentally disordered, it is necessarily true that other people are relatively more at risk from the mentally disordered than if they are excluded. Furthermore, if our definition of a psychopathic disorder requires abnormally aggressive or seriously irresponsible conduct, as it does under the 1983 Act, it is inevitable that people within the definition will often have been violent. Such a concept is bound to produce such a statistical finding, the whole aim being to detain those who, though not mentally ill, put others at significant risk. Conversely, if such people are excluded, the level of violence committed by what may be called the antisocial element in society will be that much greater, and the contribution of the mentally disordered that much less.

The definition of mental disorder in the 1983 Act includes people categorized as having a psychopathic disorder, but does not include people by reason only of promiscuity, immoral conduct, sexual deviancy or dependence on alcohol or drugs. It is clear, however, from the draft Bill, that the Government considers that such persons have a mental disorder. By implication, it counts them as part of the group of mentally disordered persons who commit violence, violence from which the public are inadequately protected.

This all-inclusive approach seems to us to be artificial and unjustified. What is the evidence that suggests that people said to be psychopaths have a disease or disorder that requires medical attention?

Kurt Schneider defined personality as 'the unique quality of the individual, his feelings and personal goals; the sum of his traits, habits and experiences and the whole system of relatively permanent tendencies, physical and mental, which are distinctive of a given individual' (Schneider, 1958). In short, personality is what makes one individual different from another: the whole system of relatively permanent abilities and tendencies distinctive of a given individual's brain. It is who I am.

This observation immediately gives rise to two important questions. Are people said to have disordered personalities injured, ill or diseased? Is the human personality a proper subject for medicine?

Although limited development of the human personality may be caused by an innate structural defect, such as mental retardation, this is rare. No one has demonstrated any injury or disease that accounts for the characteristics of those with highly dissocial personalities (or the characteristics of their counterparts: empathic, law-abiding citizens).

Although this is also the case with schizophrenia, there are important differences. Schizophrenia is a process that, without intervention, develops and interferes with the body in certain characteristic ways. It results in a marked deterioration in the individual's level of mental functioning, and this implies significant corresponding structural or physiological changes.

If the brains of people classed as psychopaths are not diseased, are they, therefore, normal? That depends upon how one defines what is normal. The mental state and behaviour of an individual said to have a personality disorder are abnormal, in the sense that they deviate from the social norm, but normal in relation to that person's own individual norm: that is, it is consistent with what is known about the person's development and functioning over time. Here, then, the individual is only abnormal by reference to a social norm, and such a deviation cannot be said to constitute a disease, because mere social deviation is not evidence of biological disorder. This requires evidence of injury or deviation from the individual norm. If there is no evidence of either, then one is simply confusing individuality with ill-health: treating as biologically abnormal an undiseased, uninjured creature living its natural life, so that medicines are pesticides.

The evidence suggests that present medical interventions have, like liberal prison regimes, the reformation of the individual as their aim. This is unacceptable, because the proper function of medical science and practice is to treat individual suffering attributable to disease or injury, not to alleviate the suffering of society, and, in the field of mental health, to treat those diseases or injuries that interfere with the development or expression of an individual's personality, not to reform his or her personality by reference to some social or political norm.

The motivation for this social control is transparent. People want to live in a cultivated society, and they cultivate society in much the same way they cultivate nature in their gardens. This involves eradicating disease in the garden, but also weeding it and controlling pests – that is, containing or destroying organisms that are doing nothing more than expressing their natures. There is nothing unique in this, for the same power is claimed over animals and unborn life, and most other things that interfere with personal survival or fulfilment. But it is why CS Lewis (1953) wrote that:

To be cured against one's will and cured of states which we may not regard as disease is to be put on a level with those who have not yet reached the age of reason or those who never will; to be classed with infants, imbeciles and domestic animals. But to be punished … because we have deserved it … is to be treated as a human person made in God's image.

Although today many people would not understand the issue in religious terms, the argument retains its inner strength: there is more human dignity in punishment than in medicalizing antisocial or violent behaviour. According to Conrad (1981), the conditions for the medicalization of deviance are that: (1) a behaviour or set of behaviours must be defined as deviant and as a problem in need of remedy by some segment of society; (2) previous or traditional forms of social control must be seen as inefficient or unacceptable, e.g. corporal punishment or penal servitude; (3) some medical form of social control must be available; (4) ambiguous organic data as to the source of the problem must exist; and (5) the medical profession must be willing to accept the deviant behaviour as within its jurisdiction.

This is an uncomfortable message for an age that is uncomfortable with the notion of punishment, the more so when the debate involves issues of responsibility and free will, and the extent to which some people's personalities do not enable them to refrain from antisocial behaviour. However, our conscious thinking and deciding are embodied in the workings of our brains, and consequently our behaviour is determined by our thinking and choosing. While determinism provides an explanation for our choices and actions, it is human beings, not deterministic rules, that cause events. The fact that an individual's personality, as determined by his or her genes and previous experiences, dictates the choice he or she makes does not mean that that person has not chosen between alternatives. Furthermore, whilst not everyone has the same capacity to eschew the wrong, this does not preclude us from judging their actions, because whether an action is harmful is not affected by its antecedents. In short, our conscious decisions and actions are matters of personal choice: each chooses what suits their personality, not that of others, and must be accountable to others for their choice. The counterpart of freedom and autonomy is accountability for acts freely and autonomously done.

Therefore the view presented here is that those people presently categorized as psychopaths are not mentally disordered, and they should be excluded from mental health legislation. We are simply medicalizing 'deviant behaviour'.

Believing this, there is no inhumanity in holding that they should be imprisoned if their offence and forensic history merit it. If we are satisfied that our prison system is the best that can be devised for the prevention of crime, and the reformation of the criminal, then we may rest satisfied that it is the best

treatment for the sort of insanity from which criminals suffer. If, on the other hand, we are not satisfied that prisons are reformative, then why this is so needs to be the principal focus of our attention (Maudsley, 1885).

What cannot be justified are mental health or social protection laws that permit the preventive detention of law-abiding citizens who are free of injury or disease. It would be unjust to detain them for crimes they have not committed and are actuarially unlikely to commit. It would be immoral, because the old maxim that 'you shall not do evil that good may come' is applicable in law as well as in morals. It would be inutile, because any impact on the rates at which serious offences are committed is likely to be marginal. There is little gain in detaining a handful of notionally dangerous civilians each year when guilt in criminal proceedings must be proved beyond all reasonable doubt, because every year we release without penalty thousands of rapists and other violent offenders. Lastly, it would be unwise, for when the public perceives that they are no safer despite such a reform, rather than realize and learn from their folly, they will demand that basic freedoms be further curtailed and the penalties made more severe.

Such demands misunderstand the functions of the law and its natural limits. It is not within the power of the law, given the venality of the times, to cleanse the Augean stable. As Montesquieu (1989) observed, in 'moderate governments, the love of one's country, shame, and the fear of blame are restraining motives, capable of preventing a multitude of crimes. Here, the greatest punishment of a bad action is conviction. ... In those states a good legislator is ... more attentive to inspire good morals than to inflict penalties'.

Only those who know the cost but not the value of our freedoms would embark upon such a journey. Nothing that has great value is without cost, and the value of anything is what one is prepared to sacrifice for it. The value attached to trial by one's peers is the financial cost of the jury system; the value of justice is demonstrated by a willingness to see the guilty go free rather than risk convicting the innocent; and the value of liberty is demonstrated by stoically bearing the many evils that liberty permits. If the defence of these freedoms was worth the sacrifice of millions during two wars, then, unless society has become wholly degraded, it must withstand the death of a few during peacetime. Such a scheme has no utility that can justify its innate immorality and the infliction of such great injustice, and it would be highly imprudent to interfere with public liberties in the name of public safety when the necessity of such a scheme has not been firmly established (Eldergill, 1999).

SHOULD PSYCHOPATHS BE DETAINED IN HOSPITAL?

If this argument is ever accepted by Parliament, it will be necessary to confer on courts alternative powers to deal with violent or sexual offenders and, in particular, that group of people for whom hospitalization will no longer be an option.

Paradoxically, the problem may best be dealt with in a manner similar to that already used in the criminal courts to try issues of insanity and unfitness to plead. The procedure would be as follows. If an offender who is not mentally ill or impaired is convicted before the Crown Court of a sexual or violent offence and, in order to protect the public from serious harm, he or she is imprisoned for a term that exceeds that commensurate with the offence, the court may empanel a jury to determine the following issue: whether they are satisfied beyond all reasonable doubt that the defendant is a person who, if released at the end of the sentence, will commit a further sexual or violent offence. If the jury are satisfied, the court shall also make a secure accommodation order, directing that the offender be detained in civilian accommodation after his or her sentence expires, until the Home Secretary or the Lifer's Panel is satisfied that the safety of others no longer requires this.

Under such a scheme, therefore, a person will be liable to indefinite detention if it is established beyond all reasonable doubt that he or she has committed a violent or sexual offence, a judge imposes an extended term of imprisonment, and a jury is satisfied beyond all reasonable doubt that the person will commit a further offence of a similar kind if released at the expiration of the sentence. Those who observe society's laws may reasonably expect to be protected from such people, as indeed they generally are at present. If the lesser of the two evils is always to be chosen, this seems to be the lesser of them and a reasonable balance of the different legitimate interests.

REFERENCES

Berlin I, Sir (1969). *Four Essays on Liberty*. Oxford: Oxford University Press.

Butler, Hudibras (1663), Part 3, Canto 3.

Conrad P (1981). On the medicalization of deviance and social control. In: Ingleby D (ed.), *Critical Psychiatry: The Politics of Mental Health*. Harmondsworth: Penguin, 111–18.

Constant B (1988). *Benjamin Constant: Political Writings*. (Translated and edited by Biancamaria Fontana.) Cambridge: Cambridge University Press.

Department of Health (2002). Draft Mental Health Bill, Cm 5538–I. London: Department of Health.

Department of Health (2004). Draft Mental Health Bill, Cm 6305–I. London: Department of Health.

Department of Health and Home Office (2000). *Reforming the Mental Health Act*. Part I: *The New Legal Framework*, Cm 5016–I; Part II: *High-risk Patients*, Cm 5016–II. London: Department of Health.

Dewey J (1897/1998). My pedagogic creed. In: Hickman L and Alexander TM (eds), *The Essential Dewey*, Vol. 1. Bloomington/Indianapolis, IN: Indiana University Press.

Dewey J (1922). *Human Nature and Conduct*. London: Allen & Unwin.

Dias RWM (1985). *Jurisprudence*, fifth edition. London: Butterworth, 109.

Eldergill AC (1997). *Mental Health Review Tribunals – Law and Practice.* London: Sweet and Maxwell.

Eldergill A (1999). Psychopathy, the law and individual rights. *Princeton University Law Journal* **III**(2):1–30. Reproduced in Eldergill A (1999). A greater evil. *The Guardian*, 20 July.

Hansard, H.C. Vol. 605, col. 276.

Home Office and Department of Health (1999). *Managing Dangerous People with Severe Personality Disorder: Proposals for Policy Development.* London: Home Office.

Jefferson T (1782). *Notes on Virginia Q.XIII, 1782. Memorial Edition* (supra), 2:164.

Jefferson T (1774). Rights of British America. In: Lipscomb AA and Bergh AE (eds), *The Writings of Thomas Jefferson*, memorial edition. Washington, DC, 1903–4.

Jefferson T (1821). Autobiography. In: Lipscomb AA and Bergh AE (eds), *The Writings of Thomas Jefferson*, memorial edition. Washington, DC, 1903–4.

Justinian, Inst., 1, 1.

Lewis CS (1953). The humanitarian theory of punishment. *University of Melbourne Law Review* 228.

Maudsley H (1885). *Responsibility in Mental Disease*, fourth edition. London: Kegan Paul, Trench & Co., 27.

Montesquieu, Baron de (1989). *The Spirit of the Laws.* Cambridge: Cambridge University Press.

Mill JS (1962). *On Liberty.* London: Wm Collins Sons and Co. Ltd.

Schneider K (1958). *Clinical Psychopathology*, fifth edition, translated by Hamilton MW. New York: Grune & Stratton.

Walker DM (1980). *The Oxford Companion to Law.* Oxford: Clarendon Press, 1093.

Part 5

MEASURING TREATMENT EFFECTIVENESS

Chapter 29

RESEARCH TOOLS

Ronald Blackburn

INTRODUCTION

The primary goal in treating personality disordered offenders is to reduce their propensity for serious antisocial behaviour, but attainment of this goal is assumed to depend on changes in the abnormal personality characteristics of which this behaviour is a function. In treatment outcome research in this area, personality measurement serves two purposes. The first is as an independent variable, such as diagnostic category, that identifies individuals who will be subject to the treatment of interest. The second is as dependent or outcome variables that reflect the dispositions to be changed through treatment.

Investigations of personality disorders in a treatment context have so far focused on their role in predicting the outcome of treatments for common clinical syndromes such as depression (Reich and Green, 1991), and there is a continuing dearth of studies dealing with the treatment of these disorders themselves (Benjamin, 1997). Similarly, personality status has often been an independent variable in treatment research with psychologically disturbed offenders, but recidivism is the most frequently used outcome criterion (Dolan and Coid, 1993; Blackburn, 2000). There is therefore little in the way of established custom and practice to guide the selection of measures for evaluating treatment efficacy in this area. This chapter emphasizes recently developed clinical instruments that may assist treatment researchers in the selection of participants, the prediction of treatment outcome, or the monitoring and assessment of personality change.

DIAGNOSTIC INSTRUMENTS

Despite explicit criteria for each of the personality disorders, research indicates that unstructured clinical interviews are not very reliable in terms of diagnostic agreement between clinicians. To ensure diagnostic reliability, structured measures involving standardized presentation and scoring are essential, and a wide range of semi-structured interviews and self-report questionnaires is now available (for detailed reviews, see Widiger and Frances, 1987; Reich, 1989; Perry, 1992; Zimmerman, 1994; Tyrer, 2000; Clark and Harrison, 2001).

SEMI-STRUCTURED INTERVIEWS

Semi-structured interviews provide a uniform assessment by eliciting personality disorder criteria through standard questions for which scoring guidelines are provided. The interviewer can ask additional questions for clarification and probe for examples. Several schedules have been developed to diagnose the personality disorder categories of the *Diagnostic and Statistical Manual of Mental Disorders* (DSM; American Psychiatric Association, 1980), the most widely investigated being the Structured

Clinical Interview for DSM-III, Axis II (SCID-II; Spitzer et al., 1987), the Structured Interview for DSM-III Personality Disorders (SIDP; Stangl et al., 1985), the Diagnostic Interview for Personality Disorders (DIPD; Zanarini et al., 1987), the International Personality Disorder Examination (IPDE; Loranger et al., 1994), and the Personality Disorder Interview-IV (PDI-IV; Widiger et al., 1995). Interviews developed to assess DSM-III personality disorders have been updated to accommodate DSM-IV (American Psychiatric Association, 1994).

The Standardised Assessment of Personality (SAP; Mann et al., 1981) provides diagnoses of personality disorder categories specified in the *International Classification of Diseases* (ICD; World Health Organization, 1979) and two speculative categories (anxious and self-conscious) based on a brief interview with an informant, and there is also an ICD-10 (World Health Organization, 1992) version of IPDE. The Personality Assessment Schedule (PAS; Tyrer, 2000) differs from other interviews in rating the social impairment associated with 24 traits drawn mainly from earlier editions of ICD, but yields ICD-10 diagnoses. The PAS can be used with either the subject or an informant, or both.

Although not producing a DSM diagnosis, the Psychopathy Checklist–Revised (PCL-R; Hare, 1996, 2003) is particularly relevant to personality disordered offenders. Psychopathic personality has traditionally been considered the major abnormality in this group, and the categories of antisocial personality disorder (APD) in the DSM and dissocial personality disorder in ICD-10 represent this construct. However, the criteria for APD fail to reflect traditional criteria of psychopathy, such as callousness or egocentricity, and research indicates the superiority of the PCL-R in predicting socially deviant behaviour. The PCL-R is now also included in several risk assessment instruments. It is scored from a semi-structured interview and a review of case notes, and divides into two oblique factors. The first measures a callous and remorseless style of relating to others, and the second measures a socially deviant lifestyle more closely related to APD. The PCL-R predicts poorer response to some forms of treatment (Hare, 2003), and there is a strong case for including this measure in any clinical research with offenders.

Interview schedules vary in structure and procedure (Zimmermann, 1994). For example, the SCID-II and DIPD organize questions by diagnostic category, whereas the SIDP and IPDE are organized by behavioural topic or theme. The former is closer to the usual psychiatric interview, but may lead to 'halo' effects whereby the subject's responses tend towards those expected. There are also variations in the matching of questions to DSM criteria, scoring methods, and the timeframe for determining presence or absence of criteria (e.g. last 5 years). A practical consideration is the training required for administration. All interviews assume prior experience in clinical interviewing, and formal training in the specific schedule is not only desirable, but also often mandatory (e.g. for the IPDE, PCL-R).

A further consideration is the duration of administration. The SAP and PAS are relatively brief, but these instruments provide less comprehensive coverage of abnormal traits than DSM-based interviews. The latter generally take from 1 to 3 hours. The time required may seem prohibitive, but a personality disorder interview needs to cover detailed features of a person's life.

Acceptable inter-rater reliabilities have been reported for all interview schedules. This does not guarantee freedom from biases when they are used by individual clinicians, and inter-rater reliabilities should always be obtained in research. There is, however, little evidence on comparative validity, and studies of concurrent validity reveal that interviews produce only moderate diagnostic agreement with other interviews (Perry, 1992; Zimmerman, 1994). Practical considerations apart, there is little to permit a choice between the available schedules.

SELF-REPORT QUESTIONNAIRES

Of several self-report questionnaires that aim to diagnose DSM personality disorders, only the Personality Diagnostic Questionnaire (PDQ; Hyler et al., 1988) and a screening questionnaire accompanying SCID-II directly assess DSM criteria; DSM-IV versions are available. The Millon Clinical Multiaxial Inventory (MCMI; Millon, 1983) provides measures of DSM categories, but the scales assess these constructs as developed in Millon's personality theory. The MCMI has been modified to accommodate changes in the DSM, the latest version being MCMI-III. It also assesses Axis I disorders.

Personality disorder (PD) scales for the Minnesota Multiphasic Personality Inventory (MMPI-1) were constructed by Morey et al. (1985) by matching available MMPI items to DSM-III concepts. A DSM-IV equivalent for the MMPI-2 has not been published. Although some MMPI personality disorder scales may be useful, they are limited by reliance on the pre-existing MMPI-1 item pool.

Questionnaires typically achieve higher reliabilities than interviews, and they agree reasonably well with other questionnaires. Agreement between the MCMI and PDQ on categorical diagnosis is low (Zimmerman, 1994). However, better correspondence is demonstrated when PDQ categories are 'dimensionalized' (see Chapter 3) and treated as continuous interval measures rather than as nominal categories (Widiger and Corbitt, 1993; Blackburn et al., 2004). McCann (1991) compared the MCMI-II and the MMPI-PD scales and found that convergence for different categories varied from high for several scales (avoidant, borderline, passive–aggressive, schizotypal) to low for others (paranoid, compulsive). Similar results were obtained in a comparison of the PDQ and MMPI-PD scales (Trull and Larson, 1994), all correlations being significant except those for schizoid and narcissistic disorders.

Diagnostic concordance between questionnaires and interviews is typically low, and questionnaires over-diagnose personality disorders by comparison with interviews (e.g. Trull and Larson, 1994). However, when all measures are treated as continuous scales, agreement is somewhat better. Trull and Larson (1994) found that all PDQ scales and all MMPI personality disorder scales except the narcissistic scale correlated significantly with their counterparts on the SIDP (median correlations of 0.43 and 0.40, respectively), indicating that the questionnaires and interview tap the same underlying constructs. Low, but significant, correlations have also been found between the MCMI-I and the SIDP (Widiger and Corbitt, 1993).

The MCMI-I was criticized for limited convergence with other measures of DSM personality disorders, but many of these criticisms were overcome by the MCMI-II (only limited data are currently available on the MCMI-III). The MCMI-II is a psychometrically sophisticated instrument and, from a review of its external validity, Widiger and Corbitt (1993) conclude that other questionnaires are unlikely to prove more reliable or valid in assessing personality disorders. A substantial literature has also developed on the use of the MCMI-II with offenders (McCann and Dyer, 1996).

LIMITATIONS OF DIAGNOSTIC INSTRUMENTS FOR TREATMENT RESEARCH

The main use of categorical diagnoses of personality disorders in treatment research is as independent variables. For example, patients may be allocated to treatment or control groups on the basis of presence or absence of personality disorder or membership in a particular category of disorder. However, the validity of individual categories of personality disorder and the classification as a whole are poor (Livesley and Jackson, 1992). The utility of diagnostic instruments is therefore inherently limited by the weak validity of the diagnostic categories they aim to represent.

One limitation is that high rates of co-occurring, or co-morbid, diagnoses are the rule rather than the exception in most clinical populations, including personality disordered offenders (Coid, 1992). This suggests that classes of disorder are neither mutually exclusive nor independent, and questions the utility of individual diagnostic categories in selecting patients for inclusion in, or exclusion from, specific treatments, because patients with a single 'pure' disorder are rare. Researchers should therefore obtain the full range of categorical diagnoses permitted by an instrument, even if the interest is primarily in a particular category.

Diagnostic instruments are also of limited use in evaluating change, because of the diagnostic decision rules. For example, a patient who met all nine criteria of borderline personality disorder prior to treatment but only five at treatment termination would nevertheless still qualify for the diagnosis. The utility of diagnostic instruments in this respect can be improved by treating the total number of criteria within a category as a dimension or continuous scale. This effectively changes measurement from the nominal level of a dichotomous category to an ordinal or interval scale, and increases statistical power. This procedure improves both the reliability and validity of assessment, and should be followed routinely.

However, the assessment of individual criteria in most diagnostic instruments is insensitive to short-term change. Because personality disorders are defined as 'enduring', the criteria are those characteristics exhibited during a minimum time frame, variously 2 years (DIPD), 5 years (SCID-II, IPDE), or 'the past several years' (PDQ). Although significant personality change is unlikely with any treatment in much less than a year, such change would not be recognized by most instruments. This is less of a problem with the MCMI or MMPI, which enquire about 'usual' behaviour patterns.

Despite these limitations, the current systems provide an international nomenclature and are the basis for communication in the research community. Treatment research will therefore usually include at least one diagnostic instrument, if only to describe the sample studied. However, the aim of clinical intervention is not to change reified abstractions such as borderline or antisocial personality, but rather to modify the pathological traits that these labels summarize, and the evaluation of outcomes demands more sensitive measures of these traits.

MEASURES OF ABNORMAL PERSONALITY TRAITS

BROAD-BAND INSTRUMENTS

Deviant personality dispositions are assessed by many traditional clinical instruments developed within clinical psychology, and also by measures of interpersonal maturity, moral development or socialization used in offender rehabilitation programmes (Blackburn, 1993). Appraisal of the relation of these to personality disorders is perhaps overdue. There are also numerous measures of specific dysfunctional traits relevant to personality disordered offenders, such as impulsivity, aggression or low self-esteem. Novaco's Anger Scale, for example, assesses cognitive, affective and behavioural components of anger, an explicit criterion of paranoid, antisocial and borderline disorders, and this scale has been used in maximum security treatment programmes (Novaco, 1997). However, several broad-band instruments have been developed that sample a range of deviant traits.

The MMPI is widely used in mental health and forensic settings in the USA, but it does not clearly separate personality traits from symptoms of mental illness. The item pool is also dominated by negative affectivity or neuroticism and introversion–extraversion, and other higher-order dimensions of personality are not well represented. Nevertheless, personality disorder scales for the MMPI-1 have already been noted, and Harkness et al. (1995) developed the Personality Psychopathology Five scales (PSY-5) for the MMPI-2 to measure broad dimensions of aggressiveness, psychoticism, constraint, negative emotionality and positive emotionality. These scales cover both normal range and personality disorder traits and have some promise as dependent measures in clinical research.

However, the MCMI and the Personality Assessment Inventory (PAI; Morey, 1991) are serious competitors to the MMPI. Both measure psychopathology more broadly, as well as personality dysfunctions, and contain scales to detect exaggerated or defensive responding. The PAI also includes several scales related to treatment need and responsiveness.

Two instruments with good psychometric properties have been developed to assess abnormal traits identifying personality disorders (Clark et al., 1996). Clark's Schedule for Nonadaptive and Adaptive Personality (SNAP) measures 15 specific trait dimensions (e.g. mistrust, entitlement, disinhibition), and Livesley's Dimensional Assessment of Personality Pathology – Basic Questionnaire (DAPP-BQ) measures 18 traits that are similar, despite varying labels (e.g. suspiciousness, narcissism, conduct problems). Although these inventories were developed independently, joint analysis reveals a high level of convergence between the traits they measure (Clark et al., 1996), and each inventory provides comprehensive coverage of the domain of abnormal personality.

Although less comprehensive, the Antisocial Personality Questionnaire (APQ; Blackburn and Fawcett, 1998) is a relatively brief broadband instrument that measures traits particularly relevant to mentally disordered offenders (self-control, self-esteem, paranoid suspicion, avoidance, resentment, aggression, social deviance, extraversion). Evidence for its validity has been obtained from patients in maximum security, and the scales correlate with measures of interpersonal style, criminality, and self-report scales of personality disorder.

DIMENSIONS OF PERSONALITY

Personality disorders can be regarded as abnormal variants of normal personality (see Chapter 3), and dimensions that describe normal personality may be useful as predictors or outcome variables in treatment research. Several dimensional systems have been proposed, but there is now a consensus that the 'Big Five' dimensions of Extraversion, Agreeableness, Neuroticism, Conscientiousness and Openness (as described in Chapter 3) are central in identifying personality variation (Widiger and Costa, 1994). Most measures of normal and abnormal personality are related to one or other of these dimensions, and they summarize relationships between the more specific abnormal traits measured by the SNAP and DAPP-BQ (Clark et al., 1996). The five-factor model is also related to personality disorders in violent offenders (Blackburn and Coid, 1998).

The most established five-factor measure is the NEO-Personality Inventory – Revised (NEO-PI-R; Costa and McCrae, 1992), for which a short version is also available. However, dimensional assessment may be too general to evaluate clinical outcome, and assessment at the level of specific traits (facets) may provide greater sensitivity to change. As well as assessing the main dimensions, the full NEO-PI-R measures specific facets relevant to antisocial populations, such as hostility, anger and impulsivity.

A further dimensional model pertinent to personality disorders is the *interpersonal circle* (IPC; Kiesler, 1996). The IPC represents interpersonal styles as a circular array (or circumplex) around two dimensions of power or control (dominance versus submission) and affiliation (hostile versus friendly or nurturant), and these styles are significant components of personality disorder. Although dominance and affiliation are related to the 'Big

Five' dimensions of Extraversion–Introversion and Agreeableness–Antagonism, respectively, measurement of the IPC may more readily capture interpersonal traits related to antisocial behaviour (Blackburn, 1998).

There are several self-report measures of the IPC, including one that incorporates other 'Big Five' dimensions (Wiggins and Pincus, 2002), but Blackburn and Renwick (1996) developed the Chart of Interpersonal Reactions in Closed Living Environments (CIRCLE) specifically to measure the IPC in forensic psychiatric in-patients through nurse observations. The CIRCLE consists of ratings of everyday social behaviours and measures eight interpersonal styles (dominance, coercion, hostility, withdrawal, submission, compliance, nurturance, gregariousness). The scales have acceptable psychometric properties, and their validity in assessing mentally disordered offenders has been established (Blackburn, 1998). Because they do not depend on patients' self-reports, they may have particular utility in monitoring treatment effects.

METHODOLOGICAL CONSIDERATIONS

SELECTION

The selection of appropriate instruments will depend on: (a) treatment objectives; (b) psychometric adequacy of relevant instruments; and (c) practical considerations such as resources available or staff qualifications. It will be apparent that there is a relatively wide choice of measures of abnormal personality that meet basic psychometric requirements and that have potential utility in evaluating a range of treatments. The measures described do not, of course, exhaust the possibilities. Treatment methods applicable to personality disorders are theoretically driven (Benjamin, 1997), and psychodynamic, cognitive and interpersonal approaches generally assume that changes in surface traits will be lasting

only when they reflect changes in deeper psychological structures such as cognitive schemata. However, the assessment of theoretical structures associated with specific models is beyond the scope of this chapter.

Because personality has both outer manifestations that are publicly observable and inner aspects known only to the individual, no single method provides a complete assessment. The methods described rely heavily on the person's own reports as elicited by either an interviewer or a standardized questionnaire. Questionnaires are relatively economical to administer, but interviews have the advantage of greater flexibility. In relying on self-reports, both approaches share methodological problems arising from the patient's defensiveness or poor self-awareness. Although it is assumed that the latter is partially offset by a skilled interviewer, this is not guaranteed, and interviews are subject to interviewer bias and halo effects. The limitations of both methods should be recognized.

Questionnaires generally yield higher prevalence rates of disorder, but tend to have high specificity (i.e. they detect most patients in the sample who do not have a disorder). Some therefore suggest that questionnaires may be most useful in categorical diagnosis as a preliminary screening-out measure, more detailed interview being reserved for those showing evidence of dysfunction on the questionnaire (Zimmerman, 1994). This has some merit in clinical practice, but the assumption that interview diagnoses are necessarily more valid is not warranted. Interviews disagree as much with each other as with questionnaires (Perry, 1992), and the greater concordance between diagnostic methods when assessments are 'dimensionalized' suggests that the diagnostic decision rules are as much a source of disagreement as any inherent properties of the measures themselves (Blackburn et al., 2004).

Hare (1996) suggests that offenders cannot be trusted to answer self-report questionnaires honestly, but there is little evidence that this is a widespread problem or that interviews successfully detect dissimulation or 'impression management'. The assumption that people have a 'true' personality that can be detected more readily by observers than by the self is also questionable. Personality assessment through self-report is concerned less with eliciting verifiable facts than with beliefs about the sort of person one is, and relies on a person's self-concept and self-representation (Hogan and Nicholson, 1988). For example, some questionnaires include measures of 'improbable virtues' to detect dissimulation, but 'lie' scales actually reflect substantive personality traits such as rigid conscientiousness. Given the similar demands of personality questionnaires and interviews, there seems to be no reason why offenders should represent themselves differently in response to one rather than the other.

An unresolved problem shared by both methods is potential distortion of personality from mood variations or co-morbid Axis I disorders such as depression. Coid (1992) showed that the latter is common among personality disordered offenders, and mood disorders may mask usual personality functioning through effects on behaviour and self-ascription (Zimmerman, 1994). Attempts to resolve this by the use of intimate informants have had mixed success (Mann et al., 1981; Zimmerman, 1994; Tyrer, 2000). However, this approach has typically involved diagnostic instruments, and informants are unlikely to possess the range of information necessary for categorical diagnosis.

Observer ratings more generally can enhance trait assessment by providing information about social behaviour not readily available to an interviewer or to subjects themselves. For example, characteristics such as interpersonal warmth, grandiosity or sadistic style are most reliably assessed through observations of the person in natural interactions. Peer and partner ratings of the 'Big Five' have been found to agree reasonably well with self-reports, and in institutions such as hospitals and prisons,

appropriately structured staff ratings can provide an equivalent source of assessment.

CONCLUSION

This chapter describes the main instruments available for the reliable assessment of personality disorders. Interviews, questionnaires, and observer ratings should be considered potentially useful sources of information about personality in their own right. Each is fallible and subject to measurement errors arising from the method itself. Instruments selected for investigating treatment should therefore draw on each of these sources.

REFERENCES

American Psychiatric Association (1980). *Diagnostic and Statistical Manual of Mental Disorders,* third edition. Washington, DC: American Psychiatric Association.

American Psychiatric Association (1994). *Diagnostic and Statistical Manual of Mental Disorders,* fourth edition. Washington, DC: American Psychiatric Association.

Benjamin LS (1997). Personality disorders: models for treatment and strategies for treatment development. *Journal of Personality Disorders* **11**:307–24.

Blackburn R (1993). *The Psychology of Criminal Conduct: Theory, Research and Practice.* Chichester: John Wiley & Sons.

Blackburn R (1998). Psychopathy and personality disorder: implications of interpersonal theory. In: Cooke DJ, Hart SJ and Forth AE (eds), *Psychopathy: Theory, Research and Implications for Society.* Amsterdam: Kluwer, 269–301.

Blackburn R (2000). Treatment or incapacitation? Implications of research on personality disorders for the management of dangerous offenders. *Legal and Criminological Psychology* **5**:1–21.

Blackburn R and Coid JW (1998). Psychopathy and the dimensions of personality disorder in violent offenders. *Personality and Individual Differences* **25**:129–45.

Blackburn R, Donnelly JP, Logan C and Renwick SJ (2004). Convergent and discriminant validity of interview and questionnaire measures of personality disorder in mentally disordered offenders: a multi-trait–multimethod analysis using confirmatory factor analysis. *Journal of Personality Disorders* **18**:129–50.

Blackburn R and Fawcett DJ (1998). The Antisocial Personality Questionnaire: an inventory for assessing deviant traits in offender populations. *European Journal of Psychological Assessment* **15**:14–24.

Blackburn R and Renwick SJ (1996). Rating scales for measuring the interpersonal circle in forensic psychiatric patients. *Psychological Assessment* **8**:76–84.

Clark LA and Harrison JA (2001). Assessment instruments. In: Livesley WJ (ed.), *Handbook of Personality Disorders: Theory, Research, and Treatment*. New York: Guilford, 277–306.

Clark LA, Livesley WJ, Schroeder ML and Irish SL (1996). Convergence of two systems for assessing specific traits of personality disorder. *Psychological Assessment* **8**:294–303.

Coid JW (1992). DSM-III diagnosis in criminal psychopaths: a way forward. *Criminal Behaviour and Mental Health* **2**:78–94.

Costa PT and McCrae RR (1992). Normal personality assessment in clinical practice: the NEO personality inventory. *Psychological Assessment* **4**:5–13.

Dolan B and Coid J (1993). *Psychopathic and Antisocial Personality Disorders: Treatment and Research Issues*. London: Gaskell.

Hare RD (1996). Psychopathy: a clinical construct whose time has come. *Criminal Justice and Behavior* **23**:25–54.

Hare RD (2003). *The Hare Psychopathy Checklist–Revised*, second edition. Toronto: Multi-Health Systems.

Harkness AR, McNulty JL and Ben-Porath YS (1995). The Personality Psychopathology Five (PSY-5): constructs and MMPI-2 scales. *Psychological Assessment* **7**:104–14.

Hogan R and Nicholson RA (1988). The meaning of personality test scores. *American Psychologist* **43**:621–6.

Hyler SE, Rieder RO, Williams JBW, Spitzer RL, Hendler J and Lyons M (1988). The Personality Diagnostic Questionnaire: development and preliminary results. *Journal of Personality Disorders* **2**:229–37.

Kiesler DJ (1996). *Contemporary Interpersonal Theory and Research: Personality, Psychopathology, and Psychotherapy*. New York: John Wiley & Sons.

Livesley WJ and Jackson D (1992). Guidelines for developing, evaluating, and revising the classification of personality disorders. *Journal of Nervous and Mental Disease* **180**:609–18.

Loranger AW, Sartorius N, Andreoli A et al. (1994). The International Personality Disorder Examination: The World Health Organization/Alcohol, Drug Abuse and Mental Health Administration international pilot study of personality disorders. *Archives of General Psychiatry* **51**:215–24.

Mann AH, Jenkins R, Cutting JC and Cowen PJ (1981). The development and use of a standardised assessment of abnormal personality. *Psychological Medicine* **11**:839–47.

McCann JT (1991). Convergent and discriminant validity of the MCMI-I and MMPI personality disorder scales. *Psychological Assessment* **3**:9–18.

McCann JT and Dyer FJ (1996). *Forensic Assessment with the Millon Inventories*. New York: Guilford Press.

Millon T (1983). *Millon Clinical Multiaxial Inventory*, third edition. Minneapolis, MN: National Computer Systems.

Morey LC (1991). *Personality Assessment Inventory*. Odessa, FL: Psychological Assessment Resources, Inc.

Morey LC, Waugh MH and Blashfield RK (1985). MMPI scales for DSM-III personality disorders: their derivation and correlates. *Journal of Personality Assessment* **49**:245–56.

Novaco RW (1997). Remediating anger and aggression with violent offenders. *Legal and Criminological Psychology* **3**:77–88.

Perry JC (1992). Problems and considerations in the valid assessment of personality disorders. *American Journal of Psychiatry* **149**:1643–5.

Reich J (1989). Update on instruments to measure DSM-III and DSM-III-R personality disorders. *Journal of Nervous and Mental Disease* **177**:366–70.

Reich J and Green AI (1991). Effect of personality disorders on outcome of treatment. *Journal of Nervous and Mental Disease* **179**:74–82.

Spitzer RL, Williams JB and Gibbon M (1987). *Structured Clinical Interview for DSM-III-R Personality Disorders*.

New York: Biometrics Research Department, New York State Psychiatric Institute.

Stangl D, Pfohl B, Zimmerman M, Bowers W and Corenthal C (1985). A structured interview for the DSM-III personality disorders: a preliminary report. *Archives of General Psychiatry* **42**:591–6.

Trull TJ and Larson SL (1994). External validity of two personality disorder inventories. *Journal of Personality Disorders* **8**:96–103.

Tyrer P (2000). *Personality Disorders: Diagnosis, Management and Course*, second edition. London: Wright.

Widiger TA and Corbitt EM (1993). The MCMI-II personality disorder scales and their relationship to DSM-III diagnosis. In: Craig RJ (ed.), *The Millon Clinical Multiaxial Inventory: A Clinical Research Information Synthesis*. Hillsdale, NJ: Erlbaum, 181–201.

Widiger TA and Costa PT (1994). Personality and personality disorders. *Journal of Abnormal Psychology* **103**:78–91.

Widiger TA and Frances AJ (1987). Interviews and inventories for the measurement of personality disorders. *Clinical Psychology Review* **7**:49–75.

Widiger TA, Mangine S, Corbitt EM, Ellis CG and Thomas GV (1995). *Personality Disorder Interview-IV: A Semistructured Interview for the Assessment of Personality Disorders*. Odessa, FL: Psychological Assessment Resources, Inc.

Wiggins JS and Pincus AL (2002). Personality structure and the structure of personality disorders. In: Costa PT and Widiger TA (eds), *Personality Disorders and the Five-Factor Model of Personality*, second edition. Washington, DC: American Psychological Association, 103–24.

World Health Organization (1979). *International Classification of Diseases,* ninth revision. Geneva: World Health Organization.

World Health Organization (1992). *International Classification of Diseases,* tenth revision. Geneva: World Health Organization.

Zanarini MC, Frankenburg FR, Chauncey DL and Gunderson JG (1987). The Diagnostic Interview for Personality Disorders: interrater and retest reliability. *Comprehensive Psychiatry* **28**:467–80.

Zimmerman M (1994). Diagnosing personality disorders: a review of issues and research methods. *Archives of General Psychiatry* **51**:225–45.

Chapter 30

TREATMENT OF SERIOUS OFFENDERS WITH PERSONALITY DISORDER: EFFECT, EFFECTIVENESS AND INDIVIDUALITY

Pamela J. Taylor

INTRODUCTION

Three questions about the possible benefits of treatment for people with personality disorder who commit serious antisocial acts or criminal offences are particularly urgent:

- What 'effect' in this constitutes context?
- Is there research evidence of relevant effect of adequate size with certain types or combinations of treatment? For the purposes of this book, the same question must be asked more specifically about the unit that is at the centre of it.
- How may research findings – which generally refer to groups – are useful in clinical practice? In other words, for any given individual, what would be the markers of success?

Underpinning these questions is the assumption that there are, or could be, reliable and valid systems for defining the pivotal problems and characteristics of personality disorder at presentation or before treatment, and then at subsequent times. There is also my preference – not always possible to indulge in readings of research – for defining personality disorder without reference to antisocial

behaviour. The category of 'antisocial personality disorder', or one of its synonyms, is unsatisfactory and tautologous. In general and in individual cases, separation of personality traits from antisocial acts enables some practical hypothesis formation about the nature of any relationship between the disorder and the offending, and thus greater clarity in setting goals for treatment. This would help all parties in the prospective treatment alliance. For offender patients, the parties may include the judiciary, other criminal justice staff and, for the UK, relevant governmental department officials. If the serious or persistent offending can plausibly be attributed, at least in part, to aspects of a personality disorder, then successful management or treatment of that personality disorder may be expected to bring about important changes in antisocial or offending behaviour. If not, then it may still be important to treat the disorder to alleviate suffering or save life, but amelioration in antisocial potential will not necessarily go with clinical improvements. Those distinctions may be explicit once assessment is complete. Blackburn (Chapter 29) and Moore (Chapter 4) cover some of the instruments available for assessment, and their strengths and pitfalls.

INSUFFICIENT ATTENTION TO THE NEGATIVE EFFECTS OF TREATMENT?

Effect cannot be adequately measured unless the goals of the treatment or intervention are clear. While the clinical ideal is that intervention should do no harm, it is acknowledged that most active treatments have recognized unwanted consequences. In clinical systems it is expected that treater and treated should be able to consider together the probabilities of benefit, and then those of discomfort or harm. This enables them to determine the likely balance of effects before the person seeking help decides whether or not to embark on treatment. The criminal justice system is not bound by such considerations.

In relation to health services, there is some consideration of the potential for harm in the settings of treatment (e.g. Goffman, 1961; Wing, 1962; Martin, 1984) inclusive of community health structures (Wing, 1990). Although, Goffman's work, for example, would apply as well to prisons as to hospitals, and there have been a number of harrowing descriptive accounts of the impact of imprisonment (e.g. Parker, 1970; Priestley, 1989), there has been little systematic study of the impact of the various settings in the criminal justice system. Further, in neither system is it clear that either specialist interventions or overall systems enter much into research consciousness in terms of potential for harm in relation specifically to people with personality disorder. This is in spite of the fact that harsh and inconsistent discipline in childhood has been implicated as one causative factor for such disorders, and the harsh and inconsistent discipline that may be a feature of secure environments could constitute a maintenance, or even exacerbatory, factor for these. Most studies of long-term prisoners are consistent in showing disruption of relationships to be

a problem, but only Bolton et al. (1976) have conducted a systematic study of the impact of imprisonment over a lengthy period of time (19 months). They showed no evidence of psychological deterioration over this period on the measures they chose. This is in contrast with a study from Scandinavia (Andersen et al., 2000), which showed damaging effects, albeit not exclusive to people with personality disorder, within a shorter time scale in a pretrial prison. Here, people who had no psychiatric disorders on entry to the prison were found to present with features that fitted with the operational criteria for disorders after a few weeks.

The reason for opening on this point about problems, and the measurement of harmful effects of treatment and management systems, is both general and specific. It is invariably arguable that reasonable goals of treatment in relation to chronic disorders are the prevention of spread of harm, the prevention of deterioration where possible and palliation where not. English mental health legislation, however, explicitly incorporates 'prevention of deterioration' as one core criterion of 'treatability' in relation to personality disorder. It is important, therefore, to be sure that hospital settings at least do not foster conditions in which disorder is exacerbated or reinforced.

'HOLDING'

Outcome studies across the whole range of treatment literature are inconsistent in the way in which they deal with people who fail to complete a course of treatment. Some would argue that unless a person has had what would generally be agreed as 'adequate' treatment, the effectiveness of the treatment for that individual cannot be measured, and people who refuse or drop out from treatment cannot be included in the final analysis in treatment trials. Others would argue that the mere fact that a treatment is found unacceptable, intolerable or unsustainable is a marker of its lack of effectiveness. For people with personality disorder who, by definition, have difficulty in maintaining a relationship, and many of whom lead chaotic lives, the attainment of being 'held' in a psychotherapeutic relationship, or within a stable, benign setting, may itself be a valid measure of effectiveness. In these terms, psychotherapy may not appear promising for people with major mental disorder. Stanton et al. (1984), for example, found that in a series of 164 people with schizophrenia who actually engaged in psychotherapy, 69 (42 per cent) failed to complete 6 months, and only one-third remained in treatment after 2 years. By these standards, the prospects for personality disorder look rosy. Whether in a setting without external constraints (the Henderson Hospital: Whiteley, 1970; Copas and Whiteley, 1976) or in prison (Gunn et al., 1978), between one-half and one-third of those regarded as suitable, and therefore also motivated, for treatment dropped out within a month; thereafter, however, there was little attrition.

Politics is never far from forensic mental health services, and a different view of 'holding' is taken by politicians, who see one of their roles as guardians of public safety. In relation to those personality disorders that are related to offending, the issue for them is prevention of further offending or harm. This is hardly a disadvantageous goal, even for the individual concerned, but politicians see incarceration as the best option here. It is extremely unlikely that harm will spread further to the general population while an afflicted individual is in prison or a secure hospital. There remains an important question: at what cost is such safety achieved? The price may include suicide, other self-harm by the individual concerned, attacks on staff or fellow residents, further deterioration in personality traits, or introduction to illicit drugs. Such additional problems may complicate the personality disorder to a point of further and perhaps greater impact than previously when the individual finally returns to the community – and most

do. Too little is known about these potential risks, although it is known that the suicide rate in prisons remains a cause for concern in the UK (Shaw et al., 2003). There is also some evidence that, in spite of a range of preventive initiatives, the suicide rate in UK prisons is continuing to rise (HM Prison Service, 2003).

PALLIATION AND PREVENTION OF DETERIORATION

As with all clinical conditions, there will be some people with personality disorder who will not improve or recover with treatment. While some of these may be 'held' in yet another sense, in that their condition gets no worse, some will deteriorate regardless of all interventions. The task then is palliation, to slow the deterioration where possible, and to limit consequences, including minimizing distress and reducing the rate or seriousness of further harm to self or others. As long as the goals and limitations are clear, this is a tolerable situation for treated and treaters. Indeed, it can even be rewarding in these circumstances to see that effort expended has maintained a defined state of health and behaviour.

Clinical and research evidence for such an outcome, however, must rely on more substantial baseline measures than even a classic change trial. Documentation of pre-intervention trends in symptoms and signs and in behaviour is needed; relevant data must reflect a lengthy period. Measures must then be continued for long enough to show that there truly is a steady state and that a trend has been arrested. Perhaps there has merely been a reduction in the slope of deterioration. How long is long enough? A decision about the length of baseline measures must, of necessity under present knowledge, be somewhat arbitrary. Diagnostic classification systems specify length of presenting aspects of disorder as fundamental to the definition, but only in terms of 'enduring' or 'longstanding'. Given that this probably means years rather than weeks or even months in most cases, in almost all cases some baseline measures will have to be made retrospectively. Ethically, intervention would probably have to start before 'ideal' length of prospective baseline data collection, although it may still be wise to allow a period of weeks or months for assessment. Indeed, English legislation (Mental Health Act (MHA), 1983), under the Interim Treatment Order, explicitly allows for up to 6 months and longer if other assessment possibilities were included, in order to set the baseline and begin the testing of 'treatability'. What can be achieved within specified periods of time? For other conditions, such as schizophrenia, there are some research-based calculations of the time in which most people might be expected to show some response to medication, and the time after which no further response would be expected, for a given treatment. Could we aim at such researched targets for personality disorder? These sorts of calculations are not yet well done in clinical practice, and research has yet to tackle these important areas for personality disorder.

GOALS FOR IMPROVEMENT

The shared goal

In regular clinical practice, the ideal is that, from the outset, clinician and patient are working towards a shared goal. After only a little negotiation, this is generally the case. In working with people with personality disorder, this is much less commonly true. When such a disorder is combined with offending, on first contact, anything more than superficial common ground in goals seems so unusual that attainment of truly shared goals can perhaps be seen as another interim outcome measure. It may be, for example, that clinician and patient can readily agree on a broad aim of the patient living freely in his or her own home, effectively and safely and feeling better, but quickly hit difficulty on the route there. The patient may not subscribe to the view that a prolonged

period of commitment to treatments of various kinds will be necessary, whether within or outside a restricted environment. Recording of the nature or extent of agreement to treatment is rarely a feature of reported research, either in notation of the absence of common ground or in evaluation of the techniques best suited for attaining this position in the shortest time. Motivational interviewing (Miller and Rollnick, 1991), which was introduced for working with people with addictive behaviours, could have a role here.

The overarching goals

The most widely reported measures of 'effectiveness' are crude, including 're-offending' and sometimes 're-hospitalization'. They tend to be reflective of the self-interest of service purchasers and providers, and even politicians. This may mean nothing more than that personality disorder outcome research is less far advanced than research into other mental disorders. Much of the early schizophrenia outcome research, for example, is reported simply in terms of re-hospitalization. For people with personality disorder who offend, reduction in the use of health or criminal justice services may be an adequate surrogate for reduction of need, but relationships between use, risk and need are rarely clear. Reduction in criminal convictions and/or imprisonment may only imply that the individual has become more skilled at evading detection; a steady state or increase in number of convictions may mask real improvement in offending behaviour, but continuing vulnerability to need for attention from services; decrease in the use of hospital services may symbolize rejection on the part of those services *and* a reason for maintained or increased use of the criminal justice system; increased use of health services may mean more suspect health, but equally, perhaps, more realistic management on the part of both the patient and the services of the patient's health problems. Better studies would make these distinctions.

Working with co-morbidity

Among those who argue against the treatability of personality disorder are those who suggest that it is only the additional presentation of a more acute disorder, such as depression, that provides any scope for treatment, and that treatment in this context will only be needed and justified on a short-term basis. There is a small but growing literature confirming the extent of co-morbidity between personality disorder and other psychiatric disorders (see Chapter 14). In addition, it is worth emphasizing here the high rates of parasuicide and completed suicide in such groups. So, treatment of co-morbid disorders is indeed a key task, with consequent reduction in relevant symptomatology as one set of acceptable outcome measures, and reduction in self-harm, even suicide, as another. Papers commenting on personality disorder as an impediment to the treatment of other disorders can be found in the literature (Reich and Green, 1991; Merson et al., 1992; Tyrer et al., 1998; Gandhi et al., 2001). Papers showing the effect of other disorders on treatment for personality disorder are less evident. Longitudinal studies that might map the effect of co-morbid disorders on personality disorder, for example in precipitating episodes of offending or other major social decompensation, would be useful. Perhaps treatment of a co-morbid disorder is all that is required to maintain social function that would be acceptable to both patient and society?

Experience on the unit at the centre of this volume, Woodstock Ward, suggests that preliminary treatment of concomitant disorders has a principal effect in enabling treatment of the personality disorder. Although the Woodstock group is too highly selected for generalization, prison surveys suggest that more attention to such issues would be important. In 1997, for example, when the English prison population was just in excess of 63 000, Singleton et al. (1998) estimated that 40 000 of the nearly 50 000 sentenced men then in prison had a personality disorder; 7 per cent of sentenced men, 10 per cent of pre-trial men and 14 per cent of women had a diagnosis of psychosis; the respective proportions for neurotic disorder were 60 per cent, 40 per cent and over 70 per cent; more than half of the men and a third of the women had alcohol use disorders; and more than 40 per cent of both men and women had illicit drug use disorders.

Personality change: passive/responsive or active and substantive?

This question accepts for the moment that there can be a change in habitual styles of construing the world and relating to others and the environment. It suggests, however, that since adverse environments are generally consistent for some individuals, an apparently persistent distortion in their relating styles may be more reflective of these environmental adversities than of core disorder. For others, there may be more fundamental disorder that has always been or has become independent of immediate environment. For the former group, after an initial reappraisal and readjustment phase, real change in personal style will emerge, but its maintenance may be dependent on sustaining the changed environment (or key elements of it), on avoidance of the reproduction of key elements of the distorting environment, or both. In other words, the change may be real, but in itself insufficient and unsustainable. Targeting relative dependency and passivity traits may be of some importance for this group, but of most importance will be an attempt to maintain ameliorating conditions, where effective, once the individuals have left the principal treatment setting. Paradoxically, for those in the sub-group with the more environment-independent disorders, if improvements can be brought about at all, longer term performance may be better.

Research, however, tends to treat people as if they are homogenous in these respects. What evidence is there to suggest that primary causative factors and maintenance factors would be better treated separately? Gunn et al.

(1978) assessed men with personality disorder and generally extensive histories of violence, and evaluated outcome after treatment in the English psychiatric prison Grendon. Over the 16 months or so undergoing treatment, the group change was from a predominance of moderate to severe, essentially neurotic, disorders to one of sub-clinical disturbances. The attitudes of the men to authority figures and offending also changed substantially. They were not violent during the treatment phase. Outside the therapeutic environment, there were only the crude, overview measures of mortality and offending available. Here, the Grendon men did no better over the next 10 years than their peers from other parts of the prison system with comparable offending histories (Robertson and Gunn, 1987). Subsequent studies have tended to support this balance of findings (e.g. Genders and Player, 1995; Newton, 1998), but with a suggestion that, taking the high risk of conviction into account, treatment duration of 18 months or more confers an advantage on reconviction rates (Taylor, 2000). Newton (1971) underscores the value of achieving a more settled and safe state while still in prison, almost regardless of longer-term outcome. One should also question why 'cure' of longstanding conditions called personality disorder should be expected when no such expectation arises in relation to others such as schizophrenia (Taylor, 1986). It would be almost unheard of to discharge someone who had been violent in the context of schizophrenia without at least attempting maintenance treatment in the community. Such attempts at treatment maintenance were rare for the men reported on after leaving Grendon Prison. Could stability of the change recorded in Grendon have been dependent on the maintenance of a more positive environment?

McCord and Sanchez (1982) compared 'the most recalcitrant of delinquents' graduating from a school that emphasized therapy (Wiltwyk) with a 'typical public reformatory'

(Lyman) run along disciplinarian lines, both in 1950s' New York. Twenty-five years later, they examined the impact of these experiences over time. About one-third of the adolescents in each group were designated 'psychopaths'. Overall, the Wiltwyk boys did better than the Lyman boys on measures of further offending, but only until the age of 25. Then there was a crossover. This difference appeared to relate to an interactional effect between placement and subsequent family influence. For graduates of the disciplinarian school, subsequent family versus other placement made no difference. For those who had been in the treatment school, overall nearly one-quarter of those who returned to their families continued to offend or resumed offending after the age of 24, but only 10 per cent of those going to other environments did so. This difference was exaggerated for a sub-group of 42 Wiltwyk boys considered to be 'psychopaths' (33 per cent compared with 8 per cent). At the least, further research on the interaction between the individual and differing steady states in his or her environment seems warranted.

THE EVIDENCE ON TREATMENT FOR PERSONALITY DISORDER

The complexities of personality disorder and its context are widely acknowledged, but research tends to focus on the value of 'a treatment' rather than on the combination of treatments that usually constitute the treatment process for any particular individual. Devising and taking account of a combination of treatments would make logical sense on the basis of the mechanisms behind and route to the personality disorders. Bateman and Fonagy (1999, 2001) in fact do that, although the emphasis is on the psychoanalytic components of the programme. Others, almost by default, achieve something similar. It seems unduly simplistic, for example, to consider the therapeutic community, whether in pure or modified form, as a single treatment. That, however, is how it is commonly represented, and, notwithstanding caveats about the difficulties in defining and sustaining its elements, that is how it has been approached in terms of research evaluation. Not only would there be theoretical sense in evaluating combined psychological and social approaches to therapies, but Stein (1993), in his review of drug treatment of personality disorders, cites a number of clinical-researcher advocates for combining appropriate medication with psychotherapy. This might perhaps reduce drop-out rates from psychotherapy, and may shorten the time to build a useful treatment alliance, but the studies testing these possibilities are not evident.

Ahmed and Seifas (1998) raised the alarm not only about the quantity and quality of treatment trials, but also about the possible lack of positive reinforcement for work in this difficult field. The psychiatric journal with the highest citation index – *Archives of General Psychiatry* – published 621 randomized controlled trials (RCTs) in the 37 years between 1959 and 1995. Only 2 per cent of these referred to personality disorder. Further, they noted a decline in publication of non-drug trials – from 21 per cent between 1959 and 1976 to 13 per cent between 1977 and 1995.

There are three systematic reviews of treatment for personality disorder, one each from the USA and UK covering 'psychotherapy' (Perry et al., 1999; Bateman and Fonagy, 2000) and the other from the UK on therapeutic communities (Lees et al., 1999). In 2001, the English Department of Health produced an 'evidence-based clinical practice guideline' on treatment choice in psychological therapies and counselling. Recommendations are weighted according to whether there is consistent evidence from systematic reviews or high-quality studies (A), at least one high-quality trial or some inconsistent findings (B), evidence from individual studies that do not meet all the criteria of 'high quality' (C), and structured expert consensus (D). There is some specific guidance

in relation to personality disorder, but at lower evidence weightings. A more general review of treatment for personality disorder has emerged in association with UK government initiatives for developing services for people with personality disorder (Bateman and Tyrer, 2002). The UK systematic review of therapeutic communities does make specific reference to offender patients; the other studies do not. There is no reason to suppose that, where offender patients have such disorders as borderline personality disorder, the disorder differs in quality or quantity from the same disorder in someone who does not go on to commit criminal offences – but such a hypothesis has not, in fact, been tested. It is certainly not clear from the non-offender studies whether, insofar as the treatments are effective for personality disorder, they would, through ameliorating the disorder, also limit offending. With this caveat, it is nevertheless important to peruse them.

It is probable that clinicians can also learn useful techniques from training packages developed in the criminal justice system. McGuire's (1995) book on 'what works' provides a comprehensive review. Most of the techniques and programmes described have been developed by non-clinicians, but they are informed by cognitive–behavioural techniques. The preoccupation, understandably for the criminal justice system, is with reduction in re-offending as the outcome. There are a number of impressive meta-analyses of such regimes (e.g. Andrews et al., 1990; Lipsey, 1995), which suggest promise in this respect. Further, given the likely high rates of personality disorder among offenders in general, and prisoners in particular, it is likely that these regimes have proved helpful for some people with personality disorder. Lösel has begun to use the language of treatment of 'psychopaths' in his reviews of them (e.g. Lösel, 1998), but it is far from clear whether they have any impact on personality and its disorders per se. It is perhaps encouraging, though, that the 20 factors he identifies (Lösel, 1995) as associated with positive outcome have a lot in common with the Bateman and Fonagy (2000) list of indicators of effective treatment of personality disorder (see also below). All that can be said for sure at present is that such regimes may offer promise and should be a focus for further research. Paradoxically, they may not work well for those who may fall within the English concept of 'Dangerous and Severe Personality Disorder' – and other high scorers on the Psychopathy Checklist (PCL; Hare, 1991; Taylor, 2002).

MEDICATION

Stein (1993) and Soloff (1992) are agreed that true treatment trials of medication for personality disorder have quashed most of the initial hopes derived from individual successes with drugs or reported open trials in the literature. As an apparently primary, or principal, treatment for personality disorder, just about all groups of psychotropic drugs have been tried, reflecting perhaps concerns about the more challenging and relatively acute presentations, perhaps co-morbidity, or maybe just the sheer complexity of personality disorder. The list includes neuroleptics, antidepressants, mood stabilizers, anticonvulsants (with that would-be panacea carbamazepine somehow straddling the last two groups) and stimulants. Benzodiazepines are now generally viewed as a bad thing, even contraindicated. After all, some people with personality disorder even ask for them! This is interesting for a group of drugs first introduced on to the market with an advertisement claiming their capacity to tame lions. In fact, they have a good record for limiting episodes of aggression (Lion, 1979), with the problem being their unpredictability for long-term use.

Cowdry and Gardner (1988) used 16 subjects as their own controls in order to test the value of most of the drug classes just listed, including benzodiazepines. Not all of the 16 tried all of the drugs. Tranylcypromine was the only drug clearly superior to placebo over a broad range of self-ratings and observer ratings for the nine patients who tried it. It may not be irrelevant that this now rarely used monoamine oxidase inhibitor antidepressant, with its accompanying dietary and drug-mixing risks, emerges on chemical analysis well within the amphetamine/stimulant range of drugs. Alprazolam, the benzodiazepine tested, was unequivocally the best drug for two of the patients, but carried the serious risk of increased occurrence of rage attacks in seven of the remaining ten who tried it. With such a small sample of patients, it can hardly be claimed that the findings are more than pointers. Such drugs must be approached with great caution for anyone with a personality disorder, but they should not be ruled out if they can be tried in safe conditions and other methods of assistance have failed.

Placebo-controlled trials of small doses of conventional neuroleptics have also given mixed results, in showing some advantage for those patients who could take them, particularly those from 'schizotypal' groups. Tolerance of the drugs was, however, rather poor, with a tendency to drop out of treatment with them (Goldberg et al., 1986; Soloff et al., 1986; Cowdry and Gardner, 1988).

Atypical neuroleptics may offer both better compliance and more effective treatment for those who persist with the course. A small, double-blind placebo-controlled trial with 28 women with borderline personality disorder showed that those who took olanzapine for 6 months had a significant advantage in terms of improvement of anxiety, anger, interpersonal sensitivity and paranoia (Zanarini and Frankenburg, 2001), but there was a high (50 per cent) drop-out rate. Bateman and Tyrer (2002) cite a 1999 conference report by Schulz and colleagues as showing reduction in the presentation of similar features in a similar sized placebo-controlled study of risperidone, but also with a similar drop-out rate. There is more limited evidence for such benefit from clozapine (Chengappa et al., 1999).

Tricyclic antidepressants have been shown to have a main effect in treating depression, although even for the treatment of depression in this context, antidepressants were not necessarily superior to neuroleptics (Soloff et al., 1986). Selective serotonin re-uptake inhibitors (SSRIs) now have their supporters, for the relief of both emotional and behavioural traits (e.g. Coccaro and Karoussi, 1997) and for personality traits per se (Ekselius and von Knorring, 1999) albeit in the context of depression.

Neither carbamazepine nor lithium, much vaunted in open studies, receive much support from controlled studies, but that may be in part because of the nature of the study designs – very small numbers with mixed diagnoses. The largest studies to date were for paranoid personality disorder (Gardner and Cowdry, 1986), with 14 subjects on carbamazepine, and for 21 female adolescents with 'emotionally unstable' personality disorder on lithium (Rifkin et al., 1972); results with respect to observed behaviour were equivocal. There is just one very small double-blind placebo-controlled trial of sodium valproate (Hollander et al., 1996), which showed some promise for this drug.

There is a small literature on the psychostimulants pemoline (now discontinued in the UK except on a named patient basis) and methylphenidate. The one double-blind placebo- controlled trial (Mattes, 1984) of the latter showed no advantage, with an interesting caveat. Previous history of drug abuse rather than childhood hyperactivity was predictive of a positive response. My reservation would be about making a diagnosis of adult attentional deficit disorder without a history of childhood hyperactivity, but this is an area that perhaps offers promise for more systematic research.

PSYCHOTHERAPY

Perry et al. (1999) completed a review of empirical studies published between 1974 and 1999 on outcome for people with personality disorder treated with psychotherapy. For inclusion in the review, the studies had to have used systematic methods to make the personality disorder diagnosis, validated outcome measures, and reported data in a way that allowed either calculation of within-condition effect sizes or determination of recovery from the personality disorder. Perry and colleagues identified 15 such studies, just three of them RCTs (Alden, 1989; Linehan et al., 1994; Winston et al., 1994). Most study subjects, and all in the RCTs, were self-referred out-patients. There was a range of personality disorder, from avoidant in the Alden study, through mixed in the Winston et al. study, to predominantly borderline in the Linehan et al. study. These RCTs also reflected a range of different treatment models: cognitive–behaviour therapy (Alden) delivered over 10 weeks, dynamic psychotherapy (Winston et al.) delivered over 40 weeks, and dialectical behaviour therapy (Linehan et al.) delivered over 52 weeks. The first two used waiting list controls, while Linehan et al. used 'treatment as usual' cases. Long-term group therapies had the highest drop-out rates (42 per cent and 51 per cent: Monroe-Blum and Marziali, 1995; Budman et al., 1996). Among the RCTs, Alden reported significant improvement of target complaints according to self-ratings, and did not include observer ratings. Winston et al. and Linehan et al. used observer ratings, the former also including self-ratings, with significant improvement in the treated groups in each case. Perry et al. made a point that may be particularly important in considering the relevance of these studies for offender patients. Across all 15 studies considered, inclusive of the two RCTs in which both measures were available, and after adjustment for sample size, the effect according to self-rating was greater than that on observer ratings. This was true for both global assessment of functioning and social adjustment scales. Effect sizes in all cases were, however, calculated as significantly above zero.

Just four of the studies reviewed, none of them RCTs, suggested 'recovery from personality disorder' (Stevenson and Meares,

1992; Hogeland, 1993; Monsen et al., 1995; Budman et al., 1996), with 52 per cent of patients recovering after just over a year, on average, in treatment. All these studies were of individual dynamic psychotherapy in some form, and the recovery rate would represent a very substantial advantage in comparison with Perry's 1993 account of the natural history of borderline personality disorder. This suggested that without specific treatment it would take more than 10 years of naturalistic follow-up for 50 per cent of borderline personality disorder patients to recover.

Perry and colleagues expressed themselves to be in favour of further RCTs, but not to the exclusion of other approaches. They also called for more standardization in treatment and outcome measures. While essential for the RCT approach, this could bring limitations for application to clinical practice. Standardization might also limit effectiveness when staff flexibility may be crucial to meeting the fluctuating needs of the patient – or maybe not. Perhaps such patients would particularly benefit from a rigid framework. These issues also need research.

Leichsenring and Leibing (2003) incorporated meta-analysis in their review, favouring psychodynamic therapy and cognitive behaviour therapy.

Bateman and Fonagy's (2000) review initially drew very similar conclusions in terms of the effectiveness of psychotherapy, but added a useful list of features that seemed to be common to at least moderately effective treatments:

- good/clear structure,
- inclusion of strategies for enhancing compliance,
- clear focus (aim),
- theoretical coherence to therapist and patient,
- long term,
- encouragement of powerful attachment between therapist and patient, with therapist active rather than passive,
- well integrated with other services.

One particular RCT (Bateman and Fonagy, 1999) is of special interest here for its focus on a multi-modal approach to treatment, somewhat akin to practice on the unit (Woodstock) described in Chapter 18. The main differences between Woodstock and the Bateman and Fonagy model are that the latter is neither coercive nor secure and its treatments are more intensively applied. The Bateman and Fonagy 'experimental' group of 19 were in 'partial hospitalization', i.e. a special 5 days a week programme, during which they received a combination of (1) once-weekly individual psychoanalytic psychotherapy; (2) three times weekly group analytic psychotherapy (1 hour each); (3) once a week expressive therapy orientated towards psychodrama techniques (1 hour); and (4) a weekly community meeting. In addition, there was a monthly case administrator review and a monthly medication review. The comparison group, also of 19, had 'standard treatment in the general psychiatric services', which consisted of regular review by a psychiatrist (on average twice a month), inpatient admission as appropriate, followed by 'partial hospitalization' focusing on problem solving, then regular out-patient follow-up by a community psychiatric nurse. There were three patients in the comparison group who were moved to the other group because of serious suicidal attempts, but three others in the psychotherapeutic group had dropped out in the first 6 months. None of these six was included in the statistical analysis. On all measures of outcome, the psychoanalytic group did significantly better, including in terms of reduction in suicidal and other acts of self-harm, improvement in mood states, fewer days of crisis hospitalization and better social and interpersonal function. The differences were generally sustained for between 6 and 18 months after the start of treatment.

Follow-up of these patients was continued for 18 months after they completed treatment (Bateman and Fonagy, 2001). This time drop-outs and patients who had crossed from standard psychiatric treatment to the special programme were included in analysis, such that there were 22 in the special programme and 19 comparison patients. The special programme patients showed continued improvement during the period compared with the others, who showed little or no change in terms of demand for and use of in-patient and out-patient treatment, or in terms of use of psychotropic medication. Most self-report measures showed that the special programme group had an advantage in terms of symptom reduction, particularly anxiety symptoms, and on a global estimate of mental state. Mean scores on the Inventory of Interpersonal Problems and the Social Adjustment Scale were the third area in which the specialist psychotherapy patients had gained significantly.

THERAPEUTIC COMMUNITIES

Lees et al. (1999) conducted a systematic review of therapeutic communities for people with personality disorder and other mentally disordered offenders. The starting date for data collection was the inception of such communities in 1940s, and the search was extended up to and including 1998, covering electronic database sources, hand searches of selected, specified journals, searches of other relevant publications, visits to specialist library sites, Internet searches, and consultation with key individuals in the field. The authors generated 8160 relevant articles, covering 181 individual named therapeutic communities in 38 different countries, but most in the USA or the UK. There was a preponderance of such communities in security – 120, compared with 84 non-secure therapeutic communities. Among this wealth of data they uncovered 11 RCTs, 10 cross-institutional or comparative studies, and 32 further studies of therapeutic communities with some control strategy in the methodology. The RCTs covered units in hospitals (Craft et al., 1964; Miles, 1969; Lehman and Ritzler, 1976; Chiesa et al., 1996; Piper et al.,

1996), two in young offender settings (Auerbach, 1977; Cornish and Clarke, 1975 – started in 1960) and four in so-called concept secure therapeutic communities, focusing on the treatment of drug misuse (Martin et al., 1995; Nielson et al., 1996; Inciardi et al., 1997; Lockwood et al., 1997). The first study (Miles, 1969), however, included no post-discharge outcome evaluation or follow-up. One of the studies remains unfinished (Chiesa, 1997). Cornish and Clarke, although completing, doubted that their methodology had been appropriate for such complex treatment. Their findings were not favourable to the therapeutic community.

Lees and colleagues then performed a meta-analysis, including all those studies in which the samples were clearly defined, there were clear outcome criteria, and raw numbers were reported. This left 8 RCTs and 21 other controlled studies. The first step of the analysis was to calculate the odds ratios (ORs) for the individual studies. According to Lees et al., the tables are set out unconventionally, such that the implied negative effect of an OR of 0.4 would translate roughly into an effect size of 2.5, which Fleiss et al. (1986) and Haddock et al. (1998) suggest is what is required to indicate a clinically significant but small outcome. Perry and Bond (2000) would style smaller effect sizes as indicating a large degree of change. It seems, perhaps, that readers must decide whether they belong to the strictly statistical or more clinically oriented camp in extrapolating from significance to importance or value. Four of the 8 RCTs, and 15 of the 21 other controlled studies in the analysis unequivocally favoured therapeutic communities, but there was some between-community variation. Taking here only the RCTs, the US study of a secure democratic setting showed significant advantage for the therapeutic community model (Auerbach, 1977: OR, 0.524; 95% confidence interval (CI), 0.28–0.98), but was equivocal in the UK model (Cornish and Clarke, 1975: OR, 1.039; CI, 0.764–2.79).

Further, the Cornish and Clarke RCT approach could not, in fact, be sustained throughout the study. It is hard to know what the practical implications of these two studies are for the treatment of personality disorder per se in the context of offending, since both included only young male offenders, i.e. in their early teens, an age at which most clinicians would eschew the diagnosis of personality disorder. Of the non-secure democratic therapeutic communites, only two survived into the meta-analysis – one of a UK unit of the 1950s and 1960s for young men between the ages of 13 and 25 years, some of whom had a low intelligence quotient (IQ) (Craft et al., 1964), and one of a USA hospital unit for men and women (Lehman and Ritzler, 1976). The former was neutral overall (OR, 1.091; CI, 0.62–5.88) and the latter showed a possible negative effect of the therapeutic community (OR, 1.5; CI, 1.08–2.08). Figures for the 'concept' therapeutic communities, which focused on drug-involved offenders, were, collectively, the most encouraging (Inciadi et al., 1997: OR, 0.35; CI, 0.233–0.526; Lockwood et al., 1997: OR, 0.132; CI, 0.079–0.221; Martin et al., 1995: OR, 0.52; CI, 0.248–1.19; Nielson et al., 1996: OR, 0.23; CI, 0.142–0.373). Of the remaining controlled studies entered into the meta-analysis, 7 of the 12 evaluating secure democratic therapeutic communities showed an advantage for the therapeutic community, as did all five of those on non-secure democratic therapeutic communities. All concept therapeutic communities were confirmed to have had a clear advantage (i.e. four RCTs and four additional controlled studies all showed significant gains for those in the therapeutic community).

The second step of the analysis was to generate a summary OR, which weighted the studies differentially in relation to the overall sample size of each, and in relation to its CIs. This yielded an apparent advantage for those eight therapeutic communities evaluated by RCT (OR, 0.464; CI, 0.392–0.548), and for each type of therapeutic community – democratic (21 studies: OR, 0.695; CI, 0.631–0.769), secure (22 studies: OR, 0.544; CI, 0.498–0.596), concept (8 studies: OR, 0.318; CI, 0.271–0.374) – with just the concept therapeutic communities reaching the figures required by Fleiss and Haddock and their colleagues, as indicated above.

So far so good, and superficially it is reassuring to know that the most prized of clinical research methods – the RCT – has been successfully applied both to psychotherapy on its own and in testing the therapeutic community model, although not everyone prizes it in these circumstances (e.g. Cornish and Clarke, 1975). Lees et al. (1999), after their exhaustive review, were less convinced of the value of the RCT in this area than Perry et al. (1999). While the therapeutic community, on the face of it, is a more complex object for research than a specified type of psychotherapy, it is arguable that the centring of such treatment within a therapeutic community rather than in the subject's regular world limits some of the variance. For research purposes specifically, this might be an advantage. In general, it is reassuring that the findings, when taken together, suggest that psychotherapy alone or in the context of the therapeutic community is beneficial for people with personality disorder, almost regardless of the details of the way in which it is implemented and of the range of people offered the treatment. The advantage is least clear, however, for adult offenders with personality disorder in a therapeutic community review.

For clinicians or researchers, one approach to clarifying the conceptualization of a therapeutic community or programme as a treatment tool, possibly for maintaining it through the treatment period and then measuring it was devised by Moos (e.g. Moos, 1997). His approach has been used to define the climate of community programmes of various kinds, but the Community Orientated Programs Environment Scale (COPES) seems to have particular application to therapeutic communities for people with personality disorder who offend. The COPES has been refined to measure the community on ten items that cluster into three principal dimensions – relationship dimensions, personal growth dimensions, and systems maintenance dimensions.

Relationship dimensions include involvement – how active and energetic members are in the programme; support – how much members help and support each other; and spontaneity – how much the programme encourages the open expression of feelings by members and staff. *Personal growth dimensions* include autonomy – how self-sufficient and independent members are in making decisions and how much they are encouraged to take leadership in the programme; practical orientation – the extent to which members learn social and work skills, and are prepared for discharge from the programme; personal problems orientation – the extent to which members seek to understand their feelings and personal problems; and anger and aggression – how much members argue with other members, become openly angry and display other aggressive behaviour. The *systems maintenance dimensions* include order and organization – how important order and organization are in the programme; programme clarity – the extent to which members know what to expect in their day-to-day routine and the explicitness of programme rules and procedures; and staff control – the extent to which the staff use measures to keep members under necessary controls.

RESEARCH WITH PEOPLE IN HIGH-SECURITY HOSPITALS BECAUSE OF PERSONALITY DISORDER AND OFFENDING

There are several studies that report outcome for patients after departure from high-security hospitals – most coming from England and Wales (e.g. Tennant and Way, 1984;

MacCulloch and Bailey, 1994; Buchanan, 1998; Steels et al., 1998; Jamieson and Taylor, 2002), but some from Canada (e.g. Rice and Harris, 1992). Each reports that, after leaving a high-security hospital, the people under the 'psychopathic disorder' classification of the mental health legislation do worse than those under a mental illness classification in terms of re-offending. One study in England and Wales (Steels et al., 1998) counter-balances this by pointing out that those under the psychopathic disorder classification are more likely to make positive social adjustments; they also note that differences in re-offending are much less when time at risk for offending is taken into account. Jamieson and Taylor (2002) found that, unlike people with mental illness, it was unusual for people with personality disorder to get stuck in institutions. Rice and Harris (1992) only included people in the follow-up who were in the community, but did not indicate length of time at risk. MacCulloch and Bailey (1994), Buchanan (1998) and Davison et al. (1999) showed that those with personality disorder under formal supervision arrangements were likely to do better than those who were not, thus qualifying the community arrangements. For all of these studies, however, the experience in the hospitals is a black box. These studies are 'outcome of hospital detention for mental disorder' studies, not treatment outcome studies. Black et al. (1995) provided a similar kind of outcome report for people with personality disorder linked with offending in ordinary psychiatric facilities, and compared them with patients who had depression, schizophrenia or surgical conditions. Steadman et al. (1998) provided a more sophisticated version of this, with a three-centre follow-up of people in managed care, confirming post-hospitalization reduction in violence for people with personality disorder, but again with no clarity on what constituted treatment, in this case in the few days that those people were in hospital, or indeed on the nature of supervision or treatment subsequently in the community.

There are just two studies that do reveal a little more about overall treatment outcome in relation to what happened within the institution, and there are also some early reports on elements within an overall treatment programme.

Rice et al. (1992) described outcome for 176 men who had spent at least 2 years in the therapeutic programme in the Canadian high-security hospital wing at Penetanguishene. The timescale over which those men were treated was the period of the most active operation of the community (January 1968 to February 1978). For all but 30 of these men, a comparison subject was selected from the forensic assessment cases referred annually to the hospital, matched on age at the time of index offence, nature of index offence and criminal history. The comparison subjects had no time in the high-security hospital other than that spent for assessment, but almost all had spent some time in prison. The mean duration of follow-up was 10.5 years, with no difference in duration between treated and control men, or 'psychopathic' and 'non-psychopathic', the former defined by a cut-off of 25 or more on the PCL-R. 'Failure' was any new charge for a criminal offence, revocation of parole, or return to the hospital for behaviour that could have resulted in criminal charges; 'violent failure' brought in the qualifier of violence on any one or more of these counts. The evidence suggested that, after treatment, there was a lower recidivism rate for 'non-psychopaths' and a higher recidivism rate for 'psychopaths'.

The message frequently conveyed from this study (Rice et al., 1992) is that people with 'psychopathy' might be harmed by treatment. It is important, however, before contemplation of any generalization of the findings, to consider the nature of the 'treatment'. The programme was almost entirely peer operated, and thus the qualifications of the 'therapists' dubious to say the least. It involved intensive 'group therapy' for up to 80 hours weekly. If it were possible to translate this into therapeutic drug levels, these men must have been on toxic doses. Patients had very little contact with professional staff, and there was, or indeed could be, little anchoring to the reality of work or education. Recreational social interaction or other activities like watching television were strictly limited. As Rice et al. rather coyly observe, 'there were several aspects of the program that might be seen to violate patients' rights by today's standards'. It is important to stress that neither Rice nor her colleagues were therapists at this time; they were simply observers. The programme included naked encounters in closed spaces, and none of it was voluntary. This is perhaps particularly relevant to the apparent findings, given that it is likely that many of these men had histories of childhood abuse. Could any lasting damage from the abuse have been compounded by such intrusive acts in therapy? Rice et al. do not specify any difference between the groups treated on this variable. It has to be accepted that the treatment was, in its time, apparently favourably reviewed on ethical and clinical grounds, at least in Canada (Canada, 1977). However, if asked now to predict the outcome of such a programme, many of us would probably do so correctly for the 'psychopaths', and would express surprise only that anyone truly benefited. It is hard to say, though, merely from reconviction figures, whether the 'non-psychopaths' really emerged unscathed.

The other studies have been with English special (high-security) hospital patients. Reiss et al. (1996) reported on the outcome of treatment for 49 young men who had been admitted between January 1972 and December 1989 to the Broadmoor specialist unit, Woodstock Ward (described in Chapter 18), and detained for treatment on that unit for at least 12 months under the legal category of psychopathic disorder. The mean age at entry was 19, offending generally serious (16 had killed), and with deviant sexual motivation in up to half of the offences. Almost half of the men had never lived independently of their families, 40 had had at least one childhood behavioural or emotional problem, 17 had had previous violence convictions, and 9 previous convictions for sex offences. Eight had psychosis as well as personality disorder. Thirty-seven were discharged from the hospital by the end of the follow-up period (January 1993); of these, 17 went to other hospitals, 12 to hostels and 8 to other community residences, but in total 30 finally made it to the community within the follow-up period. The mean length of Broadmoor Hospital stay for them was 7.8 years (standard deviation (SD) 3.5 years). Two patients, one while in a secure unit placement and one while in the community, had killed, two others were convicted of serious offences and six of lesser offences. Of the 28 patients for whom full follow-up information was available in the community (mean follow-up 4.7 years, SD 3.0 years), 25 had 'good' social outcomes as indicated by steady employment, stable accommodation, relationship status and abstinence from drugs or alcohol; none of these had re-offended.

Reiss and colleagues' work was a retrospective, naturalistic study with no attempt to invoke a comparison group. Subsequent reports in an expanded group of 89 young men have focused on the potential predictive value of the PCL-R, but with return to the more usual position of not specifying treatments. Whilst still in hospital, a score of 25 or more on the scale showed some correlation with poorer outcome, including continued need for seclusion or special care, and less improvement in social functioning (Reiss et al., 1999). Seventy of this group of patients left special hospital, inclusive of 11 in the 'psychopathy' group. Psychopathy score did not correlate with outcome beyond the hospital (Reiss et al., 2000). Why should there be a difference in possible predictive power according to environment? A later, independent, study, but with some possible overlap of the samples, yields a possible

clue in that a high PCL-R score was associated with early drop-out from treatment in this hospital setting (Collins et al., in preparation). This is similar to findings in Canadian prisoner (Ogloff et al., 1990) and US state hospital groups (Hill et al., 1996). Such simple observation, however, masked two distinct groups in our hospital study. Patients with co-morbid psychosis who departed treatment in a violent episode constituted one sub-group; in the other, there was no evidence of psychosis, but the patients did not engage with treatment. One or two of the latter, however, had resumed treatment even within the 2 years of the study.

Other studies on Woodstock Ward have focused on building methods of evaluating treatments prospectively, and on elements of treatment and specific tasks rather than overall outcome. Group work on improving sexual knowledge was shown to be effective in this respect, for sex offenders and non-sex offenders alike (Quayle et al., 1998). A study evaluating the measures of outcome (Quayle and Moore, 1998) emphasized the importance of placing apparently more objective and quantifiable measures in their clinical context. Group mean scores did not necessarily reflect individual variation. Of importance in interpreting outcome studies, individual changes in scores on standard rating scales taken out of context could be very misleading. An apparent increase in anger after an anger management group, for example, reflected a need for further work, but also indicated significant improvement rather than deterioration. One man increased his score as he shed his denial of the problem. Reiss et al. (1998) described the outcome of a week-long drama therapy programme for 12 of the young men. For these men, there was not only an apparent reduction in anger, but also indirect corroboration of an increase in attempts to control that anger.

Low et al. (2001) focused on the smaller group of women in high-security hospital. One of the most important problems for this group is repeated self-harm. As noted above,

Linehan and colleagues (1994) had, in an RCT, shown a beneficial effect from dialectical behaviour therapy for people with borderline personality disorder, inclusive of a beneficial effect on parasuicide. The treatment consists of weekly, individual psychotherapy focusing on motivation, considering any episodes of self-harm, and reducing behaviour that may interfere with therapy, but has an emphasis on acceptance of the patient's experience rather than on the necessity for change. This weekly individual work is combined with group training in behavioural skills, including emotional regulation, interpersonal effectiveness and distress tolerance. In Rampton secure hospital, 17 women for whom deliberate self-harm was a major problem were referred for this treatment. Three did not meet the criteria for borderline personality disorder, one returned to prison, and three dropped out of the treatment within the first 4 months, so the outcome report is limited to ten patients. The ten were of average age 28.7 years and average length of stay in Rampton of 4.5 years. There was no change in parasuicidal behaviours during the first 3 months (quarter) of treatment, but in each of the three subsequent quarters, rates were significantly lower than at baseline, and paralleled by a decrease in dissociative experiences and an increase in survival and coping beliefs. Depression, suicidal ideation and impulsiveness also improved. The 6-month follow-up showed a rebound on first cessation of treatment, but then recovery to well above baseline levels by the second half of the period. Further evaluation would seem worthwhile in this special setting of what appears to be a promising intervention for a very damaging set of behaviours in the context of personality disorder.

CONCLUSIONS AND DIRECTIONS FOR FURTHER WORK

In order to devise and deliver effective treatment for people with personality disorder, it would be useful to have answers from detailed assessments to a set of questions:

- What factors gave rise to the disorder?
- What factors maintain it?
- What factors exacerbate it?
- What among such factors could be changed?
- What among such factors could bring about useful clinical change?

And, for offender patients only:

- To what extent is such change likely to be associated with a reduction in offending?

Each offers scope for clarifying the intervention points.

In order to measure the effectiveness of the treatment, the treatment itself must be defined in various ways. This is as true for clinical practice as for research. Definition is relatively straightforward with drugs. For psychotherapy, definition can to an extent be done by the school of psychotherapy, and then further detailed by the qualifications and experience of the therapists, and by 'dose' in the sense of length, frequency and cumulative duration of sessions. However well defined the school of therapy, the tool remains to a large extent the individual practising it. There is literature on qualities in therapists and outcome in relation to schizophrenia (Whitehorn and Betz, 1954, 1960). A larger literature on expressed emotion (EE) in carers (e.g. Bebbington and Kuipers, 1994) in relation to schizophrenia has been extended to staff working with people with long-term mental illness (Moore et al., 1992) and to the study of relationships within forensic services (Moore et al., 2002). In this forensic study, perhaps predictably, a high proportion of the relationships between nursing staff and patients were rated 'high' EE on the basis of criticism and hostility. Staff tended to be less critical of patients with positive psychotic symptoms (e.g. auditory hallucinations) than of those who were verbally argumentative or aggressive.

The histories of inconsistent and harsh discipline and often frank abuse among so many people with personality disorder perhaps underscore the potential of monitoring staff function. Patients with personality disorder can be provocative, and staff may not respond consistently, or may do so with hostility. A climate reinforcing pathology could thus easily be generated. Expressed emotion could be recorded at the beginning of contact with the patient and as the relationship develops. It would be as important for documenting the impact of the patient as for the early identification of the development of possible countertherapeutic attributes in the therapist. It might thus be possible to prevent or limit the potential for the 'malignant alienation' (Watts and Morgan, 1994) of putative therapists that may be at the heart of the reason why so few people with personality disorder seem to be in treatment.

Where the community is the tool, some measure of it that is reliable and repeatable is important for measuring the consistency of environment. The work of Moos (e.g. 1997), already mentioned, is particularly useful here. With consistency of skills and style of presentation in the therapist and/or the unit, any change in the patient may be more reliably attributable to treatment, and lack of change to 'treatment resistance'; failure to monitor the tools of treatment may result in failure to recognize the reasons behind fluctuations in effectiveness. The patient who fails to respond might be presumed to be untreatable, but may, in fact, be inadequately or inappropriately treated.

For research and clinical practice alike, measures of the strengths and weaknesses of the individual to be treated are essential in comprehensive baseline measures, preferably collected over time, and subsequently as measures to test for change. Both the tools and the context for delivering such assessments are dealt with in detail elsewhere (see Chapters 4 and 29). Within a clinical setting conducive to achieving this, assessment can merge almost imperceptibly into treatment. It is useful at the outset to generate a statement of what is and is not held in common between therapists and patient, and also of goals, tasks, pace of work and minimum and maximum expected achievements. Both parties (patient and therapist/clinical team) can benefit. Formal, multifaceted monitoring of progress is vital, but is the feedback of that to the patient a therapeutic tool, or unhelpful pressure and does the answer to this clinical question depend on whether the feedback is positive or negative? Commonly, clinicians make assumptions about practice, when further research questions about such relatively simple knowledge might better serve patients and staff.

Few, if any, people with personality disorder can tackle all of their problems simultaneously, and few clinicians have the ability to help them do so, even if it were appropriate to try. Does piecemeal work inevitably add up to the whole? Does it matter in what order work is attempted? It seems logical to treat co-morbid conditions first, including possibly, primary aetiological disorders if present, such as minimal brain damage/adult hyperactivity disorder, but does even that pattern require clearer demonstration in research? A more complex question centres on how it may be possible to test for generalizability of any recorded improvements. In larger treatment settings, like the English special hospitals, or in prisons, some attempt may be made by asking patients to repeat certain pieces of work outside their core group. In special hospitals, for example, patients may complete, say, an anger management group within the core treatment package of their main ward or unit, but, having done that successfully, may be asked to repeat the work in a group drawn from patients hospital-wide, who are therefore unfamiliar to them. Another advantage of a larger hospital setting is that patients can be observed in such a wide range of circumstances – not only at leisure in the core unit, and in a wide range of treatments there, but also in education, in work, at social functions, with family and others in and out of the hospital, and so on. Reports from workers in the various areas are collated as qualitative material, but could that process be done more effectively?

Limitations to measuring the effectiveness of treatment include those related to the reliability of the measurements and to the vulnerability of some of them to therapeutic or social context. Other limits may lie in the complexities of the systems in which they are expected to function. In addition, for research, there are the problems of small sample sizes, low turnover and the length of follow-up required to provide evidence to satisfy our own professional standards of safety and well-being, as well as the further interest with respect to offender patients from the lay public and their politicians. Given that individual differences are perhaps less impaired by personality pathology than some of the major mental illnesses, and given the model of comprehensive but staged working suggested by these questions, it may become increasingly possible, even necessary, to use each patient as his or her own control. The standard process of randomization of individuals to groups is possible, even in a field additionally entangled with legal constraints. This methodology, however, while allowing for background social complexity, is at its best when the target for investigation is a fairly simple, easily measured, single variation in treatment for classic cases of the given disorder.

The evidence is growing in favour of a range of treatments for personality disorder, whether delivered separately or together. The American Psychiatric Association (2001) has gone as far as issuing practice guidelines for the treatment of patients with borderline personality disorder. In my view, the evidence is not yet far ranging enough to offer detailed evidence-based guidance for the likelihood of a particular treatment being effective for a particular person within offender patient groups. For such people, presenting personality disorders are rarely in 'pure form', and are more likely than not to be complicated by co-morbid illness and/or substance use disorders.

It makes sense, therefore, in each clinical case to offer extended assessment and a package of treatments tailored to the problems *and strengths* identified. It may be that medication and the more cognitive of the psychotherapies have a primary effect on co-morbid conditions and specific problems, and the more psychodynamically oriented treatments – individually, in groups or communities – are closer to treatments for characterological change. It may be that with ever-more sophisticated research methods we can tease these matters out further. For the patients, clinicians and their societies, however, the key criteria for a treatment package are that it should render the patient less distressed, demonstrably more functional and more prosocial.

REFERENCES

Ahmed I and Seifas R (1998). Randomized controlled trials (1959–1995): a prevalence study. *Archives of General Psychiatry* **55**:754–5.

Alden L (1989). Short-term structured treatment for avoidant personality disorder. *Journal of Consulting and Clinical Psychology* **56**:756–64.

American Psychiatric Association (2001). Practice guidelines for the treatment of patients with borderline personality disorder. *Americal Journal of Psychiatry* **158**(10), Supplement.

Andersen HS, Sesstoft D, Lillebaek T, Gabrielsen G, Hemmingsen R and Kramp P (2000). A longitudinal study of prisoners on remand. Psychiatric prevalence, incidence and psychopathology in solitary vs. non-solitary confinement. *Acta Psychiatrica Scandinavica* **102**:19–25.

Andrews DA, Zinger I, Hoge RD, Bonta D, Gendreau P and Cullen FT (1990). Does correctional treatment work? A clinically relevant and psychologically informed meta-analysis. *Criminology* **28**:369–404.

Auerbach AW (1977). The role of the therapeutic community 'street prison' in the rehabilitation of youthful offenders. PhD dissertation, George Washington

University, cited in Lees J, Manning N and Rawlings B (1999). *Therapeutic Community Effectiveness.* York: NHS Centre for Reviews and Dissemination, 126, 184.

Bateman A and Fonagy P (1999). Effectiveness of partial hospitalization in the treatment of borderline personality disorder: a randomized controlled trial. *American Journal of Psychiatry* **156**:1563–9.

Bateman A and Fonagy P (2000). Effectiveness of psychotherapeutic treatment of personality disorder. *British Journal of Psychiatry* **177**:138–43.

Bateman A and Fonagy P (2001). Treatment of borderline personality disorder with psychoanalytically oriented partial hospitalisation: an 18-month follow-up. *American Journal of Psychiatry* **158**:36–42.

Bateman AW and Tyrer P (2002). Effective management of personality disorder. Appendix to *Personality Disorder, No Longer a Diagnosis of Exclusion.* London: Department of Health (www.nimhe.org.uk).

Bebbington P and Kuipers L (1994). The predictive utility of expressed emotion in schizophrenia: an aggregate analysis. *Psychological Medicine* **24**:707–18.

Black DW, Baumgard CH and Bell SE (1995). The long-term outcome of antisocial personality disorder compared with depression, schizophrenia, and surgical conditions. *Bulletin of the American Academy of Science and the Law* **23**:43–52.

Bolton N, Smith FV, Heskin KJ and Bannister PA (1976). Psychological correlates of long term imprisonment IV. A longitudinal analysis. *British Journal of Criminology* **16**:38–47.

Buchanan A (1998). Criminal conviction after discharge from special hospital: incidence in the first ten years. *British Journal of Psychiatry* **172**:472–7.

Budman S, Demby A, Soldz S and Merry J (1996). Time-limited group psychotherapy for patients with personality disorders: outcome and drop-outs. *International Journal of Group Psychotherapy* **46**:357–77.

Canada (1977). Proceedings of the Subcommittee on the Penitentiary System in Canada. Standing Committee on Justice and Legal Affairs. House of Commons, Second Session of the Twentieth Parliament. March 8, 1977. Cited in Rice et al. (1992) – vide infra.

Chengappa KNR, Ebeling T, Kang JS, Levine J and Parepally H (1999). Clozapine reduces severe self-mutilation in psychotic patients with borderline personality disorder. *Journal of Clinical Psychiatry* **60**: 477–84.

Chiesa M (1997). A combined in-patient/out-patient programme for severe personality disorders. *Therapeutic Communities* **18**:297–309.

Chiesa M, Iacoponi E and Morris M (1996). Changes in health service utilization by patients with severe personality disorders before and after inpatient psychosocial treatment. *British Journal of Psychotherapy* **12**:501–12.

Coccaro EF and Karoussi RJ (1997). Fluoxetine and impulsive aggressive behavior in personality-disordered subjects. *Archives of General Psychiatry* **54**:1081–8.

Collins TC, Moore E and Taylor PJ (in preparation). PCL-R scores and engagement in treatment in a special hospital unit dedicated for young male offenders with personality disorder.

Copas JB and Whiteley JS (1976). Predicting success in the treatment of psychopaths. *British Journal of Psychiatry* **129**:388–92.

Cornish DB and Clarke RVG (1975). *Residential Treatment and its Effects on Delinquency.* London: HMSO.

Cowdry R and Gardner DL (1988). Pharmacotherapy of borderline personality disorder. *Archives of General Psychiatry* **45**:111–19.

Craft M, Stephenson G and Granger C (1964). A controlled trial of authoritarian and self-governing regimes with adolescent psychopaths. *American Journal of Orthopsychiatry* **34**:543–54.

Davison SE, Jamieson E and Taylor PJ (1999). Route of discharge for special (high security) hospital patients with personality disorder. *British Journal of Psychiatry* **175**:224–7.

Ekselius L and van Knorring L (1999). Changes in personality traits during treatment with sertraline or citalopram. *British Journal of Psychiatry* **174**:444–8.

Fleiss JC, Williams JBW and Dubro AF (1986). The logistic regression analysis of psychiatric data. *Journal of Psychiatric Research* **20**:145–209.

Gandhi N, Evans K, Lamont A and Harrison Read P (2001). A randomized controlled trial of community-oriented and hospital-oriented care for discharged psychiatric patients: influence of personality disorder on police contacts. *Journal of Personality Disorders* **15**:94–102.

Gardner DL and Cowdry RW (1986). Positive effects of carbamazepine on behavioral dyscontrol in borderline personality disorder. *American Journal of Psychiatry* **143**:519–22.

Genders E and Player E (1995). *Grendon: A Study of a Therapeutic Prison.* Oxford: Oxford University Press.

Goffman E (1961). *Asylums.* Anchor Books. Reprinted in 1968 by Penguin Books, Harmondsworth.

Goldberg SC, Schulz SC, Schellz PM et al. (1986). Borderline and schizotypal personality disorders treated with low-dose thiothixine vs placebo. *Archives of General Psychiatry* **43**:680–6.

Gunn J, Maden T and Swinton M (1991). Treatment needs of prisoners with psychiatric disorders. *British Medical Journal* **303**:338–40.

Gunn J, Robertson G, Dell S and Way C (1978). *Psychiatric Aspects of Imprisonment.* London: Academic Press.

Haddock CK, Rindskopf D and Shadish WR (1998). Using odds ratios as effect sizes for meta-analysis of dicholomous data: a timer and issues. *Psychological Methods* **3**:339–53.

Hare R (1991). *The Hare Psychopathy Checklist – Revised.* Toronto: Multi-Health Systems.

Hill LD, Rogers R and Bickford NE (1996). Predicting aggressive and socially disruptive behaviour in a maximum security forensic psychiatric hospital. *Journal of Forensic Sciences* **41**:56–9.

HM Prison Service, Safer Custody Group (2003). Self inflicted deaths: trends. *Safer Custody News,* July.

Hogeland P (1993). Personality disorders and long-term outcome after brief dynamic psychotherapy. *Journal of Personality Disorder* **7**:168–81.

Hollander E, Grossman R, Stein DJ and Kwon J (1996). Borderline personality disorder and impulsive-aggression: the role for divalproex sodium treatment. *Psychiatric Annals* **26**:s464–9.

Inciardi JA, Martin SS, Butzin CA, Hooper RM and Harrison LD (1997). An effective model of prison-based treatment for drug-involved offenders. *Journal of Drug Issues* **27**:261–78.

Jamieson L and Taylor PJ (2002). Mental disorder and perceived threat to the public: people who do not return to community living. *British Journal of Psychiatry* **181**:395–405.

Lees J, Rawlings B, George K, Manning N and Rawlings B (1999). *Therapeutic Community Effectiveness: A Systematic International Review of Therapeutic Community Treatment for People with Personality Disorders and Mentally Disordered Offenders.* York: York Publishing Services.

Lehman A and Ritzler B (1976). The therapeutic community inpatient ward: does it really work? *Comprehensive Psychiatry* **17**:755–61.

Leichsenring F and Leibing E (2002). The effectiveness of psychodynamic therapy and cognitive behavior therapy in the treatment of personality disorders: a meta-analysis. *American Journal of Psychiatry* **160**:1223–32.

Linehan MM, Tutek DA, Heard HL and Armstrong HE (1994). Interpersonal outcome of cognitive behavioral treatment for chronically suicidal borderline patients. *American Journal of Psychiatry* **151**:1771–6.

Lion JR (1979). Benzodiazepine in the treatment of aggressive patients. *Journal of Clinical Psychiatry* **40**:70–1.

Lipsey MW (1995). What do we learn from 400 research studies on the effectiveness of treatment with juvenile delinquents? In: McGuire J (ed.), *What Works: Reducing Re-offending.* Chichester: John Wiley & Sons, 63–78.

Lockwood D, Inciardi JA, Butzin CA and Hooper RM (1997). The therapeutic community continuum in corrections. In: de Leon G (ed.), *Community as Method. Therapeutic Communities for Special Populations and Special Settings.* Westport, CT: Praeger, Ch 6, 87–96.

Lösel F (1995). The efficacy of correctional treatment. A review and synthesis of meta-evaluations. In: Maguire J (ed.), *What Works: Reducing Reoffending.* Chichester: Wiley.

Lösel F (1998). Treatment and management of psychopaths. In: Cooke DJ, Forth AE and Hare RD (eds), *Psychopathy: Theory, Research and Implications for Society.* Dordrecht: Kluwer, 303–54.

Low G, Jones D, Duggan C, Power M and MacLeod A (2001). The treatment of deliberate self-harm in borderline personality disorders using dialectical behaviour therapy – a pilot study in a high security hospital. *Behavioural and Cognitive Psychotherapy* **29**:85–92.

MacCulloch MJ and Bailey J (1994). Judgements of dangerousness and release decisions in special hospitals. *Issues in Criminological and Legal Psychology* **21**:76–83.

Martin JP (1984). *Hospitals in Trouble.* Oxford: Blackwell.

Martin SS, Butzin CA and Inciardi JA (1995). Assessment of a multistage therapeutic community for drug-involved offenders. *Journal of Psychoative Drugs* **27**:109–16.

Mattes JA (1984). Carbamazepine for uncontrolled rage outburst. *Lancet* **ii**:1164–5.

McCord W and Sanchez J (1982). The Wiltwyck–Lyman Project: a twenty-five year follow-up study of milieu therapy. In: McCord WM (ed.), *The Psychopath and Milieu Therapy.* New York: Academic Press, 229–64.

McGuire J (ed.) (1995). *What Works: Reducing Reoffending – Guidelines from Research and Practice.* Chichester: John Wiley & Sons.

Merson S, Tyrer P, Onyett S, Lack S, Birkett Lynch S and Johnson T (1992). Early intervention in psychiatric emergencies. *Lancet* **339**:1311–14.

Miles AE (1969). The effects of a therapeutic community on the interpersonal relationships of a group of psychopaths. *British Journal of Criminology* **9**:22–38.

Miller WR and Rollnick S (1991). *Motivational Interviewing.* New York: Guilford.

Monroe-Blum H and Marziali E (1995). A controlled trial of short-term group treatment for borderline personality disorder. *Journal of Personality Disorders* **9**:190–8.

Monsen JT, Odland T and Eilertsen DE (1995). Personality disorders: changes and stability after intensive psychotherapy focusing on affect consciousness. *Psychotherapy Research* **5**:33–48.

Moore E, Ball RA and Kuipers L (1992). Expressed emotion in staff working with the long-term adult mentally ill. *British Journal of Psychiatry* **161**:802–8.

Moore E, Yates M, Mallindine C et al. (2002). Expressed emotion in relationships between staff and patients in forensic services: changes in relationship status at 12 month follow-up. *Legal and Criminological Psychology* **7**:203–18.

Moos RH (1997). *Evaluating Treatment Environments. The Quality of Psychiatric and Substance Abuse Programs*, 2nd edition. New Brunswick, NJ: Transaction.

Newton M (1971). *Reconviction after Treatment at Grendon.* Home Office Chief Psychologist Report Series B, No. 1. Reprinted in abridged version in Shine J (ed.) (2000). *A Compilation of Grendon Research.* Aylesbury: HMP Grendon, 205–19.

Newton M (1998). Changes in measures of personality, hostility and locus of control during residence in a prison therapeutic community. *Legal and Criminal Psychology* **3**:209–23.

Nielson AL, Scarpitti FR and Inciardi JA (1996). Integrating the therapeutic community and work

release for drug-involved offenders. The Crest Program. *Journal of Substance Abuse Treatment* **13**:349–58.

Ogloff J, Wong S and Greenwood A (1990). Treating criminal psychopaths in a therapeutic community programme. *Behavioral Sciences and the Law* **8**:81–90.

Parker A (1970). *The Frying Pan.* London: Hutchinson.

Perry JC (1993). Longitudinal studies of personality disorders. *Journal of Personality Disorder* **7**(Suppl.):63–85.

Perry JC, Banon E and Ianni F (1999). Effectiveness of psychotherapy for personality disorders. *American Journal of Psychiatry* **156**:1312–21.

Perry JC and Bond M (2000). Empirical studies of psychotherapy for personality disorders. In: Gunderson JG and Gabbard GO (eds), *Psychotherapy for Personality Disorders.* Washington, DC: American Psychiatric Press.

Piper WE, Rosie JS, Joyce AS and Azim HFA (1996). *Time-limited Day Treatment for Personality Disorders. Integration of Research and Practice in a Group Program.* Washington, DC: American Psychological Association.

Priestley P (1989). *Jail Journeys: The English Prison Experience 1918–1990.* London: Routledge and Kegan Paul.

Quayle M, Deu N and Giblin S (1998). Sexual knowledge and sex education in a secure hospital setting. *Criminal Behaviour and Mental Health* **8**:S66–76.

Quayle M and Moore E (1998). Evaluating the impact of structured groupwork with men in a high security hospital. *Criminal Behaviour and Mental Health* **8**:S77–92.

Reich JH and Green AI (1991). Effect of personality disorders on outcome of treatment. *Journal of Nervous and Mental Disease* **179**:74–8.

Reiss D, Grubin D and Meux C (1996). Young 'psychopaths' in special hospital: treatment and outcome. *British Journal of Psychiatry* **168**:99–104.

Reiss D, Grubin D and Meux C (1999). Institutional performance of male 'psychopaths' in a high security hospital. *Journal of Forensic Psychiatry* **10**:290–9.

Reiss D, Meux C and Grubin D (2000). The effect of psychopathy on outcome in high security patients. *Journal of the American Academy of Psychiatry and the Law* **28**:309–14.

Reiss D, Quayle M, Brett T and Meux C (1998). Dramatherapy for mentally disordered offenders: changes in levels of anger. *Criminal Behaviour and Mental Health* **8**:139–53.

Rice M and Harris GT (1992). A comparison of criminal recidivism among schizophrenic and nonschizophrenic offenders. *International Journal of Law and Psychiatry* **15**:397–408.

Rice ME, Harris GT and Cormier CA (1992). An evaluation of a maximum security therapeutic community for psychopaths and other mentally disordered offenders. *Law and Human Behavior* **16**:399–412.

Rifkin A, Quitkin F, Carillo C, Blumberg AG and Klein DF (1972). Lithium carbonate in emotionally unstable character disorders. *Archives of General Psychiatry* **27**:519–23.

Robertson G and Gunn J (1987). A ten-year follow-up of men discharged from Grendon Prison. *British Journal of Psychiatry* **151**:674–8.

Shaw J, Appleby L and Baker D (2003). *Safer Prisons*. National Confidential Inquiry. Manchester. London: Stationery Office.

Singleton N, Meltzer H, Gatward R, with Coid J and Deasy D (1998). *Psychiatric Morbidity among Prisoners in England and Wales*. London: The Stationery Office.

Soloff P (1992). Pharmacologic therapies in borderline personality disorder. In: Paris J (ed.), *Borderline Personality Disorder: Etiology and Treatment*. Washington, DC: American Psychiatric Press, 319–48.

Soloff PH, George A and Nathan RS (1986). Progress in pharmatherapy of borderline disorders: a double-blind study of amitryptiline, haloperidol and placebo. *Archives of General Psychiatry* **43**:691–7.

Stanton AH, Gunderson JG, Knapp PH, Frank AF, Vannicelli Schnitzer R and Rosenthal R (1984). Effects of psychotherapy in schizophrenia 1. Design and implementation of a controlled study. *Schizophrenia Bulletin* **10**:520–62.

Steadman HJ, Mulvey EP, Monahan J et al. (1998). Violence by people discharged from acute psychiatric inpatient facilities and by others in the same neighborhoods. *Archives of General Psychiatry* **55**:393–401.

Steels M, Roney G, Larkin E, Jones P, Croudace T and Duggan C (1998). Discharged from hospital: a comparison of the fates of psychopaths and the mentally ill. *Criminal Behaviour and Mental Health* **8**:39–55.

Stein G (1993). Drug treatment of the personality disorders. In: Tyrer P and Stein G (eds), *Personality Disorder Reviewed*. London: Gaskell, 262–304.

Stevenson J and Meares R (1992). An outcome study of psychotherapy for patients with borderline personality disorder. *American Journal of Psychiatry* **149**:358–62.

Taylor PJ (1986). Psychopaths and their treatment. *Journal of the Royal Society of Medicine* **79**:693–5.

Taylor PJ (2002). The institutionalisation of a concept. *Criminal Behaviour and Mental Health* **12**:s5–11.

Taylor R (2000). A seven year reconviction study of HMP Grendon Therapeutic Community. In: Shine J (ed.), *A Compilation of Grendon Research*. Aylesbury: HMP Grendon, 255–63.

Tennant G and Way C (1984). The English special hospitals: a 12–17 year follow-up study. *Medicine, Science and Law* **24**:81–91.

Tyrer P, Evans K, Gandhi N, Lamont A, Harrison-Read P and Johnson T (1998). Randomised controlled trial of two models of care for discharged psychiatric patients. *British* **316**:106–9.

Watts D and Morgan G (1994). Malignant alienation. *British Journal of Psychiatry* **164**:11–15.

Whitehorn JC and Betz B (1954). A study of psychotherapeutic relationships between physicians and schizophrenic patients. *American Journal of Psychiatry* **111**:321–31.

Whitehorn JC and Betz BJ (1960). Further studies of the doctor as a crucial variable in the outcome of treatment with schizophrenic patients. *American Journal of Psychiatry* **117**:215–23.

Whiteley JS (1970). The response of psychopaths to a therapeutic community. *British Journal of Psychiatry* **116**:517–29.

Wing JK (1962). Institutionalism in mental hospitals. *British Journal of Social and Clinical Psychology* **1**:38–51.

Wing JK (1990). The function of asylum. *British Journal of Psychiatry* **157**:822–7.

Winston A, Laikin M, Pollack J, Samstage LW, McCullough L and Muran JC (1994). Short-term psychotherapy of personality disorders. *American Journal of Psychiatry* **151**:190–4.

Zanarini MC and Frankenburg FR (2001). Olanzapine treatment of female borderline personality disorder patients: a double-blind, placebo-controlled pilot study. *Journal of Clinical Psychiatry* **62**:849–54.

CONCLUSION

TREATING PERSONALITY DISORDER: TOWARDS A FUTURE OF MORE MUTUALLY SATISFACTORY AND REWARDING OUTCOMES

Pamela J. Taylor, Chris Newrith and Clive Meux

SHIFTING THE PERSPECTIVE

What do you think is important in a treatment service for people with personality disorder? A majority of patients detained in a high-security hospital under the English legal category of 'psychopathic disorder' were willing and able to give coherent opinions (Ryan et al., 2002). It is arguable that they were in a particularly good position to do so because of their experience. Forty-eight of the 49 men and 8 of the 12 women had served a prison sentence, while 25 of the men and 11 of the women had had some in-patient hospital treatment prior to high-security hospitalization. At the time of the study, the median length of stay in the high-security hospital had been just over 6 years for the men and 4 years for the women. Most had had experience there of at least one kind of psychotherapy. These people wanted small (maximum 15 places), purpose-designed units, with domestic-style accommodation, which were not exclusive to people with personality disorder, and treatment. They did not like what they had experienced in prison

because, they said, there had been no treatment for them there, and there was a likelihood of violence and bullying. There was, however, one thing that many preferred about prison – the determinacy (in most cases) of a prison sentence. They were generally positive about hospital, except for the indeterminacy of their detention there. A few preferred the greater isolation they considered they could achieve in prison. Men were more likely than women to say that individual psychotherapy had helped them; patients who had co-morbid mental illness were less likely to appreciate group psychotherapy. A strong theme centred on staff qualities. When asked to list at least three qualities they thought would be necessary in staff for treatment to take place, not quite half wanted their staff to be experienced. With one exception, no other quality was mentioned by more than a fifth of the patients. The exceptional quality, volunteered by more than 80 per cent of the patients, was that staff must have a caring and understanding attitude.

Caring and understanding attitudes are among the experiences that have generally been in short supply through the lifetime of people with personality disorder. For some, this may have been the primary problem, resting in dysfunctional families and/or communities, with the disorder founded in pathologies of attachment (Chapter 6, McGauley and Rubitel) or social adversity (Chapter 10, Maughan). In extremes of social adversity it can be difficult to dissect out the extent to which the disorder emerges as a form of post-traumatic disorder (Chapter 15, Reiss), maladaptive learning (Chapter 11, Quayle and Moore), or an imbalance between capacity for action and capacity for thinking (Chapter 13, Skogstad) or, in reality, some combination of these. For others, the primary cause may have been in organic pathology (Chapter 7, Blair; Chapter 8, Bhagwagar and Cowen; Chapter 9, Fenton; and Chapter 16, Toone and Young). While any such problem could exert a directly adverse effect on development, early differences or disabilities could have rendered sufferers sufficiently unusual to provoke frequent rejection and stigmatization from all around them, including parents and peers, teachers and others in positions of trust and authority. Even for this organically disadvantaged group, social responses might have been the determining factor for adult outcome. In a close parallel, Theilgaard (1984), in showing that violence is not a cardinal feature of men with an extra Y chromosome, nevertheless identified a subgroup of such men reporting more aggression, and who had been arrested but not convicted more than controls. The XYY men were significantly more likely to have reported their childhood as poor on a number of measures, but inclusive of having been selected by their peers 'as a challenge' for fights in the playground. That finding related to people who merely looked unusually large. When people fail to relate warmly, when they are apparently rejecting help offered, and when they do horrible things to themselves and to others, it is very difficult for any of us to sustain caring and understanding attitudes. Indeed, from time to time some professional staff have even expressed a fear that in doing so, one may have become contaminated or manipulated.

THERAPIST QUALITIES AND QUALITY

Bowers (2002) is among the few who have studied staff attitudes. In hospitals, including high-security hospitals, the people with whom patients have most contact, other than with each other, are nurses. In embarking on qualitative research with nurses working in the English high-security hospitals with patients who have personality disorder, Bowers was clear about the horrible nature of the acts qualifying the patients' admission there. He noted that, in the privacy of a research interview, some nurses, while acknowledging that they 'wouldn't say [such things] out loud', could not help but describe some of their patients with personality disorder as 'bad', 'evil' or 'monstrous'. Bowers was able to extract from the narratives the qualities in patients that were most likely to attract such negative adjectives:

- they had not been abused as children,
- their index offence had been serious violence against vulnerable victims,
- their offence had been planned in advance and involved torture,
- they refused treatment in hospital,
- they showed no remorse,
- they appeared to be nice people.

These characteristics seem very similar to the defining features of a 'Hare psychopath' (Hare, 1991), and perhaps provide an indication of the extent to which apparently objective ratings may depend on the reactions of the observer/rater.

A further paragraph of Bowers' book is particularly telling of the difficulties and triumphs in working with such patients:

They bully, con, capitalize, divide, condition, and corrupt those around them. They make complaints over inconsequential or non-existent issues ... . They can be seriously violent over unpredictable and objectively trivial events, or may harm and disfigure themselves in ways that have an intense emotional impact on staff. If this were not enough, they behave in the same way towards each other, provoking serious problems that the staff have to manage and contain. On top of that the staff have to come to terms with the committed offences ... *Yet there are some staff who manage in a more positive fashion than others* (our italics).

Bowers goes on to describe the coping strategies of those more positive staff who offered him more personal cognitive strategies for dealing with their relationships with patients with personality disorder. These broadly fell into two categories – moral commitments and beliefs about disorder. Examples of the former were 'professionalism' – the idea that professionals provide a high-standard service regardless of who the client is – and 'universal humanity' – recalling that patients with personality disorder are members of the human race and therefore deserving of human rights, compassion and pity. Examples of disorder beliefs included 'behaviour/person split' – drawing a distinction between the behaviour as bad and the person, who is not; 'understand' – creating or accepting a model for understanding mental state and behaviour associations; and 'belief in treatment efficacy'. He then acknowledges how the whole institution may become perverse, abandoning or persecuting its staff, and makes clear recommendations to counter this, emphasizing training and supervision.

It is one thing, however, for people to admit, in private, to researchers that they may have personal difficulties in working with offenders who have personality disorder and, at arms length, to be creative about solutions. How can we identify, in the heat of practice, attitudes that threaten to compromise our skills? It is arguable that it would be useful to have

more power at our disposal in this respect than reliance on our colleagues to notice such problems or, even if they do, to enter the dangerous territory of telling us.

IMPROVING MAINTENANCE OF THE ENVIRONMENT FOR POSITIVE CHANGE

It seems increasingly to be acceptable, even expected, that supervision for the staff most in contact with residents or patients on a dedicated personality disorder unit will be available from trained psychotherapists and/or senior staff who are independent of the management structure of that unit. Independence of such supervision from line management is likely to be important so that people feel as little threat as possible from being candid. An interesting question follows, however, about the extent to which clinical managers, and perhaps senior managers in the organization as a whole, should nevertheless take part in this process. There is the possible value that, by doing so, they would be demonstrating leadership in the process by their active participation in supervision. Perhaps more fundamentally, could service or institutional managers also be able to protect themselves and the organization against maladaptive 'institutionalized attitudes' by such participation? In the UK, the concept of institutionalization of attitudes as a prime factor in creating an adverse working environment was most memorably introduced by the inquiry into the police investigation of the homicide of a young Anglo-Caribbean man, Stephen Lawrence (MacPherson et al., 1999). Recalling the earlier Scarman Inquiry, the MacPherson team agreed '... practices may be adopted by public bodies as well as private individuals which are unwittingly discriminatory against ...'. Here, the issue was 'institutional racism', but the definition may be helpful for institutions delivering services for people with major mental disorders, including personality disorder. It incorporates recognition that collective attitudes to them may be discriminatory, and not conducive to effective assessment and management of the challenges they pose, and yet not be fully conscious. Perhaps such attitudes need all the more attention if people are not fully aware of them.

We have known for decades, from research data, that institutional culture can affect the ability of clinicians to deliver effective treatment to people with major mental disorder (e.g. Wing and Brown, 1970): 'A substantial proportion of the morbidity shown by long-stay schizophrenic patients in mental hospitals is a product of their environment'. Perhaps we have had insufficient mental agility to translate this work, done in relation to the interaction between staff, their institution and people with schizophrenia, into the same sort of setting but where the primary disorder is personality disorder. We have barely considered the possibility that, with respect to a mental disorder, the presentation of 'institutionalism' is likely to be affected by the nature of that disorder. Thus, where the main disorder is residual schizophrenia, the institutional response is dominated by and reinforcing of the predominant presentations of anhedonia, anergia and anomie (e.g. Wing, 1990), but what if the main disorder is one of personality disorder, and the main presentation of antisocial traits? The risk is that the unhealthy institution may reinforce those delinquencies and perhaps, in turn, become delinquent. There is little or no research quality data to this effect, but underneath the rhetoric of the public inquiries into one of the English high-security hospitals (e.g. Blom-Cooper et al., 1992), some of the evidence suggests this. Perhaps more powerfully, the very concept of the therapeutic community, and the evidence of its effectiveness for various conditions, including personality disorder (Lees et al., 1999), provides evidence for the power of environment – this time the 'good environment'. However, a positive culture of this kind can only be

sustained with appropriate attention to staff and the environment in which they work and their patients live.

A FUTURE OF IMPROVEMENT IN MEASURES OF THE THERAPEUTIC RELATIONSHIP

Can recognition of staff needs, and work to meet them, be delivered in a more systematic or evidence-based way than is generally employed at present? One route to assessing the extent of the challenge to therapeutic relationships lies in the concept and measurement of expressed emotion (EE). This concept emerged as a way of describing characteristics in relationships between relatives of a person with schizophrenia and that person. It is explicit that such characteristics have the potential for effect on outcome (e.g. Bebbington and Kuipers, 1994). The original rating tool, the Camberwell Family Interview (CFI), requires lengthy training, then long interviews and time-consuming approaches to rating (Vaughn and Leff, 1976). Subsequently, Magaña et al. (1986) developed a screening instrument requiring rating only of a 5-minute speech sample. The subject is asked to talk for 5 minutes about his or her relationship with a designated person with a mental health problem. Moore and Kuipers (1999) applied the technique to staff relationships with patients, allowing five prompts:

1. What kind of a person is 'X'?
2. How easy has it been to get to know 'X'?
3. What is it like to work with 'X'?
4. What kind of things does 'X' do that are hard for you to deal with?
5. What kinds of things do you value/appreciate about 'X'?

Ratings are made on four sub-scales: the initial statement, which is scored as negative, neutral or positive; the quality of the relationship, scored along a five-point scale from strongly negative (1) to strongly positive (5); the number of critical comments and the number of positive remarks, both scored as in the CFI. They found that the measure reliably identified negatively charged relationships among staff working with general psychiatric patients in a day hospital service. Subsequently, with others, they have applied the technique to staff working with offender patients, and found it similarly helpful (Moore et al., 2002). Half of the latter sample had a personality disorder, with or without complicating psychosis, suggesting that the technique may indeed be useful for work with this group. It is important to stress the nature of the measure here, not least because it might enable it to become part of routine future practice. Although the measure is of a staff response, it is reflective of emergent qualities in the relationship with a particular patient, and only that. It is not indicative of primary personality traits in the staff member, nor of general relationship problems. It indicates a problem to be managed as part of the therapeutic process with the specific patient considered.

Our emphasis on staff attitudes and needs is important in itself, but also representative of the overall structure of this book. It was practical experience on Woodstock that made us aware of our own vulnerabilities, research in the hospital as a whole that tended to confirm their likely wider importance, and attention to the effort to recognize, assess, manage and use them by drawing on the literature that led us to understand their probable core importance for any personality disorder service anywhere. Effective processing of our responses to the dysfunctional and sometimes toxic relationship qualities of people with personality disorder not only paves the way to the provision of an appropriate substrate for engaging them in many of the processes of assessment and treatment described in earlier chapters, but can also be an integral part of the process. The dynamic psychotherapies rely on such process, but have been much criticized by many who have not endured the years of training necessary as apparently reliant on mystique rather than

science. There are also claims that they are far too long and expensive for the troubled masses, who cannot afford to pay their own therapy bills. A transparent, systematic and largely jargon-free approach to psychodynamic assessment, 'Operational Psychodynamic Diagnostics' (OPD), developed in Heidelberg, Germany for people with somatizing disorders (OPD Task Force, 2001), holds considerable promise for assessing readiness for treatment, identifying the focus or foci for psychotherapy, and monitoring qualities emergent in the therapeutic relationship. In order to use the assessment, it is necessary to have undergone training in all its aspects, but it is not necessary to have trained in psychodynamic psychotherapy, and every effort has been made to use terminology that is free of psychoanalytic 'jargon'. Measures are made across five axes.

Axis V need hardly detain us, since it simply maps on to the *International Classification of Diseases*, tenth revision (ICD-10; World Health Organization, 1992) or *Diagnostic and Statistical Manual of Mental Disorders*, fourth edition (DSM-IV; American Psychiatric Association, 1994). Axis IV systematizes the description of internal personality structure in terms of level of integration across five characteristics: self-perception, self-regulation, capacity for exercising defence mechanisms, ability to differentiate between internal and external reality, and ability to adapt to and communicate with others. Preliminary work with serious offender patients with personality disorder suggests a tendency to 'floor effects', with ratings towards the disintegrated end of the spectrum, but we have yet to run formal trials. Axis III requires identification of the principal pattern of internal conflict, notation of conflictual external stress, if present, and mode of mental processing (passive or active, the latter including frankly aggressive modes). Those offender patients with the most severe personality disorders may struggle to recognize internal conflict; a risk for the rater here then becomes the possibility of projecting onto the prospective patient the conflict that he or she 'ought to have'.

Most patients will show varying levels of conflict with external stressors. The latter, for this group, are likely to range from experience of the most recent or serious offence (which, contrary to popular belief, leaves many such patients traumatized), through difficulties acclimatizing to incarceration and close proximity to people with similar disorders, to the battles they have and perceive themselves as having with a stigmatizing society and coercive authorities. Axis II is of most interest in terms of recognizing how relationships become defined. Pure self-experience is not rated here, but rather those experiences, whether or not including conflicts, that are recognized at the interpersonal level.

Interpersonal relationships require rating from each of four interpersonal positions: the patient's experience of him/herself, the investigator/therapist's experience of the patient, the patient's experience of others, *and* the investigator/therapist's experience of him/herself during interaction with the patient. The ratings are explicitly to be of repeated or continuous experiences from these four perspectives: '*time and again* the ... experiences ... him/herself in such a way that s/he is ... .' (our italics). The 30 items, constituting 13 clusters, are the same for each position (e.g. item 'much admiring and idealizing'; item 'attacking and threatening'; cluster 'controlling'; cluster 'reacting as offended'). In the final stage of rating, up to three main items or clusters are selected for each position, which may be used as they are, or to lead into a more traditional dynamic formulation, or to represent active and passive modes in an interpersonal circumplex model. In the latter case, the horizontal axis would be from affiliation to alienation (attack to active love in the active mode; recoil to reactive love in the reactive) and the vertical axis the independence dimension (from allowing autonomy to control in the active mode; assert to submit in the reactive).

It is too early to say whether this approach will be as helpful in practice as it appears at face value. It will be for future research to determine this, and to evaluate the extent to which the staff contribution to interpersonal relations in these terms relates to therapeutic engagement and long-term outcome. Complementary inquiry could be about the extent to which recognition of the staff position can lead to effective/more effective staff support, supervision and training systems that will enhance the prospect of such engagement and, ultimately, therapeutic success.

BETTER MEASURES OF READINESS FOR TREATMENT?

Shifting the focus from staff, but not yet moving on from 'OPD', Axis I merits mention too. It provides for the assessment of 'treatability'. In the UK, the concept of treatability was introduced into the Mental Health Act 1983 (for England and Wales) expressly to limit powers of compulsory detention for treatment for people under the legal categories of psychopathic disorder and mental impairment. In legal terms, the definitions of these two conditions are the same, except that the latter is explicitly a developmental disorder with impairment of intelligence, but for the former, impairment of intelligence is allowed within the definition, though not required. The 2002 special supplement (1) of the *Journal of Intellectual Disability Research* seems indirectly to endorse this close relationship, at least in terms of underscoring the difficulties in defining the boundaries of intellectual disability and the limited evidence base for effective treatment (Fraser, 2002). Johnston (2002), in the same supplement, adds cautions about the specificity of risk assessment in a learning disabled group. If only there were such circumspection in relation to personality disorder, for which there is almost an in-built bias towards assuming risk of harm to others.

The 'treatability principle' in the legislation means that it is only possible to detain a person with mental impairment or personality ('psychopathic') disorder if treatment can be expected to alleviate the disorder or at least prevent deterioration. There have been cases for which clarification has been sought in a higher court on the meaning of treatment and treatability in law (e.g. *Cannons Park*), but the evidence base for a treatability concept, and how to assess it, is weak. As a result, it is thought that some people who would have benefited from treatment in hospital have been excluded on these grounds, and, in England and Wales, occasionally independent mental health review tribunals have accepted that a person originally detained as treatable is no longer considered to be so. In these circumstances, as there are no legal grounds for continued detention, regardless of any risk to the person concerned or to the public, the order for detention must be discharged. The practical effect of this is that the individual sufferer not only leaves in-patient treatment, but also abandons, and is often abandoned by, out-patient mental health services. On both health and safety grounds, therefore, there is a need to improve the determination of treatability. A similar need is arguable on economic grounds. It seems ironic that with the prospect of improvements in the assessment of this elusive quality, proposed legislative reform in England and Wales threaten its removal. Only the requirement for treatment *availability* will remain as a result of human rights legislation. By contrast, in the Netherlands, a treatability criterion is being introduced in the TBS system, where a risk reduction model for release is proving very expensive (Drost, 2005).

It is possible, then, that OPD Axis I could provide for improvements in the assessment of treatability of personality disorder. Further, in conjunction with the other axes, it may enable more accurate focus of treatment. It seems likely, however, that, before such progress can be achieved for offenders with personality disorder, this Axis needs modification to reflect some of the issues more specific to them. Many of the characteristics likely to predispose to treatability, such as motivation for treatment, were already included in the original manual (OPD Taskforce, 2001). Others more specific to these groups were not, such as the nature of any index offending, the place of residence at the time of assessment – possibly prison, beliefs about alternatives, e.g. hospital as a 'softer option'; or real or perceived coercion into treatment. These items have been incorporated for the second edition of the manual (OPD Taskforce, 2006).

People with more severe disorders may initially lack the capacity to recognize the depth of their problems or to be consistent in their motivation for change. Lack of capacity is readily accepted as a possibility for a person at the height of a psychotic episode, and this would also be the case for someone with an intellectual or learning disability, but capacity is rarely considered in relation to personality disorder. A future task may therefore be to develop tools to assist in the measurement of capacity for decision making and behavioural control specifically appropriate to personality disorder. It is for people who have impaired capacity because of such disorder that a coercive framework in legislation may be helpful in facilitating a path to treatment. We use the terminology 'coercive framework' deliberately, because, although this book focuses on treatment in a secure hospital, coercion into treatment need not necessarily mean detention in an institution. Furthermore, perhaps particularly in relation to personality disorder, it is often not only the designated patient who needs binding into the arrangement. Once there is a legal requirement for a person to have treatment and supervision, there is also a requirement that it must be provided; regular formal reviews, which are required in a compulsory framework, may also provide safeguards that the treatment and supervision are and remain appropriate to need.

RISKS AND BENEFITS OF PERSONALITY DISORDER AS A DISORDER ATTRACTING PUBLIC AND POLITICAL INTEREST

The uncertainties about the management and treatment of people with personality disorder mean that, for the foreseeable future, it will be almost impossible to disregard the politics surrounding the condition. When the process of devolution of much of the government of the UK to its constituent countries started, the first piece of legislation passed by the first devolved parliament (in Scotland) was very specific and about personality disorder. The over-arching British government has received much criticism for creating a moral panic in England and Wales, promulgating the idea that the countries contain 2400 people they describe as suffering from 'DSPD' – 'dangerous and severe personality disorder' (Home Office, Department of Health, 1999). Depending on perspective, this followed or was associated by accident with a high-profile multiple assault and double murder in 1998. A man, recently discharged from a psychiatric hospital, allegedly with an untreatable personality disorder, was convicted of the offences, but the convictions were set aside; he was reconvicted at retrial, but has lodged a further appeal against the convictions. Seven years later, in 2005, an independent inquiry into events surrounding his discharge has still not been published; some wonder if this could be because it does not condemn the healthcare workers who briefly looked after this man, or the current legislative system.

In theory, 'DSPD' would be so terrible that its sufferers would need to be segregated in new, specialist services spread between high-security prisons and high-security hospitals. Publication of a first draft Mental Health Bill in 2002, although abandoning all reference to 'DSPD' by this name, created a definition of mental disorder so broad that it became hard to know who would be excluded: '"Mental disorder" means any disability or disorder of mind or brain which results in an impairment or disturbance of mental functioning'. This Bill also removed treatability criteria per se, although, bound by the European Convention on Human Rights and consequent British human rights legislation, the Bill allows that it would be illegal to detain someone for treatment if no treatment were available. Proposed legal enshrinement of expectations about information sharing, where at least the doctor–patient relationship has carried an expectation of confidentiality, creates further alarm. A clinically taken decision to override aspects of confidentiality in an occasional situation of high risk of serious harm has long been accepted as ethical; a requirement to breach confidentiality routinely on suspicion of a 51 per cent risk of harm (or higher), calculated on the basis of imperfect risk assessment tools, is quite another. The Bill has united clinicians, patients, families and mental health lawyers, and many more besides, in opposition to it. A further draft Bill of 2004 is little changed. Drafting of the Bill and accompanying Codes of Practice continues, but in early 2006, Parliament has not yet passed the legislation.

Yet, while one aspect of political intervention has caused so much concern, without political interest in a problem, progress can rarely be made. Such interest can create enormous opportunities, through renewal of professional attention to a problem, by provision of funds to develop services and research, and by providing a focus for the co-ordination of such initiatives. In Britain, early emphasis on criminological, regime-based models for assessment and treatment raised further concerns (Taylor, 2002), but the English Department of Health has subsequently begun to demonstrate a more active role with its governmental criminal justice partner – the Home Office – in part marked by its document *Personality Disorder: No Longer a Diagnosis of Exclusion* (National Institute for Mental Health in England, 2003).

It is good news if, as a society, we can acknowledge personality disorder as a mental disorder like any other. This may deflect some of the expressed anxiety among people who suffer with personality disorder that the act of seeking help could put them at risk of adverse labelling, or undue constraints. It could also lead to better treatment and research programmes and attract high-calibre professionals to the field.

FUTURE RESEARCH DIRECTIONS

So what are the indications for research in the future? Although the core of this book is about the treatment of personality disorder once established *and* associated with serious antisocial behaviour, prevention of the disorder, where possible, must be a primary consideration for the wider community. Primary prevention cannot, however, be ignored, even by people who construe themselves primarily as therapists. Many patients have dependent children. The genetics of personality disorder are not yet well documented or understood; many parents with such disorders have a lifestyle that could inflict environmental damage on their offspring, even in utero, for example through poor nutrition, smoking or substance misuse. The extent to which this may directly cause personality disorder or act more by interaction with other factors, including genetic factors, is unclear; people with personality disorder may be disproportionately unlikely to be able to meet the demands of rearing children, for a variety of reasons. Perhaps they lack many of the skills, which in any case many themselves never experienced at first hand; perhaps the very seriousness of their position, with their disorder and its attendant antisocial behaviour, has necessitated their removal from their family as well as from wider society; some may never have experienced any sense of attachment in the first place.

We have seen little or no reference in any material about the treatment of personality disorder to the effect that the therapists of those with the personality disorder must enquire about the needs of dependent children, and perhaps also include them in a holistic treatment plan. Assumptions that the needs of such children might be identified and met by other routes are unsafe. We saw the whole range of difficulties on Woodstock. There were young men who, in a one-night stand, had fathered a child they had never seen, but also young men who cared deeply about their children, but, perhaps because of a seriously violent relationship with their partner, were barred from seeing those children. There were men who persisted, in accordance with the child's wishes and external validation of the interests of the child, in the struggle to build a relationship with a child who would otherwise have had only the possibility of nursing a dark secret about a murderer or criminal for a father. The children of only some of the men had received independent help with this. There are some data on the enormous disadvantage to a child of an absent father (e.g. Wilson, 1987), and we can infer disadvantage from having an abusive or murderous one at home. For the most part, the men were not the primary caretakers when separated from their child; women in such circumstances often were, with the added implications for the children of having to accommodate to a new living environment when their mother went into hospital or prison.

Harrington and Bailey (2003) have reviewed the evidence on interventions for the prevention of antisocial personality disorder. They take a broad, systems view, exploring evidence for the effectiveness of universal programmes as well as more targeted initiatives. They are cautious about the evidence for the universal programmes, which have tended to show up well in small-scale studies, but show small effects in large-scale studies or meta-analyses. The reasons for this may include the difficulties in sustaining them, and the limitation to 'low-dose' interventions when delivered on a large scale. Notwithstanding the risk of stigma, they rather advocate more targeted interventions towards children or adolescents already showing behaviours or disorders and/or in situations known to be associated with higher risk of subsequent development of adult personality disorder. A simplistic proposal might be that children of men or women with established personality disorder, particularly when this is associated with antisocial behaviour, would be candidates. There is a steady growth of literature, however, which may allow even better focus.

The Woodstock approach to treatment follows from recognition of the complexity of disorders of personality and their impact, and by the same token the developmental pathways towards such a state. Nevertheless, there is a risk that by giving some of the models for understanding the development of disorders of personality in separate chapters, we have not emphasized the interactions between causal factors enough. There has been a tendency in research and in literature generally to adopt unitary models, and to simplify, not least because scientific method is generally best suited to testing simple models. Nevertheless, there is a growth in the literature that does offer evidence on interactions and complex models, well founded in substantial longitudinal cohort studies, and this is surely the future for better understanding of the nature and timing of early interventions. Caspi et al. (2002), for example, tested genotype–environment interactions in all the males in the Dunedin birth cohort, using data prospectively collected from birth to age 26. They note that childhood maltreatment is a universal risk factor for antisocial personality and violent behaviour, but that there are nevertheless large differences between children in their response to maltreatment. Monoamine oxidase A (MAO-A) is a neurotransmitter that has previously been linked to violent behaviour (Brunner et al., 1993). Caspi and colleagues found that having the X-linked gene for MAO-A moderated the effect of having been maltreated. Those with a genotype conferring high levels of MAO-A expression were less likely to develop antisocial behaviour problems.

They are cautious about the implications, however, and call for replication before applying such findings in practice. Reference to genotypes could once again raise fears of eugenics, and indeed one of us and some of the Caspi and Moffitt group contributed to earlier, extensive consideration of the ethical implications of such work (Nuffield Council on Bioethics, 1998, 2002). To be purely practical too, it remains the case that the findings still leave us to work with probabilities rather than certainties, but the principle of gathering evidence about important interactions with a longer-term aim of improving the nature and specificity of the help that can be offered to people seems sound.

New and improving techniques for investigating brain activity are likely to provide another area for future research development. Already, with the application of functional imaging techniques, there is some indication of differences in brain activation under certain circumstances and when presented with different tasks (e.g. Das et al., submitted; see also Chapter 7). Response inhibition is an important ability, which may be compromised in people with personality disorder, and for which there appears to be some organic basis (e.g. Vollm et al., 2004; Kumari et al., submitted). Still improving resolution of images, and newer technology that will offer clarity of activity measures in real time, and that does not require the person being tested to be fully encased in a potentially claustrophobia-inducing machine, hold out yet more promise. It is perhaps, as yet, less clear how such developments will inform clinical practice, save perhaps to underscore that some such disorders have some 'physical reality', and that expectations of social and/or psychological treatments may have to be adjusted accordingly. It is not impossible, though, that findings from brain imaging will also assist in identifying the pathway by which an individual has come to a particular state, and even, therefore, a pathway out of it. Such findings may also help focus more preliminary interventions, for example indicating a route for the stabilization of more apparently impulsive disruptions of engagement in assessment or treatment, and more psychological assessment packages can be supported with truly relevant physical tests. Further, for patients with whom there may be concern about the possible dissimulation, it may even be feasible to provide outcome evidence of functional change in brain activity as well as apparent change in self-report, or on questionnaires and psychological tests.

Questions about whether personality can change, in what aspects and how to demonstrate any such change reliably remain only partially resolved. In seeking answers to these, Duggan (2004) draws on the Costa and McCrea (1980) model of personality, which distinguished between 'basic tendencies' and 'characteristic adaptations'. This fits well with the attempt one of us made elsewhere (see Chapter 30) to distinguish between the possibility on the one hand of apparent improvement because of better fit of environment and social structures to need and, on the other, real change, which will be generalizable to other settings. Duggan goes on to commend multiple measures of change, as do we, but to observe how limited even this approach can be if there is failure to take into account that when some aspects of the person's pathology change for the better, there may not be concordant changes in other areas. He seems to find that discouraging, but observation of such partial or contradictory changes may be what we need to help distinguish between mere re-adjustment and good-enough change.

Just as more complex models are beginning to emerge as testable with respect to pathways in to personality disorder, so the future may bring something similar for pathways out. It is very important to know about the natural history of a condition in order to test the impact of treatment. Some have suggested that the natural course of personality disorder could be towards maturation and improvement, if only the sufferer can be sustained through the years of peak disturbance (e.g. Stone, 1990). Discovery of pathways out of personality disorder will take time and large samples. Some of the birth or childhood cohort studies will be sustained for long enough for some clearer answers to emerge. The men in the Cambridge delinquency study (e.g. Farrington, 2003), for example, are now in their forties, the men and women in the Dunedin birth cohort (e.g. Moffitt et al., 2001) in their thirties. A limitation of such studies, however, as would be expected from true community sampling, is that the sub-groups with clinically important pathology are very small. Substantial long-term studies of people who have been treated are essential, and there are a few (e.g. Paris and Zweig-Frank, 2001), but they are limited by substantial attrition in numbers 'surviving'. They are also becoming harder to envisage, in Britain at least, in a new increasingly bureaucratic climate of research ethics, perhaps also biased in the patient/service user rights it protects. Many people with personality disorders may be among those least likely to have the ability to sustain long-term compliance with a research project, or the wish to do so. It would not be surprising if people were keen to put the experience of a long period of residence in secure accommodation behind them. It is necessary, however, to find a way through these difficulties, because such people need research to improve their health outcomes. Perhaps a partial answer lies in the fact that most of our residents, and many other patients/service users, are themselves enthusiastic about becoming more involved with research at the design stage, and beginning to show initiative in this.

THE HEALTH ECONOMICS OF PERSONALITY DISORDER

Another matter for the future, which we, like most, have barely considered so far, lies in the economics of the disorder. Woodstock is an expensive service, as is any other in a secure hospital setting. Furthermore, not only do patients require a long period of treatment in such services, but most will also need long-term maintenance treatment and an integrated package of lengthy social care. Additional systems often exist for monitoring more serious offenders in the community, regardless of treatment outcome, systems that are largely independent of clinical or social supervision. In England and Wales, the Home Office dedicates whole departments to such monitoring, while more local arrangements are now focused on the provision of 'multi-agency public protection panels' (MAPPPs), the agencies including health services, social services, other local authority service representatives, such as housing officers, the probation service and police. Care may be needed for the individual's family or close associates as well as for the individual him/herself. If specialist treatment for personality disorder is to become much more widely available, not only for lesser offenders but also for the great majority of people with personality disorder who do not commit criminal offences, that too will be at considerable cost. Given finite resources, other costly services will have to be reduced or stopped in order to fund new developments. This concept is alien to many clinicians. The location of funds for new or improved services may partly lie in understanding the costs of not treating.

There is to date no clear idea of such costs, but evidence only from people who enter offender services would suggest that the financial burden from untreated personality disorder is considerable. Cohen et al. (1994) showed how to approach the task of counting this group of costs. This is far from straightforward. Whenever an offence is committed, there are direct criminal justice costs to police and, once charges have been made, to a range of other criminal justices services, including the courts. Any conviction results in a sentence, which is more or less expensive according to the level of supervision required, with prison

costs if a penal sentence is incurred. In England and Wales in 2004, more than 75 000 people are imprisoned at any one time; in 1987, more than three-quarters were considered to have a diagnosis of personality disorder, and there is no reason to believe that this proportion has changed (Singleton et al., 1998). Cohen and colleagues, however, note additional, indirect costs. These may include loss to the economy because the offender is not employed, as well as the victim's costs, perhaps in hospital treatment, compensation, loss of earnings. If the offence was a homicide, the cost of the loss of the victim to the economy may also be considerable; relatives of the victim may also have lost time from work, may be traumatized and using services, or, where there were dependent children, the financial burden of rearing them may also fall on the community. It is not difficult to see how enormous the costs of failure to treat could become for an offender group. Even for those who never offend, there are all the costs, commonly occurred by offender patients too, of chronic, relapsing disorders, with frequent demands for services when in a health or social crisis. Indeed, one outcome measure that has been applied to non-offenders using personality disorder services is number of uses of other services in crisis. A marker of successful treatment, in these terms, is reduction in the use of emergency/out-of-hours services.

There is a long way to go in understanding the health economics of personality disorder. A complete picture will include not only costs, but also quality of life for those who have the disorder and that of their immediate associates, particularly any children.

CONCLUSION

'Treatability' of personality disorder rests in part with the patient, but in part also with others. The range of disorders we have come to call personality disorder present as disorders of interpersonal relationships. Friction with and alienation from others may have caused such disorders, and are likely to maintain them; much more knowledge is needed about how to maintain a therapeutic environment. To return to our opening chapter, 'starting is easy ...'. The effect of personality disorders, however, can be ameliorated if the individual sufferer can be held in appropriately skilled professional and healthy peer relationships. Questions remain about the nature and extent of improvement for people with personality disorder after such holding, and with more specific treatments, and the extent, therefore, to which some of those whose capacity to engage in treatment is impaired should be coerced into that treatment. We need more sophisticated outcome measures, inclusive of the health economics of the disorder, as well as the already accepted need to find ways of being sure of change and containing the risk of further harm to health or life. In this chapter we have just touched on the range of gaps to be filled and offered a few examples of ways forward. In Britain, a better future for the treatment of people with personality disorder, especially those whose disorders render them a danger to themselves or others, seems a bit closer given government interest and funding, renewed clinical interest on the part of many, the application of new research technologies and the construction of more complex models for testing developmental pathways and clinical outcomes. Our main interest is in the subgroup of people with personality disorder who commit serious offences, but, as with other major mental disorders, most sufferers will not also become criminals. Over-emphasis on the dangers for the general public from people with personality disorders (even from the flamboyant group), with requirements for infallible systems of care and treatment and/or mental health law which veers towards preventive detention, could damage the fragile positive potential of the developments outlined here.

REFERENCES

American Psychiatric Association (1994). *Diagnostic and Statistical Manual of Mental Disorders,* fourth edition. Washington, DC: American Psychiatric Association.

Bebbington P and Kuipers L (1994). The predictive utility of Expressed Emotion in schizophrenia: an aggregate analysis. *Psychological Medicine* **24**:707–18.

Blom-Cooper L, Brown M, Dolan R and Murphy E (1992). *Reports of the Committee of Inquiry into the Complaints about Ashworth Hospital*, CM2028 1–11. London: HMSO.

Bowers L (2002). *Dangerous and Severe Personality Disorder. Response and Role of the Clinical Team.* London/New York: Routledge.

Brunner HG, Nelan M, Breakefield XO, Ropers HH and van Oost BA (1993). Abnormal behaviour associated with a point mutation in the structural gene for monoamine oxidase A. *Science* **262**:578.

Caspi A, McClay J, Moffitt TE et al. (2002). Role of genotype in the cycle of violence in maltreated children. *Science* **297**:851–4.

Cohen MA, Miller TR and Rossman SB (1994). The cost and consequences of violent behavior in the United States. In: Reiss AJ and Roth JA (eds), *Understanding and Preventing Violence* Vol. 4, Washington, DC: National Academy Press, 67–216.

Costa PT and McCrae RR (1980). Still stable after all these years: personality as a key to some issues in aging. In: Baltes PB and Brim OG (eds), *Life-span Development and Behaviour.* San Diego, CA: Academic Press, Vol. 3, 65–102.

Das M, Kumari V, Taylor PJ et al. (submitted). A functional MRI investigation of anticipatory fear among violent men with schizophrenia or personality disorder. (Contact taylorpj2@cardiff.ac.uk for further information.)

Drost M (2005). Debate on policy and legislation from an international perspective at *The NoMS International Conference on the Management and Treatment of Dangerous Offenders*, York, UK, September 2005.

Duggan C (2004). Does personality change and, if so, what changes? *Criminal Behaviour and Mental Health* **14**:5–16.

Farrington DP (2003). Key results from the first 40 years of the Cambridge Study in Delinquent Development. In: Thornberry TP and Krohn MD (eds), *Taking Stock of Delinquency: A Overview of Findings from Contemporary Longitudinal Studies.* New York: Kluwer/Plenum, 137–83.

Fraser WI (2002). Executive summary. *Journal of Intellectual Disability Research* **46**(Suppl. 1):1–5.

Hare RD (1991). *The Hare Psychopathy Checklist – Revised (PCL-R).* Toronto, Ontario: Multi-Health Systems.

Harrington R and Bailey S (2003). The scope for preventing antisocial personality disorder by intervening in adolescence. *Criminal Behaviour and Mental Health* **13**:75–81. (A longer version of this work is available through the British Department of Health National Programme on Forensic Mental Health Research and Development Committee: http://www.dh.gov.uk/forensicmentalhealth.)

Home Office, Department of Health (1999). *Managing Dangerous People with Severe Personality Disorder: Proposals for Policy Development.* London: Department of Health.

Johnston SJ (2002). Risk assessment in offenders with intellectual disability: the evidence base. *Journal of Intellectual Disability Research* **46**(Suppl. 1): 47–56.

Kumari V, Das M, Taylor PJ et al. (submitted). Association between violent behaviour and impaired prepulse inhibition of the startle response in personality disorder and schizophrenia. (Contact taylorpj2@cardiff.ac.uk for further information.)

Lees J, Manning N and Rawlings B (1999). *Therapeutic Community Effectiveness. Systematic Review of Therapeutic Community Treatment for People with Personality Disorders and Mentally Disordered Offenders.* CRD Report 17. York: NHS Centre for Reviews and Dissemination.

MacPherson W, Cook T, Sentamu J and Stone R (1999). *The Stephen Lawrence Inquiry.* Cm4262-1-11. London: The Stationery Office.

Magaña AB, Goldstein MJ, Karno M, Miklowitz DJ, Jenkins J and Falloon IRH (1986). A brief method for assessing Expressed Emotion in relatives of psychiatric patients. *Psychiatry Research* **17**:203–12.

Moffitt TE, Caspi A, Rutter M and Silva PA (2001). *Sex Differences in Antisocial Behaviour: Conduct Disorder, Delinquency and Violence in the Dunedin Longitudinal Study.* Cambridge: Cambridge University Press.

Moore E and Kuipers E (1999). The measurement of Expressed Emotion in relationships between staff and service users: the use of short speech samples. *British Journal of Clinical Psychology* **38**:345–56.

Moore E, Yates M, Mallindine C et al. (2002). Expressed Emotion in relationships between staff and patients in forensic services: changes in relationship status at 12 month follow-up. *Legal and Criminological Psychology* **7**:203–18.

National Institute of Mental Health in England (2003). *Personality Disorder: No Longer a Diagnosis of Exclusion.* Leeds: Department of Health.

Nuffield Council on Bioethics (1998). *Mental Disorders and Genetics: The Ethical Context.* London: Nuffield Council on Bioethics.

Nuffield Council on Bioethics (2002). *Genetics and Human Behaviour: The Ethical Context.* London: Nuffield Council on Bioethics.

OPD Taskforce (2001). *Operational Psychodynamic Diagnostics.* Seattle, Toronto, Bern, Gottingen: Hogrefe & Huber.

OPD Taskforce (2006). *OPD-2 Das Manual für Diagnostik und Therapieplanung.* Bern: Verlag Hans Huber.

Paris J and Zweig-Frank H (2001). A 27-year follow-up of patients with personality disorder. *Comprehensive Psychiatry* **42**:482–7.

Ryan S, Moore E, Taylor PJ, Wikinson E, Lingiah T and Christmas M (2002). The voice of detainees in a high security setting on services for people with personality disorder. *Criminal Behaviour and Mental Health* **12**:254–68.

Singleton N, Meltzer H, Gatward R, Coid J and Deasy D (1998). *Psychiatric Morbidity among Prisoners in England and Wales.* London: The Stationery Office.

Stone MH (1990). *The Fate of Borderline Patients.* New York: Guilford.

Taylor PJ (2002). Personality disorder: the institutionalisation of a concept. *Criminal Behaviour and Mental Health* **12**:S5–11.

Theilgaard A (1984). A psychological study of the personalities of XYY and XXY men. *Acta Psychiatrica Scandinavica* **69**, Supplimentum 315.

Vaughn CE and Leff JP (1976). The measurement of Expressed Emotion in the families of psychiatric patients. *British Journal of Psychology* **15**:157–65.

Völlm B, Richardson P, Stirling J et al. (2004). Neurobiological substrates of antisocial and borderline personality disorder: preliminary results of an fRMI study. *Criminal Behaviour and Mental Health* **14**:39–54.

Wilson WJ (1987). *The Truly Disadvantaged: The Inner City, the Individual and Public Policy.* Chicago, IL: Chicago University Press.

Wing JK (1990). The functions of asylum. *British Journal of Psychiatry* **157**:822–7.

Wing JK and Brown GW (1970). *Institutions and Schizophrenia.* Cambridge: Cambridge University Press.

World Health Organization (1992). *International Classification of Diseases,* tenth revision. Geneva: World Health Organization.

CASE LAW

Cannons Park

R v. Cannons Park Mental Health Review Tribunal, ex parte A [1993] Court of Appeal [1994] Times Law Report 2.3.1994.

APPENDICES

WHO CARE'S WHAT HAPPEN'S

IT'D NOT THERE

I'M JUST A NVMBER TO THEM ALL!

IF I KILL! WHO'S TO BLAME?

IT'S YOVR'S YOU DIDN'T HELP WHEN I ASK FOR IT.

WHY ME? WHAT HAVE I DON TO DESERVE IT! IS IT A TEXT WILL I PASS OR FAIL

DO THE WORLD WANT TO HELP ME?

NO IS THE ANSWER

NO ONE LISTENS WHEN I CALL OVT FOR

HELP

WHY?

IT'S BEING UNSVRE OF THE PERSON THEY BECOME SCARED OF THEM SO THEY RUN AWAY FORM THEM.

WHAT'S THE ANSWER TO IT ALL?

LOCK THEM VP.

THEY ARE ANIMALS

PROBLEM!

WHY DON'T YOU UNDERSTAND ME?

WHEN I SCREAM DO I SCARE YOU WITH MY ILLNESS.

WHY DO WE NOT ASK FOR

HELP!

INTRODUCTION

Contained in the appendices are additional issues that may be of interest to the reader. The editors, mindful that the vast majority of this text describes treatment from the narrow perspective of UK-based practice, invited overseas colleagues to describe the salient issues pertaining to the models of care employed in their country in treating offenders with clinically important personality disorders. These examples are not intended to be exhaustive, but are provided mainly to emphasize the point that culture and social climate will affect the way in which such people are regarded and the nature and extent of the treatment offered. We also wanted to include some different perspectives to underscore our view that although we perceive our model as eclectic and holistic, other models should also prove stimulating and thought provoking, and that in the spirit of TS Eliot, '...the end of all our exploring/ will be to arrive where we started/and know the place for the very first time'.

From the Netherlands, Dr Peter Greeven of the Ministry of Justice recounts the evolution of the Dutch special hospital order, the TBS Act, and the wider effect this has had on Dutch forensic psychiatry, particularly from the viewpoint of efficiency and increased financial accountability. Then, from Denmark, Dr Peter Gottlieb describes the manner in which tensions between organic and functional psychiatry, and psychological and pharmacological approaches, were tackled in the Danish system. He describes how legislative changes to Section 69 – the hospital treatment order – of the Danish Penal Law led to a revision in practices, this last point being demonstrated by specific examples from the Herstedvester Detention Centre.

Finally, a fascinating transatlantic perspective is provided by Drs Zoe Hilton, Grant Harris and Marnie Rice from the Oak Ridge Maximum Security Hospital in Penetanguishene, Ontario, Canada. In this setting, a variety of therapeutic approaches are subjected to rigorous evaluation, and are, as a result, being continually refined. All three of the units described have had to face up to the challenges of recent political and social changes, and to evaluate changes in practice as they adapted their treatment programmes to new research findings and external pressures. At a time when we are beginning to do so too, it is particularly useful to have sight of their experiences.

Appendix 1

FORENSIC PSYCHIATRY IN THE NETHERLANDS: RECENT DEVELOPMENTS

Peter Greeven

According to the Dutch Criminal Code, a person who has committed a criminal offence for which he or she cannot be held responsible because of defective development or a psychiatric disorder can be admitted to a psychiatric hospital or placed under a special hospital order, the so-called 'Terbeschikkingstelling' (TBS). The objective of this appendix is to provide an outline of the history of TBS legislation and of the current developments in forensic psychiatry in the Netherlands.

HISTORY

Since its introduction in 1928, the TBS Order, which deals with detention under a special hospital order of the Dutch Criminal Code, intended to protect society against mentally disordered offenders, has been the subject of much attention from both the criminal justice system and public opinion. According to Franke (1995), the TBS Order is one of the most intrusive sanctions in Dutch law. Uncertainty about the length of the period of deprivation of liberty, as well as intrusion into the patient's life and restrictions on his or her freedom of movement, stand out the most. Three distinct periods in the development of the TBS Order can be distinguished during the past century (Van Marle, 1998).

The first period was based on the so-called 'Psychopath Act' (Psychopathen Wetten), in which compulsory treatment was imposed on offenders who, when committing a serious crime, were suffering from 'a pathological disturbance of their mental faculties'. Depending on progress in treatment and concomitant decrease or increase of public danger, the hospital order could be of indefinite duration. The courts tended to rely on this order, because it was a measure whereby the safety of others was guaranteed for a long time. In the 1930s, the government tried to limit execution of the TBS Order, because global economic recession required it to economize.

The second period was influenced by new ideas that developed in the criminal justice system after World War II, mainly as a consequence of the fact that a significant number of the Dutch policy makers had themselves been imprisoned during the war. As a result of their experiences, they developed an 'open' and 'advanced' view on the criminal justice system and on the implementation and objectives of imprisonment. In the post-war climate, the initiatives of the so-called 'Utrecht School' to develop a more humane way of dealing with mentally disturbed offenders fell on fertile soil (Beyaert, 1992). The focus of the 'Utrecht School' was on a positive perspective, for example that mentally disordered offenders need to be taught new skills in order to function socially and to become less dangerous. This positive perspective was reflected in the execution of the TBS Order and, as a result, the number of orders imposed increased to about 400 a year.

To ensure that the TBS Order was only executed in cases in which the risk of serious recidivism was high, and to improve efficiency, a forensic psychiatric observation facility and a forensic selection institute were erected around 1950. Despite these two new facilities, the number of TBS patients increased at the end of the 1950s to more than 2000, which prompted the policy makers to demand that the courts focus more on protecting the public and invoke the TBS Order only in cases involving serious violence.

These developments, in combination with the need to safeguard the legal rights of TBS patients, formed the basis for the 1986 TBS Act. The new act tightened up the statutory regulation of the order by demanding new material conditions for its execution. The most important of these new conditions were that the crime should carry a minimum sentence of 4 years' imprisonment and have an aspect of personal and public safety. A specific condition of the TBS Order is that it can only be imposed if necessary on the grounds of protecting the safety of others and the general safety of people and property. It was expected that these new conditions would help to reduce the number of TBS patients, but they turned out to mark the beginning of the third period of development.

THE TBS ACT SINCE 1986

For a number of reasons, the TBS Order has come under considerable pressure in the last decade. One of these reasons seems to be related to the new conditions for its execution. As the TBS Order has been invoked since 1986 only for mentally disordered offenders who have committed very serious and violent crimes, and for whom there is a high risk of recidivism, the time needed for inpatient treatment has increased. During the same period, psychopathology has changed, and nowadays most forensic patients have multiple pathology, e.g. substance abuse, severe personality disorder and/or psychosis. More then one-third of TBS patients are sexual offenders and suffer from paraphilias. This again requires more prolonged inpatient treatment, as well as aftercare facilities that offer intensive control. Other reasons may relate to sociological developments. There has been an increase in the serious and violent crimes committed by psychiatric patients, mainly as a result of the fact that, in general mental health care, chronic psychiatric patients are being discharged from their institutions (Van Panhuis, 1997). This finding may indicate that TBS hospitals have been taking over the custodial task of general psychiatric hospitals and are becoming asylums for chronic and dangerous psychiatric patients. Another reason might be demographic. According to the latest figures, the percentage of TBS patients with a non-Dutch cultural background has increased to 31 per cent (Van Emmerik, 2003). This group of mentally disordered offenders needs a different treatment approach, which still remains to be developed. The more severe pathology of TBS patients, in combination with a more dangerous profile, has also had a major influence on the transfer of mentally disordered offenders to the aftercare facilities of general psychiatric institutions or other social services. For a considerable proportion of the current population of TBS patients, termination of the TBS Order will only be justified if they can be transferred to aftercare facilities, and it has been found that the transfer of patients to such facilities within general mental health care and alternative services frequently encounters major difficulties (Greeven, 1997).

These developments not only increased the pressure on capacity, but also had a major influence on the average period of in-patient treatment, which, in the last decade, has increased to approximately 7 years. This, in combination with the increase in the number of TBS Orders invoked by the court, is one of the main reasons for the stagnation of the TBS system. Since 1990, the number of TBS patients has almost tripled (from 500 in 1990 to 1500 in 2003), and the latest forecasts of the capacity required show a steady increase for the years to come (Moolenaar et al., 2002). The Ministry of Justice and mental health institutions built three new forensic psychiatric hospitals and increased in-patient capacity, but, as a consequence of the above, the system is becoming overburdened. Currently, approximately 200 TBS patients are waiting in prison to be admitted to forensic psychiatric hospitals. In the meantime, with the assistance of the legal aid system, these patients have been successful in claiming and obtaining compensation from the Ministry of Justice for the delay in their admission to hospital. The ministry now has to pay every TBS patient approximately £25 for every day they wait in prison to be admitted to a forensic psychiatric hospital. The resulting public outcry has forced the Ministry of Justice to come up with a solution to the shortage in capacity.

INTER-DEPARTMENTAL INVESTIGATIONS AND FUTURE DEVELOPMENTS

Since the beginning of the 1990s, the discussion has shifted from an academic dispute between judicial and forensic psychiatric opinions on the treatment of mentally disordered offenders, towards the financial demands of treatment on society and its effectiveness. The Ministry of Justice must provide proof of the effectiveness of the TBS system, while at the same time the system is confronted with different, autonomous developments, causing numerous problems in the execution of TBS

Orders. Therefore, in the past 7 years, two inter-departmental task forces have been appointed to investigate the TBS system and the facilities available for mentally disordered offenders.

In 1996, the first inter-departmental task force published a report that proposed the reduction of in-patient treatment, in combination with increased pressure on the forensic psychiatric hospitals to work more effectively (Interdepartementaal Beleids Onderzoek, 1996). It also proposed, for the first time in the history of the Dutch TBS system, creating non-treatment units for mentally disordered offenders who show no improvement as a result of any previous treatment. Although the motive behind this proposal seemed understandable, at an ideological level it meant shifting from the positive perspective on which the TBS Order had been based since World War II. In 1999, the first facility of this type (a so-called 'long-stay unit') was opened, and recently a second one was built in Nijmegen. Two other facilities are under development in a shared project with the Ministry of Public Health. The aims of long-stay units are multiple: protecting society from the risk of criminal offences by these 'chronic' patients; providing the patients with proper care in order to optimize their quality of life; removing them from regular forensic psychiatric units where intensive treatment is provided (and thus increasing capacity); and providing care at a lower cost compared to regular forensic treatment units (Greeven, 2002).

The proposals from the second inter-departmental task force, however, were more radical then had been expected (Interdepartementaal Beleids Onderzoek TBS, 1998). This task force focused on the possibility of reducing the in-patient treatment period for certain categories of TBS patients without increasing the rate of recidivism. It concentrated on two consecutive phases of the TBS system: admission and the in-patient treatment period. The task force made recommendations for a more transparent and efficient decision-making process for the execution of the TBS Order. It also demanded the introduction of quality standards for the 'Pro-Justitia' reports on mentally disordered offenders, and a transparent protocol for the legal process of execution. It was felt that whether or not patients ended up in the TBS system depended on too many variables.

The conclusions that related the possible ways to reduce the in-patient treatment period in TBS hospitals have led to constructive debate. The task force stated that, at 7 years, the in-patient treatment period was much longer than would be expected. Moreover, not one of the consulted specialists was able to differentiate patient categories on the basis of treatment and the risk of recidivism, based on empirical data. The investigation also questioned the scientific 'state of the art' in Dutch forensic psychiatry and, by doing so, questioned social and public support. It became evident that in Dutch forensic psychiatry there are many different treatment models based on different theoretical and historical perspectives, but none of them has been subjected to thorough scientific research. In fact, so far, only one empirical study has been conducted on the outcome of the treatment of TBS patients with severe personality disorder pathology during the in-patient treatment period (Greeven, 1997). This study showed that about one-third of the sample demonstrated a clinically significant improvement after 2 years of in-patient treatment. However, the small sample size makes it difficult to generalize these findings, and the study design needs to be improved – for example, it would be preferable to set up a controlled study involving different institutions.

In addition, the Research and Documentation Centre of the Ministry of Justice conducted a series of studies on the rate of recidivism after termination of treatment in the TBS system. Comparison of these studies reveals evidence of a general gradual decline in recidivism, to a level of just over 50 per cent of patients committing 'any offence' after termination of treatment in TBS. However, recidivism rates of more serious (sexually) violent crimes after termination of treatment in TBS remain stable, at levels between 15 and 20 per cent (Leuw, 1999). Over the years, about one in seven mentally disordered offenders treated under a TBS Order can be considered a failure in terms of the essential goal of the system – preventing serious violent crimes in the future.

It is small wonder that most of the recommendations of the interdepartmental TBS task forces focused on improvement in quality and efficiency. To improve the quality of treatment and the scientific 'state of the art', a national research centre exclusively for forensic psychiatry needed to be erected, with the aim of co-ordinating empirical research and developing a national programme of forensic mental health research. Such a centre, the so-called Expertise Centre for Forensic Psychiatry (EFP), has been active since January 2003, based in Utrecht. The EFP was set up as a joint project by the Ministry of Justice, the Ministry of Health and the forensic psychiatric hospitals. The effectiveness of the TBS Order should be the subject of constant study to enable the legitimacy of the order to be tackled directly.

To improve efficiency, the forensic psychiatric hospitals themselves will be held responsible for the selection of TBS patients. As a consequence, the Dr F.S. Meijers Institute in Utrecht, which has been responsible for selection for half a century, has been transformed into a regular forensic psychiatric hospital. It is expected that a more randomized selection of patients will result in comparable populations in all forensic psychiatric hospitals, therefore making it possible to compare both the input and output variables of the hospitals and to stimulate new developments by using benchmark mechanisms. The selection of patients is now computer based, in four main categories: personality disordered offenders, offenders with schizophrenia and psychosis, mentally disabled offenders, and extremely dangerous offenders. Even more radical is the introduction of a new financial system on the basis of which day-reimbursement will be more or less halved for every TBS patient after 6 years of in-patient treatment. It is hoped that this financial consequence will stimulate the forensic psychiatric hospitals to reduce the in-patient treatment period and force them to develop new ways of re-socialization and to create aftercare facilities in co-operation with general mental health institutions.

CONCLUSION

Over the last century, no matter what measures policy makers introduced, the number of forensic psychiatric patients in the Netherlands seemed to increase at certain periods in time. In most cases, the financial demands of the TBS system on society were the policy makers' major concern, and the reasons behind the 'periods of increase' have been more or less ignored. On the other hand, the positive aspects of the order are attractive. It provides a means to remove mentally disordered offenders who have committed a serious violent crime from society for an indefinite period of time, while a judicial review is carried out by the criminal court every 1 or 2 years to determine whether the threat to society warrants further detention (Van Marle, 2002). As stated above, as a consequence of certain developments in the Netherlands, the number of mentally disordered offenders increased spectacularly, resulting in an increase in the implementation of the TBS Order that will probably continue for the coming years. The result of all this is an increasing number of TBS patients and a declining number of discharges from the forensic psychiatric hospitals, creating bottlenecks in the TBS system. At the same time, this pressure created a climate of change in the forensic psychiatric hospitals, an urgent need to co-operate with general mental health

care institutions, and a need to introduce a 'state of the art' in mental health care. In the past decade, general mental health care (including psychiatry) has focused on the development and implementation of care programmes based on empirical research (evidence-based medicine). These developments in mental health care have also been forced by financial and practical motives, and it seems that in forensic psychiatry we are at the beginning of similar developments. Especially in the Netherlands, where the TBS Act is based on the humanistic principle that treatment and re-socialization are preferable to repression and retribution, it is necessary to learn more about effective methods of intervention. Care programmes and the introduction of the concept of evidence-based medicine into forensic psychiatry will be the first steps forward. At present, a task force is working on the development of three forensic psychiatric care programmes (for sexual offenders, personality disordered offenders, and offenders with schizophrenia). At the same time, another task force, chaired by the EFP, is working on the validation and implementation of different risk assessment instruments. The implementation of the above-mentioned programmes and instruments will provide a good opportunity to establish a base for empirical research in forensic psychiatry in the Netherlands at the beginning of the twenty-first century.

REFERENCES

Beyaert FHL (1992). Forensic psychiatry in the Netherlands: retrospect and prospect. *Journal of Forensic Psychiatry* **3**:251–60.

Emmerik JL van (2003). TBS-gestelden: een gemêleerd gezelschap. In: Groen H and Drost M (eds), *Handboek Forensische Geestelijke Gezondheidszorg.* Utrecht: De Tijdstroom, 33–50.

Franke H (1995). *The Emancipation of Prisoners: A Socio-historical Analysis of the Dutch Prison Experience.* Edinburgh: Edinburgh University Press.

Greeven PGJ (1997). *Treatment Outcome in Personality Disordered Forensic Patients: An Empirical Study.* Deventer: Gouda Quint.

Greeven PGJ (2002). Effectivity of the TBS: What works? TBS Conference, Noordwijkerhout, The Netherlands.

Interdepartementaal Beleids Onderzoek (1996). *Doelmatig Behandelen: Financieringssysteem van Forensisch Psychiatrische Hulpverlening.* The Hague: Ministry of Justice.

Interdepartementaal Beleids Onderzoek TBS (1998). Over stromen. In: *Door – en Uitstroom bij de TBS.* The Hague: Ministry of Justice.

Leuw E (ed.) (1999). *Recidive na de TBS: Patronen, Trends en Processen en de Inschatting van Gevaar.* The Hague: Ministry of Justice-WODC.

Marle HJC van (1998). De bedwongen populariteit van de TBS. In: Buruma Y, Coppens E and Groenendijk C (eds), *Recht door de Eeuw.* Deventer: Kluwer, 239–61.

Marle HJC van (2002). The Dutch Entrustment Act: its principles and innovations. *International Journal of Forensic Mental Health* **1**:83–92.

Moolenaar DEG, Tulder FP van, Huijbregts GLAM and Heide W van der (2002). *Prognose van de Sanctiecapaciteit tot en met 2006.* The Hague: Ministry of Justice-WODC.

Panhuis PJA van (1997). *The Psychotic Patient in the TBS.* Deventer: Gouda Quint.

A SHORT NOTE ON THE TREATMENT OF PERSONALITY DISORDER IN DANISH FORENSIC PSYCHIATRY

Peter Gottlieb

As in other countries, recent trends in the use of the Danish psychiatric health services have meant that the available resources have been progressively allocated to those services that provide treatment for the major mental disorders. At a meeting of the Danish Psychiatric Society in the autumn of 1999 it was argued that it was time for a re-examination and re-evaluation of the treatment of neuroses, personality disorders, substance abuse and other 'minor' mental (i.e. non-psychotic disorders) in public health. The tendency of psychiatrists during recent decades either to neglect this field totally or to let other disciplines take over needed to be stopped, as it is in the psychiatric profession that one finds the qualifications needed to address these disorders.

This re-examination is occurring in the context of significant developments in the treatment of non-psychotic individuals. First, there is an increasing interest in somatization disorders; second, there is a growing awareness of the special problems and needs of immigrant populations and, third, colleagues in the USA appear to have a particular interest in symptoms of anxiety and depression in patients who would not be regarded as psychotic cases. As a result, the relationship between biological and psychological treatment modalities is now

being addressed more openly than perhaps at any other time since the introduction of antipsychotics, making it increasingly possible to connect psychotherapy more closely with mainstream psychiatry. This in turn might indicate that treatments for non-psychotic disorders may begin to receive more attention than has recently been the case.

In the autumn of 1999, Danish forensic psychiatrists met to discuss the topic of psychiatric evaluations for courts of law. Included was a presentation on Section 69 of the Danish Penal Law. As a consequence of the application of this legislation, practically all psychotic offenders are sentenced with treatment orders rather than punishment. According to Section 69, it is also possible that people suffering from non-psychotic psychiatric disorders may be sentenced to treatment instead of punishment, but only if the court considers that treatment is more likely than punishment to prevent criminal relapse. The likelihood of an offender being directed to a treatment centre instead of a punishment centre seems to be greater the more psychotic in nature his or her psychiatric diagnosis and the less severe the crime. Thus, even though many forensic patients do indeed possess psychopathic traits, the more clear cases of personality disorder are only rarely treated in psychiatric settings, as most individuals with a diagnosis of psychopathy are sent to prison.

Treatment of prison inmates is provided in the special prison of the Herstedvester Detention Centre, a security institution whose goal is rehabilitation. It is in this prison that offenders who have committed the most serious crimes (including sexual crimes) and who are most in need of psychological and psychiatric help serve their sentences. Psychodynamically orientated therapy is offered alongside day-to-day educational and vocational activities. The psychotherapists regard their job as focused on the offenders' deficit in the capacity for empathy. This lack of empathy – regardless of whether biological or psychological in origin – means that the treatment must teach rules, or otherwise convey how to behave socially, and help the person with the deficit to become realistic and to come to terms with his or her deficit rather than hope to be 'cured'.

A small minority of the inmates at Herstedvester pose an ethical dilemma for the therapists. These are the individuals who have been sentenced to time-indeterminate detention because of dangerous sexual criminality with a high risk of recidivism. In many cases their only way to freedom is to submit to chemical castration with antihormones. The dilemma is that neither this nor time-indeterminate detention is a good solution, but, for the individuals in question, no other reasonable alternatives are currently available.

In the more mainstream prison system, there is a growing interest in the use of cognitive measures to try to help the inmates to learn to adjust socially instead of creating trouble for themselves by using 'solutions' that include violent or threatening behaviour. This activity is very deliberately not labelled 'therapy', even though it certainly may have therapeutic qualities.

The number of forensic patients in the Danish psychiatric system seems to be ever increasing, and has now reached a total of some 1500 (the national population amounts to 5 million). The existing seven specialist units for forensic patients contain some 200 beds in all and treat some 100 out-patients as well. The remaining forensic patients, i.e. about three-quarters of the total, are treated in the general psychiatric setting. The specialist forensic units see it as their task to treat those forensic patients who cause the greatest challenge, whether because of legal, security or therapeutic difficulties.

Only one of the special forensic units in the psychiatric system has more than 15 years of experience, the other six still being in a developmental phase. In all seven units, however, the awareness of the special demands that forensic patients place on the milieu in wards is increasing.

The largest of the forensic units, that of St Hans Hospital, comprises several different wards, each with its own profile. Thus, different levels of security can be offered, from a ward with double doors, securely locked windows, highly developed alarm systems etc., to a ward where the staff are only present from Monday to Friday in the daytime. Since being founded in 1989, the unit has worked on adjusting the liberties and boundaries as sensibly as possible to meet the needs of the patients. There is a constant awareness of the double task of providing acceptance and understanding *and* providing the secure and safe limits needed by chaotic individuals. The goal is to provide safe surroundings at different levels of security within which professional contact with the staff can be established, allowing for appropriate therapeutic activities to take place.

As an example of this need to be adaptive, in the various settings, different types of *milieu therapy* take place. In the most secure wards, patient groups are termed 'thematic', which means that the task of the groups is very much defined from the start. The task may cover very different subjects, from the reading of a fairy tale to the production of pottery, the essential need being that not much unstructured space is left in which the focus of the group may be lost. The group in one of the more open wards is called a 'conversation group', the content being very much dependent on the material patients bring to it.

Regarding other issues, e.g. the freedom to leave the ward, have visitors, go to Copenhagen etc., there is a gradual progression from the more to the less restrictive wards reflecting the level of the patients' capacity for autonomous functioning. The best functioning patients are discharged from the unit to continue their court-ordered treatment in an out-patient setting, ideally with the same doctor and social worker as during the last part of their in-patient stay.

Retrospectively, it is clear that since its start in 1989, the milieu of the St Hans Forensic Psychiatric Unit has gradually become more focused on the individual responsibility of the patients and their social adaptation, with less emphasis on their psychotic illness per se. For example, 10 years ago, not all incidents of law breaking committed by the patients would be reported to the police, as it was often argued that the patient – because of his or her illness – was to remain at the hospital in any case. Today, the attitude is that the law should be respected inside as well as outside the hospital, meaning that all offences that would be reported to the police if they happened anywhere else are also to be reported if committed inside the hospital. Likewise, the increasing acknowledgement of the patients as responsible individuals has meant that single rooms are about to replace larger rooms for all patients in the unit. This development makes it possible for private belongings such as television sets, personal computers (without connection to the Internet) and personal furniture may be installed, and that the patients may be given their own copies of the keys to their rooms. Of course, the patients, in order to obtain and make use of these and other freedoms, will have to demonstrate that they are capable of taking the necessary responsibility, and the staff must be able to strike an empathic balance between trust and control.

Thus it is hoped that a change from a depersonalizing asylum to a maturing and socializing institution is taking place. Hence, while the earlier mentioned steady increase in the number of forensic psychiatric patients is due to an increase in the number of patients who have received a diagnosis of psychosis, and particularly schizophrenia, treatment is becoming more and more focused on the personality disordered aspects of the patients.

Appendix 3

TREATMENT APPROACHES AT OAK RIDGE, THE MAXIMUM-SECURITY HOSPITAL AT PENETANGUISHENE, ONTARIO

N. Zoe Hilton, Grant T. Harris and Marnie E. Rice

Oak Ridge was built in the 1930s as a maximum-security facility to house the 'criminally insane' for long periods of custody. Its maximum capacity was about 300 beds, but since the mid-1980s the beds have been reduced to 140 by transforming patient rooms into offices. Currently, about half the admissions to Oak Ridge come from courts, in the form of 30–60-day remands for psychiatric assessments of adjudicative competence or criminal responsibility. In most respects, the assessment population resembles that of a Canadian federal prison. The men detained at Oak Ridge for treatment, however, comprise a more severely mentally disordered group: about two-thirds have a primary diagnosis of a psychosis, and one-quarter a personality disorder. Most have been charged with an offence of violence against persons. In decreasing order of frequency, these men include those found not criminally responsible or unfit, mentally ill offenders from provincial or federal prisons, and patients involuntarily certified (civilly committed) under the Ontario Mental Health Act but difficult to manage in less secure psychiatric hospitals or facilities for developmentally disabled adults (Quinsey et al., 1998, 2005).

Since the 1960s, Oak Ridge has had two kinds of treatment programme. One approach, designed for lower functioning and violent patients, combined ward-based token economies with security principles (Quinsey and Sarbit, 1975; Quinsey, 1981). Originally, patients began on highly secure, minimum privilege wards where more immediate and tangible rewards were used to reduce assaultiveness and to improve hygiene, mood, co-operation and work habits. As patients improved, they moved to less secure, higher privilege wards where rewards were delayed, and much of the day was spent in off-ward workshops. Over time, the programme increasingly relied on response cost, a punitive treatment model (Harris and Rice, 1992). Ward transfers and other rewards ultimately became independent of patient performance in the behavioural programme (Rice and Harris, 1993). A long-term follow-up of patients treated in this programme was unable to show that the treatment reduced subsequent violent behaviour (Rice et al., 1990).

The other kind of programme has emphasized verbal, insight-oriented, emotionally evocative therapy in various forms. This approach was used most extensively in the Social Therapy Unit (STU) in the late 1960s to early 1980s, which treated personality disordered and psychotic patients in roughly equal proportions. Both disorders were viewed as stemming from disturbed interpersonal relationships that could be ameliorated through extended and intense social interactions, obliging patients to face the consequences of their antisocial interaction styles. A long-term follow-up of graduates of this therapeutic community showed an interaction of treatment and psychopathy on violent recidivism. Treatment was associated with lower violent recidivism rates for non-psychopathic offenders (compared with similar men who were sent to prison), but higher rates of violent recidivism for psychopathic offenders (Rice et al., 1992; Harris et al., 1994). For political reasons, the programme had ceased before this outcome research was conducted.

Beginning in the early 1970s, specialized sex offender treatment was also provided, first for child molesters and later including rapists. Follow-up studies failed to show that the treatment reduced violent and sexual recidivism (Rice et al., 1991).

Throughout the 1980s, Oak Ridge underwent a succession of reformations aimed at reviving moribund treatment programmes. The hope was to achieve levels of therapeutic integrity that could be shown to reduce violent recidivism. Many of these changes were inspired by the remarkable success reported for behavioural and psychosocial treatments (e.g. Paul and Lentz, 1977) and, in the mid-1980s, the predominant therapeutic model of care in Oak Ridge was a social learning model. This was characterized, for example, by the recruitment of non-medical directors (psychologists, a social worker, an occupational therapist) for each of four Oak Ridge units.

Since that time, shifts in treatment philosophy and staffing changes have increased the emphasis on a traditional medical model. Nurses are the clinical administrators of three of the current four units and approximately 90 per cent of all clinical staff are nurses. There is enthusiastic support given to the prescription of novel drugs (Hector, 1998). Otherwise, the primary means to deal with aggression are various forms of seclusion and restraint (Hilton and Simmons, 1999). Most patients spend little or no time engaged in structured therapeutic efforts aimed at the 'criminogenic' problems that brought them to Oak Ridge. Currently, it could be fairly said that the primary therapeutic approach in Oak Ridge is the delivery of psychotropic medication.

This is not to say that there are no psychosocial therapies provided. A minority of clinicians, whether or not from medically oriented disciplines, offer a wide range of activities to patients. For example, on any given day, at least half of all patients participate in some recreational activities, which range from skills-oriented therapeutic recreation to diversion and entertainment. Almost a third of patients engage in some vocational training, ranging from hour-long to full-day programmes. Occupational therapy, social work and psychology staff members provide programmes for small groups in addictions awareness, discharge planning, anger management, symptom management, and social skills training. It is fair to say, however, that despite some empirically based practice (Rice et al., 2004) and the clear evidence favouring psychosocial treatments that adhere to the basic principles of risk and needs as expounded by Gendreau (1996), even in addition to successful medication (Menditto et al., 1996), few of the institution's resources are currently devoted to such treatments. Clearly, there is opportunity for improvement. Suggestions for increasing evidence-based treatment in Oak Ridge and the Ontario forensic system as a whole have been proposed (Rice et al., 2004; Seto et al., 2001).

Throughout its history, the institution's administration (supported by the Provincial government) has demonstrated a commitment to research and evaluation unparalleled elsewhere in the world (cf. Rice and Harris, 1993; Quinsey et al., 1998). Oak Ridge entered the new millennium with renewed commitment to evidence-based practice that will depend not only on the conduct of research and evaluation, but also on the implementation of empirically determined best practices.

REFERENCES

Gendreau P (1996). Offender rehabilitation: what we know and what needs to be done. *Criminal Justice and Behavior* **23**:144–61.

Harris GT and Rice ME (1992). Reducing violence in institutions: maintaining behavior change. In: Peters DeV, McMahon RJ and Quinsey VL (eds), *Aggression and Violence Throughout the Life Span*. Newbury Park, CA: Sage, 261–82.

Harris GT, Rice ME and Cormier CA (1994). Psychopaths: is a therapeutic community therapeutic? *Therapeutic Communities* **15**:283–300.

Hector RI (1998). The use of clozapine in the treatment of aggressive schizophrenia. *Canadian Journal of Psychiatry* **43**:466–72.

Hilton NZ and Simmons JL (1999). Adverse effects of poor behavior management of an inpatient's difficult behavior. *Psychiatric Services* **50**:964–6.

Menditto AA, Beck NC, Stuve P et al. (1996). Effectiveness of clozapine and a social learning program for severely disabled psychiatric inpatients. *Psychiatric Services* **47**:46–51.

Paul GL and Lentz RJ (1977). *Psychosocial Treatment of Chronic Mental Patients: Milieu versus Social-learning Programs.* Cambridge, MA: Harvard University Press.

Quinsey VL (1981). The long term management of the mentally disordered offender. In: Hucker SJ, Webster CD and Ben-Aron M (eds), *Mental Disorder and Criminal Responsibility*. Toronto: Butterworths, 137–55.

Quinsey VL, Harris GT, Rice ME and Cormier CA (1998). *Violent Offenders: Appraising and Managing Risk.* Washington, DC: American Psychological Association.

Quinsey VL, Harris GT, Rice ME and Cormier CA (2005). *Violent Offenders: Appraising and Managing Risk*, second edition. Washington, DC: American Psychological Association.

Quinsey VL and Sarbit B (1975). Behavioral changes associated with the introduction of a token economy in a maximum security psychiatric institution. *Canadian Journal of Criminology and Corrections* **17**:177–82.

Rice ME and Harris GT (1993). Ontario's maximum security hospital at Penetanguishene: past, present, and future. *International Journal of Law and Psychiatry* **16**:195–215.

Rice ME, Harris GT and Cormier CA (1992). Evaluation of a maximum security therapeutic community for psychopaths and other mentally disordered offenders. *Law and Human Behavior* **16**:399–412.

Rice ME, Harris GT, Cormier CA, Lang C, Coleman G and Smith Krans T (2004). An evidence-based approach to planning services for forensic psychiatric patients. *Issues in Forensic Psychology* **5**:13–49.

Rice ME, Quinsey VL and Harris GT (1991). Sexual recidivism among child molesters released from a maximum security psychiatric institution. *Journal of Consulting and Clinical Psychology* **59**:381–6.

Rice ME, Quinsey VL and Houghton R (1990). Predicting treatment outcome and recidivism among patients in a maximum security token economy. *Behavioral Sciences and the Law* **8**:313–26.

Seto MC, Lalumière, ML, Harris GT et al. (2001). Demands on forensic mental health services in the province of Ontario. Report prepared for the Ontario Ministry of Health and Long-Term Care.

INDEX

Notes: Page numbers in **bold** denote figures and tables. Please also note that as the subject of this book is personality disorder, entries under this heading have been kept to a minimum and main entries all refer to this subject unless otherwise stated.

Abbreviations used in subentries: ADHD = attention deficit hyperactivity disorder; PTSD = post-traumatic stress disorder.